Heritage Auction Galleries
proudly presents

Summer F.U.N. Signature Auction #442

July 12-13, 2007 | West Palm Beach, Florida

Preliminary Exhibition of Lots

Marriott Inner Harbor | 110 S. Eutaw | Oriole Room | Baltimore, Maryland 21202

Wednesday, June 27 ....9 am-7 pm ET

Baltimore Convention Center | Halls A&B Booth 153, 154, 155 | One West Pratt St. | Baltimore, Maryland 21202

Thursday, June 28 ....9 am-7 pm ET
Friday, June 29 ....9 am-7 pm ET
Saturday, June 30 ....9 am-12 pm ET

Main Exhibition of Lots

Palm Beach County Convention Center | Room 1 D, E | 650 Okeechobee Blvd. | West Palm Beach, Florida 33401

Wednesday, July 11 ....9 am-7 pm ET
Thursday, July 12 ....8 am-6:30 pm ET
Friday, July 13 ....8 am-6:30 ET

Live, Internet & Mail Bid Auction #442

Palm Beach County Convention Center | Room 1 B, C | 650 Okeechobee Blvd. | West Palm Beach, Florida 33401

Session 1 .... Thursday, July 12 .... 1 pm ET .... Lots 1-641
Session 2 .... Thursday, July 12 .... 6:30 pm ET .... Lots 642-1805
Session 3 .... Friday, July 13 .... 1 pm ET .... Lots 1806-2230
Session 4 .... Friday, July 13 .... 6:30 pm ET .... Lots 2231-3362

Lots are sold at the approximate rate of 200 per hour, but it is not uncommon to sell 150 lots or 300 lots per hour. Please plan accordingly so that you don't miss the items you are bidding on.

This auction is subject to a 15% Buyer's Premium.

The World's #1 Numismatic Auctioneer
HERITAGE HA.com
Auction Galleries

3500 Maple Avenue, 17th Floor, Dallas, Texas 75219
214-528-3500 | 800-US COINS (872-6467)

LOT SETTLEMENT AND PICKUP
Room 1 D, E
Friday, July 13, 10 am-1 pm ET
Saturday, July 14, 9 am-12 pm ET

Direct Client Service Line: Toll Free 1-866-835-3243 | e-mail: Bid@HA.com
View full-color images at HA.com/Coins

THIS AUCTION IS CATALOGED AND PRESENTED BY HERITAGE NUMISMATIC AUCTIONS, INC.
Auctioneer: Samuel Foose AU3244
Heritage Numismatic Auctions, Inc. Florida License AB0000665
Cataloged by Mark Van Winkle, Chief Cataloger;
Brian Koller, Catalog Production Manager; Mark Borckardt, Senior Cataloger;
Jon Amato, John Beety, Bruce Lorich, John Salyer, Dennis Tarrant
Photography and Imaging by Jody Garver, Chief Photographer;
Joel Gonzalez, Colleen McInerney
Production and design by Cindy Brenner, Katie Brown, Lisa Fox, Kelley Norwine, Matt Pegues
Operations by Cristina Gonzalez, Alma Villa, Miguel Reynaga Sr., Edna Lopez, Celeste Robertson, Maria Flores

---

FAX BIDS TO
214-443-8425

FAX DEADLINE
Wed., July 11, Noon CT

INTERNET BIDDING
Closes at 10 PM CT before the session on sale

Auction Results
Available Immediately at our website:
HA.com/Coins

AUCTION #442

Steve Ivy
CEO
Co-Chairman
of the Board

Jim Halperin
Co-Chairman
of the Board

Greg Rohan
President

Paul Minshull
Chief Operating
Officer

The World's #1 Numismatic Auctioneer

HERITAGE HA.com
Auction Galleries

3500 Maple Avenue, 17th Floor | Dallas, Texas 75219
Phone 214-528-3500 | 800-872-6467
HA.com/Coins | e-mail: Bid@HA.com

HERITAGE AUCTION GALLERIES

THE REUBEN REINSTEIN COLLECTION | THE SILVER FOX COLLECTION | THE GARY VANEK COLLECTION

Dear Bidder,

Heritage is proud to be the *Official Auctioneer* of the Inaugural Summer F.U.N. convention in West Palm Beach. F.U.N.'s wonderful conventions held every January are traditionally the best-attended shows in the country, and we are looking forward to supporting this new event. Last January at F.U.N., Heritage set the new world record for the most valuable numismatic auction ever held (beating our old record, also set at a F.U.N. event!). We expect this new event to grow rapidly in popularity.

Heritage has ready clients for coins and notes valued in the $500 to $5,000 range, as well as million dollar rarities. In our 2007 record event – $78 million – 70% of the lots sold for less than $5,000! One of the reasons that F.U.N. auctions are so popular is that we offer a wide range of quality coins, both as to series and values. This catalog enjoys an equally diverse range of wonderful coins.

More than 200 consignors agreed with us, and placed their important coins in this auction. Among the anchor collections are:

THE REUBEN REINSTEIN COLLECTION

A marvelous collection of Morgan dollars comes to us through Laird A. Lile, the court-appointed personal representative of the estate of Reuben Reinstein. Mr. Reinstein was an avid collector of many years standing, whose discriminating eye is clearly evident in these coins. Among his outstanding Morgans are his 1893-CC MS65 NGC, 1893-O MS65 NGC, 1894 MS65 PCGS, 1895 PR65 Cameo NGC, and an 1896-O MS65 NGC.

THE SILVER FOX COLLECTION

From one of our international clients comes a wonderful selection of Gem Morgan dollars and Classic Commemoratives. The consignor started collecting world stamps at the age of 10, a natural attraction since his father's business received much mail from worldwide suppliers and customers. An interest in world coins soon followed; as his father traveled widely, pocket change always yielded "those odd and interesting coins, some so worn you could hardly make out the dates, but intriguing just the same." The consignor was introduced to the thrill of discovery, appreciation of art, knowledge of the world, the joy of completing collections, and even the frustration of some pursuits that could never be completed. In short, a true collector was created.

Such interests led to collegiate majors in architecture and art history. "Great civilizations always leave behind great sculptures, not just in marble but on their coinage. U.S. coinage is no exception to such mini-sculptures. Engravers and sculptors like Morgan, Barber, Saint-Gaudens, Brenner, Fraser, and Weinman were among the best transmitting their stories on these round -- and sometimes very small -- surfaces." He decided to "focus on Morgan dollars, compelling as a massive coin with impressive detail; the enjoyment of finding blazing white and eye appealing coins only grew over time." A purist, he believed that "Mint State" meant untoned ("Did the coins leave the mint rainbow colored?") and sought the whitest examples accordingly.

The consignor also enjoyed coins with historical significance, and turned his attention to completing a Gem 144-piece set of Commemoratives. "They tell a story, attracting people who might otherwise not collect at all. Every one is chock full of cultural details. While each is a Gem, what counted was the eye-appeal of the coin and not the holder." The consignor sought the best and the brightest of their grade.

A firm believer that the most fun of the hunt is the chase and not the catch, the consignor is selling these beloved coins to pursue other collections. He takes great pleasure knowing that so many people will be able to enjoy his coins on the floor, through the catalog, or over the Internet. Specialists in both series will find much of interest.

THE GARY VANEK COLLECTION

The single finest known 1916 half dollar highlights the collection assembled by Gary Vanek, and provides a glimpse into the strategy this dedicated numismatist followed over the course of his collecting career. Any one of the several hundred coins consigned by Mr. Vanek will exhibit superlative eye appeal, quite often mixed with rarity (both conditional and mintage). Mr. Vanek concentrated on quality coins whenever and wherever encountered, not on particular series.

Mr. Vanek began collecting as a young teenager, when his uncle gave him a Lincoln wheat cent Whitman blue folder, which he worked hard at filling. By his reckoning, however, he became a serious numismatist around 1987, when he became determined to buy the best – and trade up even higher when necessary or possible. Included in the Vanek Collection are a wide variety of high quality and desirable coins, with proof Morgan dollars, proof and prooflike gold, intriguing errors (one a rare double struck 1921-S Morgan dollar with the second strike 90% off-center), rare patterns, first year of issue coins, and world coins gathered during his extensive travels.

We invite you to join us in West Palm Beach for this first 'Summer F.U.N.' Enjoy the wonderful spirit of collegiality that F.U.N. shows are known for, and make some new friends – as we count the many fine folks in the F.U.N. organization.

I also hope that you will enjoy the many beautiful and irresistible coins in this catalog. I wish you the best of bidding success. If you can join us, please stop by the Heritage tables in West Palm Beach and say "Hello." If not, we still welcome your participation by Internet, telephone, mail, fax, or agent.

Sincerely,

Greg Rohan

President

TERMS AND CONDITIONS OF AUCTION

Auctioneer and Auction:
1. This Auction is presented by Heritage Auction Galleries, a d/b/a/ of Heritage Auctions, Inc., or their affiliates Heritage Numismatic Auctions, Inc. or Currency Auctions of America, Inc., d/b/a as identified with the applicable licensing information on the title page of the catalog or on the HA.com Internet site (the "Auctioneer"). The Auction is conducted under these Terms and Conditions of Auction and applicable state and local law. Announcements and corrections from the podium and those made through the Terms and Conditions of Auctions appearing on the Internet at HA.com supersede those in the printed catalog.

Buyer's Premium:
2. On bids placed through Heritage, a Buyer's Premium of fifteen percent (15%) will be added to the successful hammer price bid on lots in Coin and Currency auctions, or nineteen and one-half percent (19.5%) on lots in all other auctions. If your bid is placed through eBay Live, a Buyer's Premium equal to the normal Buyer's Premium plus an additional five percent (5%) of the hammer price will be added to the successful bid up to a maximum Buyer's Premium of Twenty Two and one-half percent (22.5%). There is a minimum Buyer's Premium of $9.00 per lot. In Gallery Auctions only, a ten percent (10%) handling fee is applied to all lots based upon the total of the hammer price plus the 19.5% Buyer's Premium.

Auction Venues:
3. The following Auctions are conducted solely on the Internet: Heritage Weekly Internet Coin, Currency, Comics, and Vintage Movie Poster Auctions; Heritage Monthly Internet Sports and Marketplace Auctions; OnLine Sessions. Signature Auctions and Grand Format Auctions accept bids on the Internet first, followed by a floor bidding session; bids may be placed prior to the floor bidding session by Internet, telephone, fax, or mail.

Bidders:
4. Any person participating or registering for the Auction agrees to be bound by and accepts these Terms and Conditions of Auction ("Bidder(s)").
5. All Bidders must meet Auctioneer's qualifications to bid. Any Bidder who is not a customer in good standing of the Auctioneer may be disqualified at Auctioneer's sole option and will not be awarded lots. Such determination may be made by Auctioneer in its sole and unlimited discretion, at any time prior to, during, or even after the close of the Auction. Auctioneer reserves the right to exclude any person it deems in its sole opinion is disruptive to the Auction or is otherwise commercially unsuitable.
6. If an entity places a bid, then the person executing the bid on behalf of the entity agrees to personally guarantee payment for any successful bid.

7. CREDIT REFERENCES:
Bidders who have not established credit with the Auctioneer must either furnish satisfactory credit information (including two collectibles-related business references) well in advance of the Auction or supply valid credit card information. Bids placed through our Interactive Internet program will only be accepted from pre-registered Bidders; Bidders who are not members of HA.com or affiliates should pre-register at least two business days before the first session to allow adequate time to contact references.

Bidding Options:
8. Bids in Signature Auctions or Grand Format Auctions may be placed as set forth in the printed catalog section entitled "Choose your bidding method." For auctions held solely on the Internet, see the alternatives on HA.com. Review at HA.com/common/howtobid.php.
9. Presentment of Bids: Non-Internet bids (including but not limited to podium, fax, phone and mail bids) are treated similar to floor bids in that they must be on-increment or at a half increment (called a cut bid). Any podium, fax, phone, or mail bids that do not conform to a full or half increment will be rounded up or down to the nearest full or half increment and this revised amount will be considered your high bid.
10. Auctioneer's Execution of Certain Bids. Auctioneer cannot be responsible for your errors in bidding, so carefully check that every bid is entered correctly. When identical mail or FAX bids are submitted, preference is given to the first received. To ensure the greatest accuracy, your written bids should be entered on the standard printed bid sheet and be received at Auctioneer's place of business at least two business days before the Auction start. Auctioneer is not responsible for executing mail bids or FAX bids received on or after the day the first lot is sold, nor Internet bids submitted after the published closing time; nor is Auctioneer responsible for proper execution of bids submitted by telephone, mail, FAX, e-mail, Internet, or in person once the Auction begins. Internet bids may not be withdrawn until your written request is received and acknowledged by Auctioneer (FAX: 214-443-8425); such requests must state the reason, and may constitute grounds for withdrawal of bidding privileges. Lots won by mail Bidders will not be delivered at the Auction unless prearranged.
11. Caveat as to Bid Increments. Bid increments (over the current bid level) determine the lowest amount you may bid on a particular lot. Bids greater than one increment over the current bid can be any whole dollar amount. It is possible under several circumstances for winning bids to be between increments, sometimes only $1 above the previous increment. Please see: "How can I lose by less than an increment?" on our website.

The following chart governs current bidding increments.

Current Bid	Bid Increment	Current Bid	Bid Increment
< $10	$1	$3,000 - $4,999	$250
$10 - $29	$2	$5,000 - $9,999	$500
$30 - $59	$3	$10,000 - $19,999	$1,000
$60 - $99	$5	$20,000 - $29,999	$2,000
$100 - $199	$10	$30,000 - $49,999	$2,500
$200 - $299	$20	$50,000 - $99,999	$5,000
$300 - $499	$25	$100,000 - $249,999	$10,000
$500 - $999	$50	$250,000 - $499,999	$25,000
$1,000 - $1,999	$100	$500,000 - $1,499,999	$50,000
$2,000 - $2,999	$200	> $1,500,000	$100,000

12. If Auctioneer calls for a full increment, a floor/phone bidder may request Auctioneer to accept a bid at half of the increment ("Cut Bid") which will be that bidders final bid; if the Auctioneer solicits bids other the expected increment, they will not be considered Cut Bids, and bidders accepting such increments may continue to participate.

Conducting the Auction:
13. Notice of the consignor's liberty to place reserve bids on his lots in the Auction is hereby made in accordance with Article 2 of the Texas Uniform Commercial Code. A reserve is an amount below which the lot will not sell. THE CONSIGNOR OF PROPERTY MAY PLACE WRITTEN RESERVE BIDS ON HIS LOTS IN ADVANCE OF THE AUCTION; ON SUCH LOTS, IF THE HAMMER PRICE DOES NOT MEET THE RESERVE, THE CONSIGNOR MAY PAY A REDUCED COMMISSION ON THOSE LOTS. Reserves are generally posted online several days prior to the Auction closing. Any successful bid placed by a consignor on his Property on the Auction floor or by telephone during the live session, or after the reserves for an Auction have been posted, will be considered an Unqualified Bid, and in such instances the consignor agrees to pay full Buyer's Premium and Seller's Commissions on any lot so repurchased.
14. The highest qualified Bidder shall be the buyer. In the event of any dispute between floor Bidders at a Signature Auction, Auctioneer may at his sole discretion reoffer the lot. Auctioneer's decision and declaration of the winning Bidder shall be final and binding upon all Bidders.
15. Auctioneer reserves the right to refuse to honor any bid or to limit the amount of any bid which, in his sole discretion, is not submitted in "Good Faith," or is not supported by satisfactory credit, numismatic references, or otherwise. A bid is considered not made in "Good Faith" when an insolvent or irresponsible person, or a person under the age of eighteen makes it. Regardless of the disclosure of his identity, any bid by a consignor or his agent on a lot consigned by him is deemed to be made in "Good Faith".
16. Nominal Bids. The Auctioneer in its sole discretion may reject nominal bids, small opening bids, or very nominal advances. If a lot bearing estimates fails to open for 40–60% of the low estimate, the Auctioneer may pass the item or may place a protective bid on behalf of the consignor.
17. Lots bearing bidding estimates shall open at Auctioneer's discretion (approximately 50% of the low estimate). In the event that no bid meets or exceeds that opening amount, the lot shall pass as unsold.
18. All items are to be purchased per lot as numerically indicated and no lots will be broken. Bids will be accepted in whole dollar amounts only. No "buy" or "unlimited" bids will be accepted. Off-increment bids may be accepted by the Auctioneer at Signature Auctions and Grand Format Auctions. Auctioneer reserves the right to withdraw, prior to the close, any lots from the Auction.
19. Auctioneer reserves the right to rescind the sale in the event of nonpayment, breach of a warranty, disputed ownership, auctioneer's clerical error or omission in exercising bids and reserves, or otherwise.
20. Auctioneer occasionally experiences Internet and/or Server service outages during which Bidders cannot participate or place bids. If such outage occurs, we may at our discretion extend bidding for the auction. This policy applies only to widespread outages and not to isolated problems that occur in various parts of the country from time to time. Auctioneer periodically schedules system downtime for maintenance and other purposes, which may be covered by the Outage Policy. Bidders unable to place their Bids through the Internet are directed to bid through Client Services at 1-800-872-6467.
21. The Auctioneer or its affiliates may consign items to be sold in the Auction, and may bid on those lots or any other lots. Auctioneer or affiliates expressly reserve the right to modify any such bids at any time prior to the hammer based upon data made known to the Auctioneer or its affiliates. The Auctioneer may extend advances, guarantees, or loans to certain consignors, and may extend financing or other credits at varying rates to certain Bidders in the auction.
22. The Auctioneer has the right to sell certain unsold items after the close of the Auction; Such lots shall be considered sold during the Auction and all these Terms and Conditions shall apply to such sales including but not limited to the Buyer's Premium, return rights, and disclaimers.

Payment:
23. All sales are strictly for cash in United States dollars. Cash includes: U.S. currency, bank wire, cashier checks, travelers checks, and bank money orders, all subject to reporting requirements. Checks may be subject to clearing before delivery of the purchases. Credit Card (Visa or Master Card only) and PayPal payments may be accepted up to $10,000 from non-dealers at the sole discretion of the auctioneer, subject to the following limitations: a) sales are only to the cardholder, b) purchases are shipped to the cardholder's registered and verified address, c) Auctioneer may pre-approve the cardholder's credit line, d) a credit card transaction may not be used in conjunction with any other financing or extended terms offered by the Auctioneer, and must transact immediately upon invoice presentation, e) rights of return are governed by these Terms and Conditions, which supersede those conditions promulgated by the card issuer, f) floor Bidders must present their card.

24. Payment is due upon closing of the Auction session, or upon presentment of an invoice. Auctioneer reserves the right to void an invoice if payment in full is not received within 7 days after the close of the Auction.
25. Lots delivered in the States of Texas, California, or other states where the Auction may be held, are subject to all applicable state and local taxes, unless appropriate permits are on file with us. Bidder agrees to pay Auctioneer the actual amount of tax due in the event that sales tax is not properly collected due to: 1) an expired, inaccurate, inappropriate tax certificate or declaration, 2) an incorrect interpretation of the applicable statute, 3) or any other reason. Lots from different Auctions may not be aggregated for sales tax purposes.
26. In the event that a Bidder's payment is dishonored upon presentment(s), Bidder shall pay the maximum statutory processing fee set by applicable state law.
27. If any Auction invoice submitted by Auctioneer is not paid in full when due, the unpaid balance will bear interest at the highest rate permitted by law from the date of invoice until paid. If the Auctioneer refers any invoice to an attorney for collection, the buyer agrees to pay attorney's fees, court costs, and other collection costs incurred by Auctioneer. If Auctioneer assigns collection to its in-house legal staff, such attorney's time expended on the matter shall be compensated at a rate comparable to the hourly rate of independent attorneys.
28. In the event a successful Bidder fails to pay all amounts due, Auctioneer reserves the right to resell the merchandise, and such Bidder agrees to pay for the reasonable costs of resale, including a 10% seller's commission, and also to pay any difference between the resale price and the price of the previously successful bid.
29. Auctioneer reserves the right to require payment in full in good funds before delivery of the merchandise.
30. Auctioneer shall have a lien against the merchandise purchased by the buyer to secure payment of the Auction invoice. Auctioneer is further granted a lien and the right to retain possession of any other property of the buyer then held by the Auctioneer or its affiliates to secure payment of any Auction invoice or any other amounts due the Auctioneer or affiliates from the buyer. With respect to these lien rights, Auctioneer shall have all the rights of a secured creditor under Article 9 of the Texas Uniform Commercial Code, including but not limited to the right of sale. In addition, with respect to payment of the Auction invoice(s), the buyer waives any and all rights of offset he might otherwise have against the Auctioneer and the consignor of the merchandise included on the invoice. If a Bidder owes Auctioneer or its affiliates on any account, Auctioneer and its affiliates shall have the right to offset such unpaid account by any credit balance due Bidder, and it may secure by possessory lien any unpaid amount by any of the Bidder's property in their possession.
31. Title shall not pass to the successful Bidder until all invoices are paid in full. It is the responsibility of the buyer to provide adequate insurance coverage for the items once they have been delivered.

Delivery; Shipping and Handling Charges:

32. Shipping and handling charges will be added to invoices. Please refer to Auctioneer's website www.HA.com/common/shipping.php for the latest charges or call Auctioneer. Auctioneer is unable to combine purchases from other auctions or affiliates into one package for shipping purposes.
33. Successful overseas Bidders shall provide written shipping instructions, including specified customs declarations, to the Auctioneer for any lots to be delivered outside of the United States. NOTE: Declaration value shall be the item(s) hammer price together with its buyer's premium.
34. All shipping charges will be borne by the successful Bidder. Any risk of loss during shipment will be borne by the buyer following Auctioneer's delivery to the designated common carrier or third-party shipper, regardless of domestic or foreign shipment.
35. Due to the nature of some items sold, it shall be the responsibility for the successful bidder to arrange pick-up and shipping through third-parties; as to such items Auctioneer shall have no liability.
36. Any request for shipping verification for undelivered packages must be made within 30 days of shipment by Auctioneer.

Cataloging, Warranties and Disclaimers:

37. NO WARRANTY, WHETHER EXPRESSED OR IMPLIED, IS MADE WITH RESPECT TO ANY DESCRIPTION CONTAINED IN THIS AUCTION OR ANY SECOND OPINE. Any description of the items or second opine contained in this Auction is for the sole purpose of identifying the items for those Bidders who do not have the opportunity to view the lots prior to bidding, and no description of items has been made part of the basis of the bargain or has created any express warranty that the goods would conform to any description made by Auctioneer.
38. Auctioneer is selling only such right or title to the items being sold as Auctioneer may have by virtue of consignment agreements on the date of auction and disclaims any warranty of title to the Property. Auctioneer disclaims any warranty of merchantability or fitness for any particular purposes.
39. Translations of foreign language documents may be provided as a convenience to interested parties. Heritage makes no representation as to the accuracy of those translations and will not be held responsible for errors in bidding arising from inaccuracies in translation.
40. Auctioneer disclaims all liability for damages, consequential or otherwise, arising out of or in connection with the sale of any Property by Auctioneer to Bidder. No third party may rely on any benefit of these Terms and Conditions and any rights, if any, established hereunder are personal to the Bidder and may not be assigned. Any statement made by the Auctioneer is an opinion and does not constitute a warranty or representation. No employee of Auctioneer may alter these Terms and Conditions, and, unless signed by a principal of Auctioneer, any such alteration is null and void.
41. Auctioneer shall not be liable for breakage of glass or damage to frames (patent or latent); such defects, in any event, shall not be a basis for any claim for return or reduction in purchase price.

Release:

42. In consideration of participation in the Auction and the placing of a bid, Bidder expressly releases Auctioneer, its officers, directors and employees, its affiliates, and its outside experts that provide second opines, from any and all claims, cause of action, chose of action, whether at law or equity or any arbitration or mediation rights existing under the rules of any professional society or affiliation based upon the assigned description, or a derivative theory, breach of warranty express or implied, representation or other matter set forth within these Terms and Conditions of Auction or otherwise. In the event of a claim, Bidder agrees that such rights and privileges conferred therein are strictly construed as specifically declared herein; e.g., authenticity, typographical error, etc. and are the exclusive remedy. Bidder, by non-compliance to these express terms of a granted remedy, shall waive any claim against Auctioneer.

Dispute Resolution and Arbitration Provision:

43. By placing a bid or otherwise participating in the auction, Bidder accepts these Terms and Conditions of Auction, and specifically agrees to the alternative dispute resolution provided herein. Arbitration replaces the right to go to court, including the right to a jury trial.
44. Auctioneer in no event shall be responsible for consequential damages, incidental damages, compensatory damages, or other damages arising from the auction of any lot. In the event that Auctioneer cannot deliver the lot or subsequently it is established that the lot lacks title, provenance, authenticity, or other transfer or condition issue is claimed, Auctioneer's liability shall be limited to rescission of sale and refund of purchase price; in no case shall Auctioneer's maximum liability exceed the high bid on that lot, which bid shall be deemed for all purposes the value of the lot. After one year has elapsed, Auctioneer's maximum liability shall be limited to any commissions and fees Auctioneer earned on that lot.
45. In the event of an attribution error, Auctioneer may at its sole discretion, correct the error on the Internet, or, if discovered at a later date, to refund the buyer's purchase price without further obligation.
46. If any dispute arises regarding payment, authenticity, grading, description, provenance, or any other matter pertaining to the Auction, the Bidder or a participant in the Auction and/or the Auctioneer agree that the dispute shall be submitted, if otherwise mutually unresolved, to binding arbitration in accordance with the commercial rules of the American Arbitration Association (A.A.A.). A.A.A. arbitration shall be conducted under the provisions of the Federal Arbitration Act with locale in Dallas, Texas. Any claim made by a Bidder has to be presented within one (1) year or it is barred. The prevailing party may be awarded his reasonable attorney's fees and costs. An award granted in arbitration is enforceable in any court of competent jurisdiction. No claims of any kind (except for reasons of authenticity) can be considered after the settlements have been made with the consignors. Any dispute after the settlement date is strictly between the Bidder and consignor without involvement or responsibility of the Auctioneer.
47. In consideration of their participation in or application for the Auction, a person or entity (whether the successful Bidder, a Bidder, a purchaser and/or other Auction participant or registrant) agrees that all disputes in any way relating to, arising under, connected with, or incidental to these Terms and Conditions and purchases, or default in payment thereof, shall be arbitrated pursuant to the arbitration provision. In the event that any matter including actions to compel arbitration, construe the agreement, actions in aid or arbitration or otherwise needs to be litigated, such litigation shall be exclusively in the Courts of the State of Texas, in Dallas County, Texas, and if necessary the corresponding appellate courts. The successful Bidder, purchaser, or Auction participant also expressly submits himself to the personal jurisdiction of the State of Texas.
48. These Terms & Conditions provide specific remedies for occurrences in the auction and delivery process. Where such remedies are afforded, they shall be interpreted strictly. Bidder agrees that any claim shall utilize such remedies; Bidder making a claim in excess of those remedies provided in these Terms and Conditions agrees that in no case whatsoever shall Auctioneer's maximum liability exceed the high bid on that lot, which bid shall be deemed for all purposes the value of the lot..

Miscellaneous:

49. Agreements between Bidders and consignors to effectuate a non-sale of an item at Auction, inhibit bidding on a consigned item to enter into a private sale agreement for said item, or to utilize the Auctioneer's Auction to obtain sales for non-selling consigned items subsequent to the Auction, are strictly prohibited. If a subsequent sale of a previously consigned item occurs in violation of this provision, Auctioneer reserves the right to charge Bidder the applicable Buyer's Premium and consignor a Seller's Commission as determined for each auction venue and by the terms of the seller's agreement.
50. Acceptance of these Terms and Conditions qualifies Bidder as a Heritage customer who has consented to be contacted by Heritage in the future. In conformity with "do-not-call" regulations promulgated by the Federal or State regulatory agencies, participation by the Bidder is affirmative consent to being contacted at the phone number shown in his application and this consent shall remain in effect until it is revoked in writing. Heritage may from time to time contact Bidder concerning sale, purchase, and auction opportunities available through Heritage and its affiliates and subsidiaries.

State Notices:

Notice as to an Auction in California. Auctioneer has in compliance with Title 2.95 of the California Civil Code as amended October 11, 1993 Sec. 1812.600, posted with the California Secretary of State its bonds for it and its employees, and the auction is being conducted in compliance with Sec. 2338 of the Commercial Code and Sec. 535 of the Penal Code.

Notice as to an Auction in New York City. These Terms and Conditions are designed to conform to the applicable sections of the New York City Department of Consumer Affairs Rules and Regulations as Amended. This is a Public Auction Sale conducted by Auctioneer. The New York City licensed Auctioneers are Kathleen Guzman, No.0762165-Day, and Samuel W. Foose, No.0952360-Day, No.0952361-Night, who will conduct the Auction on behalf of Heritage Auctions, Inc. ("Auctioneer"). All lots are subject to: the consignor's right to bid thereon in accord with these Terms and Conditions of Auction, consignor's option to receive advances on their consignments, and Auctioneer, in its sole discretion, may offer limited extended financing to registered bidders, in accord with Auctioneer's internal credit standards. A registered bidder may inquire whether a lot is subject to an advance or reserve. Auctioneer has made advances to various consignors in this sale.

Rev. 2_15_07

ADDITIONAL TERMS AND CONDITIONS OF AUCTION

COINS and CURRENCY TERM A: Signature Auctions are not on approval. No certified material may be returned because of possible differences of opinion with respect to the grade offered by any third-party organization, dealer, or service. No guarantee of grade is offered for uncertified Property sold and subsequently submitted to a third-party grading service. There are absolutely no exceptions to this policy. Under extremely limited circumstances, (e.g. gross cataloging error) a purchaser, who did not bid from the floor, may request Auctioneer to evaluate voiding a sale: such request must be made in writing detailing the alleged gross error; submission of the lot to the Auctioneer must be pre-approved by the Auctioneer; and bidder must notify Ron Brackemyre (1-800-872-6467 ext. 312) in writing of such request within three (3) days of the non-floor bidder's receipt of the lot. Any lot that is to be evaluated must be in our offices within 30 days after Auction. Grading or method of manufacture do not qualify for this evaluation process nor do such complaints constitute a basis to challenge the authenticity of a lot. AFTER THAT 30-DAY PERIOD, NO LOTS MAY BE RETURNED FOR REASONS OTHER THAN AUTHENTICITY. Lots returned must be housed intact in their original holder. No lots purchased by floor Bidders may be returned (including those Bidders acting as agents for others) except for authenticity. Late remittance for purchases may be considered just cause to revoke all return privileges.

COINS and CURRENCY TERM B: Auctions conducted solely on the Internet THREE (3) DAY RETURN POLICY: Certified Coin and Uncertified Currency lots paid for within seven days of the Auction closing are sold with a three (3) day return privilege. Third party graded notes are not returnable for any reason whatsoever. You may return lots under the following conditions: Within three days of receipt of the lot, you must first notify Auctioneer by contacting Client Service by phone (1-800-872-6467) or e-mail (Bid@HA.com), and immediately ship the lot(s) fully insured to the attention of Returns, Heritage, 3500 Maple Avenue, 17th Floor, Dallas TX 75219-3941. Lots must be housed intact in their original holder and condition. You are responsible for the insured, safe delivery of any lots. A non-negotiable return fee of 5% of the purchase price ($10 per lot minimum) will be deducted from the refund for each returned lot or billed directly. Postage and handling fees are not refunded. After the three-day period (from receipt), no items may be returned for any reason. Late remittance for purchases revokes these Return privileges.

COINS and CURRENCY TERM C: Bidders who have inspected the lots prior to any Auction will not be granted any return privileges, except for reasons of authenticity.

COINS and CURRENCY TERM D: Coins sold referencing a third-party grading service are sold "as is" without any express or implied warranty, except for a guarantee by Auctioneer that they are genuine. Certain warranties may be available from the grading services and the Bidder is referred to them for further details: ANACS, P.O. Box 182141, Columbus, Ohio 43218-2141; Numismatic Guaranty Corporation (NGC), P.O. Box 4776, Sarasota, FL 34230; Professional Coin Grading Service (PCGS), PO Box 9458, Newport Beach, CA 92658; and Independent Coin Grading Co. (ICG), 7901 East Belleview Ave., Suite 50, Englewood, CO 80111.

COINS and CURRENCY TERM E: Notes sold referencing a third-party grading service are sold "as is" without any express or implied warranty, except for guarantee by Auctioneer that they are genuine. Grading, condition or other attributes of any lot may have a material effect on its value, and the opinion of others, including third-party grading services such as PCGS Currency, PMG, and CGA may differ with that of Auctioneer. Auctioneer shall not be bound by any prior or subsequent opinion, determination, or certification by any grading service. Bidder specifically waives any claim to right of return of any item because of the opinion, determination, or certification, or lack thereof, by any grading service. Certain warranties may be available from the grading services and the Bidder is referred to them for further details: Paper Money Guaranty (PMG), PO Box 4711, Sarasota FL 34230; PCGS Currency, PO Box 9458, Newport Beach, CA 92658; Currency Grading & Authentication (CGA), PO Box 418, Three Bridges, NJ 08887. Third party graded notes are not returnable for any reason whatsoever.

COINS and CURRENCY TERM F: Since we cannot examine encapsulated coins or notes, they are sold "as is" without our grading opinion, and may not be returned for any reason. Auctioneer shall not be liable for any patent or latent defect or controversy pertaining to or arising from any encapsulated collectible. In any such instance, purchaser's remedy, if any, shall be solely against the service certifying the collectible.

COINS and CURRENCY TERM G: Due to changing grading standards over time, differing interpretations, and to possible mishandling of items by subsequent owners, Auctioneer reserves the right to grade items differently than shown on certificates from any grading service that accompany the items. Auctioneer also reserves the right to grade items differently than the grades shown in the prior catalog should such items be reconsigned to any future auction.

COINS and CURRENCY TERM H: Although consensus grading is employed by most grading services, it should be noted as aforesaid that grading is not an exact science. In fact, it is entirely possible that if a lot is broken out of a plastic holder and resubmitted to another grading service or even to the same service, the lot could come back with a different grade assigned.

COINS and CURRENCY TERM I: Certification does not guarantee protection against the normal risks associated with potentially volatile markets. The degree of liquidity for certified coins and collectibles will vary according to general market conditions and the particular lot involved. For some lots there may be no active market at all at certain points in time.

COINS and CURRENCY TERM J: All non-certified coins and currency are guaranteed genuine, but are not guaranteed as to grade, since grading is a matter of opinion, an art and not a science, and therefore the opinion rendered by the Auctioneer or any third party grading service may not agree with the opinion of others (including trained experts), and the same expert may not grade the same item with the same grade at two different times. Auctioneer has graded the non-certified numismatic items, in the Auctioneer's opinion, to their current interpretation of the American Numismatic Association's standards as of the date the catalog was prepared. There is no guarantee or warranty implied or expressed that the grading standards utilized by the Auctioneer will meet the standards of any grading service at any time in the future.

COINS and CURRENCY TERM K: Storage of purchased coins and currency: Purchasers are advised that certain types of plastic may react with a coin's metal or transfer plasticizer to notes and may cause damage. Caution should be used to avoid storage in materials that are not inert.

COINS and CURRENCY TERM L: NOTE: Purchasers of rare coins or currency through Heritage have available the option of arbitration by the Professional Numismatists Guild (PNG); if an election is not made within ten (10) days of an unresolved dispute, Auctioneer may elect either PNG or A.A.A. Arbitration.

WIRING INSTRUCTIONS:
Bank Information: JP Morgan Chase Bank, N.A., 270 Park Avenue, New York, NY 10017
Account Name: HERITAGE NUMISMATIC AUCTIONS MASTER ACCOUNT
ABA Number: 021000021
Account Number: 1884827674
Swift Code: CHASUS33

CHOOSE YOUR BIDDING METHOD

Mail Bidding at Auction

Mail bidding at auction is fun and easy and only requires a few simple steps.

1. Look through the catalog, and determine the lots of interest.
2. Research their market value by checking price lists and other price guidelines.
3. Fill out your bid sheet, entering your maximum bid on each lot using your price research and your desire to own the lot.
4. Verify your bids!
5. Mail Early. Preference is given to the first bids received in case of a tie. When bidding by mail, you frequently purchase items at less than your maximum bid.

Bidding is opened at the published increment above the second highest mail or Internet bid; we act on your behalf as the highest mail bidder. If bidding proceeds, we act as your agent, bidding in increments over the previous bid. This process is continued until you are awarded the lot or you are outbid.

An example of this procedure: You submit a bid of $100, and the second highest mail bid is at $50. Bidding starts at $51 on your behalf. If no other bids are placed, you purchase the lot for $51. If other bids are placed, we bid for you in the posted increments until we reach your maximum bid of $100. If bidding passes your maximum: if you are bidding through the Internet, we will contact you by e-mail; if you bid by mail, we take no other action. Bidding continues until the final bidder wins.

Mail Bidding Instructions

1. **Name, Address, City, State, Zip**
   Your address is needed to mail your purchases. We need your telephone number to communicate any problems or changes that may affect your bids.

2. **References**
   If you have not established credit with us from previous auctions, you must send a 25% deposit, or list dealers with whom you have credit established.

3. **Lot Numbers and Bids**
   List all lots you desire to purchase. On the reverse are additional columns; you may also use another sheet. Under "Amount" enter the maximum you would pay for that lot (whole dollar amounts only). We will purchase the lot(s) for you as much below your bids as possible.

4. **Total Bid Sheet**
   Add up all bids and list that total in the appropriate box.

5. **Sign Your Bid Sheet**
   By signing the bid sheet, you have agreed to abide by the Terms of Auction listed in the auction catalog.

6. **Fax Your Bid Sheet**
   When time is short submit a Mail Bid Sheet on our exclusive Fax Hotline. There's no faster method to get your bids to us *instantly*. Simply use the **Heritage Fax Hotline number: 214-443-8425**.

   When you send us your original after faxing, mark it "Confirmation of Fax" (preferably in red!)

7. **Bidding Increments**
   To facilitate bidding, please consult the following chart. Bids will be accepted on the increments or on the half increments.

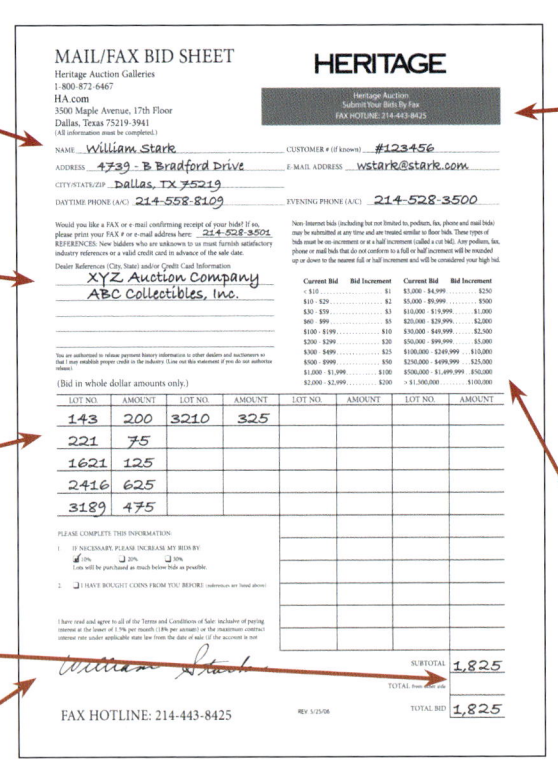

The official prices realized list that accompanies our auction catalogs is reserved for bidders and consignors only. We are happy to mail one to others upon receipt of $1.00. Written requests should be directed to Customer Service.

10_5_06

CHOOSE YOUR BIDDING METHOD (CONT'D.)

Interactive Internet Bidding

You can now bid with Heritage's exclusive *Interactive Internet* program, available only at our web site: HA.com. It's fun, and it's easy!

1. Register online at: **HA.com**
2. View the full-color photography of every single lot in the online catalog!
3. Construct your own personal catalog for preview.
4. View the current opening bids on lots you want; review the prices realized archive.
5. Bid and receive immediate notification if you are the top bidder; later, if someone else bids higher, you will be notified automatically by e-mail.
6. The *Interactive Internet* program opens the lot on the floor at one increment over the second highest bid. As the high bidder, your secret maximum bid will compete for you during the floor auction, and it is possible that you may be outbid on the floor after Internet bidding closes. Bid early, as the earliest bird wins in the event of a tie bid.
7. After the sale, you will be notified of your success. It's that easy!

Interactive Internet Bidding Instructions

1. **Log Onto Website**
   Log onto **HA.com** and choose the portal you're interested in (i.e., coins, comics, movie posters, fine arts, etc.).

2. **Search for Lots**
   Search or browse for the lot you are interested in. You can do this from the home page, from the Auctions home page, or from the home page for the particular auction in which you wish to participate.

3. **Select Lots**
   Click on the link or the photo icon for the lot you want to bid on.

4. **Enter Bid**
   At the top of the page, next to a small picture of the item, is a box outlining the current bid. Enter the amount of your secret maximum bid in the textbox next to "Secret Maximum Bid." The secret maximum bid is the maximum amount you are willing to pay for the item you are bidding on (for more information about bidding and bid increments, please see the section labeled "Bidding Increments" elsewhere in this catalog). Click on the button marked "Place Absentee Bid." A new area on the same page will open up for you to enter your username (or e-mail address) and password. Enter these, then click "Place Absentee Bid" again.

5. **Confirm Absentee Bid**
   You are taken to a page labeled, "Please Confirm Your Bid." This page shows you the name of the item you're bidding on, the current bid, and the maximum bid. When you are satisfied that all the information shown is correct, click on the button labeled, "Confirm Bid."

6. **Bidding Status Notification**
   One of two pages is now displayed.

   a. If your bid is the current high bid, you will be notified and given additional information as to what might happen to affect your high bidder status over the course of the remainder of the auction. You will also receive a Bid Confirmation notice via email.

   b. If your bid is not the current high bid, you will be notified of that fact and given the opportunity to increase your bid.

10_5_06

Heritage Auction Galleries Staff

Steve Ivy - Co-Chairman and CEO

Steve Ivy began collecting and studying rare coins in his youth, and as a teenager in 1963 began advertising coins for sale in national publications. Seven years later, at the age of twenty, he opened Steve Ivy Rare Coins in downtown Dallas, and in 1976, Steve Ivy Numismatic Auctions was incorporated. Steve managed the business as well as serving as chief numismatist, buying and selling hundreds of millions of dollars of coins during the 1970s and early 1980s. In early 1983, James Halperin became a full partner, and the name of the corporation was changed to Heritage Rare Coin Galleries. Steve's primary responsibilities now include management of the marketing and selling efforts of the company, the formation of corporate policy for long-term growth, and corporate relations with financial institutions. He remains intimately involved in numismatics, attending all major national shows. Steve engages in daily discourse with industry leaders on all aspects of the rare coin/currency business, and his views on grading, market trends and hobby developments are respected throughout the industry. He serves on the Board of Directors of the Professional Numismatists Guild (and was immediate past president), is the current Chairman of The Industry Council for Tangible Assets, and is a member of most leading numismatic organizations. Steve's keen appreciation of history is reflected in his active participation in other organizations, including past or present board positions on the Texas Historical Foundation and the Dallas Historical Society (where he also served as Exhibits Chairman). Steve is an avid collector of Texas books, manuscripts, and national currency, and he owns one of the largest and finest collections in private hands. He is also a past Board Chair of Dallas Challenge, and is currently the Finance Chair of the Phoenix House of Texas.

James Halperin - Co-Chairman

Jim Halperin and the traders under his supervision have transacted billions of dollars in rare coin business, and have outsold all other numismatic firms every year for over two decades. Born in Boston in 1952, Jim attended Middlesex School in Concord from 1966 to 1970. At the age of 15, he formed a part-time rare coin business after discovering that he had a knack (along with a nearly photographic memory) for coins. Jim scored a perfect 800 on his math SATs and received early acceptance to Harvard College, but after attending three semesters, he took a permanent leave of absence to pursue his full-time numismatic career. In 1975, Jim personally supervised the protocols for the first mainframe computer system in the numismatic business, which would catapult New England Rare Coin Galleries to the top of the industry in less than four years. In 1983, Jim merged with his friend and former archrival Steve Ivy, whom Jim had long admired. Their partnership has become the world's largest and most successful numismatic company, as well as the third-largest auctioneer in America. Jim remains arguably the best "eye" in the coin business today (he won the professional division of the PCGS World Series of Grading). In the mid-1980s, he authored "How to Grade U.S. Coins" (now posted on the web at www.CoinGrading.com), a highly-acclaimed text upon which the NGC and PCGS grading standards would ultimately be based. Jim is a bit of a Renaissance man, as a well-known futurist, an active collector of EC comics and early 20th-century American art (visit www.jhalpe.com), venture capital investor, philanthropist (he endows a multimillion-dollar health education foundation), and part-time novelist. His first fictional novel, "The Truth Machine," was published in 1996 and became an international science fiction bestseller, and was optioned for movie development by Warner Brothers. Jim's second novel, "The First Immortal," was published in early 1998 and immediately optioned as a Hallmark Hall of Fame television miniseries. Jim is married to Gayle Ziaks, and they have two sons, David and Michael. In 1996, with funding from Jim and Gayle's foundation, Gayle founded Dallas' Dance for the Planet, which has grown to become the largest free dance festival in the world.

Greg Rohan - President

At the age of eight, Greg Rohan started collecting coins as well as buying them for resale to his schoolmates. By 1971, at the age of ten, he was already buying and selling coins from a dealer's table at trade shows in his hometown of Seattle. His business grew rapidly, and by 1985 he had offices in both Seattle and Minneapolis. He joined Heritage in 1987 as Executive Vice-President and Manager of the firm's rare coin business. Today, as an owner and as President of Heritage, his responsibilities include overseeing the firm's private client group and working with top collectors in every field in which Heritage is active. Greg has been involved with many of the rarest items and most important collections handled by the firm, including the purchase and/or sale of the Ed Trompeter Collection (the world's largest numismatic purchase according to the Guinness Book of World Records), the legendary 1894 San Francisco Dime, the 1838 New Orleans Half Dollar, and the 1804 Silver Dollar. During his career, Greg has handled more than $1 billion of rare coins, collectibles and art, and provided expert consultation concerning the authenticity and grade condition of coins for the Professional Coin Grading Service (PCGS). He has provided expert testimony for the United States Attorneys in San Francisco, Dallas, and Philadelphia, and for the Federal Trade Commission (FTC). He has worked with collectors, consignors, and their advisors regarding significant collections of books, manuscripts, comics, currency, jewelry, vintage movie posters, sports and entertainment memorabilia, decorative arts, and fine art. Additionally, Greg is a Sage Society member of the American Numismatic Society, and a member/life member of the PNG, ANA, and most other leading numismatic organizations. Greg is also Chapter Chairman for North Texas of the Young Presidents' Organization (YPO), and is an active supporter of the arts. Greg co-authored "The Collectors Estate Handbook," winner of the NLG's Robert Friedberg Award for numismatic book of the year. Mr. Rohan currently serves on the seven-person Advisory Board to the Federal Reserve Bank of Dallas, in his second appointed term. He and his wife, Lysa, are avid collectors of rare wine, Native American artifacts, and American art.

Paul Minshull - Chief Operating Officer

As Chief Operating Officer, Paul Minshull's managerial responsibilities include integrating sales, personnel, inventory, security and MIS for Heritage. His major accomplishments include overseeing the hardware migration from mainframe to PC, the software migration of all inventory and sales systems, and implementation of a major Internet presence. Heritage's successful employee-suggestion program has generated 200 or more ideas each month since 1995, and has helped increase employee productivity, expand business, and improve employee retention. Paul oversees the company's highly-regarded IT department, and has been the driving force behind Heritage's web development, now a significant portion of Heritage's future plans. As the only numismatic auction house that combines traditional floor bidding with active Internet bidding, the totally interactive system has catapulted Heritage to the top rare coin website (according to Forbes Magazine's "Best of the Web"). Paul was born in Michigan and came to Heritage in 1984 after 12 years as the General Manager of a plastics manufacturing company in Ann Arbor. Since 1987, he has been a general partner in Heritage Capital Properties, Sales Manager, Vice President of Operations, and Chief Operating Officer for all Heritage companies and affiliates since 1996. Paul maintains an active interest in sports and physical fitness, and he and his wife have three children.

Todd Imhof - Vice President

Unlike most professional numismatists, Todd Imhof did not start as a coin collector. Shortly after graduating college in 1987, Todd declined an offer from a prestigious Wall Street bank to join a former high school classmate who was operating a small rare coin company in the Seattle area. The rare coin industry was then undergoing huge changes after the advent of certified grading and growing computer technologies. Being new to the industry, Todd had an easier time than most embracing the new dynamics. He soon discovered a personal passion for rare coins, and for working with high-level collectors. Through his accomplishments, Todd enjoys a reputation envied by the entire numismatic community. During his earlier tenure with Hertzberg Rare Coins, it was named by Inc. magazine as one of the nation's fastest growing private companies 1989-1991. In 1991, Todd co-founded Pinnacle Rarities, Inc., a boutique-styled firm that specialized in servicing the rare coin industry's savviest and most prominent collectors. At 25, he was among the youngest people ever accepted into the Professional Numismatists Guild, and currently serves on its Consumer Protection Committee. In 1992, he was invited to join the Board of Directors for the Industry Council for Tangible Assets, serving as its Chairman 2002-2005. Todd served as Pinnacle's President until his decision to join Heritage in 2006. In the Morse Auction, he became the only person in history to purchase two $1mm+ coins during a single auction session! Todd serves Heritage's Legacy clients, many of whom had previously sought his counsel and found his expertise and integrity to be of great value. Todd really understands what collectors are trying to accomplish, and he has an uncanny ability to identify the perfect coins at the right prices while navigating complex and difficult deals with unsurpassed professionalism.

Leo Frese - Executive VP - Numismatic Auctions

Leo has been involved in numismatics for nearly 40 years, a professional numismatist since 1971, and has been with Heritage for over 20 years. He literally worked his way up the Heritage "ladder" through dedication, hard work, and a belief that the client is the most important asset Heritage has. He worked with Bob Merrill for nearly 15 years and now is the Director of Consignments. Leo has been actively involved in assisting clients sell nearly $500,000,000 in numismatic material. Leo was recently accepted as a member of PNG, is a life member of the ANA, and holds membership in FUN, CSNS, and other numismatic organizations. He believes education is the foremost building block in numismatics. Leo encourages all collectors to broaden their horizons, be actively involved in the hobby, and donate freely to YN organizations. Leo's interests include collecting Minnesota pottery and elegant Depression glass. Although travel is an important element of his job, he relishes time with his wife Wendy, children Alicen and Adam, and son-in-law Jeff.

David Mayfield - Consignment Director

David has been collecting and trading rare coins and currency for over 35 years. A chance encounter with his father's coin collection at the age of nine led to his lifetime interest. David has been buying and selling at coin shows since the age of 10. He became a full time coin & currency dealer in the mid-80s. David's main collecting interest is in all things Texas, specializing in currency and documents from the Republic of Texas. Being a sixth generation Texan whose family fought for Texas' independence has only increased the value and meaning of these historical artifacts for him. After more than two decades of marriage, David and Tammy have two wonderful sons, Brian and Michael.

Jim Jelinski - Consignment Director

A collector since age 8, Jim has been involved in numismatics over 5 decades, progressing from humble collector to professional dealer and educator. He is a Life Member of the *American Numismatic Association*, the *American Numismatic Society*, and other state and national organizations. Starting as Buyer for Paramount International Coin Corporation in 1972, he opened Essex Numismatic Properties in 1975 in New Hampshire. Later, positions at M.B. Simmons & Associates of Narberth, Pennsylvania included Director of Sales, Director of Marketing and Advertising, and Executive Vice President. In 1979, he reorganized Essex in Connecticut and, as Essex Numismatics, Inc., worked as COO and CFO. He joined the staff at Heritage as Senior Numismatist and Consignment Coordinator. Jim has two sons, and is actively involved in his church, and community; he just completed his 20th season of coaching youth athletics, and working in Boy Scouting as a troop leader and merit badge counselor. He has been a fund raiser for Paul Newman's "Hole in the Wall Gang" camp for terminally ill children, and for Boy Scouts. His personal diversions include fly fishing, sky diving, cooking, and wine collecting.

Sam Foose - Consignment Director and Auctioneer

Sam's professional career at Heritage divides neatly into two parts. Sam joined Heritage Numismatic Auctions, Inc. in 1993 as an Auction Coordinator. Over the next five years, Sam ran the day-to-day auction operations, ultimately rising to Assistant Auction Director, and began calling auctions. After serving as a Senior Manager and Consignment Director in other collectible fields outside of numismatics, Sam returned to Heritage in 2002 as a Consignment Director in time to help Heritage's expansion into other collectibles. Sam travels the country assisting clients who wish to liquidate their collections of coins, paper money, decorative arts, and sports collectibles. To Sam, helping consignors make the best decisions to maximize their returns from auctioning their properties is the most rewarding part of his job. Sam holds auction licenses in several jurisdictions, and has hammered in excess of $250 million in collectibles as one of Heritage's primary auctioneers. During his free time, Sam enjoys his wife (Heather) and two children (Jackson and Caroline), gardening, golf, grilling, and sports.

David Lisot - Consignment Director

David Lisot is in his fourth decade as a numismatist, writer, researcher, publisher, cataloger, public speaker, and website creator. His expertise includes US & world coins and paper money, gemstones, jewelry, stamps, pocket watches, art, postcards, cigar label art, and antique advertising. David is Director of Heritage's Coin Club Outreach program and a Consignment Director. An accomplished videographer and television producer, David produced the award-winning documentaries, *Money, History in Your Hands, Era of Hometown Bank Notes* for the Higgins Money Museum, and video productions for Heritage. He has videotaped over 750 lectures and presentations about coins and collecting as seen on Coinvideo.com. David was featured in the PBS series, *Money Moves* with Jack Gallagher, as a reporter for FNN, and as founder of CoinTelevision.com. David served as an ANA Governor and is a member of many numismatic organizations. He is a Philosophy graduate of the University of Colorado in Boulder, and a Graduate Gemologist from the GIA. David is married with two children, and enjoys travel, history, exercise, and religious studies.

Bob Marino - Consignment Director & Senior Numismatist

Bob started collecting coins in his youth, and started selling through eBay as the Internet became a serious collector resource. He joined Heritage in 1999, managing and developing Internet coin sales, and building Heritage's client base through eBay and other Internet auction websites. He has successfully concluded more than 40,000 transactions on eBay, selling millions of dollars of rare coins to satisfied clients. Many collectors were first introduced to Heritage through Bob's efforts, and he takes pride in dealing with each client on a personal level. Bob is now a Consignment Director, assisting consignors in placing their coins and collectibles in the best of the many Heritage venues – in short, maximizing their return on many of the coins that he sold to them previously! Bob and his family moved to the DFW area from the Bitterroot Valley in Western Montana. He enjoys spending time with his family, woodworking (building furniture), and remodeling his house.

Charles Clifford - Consignment Director
Charles has been involved with collectibles for over 35 years. His first venture with coins began in the 1970s when he drove to banks all over North Texas buying bags of half dollars to search for the 40% silver clad coins. He has worked as a bullion trader, a rare coin buyer, worked in both wholesale and retail sales, served as a cataloger, and has traveled to hundreds of coin and sports card conventions across the country. Charles also has the distinction of working with Steve Ivy over four decades! Currently he is assisting clients obtain top dollar for the items they have for sale, either by direct purchase or by placing their material in auction. He appreciates Heritage's total commitment to "World Class Client Service" and the "Can Do - Nothing is Impossible" attitude of management and each and every employee. He enjoys collecting hand-blown Depression glass and antique aquarium statues.

Mike Sadler - Consignment Director
Mike Sadler joined the Heritage team in September 2003. Mike attended the United States Air Force Academy, earning a degree in civil engineering and pinned on his silver wings in June 1985. After seven years flying various aircraft, he joined American Airlines where he still pilots. More than once, Mike has surprised Heritage employees serving as their pilot while they flew to shows, conventions, and to visit clients. Like so many of our clients, Mike started putting together sets of coins from circulation when he was a small boy, and that collection grew to go to the auction block with Heritage in January 2004. Before coming to Heritage, his unlimited access to air travel enabled him to attend coin shows all around the country. He gained a tremendous knowledge of rare coins and developed an outstanding eye for quality. He is a trusted friend and colleague to many of today's most active collectors. Having been a collector for so long, and a Heritage consignor himself, Mike understands the needs of the collector and what Heritage can offer. Mike is married, has three children, and enjoys coaching and playing lacrosse

David Lewis - Consigment Director
David Lewis joined Heritage in 2005 as a numismatist, with an extensive numismatic background in wholesale, retail, and internet sales. David's current duties are focused on Heritage's website features, especially "Ask an Expert" and "Coins and Currency Questions", as well as telephone consignments and purchases of rare coins and collections. David is a 22-year veteran of the United States Air Force, and has more than 5000 hours of flight-time as an Airborne Mission Supervisor and Hebrew linguist. David is the winner of the Numismatic Guarantee Corporation's 2004 and 2005 Best Presented Registry Set Awards, and is an avid collector of Washington Quarters and quarter varieties. He holds membership in the ANA, CSNS, and the Barber Coin Collectors Society, among other organizations. David's interests include flying, world travel, history, and collecting Art Deco ceramics and antiques.

Katherine Kurachek - Consignment Director
Katherine grew up in Sarasota, Florida, graduated from the University of Mississippi in 1993 as an art major, and then resided in Colorado (where she opened a pizzeria!) before moving to Dallas. Acting on a suggestion from her father, an avid collector of type coins and a client of Steve Ivy for more than two decades, Katherine came to Heritage in January 2003. She worked alongside Leo Frese for several years, honing her experience in dealing with the numismatic wholesale trade. Taking care of the needs of our dealer-consignors includes soliciting the consignments, inputting the material into our computer systems, and ensuring the smooth flow of the consignment through the many production processes. Katherine is now frequently traveling to coin shows to represent Heritage and service her dealer accounts.In her spare time, she enjoys gardening, golf, hiking, fly-fishing, and walking her two Akitas (Moses and April). Katherine has finally inherited her father's love of these pieces of history, and currently collects love tokens and counterstamps.

Robert Phillips - Consignment Director
Robert developed his lifelong passion for coin collecting in 1st grade after his grandmother gave him a Whitman Lincoln Cent folder for his 6th birthday. He has since expanded his collecting interests to include all U.S. coins and paper money, as well as those of Australia and Spain. His collecting fervor extends to boomerangs, Colt and Smith & Wesson revolvers, and Cadillac memorabilia. Robert worked through college in a pawnshop, and regularly attended gun, coin and antique shows to buy, sell, and trade. After earning undergraduate & advanced degrees in a technical scientific field, he spent the next 15 years negotiating and fulfilling contracts with government entities across the U.S. As a physical fitness buff, Robert enjoys jogging & bodybuilding, while his favorite leisure activities include water surfing, trap and skeet shooting, genealogy, and his various collecting interests. His wife, Natividad, a Professor of Romance Languages, is a native of Barcelona, and an avid art enthusiast. Together, Robert and Natividad have visited most of the world's premier art museums, including the Louvre, Vatican, Prado and Uffizi.

Harvey Gamer - Consignment Director
Harv Gamer has been collecting coins since the mid-1950s, but unlike most young collectors then, he pursued world coins. Selling his first coin for a profit in 1958, he began dealing as a California teenager. After high school, Harvey joined the USAF in 1967. After his service, he started on the coin show circuit, traveling regularly around the U.S. and Canada. In more recent years, Harv operated his own coin store in Canada. When his wife was offered a job transfer to Dallas, Harv joined the Heritage team. He just celebrated his 25th ANA anniversary, and is also a member of CNA, CNS, AINA, TAMS, and NTCA. Harv has been a Contributor to the *Standard Catalog of United States Tokens 1700-1900* by Russ Rulau and *American and Canadian Countermarked Coins* by Dr. Gregory Brunk.

Mark Van Winkle - Chief Cataloger
Mark has worked for Heritage (and Steve Ivy) since 1979. He has been Chief Cataloger since 1990, and has handled some of the premier numismatic rarities sold at public auction. Mark's literary achievements are considerable. He was editor of *Legacy* magazine, won the 1989 NLG award for Best U.S. Commercial Magazine, and the next year won another NLG award for Best Article with his "Interview With John Ford." In 1996 he was awarded the NLG's Best Numismatic Article "Changing Concepts of Liberty," and was accorded a third place Heath Literary Award that same year. He has done extensive research and published his findings on Branch Mint Proof Morgan Dollars, in addition to writing numerous articles for *Coin World* and *Numismatic News*. Mark has also contributed to past editions of the *Red Book*, and helped with the Standard Silver series in Andrew Pollock's *United States Patterns and Related Issues*. He was also a contributor to *The Guide Book of Double Eagle Gold Coins*.

Mark Borckardt - Senior Cataloger
Mark started attending coin shows and conventions as a dealer in 1970, and has been a full-time professional numismatist since 1980. He received the Early American Coppers Literary Award, and the Numismatic Literary Guild's Book of the Year Award, for the *Encyclopedia of Early United States Cents, 1793-1814*, published in 2000. He serves as a contributor to *A Guide Book of United States Coins*, and has contributed to many references, including the Harry W. Bass, Jr. Sylloge, and the *Encyclopedia of Silver Dollars and Trade Dollars of the United States*. Most recently, he was Senior Numismatist with Bowers and Merena Galleries, serving as a major contributor to all of that firm's landmark auctions. Mark is a life member of the A. N. A., and an active member of numerous organizations. He is an avid collector of numismatic literature, holding several thousand volumes in his library, as well as related postcards and ephemera. He is an avid bowler, carrying an 200+ average, and with seven perfect 300 games. Mark is a graduate of the University of Findlay (Ohio) with a Bachelors Degree in Mathematics. Mark and his wife have a 20-something year old son, and twin daughters who are enrolled at Baylor.

Brian Koller - Cataloger & Catalog Production Manager
Brian's attention to detail ensures that every catalog, printed and on-line, is as error free as technology and human activity allows. In addition to his coin cataloging duties, he also helps with consignor promises and client service issues. Brian has been a Heritage cataloger since 2001, and before that he worked as a telecom software engineer for 16 years. He is a graduate of Iowa State University with a Bachelor's degree in Computer Engineering, and is an avid collector of U.S. gold coins. Brian's numismatic footnote is as discoverer of a 1944-D half dollar variety that has the designer's monogram engraved by hand onto a working die. In addition to describing many thousands of coins in Heritage catalogs, Brian has written more than one thousand reviews of classic movies, which can be found on his website, filmsgraded.com.

John Salyer - Cataloger
John has been a numismatist and coin cataloger with Heritage since 2002. He began collecting Lincoln Cents, Jefferson Nickels, Mercury and Roosevelt Dimes, and Franklin Halves at the age of eleven, as a sixth-grader in Fort Worth; his best friend was also a collector, and his dad would drive them to coin shops and flea markets in search of numismatic treasures. The two youngsters even mowed lawns together in order to purchase their coins, which were always transferred into Whitman folders. John graduated from the University of Texas with a bachelor's degree in English. Prior to his numismatic employment, he worked primarily within the federal government and for several major airlines. His hobbies include playing guitar and collecting antique postcards; an avid golfer, he also enjoys spending time on the links. John has enjoyed making his former hobby his current occupation, and he still actively collects coins.

Jon Amato - Cataloger
Jon has been with Heritage since 2004. He was previously a Program Manager in the NY State Dept. of Economic Development, and an Adjunct Professor at the State University of New York at Albany, where he taught economic geography, natural disasters assessment, and environmental management. Jon is currently writing a monograph on the draped bust, small eagle half dollars of 1796-1797; his research included surveying more than 4,000 auction catalogs, recording the descriptions, grades, and photos of 1796-1797 halves. He published an article entitled "Surviving 1796-1797 Draped Bust Half Dollars and their Grade Distribution," in the *John Reich Journal*, February 2005, and also wrote "An Analysis of 1796-1797 Draped Bust Half Dollars," in *The Numismatist*, Sept. 2001. Jon belongs to many numismatic organizations, including the ANA, ANS, John Reich Collectors Society, and the Liberty Seated Collectors Club, and has made several presentations at ANA Numismatic Theaters. He earned a bachelor's degree from Arizona State University, an M.A. from the S. U. N. Y. at Buffalo, and a Ph. D. from the University of Toronto.

Greg Lauderdale - Cataloger
Greg grew up in Dallas, and began working in a coin shop there in 1979. His interest in numismatics and his trading skills blossomed, and he became a Life Member of the ANA only two years later in 1981. During the 1980s, he conducted several coin auctions in the Dallas Area, including several for the Dallas Coin Club show. He first contracted with Heritage to help write the 1985 Baltimore ANA catalog. He joined Heritage full-time in September of 1985, working as a cataloger and a coin buyer. Greg "left" Heritage in 1988 to develop his personal rare coin company, but has continued to split his time between cataloging for Heritage and trading on eBay from his new home in Maui. Greg has also developed into quite a 'presence' in the world of rare and early Hawaiian postcards. For bidders who attend Heritage's auctions, Greg can often be seen working at the front table – one of the few catalogers in America who is actively involved in the selling process!

John Beety - Cataloger
John grew up in Logansport, Indiana, a small town associated with several numismatic luminaries. Highlights as a Young Numismatist include attending Pittman III, four ANA Summer Seminars (thanks to various YN scholarships), and placing third in the 2001 World Series of Numismatics with Eric Li Cheung. He accepted a position with Heritage as a cataloger immediately after graduation from Rose-Hulman Institute of Technology, after serving an internship at Heritage during the summer of 2004. In addition to his numismatic interests, he enjoys many types of games, with two state junior titles in chess and an appearance in the Top 20 Juniors list of the World Blitz Chess Association.

Steven R. Roach, J.D. - Director, Trusts and Estates
As both a licensed attorney and a seasoned numismatist, Steve is in a unique position to help heirs, nonprofit institutions, attorneys, and advisors with their collectible assets. In his more than 15 years in the coin industry, he has worked with many of the best, including positions at Heritage as a senior grader and numismatist, ANACS as a grader, and stints with Christie's and Spink-America in New York, and PCGS in Los Angeles. Steve writes the popular "Inside Collecting" column in Coin World, and has received two Numismatic Literary Guild (NLG) awards. He received his JD from The Ohio State University Moritz College of Law. He was a judicial extern to United States District Court Judge Gregory Frost, and a summer research fellow for the American Bar Association Section on Dispute Resolution in Washington, D.C. Steve received his BA with high honors from the University of Michigan with a dual degree in the History of Art and Organizational Studies, receiving the Tappan award for outstanding performance in the History of Art program, and studied in Florence, Italy. He is a life member of the American Numismatic Association, and a member of the American Bar Association, the Dallas Bar Association, the Dallas Association of Young Lawyers, and the Dallas Estate Planning Council.

Norma L. Gonzalez - VP of Operations - Numismatic Auctions
Born in Dallas, Texas, Norma joined the U.S. Navy in August of 1993. During her five-year enlistment, she received her Bachelor's Degree in Resource Management and traveled to Japan, Singapore, Thailand and lived in Cuba for three years. After her enlistment, she moved back to Dallas where her family resides. Norma joined Heritage in 1998; always ready for a challenge, she spent her days at Heritage and her nights pursuing an M. B. A. She was promoted to Vice President in 2003. She currently manages the operations departments, including Coins, Currency, World & Ancient Coins, Sportscards & Memorabilia, Comics, Movie Posters, Pop Culture and Political Memorabilia. Norma enjoys running, biking and spending time with her family. In February 2004 she ran a 26.2-mile marathon in Austin, Texas and later, in March she accomplished a 100-mile bike ride in California.

Kelley Norwine - VP - Marketing
Born and raised in South Carolina, Kelley pursued a double major at Southern Wesleyan University, earning a BA in Music Education and a BS in Business Management. A contestant in the Miss South Carolina pageant, Kelley was later Regional Manager & Director of Training at Bank of Travelers Rest in South Carolina. Relocating to Los Angeles, Kelley became the Regional Manager and Client Services Director for NAS-McCann World Group, an international Advertising & Communications Agency where she was responsible for running one of the largest offices in the country. During her years with NAS Kelley was the recipient of numerous awards including Regional Manager of the Quarter and the NAS Courage and Dedication award. After relocating to Dallas, Kelley took a job as Director of Client Services for TMP/Monster Worldwide and joined Heritage in 2005 as Director of Client Development. She was named VP of Marketing for Heritage in 2007. A cancer survivor, Kelley is an often-requested motivational speaker for the American Cancer Society. In her spare time, she writes music, sings, and plays the piano.

John Petty - Director - Media Relations
John Petty joined Heritage in 2001 as the first employee of the newly-formed Heritage Comics division, anxious to join the exciting auction industry. A passionate collector, comics historian, and Overstreet advisor, John had a life-long interest in comics. In 2004, John became the Director of Media Relations, and now handles public relations, copywriting, and media affairs for Heritage Auction Galleries. He also works on special assignments such as magazine articles, book projects, and TV productions. John is also one of Heritage's popular auctioneers, and can frequently be seen calling Movie Poster, Entertainment, and Fine & Decorative Art auctions. Currently, John co-writes monthly columns for both *The Comics Buyers Guide* and *Big Reel Magazine*. Originally from the New York area, John now lives in Texas with Judy, his significant other, two dogs, and three cats. He holds a Bachelor of Music degree in Voice from Baldwin-Wallace College in Berea, Ohio. In his spare time, John enjoys leather carving, silent movies, and Celtic music.

Marti Korver - Manager - Credits/Collections
Marti has been working in numismatics for more than three decades. She was recruited out of the banking profession by Jim Ruddy, and she worked with Paul Rynearson, Karl Stephens, and Judy Cahn on ancients and world coins at Bowers & Ruddy Galleries, in Hollywood, CA. She migrated into the coin auction business, running the bid books for such memorable sales as the Garrett Collection and representing bidders as agent at B&R auctions for 10 years. She also worked as a research assistant for Q. David Bowers for several years. Memorable events included such clients (and friends) as Richard Lobel, John Ford, Harry Bass, and John J. Pittman. She is married to noted professional numismatist and writer, Robert Korver, (who is sometimes seen auctioneering at coin shows) and they migrated to Heritage in Dallas in 1996. She has an RN daughter (who worked her way through college showing lots for Heritage) and a son (who is currently a college student and sometimes a Heritage employee) and a type set of dogs (one black and one white). She currently collects kitschy English teapots and compliments.

DENOMINATION INDEX

Early American Coins 1-13
Half Cents 14-21
Large Cents... 22-51
Small Cents 52-225
Two Cent Pieces 226-238
Three Cent Silver 239-256
Three Cent Nickels 257-283
Nickels 284-453
Half Dimes 454-492
Dimes.. 493-626
Twenty Cent Pieces 627-641
Quarters 642-846
Half Dollars... 847-1138
Silver Dollars 1139-1206, 1231-1920, 2217-2224
Trade Dollars 1207-1230
Gold Dollars... 2274-2330
Quarter Eagles 2331-2441
Three Dollar Pieces 2442-2486
Half Eagles 2487-2658
Eagles 2659-2801
Double Eagles 2802-3321
Territorial Gold 2225-2230, 3322-3362
Silver Commemoratives 1921-2104
Gold Commemoratives 2105-2164
Patterns... 2231-2273
Modern Issues 2165-2192
Coins of Hawaii... 2193-2196
Errors 2197-2211
Proof and Mint Sets 2184, 2186-2188, 2212-2216

A WORLD OF COLLECTIBLES

Paquet Liberty Double Eagle
Realized: $1,610,000
August 14, 2006

Babe Ruth Game Worn Jersey
Realized: $657,250
October 27, 2006

HERITAGE IS THE WORLD'S LARGEST Collectibles Auctioneer, with on-staff experts in a variety of fields, including:

- Coins
- Currency
- Fine Art
- Decorative Arts
- Comic Books
- Original Comic Art
- Sports Memorabilia
- Political Memorabilia & Americana
- Entertainment & Music Memorabilia
- Jewelry & Timepieces
- Vintage Movie Posters
- Character Memorabilia & Vintage Toys
- Autographs & Rare Manuscripts
- And Much More!

Thomas Moran Oil Painting
Realized: $567,625
November 8, 2006

Pre-Columbian Gold Figure
Realized: $155,350
September 28, 2006

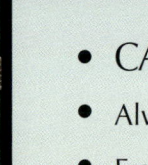

Kurt Cobain Guitar
Realized: $131,450
April 15, 2006

- **CASH FOR YOUR ITEMS**
- Always Accepting Consignments
- Free Appraisals by Appointments

Mickey Mouse Poster
Realized: $138,000
March 18, 2006

Whatever your area of interest, Heritage can help! Interested in selling the collection you've spent years putting together? Call one of our expert Consignment Directors today at 1-800-872-6467 and find out how easy it is to turn your treasures into cash.

And be sure to visit HA.com, where you can explore all of our exciting categories and join our on-line community of 275,000 members, all of whom enjoy a host of benefits that only Heritage can offer!

To receive a complimentary catalog of your choice, register online at HA.com/CAT7013, or call 866-835-3243 and mention reference #CAT7013.

Annual Sales Exceeding $500 Million • Over 300,000 Registered Online Bidder-Members

3500 Maple Ave, 17th Floor • Dallas, Texas 75219 • 214-528-3500 • 800-872-6467 • HA.com

Auctioneer: John Petty, TX license #00013740

HERITAGE HA.com
Auction Galleries

SESSION ONE

Live, Internet, and Mail Bid Signature Auction #442
Thursday, July 12, 2007, 1:00 PM ET, Lots 1-641
West Palm Beach, Florida

A 15% Buyer's Premium ($9 minimum) Will Be Added To All Lots

Visit HA.com to view full-color images and bid.

COLONIALS

VF Details Noe-27 Oak Tree Threepence

1 **1652 Oak Tree Threepence—Tooled—NCS. VF Details.** Crosby 5-B, Noe-27, R.5. 16.7 gns. This full weight threepence has intact legends and bold centers. A mint-made clip is present at 3 o'clock, and both sides have greater wear along the border of the clip. Hairlined, but with little evidence of tooling. The obverse beads near the letter E more closely resemble Noe-27.1 than Noe-27, and this may be the cause of the NCS designation. Listed on page 36 of the 2007 Guide Book. (#18)

Scarce Noe-29 Pine Tree Shilling XF40

2 **1652 Pine Tree Shilling, Small Planchet XF40 NGC.** Crosby 14-R, Noe-29, R.3. 70.98 gns. A deep steel-gray example with an even strike and only a hint of verdigris. Late dies with slender cracks across the obverse border. The obverse is misaligned toward 10 o'clock, and the reverse is misaligned toward 12 o'clock, but the tree, date, and denomination are intact. On each side, about one-third of the peripheral letters are partly off the flan. Slightly wavy, as made. Listed on page 37 of the 2008 Guide Book. (#24)

3 **1758-A French Colonies Sou Marque VF35 PCGS.** Breen-417, V-39a, R.5. Second semester with dot under the D in LUD. Problem-free for the grade, with ample silvering within the legends and design. A few flecks of debris ensure the originality. Listed on page 51 of the 2008 Guide Book. (#158604)

1766 William Pitt Halfpenny AU50

4 **1766 Pitt Halfpenny AU50 PCGS.** Breen-251. William Pitt, beloved in England as "The Great Commoner," was hailed on the American side of the Atlantic as well. This was due to his opposition to the hated Stamp Act, which taxed commerce with the colonies. A medium brown representative with moderate wear and evenly striated surfaces. Listed on page 48 of the 2008 Guide Book. (#236)

5 **1787 Massachusetts Half Cent XF45 PCGS.** Ryder 4-C, R.2. A deep brown piece with a faint but fully legible HALF CENT. All other legends are bold. Moderate build-up is present, and close examination locates a few old field abrasions. Listed on page 57 of the 2008 Guide Book. (#296)

6 **1787 Connecticut Copper, Laughing Head—Corroded—NCS. AU Details.** M. 6.2-M, R.4, significantly scarcer than the usual M. 6.1-M Laughing Head dies. The usual die state for M. 6.2-M with an obverse crack to the rim at 6:30. A boldly struck and well centered mahogany-brown representative with minor peripheral granularity and three obverse planchet flaws between 3 and 6 o'clock. The seated effigy has a couple of parallel marks on the legs. Listed on page 59 of the 2008 Guide Book. (#358)

Desirable 1787 Seated Left Nova Eborac MS62

7 **1787 Nova Eborac Copper, Seated Left MS62 Brown PCGS.** Breen-986. Golden-brown and gunmetal-gray embrace this boldly defined Nova Eborac. Traces of the original mint color reside within protected areas. A mint-made edge flaw at 1:30 does not impact the design. Struck perhaps 5% off center, toward 7 o'clock. Listed on page 65 of the 2007 Guide Book. Population: 3 in 62, 4 finer (5/07). (#478)

8   **1787 Vermont Copper, BRITANNIA XF45 PCGS.** RR-13, Bressett 17-V, R.1. A popular variety caused when a counterfeit British halfpenny reverse die was paired with a genuine Vermont obverse die. A pleasing deep golden-brown and mahogany example. The reverse legends are blurry, as always, but the obverse is bold. Listed on page 68 of the 2008 *Guide Book*. (#554)

9   **1787 Vermont Copper, BRITANNIA XF45 PCGS.** RR-13, Bressett 17-V, R.1. This medium brown representative lacks the bold die crack on the neck seen on a different XF45 example in the present auction. The reverse has abrasions at 11:30 and 3 o'clock. Listed on page 68 of the 2008 *Guide Book*. (#554)

10 **1783 Nova Constellatio Copper, Blunt Rays AU55 PCGS.** Crosby 3-C, R.3. The only 1783-dated variety with the CONSTELATIO spelling. Intermingled olive and mahogany patina, with clear details and clean surfaces aside from a few wispy slide marks above the S in US. Struck with nearly medal turn. Listed on page 52 of the 2008 *Guide Book*. (#807)
Ex: Baltimore Signature, (Heritage, 7/03), lot 5081.

11 **1787 Fugio Cent, STATES UNITED, Cinquefoils VF20 PCGS.** Newman 12-M.1, R.4. A scarce die marriage. Richly detailed for the grade, particularly on MIND YOUR BUSINESS and the left side of the sundial. The centers have minor planchet flaws, and a small depression is noted at 2 o'clock on the obverse. Struck from clashed dies. Listed on page 83 of the 2008 *Guide Book*. (#883)

12 **1787 Fugio Cent, STATES UNITED, Eight-Pointed Stars—Corroded—ANACS. AU55 Details.** Newman 15-Y, R.3. This variety receives its own Guide Book listing, since it is the sole marriage with two eight-pointed stars on the reverse label. A radial obverse die crack is present at 4:30, but there is no die break yet on the 5 o'clock reverse ring. The obverse is unusually sharp except for the U in FUGIO, which may have been weakened by a possible counterpunch opposite. The dark brown surfaces exhibit a whisper of verdigris. (#898)

13 **1795 Washington Grate Halfpenny, Large Buttons, Reeded Edge MS63 Red and Brown PCGS.** Ex: Benson. Baker-29AA. Deep sea-green consumes the fields and the portrait, but substantial salmon-pink fills the legends and outlines the devices. The lower left reverse has a few curved planchet abrasions, as struck. (#747)
Ex: Benson Collection, Part I (Ira & Larry Goldberg, 2/01), lot 127; earlier purchased from Ira S. Reed in July 1944 for $5.

HALF CENTS

14 **1793—Corroded, Scratched—ANACS. Good 4 Details.** C-2, B-2, R.3. The granular ebony fields contrast with the tan-brown devices. The portrait has myriad wispy marks from verdigris removal. The reverse rim has a small nick at 5:30. EAC 3. (#1000)

15 **1802/0 Reverse of 1802 VG10 PCGS.** C-2, B-2, R.3. A deep brown better date half cent with bold legends aside from softer definition on HALF CENT. The reverse has a couple of faint, thin marks and the borders are mildly granular. EAC 5. (#1057)

16 **1806 Small 6, No Stems—Defective Planchet—AU58 ANACS.** C-1, B-3, R.1. A satiny mahogany-brown half cent with only trivial contact. A small rim defect is noted at 4 o'clock. Slightly soft on the bust tip and on the M in AMERICA. Struck from moderately rotated dies. EAC 40. (#1093)

17 **1809/6 AU53 PCGS.** C-5, B-5, R.1. Manley Die State 1.0. Primarily golden-brown with occasional glimpses of steel-blue on the cheek, bust tip, and reverse field. Three parallel hair-thin marks are present on the portrait. EAC 35. (#1126)

18 **1810 MS62 Brown NGC.** C-1, B-1, R.2, the only variety. Sharply struck in the centers, with some softness noted along the peripheries. Lustrous and appealing, with deep reddish-brown coloration and few marks. Census: 5 in 62, 5 finer (6/07). EAC 50. (#1132)

19 **1828 13 Stars MS64 Brown PCGS.** C-3, B-2, R.1. The obverse has light brown surfaces with clear red accents, while the reverse has similar color at the periphery with a medium brown center. Nicely struck and luminous with a single darkly toned hair curl just below the headband. In a green label holder. EAC 50. (#1147)

20 **1835 MS65 Brown NGC.** C-1, B-1, R.1. The surfaces of this lovely later Classic Head example display warm mahogany and rosewood tones with a touch of violet on the reverse. Well-defined overall with only a touch of softness on the hair. EAC 60. (#1168)
From The Vanek Collection.

21 **1851 MS64 Brown PCGS.** C-1, B-1, R-1. A beautiful chocolate-brown near-Gem. Well struck aside from the leaves opposite Liberty's high relief shoulder. Housed in a first generation holder. EAC 60. (#1224)

LARGE CENTS

Nicely Detailed Chain AMERICA Cent, Fine Details, S-3

22 **1793 Chain AMERICA—Damaged—NCS. Fine Details.** S-3, B-4, Low R.3. The R in LIBERTY is high, large, and leans right, and AMERICA is spelled out in full. Medium to dark brown surfaces display several small, shallow punch marks scattered over both sides. Fortunately, these do not, for the most part, interfere with the design detail, that shows up rather nicely. EAC 5. (#1341)

Sharply Defined 1793 S-3 Chain Cent

23   **1793 Chain AMERICA AU53 PCGS.** S-3, B-4, Low R.3. The obverse surface has countless minute defects that are almost entirely planchet flaws, in our opinion, representing an improperly refined strip of copper, a common problem in the first year of Mint operations. A few tiny rim bumps are visible, and these appear to be the only post-strike imperfections.

In direct opposition to the obverse, the reverse surface is nearly flawless. Only a few minute defects, rim flaws, and abrasions can be seen. Both sides have lovely medium brown color with traces of darker steel color on the high points. Considerable original mint frost remains, with splashes of lighter tan on the reverse, faded from original mint red.

This example is a later die state. The obverse has prominent clash marks around and below the bust, and the reverse is flowlined with field roughening below UNITED STATES.

There is no question among specialists that Sheldon-3 is the most common Chain cent. Current rarity ratings for the Chain cent varieties suggest that the total surviving population of all varieties is 900 to 1,000 coins, with 400 to 500 examples of the S-3 and about 500 to 600 of all other varieties combined. Working under the assumption that the current rarity ratings are reasonably accurate, we can surmise that the original mintage occurred in about the same proportion. Approximately 18,000 examples of this die marriage were coined, with another 18,000 of the other three Sheldon numbers. EAC 40. (#1341)

24 **1793 Wreath Cent—Vine and Bars, Corroded—NCS. Good Details.** S-6, B-7, R.3. The "Sprung Die" with a mint-made obverse bulge in the field near 9 o'clock; this shows up better without a glass. Medium brown surfaces are moderately corroded. Part of Liberty's eye shows, as does the top of the 9 in the date. On the reverse, most of the wreath is outlined, as is ONE CENT; about a third of the peripheral lettering is clear. EAC 3. (#1347)

25 **1793 Wreath—Vine and Bars, Damaged—NCS. VG Details.** S-11a, B-16a, High R.4. A significantly worn but legible representative of this desirable Wreath cent variety, distinguished by the right-leaning trefoil below the bust and the vine and bars design of the edge. The chocolate-brown surfaces display a number of depressions and bruises, including one that obscures the 1 of the date and the tips of Liberty's hair, though the overall appearance is pleasing. EAC 4. (#1347)

VF Details S-9 1793 Wreath Cent

26 **1793 Wreath Cent—Vine and Bars, Corroded—NCS. VF Details.** S-9, B-12, R.2. A minutely granular mahogany-brown representative of this famous and important early copper type, struck only in year 1793. The obverse has unimportant planchet flaws beneath the chin and near the rim at 11 o'clock, but both sides are surprisingly free from abrasions. EAC 8. (#1347)

27 **1794 Head of 1794 VG10 ANACS.** S-30, B-12, R.1. The "First Marred Field" variety, equally distinctive for the bold die crack through the R in AMERICA. Deep golden-brown surfaces are smooth and only faintly abraded. The upper reverse is softly defined, as often seen with the marriage. EAC 7. (#901374)

28 **1794 Head of 1794—Corroded—ANACS. VF30 Details.** S-47, B-39, R.4. The medium brown fields and devices are pitted, slightly more extensively on the reverse. But all legends are clear, as are the important details of the portrait and wreath. EAC 10. (#901374)

29 **1794 Head of 1794—Corroded—NCS. XF Details.** S-22, B-6, R.1. The familiar "Mounds Reverse" with the reverse die sinking above the N in ONE. Moderately granular with a somewhat rougher texture on OF and the CA in AMERICA. Perhaps lightly burnished to smooth the surfaces, and the obverse rim has a minor ding at 8 o'clock. EAC 12. (#901374)

Choice XF S-44 1794 Cent

30 **1794 Head of 1794 XF45 PCGS.** S-44, B-33, R.1. Breen Die State V with cracks through the 17 in the date and the EN in CENT. A charming chocolate-brown example of this widely collected Liberty Cap date. The hair is detailed and displays glimmers of luster. Minor marks on the right obverse field and the obverse rim at 12 and 3 o'clock are barely worthy of mention. EAC 20. (#901374)

Sharp 1794 S-55 Cent, AU53 Details

31 **1794 Head of 1794—Corroded—ANACS. AU53 Details.** S-55, B-47, R.2. Both sides have deep steel-brown color with minor surface roughness and additional patches of deep red and green porosity on both sides. This variety is immediately recognized by the distinct misplacement of the A in STATES that is high and leans sharply to the left. EAC 15. (#901374)

Double Struck 1795 S-78 Cent

32 **1795 Plain Edge, Double Struck—Corroded—ANACS. VF20 Details.** S-78, B-8, R.1. Although the surfaces are dark steel with lighter tan on the devices, exhibiting moderate corrosion on both sides, the double strike trumps the quality. Doubling is visible on both sides, the first strike centered and the second strike approximately 10% off center toward 10 o'clock. We could use a lot of words to describe this piece, or we could simply suggest examination of the picture, and the coin if possible. EAC 8. (#1380)

1796 Liberty Cap Cent, S-87, VF20

33 **1796 Liberty Cap VF20 PCGS.** S-87, B-8, R.3. On this variety, the 6 is low and close to the 9, the mouth is open and the lips are unfinished, and there is a double leaf to the left of ONE. Light to medium tan patination bathes both sides, and the design elements exhibit nice definition for the grade. Some minor roughness on the reverse is mentioned for complete accuracy. EAC 12. (#1392)

34 **1798/7—Damaged, Burnished—NCS. VF Details.** S-152, B-13, R.2. The left top of the underdigit 7 is distinct, and the crossbar of the E in AMERICA is connected with the upper pendant, which ends in a sharp point. A few small, shallow punch marks are noted on each side, and the medium to dark brown surfaces have a glossy appearance. Sharp definition is visible on the design elements, which are well centered on the planchet. The dentils are complete, and for the most part quite strong. EAC 12. (#1440)

35 **1803 Small Date, Small Fraction XF40 PCGS.** S-254, B-13, R.2. The corner of the 3 touches the drapery; the reverse shows a short fraction bar too far right, covering the last 0 but not the 1. Pleasing medium brown color bathes smooth, minimally abraded surfaces. Sharp detail on the design elements, with all of the dentilation showing. A very nice early large cent. EAC 20. (#1482)

36 **1803 Small Date, Large Fraction—Corroded—ANACS. XF45 Details.** S-257, B-16, R.2. A sharply detailed Draped Bust cent whose golden-brown and steel-blue surfaces are mildly to moderately porous. Small marks are found on the obverse at 3 o'clock on the reverse near 6 o'clock. EAC 15. (#1485)

37 **1813—Cleaned—ANACS. AU53 Details.** S-292, B-2, R.2. A smooth mahogany-brown cent with glimpses of golden-brown luster in selected areas. The stars have soft centers, partly due to die wear, but the major devices are bold. Mildly and inoffensively cleaned. EAC 25. (#1570)

Lovely Select 1814 Crosslet 4 Cent, S-294

38 **1814 Crosslet 4 MS63 Brown NGC.** S-294, B-1, R.1. This variety is attributed by the crosslet 4 in the date; the S-295 variety has a large plain 4. Walter Breen, in his *Encyclopedia of Early United States Cents, 1793-1814*, cites Robert Julian's research in saying: " ... Chief Coiner Adam Eckfeldt delivered 357,830 cents to Mint Treasurer Benjamin Rush on October 27, exhausting the Mint's supply of cent blanks." Breen goes on to say: "Unsurprisingly, gem uncirculated 1814s are unobtainable, though both varieties of this date are plentiful in all lower grades."

This Brown Select example displays highly attractive glossy medium brown surfaces that exhibit sharply struck design elements. Most of the dentilation shows on both sides, and is for the most part quite bold. Each face is devoid of significant contact marks, spots, or corrosion. In other words, a truly outstanding specimen. Census: 16 in 63 Brown, 11 finer (6/07). EAC 55. (#1573)

39 **1814 Plain 4 AU50 PCGS.** S-295, B-2, R.1. Breen Die State XIII. A die break beneath the chin gives Liberty a bearded appearance. A mahogany-brown example with lighter golden-brown luster in protected areas. A few moderate marks are made inconspicuous by the toning. EAC 40. (#1576)

Pleasing 1817 13 Stars Cent, N-13, MS65

40 **1817 13 Stars MS65 Brown PCGS.** N-13, R.1. The variety is confirmed by the point of the coronet midway between stars 5 and 6, a double dentil left of the first 1 in the date, and a die scratch from the base of I to the back of the C in AMERICA. Exquisite definition is visible on the design elements, and light brown patina reveals traces of underlying gold. Well preserved surfaces reveal no roughness or significant marks. EAC 60. (#1594)

41 **1821—Corroded—ANACS. AU55 Details.** N-2, R.1. A scarcer date with only two die varieties, neither of which participated in the Randall Hoard. This sharply struck and unabraded representative has several areas of subtle granularity on both sides. EAC 20. (#1621)

42 **1828 Large Narrow Date MS63 Brown NGC.** N-2, R.2. The final A in AMERICA nearly touches the stem, characteristic of this Newcomb marriage. A crisply struck and impressively unabraded representative with rich golden-brown fields and walnut-brown devices. EAC 55. (#1654)

43 **1837 Plain Cords, Medium Letters MS65 Brown NGC.** N-3, R.1. Blended olive and tan-brown embrace the obverse, while the reverse has powder-blue and rose-red shades. A lustrous and crisply struck Gem limited only by whispery grazes on the cheek and a spot near the R in AMERICA. EAC 60. (#1735)

44 **1838 MS65 Brown NGC.** N-4, R.2. Noyes Die State A. The curved line at the lower obverse rim is diagnostic. An unworn Gem, well-preserved overall with blue and violet accents that grace the medium-brown surfaces. As sometimes seen, softness is evident on the left-side stars. EAC 60. (#1741)

45 **1838 MS65 Brown PCGS.** N-6, R.1. A bold die line from the leaf tip near the R in AMERICA confirms the die marriage. A chocolate-brown beauty that has unmarked surfaces and a bold central strike. Slightly soft on the left borders and upper stars. Darker and a bit granular above stars 6 and 7 and on STATES OF. Certified in an old green label holder. EAC 60. (#1741)

46 **1838 MS66 Brown PCGS.** N-7, R.1. Recognized by a noticeable die scratch that extends to the base of the F of OF, and multiple center alignment dots that are visible on the reverse. A wonderfully produced and preserved Coronet cent that shows pinpoint sharpness on the motifs. Hints of mint orange peek through attractive medium brown patina. EAC 62. Population: 9 in 66 Brown, 0 finer (5/07). EAC 62. (#1741)

47 **1853 MS66 Brown NGC.** N-25, R.1. Grellman Die State b. Mint orange glows from selected protected areas, although chocolate-brown toning prevails. An undisturbed and satiny Premium Gem that has a well struck portrait. EAC 60. (#1901)

48 **1853 MS66 Brown NGC.** N-18, R.1. Grellman Die State b. Orange-red outlines design recesses, while the open fields and portrait are steel-blue. A sharply struck and remarkably unabraded Premium Gem. EAC 63. (#1901)

49 **1855 Upright 5s MS65 Brown PCGS.** N-7, R.1. Grellman Die State d, with no clashmark over the N in CENT. The date is lightly entered into the working die, but the strike is otherwise crisp. The lustrous medium brown surfaces are free from consequential marks. EAC 60. (#1907)

50   1856 Slanted 5 MS65 Red and Brown PCGS. N-2, R.1. Grellman Die State f. Boldly struck save for the upper obverse stars, and only minor carbon is present. Incorrectly designated by PCGS as an Upright 5 variety. Population: 31 in 65 Red and Brown, 1 finer (5/07). EAC 63. (#1923)

PROOF LARGE CENT

Outstanding 1848 Cent, PR66 Red and Brown Low R.6 A Proof-Only Variety

51   1848 PR66 Red and Brown NGC. Ex: P. Kaufman. N-19, Low R.6. A proof only variety. Walter Breen, in his Encyclopedia of United States and Colonial Proof Coins, presents a roster of 16 pieces, but then says: " ... I have excellent reason to believe that this enumeration is far from complete."
This Premium Gem has impressive quality obverse and reverse surfaces. There is a fine irregular line across the 1 in the date just above the base. The reverse has a fine die line on the rim over TED. Intermingled mint orange color with hints of blue toning resides on the obverse, and rich reddish-orange color with light blue on the reverse. It is sharply struck with slight cameo contrast. The surfaces on both sides are well preserved. Census: 2 in 66 Red and Brown, 0 finer (6/07). EAC PR63. (#1974)

FLYING EAGLE CENTS

52   1857 MS64 PCGS. Beige and violet-tinged tan are the predominant colors on this lovely Choice example. Solidly defined and immensely appealing with a single carbon fleck on the eagle's left wing. (#2016)

53   1857 MS64 PCGS. This chestnut-gold near-Gem has a precise strike with sharp definition on the peripheries of the eagle. Smooth fields conceal a subtle retained lamination northwest of the date. (#2016)

54   1857 MS64 NGC. This orange-red near-Gem is sharply struck, since only the lower leaf cotton leaf shows any signs of weakness. Nearly free from contact, and only minor gray freckles on the upper reverse field stand in the way of an even higher grade. (#2016)

55   1857 MS64 NGC. The sunset-orange surfaces of this lovely near-Gem have glints of ruby-red and lemon-gold. A solidly struck representative of this first official small cent issue. (#2016)

56   1857 MS64 PCGS. Boldly struck with just a touch of weakness along the bottoms of ED STAT, and on both of the reverse N's. The obverse is primarily light tan, with amber-orange across much of the reverse. A small spot is observed near the reverse rim at 3 o'clock. (#2016)

Wonderful 1857 Gem Cent

57   1857 MS65 PCGS. This popular issue was initially heavily saved because of its novelty. The Gem presented in this sale is exceptionally well struck for the type. The eagle's plumage is crisp, save for minor softness on the end of the tail feathers. The entire reverse wreath is also sharp. Lustrous surfaces exhibit pretty golden-tan color, and are free of mentionable marks. A wonderful type coin! (#2016)

Colorful Gem 1857 Flying Eagle Cent

58   1857 MS65 PCGS. This unabraded Gem has lime-green, peach, and rose-red toning. Each side has a tiny spot near 9 o'clock, but the satiny surfaces are nonetheless exceptional. Well struck on the eagle, and the wreath is also bold with only a hint of softness on the lowest right cotton leaf. (#2016)

59   1857 Doubled Die Obverse MS63 NGC. VP-001, FS-002, Snow-4. The eagle's beak and the CA in AMERICA are among the die doubled elements. A sharply struck and satiny tan-brown piece with pleasing surfaces. VP-001 Census: 8 in 63, 13 finer (5/07). (#2017)

60   1857 Doubled Die Obverse MS63 NGC. VP-001, FS-002, Snow-4. Wide die doubling on the first S in STATES is a pick-up point for this popular *Cherrypickers'* variety. This boldly impressed cent is smooth aside from a luster graze above the left (facing) wing. VP-001 Census: 8 in 63, 13 finer (5/07). (#2017)

61   **1858 Large Letters MS64 PCGS.** Low Leaves, Closed E in ONE. This tan-gold near-Gem has satin luster, and the strike is bold aside from the O in ONE. Interesting die cracks are noted on the bow and the right wreath end. (#2019)

Lustrous MS65 Large Letters 1858 Flying Eagle Cent

62   **1858 Large Letters MS65 PCGS.** High Leaves Reverse. Closed E in ONE. The Large and Small Letters obverse have long been recognized by collectors and have been listed in the Red Book since the first edition. Gem examples are scarce. This is a lovely example that has lustrous, pale honey-tan surfaces. Sharp but not fully struck, close magnification reveals a couple of tiny specks of carbon on each side, but there are no obvious or mentionable abrasions. (#2019)

63   **1858 Small Letters MS64 PCGS.** Low Leaves, Open E in ONE. An evenly struck and lustrous Choice type coin with unmarked surfaces and a few pinpoint flyspecks. Minor rim die breaks are present on the reverse between 1 and 3 o'clock. (#2020)

Sparkling MS66 Small Letters
1858 Flying Eagle Cent

64   **1858 Small Letters MS66 PCGS.** Low Leaves Reverse, Closed E in ONE. It was the Act of February 21, 1857 that authorized the new small cents, struck in copper-nickel, although obviously the change was under consideration earlier, as indicated by the existence of pieces dated 1856. The coinage of half cents was discontinued by this same legislation. There is often discussion in numismatic circles regarding the status of the 1856 Flying Eagle cents: Are they patterns or regular issue coins? As Congress had not authorized the small cent until 1857, any pieces made in 1856 are unquestionably patterns, although they are often collected as part of the regular series.

The first design entry for the new smaller-size one cent coinage was the Flying Eagle design, attributed to James Barton Longacre. Several designs were tried on pattern pieces during the mid-1850s before this motif was chosen. Twenty years earlier, Christian Gobrecht chose a similar eagle in flight for the reverse of his silver dollar design in 1836. For the small cents, the design was short-lived, issued only from 1856 to 1858 with two hubs used for the final year. Current PCGS population data indicates that the Small Letters coins represent only about 30% of all 1858 Flying Eagle cents. This example is a splendid Premium Gem with fully brilliant satin luster. Both sides have attractive golden-tan color with faint pinkish accents on the obverse. A few tiny planchet flakes are evident, but there are no post-mintage defects worthy of mention. Population: 8 in 66, 0 finer (4/07). (#2020)

PROOF FLYING EAGLE CENTS

Classic 1856 Flying Eagle Cent PR64

65 1856 PR64 PCGS. Snow-9. The usual dies for proofs of this coveted and historic issue, and a later state with a slender vertical die crack beneath the tip of the eagle's claw. A chocolate-brown near-Gem with glimpses of peach-gold within the legends and about the devices. Careful inspection with the aid of a loupe locates an infrequent pinpoint carbon fleck, but there are no abrasions or planchet defects. The strike is full, even on the often suspect extremities of the eagle, and on the cotton leaves that on business strikes rarely exhibit full veins. Many collectors still in need of an 1856 Flying Eagle cent have waited for years for the "right" coin to come along, and this mark-free, razor-sharp specimen could be the one. (#2037)

Lovely Choice Proof 1856 Flying Eagle Cent

66 1856 PR64 NGC. Snow-9. The usual proof variety, identified by a tiny spike on the left ribbon end and a faint die line that lies parallel to the I in UNITED. This is an unusually attractive piece, because it displays multi-color bands of orange, forest-green, and gold. As expected of a proof striking, the features are razor-sharp, even on the eagle's extremities and the veins of the cotton leaves. This gently mirrored near-Gem is impressively devoid of marks, and would be the highlight of a Flying Eagle and Indian cent collection. As a date, the 1856 has the lowest mintage of any small cent, and since it introduced the denomination, its historical significance is assured. (#2037)

INDIAN CENTS

67 1859 MS64 PCGS. Resplendent luster sweeps across this light chestnut-tan near-Gem. A well struck type coin with interesting obverse rim die breaks between 3 and 6 o'clock. (#2052)

68 1859 MS64 NGC. Chocolate-brown, pale orange, and lilac shades enrich this satiny and unabraded near-Gem. The strike is precise, as is customary for the single-year type. (#2052)

69 1859 MS64 PCGS. A lovely representative of this one-year type, Choice with pale straw-gold surfaces overall and a splash of deeper color at the STA of STATES. Few flaws are evident on the well struck obverse, though a handful of abrasions in the reverse fields preclude a finer grade. (#2052)

70 1859 MS64 NGC. This is a pleasing near-Gem example of the first-year 1859 Indian cent, the only issue in the series with the Laurel Wreath Without Shield reverse. Well struck and lustrous with rich reddish coppery-brown coloration and minimal surface marks. (#2052)

Light-Colored 1859 Indian Cent, MS65

71   **1859 MS65 PCGS.** A highly lustrous example of this scarce, one-year type coin. The obverse is fully struck, but there is slight softness of detail on the reverse. The surfaces of this piece are pale honey-gold and show little mellowing of the original light color. Always in demand as both a business strike and a proof. Certified in a green label holder. (#2052)

MS66 1859 Indian Cent With Semi-Reflective Fields

72   **1859 MS66 PCGS.** An important Premium Gem of this always-needed one-year type. Sharply struck with full definition on the diamonds. The lustrous surfaces display a light golden-tan patina and the fields have a confirmed semi-prooflike glimmer on each side. A few unobtrusive marks in the upper left obverse and upper reverse fields do not distract in the least from the great eye appeal of this one-year type coin. Population: 15 in 66, 0 finer (3/07). (#2052)

73   **1860 MS66 NGC.** A Rounded Bust representative with the new reverse, which features an oak wreath divided by a shield at the top. The devices have sharp definition, and the shining surfaces are copper-orange with a splash of rouge. Well preserved with excellent eye appeal. Census: 35 in 66, 3 finer (5/07). (#2058)

74   **1861 MS65 PCGS.** The prooflike obverse exhibits subtle peach and gold toning. The satiny reverse is light tan-gold. A mark-free Gem with minimal carbon and a pleasing strike. (#2061)

Surprising MS66 1861 Copper-Nickel Cent

75   **1861 MS66 PCGS.** The golden-orange surfaces of this lovely Premium Gem, surprisingly, much more resemble the typical color of a late-series bronze cent, rather than the more-brownish surfaces on the typical copper-nickel cent. This piece is sharply struck save for the foremost feather tip, and visible distractions, as expected from the grade, are virtually nonexistent. PCGS has graded only nine pieces finer (4/07). (#2061)

Challenging 1861 Copper-Nickel Cent, MS67

76   **1861 MS67 PCGS.** Exceedingly lustrous with spot-free, almost perfect surfaces. The strike is just short of complete, being a trifle soft at the tips of the first three feathers in the headdress, and the light tan obverse color takes on a slightly deeper hue on the reverse. The 1861 was the lowest mintage issue of the brief copper-nickel Indian type. Population: 8 in 67, 1 finer (5/07). (#2061)

77   **1862 MS65 PCGS.** Boldly detailed on the reverse but somewhat soft on the Liberty's headdress, hair, and ribbon. Satin luster warms the carefully preserved, unmarked surfaces. (#2064)

Attractive 1862 Copper-Nickel Indian Cent MS66

78   **1862 MS66 NGC.** Boldly struck, save for minor softness on the upper feather tips of the headdress, with gleaming luster and lovely golden-tan coloration that is slightly deeper-than-usual, for the type. A tiny center dot (as struck) resides between the E and N of CENT on the reverse. Minimally marked, with a few trivial nicks noted near Liberty's ear. Census: 28 in 66, 5 finer (6/07). (#2064)

Splendid Premium Gem 1862 Copper-Nickel Cent

79   **1862 MS66 PCGS.** This is a simply splendid Premium Gem example from the first year of the copper-nickel (also called the Oak Wreath With Shield) type of Indian cent. Well struck, lustrous, and virtually unmarked, with pleasing golden-tan coloration. According to *A Guide Book of United States Type Coins* (2005): "For reasons that are not clear today, Mint Director James Ross Snowden found the laurel wreath reverse of the 1859 cent to be unsatisfactory and directed that patterns be made for a new style. In 1860, this new style became the standard." Population: 49 in 66, 7 finer (6/07). (#2064)

80   **1863 MS65 PCGS.** Boldly struck and lustrous, with pleasing light tan coloration and a blemish-free reverse. A couple of tiny nicks are observed on Liberty's face (with a magnifier), along with an interesting pebbly texture (as struck) on the neck. (#2067)

Glossy, Superb Gem 1864-L Cent

81 1864 L On Ribbon MS67 Brown NGC. The 1864-L was not saved in large numbers and, consequently, is not generally found in high grades, most likely because the addition of Longacre's initial was not readily discernible to the general public. This piece, however, is a splendid example with undisturbed, glossy brown surfaces. Unlike many of the high grade survivors known, this piece displays full detail and minute flecks of ruby and sapphire color in the fields. Strong clash marks are noted on the obverse, but little evidence of clashing is noted on the reverse. This is the only Superb Gem of this issue graded by either NGC or PCGS in any color category (4/07). (#2079)

Sharply Struck 1864 With L Near-Gem Cent

82 1864 L On Ribbon MS64 Red PCGS. Copper-gold color graces lustrous surfaces on this near-Gem cent, and the design elements benefit from a sharp strike, including clarity on all four diamonds. Devoid of mentionable contact marks; a couple of light flecks are noted on each side. The new With L design is found on all Indian Head cents from this issue onwards. Population: 46 in 64 Red, 38 finer (6/07). (#2081)

83 1866 MS64 Red PCGS. This near-Gem is lustrous and well struck, save for minor weakness on some of the obverse and reverse denticles. The salmon-colored surfaces betray hints of speckled darker patina on the upper half of the obverse. Surface marks are nonexistent. Population: 40 in 64 Red, 28 finer (6/07). (#2087)

84 1867 MS65 Red and Brown PCGS. A pleasing woodgrain finish is presented on both sides of this well preserved Gem. All of the design features are crisply impressed and surface blemishes are nonexistent. A lustrous and attractive example; housed in an earlier PCGS holder with a yellow-green label. Population: 37 in 65, 1 finer (6/07). (#2089)

85 1868 MS64 Red PCGS. A satiny and unabraded near-Gem with straw-gold and pumpkin-orange surfaces. Well struck aside from the feather tips. A few toning flecks on the lower right reverse limit the grade. Population: 55 in 64 Red, 33 finer (4/07). (#2093)

86 1869 MS64 Red PCGS. Highly lustrous with beautiful lime-green and peach-red coloration, this near-Gem scores very high in the eye appeal department. Lacking any discernible marks on either side, it also seems conservatively graded at the current level. Rick Snow observes that few Indian cent collectors realize how rare this date really is, in his *Guide Book of Flying Eagle and Indian Cents*. Population: 41 in 64 Red, 35 finer (6/07). (#2096)

87 1870 MS66 Brown PCGS. Sharply struck with essentially full definition on all of the design elements. The highly lustrous surfaces reveal cobalt-blue and red-gold color on the obverse, with mint-orange and magenta toning on the reverse. Exquisitely preserved and free of marks. A lovely Premium Gem Indian cent, and highest-graded example of this issue at PCGS, with the Brown color designation. Population: 1 in 66 Brown, 0 finer in Brown at either service (6/07). (#2097)

88 1870 MS64 Red and Brown PCGS. Better struck than usual on the obverse, with crisp detailing on all of the feather tips of the headdress. The lustrous reddish-tan surfaces are without distracting marks, but scattered carbon flecks limit the grade. (#2098)

89 1870 MS64 Red PCGS. Shallow N in ONE (Type of 1869.) Lovely bronze-green and fire-red coloration adorns this appealing Indian cent. A lustrous near-Gem with a reasonable strike. Nearly pristine aside from a faint abrasion on the neck. Population: 68 in 64 Red, 33 finer (6/07). (#2099)

90 1871 MS64 Red and Brown PCGS. All of the design elements are well struck, including the feather tips of Liberty's headdress, and satin luster is especially noticeable near the devices. Some definite browning occurs on each side, but the piece is still desirable as a near-Gem. Housed in a green label PCGS holder. (#2101)

Attractive Red Near-Gem 1872 Cent

91 1872 MS64 Red PCGS. Attractive orange-gold color adorns both sides of this near-Gem Indian cent, each of which is devoid of mentionable abrasions or spots. We note sharp definition on the design features; three and a half diamonds show clearly on this specimen. Richard Snow (2006) contends that: "Aside from the 1877, this is the toughest date to find today." Population: 45 in 64 Red, 15 finer (6/07). (#2105)

Exceptional, Full Red MS65 1872 Indian Cent

92 1872 MS65 Red PCGS. The 1872 is a widely recognized, semi-key date in the Indian cent series. Just over 4 million pieces were struck, but that only tells part of the story of this date's scarcity. According to Rick Snow in his *Flying Eagle & Indian Cents* reference: "A low mintage date to begin with, the scarcity of this date can be additionally attributed to excessive meltage. Vast amounts of cents were recoined during 1873-75." One thing leads to another in the case of this date. Because it is a lower mintage date and large (but unknown) numbers were melted, there were obviously fewer pieces set aside in all grades and especially in high grades. Combining the population data from both major services shows that only 17 Gems have been certified (13 by PCGS and four by NGC), and only two are finer (5/07). This is a lovely full red Gem. The surfaces are bright, even orange-gold on each side. The only hint of color other than the original red is faint oil-slick iridescence that is visible with magnification on the reverse. The striking details are strong throughout with sharp definition on the tips of the feathers of the headdress and four full diamonds. An important and valuable coin for the collector of high grade Indian cents. (#2105)

Lovely MS66 Red and Brown 1873 Closed 3 Indian Cent

93 1873 Closed 3 MS66 Red and Brown NGC. Ex: Jules Reiver Collection. An example of the slightly scarcer Closed 3 variety, coined early in the year. Sharply struck with satiny luster. The surfaces are essentially full red, with just a trace of tan at the lower reverse. Truly a remarkable Premium Gem example. Census: 12 in 66, 0 finer (5/07). (#2110)

94 1874 MS64 Red PCGS. This is a highly lustrous near-Gem that displays wheat-gold coloration and well impressed design elements. A few wispy obverse blemishes and light scattered carbon flecks limit the grade. Population: 67 in 64 Red, 33 finer (6/07). (#2120)

95 1877 Good 6 PCGS. Although quite extensively worn, this smooth dark olive piece has wonderful surfaces for the grade. In fact, it is only with magnification that any surface marks can be seen. There are not spots, and only traces of verdigris around a few devices. The tops of several letters in LIBERTY can be seen. (#2127)

96 1877—Corroded, Cleaned—ANACS. VG8 Details. This chocolate-brown key date cent shows little evidence of a past cleaning, but the obverse border has four small spots, one of which is beneath the 77 in the date. (#2127)

97 1877—Cleaned—ANACS. VF20 Details. This Shallow N key date cent has non-deceptive bright orange-gold and lilac patina. All letters in LIBERTY are legible, and only the B and Y are weak. (#2127)

Pleasing 1877 Choice AU Cent

98 1877 AU55 PCGS. This Choice AU key date cent has only a trace of friction on the highpoints. Intermingled streaks of tan and dark brown patina enrich the nearly unabraded surfaces, and the design elements are well impressed; three of the diamonds are crisply impressed. Liberty's neck has a faint pinscratch, otherwise completely problem-free. (#2127)

Famous 1877 Cent MS64 Red and Brown

99 1877 MS64 Red and Brown PCGS. Orange-red occupies the obverse field, while the portrait is ruby-red. The reverse is about equally divided into areas of gold, fire-red, lilac, and steel-blue. This key date cent has pleasing luster and lacks remotely relevant contact. A good strike, although the right border and a few feathertips are incompletely brought up. (#2128)

Key-Date 1877 Cent, MS64 Red

Full Red MS65 1877 Indian Cent

100 **1877 MS64 Red PCGS.** Richard Snow (2006) writes: " ... the purported original mintage of this date (852,500 business strikes) appears to be way too high compared to the number of observed surviving examples. An upper estimate of 200,000 coins struck seems more accurate." The near-Gem example in this lot displays lustrous copper-gold surfaces devoid of any abrasions or unsightly spots, though for complete accuracy we mention some scattered light flecks on the reverse. Occasional minor strike softness is noted, including incomplete definition on the diamonds. This is not unusual, as Snow indicates: " ... the diamond detail for this issue is typically shallow." Housed in a green-label holder. Population: 40 in 64 Red, 27 finer (6/07). (#2129)

101 **1877 MS65 Red PCGS.** Although the 1909-S Indian cent has a lower mintage than the 1877, the latter is regarded as the key to the series, since few pieces were set aside, while the 1909-S was hoarded to some degree due to the change in designs that year. When encountered, 1877 cents are usually in well worn grades, and often corroded. High grade, full Red examples are under great demand from collectors of this popular series. This highly lustrous Gem features gold centers, bordered by reddish-orange color near the rims. The strike is decidedly above average, and surface imperfections, such as a tiny mint-made planchet flaw in the field near the chin, are unimportant. As usual for business strikes for this important issue, the N in ONE is shallow, unlike proof 1877 cents, which feature a bold N in ONE. In fact, the business strike 1877 marks the final appearance of the shallow N reverse subtype, which had begun to be phased out in 1870. Population: 21 in 65, 6 finer (3/07). (#2129)

102 **1882 MS65 Red PCGS.** This pinpoint-sharp Gem has satiny luster and is virtually void of contact. A few faint lilac streaks deny perfection. Certified in an old green label holder. (#2144)

103 **1882 MS65 Red PCGS.** Snow-1. The 8s in the date are widely repunched within the upper loops. This Gem boasts a sharp strike, although the upper three feather tips in the headdress are not completely defined. Each side displays lovely crimson and lime-green coloration and effulgent luster, along with a few scattered flyspecks. Population: 69 in 65 Red, 22 finer (6/07). (#2144)

Bright, Lustrous MS66 Red 1882 Indian Cent

104 **1882 MS66 Red PCGS.** Ex: Richard Collection. Simply extraordinary quality for a business strike Indian cent. Both sides are smooth enough to warrant consideration at an even higher grade level. There are virtually no bothersome carbon flecks, and the surfaces are alive with bright, glossy golden-red luster that is a little deeper in shade on the obverse. Population: 20 in 66, 2 finer (3/07). (#2144)

105 **1884 MS65 Red PCGS.** This meticulously struck and lustrous Indian cent alternates between orange-red and yellow-gold. Wispy contact on the cheekbone precludes a finer grade. Encapsulated in a green label holder. (#2150)

106 **1886 Type Two MS64 Red and Brown PCGS.** Moderately frosty in texture, both sides are powerfully impressed with no singularly bothersome abrasions. The deep red-brown and violet toning is highly attractive. A couple of small marks on the obverse limit the grade. Population: 93 in 64 Red and Brown, 16 finer (6/07). (#92155)

Attractive 1889 Red Gem Cent

107 **1889 MS65 Red PCGS.** This MS65 Red Indian cent is well defined throughout with even, glowing mint red luster over each side. All four diamonds are bold. Devoid of contact marks, though a handful of light flecks are visible on both obverse and reverse. With respect to survivability of this issue, Richard Snow (2006) says: "As with other dates of this era, these were workhorse coins that stayed in circulation long after the design was changed in 1909. High-grade examples survived only by chance." Population: 31 in 65 Red, 6 finer (6/07). (#2174)

108 **1891 MS65 Red NGC.** A vibrant orange-red Gem that only shows a couple of tiny specks of carbon at the margins and a pair of small marks in the left obverse field. Well-defined overall, though slight weakness is noted on the tips of the feathers. NGC has graded just three finer pieces with Red surfaces (5/07). (#2180)

109 **1892 MS65 Red PCGS.** Bold orange color dominates much of the obverse, while the portrait and the reverse have paler salmon surfaces. Solidly struck with a single carbon spot above the E in ONE. Despite a mintage of over 37 million pieces, Red Gems remain elusive. Population: 52 in 65 Red, 12 finer (5/07). (#2183)

110 **1893 MS65 Red PCGS.** This is a flaming Gem example that is boldly struck and displays beautiful fire-red and chartreuse coloration on both sides. Surface marks are nonexistent and scattered flyspecks on the upper reverse are not overly distracting. Population: 72 in 65 Red, 22 finer (6/07). (#2186)

111 **1904 MS66 Red NGC.** Fiery reddish-orange gives way to lemon and sunset colors near the periphery. This crisply struck Premium Gem has four full diamonds on the ribbon. Census: 25 in 66 Red, 1 finer (6/07). (#2219)

112 **1909-S MS64 Brown PCGS.** The obverse is mostly deep olive-brown and golden-brown, although a streak of the initial gold color is present near 12 o'clock. The reverse is more red than brown, despite the Brown designation. This unabraded near-Gem is well struck aside from the tips of the uppermost feathers. (#2238)

Splendid 1909-S Key-Date Indian Cent, MS64 Red

113 **1909-S MS64 Red PCGS.** The 1909-S Indian cent was saved as the last of its issue, making its rarity much lower than the low-mintage coins of earlier years (Richard Snow, 2006). Nevertheless, it is a popular date in the Indian Head cent series, and is necessary for the completion of a date/mintmark collection. The near-Gem example offered in this lot possesses an attractive copper-brass-gold coloration, and is sharply struck, including crisp delineation on all of the diamonds. A few minuscule marks and flecks preclude full Gem status. (#2240)

PROOF INDIAN CENTS

Attractive 1863 Cent, PR65

114 **1863 PR65 PCGS.** It is estimated that 460 or so proof cents were struck in 1863. Relatively few apparently survived in PR65 and finer levels of preservation, at least according to certified population/census figures. Razor-sharp definition shows on the design features of this well preserved specimen. Both sides are bathed in orange-tan patina, with a good amount of field-motif contrast, especially when the coin is rotated under a light source. Population: 24 in 65, 7 finer (6/07). (#2262)

Beautiful Gem Proof 1864 Copper-Nickel Cent

115   1864 Copper-Nickel PR65 PCGS. This issue, the lowest-mintage copper-nickel Indian Head proof cent, also has the highest mintage for any of the three varieties of proof cents for the year. This well-preserved example offers pleasing copper-orange color and minimal carbon. The solidly struck devices offer subtle contrast with the fields, though this does not appear as a cameo effect. Population: 43 in 65, 10 finer (5/07). (#2265)

Gem Cameo Proof 1864 Copper-Nickel Cent

116   1864 Copper Nickel PR65 Cameo PCGS. This amazing proof has exceptional light tan color, consistent with the composition of the copper-nickel cents. The well-preserved surfaces are fully mirrored with highly lustrous and frosty devices. The result is a delightful cameo appearance that is highly desired by collectors of proof coinage. Population: 16 in 65 Cameo, 7 finer (6/07). (#82265)

Red and Brown PR66 1864 Bronze Cent

117   1864 Bronze No L PR66 Red and Brown PCGS. While the bronze No L proof cents of 1864 are less common than their copper-nickel cousins, they are certainly more available than the bronze proofs that bear Longacre's initial. This glowing reddish-tan proof is among the finest survivors from an estimated mintage of 150 specimens, boldly impressed and immensely appealing. Population: 14 in 66, 1 finer (3/07). (#2277)

Exceptional 1865 Cent, PR64 Red

118   1865 PR64 Red PCGS. Richard Snow (2006) says of the 1865 proof cent: "This is one of the tougher dates in the early Indian Head series. ... It usually is found with streaky red-brown colors. Full red examples are very hard to locate, especially without spots and problems. Cameos are very rare." The near-Gem in this lot displays gorgeous reddish-gold color imbued with wisps of light green. Excellent definition on the design elements has resulted from a solid strike, and strong contrast is noted when the piece is tilted beneath a light source. Close scrutiny reveals no unsightly spots, stains, or significant contact marks. Population: 16 in 64 Red, 9 finer (6/07). (#2284)

119   1866 PR65 Red and Brown PCGS. A well-defined and appealing Gem representative of this post-war Indian cent issue, predominantly mahogany-brown with elements of orange. The surfaces retain an attractive gleam. Population: 43 in 65 Red and Brown, 5 finer (6/07). (#2286)

120   1867 PR65 Red and Brown PCGS. This exquisitely struck straw-gold and olive Gem is close to full red, although the obverse has a few pinpoint carbon flecks. Encased in a green label holder. Just 625+ proofs were struck. (#2289)

121   1868 PR65 Red and Brown PCGS. This exactingly struck Gem has attractive honey-gold and sea-green toning. The dies are only a few degrees from medal turn. Housed in a green label holder.

From The Vanek Collection. (#2292)

122   1868 PR64 Red PCGS. Fully struck and pristine, with reflective fields and lovely mint orange color on the devices. The dies are rotated nearly 180 degrees, as often seen on proofs of this date. A scarce, low mintage issue of 600 pieces. Population: 28 in 64 Red, 9 finer (6/07). (#2293)

Gem Proof 1874 Cent, PR65 Red Cameo

123   1874 PR65 Red Cameo NGC. A search through the population figures at the major grading services reveals that only eight proof 1874 cents have received both the Red and Cameo designations. To date, no coin of the date has been designated as Red and Ultra or Deep Cameo, so collectors of contrasted proof Indian cents will be well-served to closely consider this coin, a glittering brick-red Gem which fully merits both of its designations. The few pinpricks that seemingly limit the grade are virtually impossible to see without a loupe, and do not adversely affect the eye appeal in the slightest. Census: 2 in 65 Red Cameo, 1 finer (6/07). (#82311)

124   1884 PR66 Red and Brown NGC. A ruby or dark crimson color quietly glows from the surfaces of this generally dark coin. The mirrored surfaces can still be seen, but are muted due to the dark overall color. Fully detailed throughout. Census: 50 in 66, 9 finer (6/07). (#2340)

125   **1884 PR67 Red and Brown PCGS.** A nearly perfect proof striking with fields that are evenly mellowed over each side. Both obverse and reverse are perfectly balanced in overall appearance, color, and degree of reflectivity. A wonderful proof Indian cent and an excellent value as a Red and Brown coin. Population: 15 in 67, 1 finer (6/07). (#2340)

126   **1885 PR66 Brown NGC.** Rose-violet, lime-green, and gold endow this exquisitely preserved Premium Gem. The date and the top of the shield lack absolute definition, but the portrait and wreath are intricate. (#2342)

Iridescent Brown 1885 Cent, PR67

127   **1885 PR67 Brown PCGS.** Both sides of this extraordinary Gem have lost virtually all signs of mint red, but have been replaced by colorful lime-green and rose iridescence. Save for a few tiny flecks of carbon, the modestly reflective surfaces are essentially as struck. Population: 8 in 67, 0 finer (3/07). (#2342)

128   **1886 Type One PR66 Brown NGC.** Lovely ruby-red, sea-green, and olive-gold patina graces this precisely struck and mark-free specimen. A few tiny carbon flecks are of little import. In a prior generation holder.
From The Vanek Collection. (#2345)

129   **1886 Type Two PR65 Brown NGC.** Rich plum-red, gold, and olive embrace this sharply struck and unblemished Gem. The Type Two features a feather tip between the CA in AMERICA, and is the key to the post-1877 proof series. (#92345)

130   **1886 Type Two PR66 Brown NGC.** Rose-red and apple-green patina emerges when this exquisite specimen is rotated beneath a light. In mid-1886 the Type One obverse, with the last feather of the headdress pointing between I and C in AMERICA, was changed to the Type Two, with the last feather pointing between C and A. (#92345)

1886 Type Two Cent, PR64 Red

131   **1886 Type Two PR64 Red PCGS.** The scarcer of the two types from 1886, this variant shows the last feather in the headdress pointing between the C and A in AMERICA, rather than between the I and C on the previous Type One coins. Full Red coins are difficult indeed and worth a large premium. This deep cherry-red example shows slight blue mellowing in the center of the obverse. A pleasing, problem-free proof with no obvious or mentionable contact marks. Population: 9 in 64, 3 finer (5/07). (#92347)

132   **1892 PR65 Red PCGS.** The well struck orange-gold surfaces are devoid of marks and offer only minor carbon. Mild field-motif contrast is visible when the piece is rotated under a light. Population: 44 in 65 Red, 15 finer (4/07). (#2365)

133   **1892 PR65 Red PCGS.** This vibrant Gem exhibits wonderful reddish-orange color with subtle variation on the reverse. Boldly impressed and practically carbon-free. Population: 44 in 65 Red, 15 finer (6/07). (#2365)

Bright Red Cameo Gem Proof 1892 Indian Cent

134   **1892 PR65 Red Cameo PCGS.** While a relatively common date as a proof, few Cameo pieces have been certified. In fact, only three such coins have been graded by PCGS with five finer (5/07). This is a splendid proof that shows deeply mirrored fields with noticeably contrasted devices. The surfaces overall are light red-orange and evenly balanced from one side to the other. (#82365)

135   **1893 PR65 Brown PCGS.** Razor-sharp definition on the design elements befits a proof strike, and lovely light brown patination yields hints of underlying red. There are no bothersome marks to report. Population: 1 in 65 Brown, 2 finer (6/07). (#2366)

136   **1897 PR66 Red PCGS.** This intricately struck crimson-orange proof is every bit the Premium Gem. The surfaces are mark-free and exhibit only minimal carbon. A lovely survivor that should see spirited bidding among advanced specialists. Certified in a green label holder. Population: 6 in 66 Red, 6 finer (4/07). (#2380)
Ex: Joseph P. Gorrell Collection (Heritage, 1/03), lot 4515.

Outstanding 1899 Cent, PR67 Red and Brown

137   **1899 PR67 Red and Brown PCGS.** 1899 proof Indian cents, with a mintage of 2,031 pieces, are readily available through the Premium Gem level. PR67 Red and Brown specimens, however, such as the coin in this lot, are quite elusive, as can be seen from the population data below. Reddish-tan hues dominate both sides, and exhibit hints of occasional lime-green. Razor-sharp definition is apparent throughout, and impeccably preserved surfaces further enhance the outstanding eye appeal. Housed in a green label holder. Population: 3 in 67 Red and Brown, 0 finer (6/07). (#2385)

138   **1901 PR67 Red NGC.** Vibrant sunset-orange color dominates the margins, while the centers have delightful lemon-gold color. A carefully preserved and sharply struck example of this later Indian Head proof cent issue, one of 1,985 specimens distributed. Census: 3 in 67 Red, 2 finer (5/07). (#2392)
From The Vanek Collection.

139   **1902 PR66 Red PCGS.** Bright copper-gold coloration is joined by ruby-red on the reverse. Exquisitely struck throughout, including razor-sharp definition on the feather ends and diamonds. A fleck or two is noted on each side. Not that many full-red specimens are extant out of a mintage of 2,018 proofs. Population: 24 in 66 Red, 9 finer (6/07). (#2395)

140 **1909 PR65 Red and Brown PCGS.** The watery surfaces are almost completely red on the obverse with attractive olive-green shades on the reverse. Subtle contrast is evident on both sides. A great survivor from the original mintage of 2,175 pieces for this final-year issue. Population: 41 in 65 Red and Brown, 15 finer (6/07). (#2415)

LINCOLN CENTS

Gem 1909 VDB Doubled Die Cent, MS65 Red

141 **1909 VDB DDO MS65 Red PCGS.** FS-012. Although not listed in the *Guide Book*, the doubling on the obverse of this variety is readily visible with a low power glass. Unlike some other varieties, eye strain is not required to see the doubling at the date and RTY. This sharply detailed example is fully brilliant with lovely orange mint color and frosty surfaces. Population: 15 in 65 Red, 7 finer (6/07). (#82425)

142 **1909-S VDB Fine 12 ANACS.** A significantly worn, yet appealing representative of this noteworthy Lincoln cent issue, predominantly chocolate-brown with deeper color at the margins. Minimally marked overall, though a horizontal abrasion crosses the lower coat. (#2426)

143 **1909-S VDB—Damaged, Cleaned—ANACS. Fine 12 Details.** Cleaned long ago, the surfaces have taken on an even brown appearance that largely conceals the hairlines. The Damaged disclaimer is from a scratch below the date and a few pinprick marks on the lower reverse. (#2426)

144 **1909-S VDB Fine 15 PCGS.** A pleasing light brown example of this key date cent. Excellent definition shows on the design elements, better than what might be expected for the grade! A small as-struck lamination on Lincoln's bust does not detract from the coin's eye appeal. A great piece for a mid-grade Lincoln cent collection! (#2426)

145 **1909-S VDB—Cleaned, Scratched—ANACS. VF20 Details.** This medium brown example has a slightly glossy portrait and a few light reverse pinscratches. A hint of verdigris is noted beneath AMERICA and above the U in UNITED. (#2426)

146 **1909-S VDB VF25 NGC.** A moderately worn representative of this prized first-year Lincoln cent issue. The glossy walnut-brown surfaces display a hint of ruby color, and the abrasions present in the fields are minor. (#2426)

147 **1909-S VDB VF30 ANACS.** Pleasing olive-brown surfaces with a few minor marks that are consistent with the grade. This is a highly desirable piece that is missing from individual collections more often than not. (#2426)

148 **1909-S VDB XF40 NGC.** A well-defined, lightly worn example of this famous key issue, predominantly walnut-brown with traces of cherrywood color. The overall visual appeal is strong for the grade and the coin would make a great cornerstone for a collection of Lincoln cents. (#2426)

149 **1909-S VDB—Scratched, Cleaned—ANACS. AU50 Details.** A close inspection is necessary to locate the horizontal pinscratch from the base of Lincoln's ear into the right obverse field. The medium brown obverse is lighter than the deep walnut-brown reverse. The cleaning is unobtrusive, and the VDB initials are sharp. (#2426)

150 **1909-S VDB—Corroded, Cleaned—ANACS. AU58 Details.** The corrosion is mostly seen on the reverse, and the hairlines from cleaning are greatly subdued by the brown patina seen over both sides. Sharply defined throughout. (#2426)

151 **1909-S VDB MS63 Brown NGC.** Well struck with attractive coloration and soft, satiny luster. The surfaces are entirely mark-free. A few faint specks of olive-green are noted on the obverse. (#2426)

152 **1909-S VDB MS63 Brown PCGS.** A blend of plum, rose, and pumpkin-orange characterizes this pleasing Select example. Well-defined with few marks visible, though light fingerprints are noted in the obverse fields of this key-date coin. (#2426)

153 **1909-S VDB MS64 Brown NGC.** Vivid magenta and amethyst color dominates both sides, while a measure of copper-orange appears near the devices. A well-defined representative of this classic issue, one that approaches the century mark. (#2426)

154 **1909-S VDB MS64 Brown PCGS.** This needle-sharp and satiny Choice key date cent is nearly void of contact, and carbon is also minimal. Golden-brown and olive with glimpses of faded mint red near the margins. (#2426)

Choice Red and Brown 1909-S VDB Cent

155 **1909-S VDB MS64 Red and Brown PCGS.** A satiny near-Gem with olive-brown centers and red-gold peripheries. Sharply struck, particularly on the VDB initials, which on many examples are blurry or in low relief. A worthy representative of this perennial collector favorite. Encapsulated in an old green label holder. (#2427)

Pleasing 1909-S VDB Cent, MS63 Red

156 **1909-S VDB MS63 Red NGC.** Glowing luster radiates from the copper-orange surfaces of this Select '09-S VDB example. A well executed strike brings out sharp definition on the design features, including full separation in all of the grains and lines of both wheat stalks, and boldness on the V.D.B. elements. A few inoffensive, light toning spots are scattered about the obverse, but both sides are devoid of significant contact marks or annoying dark carbon spots. (#2428)

Full Red MS64 1909-S VDB Cent

157 **1909-S VDB MS64 Red NGC.** Sharply defined on each side with the strength of strike that is usually seen on this first-year issue. The luster is bright and orange-red in color on this famous and popular key-date issue. A few minor spots of dark toning are visible (with magnification) on the reverse of this near-Gem cent. (#2428)

Attractive 1909-S VDB Cent, MS64 Red

158 **1909-S VDB MS64 Red PCGS.** The 1909-S VDB was widely hoarded at the time of its release, making Uncirculated coins, even fully red Gems, fairly available. That said, these coins sell quickly to those putting together a date and mintmark set, or to those that are simply fascinated by the issue. The near-Gem red specimen we offer in this lot displays bright orange surfaces and sharply impressed motifs. Slightly darker toning spots that pepper both sides limit the grade. Still, a very attractive representative of this coveted issue. (#2428)

Lovely Near-Gem 1909-S VDB, MS64 Red

159 **1909-S VDB MS64 Red PCGS.** The mere mention of "SVDB" brings special thoughts and fond memories to nearly all collectors and numismatists. That is because Lincoln cents are generally the first coins that youngsters collect. Rekindle that childhood collecting interest with this coin, a fully lustrous near-Gem with brilliant orange and gold color. (#2428)

Gem 1909-S VDB Cent, Full Red Surfaces

160 **1909-S VDB MS65 Red PCGS.** The popularity of the S-VDB is a constant in U.S. numismatics. Worth a premium as soon as they were minted, considerable numbers were set aside in high grade. However many were set aside is not enough to satisfy collector demand for this one-year type. This piece shows blazing mint red color with just a touch of pale olive on each side. Strongly defined throughout. A lovely Gem example of this important early Lincoln cent. (#2428)

Handsome Red Gem 1909-S VDB Cent

161 **1909-S VDB MS65 Red PCGS.** The 1909-S VDB has the lowest business strike mintage of any Lincoln cent issue, and is the scarcer of the two issues that constitute the briefly produced VDB reverse subtype. This lustrous green-gold Gem is boldly struck and unabraded. A minor lamination is noted near the M in AMERICA. (#2428)

Outstanding 1909-S Red Gem Cent

162 **1909-S VDB MS65 Red PCGS.** Light orange and gold streaks invigorate this lustrous and meticulously struck Gem. The VDB initials are boldly impressed, unlike some Uncirculated examples seen. Close inspection reveals no significant contact marks or unsightly spots. Encased in a green label holder. David Lange (2005) writes: "The Holy Grail for Lincoln cent collectors, the acquisition of a 1909-S VDB cent usually marks the completion of the series." (#2428)

Gorgeous 1909-S VDB, MS66 Red

163 **1909-S VDB MS66 Red ICG.** The 1909-S VDB cent was widely hoarded at the time of its release, and even Mint State coins are available to collectors. Carl Herkowitz, in a November 1995 article in *The Numismatist*, elaborates on this situation: "The vast majority of the 484,000 minted were pounced upon like no other United States coin and kept as centerpieces, as trophies. A virtual flood tide of citizens from all walks of life seized these talismans from circulation in a half-century-long ... frenzy, and relatively few pieces were lost to the rigors of chance." This Premium Gem Red specimen displays beautiful copper-gold luster with hints of light green undertones and occasional blushes of light crimson. The strike is exquisite, bringing crisp definition to the design elements. Close scrutiny with a glass reveals no mentionable abrasions or spots. Unbelievable technical quality and aesthetic appeal. (#2428)

164 **1909 MS66 Red PCGS.** Intense luster and beautiful sunset-orange and mint-green coloration are the hallmarks of this lovely Premium Gem cent. The exquisitely preserved surfaces are unblemished, and show just a few traces of carbon. From the first year of the long-lived Lincoln cent series. (#2431)

165 **1909-S MS65 Red and Brown ICG.** This is one of the more attractive examples of the 1909-S Lincoln cent that we have ever encountered. Fully Red coins are generally preferred by serious collectors, but this example suffers not at all in the eye appeal department, despite some definite browning on each side. Well struck, lustrous, and free of surface distractions. (#2433)

166 **1909-S MS65 Red and Brown PCGS.** Beautiful copper-gold color, laced with occasional wisps of light tan, is evenly distributed over impeccably preserved surfaces. Except for weakness in the right wheat stalk, the design elements are well impressed. (#2433)

167 **1909-S MS65 Red NGC.** The sunset-orange surfaces of this first-year San Francisco example display hints of lime color at the margins. Well-defined save for the top of the O in ONE with isolated carbon in the open peripheral regions. (#2434)

168 **1909-S MS65 Red PCGS.** The lustrous fields have a distinctly matte-like, fine grain texture that is quite attractive. The tan-gold coloration achieves a mild woodgrain appearance over the obverse. A well struck and unabraded Gem from the first year of the Lincoln cent type. (#2434)

Attractive 1909-S Cent, MS66 Red

169 **1909-S MS66 Red PCGS.** While the 1909-S sits within the shadow of the famous 1909-S VDB, it is nevertheless a semi-key date within the Lincoln cent series. The Premium Gem example that we offer here displays pleasing luster and brass-gold color that gives hints of apricot, especially on the reverse. All of the design elements benefit from a solid strike. Full Red specimens are rare in higher grades. (#2434)

170 **1909-S S Over Horizontal S MS66 Red and Brown ANACS.** FS-012.3. This curious mintmark variant actually constitutes a large percentage of high quality 1909-S Lincoln cents. The impeccably smooth surfaces have mellowed to a relatively uniform amber-brown. Close inspection locates unimportant peripheral carbon. (#92433)

171 **1909-S S Over Horizontal S MS65 Red PCGS.** FS-012.3. This copper-orange cent displays the anomalous mintmark that distinguishes the variety. Solidly struck with only light marks, though the outer reverse displays minor carbon. Still, a pleasing example of this early Lincoln cent variety. (#92434)

172 **1909-S S Over Horizontal S MS65 Red PCGS.** FS-012.3. The undermintmark feature is easy to see on this example. Well struck with shimmering luster and beautiful tan-gold coloration. Free of marks or abrasions, with just a few tiny specks that deny perfection. A fabulous Gem example of this scarce variety. (#92434)

173 **1910-S MS65 Red PCGS.** In its second year of Lincoln cent production, San Francisco issued just over 6 million pieces. This lustrous copper-orange Gem has an exquisite strike and a nearly carbon-free appearance. Only faint marks in the fields preclude a finer grade. (#2440)

Red Gem 1912-D Lincoln

174 **1912-D MS65 Red PCGS.** This second-year Denver Mint cent is satiny and decisively struck with luminous brick-red fields. The portrait highpoints have a whisper of ruby-red. Essentially void of contact, and only trivial carbon emerges with the aid of a loupe. Encased in a green label holder. (#2455)

175 **1912-S MS65 Red and Brown NGC.** This is a truly impressive Lincoln cent that displays rich coloration and beautiful satin luster. The crisp striking details are perhaps its most noteworthy attribute, as the detail on Lincoln's portrait seems complete. The surfaces are unmarked and show minimal carbon. Census: 33 in 65 Red and Brown, 4 finer (6/07). (#2457)

176 **1912-S MS64 Red NGC.** The West Coast demonstrated less demand for cents than the East in 1912; Philadelphia produced over 68 million cents, while the mintage for San Francisco was slightly over 4.4 million pieces. This dusky orange cent has pleasing detail and generally well-preserved surfaces. A few areas in the pebbly obverse fields have begun to turn. Census: 40 in 64 Red, 20 finer (5/07). (#2458)

177 **1914-D AU55 PCGS.** With a mintage of under 1.2 million pieces and little awareness of that low production, the vast majority of 1914-D cents entered circulation, and in higher grades, the price of a 1914-D cent rivals or even exceeds its 1909-S VDB counterpart. This modestly worn, pleasing example offers strong detail and lovely nutmeg-brown color with a touch of gold on the lower left wheat ear. A lovely piece that would fit well in a similarly graded date set. (#2471)

MS63 Brown 1914-D Cent

178 **1914-D MS63 Brown PCGS.** A satiny chocolate-brown key date cent whose unmarked fields and boldly struck devices ensure impressive eye appeal. The 1914-D has the third lowest mintage of the series, behind the 1909-S VDB and the 1931-S. However, Mint State examples of the latter two issues were saved in significantly greater numbers. (#2471)

1914-D Key-Date Cent, MS66 Brown

179 **1914-D MS66 Brown NGC.** The 1914-D is an important key-date in the Lincoln cent series. In referring to this issue, David Lange (2005) writes: "Mint State coins of any quality are now and always have been in short supply. Gems of any color are very scarce; fully red gems are rare." A mix of light brown and sky-blue patination adheres to semi-glossy surfaces, and is joined by blushes of crimson and copper-gold on the reverse. A well executed strike results in sharp design element definition. Both sides are devoid of mentionable contact marks or unsightly spotting. A truly wonderful specimen that will add outstanding quality and appeal to a high-grade Lincoln cent collection. (#2471)

Key 1914-D Cent MS64 Red and Brown

180 **1914-D MS64 Red and Brown PCGS.** This boldly struck key date cent is impressively free from abrasions, and displays unencumbered satin sheen. The obverse is more red than brown, while the obverse is orange and sea-green along with a prominent blush of deep ruby-red. Certified in an old green label holder. (#2472)

Choice Red and Brown 1914-D Cent

181 **1914-D MS64 Red and Brown PCGS.** A satiny and unabraded near-Gem of this desirable low mintage issue. Dusky gold alternates with cherry-red and olive. The strike is intricate, and the absence of relevant carbon confirms the eye appeal. Given the cost of a spot-free full red example, the present piece provides a collectible alternative. (#2472)

182 **1914-S MS64 Red and Brown PCGS.** Though not as celebrated as its D-mint counterpart, the 1914-S cent presents a legitimate challenge in finer grades. Streaks of orange and glints of ruby punctuate the otherwise violet-brown surfaces of this near-Gem, well struck and free of major distractions. (#2475)

Exceptional 1914-S Semi-Key Cent, MS65 Red

183 **1914-S MS65 Red NGC.** The 1914-S is among the scarcest of the semi-key dates in the Lincoln cent series. High-grade pieces are in relatively short supply due to problems in producing the coins. More specifically, cent specialist David Lange (2005) writes: "Problems with the planchet stock have caused many specimens across the entire grade spectrum to display signs of corrosion and other discoloration." The elusiveness of full Red Gem specimens is evident from the census/population data that shows just 38 MS65 coins, and a mere two finer (6/07). The exceptional Red Gem in this lot displays bright gold surfaces that exhibit sharply struck design elements. Impressively preserved on both sides, with no mentionable spots, discoloration, or stains. Census: 5 in 65 Red, 0 finer (6/07). (#2476)

184 **1915-S MS64 Red and Brown PCGS.** The satiny surfaces of this unabraded cherry-red and orange-gold near-Gem have mellowed only slightly. The strike is absolute except on the top of the O in ONE. Infrequent pinpoint carbon is all that limits the grade. (#2484)

Sharp 1917 Doubled Die Obverse Cent, XF45

185 1917 Doubled Die Obverse XF45 PCGS. FS-013. Clear doubling is seen on WE TRUST and the 9 and 7 of the date. Medium brown color with hints of underlying red covers the surfaces of both obverse and reverse. Nice definition is apparent on the design features, including near-complete separation in the lines and grains of the wheat stalks. David Lange (2005) writes that: "This variety is illustrated in ... the *Red Book*, also in Walter Breen's ... *Encyclopedia*. This assures that it will always be in demand and command a premium price when properly attributed." (#92495)

186 1917-D MS65 Red and Brown PCGS. This is a highly attractive Lincoln cent with deep blue and red color over the matte-like surfaces. Well struck and lacking contact marks or excessive carbon. A conditionally scarce Gem example. Population: 25 in 65 Red and Brown, 1 finer (6/07). (#2499)

Gorgeous 1921 Cent, MS66 Red

187 1921 MS66 Red PCGS. 1921 Mint State cents are relatively plentiful in all color designations. Even fully Red pieces are available, but as David Lange (2005) says: " ... these frequently fall short of the gem category because of spotting or indifferent striking quality." The MS66 Red example offered here does not fit this profile. A solid strike emboldens the design features, including sharp delineation in Lincoln's hair and bowtie, and on the grains and lines of both wheat stalks. Impeccably preserved surfaces exude intense luster, and display gorgeous golden color with splashes of golden-orange on the obverse. Population: 63 in 66 Red, 11 finer (6/07). (#2533)

188 1922-D MS65 Red NGC. The bright orange-red fields display crimson overtones. The surfaces are carefully preserved with no distracting blemishes or carbon. A pleasing representative of the only 1922-dated cent issue. (#2539)

189 1922 No D Strong Reverse Fine 12 PCGS. Die Pair 2. Though the wheat ears actually show little definition on the reverse, other die diagnostics confirm the pair. This chocolate-brown coin's significant wear further enhances the pillowy, blurred effect found on the obverse. (#3285)

Key 1922 No D Lincoln Cent XF40

190 1922 No D Strong Reverse XF40 PCGS. FS-013.2. Die Pair 2. The lines of the wheat ears are sharp, and there is much more overall striking detail on the reverse than on the obverse. The greenish-tan surfaces only show a few minor marks. A scarce and popular key issue which is noted on page 115 of the 2008 *Guide Book*. (#3285)

XF Strong Reverse 1922 No D Cent

191 1922 No D Strong Reverse XF40 PCGS. FS-013.2. Die Pair 2. A chocolate-brown beauty with a bold reverse and blurry obverse definition, diagnostic for this key *Guide Book* variety. The PCGS holder is a bit scuffy, but the coin itself is problem-free aside from a fleck or two of debris along the reverse border. (#3285)

Desirable 1922 No D Strong Reverse Cent MS62 Red and Brown

Important Red Gem 1923-S Cent

192 **1922 No D Strong Reverse MS62 Red and Brown PCGS.** The most popular variety of no-D cent is the one coined from Die Pair 2, which is the one that commands the highest price. This die pair possesses a brand-new reverse die with no wear, hence the "Strong Reverse" label. PCGS has seen only 13 Strong Reverse Red and Brown examples (6/07).

This MS62 Red and Brown specimen displays considerable mint orange intermixed with light tan patination. The obverse exhibits the typical low-relief, weakened design elements resulting from abrasive polishing of the die to remove clash marks, which in the process removed the mintmark. The reverse design features are sharp, as expected. A few minor handling marks are noted, especially on the obverse, but none are serious distractions. A couple of light, minute flecks are seen on the reverse. (#3286)

193 **1923 MS66 Red PCGS.** A magnificent razor-sharp Premium Gem with dazzling luster and exceptional eye appeal. Devoid of marks, and carbon is minimal. Population: 77 in 66 Red, 13 finer (5/07). (#2545)

194 **1923-S MS64 Red and Brown PCGS.** Dusky orange-red and olive grace this satiny near-Gem. Well struck save for the AM in AMERICA. The upper reverse has a couple of minuscule specks of lacquer. (#2547)

195 **1923-S MS65 Red NGC.** In the 1950s, when Lincoln cents were principally collected from pocket change, no one regarded the 1923-S as a key to a high grade collection. Certainly, the 1923-S was considered a better date, but one that could be found (in worn grades) with sufficient searching. As quality and specialization became increasingly important, the 1923-S rose in significance. PCGS published population reports that pointed out the rarity of the '23-S in full Red. Registry sets were formed, focusing demand on the '23-S and other difficult branch mint issues from the teens and twenties. Today, a '23-S with consistent orange-red color and smooth, nearly carbon-free surfaces is a coveted opportunity for the Lincoln enthusiast. The present Gem has these features, and in addition, the strike is sharp save for minor blending on the right border of the right wheat ear. Census: 2 in 65 Red, 0 finer (5/07). (#2548)

196 **1924-D MS65 Red and Brown PCGS.** A sharply struck and attractive Gem example of this Roaring Twenties issue, largely chocolate-brown on the obverse with a blend of orange and ruby on the reverse. Tied for the finest certified Red and Brown example graded by PCGS (5/07). (#2553)

197 **1924-D MS64 Red PCGS.** Well struck for the issue, with pleasing satin luster and attractive coloration. Faint toning streaks are noted on each side, but surface blemishes are nearly nonexistent. According to David Lange (2005): "A semi-key date in all grades, 1924-D is scarce and always in demand." (#2554)

198 **1925 MS67 Red NGC.** Attractive copper-gold patina embraces fully lustrous surfaces. The design elements are adequately struck, and a couple of minuscule reverse flecks are mentioned only for the sake of accuracy. Census: 26 in 67 Red, 0 finer (6/07). (#2560)

Colorful Gem 1925-S Cent

199 1925-S MS65 Red and Brown NGC. This unabraded Gem is well struck aside from minor incompleteness on the O in ONE. Lemon, olive, and peach consume the obverse, while the reverse is mostly rose-red with peripheral yellow-gold. A few tiny ebony flecks are of little import. Certified in a prior generation holder. (#2565)

200 1931-D MS65 Red PCGS. Boldly struck with attractive pink-red toning and well-preserved surfaces that are nearly undisturbed by even the smallest of abrasions. A lovely example of the "other" branch mint cent issue of 1931, one with significantly lower populations in Gem Red than the 1931-S. (#2617)

201 1931-S MS66 Red and Brown NGC. David Lange (2005), discussing the 1931-S cents, writes: "Mint State coins of average to choice quality are readily available due to widespread hoarding during the early 1930s. Gems are more elusive, since these hoarded coins were subject to poor storage methods and environmental hazards. In addition, most have less than perfect strikes." This Premium Gem displays considerable mint orange imbued with whispers of light tan. The design elements were subjected to a better-than-average strike, though some softness is noted in Lincoln's hair and beard. The grains and lines of the wheat stalks, on the other hand, are clearly defined. A few light flecks are visible on the obverse. (#2619)

202 1931-S MS65 Red PCGS. A lustrous pumpkin-orange Gem, essentially void of abrasions but with a couple of small areas of gray color on the lower half of the reverse. This issue's atypically low mintage drew the attention of collectors then and continues to do so today. Housed in a green label holder. (#2620)

Important 1936 Doubled Die Cent, MS63 Red and Brown

203 1936 Doubled Die Obverse MS63 Red and Brown PCGS. FS-014. This piece is identified on the holder as Type One. It is the most important of three doubled die varieties listed in the *Cherrypicker's Guide*, and carries its own listing in the current *Guide Book*. Doubling can be seen at the date, LIBERTY, the motto, and even Lincoln's bow tie. Both sides have satiny luster with considerable orange mint color, blended with pale blue and light olive. (#82649)

204 1943-D/D MS65 PCGS. FS-019. The most dramatic repunched mintmark variety for the 1943-dated zinc-plated steel cents. The secondary mintmark is fully outlined and widely shifted southwest. The variety is both listed and photographed in the 2008 Guide Book. Intricately struck, lustrous, and splendidly smooth. (#2715)

205 1944-D/S MS64 Red PCGS. FS-020. OMM #1. *Cherrypickers'* gives this variety a five-star interest rating, partly because it is listed in the Guide Book. A lustrous and well struck pumpkin-gold near-Gem with minor carbon limiting the grade. (#2728)

Lovely 1955 Doubled Die Cent, MS63 Red and Brown

206 1955/55 Doubled Die Obverse MS63 Red and Brown PCGS. The famous doubled die of 1955 is possibly the most important doubled die variety listed in the Guide Book. This piece has splendid surfaces with full satin luster. Both sides have considerable reddish-orange mint color that is accompanied by pale blue and brown toning. A single small spot can be seen on the reverse. (#2826)

1955/55 Doubled Die Obverse Cent MS64 Red and Brown

207 1955/55 Doubled Die Obverse MS64 Red and Brown PCGS. The first 1955 doubled die specimens turned up in Massachusetts in late 1955, and also in upstate New York. David Lange (2005) writes that: "Quite a few were found sealed within packages of cigarettes dispensed from vending machines. With these packs then priced at 23 cents each, change of a quarter was already provided by the cigarette manufacturer along with the cigarettes to avoid the nuisance of loading cents separately into their machines." Spectacular doubling is readily visible on all obverse letters and digits. Whispers of light tan, sky-blue, and crimson visit copper-gold surfaces that are devoid of blemishes, and a sharp strike results in strong design feature detail.(#2826)

Attractive 1955/55 Doubled Die Obverse, MS64 Red

208 1955/55 Doubled Die Obverse MS64 Red PCGS. FS-021.8. A lovely coin from the standpoint of aesthetic appeal, both sides are richly colored in copper-gold luster that brightens slightly in the fields. A sharp strike brings out great detail on the design elements. The smooth surfaces are at the threshold of a full Gem rating. On a historical note, David Lange (2005) writes: "Several years passed before these coins acquired much of a premium, but they were firmly established as a popular addition to the Lincoln series by 1960." (#2827)

209 **1956-D MS66 Red PCGS.** FS-022. RPM #8. Early die state. The mintmark is repunched directly south, with such a dramatically wide spread that the two mintmarks are fully separated. The secondary mintmark is weak but completely outlined. A lustrous straw-gold Premium Gem. A diagonal slide mark at 4 o'clock on the reverse is of little import. (#2839)

210 **1961-D MS67 Red NGC.** A gorgeous orange-red Superb Gem with virtually immaculate preservation. Well struck aside from the centers of a few steps. Census: 43 in 67 Red, none finer (5/07). (#2875)

211 **1963-D MS67 Red NGC.** Ex: Omaha Bank Hoard. This amazing cent has exquisite orange mint luster with satiny surfaces. In fact, the fields are nearly prooflike in appearance, with visible reflectivity. Seldom do such coins appear in the numismatic marketplace. PCGS has never graded an example of this date so high, with just two certified by NGC, and none any finer (6/07). (#2887)

212 **1972/72 Doubled Die MS65 Red NGC.** FS-033.3. The lustrous surfaces of this doubled die Lincoln cent display deep fire-red toning, with occasional hints of steel-gray. A shallow planchet flaw is noted adjacent to the T in CENT. Splashes of ruby and steel-green patina are noted in the obverse fields. A fingerprint fragment is noticeable on the lower half of the reverse. (#2950)

213 **1972/72 Doubled Die MS66 Red PCGS.** FS-033.3. Die #1. A satiny Premium Gem, this lovely piece has brilliant pinkish-orange mint color with pristine surfaces. This is a "naked eye" doubled die variety, with doubling that does not require magnification to view. (#2950)

PROOF LINCOLN CENTS

214 **1909 PR65 Red and Brown NGC.** The finely faceted surfaces showcase an attractive blend of lemon-gold, umber, and orange colors. Boldly defined with tremendous eye appeal and minimal carbon. Census: 40 in 65 Red and Brown, 22 finer (6/07). (#3304)

215 **1912 PR65 Red and Brown NGC.** An intricately detailed proof, this piece has satiny luster with silvery surfaces that blend bright orange, dark brown, and pale blue color. The squared rims and bold lettering that appears to sit on top of the matte fields characterize the early proof Lincoln cents. (#3313)

216 **1913 PR65 Red PCGS.** An especially attractive Gem proof with matte surfaces that exhibit satiny luster and actually display a trace of reflectivity in the fields. As it should be, every detail is intricately defined. (#3317)

217 **1914 PR66 Brown PCGS.** Fully struck and pristine, with lovely matte proof surfaces that show electric-green and brown toning on the obverse, with satiny brown color across the reverse. Population: 10 in 66 Brown, 0 finer at either service (6/07). (#3318)

218 **1915 PR65 Brown NGC.** The 1915 and 1916 issues tie for the lowest-mintage matte proof cents offered to the general public, with just 1,150 specimens each. The orange-brown surfaces of this softly shimmering cent have unusual vitality, and the portrait has crisp detail. (#3321)

219 **1915 PR64 Red PCGS.** Fully struck and well preserved, with rich coloration and lovely matte-like surfaces. Faint carbon flecks and streaks limit the grade. Population: 14 in 64 Red, 28 finer (6/07). (#3323)

220 **1950 PR65 Red Cameo PCGS; 1951 PR65 Red PCGS,** a small spot near the ear; **1952 PR65 Red Cameo PCGS; 1953 PR65 Red Cameo PCGS; 1954 PR66 Red Cameo PCGS; 1955 PR67 Cameo PCGS,** in a green label holder; **1956 PR67 Deep Cameo PCGS; 1957 PR67 Red Cameo PCGS; 1958 PR67 Cameo PCGS,** minor obverse flyspecks; **1959 PR67 Red Cameo PCGS; 1960 Small Date PR67 Red Cameo PCGS; 1961 PR67 Red Deep Cameo PCGS; 1962 PR68 Deep Cameo PCGS; 1963 PR69 Deep Cameo PCGS,** two pinpoint flecks; **1964 PR69 Deep Cameo PCGS; 1968-S PR67 Red Deep Cameo PCGS; 1968-S PR68 Red Deep Cameo PCGS,** a couple of flecks; **1969-S PR68 Red Deep Cameo PCGS;** and a **1970-S Large Date PR65 Red PCGS,** lovely orange-red and lime obverse patina. (Total: 19 coins) (#83359)

221 **1950 PR66 Cameo PCGS.** This peach-gold Premium Gem also has glimpses of ice-blue and aquamarine. The strike is decisive, and the surfaces are virtually mark-free. Certified in an old green label holder. (#83359)

222 **1960 Large Over Small Date PR67 Red PCGS.** FS-025. Fivaz and Stanton rate this as "the more popular" of two proof Large Over Small Date varieties for the year, distinguished by the precisely concentric zeroes in the date. This gleaming Superb Gem offers bold detail and vivid, original copper-orange color. Population: 45 in 67 Red, 16 finer (6/07). (#3410)

223 **1960 Small Over Large Date PR67 Red PCGS.** Though two distinct, major Large Date Over Small Date varieties are known to proof Lincoln cent collectors, only one doubled die of note has the opposite pattern. This flashy, originally colored 1960 cent's date has the smaller numerals floating atop larger versions. Boldly struck with powerful visual appeal. (#3413)

224 **1971-S Doubled Die Obverse, Type Two, FS-032 PR67 Red NGC.** The date, GOD, and LIBERTY are prominently die doubled. FS-032 is the sole '71-S DDO with significant die doubling on the date. A lovely and unabraded pumpkin-gold specimen that boasts an intricate strike. A carbon fleck is noted above the first U in PLURIBUS. (#3533)

225 **1971-S Doubled Die Obverse, Type Two, FS-032 PR67 Red PCGS.** LIBERTY, GOD, and the date are boldly die doubled. This is a key issue among the varieties in the PCGS Set Registry. This example is a lovely Superb Gem with fire-red centers and yellow-gold margins. Faint flecks are found near the E in ONE. Population: 19 in 67, 2 finer (6/07). (#3533)

TWO CENT PIECES

226 **1864 Small Motto MS61 Brown NGC.** FS-000.5. The design elements are a bit softly struck on each side. Even brown patina covers the surfaces and has subdued the original mint luster. A few light marks are seen in the center of the reverse. (#3579)

227 **1864 Small Motto MS64 Brown NGC.** FS-000.5. The Small Motto is a key to the two cent series, and some consider it to be a pattern issue. This piece is sharply struck on each side. The surfaces retain a surprising amount of red color, especially for a coin that is technically considered Brown by NGC. A pleasing, upper-end example of this important issue. (#3579)

228 **1867 MS64 Red NGC.** Gorgeous orange-gold color occupies both faces of this near-Gem Red two cent piece. A well executed strike results in nice, uniform definition on the design elements. Devoid of significant marks or any unsightly spotting. A light, inoffensive toning spot is noted on the base of the 2. Census: 15 in 64 Red, 11 finer (6/07). (#3593)

229 **1867 Doubled Die Obverse AU55 NGC.** FS-101, formerly FS-003. The pickup point for the wide die doubling is IN GOD WE TRUST, although nearby design elements are also doubled. A briefly circulated chocolate-brown representative that has an attractive appearance. (#3594)

230 **1867 Doubled Die Obverse—Cleaned—ANACS. MS60 Details.** FS-101, formerly FS-003. Die #1. IN GOD WE TRUST is widely die doubled. This lustrous example is recolored orange-red, and a shallow lamination is present east of the date. The final letters in AMERICA are softly struck, perhaps due to a partly clogged die. (#3594)

231 **1869 MS65 Red NGC.** A decisively struck brick-red Gem with pleasantly mark-free surfaces. Carbon is also inconsequential. By 1869, the mintages for this type had dwindled significantly from the 1864 heyday, limiting the number of full Red survivors. Census: 17 in 65 Red, 2 finer (6/07). (#3605)

PROOF TWO CENT PIECES

232 **1864 Large Motto PR64 Brown PCGS.** Iridescent bluish-gold fields accentuate light tan motifs, especially when the coin is tilted under a light source. A well executed strike leaves excellent definition on all of the design features. Close examination reveals no significant contact marks or unsightly spotting. Population: 11 in 64 Brown, 9 finer (4/07). (#3621)

233 **1864 Large Motto PR65 Brown NGC.** Decisively struck with a touch of flash and distinctive coloration. The obverse has a blend of lime-green and lemon-gold patina, while the reverse displays deeper, slightly streaky pumpkin-orange and walnut-brown toning. Immensely appealing. (#3621)

234 **1867 PR64 Red and Brown NGC.** Choice with vibrant pumpkin-orange surfaces on the obverse and just enough brown on the reverse to deny a full Red designation. Modest carbon is noted at the upper obverse periphery, and a few small hairlines are noted in the fields. (#3634)

235 **1867 PR65 Red and Brown PCGS.** An orange-gold Gem with hints of violet-red toning across the open fields. Sharply struck, unabraded, and only limited in grade by peripheral minuscule carbon flecks. Only 625+ proofs were struck. (#3634)

236 **1868 PR66 Red and Brown NGC.** Rose and lemon-gold alternate across this boldly struck and unabraded Premium Gem. Two minuscule obverse carbon flecks are noted near 9 o'clock. A mere 600+ proofs were struck. (#3637)

237 **1868 PR64 Red PCGS.** This intricately struck and unabraded Choice proof is mostly yellow-gold, although minor carbon and blushes of cherry-red are also present, particularly near the date. Housed in a green label holder. Population: 31 in 64 Red, 31 finer (4/07). (#3638)
From The Vanek Collection.

Gorgeous 1870 Two Cent, PR66 Red

238 **1870 PR66 Red NGC.** Somewhat over 1,000 proof two cent pieces were produced in 1870. NGC and PCGS combined have assigned the full Red color designation to approximately 140 specimens, primarily through the Gem level of preservation. Blazing mint orange exudes from both sides of this wonderful two center, and sharp design elements prevail. A small toning spot is noted on the right-side wreath. Census: 11 in 66 Red, 2 finer (6/07). (#3644)

THREE CENT SILVER

239 **1853 MS65 PCGS.** This beautifully smooth and lustrous Gem has a few dabs of russet patina on the reverse. The centers are well struck, particularly the shield. The base of the 3 in the date and a couple of peripheral stars lack absolute definition. (#3667)

240 **1856 MS64 PCGS.** Choice with potent, swirling luster. The reverse surfaces are largely untoned, though the fields have specks of green-gray at the left obverse. The centers have pleasing definition, though the peripheral devices are softly struck. An attractive example of this second-type issue. (#3672)

241 **1856 MS64 PCGS.** Pumpkin-gold, ruby-red, and aquamarine patina endows this refreshingly mark-free near-Gem. The shield is sharply impressed for a business strike, although portions of the peripheries are incomplete. (#3672)

Pleasing 1856 Three Cent, MS65

242 **1856 MS65 PCGS.** This little Gem trime displays a medley of pastel mauve, gold, and sky-blue patination on the obverse, while the reverse takes on deep forest-green and purple. A sharper strike than usually seen on the 1854-1858 design type (Type Two) brings up generally strong definition on the motifs. David Bowers (1988) writes that: "Of all three types of the silver three cent denomination, the 1854-58 style is the most difficult to locate. Few Uncirculated pieces were saved at the time of issue, so pieces in Mint State are quite rare today." Population: 21 in 65, 3 finer (5/07). (#3672)

Lustrous 1856 Three Cent Silver, MS65

243 **1856 MS65 NGC.** A lustrous and well preserved cream-gray Gem. Sharply struck on the major devices; softness is noted on the peripheral elements. A few interesting die lines (as made) intersect near the shield border, and clashmarks occur on the reverse. Quite scarce at the MS65 level, and in demand as a high grade example of the scarce Variety Two design. Census: 15 in 65, 4 finer (6/07). (#3672)

244 **1857 MS64 PCGS.** Peach, apple-green, and plum-red shadings enrich this Type Two trime. The smooth surfaces ensure the eye appeal. The centers are boldly brought up, while the margins show isolated softness. (#3673)

245 **1861 MS66 PCGS.** Nearly half a million business strike three cent silver pieces were struck in 1861. PCGS and NGC have certified close to 140 coins in Premium Gem, the level of preservation of the specimen in this lot. Highly lustrous, nicely preserved surfaces display a medley of gray, cobalt-blue, and faint reddish-gold patination. All of the design features are impressively struck. Population: 67 in 66, 22 finer (6/07). (#3679)

246 **1862 MS65 PCGS.** Splotches of cobalt-blue, golden-tan, and lavender gravitate to the margins of this lustrous Gem trime. Generally well struck, save for the usual weakness in the reverse leaves. There are no significant marks to report. (#3680)

247 **1862/1 MS65 PCGS.** FS-007. The upright of the 1 is visible near the left edge of the 2. This trime has charming toning, with red, violet, and blue over somewhat reflective surfaces. Struck from clashed dies. (#3681)

248 **1864 MS62 NGC.** Crisply struck with glassy, prooflike fields and speckled russet and green patina on both sides. A few wispy pinscratches and carbon flecks restrict the grade. Only 12,000 pieces were struck of this reduced Civil War issue, at a time when silver and gold coins were widely hoarded. (#3684)

249 **1870 MS64 PCGS.** Of the 3,000 business strike trimes coined for this year, many found the melting pot, and survivors are few today. This silver-gray Choice example offers pleasing detail and strong, partially reflective luster. Highly appealing. Population: 15 in 64, 12 finer (5/07). (#3691)

PROOF THREE CENT SILVER

250 **1860 PR64 PCGS.** Walter Breen (1977) writes of the 1860 proof trime: "Survivors represent only a small minority of the original mintage (1,000 pieces). Some 538 sold ... the rest melted." Lilac and cobalt-blue patina covers both sides of this near-Gem, and a well executed strike brings up most of the design features, except for softness in some of the reverse stars and the leaves. A linear strike-through is located along the left border of the reverse. Population: 30 in 64, 6 finer (4/07). (#3709)

251 **1863 PR63 Cameo PCGS.** Light gold toning visits the reflective fields. The devices are delicately frosted. Struck from clashed dies. Only 460 proofs were produced for this Civil War date. (#83712)

252 **1865 PR63 PCGS.** Gold, rose, and olive toning envelop this decisively struck and unabraded specimen. Only 500 proofs and 8,000 business strikes were issued for this scarce Civil War date. (#3715)

253 **1867 PR65 PCGS.** Deep lavender, midnight-blue, and aqua toning dominates this razor-sharp Gem. A hair-thin lintmark is present beneath the ST in STATES. Encapsulated in a green label holder. Just 625 proofs were struck. Population: 55 in 65, 22 finer (6/07). (#3717)

254 **1868 PR64 PCGS.** Apple-green and salmon-pink patina embrace this beautiful needle-sharp near-Gem. A scant 600 proofs were struck. Certified in a green label holder. (#3718)
From The Vanek Collection.

255 **1871 PR66 NGC.** A flashy specimen with lovely ice-blue, rose-red, and gold toning. Sharply struck aside from the arrows ribbon and selected portions of the shield. Only 960 proofs were struck. Census: 17 in 66, 13 finer (5/07). (#3722)

Exquisite 1872 Three Cent Silver, PR66

256 **1872 PR66 PCGS.** A thin coat of iridescent reddish-gold color is joined by an occasional speckle of cobalt-blue, and the exquisite design delineation befits a proof striking. There are no significant marks on either side. Frosted motifs offer a pleasing contrast with deeply mirrored fields. The 1872 proof issue, with a mintage of 950 pieces, is in demand from date collectors, as only 1,000 business strikes were produced. Population: 14 in 66, 2 finer (6/07). (#3723)

THREE CENT NICKELS

257 **1872 MS66 PCGS.** Lustrous surfaces display a haze of golden-gray patination and well struck design elements, except for weakness in some of the lines of the III. There are no mentionable marks to report. Population: 11 in 66, 0 finer (4/07). (#3738)

258 **1880 MS66 PCGS.** This impressive three cent nickel is well struck and immaculately preserved. Each side is draped with bluish-gray toning that yields to pretty golden highlights near the peripheries. A low mintage issue that remains surprisingly available in high grades. (#3748)

Rare Business Strike 1887 Three Cent Nickel, MS65

259 **1887 MS65 NGC.** One of the rare business strikes from this date, and worth a significant premium in all grades. To underscore that last statement, the Red Book lists a value of $250 for the 1887 in Good 4! This is a definite business strike that lacks any reflectivity in the fields. Also, there is slight striking weakness on the fluted left column of the Roman numeral on the reverse—a trait usually only seen on business strikes. Brilliant throughout, the mint luster swirls around each side. The only defect is a planchet flake out of the center of the reverse. Census: 21 in 65, 4 finer (6/07). (#3755)

PROOF THREE CENT NICKELS

Lovely 1865 Three Cent Nickel, PR65 Cameo

260 **1865 PR65 Cameo PCGS.** One of two candidates for the lowest-mintage proof three cent nickel issue, alongside the proof-only 1877, both of which have estimated mintages of slightly over 500 pieces. Strongly reflective with pleasing detail and distinct contrast evident on each side, particularly the gold-tinged reverse. A large area of the portrait exhibits vibrant sunset-orange color as well. Population: 18 in 65 Cameo, 24 finer (4/07). (#83761)

Pleasing 1866 Three Cent Nickel, PR66 Cameo

261 **1866 PR66 Cameo NGC.** The 1866 three cent nickel comes with a reported mintage of 725 pieces. NGC and PCGS have assigned the Cameo designation to approximately 80 pieces. Frosty design elements are sharply impressed, and present a strong contrast with the deeply mirrored fields. Hints of speckled tan-gold adhere to well preserved surfaces. Census: 10 in 66 Cameo, 1 finer (6/07). (#83762)

262 **1867 PR65 Cameo PCGS.** This lovely Gem displays cameo contrast which is unimprovably strong on both sides. The design details are completely struck and the surfaces are impeccably preserved. The 1867 is a very scarce and sought-after issue in the proof three cent nickel series. Population: 13 in 65 Cameo, 17 finer (6/07). (#83763)

263 **1868 PR64 PCGS.** A well struck near-Gem with an aquamarine obverse and medium orange-gold, lime, and powder-blue toning on the reverse. The *Guide Book* reports a proof mintage of only 600+ pieces. Housed in a green label holder. (#3764)
From The Vanek Collection.

264 **1869 PR66 Ultra Cameo NGC.** A boldly struck and nearly immaculate Premium Gem that boasts flashy fields and obvious white-on-black contrast. Census: 8 in 66 Ultra Cameo, 1 finer (5/07). (#93765)

265 **1870 PR65 PCGS.** This flashy Gem has pastel sun-gold patina. Well struck save for the right center of the first denominational column. The initial dates in the series are scarce in proof, relative to the post-1877 issues. Population: 59 in 65, 7 finer (4/07). (#3766)

266 **1871 PR66 PCGS.** This is a lovely Premium Gem proof that exhibits nearly unimprovable quality. The design elements are crisply struck and the surfaces are essentially untoned, save for a touch of color on Liberty's cheekbone. A small window of prooflikeness, from die polish, is noted near the upper right obverse border, between OF and AMERICA. Population: 23 in 66, 0 finer (4/07). (#3767)

267 **1873 Closed 3 PR66 Cameo PCGS.** All of the 1,100 proofs of this year were struck with a "Closed" 3 in the date. The later Open 3 dies were only used for business strikes. This is a lovely Premium Gem with obvious cameo contrast on both sides. The design details are crisply rendered and the surfaces are immaculately preserved. Population: 8 in 66 Cameo, 1 finer (6/07). (#83769)

268 **1876 PR66 Cameo PCGS.** An exceptional, sharply contrasted proof striking from this popular year. The fields are unfathomable in their deep reflectivity and the devices are thickly frosted. Virtually defect-free. Each side shows a light layer of rose-gray patina. Population: 11 in 66, 0 finer (6/07). (#83772)

Key 1877 Three Cent Nickel, PR64

269 **1877 PR64 NGC.** The 1877, along with the 1865, are the two keys to the three cent nickel series. Only 510 pieces were struck of the 1877, and all were proofs. Shallowly mirrored, as often seen. The surfaces are covered with fine, streaky gray-lilac toning on each side. Fully struck, of course, as expected from a proof. (#3773)

270 **1878 PR65 NGC.** A pleasing Gem specimen from the second of three proof-only three cent nickel issues, this one with a mintage of 2,350 pieces. Luminous with sun-gold patina over the obverse and the outer reverse and soft mint-green color that drapes the center of the reverse. (#3774)
From The Vanek Collection.

271 **1878 PR65 NGC.** Sharply struck and immaculately preserved, the essentially color-free surfaces show mildly reflective fields and a faint cameo-like effect on both sides. There are no distracting marks or hairlines to report. A scarce, proof-only issue with a mere 2,350 pieces produced. (#3774)

272 **1881 PR66 Cameo NGC.** An untoned and highly attractive proof striking. Excellent contrast is seen on each side and there are no mentionable marks on this high grade piece. (#83777)

273 **1881 PR67 Cameo NGC.** Deeply reflective, essentially untoned fields and boldly impressed devices converge on this carefully preserved later three cent nickel proof. Appealing with distinct contrast. Census: 26 in 67 Cameo, 7 finer (5/07). (#83777)

274 **1881 PR67 ★ Cameo NGC.** This dazzling Superb Gem proof exhibits stark field-to-device contrast on each side, between the richly frosted devices and the jet-black fields. Fully struck and impeccably preserved. NGC Census: 3 in 67 ★ Cameo, 2 in 68 ★ Cameo, none finer (6/07). (#83777)

275 **1882 PR67 Cameo PCGS.** This glittering Superb Gem proof displays razor-sharp striking details and stark cameo contrast on both sides. Impeccably preserved and seemingly pristine, with unimprovable eye appeal. Population: 50 in 67 Cameo, 4 finer (6/07). (#83778)

276 **1883 PR66 NGC.** This issue's proof mintage of 6,609 pieces, the highest for any three cent nickel, is larger than the business strike mintage, which consisted of 4,000 examples. Well-defined with pleasing reflectivity and elegant gold-rose patina over each side. (#3779)

277 **1883 PR66 PCGS.** Light lilac streaks cross the obverse of this fully struck Premium Gem. The reverse is nearly untoned. A low mintage date, but nonetheless collectible in high quality. Encapsulated in an old green label holder. (#3779)

278 **1884 PR67 ★ Cameo NGC.** The brilliant obverse has dramatically profound white-on-black contrast between the icy devices and the glittering field. The wreath is also frosty, although the three columns lack sufficient contrast to merit an Ultra Cameo designation. (#83780)

279 **1885 PR67 NGC.** The portrait and wreath are delicately frosted, and appear to provide cameo contrast, although there is no such designation on the NGC insert. The mirrored fields are unabraded, and this Superb Gem is essentially bereft of toning. Census: 19 in 67, 0 finer (5/07). (#3781)

280 **1886 PR66 PCGS.** This satiny proof-only Premium Gem displays a hint of gold patina, although many would regard it as brilliant. Boldly struck, beautiful, and encapsulated in a green label holder. (#3782)

281 **1886 PR67 NGC.** Brilliant surfaces reveal moderate reflectivity in the fields, and lightly frosted motifs. Well struck, including full definition in the III. Both sides are impeccably preserved. (#3782)

282 **1888 PR66 PCGS.** A meticulously struck Premium Gem with smooth and lustrous silver-gray and chestnut-gold surfaces. Scarce in such quality. (#3785)

283 **1889 PR67 PCGS.** Blushes of tan-gold toning adorn the centers of this final-year Superb Gem. The strike is intricate except for the denticles. Only microscopic carbon denies perfection. Population: 49 in 67, 1 finer (4/07). (#3786)

SHIELD NICKELS

284 **1866 Rays MS65 PCGS.** Honey-gold toning graces this lustrous Gem. The obverse is remarkably preserved, and the reverse has only faint contact near the lower border. A few of the stars near 6 o'clock are typically brought up. (#3790)

285 **1867 Rays MS64 PCGS.** Fewer than 10% of the nickels struck in 1867 were of the Rays variety, and the piece offered here is a wonderful example of the short-lived design type. The well-defined devices and quicksilver fields are generally distraction-free. A splash of peach toning at the upper obverse rim draws attention to a heavy die crack that nearly encircles that side, while the center of the reverse has a blush of similar color. (#3791)

286 **1867 No Rays MS65 NGC.** During its early years, the Shield nickel was plagued with production problems, due at least partly to the hardness of the metal. This can be illustrated on the current example by reference to the spindly die cracks that are noticeable on the obverse. Lustrous and well preserved, this is still an attractive and conditionally scarce Gem example. Census: 96 in 65, 28 finer (6/07). (#3794)

287 **1867 No Rays MS65 PCGS.** This is a lovely, lustrous Gem Shield nickel from the second year of the series; and the first year of the No Rays type. Generally well detailed except for minor softness on the shield's vertical stripes. Bright, essentially untoned, and free of distracting marks. A few spidery die cracks are observed on the obverse. Population: 69 in 65, 9 finer (6/07). (#3794)

288 **1869 MS66 NGC.** The 6 and 9 in the date are repunched relatively widely, but this particular variety appears unlisted in the *Cherrypickers' Guide*. A lustrous and lightly toned Premium Gem that lacks visible marks or carbon. Census: 13 in 66, 3 finer (5/07). (#3796)

Fabulous 1873 Open 3 Nickel, MS66

289 **1873 Open 3 MS66 PCGS.** This is a fabulous Premium Gem Open 3 Shield nickel. Both sides are awash in bright luster, and yield untoned surfaces that have been well cared for. A powerful strike emboldens the design elements, resulting in complete separation in the horizontal and vertical lines of the shield and in the star radials. David Bowers (2006) writes of the 1873 that: " ... choice and gem mint state coins are very elusive. When located, the problems of striking and eye appeal arise. In short, finding a nice specimen ... will be a challenge." As we have seen, Bowers' comments are not germane for the present piece. Population: 5 in 66, 0 finer (6/07). (#3800)

Exceptional 1875 Gem Five Cents

290 **1875 MS65 NGC.** David Bowers (2006), writing about the 1875 nickel, indicates that: "Quality is elusive for this date" because of poor planchet preparation. The Gem offered here deviates from this profile. Its light gray surfaces yield soft luster and sharply impressed design features. A couple of light obverse flecks are noted for complete accuracy. Census: 24 in 65, 5 finer (6/07). (#3804)

PROOF SHIELD NICKELS

291 **1866 Rays PR62 NGC.** Pastel sky-blue and salmon-pink toning endows this boldly struck specimen. A tiny obverse spot near 3 o'clock is noted, and a subtle granular area is found on the reverse near the stop at 4:30. Only 600+ proofs were struck, and those pieces are under strong demand from proof type set collectors. (#3817)

Cameo PR64 1866 Rays Nickel

292 **1866 Rays PR64 Cameo NGC.** The Rays type was struck for only two years, and since the proof 1867 Rays is a famous rarity, proof type demand is focused on the 1866, which has a low mintage of 600+ pieces. This brilliant specimen has a good strike with only slight central incompleteness. Faintly granular on the obverse near 3 o'clock and on the upper left reverse. Census: 12 in 64 Cameo, 51 finer (6/07). (#83817)

293 **1869 PR65 NGC.** Most of the design elements are sharply struck, except for several of the stars on the reverse. The obverse is untoned and seems pristine. The reverse shows a few russet toning specks and a couple of tiny planchet flaws. (#3823)

294 **1869 PR65 NGC.** A wondrous Gem with reflective devices and deeply mirrored fields, this piece retains full nickel-gray brilliance on both sides. The top star on the reverse is a trifle weak, but all other design elements on each side are bold. From an unknown but doubtless small proof mintage, likely only a few hundred coins. (#3823)

295 **1869 PR65 Cameo PCGS.** A hint of golden-tan in the centers is the only toning on this lovely Gem. Boldly struck with appreciable contrast. Population: 8 in 65 Cameo, 10 finer. (6/07) (#83823)

Scarce Cameo 1870 Shield Nickel, PR66

296 **1870 PR66 Cameo PCGS.** A splendidly preserved cameo that is nicely mirrored in the fields. The reverse displays subtle shadings of lilac and rose, while there is almost no color to be seen on the obverse. Contrast on coins from this era is more a matter of chance than design, as most were created from a fresh set of dies and not intentionally produced for aesthetic appeal. Population: 14 in 66 Cameo, 0 finer (4/07). (#83824)

297 **1872 PR66 NGC.** Lightly toned over each side. The fields display bright reflectivity. Sharply struck except on the upper horizontal shield lines. (#3826)

298 **1872 Doubled Die Obverse PR66 NGC.** Fletcher-06. The annulet is doubled south, with the doubling visible to the unaided eye. A satiny and nearly untoned Premium Gem. Only 950+ proofs were struck. (#3826)

299 **1873 Closed 3 PR65 NGC.** All 1873 proof nickels are the Closed 3 variety. A moderately reflective and sharply struck Gem that has delicate reddish-gold patina over the surfaces. A spot of dark toning is noted below the date. (#3827)

300 **1875 PR65 PCGS.** Well struck with a pleasingly reflective appearance. An attractive, essentially untoned specimen with clean surfaces and great eye appeal. Population: 56 in 65, 9 finer (4/07). (#3829)

301 **1876 PR66 PCGS.** A crisply struck centennial coin with lovely blue and gold toning over each side. A small dark spot is noted in the center of the shield. PCGS has certified just one finer non-Cameo specimen (6/07). (#3830)

Cameo PR65 1877 Shield Nickel
A Rare Proof-Only Year

302 **1877 PR65 Cameo PCGS.** Key issue in the Shield nickel series with only 510 pieces believed struck, all proofs. This and the following year are both proof-only issues and both are predictably elusive in any grade. This piece has the added element of sharp cameo contrast between the devices and the deeply mirrored fields. Just the slightest overlay of tan patina can also be discerned on each side of this lovely and problem-free Gem. Population: 27 in 65, 28 finer (5/07). (#83831)

303 **1878 PR62 ANACS.** Rose-gold and olive-green toning confirms the originality of this satiny specimen. Sharply struck save for minor blending on a few of the horizontal shield lines. A small spot is noted near the M in AMERICA. A popular proof-only date. (#3832)

304 **1878 PR65 PCGS.** This well struck proof-only Gem has medium golden-gray toning and refreshingly smooth surfaces. Encased in a first generation holder. (#3832)

305 **1878 PR66 NGC.** A glut of minor coinage stalled production of low-denomination pieces in the late 1870s, and the 1878 nickel, like the 1877 before it, was a proof-only issue. This coin displays strong detail and attractive luster beneath dappled green-gold and silver-gray patina. *From The Vanek Collection.* (#3832)

306 **1879 PR65 NGC.** Solidly struck and well preserved, with reflective fields and a rich layer of olive and rose patina across both sides. A planchet flaw resides between OF and AMERICA on the upper reverse, crossing through the outer left foot of A. Post-striking distractions are absent. *From The Vanek Collection.* (#3833)

307 **1879 PR67 NGC.** This is a clean, well struck, untoned Superb Gem proof. The surfaces are unimprovable and virtually pristine. A great example of this low total mintage date. Census: 10 in 67, 1 finer (6/07). (#3833)

308 **1879/8 PR67 NGC.** Breen-2514, "Very Scarce." An overdate variety which is listed both in Breen and in the *Guide Book*. This Superb Gem example is sharply struck and seemingly pristine, with untoned surfaces that exhibit flashy reflectivity in the fields. (#3834)

309 **1879/8 PR66 Cameo PCGS.** Breen-2514, "Very Scarce." One of four distinct date varieties for the 1879 proof Shield nickel, according to Mr. Breen. This Premium Gem is well struck and shows the overdate feature very nicely. Free of distractions and showing a pleasing, if mild cameo contrast on both sides. Population: 25 in 66 Cameo, 7 finer (6/07). (#83834)

310 **1881 PR66 PCGS.** Ice-blue and peach tints visit this satiny and fully struck Premium Gem. Minor carbon along the right border denies an even finer grade. Collectors often select proofs to represent this low mintage date. (#3836)

311 **1881 PR66 PCGS.** Speckles of gold color are evenly distributed over both sides of this Premium Gem, which illustrates cameo tendencies when the piece is rotated under a light source. The design elements are well brought up and uniformly struck throughout. There are no significant marks to report. Housed in a green-label holder. (#3836)

312 **1881 PR66 Cameo NGC.** The glassy fields display traces of gold toning. The devices are well struck, and the shield is frosted. A small mint-made planchet flaw is noted between the final two vertical shield stripes. A low mintage date. Census: 36 in 66 Cameo, 22 finer (5/07). (#83836)

313 **1882 PR66 PCGS.** A light honey-gold Premium Gem with peripheral obverse aqua tints. This well struck proof type coin has smooth surfaces and satiny luster. (#3837)

314 **1882 PR67 Cameo NGC.** Fully struck and brilliant, with glassy mirrored fields and marvelously frosted devices. Free of troublesome marks or hairlines. Conditionally scarce and unavailable any finer, with the Cameo designation. Census: 20 in 67, 0 finer at either service (6/07). (#83837)

315 **1883 PR66 PCGS.** This Premium Gem proof has rich gold toning, rather deep in nature. It is a sharply struck piece with fully mirrored fields and considerable contrast, although the toning prevents a Cameo designation. (#3838)

316 **1883 PR67 NGC.** An immaculately preserved Superb Gem example of this final year Shield nickel issue. The moderately reflective surfaces show machine doubling on the obverse lettering and, except for a slight degree of golden toning on the obverse, appear essentially as struck. Census: 42 in 67, 1 finer (6/07). (#3838)

LIBERTY NICKELS

Choice Mint State 1885 Liberty Nickel

317 **1885 MS64 PCGS.** An irresistible coin, this blazing Mint State 1885 nickel has bright nickel-gray surfaces with frosty luster and sharp details. In all grades, business strike 1885 Liberty nickels rank among the most important regular issue coins in the series. Population: 73 in 64, 50 finer (6/07). (#3846)

Appealing 1887 Premium Gem Nickel

318 **1887 MS66 NGC.** While the 15 million-plus mintage 1887 nickel is readily available in all grades, David Bowers (2006) indicates that quality can be a problem with high-grade coins: "Many Mint State coins have granular surfaces from dies that remained in service too long." This MS66 specimen does reveal minor granularity, especially at the reverse periphery. This does not, however, detract from the coin's pleasing eye appeal that results from warm gold and blue-gray patina resting on highly lustrous surfaces exhibiting sharply struck design elements. The only mentionable flaws are a couple of small spots at the D of UNITED. Census: 17 in 66, 0 finer (5/07). (#3848)

Lustrous MS66 1888 Liberty Nickel

319 **1888 MS66 PCGS.** Heavy die flow around the margins on each side give this piece a matte-like appearance. Fully struck with complete definition on the left ear of corn. Pale gray and lilac color can be seen on each side when closely examined, but the coin generally presents as untoned. Population: 8 in 66, 0 finer (6/07). (#3849)

320 **1889 MS65 NGC.** Blended sun-gold and dove-gray toning invigorates this lustrous and clean-cheeked Gem. A couple of stars and the left ear of corn are incompletely brought up. (#3850)

321 **1889 MS65 PCGS.** Sharply struck, the surfaces display just the slightest overlay of pale gray-rose-lilac toning. Excellent luster. (#3850)

322 **1891 MS65 PCGS.** A hint of gold patina enhances this highly lustrous and unblemished Gem. The strike is sharp aside from a couple of star centers. Population: 60 in 65, 12 finer (4/07). (#3852)

323 **1893 MS65 PCGS.** Most of the design elements are well defined, except for the reverse left ear of corn and the first two obverse stars. The steel-gray surfaces display shimmering luster and are essentially blemish-free. Population: 68 in 65, 12 finer (6/07). (#3854)

324 **1894 MS64 PCGS.** This satiny example is an excellent representative of the Liberty nickel type, at the near-Gem level of preservation. Essentially untoned, except for a touch of golden color near the lower obverse border. A couple of tiny marks are noted on Liberty's cheekbone. (#3855)

325 **1898 MS65 PCGS.** Delicate golden-gray patina rests on highly lustrous surfaces that exhibit sharply impressed design features. A few minute abrasions are noted over each side. Population: 60 in 65, 17 finer (4/07). (#3859)

326 **1899 MS65 PCGS.** An olive-gray Gem with a well preserved reverse and only minor obverse contact. The left obverse denticles are slightly soft, as is the left ear of corn, but the stars and curls are nicely defined. (#3860)

327 **1899 MS65 PCGS.** Bright mint luster underlies and enlivens the gray-rose toning that covers each side. Just a bit weakly struck. (#3860)

328 **1903 MS66 PCGS.** Light gold toning adorns this thoroughly lustrous Premium Gem. Careful inspection fails to locate any abrasions. The strike is crisp except for star 7 and the left ear of corn. Population: 69 in 66, 2 finer (6/07). (#3864)

329 **1903 MS66 PCGS.** Brilliant and fully struck with superior mint luster. A wonderful type coin. Population: 69 in 66, 2 finer (6/07). (#3864)

330 **1904 MS66 PCGS.** The untoned obverse gives way to light champagne color on the reverse. A sharply struck and well preserved Premium Gem. Population: 62 in 66, 0 finer (6/07). (#3865)

331 **1905 MS65 NGC.** From a high mintage of nearly 30 million pieces, relatively few have survived as Gems. This example has beautiful luster and equally appealing champagne-gray coloration. Softly struck on the obverse stars, and on the lower left segment of the reverse wreath; but exquisitely preserved and distraction-free. (#3866)

332 **1908 MS65 PCGS.** A lovely Gem example of this later Liberty Head nickel issue, well-defined in the centers with pleasing luster. Delicate pink and peach patina graces the obverse, while vivid orange toning covers much of the left reverse. (#3869)

333 **1908 MS65 PCGS.** Alluring satiny iridescence radiates from both sides of this sparkling Gem. Just a touch of toning mitigates the steel-gray color. The unmarked surfaces reveal crisply struck central elements, although the left ear of corn and star 1 are soft. Population: 69 in 65, 11 finer (4/07). (#3869)

334 **1911 MS65 PCGS.** Champagne-gold patination is imbued with hints of sky-blue, and covers lustrous surfaces. Well struck, save for minor softness in some of the leaves left of the bowknot. There are no significant marks on either side. (#3872)

Choice Mint State 1912-S Liberty Nickel

335 **1912-S MS64 PCGS.** This is the only San Francisco Mint nickel of the Liberty Head design, and the first issue of the denomination at that mint. A deeply toned example with lilac and gold color over dark gray surfaces. This piece is nicely detailed with strong definition on all aspects of the obverse and reverse design. (#3875)

PROOF LIBERTY NICKELS

336 **1883 No Cents PR66 ★ Cameo NGC.** The devices are icy throughout, even on Liberty's cheek and neck, which on other proof examples sometimes lack contrast. The strike is also exemplary, and the nearly brilliant surfaces display only infrequent pinpoint carbon. (#83878)

337 **1883 No Cents PR65 Deep Cameo PCGS.** Radiant frost dominates the legends and devices. Unlike sometimes seen, there is no dissipation of the frost across Liberty's face and neck. The darkly mirrored fields ensure prominent white-on-black contrast. A gorgeous one-year proof type coin. Population: 1 in 65 Deep Mirror, 4 finer (5/07). (#93878)

338 **1883 With Cents PR65 Cameo NGC.** Frosty devices provide favorable contrast with the darkly mirrored fields. Untoned aside from pearl-gray freckles on the central reverse. Boldly struck and beautiful. Census: 32 in 65 Cameo, 24 finer (5/07). (#83881)

339 **1884 PR65 PCGS.** FS-013.8. The 18 in the date is widely repunched. A penetratingly struck Gem with consistent chestnut-gold toning. Beautifully preserved, and encased in an old green label holder. (#3882)

340 **1886 PR65 NGC.** Nicely struck with just a bit of softness on a couple of the obverse stars, this specimen displays glassy reflectivity in the fields and attractive light-green toning with light streaks of red-orange patina near the center of each side. Unimpaired by contact marks or hairlines. (#3884)
From The Vanek Collection.

341 **1886 PR66 Cameo NGC.** A flashy specimen whose light gold toning contributes further to the eye appeal. A well struck and beautiful representative of this lower mintage date. Census: 18 in 66 Cameo, 3 finer (5/07). (#83884)

342 **1889 PR67 NGC.** Ice-blue at the periphery with bluish-green color at the centers and occasional amber-orange accents on each side. The devices display excellent detail, and the surfaces are exceptionally well preserved, as one would expect for the grade. Highly appealing. Census: 16 in 67, 1 finer (6/07). (#3887)

343 **1893 PR65 Cameo PCGS.** This piece shows unusually deep, mirror-like reflectivity in the fields. Each side is well balanced in overall appearance with good mint frost over the devices and a slight accent of color. Population: 13 in 65, 19 finer (6/07). (#83891)

344 **1898 PR65 Cameo NGC.** The legends and devices are evenly frosted, unlike some pieces seen with less frost on the face and neck of Liberty. The strike is needle-sharp, and only a whisper of carbon limits the grade. Census: 14 in 65 Cameo, 18 finer (5/07). (#83896)

345 **1901 PR67 NGC.** A strongly reflective, decisively struck example of this mid-date issue. The outer zones exhibit moderate-thickness olive-gold patina, while the centers are largely untoned. Census: 27 in 67, 3 finer (5/07).
From The Vanek Collection. (#3899)

346 **1903 PR65 NGC.** This is an outstanding Gem proof example with razor-sharp striking details and intense, watery reflectivity in the fields. A touch of streaky patina in the left obverse field is not distracting. Hairlines or contact marks are nonexistent. (#3901)
From The Vanek Collection.

347 **1905 PR65 PCGS.** Gold and crimson dominate the reverse, but cling to the margins of the obverse. Exquisitely impressed throughout, as befits a proof strike. No bothersome marks are apparent. Population: 90 in 65, 47 finer (6/07). (#3903)

348 **1905 PR66 PCGS.** A brilliant Premium Gem proof with unbelievably deep, watery reflectivity in the fields and razor-sharp striking details. The surfaces seem pristine, or nearly so. The reverse devices are lightly frosted, producing a distinct white-on-black contrast. Population: 37 in 66, 10 finer (6/07). (#3903)

349 **1909 PR66 PCGS.** Fully struck and untoned, with splendidly preserved steel-gray surfaces. The fields are satiny rather than reflective, typical of later strikes from proof dies. A truly lovely Premium Gem. (#3907)

350 **1909 PR67 NGC.** Fully struck and virtually pristine with sparkling, beautifully reflective, light honey-gold surfaces. A magnificent Superb Gem proof. Census: 85 in 67, 6 finer (6/07). (#3907)

351 **1909 PR67 NGC.** Fully struck with glittering prooflike fields and bright untoned surfaces that yield a mild cameo-like effect on each side. This Superb Gem seems pristine, even under close inspection with a magnifier. Census: 85 in 67, 6 finer (6/07). (#3907)

352 **1909 PR67 NGC.** Moderately mirrored and nearly untoned with traces of lilac haze on each nearly immaculate side. NGC has certified only six specimens finer (6/07). (#3907)

353 **1909 PR66 Cameo PCGS.** This intricately struck Premium Gem exhibits dusky and consistent tan-gold toning. The flashy fields appear immaculate. Population: 44 in 66 Cameo, 9 finer (4/07). (#83907)

354 **1909 PR66 Cameo NGC.** This is a simply stunning Cameo! Both sides yield a white-on-black appearance when the piece is viewed from directly overhead. Razor sharp definition complements the Cameo, as do immaculately preserved surfaces. Census: 35 in 66, 32 finer (6/07). (#83907)

Outstanding 1911 Nickel, PR67 Cameo

355 **1911 PR67 Cameo NGC.** The 1911 nickel had a proof mintage of 1,733 pieces, of which several hundred specimens have been certified by NGC and PCGS. The two services have given fewer than 90 coins a Cameo designation. This Superb Gem Cameo yields outstanding field-motif contrast at all angles of view. Untoned surfaces are impeccably preserved, and exhibit crisply struck design elements. Census: 9 in 67 Cameo, 0 finer (6/07). (#83909)

BUFFALO NICKELS

356 **1913 Type One MS67 PCGS.** An orange-peel texture is common on both sides, and is frequently seen on examples of this first-year Buffalo nickel issue. Gold, olive, and steel-blue colors are the most prominent. An immaculately preserved and seemingly pristine Superb Gem. (#3915)

357 **1913 Type One MS67 NGC.** A splendid gold-tinged example of the famous one-year Type One design, well-defined with effusive luster and only the tiniest of flaws. NGC has graded just nine coins finer (5/07). (#3915)
From The Vanek Collection.

358 **1913-D Type One MS66 PCGS.** This sharply struck Type One nickel has light gunmetal-gray and rose-gold toning. Unobtrusive contact on the front leg and nostril decides the grade. Essential for a Denver Mint type set. (#3916)

359 **1913-D Type Two MS65 PCGS.** This first-year Denver Mint Gem displays attractive, coppery toning and shimmering luster across both sides. The piece shows a decent strike, with typical softness noted over the centers and on the bison's head, and remarkably clean surfaces overall. (#3922)

360 **1913-S Type Two AU53 NGC.** This lightly circulated nickel displays golden-gray patination on bright surfaces, and the design features are nicely defined. We mention a small scrape on the date, and another on the lower large feather. (#3923)

361 **1913-S Type Two AU55 NGC.** A well struck, lightly circulated gold-gray representative of this lowest-mintage first-year Buffalo nickel issue. The still-lustrous fields contrast with slightly dulled devices that display subtle rose overtones. (#3923)

362 **1913-S Type Two AU58 NGC.** A gunmetal-gray and chestnut near-Mint example of this famous low mintage variety. The hipbone displays slight friction, but luster shimmers across the unmarked surfaces. (#3923)

363 **1913-S Type Two MS61 NGC.** Softly struck with nice satin luster and attractive rose-tan coloration over both sides. Any surface marks are too small to notice without a magnifying glass. One of the key dates in the Buffalo nickel series at all levels of preservation. (#3923)

364 **1913-S Type Two MS62 NGC.** More sharply struck than usual, for this key Buffalo nickel issue. The grayish-olive surfaces are essentially untoned. Surface marks are minimal. (#3923)

365 **1914/3 AU58 ANACS.** FS-014.87. Late Die State. This is an attractive AU representative with a satiny appearance and light greenish coloration with a few minor toning streaks. Abrasions are nonexistent on both sides. Relatively few examples of this subtle overdate variety have been authenticated by NGC, PCGS and ANACS. (#93924)

366 **1914-D MS65 PCGS.** Both sides exhibit satin luster and are tinted a delicate antique-gold and steel-blue on the reverse. The dove-gray obverse remains untoned. Both sides of the piece are free of distractions. A difficult early Buffalo nickel issue at all grade levels, and a particularly attractive Gem example, in a green label PCGS holder. (#3925)

367 **1914-D MS65 PCGS.** Bright lustrous surfaces display whispers of light beige, powder-blue, and light gray color. Generally well struck, except for softness in the lower parts of the date, as is typical for this issue. Both sides are free of significant marks. (#3925)

368 **1914-S MS64 NGC.** The satiny surfaces glow beneath canary-yellow and gold-gray patina. This Choice example is well-defined for the issue, with only slight weakness at the Indian's temple and the bison's shoulder. A lovely example of this second-year issue. (#3926)

369 **1915-D MS65 PCGS.** Slightly soft over the centers and on the bison's head, but otherwise boldly struck. The olive-gray surfaces reveal a few russet specks upon close examination. A lustrous, well preserved Gem. Conditionally scarce at MS65, and rare any finer. (#3928)

Rare 1915-S Premium Gem Nickel

370 **1915-S MS66 PCGS.** The 1915-S nickel is a scarce date, and rare in the better grade levels of Mint State. The issue also tends to be poorly struck. This Premium Gem displays dazzling luster and a thin coat of gold, lilac, and light blue patina. The strike is much better than average, with no areas showing hints of weakness. Well preserved throughout. Population: 26 in 66, 3 finer (6/07). (#3929)

371 **1916 MS66 PCGS.** An original-looking specimen with lovely sky-blue, rose, olive, and gold toning. A few tiny marks are seen around the Indian's mouth. Overall, a well struck and eye-catching Premium Gem. (#3930)

372 **1916 MS66 PCGS.** The devices exhibit razor-sharp definition that brings up every design element. Satiny and lightly toned, with pleasing peripheral toning and immaculate surfaces. One of the more available issues of the 1910s, the 1916 is, nonetheless, a scarce issue at the Premium Gem level of preservation. (#3930)

Choice AU 1916 Doubled Die Nickel

373 1916 Doubled Die Obverse AU55 NGC. FS-016. This variety is an extremely important issue in the Buffalo nickel series, and is accorded the special honor of its own listing in the *Guide Book* where it has been listed since the late 1970s. While many varieties have been added to the listings of this annual reference in recent years, the '16 doubled die nickel, the '55 doubled die cent, and a few others have been included for many years.

This is a pleasing example with sharp doubling on the obverse. Both sides retain nearly full mint luster beneath dark gray-gold toning with hints of iridescence. Although a few faint surface marks are evident, neither side has any noticeable distractions to be concerned about.

While doubled die varieties exist in nearly every series of copper, nickel, silver, and gold coinage, few are as dramatic as this example. Some of the more visible doubled dies, such as the 1873 Indian cent, the 1955, 1969-S, 1972, 1983, and 1984 Lincoln cents, and this 1916 nickel, are listed in the *Guide Book*. There are many other doubled die varieties that are less obvious, and these are listed in important references such as Breen's *Complete Encyclopedia*, and the *Cherrypickers' Guide* by Fivaz and Stanton.

In *The Complete Guide to Buffalo Nickels*, David Lange notes that this important variety has been known since its first publication in the July 1962 issue of *The Numismatic Scrapbook* magazine. The discovery was announced by Herbert Perlin of Pomona, California, and yet the variety was not familiar with most collectors until the 1970s when it was described in the September 1976 issue of *The Coin Dealer Newsletter*. It is fascinating to ponder why a variety of this magnitude, struck in Philadelphia, was discovered on the other side of the country. (#3931)

374 **1916-S MS64 PCGS.** Well struck and lustrous, with champagne-gold and olive toning on the obverse, and steel-blue reverse color that yields to golden accents along the left border. A handful of minor marks on the bison's shoulder seemingly prevent a Gem grade designation. (#3933)

375 **1916-S MS65 PCGS.** This lustrous walnut-brown and steel-gray Gem is pleasantly unperturbed by contact. The centers show minor incompleteness, but the date, mintmark, tail, horn, and LIBERTY are well struck. Population: 74 in 65, 30 finer (4/07). (#3933)

376 **1917 MS66 PCGS.** Apricot and olive toning invigorates this lustrous and mark-free Premium Gem. Well struck save for the unavoidable minor incompleteness above the braid. Housed in a green label holder. (#3934)

377 **1917 MS66 PCGS.** Sharply struck and untoned, with lustrous, amazingly clean surfaces that have a pleasing satiny glow. A beautiful premium Gem. Population: 123 in 66, 12 finer (6/07). (#3934)

378 **1917-S MS64 PCGS.** This near-Gem is extremely impressive for the grade, with crisply defined motifs and smooth, virtually pristine surfaces. Untoned with even olive-gray coloration and slightly muted luster that precludes a finer grade assessment. (#3936)

379 **1918 MS65 PCGS.** The low survival rate of this high-mintage issue is surprising, but it seems clear that few were saved from circulation. Currently, less than a thousand pieces have been certified in Mint State by NGC and PCGS combined (4/07). This Gem example is lustrous and nearly pristine, with light rose and mint-green toning. Surface marks are essentially nonexistent. (#3937)

380 **1918-D MS64 NGC.** This satiny and unabraded near-Gem displays a few pinpoint cream-gray flecks and the expected minor incompleteness of strike in the centers. Early branch mint Type Two nickels are invariably scarce in such quality. (#3938)

Bright 1918-D Gem Five Cent

381 **1918-D MS65 PCGS.** The 1918-D nickel, while common in lower grades, is a rarity in MS65 and higher levels of preservation, especially with a "decent strike" (David Bowers, 2007). Bright luster adorns the essentially untoned surfaces of this lovely Gem. The strike is well impressed throughout, and there are no significant marks to report. Population: 66 in 65, 22 finer (6/07). (#3938)

382 **1918/7-D Good 6 PCGS.** Although this silver-gray key date nickel is well circulated, the mintmark is bold, and all four digits in the date can be discerned by the naked eye. The thick horizontal and downward stroke of the 7 is evident. The bison displays a few faint hairlines. (#3939)

Popular 1918/7-D Nickel, VF20

383 **1918/7-D VF20 NGC.** This overdate Buffalo nickel has been known for a great many years and examples are always welcomed by advanced collectors of the series. In The Complete Guide to Buffalo Nickels, David Lange writes: "The 1918/7-D overdate certainly rivals the 1916 DDO and the 1937-D 3-leg nickel for the title of most popular and highly sought variety in the series." This piece is a pleasing light gray representative with traces of darker steel toning on each side. The quality of the surfaces are consistent with the grade. (#3939)

Well-Detailed 1918/7-D Nickel, XF Details

384 **1918/7-D—Acid Etched—NCS. XF Details.** FS-016.5. This is a curious coin, not only for the overdate feature but also for the acid etching. When viewing this piece, one has to ask: Why? On some AG-Good coins acid etching really does bring out the date. Such treatment certainly lessens the value, but at least the date is verifiable. But this piece has strong striking definition on each side. The overdate feature is especially sharp with both the 8 and 7 pronounced. The overall surfaces on each side have a "wavy" appearance from the acid treatment. Just the slightest trace of toning is present. (#3939)

385 **1920 MS66 PCGS.** A lovely example of this postwar issue, solidly struck with swirling luster and colorful patina. Ice-blue patina graces the centers, while deeper green-gold color appears at the margins. PCGS has graded just eight coins finer (5/07). (#3944)

Beautiful 1920 Superb Gem Nickel

386 **1920 MS67 NGC.** The 1920 nickel, with a mintage of more than 63 million pieces, is a fairly common date through the MS64 level. Even Gem and Premium Gems can be obtained with a little patience and searching. However, Superb Gem examples, such as the one in the current lot, are very elusive. Indeed, NGC and PCGS combined have seen fewer than 15 MS67 pieces, and none finer. A thin coat of iridescent ice-blue, lilac, and yellow-gold patina adheres to radiantly lustrous surfaces that are free of mentionable marks. Unlike frequently seen 1920 specimens that are softly struck, this coin exhibits well defined motifs. A simply beautiful Buffalo nickel! Census: 5 in 67, 0 finer (6/07). (#3944)

387 **1920-D MS64 PCGS.** Lilac and khaki-gold toning embrace this attractive branch mint Buffalo nickel. The reverse appears immaculate, and the obverse has only a few minute ticks. Well struck aside from the bison's hair. Encapsulated in a green label holder. (#3945)

388 **1921-S XF45 NGC.** Light grayish-tan with speckled russet and iridescent aqua toning. Evenly worn with only the tip of the bison's horn lacking complete definition. A rare XF example of this desirable S-mint Buffalo nickel. (#3948)

389 **1921-S AU58 ANACS.** Light golden-gray patination adheres to remarkably clean surfaces on this high-end AU Buffalo. Much better struck than usually seen. A somewhat scarce date in all grades (David Bowers, 2007). (#3948)

390 **1924-D MS64 PCGS.** David Lange notes regarding this issue that fully struck pieces may be unknown. The current offering certainly shows the flatness that he also mentions, on the bison's head, but most of the remaining design elements are boldly rendered. Even olive-gray toning and satin luster are found on both sides, and the surfaces are pristine. (#3952)

391 **1925-S MS63 PCGS.** Pastel gold, blue, and lilac patina covers lustrous surfaces. Weakly struck in some areas, as typical for the issue. Devoid of mentionable marks. (#3956)

392 **1926 MS66 PCGS.** Gold-champagne patination rests on highly lustrous surfaces that exhibit sharply impressed design features. Both sides are quite well preserved. (#3957)

393 **1926 MS66 PCGS.** A shining Premium Gem representative of this well-produced issue, solidly detailed with powerful visual appeal. The surfaces have ice-blue patina in the centers and pastel yellow color at the margins. (#3957)

Imposing Superb Gem 1926 Nickel

394 **1926 MS67 NGC.** This Superb Gem has satiny luster and exceptional aesthetic appeal. Both sides have gorgeous lilac-blue toning with lovely gold color at the edge. The reverse is fully struck, and the obverse is completely brought up with the exception of the hair above the braid. Only one finer example has been certified by NGC. Census: 12 in 67, 1 finer (5/07). (#3957)

395 **1926-S—Obverse Scratched, Improperly Cleaned—NCS. AU Details** The 1926-S has the lowest mintage (970,000 pieces) of any regular issue in the Buffalo nickel series. AU coins are difficult to locate, and Mint State examples are scarce to rare. Bright, lightly toned surfaces reveal a few shallow scratches on the lower obverse of this AU Details specimen. All of the design elements show good definition. The scratches are not that bad, and the cleaning was light. Interested bidders should not be intimidated by these minor flaws. (#3959)

Lightly Toned 1927-S Nickel, MS64

396 **1927-S MS64 NGC.** Ex: Richmond Collection. David Lange (2000) notes that the 1927-S "... is genuinely rare in choice and gem condition." This near-Gem possesses pleasing luster with a coating of iridescent pastel rainbow patina. Well struck, except for minor softness in the hair on the bison's head. A couple of small darker toning spots are noted on each side. (#3962)

397 **1928 MS66 PCGS.** Lustrous and very well struck, with just a touch of weakness of the bison's tail and above the knot in the Indian's hair braid. Pleasing steel-blue toning over each side with hints of salmon near the centers. The surfaces are unmarked, with a few scattered toning specks. (#3963)

398 **1928 MS66 PCGS.** This is a bright, highly lustrous, untoned Premium Gem with boldly defined design elements and well preserved surfaces that are near-pristine. A lovely example of this Buffalo nickel issue from the Philadelphia Mint, with an original mintage figure in excess of 23 million pieces. Relatively few of those coins survive at this lofty level of preservation, however. (#3963)

399 **1928-S MS64 PCGS.** Satiny and well detailed, with deep rose and olive toning on the reverse. A few small abrasions are noted on each side, with the aid of a magnifier. The '28-S is similar to the other mintmarked Buffalo nickels from the 1920s, as an important strike rarity. (#3965)

Well Struck 1928-S Nickel, MS65

400 **1928-S MS65 PCGS.** According to David Lange (2000), most 1928-S nickels " ... display a general softness in the date, the mintmark and the bison's forehead." Not so the specimen in this lot! An attentive strike brought out strong definition in the design features, including those elements alluded to above. Lustrous surfaces show a thin coat of champagne color, and are devoid of bothersome marks. Population: 57 in 65, 5 finer (6/07). (#3965)

401 **1929 MS66 PCGS.** Shimmering luster bathes this lovely gunmetal-gray Premium Gem. The strike is good for the type, and only trivial marks are detected. The fields possess an orange-peel texture, as provided by long-used dies. (#3966)

402 **1930-S MS66 PCGS.** Boldly struck on the obverse but very soft on the bison. Intensely lustrous and essentially untoned with minimal marks on either side. PCGS has only graded four pieces finer (4/07). (#3970)

403 **1931-S MS66 PCGS.** Boldly struck, except over the obverse center, with lustrous surfaces that display golden-green color on the obverse and bluish-gray patina on the reverse. Immaculately preserved and seemingly pristine on both sides. (#3971)

404 **1934 MS66 PCGS.** This silver-gray Gem offers fully lustrous, blemish-free surfaces and suitably bold striking definition. Scarce in finer grades, as PCGS has graded only 19 pieces higher (5/07). (#3972)

405 **1934-D MS65 PCGS.** Gold, lilac, and olive tints enrich this mildly prooflike Gem. Nearly unabraded, but the centers and tail are a bit soft, as usual for the issue. Encapsulated in a green label holder. (#3973)
From The Vanek Collection.

406 **1934-D MS65 PCGS.** Satiny and lightly toned, with attractively bright, lustrous surfaces. Very softly struck over the centers, with noticeable doubling on the date and an interesting strike-through near TES OF along the upper reverse. A well preserved Gem that is blemish-free. (#3973)

Semi-Key 1934-D Nickel, MS66

407 **1934-D MS66 PCGS.** One of the better known strike rarities in the Buffalo nickel series, this issue is from the 1930-38 Short Set. Very few sharply struck Gem examples have been certified by either of the major services over the past ten years, and it seems that this issue's semi-key status is now well assured. This is a well defined coin that has satiny luster and is lightly and attractively toned on each side. Population: 38 in 66, 0 finer (6/07). (#3973)

408 **1935-D MS66 PCGS.** Satiny and well struck, with just a touch of softness on 18 in the date, just above the Indian's hair braid, and along the tops of ED STATES. The gray-green surfaces are imbued with rose accents near the reverse center. A great, unblemished Premium Gem. (#3975)

409 **1936 MS67 PCGS.** The certified population of the 1936 at the MS67 level is surprisingly low for a common P-mint issue with a sizeable original mintage of 119 million pieces. The otherwise apricot-orange toning yields to silver-lilac tinting in select areas toward the centers. Both sides exhibit a sharp strike that is free of criticism, and the surfaces are also devoid of bothersome abrasions. Population: 75 in 67, 0 finer (6/07). (#3977)

410 **1936-D MS67 PCGS.** Generally well struck with lovely olive-rose-gray coloration that is distributed evenly over both sides. Only the tops of the bison's head and shoulder reveal minor striking weakness. Broad mechanical doubling is apparent on the date. The lustrous surfaces are virtually pristine. Population: 56 in 67, 2 finer (5/07). (#3978)

411 **1936-S MS66 PCGS. FS-020.** The mintmark is sharply repunched southeast. Tan-gold patina graces this satiny and well preserved Premium Gem. The strike is precise with the usual exception of the hair immediately above the braid. PCGS does not track populations for FS-020, but NGC has certified only two pieces as MS66 with none finer (6/07). (#3979)

412 **1937-D Three-Legged VF35 NGC. FS-020.2.** Moderately worn with drab reddish-brown and gray coloration and a handful of noticeable marks on each side. A Choice VF example of everybody's favorite Buffalo nickel variety. (#3982)

413 **1937-D Three-Legged—Cleaned—ANACS. XF40 Details. FS-020.2.** This cream-gray and walnut-tan key date nickel has a few faint hairlines on the bison, but most collectors would overlook such a minor impairment. (#3982)

414 **1937-D Three-Legged—Scratched—ANACS. XF40 Details. FS-020.2.** A satiny gunmetal-gray key date nickel with a small rose-red spot at 11 o'clock on the reverse and a thin but relatively lengthy vertical pinscratch within the Indian's hair. (#3982)

415 **1937-D Three-Legged XF40 NGC. FS-020.2.** Supposedly created by a Mr. Young, by excessively polishing a die to erase clash marks, this famous Buffalo nickel type has been advertised on the back of cereal boxes and marketed in other ways that have made it familiar even to non-numismatists—thereby increasing its value at nearly all grade levels. This XF example is well detailed but shows some drab toning and bits of dark-green verdigris on each side. Even so, it is still a highly desirable item as an authenticated example of the so-called Three-Legged Buffalo nickel. (#3982)

416 **1937-D Three-Legged XF45 NGC. FS-020.2.** This attractive example displays very smooth surfaces that are evenly worn and still exhibit noticeable luster remnants. Both sides have a sort of creamy-gray appearance. A handful of small abrasions are noted on the bison. (#3982)

417 **1937-D Three-Legged AU50 PCGS. FS-020.2.** One of the most famous varieties in all of American numismatics. Hints of luster are visible beneath light gray patina on this Three-Legged specimen, and excellent detail appears on the design elements. A few light circulation marks on each side are not bothersome. (#3982)

418 **1937-D Three-Legged AU53 NGC. FS-020.2.** This lightly circulated example is free of severe marks and reveals mostly gunmetal-gray color on both sides. A famous Buffalo nickel variety that is desired by every collector of this immensely popular series. (#3982)

419 **1937-D Three-Legged AU53 NGC. FS-020.2.** Nicely detailed and with plenty of luster for the grade, this is an attractive AU example of the famed Three-Legged Buffalo nickel. Lightly worn, with evidence of minor die erosion and a few small marks on the reverse. (#3982)

420 **1937-D Three-Legged AU55 NGC. FS-020.2.** Light, even friction over the highpoints explain the AU55 grade. Pale gray-olive color is slightly deeper in hue around the margins and within the recesses of the design. An attractive example of this popular Buffalo nickel. (#3982)

421 **1937-D Three-Legged AU58 NGC. FS-020.2.** Rich dove-gray and tan toning blankets this satiny and boldly defined key date nickel. The diagnostic trail of die lumps beneath the bison's flank confirms this popular mint error. (#3982)

422 **1937-D Three-Legged AU58 NGC.** Just a hint of highpoint friction is seen on each side of this beautiful Three-Legged Buffalo nickel. Unlike most seen, this piece has concentric rings of iridescent toning around the margins and light golden-rose centers. A few shallow field marks are present, but these are noticeable only with magnification. (#3982)

Lightly Toned 1937-D Three-Legged Nickel, MS61

423 **1937-D Three-Legged MS61 NGC.** John Wexler et al (2007), write that: "The rarity of this coin is almost always overstated. It is not rare, or for that matter, even scarce. Thousands exist. The high values are the result of very high demand." The above statement notwithstanding, it is expected that this MS61 will bring about spirited bidding. Glowing surfaces display pleasing golden-gray patina that exhibit well struck devices, save for minor softness in the hair on the bison's head. A few unobtrusive marks do not disturb. A nice piece for the grade designation. (#3982)

Pleasing 1937-D Three-Legged Five Cent, MS61

424 **1937-D Three-Legged MS61 NGC.** FS-020.2 The 1937-D Three-Leg nickel, according to David Lange (2000), " ... was evidently discovered by, or at least first publicized by, C.L. 'Cowboy' Franzen. He was advertising them for sale in *The Numismatic Scrapbook Magazine* as early as 1937-38." The MS61 specimen offered in this lot exhibits light to medium gray toning with red-gold accents. The design elements are generally well impressed, though there is minor softness in the hair at the bison's forehead. The date, LIBERTY, the horn, and mintmark are sharp. All in all, a very pleasing example for the grade, that is perhaps somewhat conservative. (#3982)

Colorful 1937-D Three-Legged Buffalo Nickel MS62

425 **1937-D Three-Legged MS62 NGC.** This is a pleasing Mint State example of this famous Buffalo nickel variety that displays noticeably finer striking details than are ordinarily seen. The reddish-olive coloration is quite attractive. The obverse is nearly blemish-free, and there are only a handful of small marks on the bison that prevent a higher grade designation. (#3982)

Lustrous MS62 Three-Legged Buffalo Nickel

426 **1937-D Three-Legged MS62 NGC.** FS-020.2. Struck from only one die pairing, and a worn out one at that, the majority of Three-Legged Buffalo nickels are weakly struck from the advanced state of the dies. This piece shows typical striking details, but it is definitely above average in terms of overall preservation of surfaces. Bright and lustrous, the pale silver-gray coloration is interspersed with occasional streaks of lilac and rose. (#3982)

Lightly Toned 1937-D Three-Legged Five Cents, MS63

427 **1937-D Three-Legged MS63 NGC.** FS-020.2. Delicate champagne-gold patina rests on the highly lustrous surfaces of this popular variety in the Buffalo nickel series. An impressive strike left strong definition on the design features, and a few light marks concealed within the central devices do not detract. David Bowers (2007) presents some historical background for the issue: "In the 1950s, nearly al coins in the marketplace were in grades such as Very Fine and Extremely Fine. ... Many hundreds of Mint Sate coins exist today. I have no idea where all of these came from. ... Perhaps a bunch of rolls turned up that included examples from this particular die." (#3982)

Satiny, Well Struck MS64 Three-Legged Nickel

428 **1937-D Three-Legged MS64 NGC.** A scarce and always sought-out issue in high grade, the Three-Legged nickel is generally found in circulated grades and seldom in mint condition. A near-Gem coin such as this is especially desirable for the collector. This piece has bright, satiny mint luster with just the slightest overlay of pale golden color. Strongly struck for the issue with especially good definition on the matted hair at the top of the bison's head. Lightly abraded, as one would expect, the only mentionable surface defect is a shallow, vertical planchet lamination on the cheek of the Native American. (#3982)

429 **1937-S MS67 PCGS.** A precisely struck and remarkably mark-free Superb Gem with delicate ice-blue and caramel-gold toning. Essentially unobtainable any finer. Population: 76 in 67, 0 finer (4/07). (#3983)

430 **1937-S MS67 PCGS.** This is a pretty Superb Gem Buffalo nickel that enjoys an abundance of eye appeal. Lustrous and sharply struck, the coin is nearly pristine. Its chief visual attribute, however, is the variegated lime-green, red, and sunset-orange coloration that adorns each side. Population: 76 in 67, 0 finer (6/07). (#3983)

PROOF BUFFALO NICKELS

431 **1936 Type One—Satin Finish PR62 PCGS.** Even golden-brown toning covers each side. The coin is downgraded because of the presence of speckles of carbon that are distributed over both obverse and reverse. (#3994)

432 **1936 Type One—Satin Finish PR65 PCGS.** Before the Mint produced the brilliant proofs of 1936, it began with a set of proofs in satin finish, slightly reminiscent of the matte proofs of the early 20th century. This crisply struck example has lovely lavender-gray peripheral toning with warm orange color in the centers. (#3994) *From The Vanek Collection.*

433 **1936 Type One—Satin Finish PR66 PCGS.** Autumn-gold and gunmetal-blue patina invigorates this needle-sharp and unabraded Premium Gem. Infrequent pinpoint carbon denies an even higher grade. Housed in an old green label holder. (#3994)

Amazing 1936 Satin Finish Nickel, PR67

434 **1936 Type One—Satin Finish PR67 PCGS.** The satin proof nickels of 1936 had the first of two finishes for the year; initial collector disapproval of the satin proofs' soft luster led to the return of the brilliant fields associated with pre-1900 coinage. This sharply struck specimen displays light golden-orange patina in the fields and essentially untoned devices. The carefully preserved surfaces approach technical perfection. (#3994)

Lightly Toned 1936 Nickel, Type Two, Brilliant Finish PR66

435 **1936 Type Two—Brilliant Finish PR66 PCGS.** According to David Lange (2000), writing about the 1936 proof nickel: "Though both the mintage and survival rate of this date greatly exceed those of all previous Buffalo nickel proofs, the demand for 1936 proofs, particularly in the brilliant finish, is tremendous." Delicate ice-blue, lilac, and beige patination adorns both sides of this Premium Gem brilliant specimen. A solid strike, befitting a proof example, leaves sharp motif detail, and close inspection reveals no significant marks or spots. Housed in a green-label holder. (#3995)

436 **1937 PR64 NGC.** Slight contrast between the devices and the fields can be seen on both sides of this Choice proof. The fields are fully mirrored. Each side has a subtle hint of champagne toning, although the surfaces are mostly brilliant nickel-gray. (#3996)

437 **1937 PR65 PCGS.** This exquisite Gem possesses an exacting strike, and the glassy almond-gold fields are void of hairlines and offer only trivial carbon. The end of the trail for the proof Buffalo nickel, although the designs were resurrected for NCLT issues within recent years. (#3996)

Exquisite 1937 Superb Gem Proof Five Cent

438 **1937 PR67 PCGS.** The 1937 proof five cent, with a mintage of 5,769 pieces, is according to David Lange (*The Complete Guide to Buffalo Nickels*), "... the most readily available of proof Buffalo nickels. Though a number of pieces have been impaired, even gems turn up with some frequency." A thin veneer of iridescent ice-blue, beige-gold, and lilac patina covers well preserved surfaces of this Superb Gem. Exquisite definition is noted on all of the design features. Housed in a green-label holder. (#3996)

Lightly Toned PR67 1937 Buffalo Nickel

439 **1937 PR67 PCGS.** Second year of the two-year issue of proof Buffalo nickels, and a consistently well-produced issue. This piece has especially strong visual appeal, a combination of deeply reflective mirrors in the fields and a subtle overlay of rose and lilac toning. Essentially a defect-free proof striking. (#3996)

JEFFERSON NICKELS

Conditionally Scarce 1938 Jefferson Nickel MS67 Full Steps

440 **1938 MS67 Full Steps NGC.** Ex: Omaha Bank Hoard. Crisply struck design elements and untoned surfaces are illuminated by a pleasing satiny sheen. Wispy die striations are noted in the fields, and a tiny nick in the lower right obverse field is seen only under magnification. Census: 3 in 67 Full Bands, 0 finer (5/07). (#84000)

441 **1938-D MS67 Full Steps PCGS.** Although the slightest merging is present, all of the steps on this example are sharp and essentially complete. The frosty surfaces have excellent gold and iridescent toning over brilliant luster. Population: 28 in 67 Full Steps, 0 finer (6/07). (#84001)

442 **1939 Reverse of 1940 MS67 Five Full Steps NGC.** Blue-green patina dominates the obverse. The reverse is honey-gray. A high quality Superb Gem of the "Straight Steps" subtype, first issued in 1939. (#894003)

443 **1939 Reverse of 1940 MS67 Full Steps PCGS.** Subtle peach, rose, and steel-blue patina. A well struck, shimmering, and exceptionally preserved Superb Gem. Population: 17 in 67 Full Steps, 0 finer (4/07). (#894003)

444 **1939 Doubled MONTICELLO MS64 PCGS.** FS-022. FIVE CENTS and MONTICELLO are broadly die doubled. This piece is well struck with a typical orange-peel texture (as made) in the fields. Streaky champagne and aqua toning occurs on each side. A few small abrasions on the reverse limit the grade. (#4004)

445 **1939 Doubled MONTICELLO MS65 PCGS.** FS-022. MONTICELLO and FIVE CENTS are widely die doubled on this popular *Guide Book* variety. Light gold and powder-blue patina invigorates this lustrous and undisturbed Gem. Population: 35 in 65, 31 finer (6/07). (#4004)

1939-S Reverse of 1940 Nickel, MS66 Full Steps

446 **1939-S Reverse of 1940 MS66 Full Steps PCGS.** Not only does this piece have virtually six full steps, but it is also an example of the 1940 reverse, a transitional hub design. The surfaces have wisps of light gold toning with satiny luster and reflective fields. Population: 13 in 66, 0 finer (3/07). (#894006)

447 **1940 MS67 Full Steps PCGS.** The surfaces are highly lustrous with attractive light gold toning on both sides. The fields appear immaculate. Jefferson's shoulder has a couple of faint lilac streaks. Population: 23 in 67, 0 finer (5/07). (#84007)

448 **1949-D/S MS66 NGC.** FS-501, formerly FS-032. According to the *Cherrypickers' Guide*, "This variety is quite rare in mint state, and highly sought after." The strike is slightly soft on the mintmark, but the diagnostic features are evident. Peach, lilac, and yellow-gold enrich this lustrous and unmarked Premium Gem. A few pinpoint flecks decide the grade. Census: 12 in 66, 0 finer (5/07). (#4039)

Rare Full Steps 1953-S Nickel, MS64

449 **1953-S MS64 Full Steps PCGS.** An extreme rarity with Full Steps, this example is lustrous and virtually untoned. Typical mushiness exists on most of the reverse details but the steps of Monticello are nicely defined. Two or three tiny marks are noted on each side. Population: 14 in 64 Full Steps, 2 finer (5/07). (#84051)

450 **1957-D MS66 Five Full Steps NGC.** Ex: Omaha Bank Hoard. Medium gold toning adorns this satiny and carefully preserved Premium Gem. Sharper than generally seen, since only the center of the lowest step is incomplete. Census: 6 in 66 5FS, 0 finer (5/07). (#84062)

451 **1962-D MS65 Five Full Steps NGC.** A satiny Gem with faint green-gold toning. The 1962-D is a formidable strike rarity within the series, seldom encountered with five unbroken steps on Monticello. As of (5/07), NGC has graded just **two** examples with Five Full Steps, and none with Six Full Steps. (#84072)

PROOF JEFFERSON NICKELS

452 **1938 PR68 NGC.** Iridescent rainbow toning gravitates to the margins of this gorgeous proof. Razor-sharp definition and exquisite preservation characterizes both obverse and reverse. Census: 8 in 68, 0 finer (6/07). (#4175)

453 **Uncertified 1971 Proof Set With No S Nickel.** Though uncertified, the No S nickel in this five-coin proof set, complete with original packaging, appears to be of at least Gem quality with appealing cameo contrast. A small spot of milky patina appears above the left wing of Monticello. The other clad pieces display a similar appearance, and the cent displays vibrant copper-orange color. (#4204)

EARLY HALF DIMES

454 **1795—Scratched, Cleaned—ANACS. VF30 Details.** This Flowing Hair half dime is unduly bright, but has partly retoned olive and pearl-gray. The moderately wavy surfaces display hair-thin marks near the B and Y in LIBERTY, beneath the second T in STATES, beneath the left (facing) wing, and on the left portion of the right wing. (#4251)

Choice AU 1795 LM-8 Half Dime

455 **1795 AU55 NGC.** V-5, LM-8, R.3. This is one of the common 1795 half dime varieties, available in all grades including Mint State. This piece, a Choice AU survivor, has deep steel and grayish-gold toning on both sides. The strike is somewhat indistinct at the centers, especially on the reverse. A small planchet lamination is hidden in the hair. The obverse die is extensively cracked as usual. (#4251)

456 **1800—Scratched, Cleaned—ANACS. Fine 15 Details.** V-1, LM-1, R.3. This slate-gray early half dime is cloudy from vertical hairlines, but does not appear to merit a "Scratched" designation. Charcoal toning outlines the legends. The stars above the eagle are softly struck, but the eagle and UNUM are boldly defined for the details grade. (#4264)

457 **1800 LIBEKTY—Cleaned, Corroded, Scratched—ANACS. XF45 Details.** V-2, LM-3, R.4. This wavy representative has bright gold and blue-green toning. The left obverse field has a few roundish depressions, and the reverse rim is abraded between 9 and 10 o'clock. Moderately granular near 1 o'clock on the reverse, and each side has a few thin marks that are more prominent near the shield. (#4265)

BUST HALF DIMES

1829 Half Dime, MS63, V-12, LM-13.1

458   **1829 MS63 NGC.** V-12, LM-13.1, R.1. Star 13 is rotated clockwise and close to the dentil, and the tip of the stem is over the serif of C. Gray, lilac, and blue patina covers lustrous surfaces, and the design elements are well struck. The dentilation is quite strong on both sides. Minor handling marks are noted on the obverse. (#4276)

459   **1830 MS64 PCGS.** V-7, LM-7, R.2. Forest-green, fire-red, and pearl-gray embrace this satiny and unmarked near-Gem. Well struck except for the left shield border. (#4277)

Frosty 1830 LM-7 Half Dime, MS66 NGC

460   **1830 MS66 NGC.** V-7, LM-7, R.2. This is a common die marriage that is generally available in almost any grade desired, including Choice Mint State. However, examples in Gem or finer quality, like this piece, are rare. This example is a sharply struck Premium Gem with frosty silver luster that is accented on both sides by peripheral gold and iridescent toning. (#4277)

Flashy Premium Gem 1831 Half Dime, LM-4

461   **1831 MS66 NGC.** V-4, LM-4, R.2. Russet-gold and lime-green toning adorns this penetratingly struck Premium Gem. The fields are moderately prooflike, although the piece is undesignated as such by NGC. The obverse field is particularly flashy. Even prolonged inspection beneath a loupe fails to locate abrasions. Outstanding quality for the date, type, or variety collector. (#4278)

Scarce LM-10.1 1832 Half Dime, MS65

462   **1832 MS65 PCGS.** LM-10.1, V-13, R.3. Attributable as a 10.1 by the faint presence of die clash marks at the throat and ear of Liberty, and the absence of a die chip above the N in UNITED. A scarce die marriage, the LM reference lists the Witham coin as a Gem from that 1977 RARCOA sale. The surfaces of this piece are toned rich sea-green with an occasional dab of rose. Sharply struck on each side, with a few inconspicuous field marks on the left portion of the obverse. (#4279)

SEATED HALF DIMES

Outstanding 1837 Large Date Half Dime, MS66

463   **1837 Large Date (Curl Top 1) MS66 PCGS.** The curl top 1 in the date confirms the Large Date. An outstanding strike brought up excellent definition on the design features, and potent luster exudes from both sides. Speckles of faint tan color visit well preserved surfaces that are devoid of mentionable marks. Population: 31 in 66, 3 finer (6/07). (#4311)

464   **1843 MS65 PCGS.** Cream-gray and golden-brown toning drapes this lustrous and intricately struck Gem. The obverse is remarkably close to pristine, while the reverse has only a couple of wispy grazes near the denomination. Population: 9 in 65, 9 finer (4/07). (#4332)

465   **1844 MS66 PCGS.** Orange-red hugs the obverse border, and lime and stone-gray fill the centers. An original and lustrous representative with a nearly immaculate reverse and an unabraded obverse field. Liberty's waist displays faint contact. Population: 12 in 66, 6 finer (6/07). (#4333)

Prooflike MS66 1847 Half Dime

466   **1847 MS66 Prooflike NGC.** At first glance, this impressive Premium Gem has every appearance of a proof strike. The fields are fully mirrored and exhibit striae usually associated with proof coins from this era. The devices have full mint frost, also common to proofs. With the date high in the field, joining the base of Liberty, and defects near most of the stars, this piece matches Breen's description of the proof variety. All of the design elements are bold, and the surfaces are brilliant with only a hint of ivory color. (#4337)

467 **1852 MS64 PCGS.** Choice and satiny beneath deep plum and silver-gray patina on the obverse, with only the latter color on the reverse. A suitably struck representative with few marks overall. Population: 38 in 64, 31 finer (6/07). (#4349)

Rarely Seen 1852-O Half Dime, MS63

468 **1852-O MS63 PCGS.** The mintage of the 1852-O was certainly sufficient with 260,000 pieces struck. One would think that a considerable number of high grade examples would have survived. However, with the coins worth more melted than in circulation, reality intervened and the vast majority of this issue was melted. This is an attractive survivor that is brilliant throughout. Well struck, except on the highpoints of a few of the leaves of the wreath. Bright, satiny mint luster. Population: 3 in 63, 13 finer (6/07). (#4350)

469 **1856 MS66 NGC.** With smooth, delicately frosted surfaces and no blemishes to report, this attractively toned example belongs in a high grade type set. The otherwise silver color yields to champagne-tinged patina on the reverse. Well struck with a hint of softness at the peripheries. Census: 38 in 66, 6 finer (5/07). (#4363)

470 **1857-O MS64 NGC.** Tawny-gold and ocean-blue endow the peripheries of this satiny and refreshingly mark-free near-Gem. Evenly struck, and worthy of personal inspection. Census: 39 in 64, 30 finer (5/07). (#4366)

471 **1858 MS65 NGC.** Deep rose-gray and cobalt-blue toning covers each side of this well struck Gem. The carefully preserved surfaces reveal satiny luster, and are nearly pristine. (#4367)

472 **1858 MS66 NGC.** A brilliant, sharply struck, and moderately prooflike Premium Gem that is kept from a finer grade by a couple of faint handling marks in the right obverse field. Struck from clashed dies. Census: 55 in 66, 21 finer (5/07). (#4367)

473 **1858 MS66 NGC.** This satiny and unabraded Seated half dime offers vivid blue-green and orange obverse toning. The reverse is cream-gray with peripheral aqua and tan shades. Slightly soft in the centers. Census: 54 in 66, 21 finer (5/07). (#4367)

474 **1860 MS65 PCGS.** V-4, Breen-3099. Repunched 1 and 0. Actually, the repunching is visible on all four digits in the date, but is more dramatic on 1 and 0. Well struck with shimmering luster and pleasing golden-tan and turquoise coloration. There are no marks or abrasions on either side of this charming Gem example. (#4377)

475 **1860-O MS66 NGC.** A lightly toned and thoroughly lustrous Premium Gem with a precise strike and exceptional eye appeal. The only New Orleans issue of the Legend Obverse type. Census: 10 in 66, 0 finer (5/07). (#4378)

476 **1862 MS66 PCGS.** A lustrous piece with slate-gray patina that has traces of gold and russet. A boldly struck example of this popular Civil War issue. Population: 33 in 66, 21 finer (5/07). (#4381)

Richly Toned MS67 1863 Half Dime
Mintage of Only 18,000 Pieces

477 **1863 MS67 PCGS.** Deep copper, aqua, and midnight-gray patina shows on the obverse, obscuring the luster in places, but not enough to diminish the grade. The toning on the reverse is dark greenish-gold with a hint of blue, with brilliant luster showing. Boldly struck for this date and highly desirable, as a scant 18,000 pieces were coined for circulation, few of which can compare to this Superb Gem example. An opportunity for the date collector to put away one of the scarcer issues in the Seated half dime series. Population: 15 in 67, 3 finer (4/07). (#4382)

Lightly Toned 1868 Premium Gem Half Dime

478 **1868 MS66 PCGS.** Gently toned in faint tan hues, this lustrous and splendidly preserved Premium Gem is among the finest survivors of its issue. Well struck except for the usual touch of weakness on the upper left cereal grains. A relatively low quantity of 88,600 pieces was produced, since silver half dimes were largely replaced in circulation by fractional currency and Shield nickels by 1868. Population: 5 in 66, 2 finer (6/07). (#4392)

479 **1870 MS65 PCGS.** The shimmering ivory-white surfaces reveal intense mint frost and careful preservation. The design elements are boldly outlined, with just a trace of softness on the upper half of Liberty. An available issue in lower grades but scarce this nice. Population: 15 in 65, 10 finer (6/07). (#4396)

Glorious 1872-S Half Dime, MS67

480 **1872-S Mintmark Above Bow MS67 NGC.** Beginning in 1870, and continuing to the middle of 1872, mintmarks were placed inside the wreath on the half dimes, reverting back to the previous position below the wreath for the remainder of 1872 and all of 1873. This example, a pristine Superb Gem, has bold design features and frosty luster. Both sides have bright silver surfaces with no evidence of toning. Census: 3 in 67, 0 finer (6/07). (#4402)

481 **1873-S MS65 PCGS.** The final year of issue, this blazing Gem has brilliant ivory color with splashes of emerald, sapphire, and ruby toning on the obverse. (#4405)

PROOF SEATED HALF DIMES

482 **1859 PR64 PCGS.** V-4. The date shows strong repunching on the bottom of all the digits (hidden by a contact mark on the 5); possibly a very early die state of V-1 or V-3. A lovely, deeply toned example of this scarce proof date, from a mintage of 800 pieces. Lavish shadings of deep purple and electric-blue adorn both sides. The fields are nicely reflective, and there are no obvious surface impairments on either side. Population: 55 in 64, 32 finer (6/07). (#4438)

Lushly Toned 1860 Half Dime PR66

483 **1860 PR66 PCGS.** Ocean-blue, gold, and cherry-red endow this colorful specimen. The strike is sharp except for the usual slight blending on the upper left portion of the wreath. A pair of hair-thin obverse marks are noted at 12 and 4 o'clock. The first year of the Legend Obverse type. Population: 7 in 66, 2 finer (4/07). (#4443)

484 **1861 PR64 NGC.** Fully struck with dynamically reflective fields and a layer of original toning across each side. A small contact mark on Liberty's jaw, and a few wispy field hairlines limit the grade of this near-Gem proof half dime, from a mintage of 1,000 pieces with a low rate of survival. Census: 26 in 64, 32 finer (6/07). (#4444)

485 **1864 PR65 Cameo PCGS.** Blue-green, orange, lavender, and russet converge on the small surfaces of this war-date half dime. The contrast is surprisingly strong, given the depth and coverage of this Gem's patina. Population: 4 in 65 Cameo, 4 finer (6/07). (#84447)

Patinated PR66 1865 Half Dime

486 **1865 PR66 PCGS.** Lush sea-green, gold, and lilac-gray toning dominates this pinpoint-sharp and unabraded Premium Gem. A pair of minute mint-made lintmarks reside beneath the date. Just 500 proofs were struck, in addition to only 13,000 business strikes. Housed in a green label holder. Population: 10 in 66, 0 finer (6/07). (#4448)

Gem Cameo Proof 1866 Half Dime

487 **1866 PR65 Cameo NGC.** Just a trace of champagne toning is evident on the obverse and reverse devices of this Gem Cameo proof. All of the design motifs on each side are boldly and intricately detailed, just as intended for the design. Date collectors often seek these Gem proofs, given the rarity of similar quality business strikes. Census: 4 in 65 Cameo, 4 finer (6/07). (#84449)

488 **1868 PR65 PCGS.** Autumn-brown patina clings to the borders. This lovely Gem has icy devices, but lacks a Cameo designation since it is housed in a green label holder. A mere 600 proofs were struck. Population: 19 in 65, 12 finer (4/07). (#4451)
From The Vanek Collection.

489 **1868 PR65 Cameo PCGS.** A flashy Gem whose deep reflectivity is undimmed by light haze. Boldly struck with pleasing contrast. Population: 4 in 65 Cameo, 3 finer (6/07). (#84451)

490 **1870 PR65 NGC.** A deep layer of original toning blankets both sides of this Gem proof half dime. Razor-sharp striking details are readily evident on all of the design elements, including the denticles. Only a faint milky patch in the right obverse field precludes an even loftier grade designation. Census: 32 in 65, 29 finer (6/07). (#4453)

491 **1871 PR66 PCGS.** Caramel-gold and sea-green are distributed across the obverse. The reverse has a golden-brown center framed by peripheral ocean-blue. Liberty's waist has a granular appearance, as made from a rusted die. A scant 960 proofs were struck. Population: 14 in 66, 1 finer (4/07). (#4454)

492 **1871 PR63 Cameo NGC.** Light golden-gray color dominates, and is accented with wisps of cobalt-blue and lavender. Sharply struck design elements enhance the Cameo contrast. A few minor handling marks define the grade. (#84454)

EARLY DIMES

1802 JR-4 Dime, Terminal Die State, Fine 15

493 **1802 Fine 15 PCGS.** JR-4, R.4. A seldom-seen variety with a mintage of only 10,975 pieces. This is the most frequently seen variety of this scarce year. The obverse is struck from the terminal die state and shows the retained rim-to-rim break that describes an arc from star 7 through BE of LIBERTY. Only a dozen or so examples are believed known with this retained cud. All the coins show lettering within the arc of the die crack, and none are smooth in this area. Weakly struck in the right center of the reverse, as usual. The light gray surfaces are accented with speckled blue and golden-rose toning on each side. A few light marks and old, shallow scratches are consistent with the grade. (#4472)

494 **1805 4 Berries—Bent, Scratched, Whizzed—ANACS. VF30 Details.** JR-2, R.2. Several faded pinscratches traverse the portrait, and other lesser marks are noted on the obverse at 4 o'clock and beneath OF. Both sides are somewhat wavy and have been whizzed to provide a consistent micro-granular appearance. (#4477)

Satiny MS62 1805 4 Berries Dime

495 **1805 4 Berries MS62 ANACS.** JR-2, R.2. Only two die varieties are known for 1805 dimes, and each receives a separate *Guide Book* listing due to different berry counts. This golden-brown and steel-gray example has shimmering luster and smooth surfaces. Each side has faint roller marks, as made, where the strike is incomplete, but post-strike distractions are nonexistent. (#4477)

1805 Ten Cents, AU53, JR-1

496 **1805 5 Berries AU53 NGC.** JR-1, R.3. A scarce variety, the less common of two varieties. This variety has five berries on the reverse. The silver-gray surfaces exhibit traces of luster in the recesses, and are quite clean for a coin that has seen some circulation. Sharp detail is noted on the design features, that are also well centered on the planchet. (#4478)

BUST DIMES

497 **1820 Medium 0—Cleaned—ANACS. MS60 Details.** JR-11, R.3. This well struck Capped Bust dime has no indication of wear. The lightly toned fields are prooflike. A U-shaped lintmark is noted on the left reverse field. Faintly hairlined but nonetheless impressive. (#4492)

498 **1828 Small Date MS63 PCGS.** JR-1, R.2. Amazingly sharp on all of the design elements, with a deep layer of red-brown and bluish-green patina over both sides. The two or three trivial marks on the obverse are minimal for the grade. One of two *Guide Book* varieties that share a combined mintage of 125,000 pieces; both varieties are scarce, especially in Mint State. (#4510)

Impressive Select Mint State 1835 Dime

499 **1835 MS63 PCGS.** JR-4, R.2. The 5 in the date is high, while the 8 and the 3 are repunched. The design elements are sharply struck throughout. Both sides are blanketed in shades of deep cobalt-blue, gold, forest-green, and purple-rose. Exquisitely preserved with substantial luster and remarkable eye appeal. (#4527)

Lustrous and Attractively Toned JR-1 1836 Dime, MS64

500 **1836 MS64 PCGS.** JR-1, R.3. Sharply struck with surprisingly strong, frosted luster beneath the delicate blue-violet, rose, and gold toning that is draped over each side. Kept from a full Gem grade only by a shallow mark on the cheek of Liberty. A lovely, high grade example of this scarcer variety. (#4528)

SEATED DIMES

Well Struck 1837 No Stars, Small Date Dime, MS64

501 **1837 No Stars, Small Date MS64 PCGS.** The 1837 Small Date is distinguished from the Large Date by the curved top of the 3 in the date versus the Large Date's flat-topped 3. Golden-gray patination bathes each side of this near-Gem. A well executed strike brings out sharp definition on the design elements, including the horizontal and vertical stripes of the shield, elements frequently weak on this date (Brian Greer, 1992). A near horizontal crack travels across part of the reverse. Population: 12 in 64, 6 finer (6/07). (#4562)

502 **1838-O No Stars AU53 NGC.** The 1838-O is essential to New Orleans type collectors, since it is the only No Stars dime from the Southern facility. It is also the first O-mint dime issue, although Breen believed that examples (such as the present coin) from a rusted obverse die were struck as late as 1839. Satiny and smooth with light rose-red and gray toning. (#4564)

Well Struck 1838 Large Stars Dime, MS65

503 **1838 Large Stars MS65 NGC.** The Large Stars 1838 dime can be distinguished from the Small Stars variety by the fact that the latter, according to Brian Greer (1992): "Always (has) a die crack through the first six stars." The Gem in this lot does not possess this crack. Essentially untoned surfaces yield strong luster and are free of disturbing marks. An impressive strike brings out nice definition on the design features. Census: 39 in 65, 34 finer (6/07). (#4568)

Beautiful 1838 Large Stars Dime MS67

504 **1838 Large Stars MS67 NGC.** Fortin-105. A lustrous and precisely struck Superb Gem whose sparkling surfaces display only a hint of gold patina. Stars 9 and 13 are boldly repunched, since stars were added by hand to the working die for this issue. (#4568)

1839 Ten Cent No Drapery, MS67

505 **1839 No Drapery MS67 NGC.** Although NGC and PCGS have each certified a few pieces at an even higher numeric grade level, this is one of the finer 1839 dimes in existence. The strike is crisp with every design element showing the boldness that was intended by the engraver. The surfaces are frosty with radiant luster shimmering through original gray and gold color with attractive iridescent accents. As a representative of a short-lived design type, this piece will appeal to the advanced type collector in addition to the date collector. Census: 14 in 67, 5 finer (6/07). (#4571)

506 **1844 VF30 ANACS.** This pleasing Choice VF dime displays light to medium gray toning that becomes slightly deeper on the reverse. The design elements are well defined, and each side is quite clean. The famed "Little Orphan Annie." (#4585)

507 **1853 Arrows MS64 NGC.** A brilliant and precisely struck Seated Liberty type coin with good luster and only a single detectable mark, a thin line near star 13. (#4603)

508 **1858-S—Scratched—ANACS. AU58 Details.** Aqua-blue borders frame the steel-gray centers. This slightly bright rare date dime has a thin mark near star 12 and several faint pinscratches near ONE DIME. Well struck with ample luster. A scant 60,000 pieces were struck. (#4618)

509 **1859-O MS64 NGC.** The pleasing design details are well defined on this originally toned near-Gem, with only a touch of weakness noted on the top of Liberty's head and on the right side obverse stars. Deep plum coloration adorns the central regions, yielding to electric-blue toning near the borders. Clash marks are noticeable near the reverse center, but abrasions are nowhere to be seen. Census: 24 in 64, 33 finer (6/07). (#4620)

510 **1859-S—Cleaned—ANACS. AU50 Details.** The deep sea-green and tan-gray surfaces are minutely granular. A splendidly detailed dime with minor incompleteness of strike on Liberty's hair and the wreath bow. A mere 60,000 pieces were struck, and since there were no serious West Coast collectors until decades later, only a few Mint State examples are known. (#4621)

511 **1862 MS65 PCGS.** A popular Civil War-era dime. While production was high, survival was low because of extensive melting of silver and gold coins during The War. This piece displays excellent mint luster and each side shows rich sea-green, rose, and gray toning. Population: 14 in 65, 13 finer (6/07). (#4635)

512 **1871 MS64 PCGS.** Powder-blue, rose-pink, and chestnut-tan adorn this carefully preserved and gently shimmering near-Gem. A good strike overall, with unimportant softness on Liberty's foot and hair. A surprisingly difficult issue in Mint State. Population: 7 in 64, 8 finer (6/07). (#4653)

513 **1875 MS65 NGC.** Tan-brown toning is generally limited to the reverse periphery. A boldly struck and satiny Gem that exhibits faint clash marks on both fields. Census: 49 in 65, 48 finer (5/07). (#4672)

514 **1875 MS66 NGC.** Deeply patinated in autumn-brown and sea-green shades, this well struck Premium Gem nonetheless displays good luster. The central reverse shows unimportant grazes. Struck from clashed dies. Census: 41 in 66, 7 finer (5/07). (#4672)

515 **1877 MS66 PCGS.** Glowing luster emanates from white surfaces that exhibit sharply struck design elements. There are no significant marks to report. Population: 10 in 66, 4 finer (6/07). (#4682)

Attractively Toned 1877 Superb Gem Dime Type Two Reverse

516 **1877 MS67 PCGS.** The more commonly seen Type Two reverse, attributed by the E in ONE being distant from the wreath. Highly lustrous surfaces display, on the obverse, waves of medium intensity golden-brown, cobalt-blue, and lavender, and pastel violet, sky-blue, and gold-yellow on the reverse. An attentive strike yields well defined and uniform definition on the design features. Impeccably preserved throughout. Population: 4 in 67, 0 finer (6/07). (#4682)

517 **1878-CC MS61 PCGS.** Boldly struck, lustrous, and essentially untoned, this silvery-white example is bright and highly attractive. A few spidery die cracks are seen on the reverse, and faint field lines are noted on each side. A low mintage final Carson City dime issue of just 200,000 coins. Population: 1 in 61, 32 finer (6/07). (#4686)

518 **1882 MS65 NGC.** Well struck for the issue, even on the often indistinct area of Liberty's head. Rose-gray and pale violet toning consumes the satiny surfaces. (#4690)

519 **1884 MS66 PCGS.** Light almond-gold toning graces this exuberantly lustrous Premium Gem. Nicely struck and beautifully preserved. Dimes were the first Seated denomination to return to plentiful production after the advent of the Morgan dollar. Population: 26 in 66, 24 finer (4/07). (#4692)

520 **1887 MS66 NGC.** Rose-pink and aquamarine dominate the obverse. Lavish blue-green toning consumes the reverse. Lustrous and unabraded with minor softness on Liberty's hair. Census: 44 in 66, 4 finer (5/07). (#4698)

521 **1889-S MS64 PCGS.** Well struck, except for the top of Liberty's head and a few of the wreath leaves, with intense satiny luster and deep brownish sea-green toning across both sides. Surface marks are minimal and nearly nonexistent. A conditionally scarce issue at this grade level. Population: 11 in 64, 3 finer (6/07). (#4703)

522 **1890-S MS64 PCGS.** Medium autumn-gold and cream-gray toning graces this lustrous and precisely struck near-Gem. Splendidly smooth and desirable. An unusual clash mark is noted beneath the DI in DIME, an interesting project for the numismatic researcher. Population: 11 in 64, 8 finer (4/07). (#4705)

523 **1891 MS66 NGC.** Electric-blue patina occupies portions of each side, competing for territory with lavender and golden-brown. Generally well struck, save for softness in Liberty's hair. Well preserved and lustrous. Census: 48 in 66, 18 finer (5/07). (#4706)

PROOF SEATED DIMES

Lovely PR66 Cameo 1863 Dime

524 **1863 PR66 Cameo NGC.** The 1863 has long been a favorite of collectors as only 460 proofs were struck in addition to a scant production of 14,000 business strikes. This is a deeply reflective proof striking that displays strongly contrasting frosted devices on each side. Light golden-gray toning accents both obverse and reverse with no imperfections visible to the unaided eye. Population: 3 in 66, 3 finer (5/07). (#84756)

525 **1864 PR66 NGC.** Ruby-red, gold, and emerald-green endow the flashy mirrors and exquisitely struck devices. This Civil War date has a minuscule proof mintage of 470 pieces. Census: 11 in 66, 6 finer (5/07). (#4757)

526 **1866 PR64 PCGS.** A precisely struck and untoned near-Gem whose glassy fields are well preserved. Since silver coins did not circulate in 1866 except in the West, only 8,000 business strikes and 725 proofs were struck. Housed in a green label holder. (#4759)

Brilliant 1875 Dime, PR66 Cameo

527 **1875 PR66 Cameo NGC.** This brilliant proof is designated Cameo by NGC, but it is a borderline Ultra Cameo with extraordinary eye appeal. Both sides are entirely devoid of toning. A faint reverse hairline just below the denomination is the only imperfection of any consequence, merely limiting the grade, keeping this beauty out of the Superb Gem category. Census: 7 in 66 Cameo, 3 finer (6/07). (#84772)

528 **1875 PR64 Deep Cameo ANACS.** Dashes of sea-green and tobacco-brown enrich the margins of this boldly struck and flashy near-Gem. The devices are thickly frosted. A mere 700 proofs were produced. (#94772)

529 **1876 PR66 NGC.** Deep electric-green toning covers both sides of this conditionally scarce Premium Gem proof. Contact-free and expertly preserved, the piece has reflective fields and sharply struck devices. Census: 4 in 66, 4 finer (6/07). (#4773)

530 **1876 PR65 Cameo NGC.** Crisply struck and free of noticeable flaws, with glassy fields and frosted devices. Deep turquoise-blue toning is noted in the fields. A few wispy hairlines in the right obverse field are easy to forgive. Census: 5 in 65 Cameo, 3 finer (5/07). (#84773)

531 **1880 PR65 Cameo PCGS.** Pleasing Cameo frost distinguishes this nicely struck Gem. Wisps of milky gray patina are present beneath the denomination, but the flashy fields are otherwise brilliant. A low mintage date. (#84777)

Splendid 1882 Dime, PR67 Cameo

532 **1882 PR67 Cameo NGC.** Eleven hundred dime proofs were reportedly struck in 1882. NGC and PCGS have graded a total of about 450 examples; fewer than 100 examples were assigned the Cameo designation, primarily between PR60 and PR65. Sharply struck, heavily frosted motifs on the Superb Proof Cameo offered in the present lot appear to float over deeply mirrored, glassy fields. Impeccably preserved surfaces are essentially color free. A truly splendid Cameo specimen! Census: 13 in 67 Cameo, 3 finer (6/07). (#84779)

Toned Proof 1882 Dime, PR67 Cameo

533 **1882 PR67 Cameo NGC.** Both sides of this Superb Cameo proof have peripheral toning that blends rich gold, cobalt-blue, and violet into a presentation of exceptional aesthetic appeal. The central obverse and reverse are mostly brilliant with only a trace of champagne color. This sharply struck Superb proof will easily delight the connoisseur. (#84779)

534 **1883 PR65 PCGS.** Needle-sharp definition is seen on the design features. Both sides are toned in light to medium gray, and reveal no significant marks. Population: 37 in 65, 36 finer (6/07). (#4780)

Superb Cameo Proof 1884 Seated Dime

535 **1884 PR67 Cameo NGC.** Both sides of this Superb proof have wonderful gold and lilac toning along the borders, framing silver brilliance at the centers. All of the design elements on both sides are bold and the surfaces are pristine. The devices have frosty luster and the fields have deep mirrors, creating the cameo appearance that is so highly prized by today's collectors. (#84781)

Beautiful 1884 PR67 Cameo Dime

536 **1884 PR67 Cameo NGC.** The 1884 proof dime was struck to the tune of 875 pieces. NGC and PCGS combined have graded several hundred examples, and given the Cameo label to approximately 85 specimens. Crisply struck, frosted motifs stand out against the backdrop of deep mirrored fields, and the white surfaces are devoid of significant marks. Census: 16 in 67 Cameo, 3 finer (6/07). (#84781)

537 **1886 PR65 NGC.** Lovely reddish-tan and mint-green toning is intermingled across both sides of this conditionally impressive Gem proof dime. The fields display vibrant reflectivity and the surfaces are exquisitely preserved. The upper obverse details are very weak, especially Liberty's head, but the remaining design elements are nicely struck. Census: 54 in 65, 42 finer (6/07). (#4783)

538 **1886 PR66 NGC.** Strongly reflective with mild contrast that is more evident on the reverse. Thin bands of tan-gold patina grace the rims, while the centers are practically untoned. A carefully preserved example that would be an excellent candidate for a proof type set.(#4783)
From The Vanek Collection.

539 **1889 PR64 Cameo PCGS.** This lovely Cameo displays color free surfaces. Frosty motifs are sharply impressed. A few minor obverse handling marks preclude Gem classification. Fewer than 30 examples have been given the Cameo designation (6/07). (#84786)

BARBER DIMES

Key AU55 Details 1895-O Dime

540 **1895-O—Cleaned—ANACS. AU55 Details.** The majority of Barber dimes grade from AG to VG, but the present piece gives little indication of actual circulation. A hairlined slate-gray example with minor striking incompleteness on selected portions of the wreath. Aside from the practically non-collectible '94-S, the 1895-O is the key date of this popular series. (#4807)

Sharp 1899-S Dime, MS65

541 **1899-S MS65 PCGS.** Splashes of reddish-gold, purple and aqua grace the obverse, while the reverse is mostly a deep shade of mottled gunmetal-blue. The design elements on this conditionally-scarce S-mint Barber dime are sharply struck. Fine roller marks are noted on Liberty's cheek. Population: 5 in 65, 11 finer (6/07). (#4820)

542 **1900-S MS64 NGC.** Sharply struck with prooflike fields and attractive light coral toning on the obverse. Deeper purple-rose, cobalt-blue and gold coloration adorns the reverse, where faint grease streaks (as made) extend diagonally beneath ONE DIME. A desirable near-Gem example of this popular turn-of-the-century issue. Census: 23 in 64, 14 finer (6/07). (#4823)

543 **1902-S MS63 NGC.** Like most Barber issues, the 1902-S is plentiful in heavily circulated grades, but difficult to locate with full mint luster. This untoned and attractive example has well struck devices and softly defined denticles. Census: 12 in 63, 20 finer (5/07). (#4829)

544 **1906-S MS66 PCGS.** One of just over 3.1 million pieces struck for this issue, which came from an eventful year for the San Francisco Mint. This solidly struck example offers pleasing luster and carefully preserved surfaces with just a touch of amber patina at the margins. Highly appealing. Population: 13 in 66, 3 finer (5/07). (#4841)

545 **1906-S MS66 NGC.** Deep sea-green and sunset-orange toning blankets both sides of this alluring Premium Gem. Boldly struck and lustrous, with blemish-free surfaces that reveal vertical striations in the reverse fields. Census: 10 in 66, 1 finer (5/07). (#4841)

546 **1908 MS66 NGC.** Well struck with shimmering, satiny luster and mostly silver-white surfaces that exhibit a few wisps of russet and pale green patina. Well preserved and virtually pristine; a conditionally scarce Premium Gem. Census: 10 in 66, 4 finer (5/07). (#4846)

547 **1908 MS66 PCGS.** A sharply struck, satiny Premium Gem with peripheral lemon, forest-green, and ruby-red toning. As is the case with the other Barber denominations, the dimes were not widely saved in the earliest years after their mintage, as most collectors of the day preferred proofs. Today's numismatist prefers matched sets of these coins, either collecting only the proof issues, or seeking out all date and mintmark issues in business strike form. Population: 13 in 66, 1 finer (6/07). (#4846)
Ex: Dr. Steven L. Duckor (Heritage, 1/06), lot 1018.

548 **1908-O MS65 PCGS.** Dusky gold and gray color on the obverse with a mostly brilliant reverse surface ringed by vivid gold and blue color. The obverse has underlying satiny luster and the reverse tends toward frosty luster. A lovely example from the penultimate year of operation for the New Orleans Mint. Population: 23 in 65, 10 finer (5/07). (#4848)

Attractive 1908-S Gem Dime

549 **1908-S MS65 PCGS.** Low to medium intensity cobalt-blue, lavender, and golden-brown patination rides over the obverse, while light gold-tan color dominates the reverse, which is framed by russet and light blue at the periphery. Sharply struck throughout. A couple of minor obverse marks are within the confines of the grade designation. Population: 16 in 65, 10 finer (6/07). (#4849)

Outstanding 1908-S Dime, MS66

550 **1908-S MS66 NGC.** While the 1908-S Barber dime is not considered a rarity, it is seldom seen in grades as fine as this. In fact, this Premium Gem is tied for the finest that NGC has certified. Both sides have pale ivory color that is accompanied by deeper gold and iridescent toning. All aspects of the design are bold. Census: 3 in 66, 0 finer (6/07). (#4849)

Conditionally Rare 1909-D Dime, MS65

551 **1909-D MS65 PCGS.** This date is a scarce one in all grades, and is usually found in lower quality, more often than not with extensive wear. This Gem is an important exception to the rule. Housed in a green-label holder, it has frosty luster that shines through deep grayish-gold and iridescent toning. Population: 6 in 65, 10 finer (6/07). (#4851)

Scarce 1910-S Premium Gem Dime

552 **1910-S MS66 NGC.** David and John Feigenbaum (1999) rate the 1910-S dime R.4 in "total mint state," and say: "We know the (1910) 'S' is scarce because of its low mintage." Dappled golden-brown and cobalt-blue toning bathes lustrous surfaces that are well preserved. The design elements are impressively struck. Census: 1 in 66, 2 finer (6/07). (#4856)

553 **1913 MS66 PCGS.** Sharply struck over the centers, with slight weakness observed on a few of the obverse peripheral letters. Bright satiny luster illuminates the silver surfaces that display a slight degree of speckled olive patina on both sides. A well preserved and entirely blemish-free Premium Gem. Population: 25 in 66, 0 finer (6/07). (#4863)

554 **1916 MS66 PCGS.** A delightful Premium Gem that sports golden-brown patina on each side, accompanied by violet on the obverse. Highly lustrous with great detail. Population: 37 in 66, 3 finer (8/06). (#4870)

PROOF BARBER DIMES

Ultra Cameo PR67 1892 Dime

555 1892 PR67 Ultra Cameo NGC. The first-year 1892 Barber proof coinage of 1,245 pieces was more than double 1891's 600 coins, but contemporary enthusiasm for the series was short-lived. An excerpt from *The Numismatist* reviewing the new Barber designs reads, in part, "These pieces have, by this time, been in the hands of our readers. The mechanical work is all that could be desired, and it is probable, that owing to the conventional rut in which our Mint authorities seem obliged to keep, that it is the best that could be done,—for after all they are not gotten up for the collector, but for general barter,—but to the numismatist or lover of the beautiful in design and art, they will be but another disappointment, hardly noticeable [sic] now because expected, and we are getting so used to them." The proof mintage plummeted in 1893 to 792 pieces, a near-40% drop.

The present example is an essential type coin, at PR67 Ultra Cameo the only coin so graded at NGC (5/07). Both sides feature deep black-on-silver contrast between the fields and devices, with no hint of toning. A small contact mark is noted on Liberty's cheek. (#94875)

556 1893 PR65 PCGS. The rich orange-gold centers are surrounded by aquamarine and ruby-red borders. A penetrating strike contributes further to the eye appeal. A scant 792 proofs were struck. (#4877)

557 1893 PR65 Cameo NGC. Frosty devices and legends validate the Cameo designation. Mostly brilliant, although gold toning is concealed on the left half of the wreath, and the portrait has three minuscule gray freckles. Only 792 proofs were struck, a reduction of 453 pieces from the introductory 1892 proof emission. (#84877)

558 1895 PR64 PCGS. A needle-sharp Choice proof dime with light golden-gray toning. The 1895 is the scarcest Philadelphia date of the series. Certified in an old green label holder. (#4879)

559 1895 PR66 PCGS. A melange of cobalt-blue, magenta, gray, and yellow-gold rest over the undisturbed surfaces. The motifs are sharply struck, and the preservation is exceptional. A scant 880 proofs were struck. Population: 31 in 66, 15 finer (5/07). (#4879)

560 1896 PR66 Cameo NGC. This fully struck specimen has a brilliant obverse. A hint of gold toning is noted on the reverse. The devices are frosty, and the fields provide satin luster. Census: 11 in 66, 11 finer (5/07). (#84880)

561 1897 PR65 NGC. Ruby-red, apple-green, ice-blue, and gold toning drapes this exquisitely struck and flashy Gem. A mere 731 proofs were struck, and the entire proof mintage of the type is less than that of the 1995-W silver eagle. (#4881)

562 1900 PR65 PCGS. Mottled orange, cobalt-blue, and ruby-red embrace this flashy Gem. The surfaces appear void of marks. A scant 912 proofs were produced. Population: 21 in 65, 29 finer (4/07). (#4884)

563 1906 PR66 NGC. The white-on-black contrast is noticeable, and the reverse on its own likely merits a Cameo designation. This exquisitely struck Premium Gem is undisturbed and stone-white. A scant 675 proofs were coined. Census: 20 in 66, 13 finer (5/07). (#4890)

564 1907 PR66 PCGS. Deeply reflective and boldly impressed. Delicate blue, gold, and orange patina adorns each side. Well cared for surfaces are devoid of blemishes. Population: 19 in 66, 10 finer (6/07). (#4891)

Lavishly Toned PR67 1907 Dime

565 1907 PR67 NGC. This Superb Proof is for the aficionado of colorfully toned coins. Variegated cobalt-blue, orange-gold, and lavender patina adorns each side, but does not in the least interfere with the reflectivity from the mirrored fields. Exquisitely struck design elements appear to be suspended over glassy fields when the coin is tilted beneath a light source. Only 575 proofs were struck. Census: 18 in 67, 0 finer (5/07). (#4891)

566 1909 PR65 PCGS. A hint of cameo contrast is created by satiny luster on the devices. The fields are completely mirrored, although the depth is subdued by toning on both sides. The obverse has light ivory color that is surrounded by peripheral iridescence, and the reverse has deep steel toning throughout. (#4893)

567 1910 PR65 PCGS. Medium-intensity cobalt-blue and rose-brown toning bathes each side. A couple of dark toning spots are also noted on each side. The surfaces are free of mentionable contact marks, and exhibit sharply defined design elements. Population: 25 in 65, 19 finer (4/07). (#4894)

Exquisite 1910 Dime, PR67

568 1910 PR67 PCGS. The 1910 dime has a relatively low mintage of 551 pieces. Walter Breen (1977) writes that: " ... several hoards exist." In any event, PCGS and NGC have certified close to 300 1910 proof ten cent examples, mainly through the PR65 grade level. The Superb Gem offered here yields a coat of light tan-gold color on the obverse, and iridescent cobalt-blue on the reverse. Immaculately preserved surfaces exhibit exquisitely struck design elements. Housed in a green-label holder. Population: 7 in 67, 2 finer (5/07). (#4894)

569 **1911 PR65 NGC.** An argument could be posed for a Cameo assignment to this Gem, although the toning, especially on the reverse, tends to subdue the contrast. This lovely piece has considerable mint brilliance on the obverse, with peripheral gold and iridescent toning. The reverse has deeper gold, lilac, and thick green toning. (#4895)

MERCURY DIMES

Incredible 1916 Dime, MS68 Full Bands

570 **1916 MS68 Full Bands PCGS.** As a first-year issue, the 1916 dime was saved in quantity, particularly in the populated cities of the East Coast, yet only a handful of survivors have the combination of bold detail and stunning visual eye appeal that this piece possesses. Both sides offer powerful luster, and the strike is sharp. The lower and left sides of the obverse display vivid sea-green, cerulean, violet, and cherry-red toning, while the reverse periphery has similar colors. The practically perfect surfaces are untoned otherwise. A delightful example that would be a wonderful addition to a high-octane Registry set. Population: 8 in 68 Full Bands, 0 finer (5/07). (#4905)

Impressive 1916 Mercury Dime MS68 Full Bands

571 **1916 MS68 Full Bands NGC.** A lovely frosty sheen envelopes the icy-white surfaces of this crisply struck Superb Gem. The fields have a pleasing matte-like texture, by design in this year only. The central reverse bands are fully split and rounded. Both sides of the piece are immaculately preserved. Census: 14 in 68 Full Bands, 0 finer (6/07). (#4905)

572 **1916-D Good 4 ANACS.** Light gray surfaces still exhibit a fair amount of detail on this Good 4 '16-D specimen. The obverse rim is virtually full, and has worn only slightly into a couple of letters; the outer portions of about half of the reverse letters have merged with the rim. A couple of inoffensive, small marks are entirely consistent with the grade designation. A great key-date piece for a low-grade Mercury dime set. (#4906)

573 **1916-D Good 4 PCGS.** This is a truly pleasing key-date representative for the grade level. Semi-bright, silver-gray surfaces are remarkably clean for a coin having seen the circulation that this Good example has. The obverse legend, motto, and date are sharp, as are most of the elements on the reverse, where about half of the peripheral letters show slight merging with the rim. Close examination reveals no mentionable marks. This piece is sure to find a home in a low to mid-grade, problem-free Mercury dime collection. (#4906)

574 **1916-D—Cleaned—ANACS. Good 4 Details.** The obverse is somewhat bright from a wipe, but the all-important date and mintmark are bold. The tops of the letters in AMERICA are partly merged into the rim. (#4906)

575 **1916-D—Counting Wheel Damage—ANACS. VG8 Details.** A silver-blue patch of fine lines near E PLURIBUS UNUM is attributed by ANACS to a pass through a mechanical coin counter. Otherwise, a pleasing cream-gray key date dime with a bold date and mintmark and some fasces definition. (#4906)

Outstanding 1916-D Dime, MS65 ★

576 **1916-D MS65 ★ NGC.** The 264,000 pieces that comprised the entire mintage of 1916-D dimes were struck in one month, November. The story of that truncated mintage, often-told but worth repeating, places every Mint Superintendent at a meeting in Washington, D.C., where the Denver chief was instructed to halt production of most denominations and concentrate on the Barber quarter, unexpectedly in demand. The result was an instantly recognized rarity, popular to this day.

The Gem offered here exhibits stellar visual appeal. The strike is solid overall, and only a tiny section at the center of the fasces keeps the piece from Full Bands status. The surfaces are slightly satiny, as is the case with a majority of Mint State examples, and display vivid patina that ranges from subtle silver-blue over the devices and parts of the fields to strawberry, gold, and blue-green color elsewhere. An incredible example of this key issue and the finest non-Full Bands piece ever offered by Heritage. Census: 1 in 65 ★, 2 finer (5/07). (#4906)

Desirable 1916-D Dime, MS61 Full Bands

577 1916-D MS61 Full Bands NGC. Like the 1909-S VDB cent, the 1916-D dime is more available in Mint State grades than some other key issues, largely due to its first-year status. Members of the general public saved examples, and so the issue has a significant proportion of higher-grade survivors. At the same time, those coins held by non-numismatists often suffered from careless handling, which helps explain the lack of Gem and better representatives.

Lange (2005) describes the 1916-D issue as "nearly always well struck, with many Mint State examples qualifying" for the Full Bands designation. On this piece, the bands of the fasces exhibit full separation and rounding as well. The surfaces offer pleasing luster and a blend of gunmetal and gold color at the margins, while the centers retain a silver-gray appearance. Wispy abrasions in the textured fields and on the devices account for the grade, though the coin would rate considerably better on visual appeal alone. (#4907)

578 1917-S MS66 Full Bands PCGS. Fully struck with marvelously smooth, nearly pristine surfaces. Essentially untoned on the obverse with several faint russet-orange streaks on the reverse. An impressive Premium Gem from the second year of the immensely popular Mercury dime series. Population: 57 in 66 Full Bands, 10 finer (4/07). (#4915)

579 1918 MS65 Full Bands PCGS. A moderately challenging early P-mint in the Mercury dime series. This piece is brilliant throughout. The strike is strong on all the design elements, including the peripheries. Bright mint luster. (#4917)

580 1918 MS65 Full Bands NGC. David Lange (2005), discussing the 1918 issue, writes that "Mint State coins are generally available, though most are weakly struck around their peripheries." Not so this Gem! The sharp strike transcends the Full Bands to encompass all of the design elements, including those on the peripheries. Splashes of golden-tan, crimson, and forest-green visit highly lustrous surfaces that are devoid of significant marks. Census: 54 in 65 Full Bands, 16 finer (5/07). (#4917)

581 1918 MS66 Full Bands PCGS. A difficult early P-mint dime to locate in high grade. This is a superlative example that has creamy-white surfaces and no abrasions to interrupt the flow of luster. Brilliant and fully struck throughout with virtually none of the peripheral weakness often seen on this issue. Population: 39 in 66, 4 finer (6/07). (#4917)

Conditionally Elusive 1918-D Dime MS64 Full Bands

582 1918-D MS64 Full Bands PCGS. Lustrous and untoned, with well preserved surfaces that are blemish-free. A small charcoal spot is noted near the lower obverse rim, below 18 in the date. The importance of this piece derives from the fully split central bands on the reverse, a condition rarely seen on 1918-D dimes. Population: 79 in 64 Full Bands, 18 finer (6/07). (#4919)

583 1918-S MS64 Full Bands PCGS. Attractive apricot and chestnut toning adorns this lustrous and carefully preserved World War I dime. A golden-brown freckle is noted at 4 o'clock on the reverse. (#4921)

Highly Lustrous 1920 Dime, MS67 Full Bands

584 1920 MS67 Full Bands PCGS. With a mintage of nearly 60 million pieces, the 1920 dime is available in all grades through MS65, and even Full Band coins are not especially scarce. Superb Gems with Full Bands, however, such as the example in this lot, are elusive. Indeed, PCGS and NGC have certified fewer than 25 such specimens, and just a couple finer. Dazzling luster emanates from immaculately preserved surfaces that show faint tan color under magnification. An impressive strike results in sharp definition throughout. Population: 12 in 67 finer, 0 finer (6/07). (#4929)

585 1920-D MS64 Full Bands NGC. A boldly impressed and largely untoned representative of this early branch mint issue. A touch of ice-blue color graces minimally marked, shining fields that display a degree of die erosion. (#4931)

586 1920-D MS64 Full Bands PCGS. Light gold and rose patina invigorates this lustrous and exactingly struck near-Gem. This beautifully preserved branch mint dime is surprisingly smooth for its grade. (#4931)

587 1920-S MS63 Full Bands PCGS. Well struck with no evidence of peripheral fadeaway. Slight amounts of speckled patina are seen on each side. A few wispy marks restrict the grade. A scarce, early S-mint Mercury dime that is relatively difficult to locate with a full strike. (#4933)

588 1921—Cleaned—ANACS. AU58 Details. The satiny luster is slightly subdued, but this smooth pearl-gray semi-key dime gives little other indication of either circulation or a past cleaning. The fields have an orange peel texture and IN GOD WE TRUST is distorted, all as made from long-in-use dies. (#4934)

589 **1924 MS66 Full Bands PCGS.** This blazing Premium Gem has frosty silver luster with pure white color on both sides. This combination of quality and color is seldom seen on these coins, and desired by so many. Population: 60 in 66, 11 finer (6/07). (#4943)

590 **1924-D MS62 Full Bands PCGS.** Light golden-brown and gunmetal-gray toning drapes this satiny and unmarked better date dime. The centers are exquisitely struck, although a few letters near the left border lack absolute definition. (#4945)

591 **1924-D MS65 Full Bands PCGS.** Lush forest-green, rose-red, and dove-gray endow this sharply struck and highly lustrous Gem. The fields appear essentially immaculate. The date is lightly strike doubled. (#4945)

592 **1925 MS65 Full Bands PCGS.** Dappled olive-green patination is evenly distributed over the obverse, but becomes concentrated at the peripheries on the reverse. A few light obverse ticks do not disturb, and lustrous surfaces exhibit sharply struck design elements that culminate in Full Bands. Population: 80 in 65 Full Bands, 29 finer (6/07). (#4949)

593 **1925-D MS64 Full Bands PCGS.** Bright and boldly struck with a few splashes of milky patina against the otherwise untoned surfaces of this 1920s D-mint piece. A handful of minor, scattered marks bar the way to a Gem grade. (#4950)

Exceptional 1925-S Full Bands Gem Dime

594 **1925-S MS65 Full Bands PCGS.** The 1925-S (5.8 million pieces produced) is not a challenging coin to locate in most grades. This date, however, is probably the most poorly struck in the entire Mercury Dime series, and even those coins that display Full Bands definition are apt to posses indistinct peripheral detail and/or numerous die polishing lines. That said, we are pleased to be offering the present Gem. Both the peripheries and the central devices are impressive for their sharpness of strike, and the frosty textured surfaces are veiled in mottled champagne-apricot patina. Solidly graded at the MS65 Full Bands level. Population: 56 in 65 Full Bands, 20 finer (6/07). (#4953)

595 **1926 MS66 Full Bands PCGS.** Glowing luster emanates from untoned surfaces, and a powerful strike left excellent definition on the design elements. In addition to full split bands, the diagonal straps on the fasces are also bold. Both faces have been well cared for. Population: 59 in 66, 14 finer (6/07). (#4955)

Toned Superb Gem 1926 Mercury Dime, Full Bands

596 **1926 MS67 Full Bands NGC.** The '26 Philadelphia issue, with its generous mintage of over 32 million pieces, is relatively common, as one would expect. All grades through MS65 are readily available, though pieces in loftier states of preservation are more elusive. The MS67 example we offer here is exquisitely struck, resulting in the Full Bands designation. The obverse fields display crimson-orange and lime-green coloration, highlighting Mercury's portrait, which is mostly untoned. A crescent of crimson-orange and lime-green toning bathes the left reverse margin. Lustrous surfaces are lovingly preserved on each side. Census: 8 in 67 Full Bands, 0 finer (6/07). (#4955)

597 **1926-D MS64 Full Bands PCGS.** The 1926-D dimes were manufactured with much more care than the notorious 1926-D Buffalo nickels. Mottled ice-blue and lilac patina greets the viewer on the obverse, while the reverse is mostly brilliant with a tinge of smoke-gray toning. The fairly deep obverse color somewhat subdues the luster, but the central bands are fully split and rounded. (#4957)

598 **1926-D MS64 Full Bands PCGS.** Lovely pastel rose-gray toning across the centers yields to sky-blue and pale golden iridescence near the peripheries. Boldly struck with appealing luster and just a few tiny nicks on the fasces that seem to limit the grade. (#4957)

Sharp 1926-D Ten Cent, MS66 Full Bands

599 **1926-D MS66 Full Bands NGC.** David Lange (2005) writes of the 1926-D dime that: "Finding one with both full bands and a fully struck legend UNITED STATES OF AMERICA will be challenging." This Premium Gem comes very close to attaining this goal: a well executed strike transcends the Full Bands to bring strong definition to all of the design elements, with the exception of minor softness in the outer parts of the letters in AMERICA. Further enhancing this coin's eye appeal is the potent luster and well preserved, essentially untoned surfaces. Census: 7 in 66 Full Bands, 0 finer (6/07). (#4957)

600 **1927-D MS66 PCGS.** Lustrous surfaces display powder-blue and beige patination, overlaid with speckles of russet. Well struck, including partial separation in the middle bands. Well preserved throughout. Population: 10 in 66, 0 finer (6/07). (#4962)

601 **1928 MS67 NGC.** Rich crimson, cobalt-blue, and amber-gold peripheral toning is seen on each side, but is more dramatic on the obverse. Fully struck and near-pristine, with fine satin luster. This is the finest-graded example at NGC, and only a single coin equals it at PCGS, with none finer at either service (5/07). (#4966)
From The Vanek Collection.

602 **1931 MS66 Full Bands PCGS.** Glowing luster issues from light golden-tan surfaces that have benefited from an exquisite strike. In addition to the Full Bands, the diagonal ones are bold, as are all of the peripheral elements. Impeccably preserved over both sides. Population: 58 in 66 Full Bands, 10 finer (6/07). (#4983)

Gem Full Bands 1931-S Dime

603 **1931-S MS65 Full Bands PCGS.** Sharply struck with bright, sparkling surfaces that display appealing golden-yellow toning. An interesting, thin russet streak traverses the left obverse border. Impressively preserved and precisely struck. A popular Great Depression issue with a mintage of only 1.8 million pieces. Population: 50 in 65 Full Bands, 39 finer (5/07). (#4987)

Exquisite 1934-D Ten Cent, MS67 Full Bands

604 **1934-D MS67 Full Bands PCGS.** David Lange (2005), in discussing the 1934-D dime, states: "Mint State examples are not rare, but those having full bands are in the minority." This sharply struck Superb Gem displays coruscating luster exuding from untoned surfaces. A few minor ticks are within the confines of the grade designation. Population: 34 in 67 Full Bands, 0 finer (6/07). (#4991)

605 **1935-D MS66 Full Bands NGC.** This lot presents an exceptional 1935-D dime, in that all of the design features are impressively struck, including not just the full middle bands, but the peripheral elements as well. Both of these areas are typically weak (David Lange, 2005). Radiant luster issues from impeccably preserved surfaces that are visited by whispers of red, gold-brown, and light green toning, especially on the obverse. Census: 30 in 66 Full Bands, 4 finer (5/07). (#4995)

606 **1937-D MS67 Full Bands PCGS.** Fully struck and immaculately preserved, this satiny dime is decorated on the obverse by dappled maroon and cyan patina. The reverse shows antique-gold and cyan coloration. Surface marks are virtually nonexistent. (#5007)

Spectacular 1938 Dime, MS68 FB

607 **1938 MS68 Full Bands PCGS.** The 1938 dime mintage from the Philadelphia Mint (22,190,000 pieces) decreased from the extremely large coinage of the previous three years. David Lange (2005) explains this: "The recession which had set in during the latter part of 1937 slowed the nation's economy throughout 1938. This fact is reflected in lower production figures for all five denominations."
  The MS68 specimen offered here displays potent luster emanating from immaculately preserved surfaces. Hints of occasional olive-green color are visible under magnification, and all of the design elements are well impressed. In addition to the full middle bands, the diagonal ones are bold as well. Population: 5 in 68 full Bands, 0 finer (6/07). (#5011)

608 **1939-S MS66 Full Bands PCGS.** A lustrous and meticulously struck Premium Gem with nearly unabraded fields. Dashes of gold toning adorn the peripheries. The reverse is moderately prooflike. (#5021)

609 **1942/1 AU50 PCGS.** FS-101, formerly FS-010.7. Dusky rose-gold and sky-gray toning confirms the originality of this richly detailed key date dime. As always, the 1 underdigit is obvious to the unaided eye. (#5036)

610 **1942/1 AU55 Full Bands PCGS.** FS-101, formerly FS-010.7. One of the most eye-catching overdates of the 20th century, the "19412" variety has been a numismatic staple for nearly six decades. This briefly circulated example offers ample remaining luster and a touch of gold against the silver-gray of the fields. Decisively struck with full separation on the bands of the fasces. (#5037)

611 **1942/1-D VF20 ANACS.** Little of the underlying 1 is visible, but the doubled 4 is diagnostic. Light gray surfaces are quite clean for the grade. A very nice example of this popular overdate. (#5040)

PROOF MERCURY DIMES

612 **1936 PR65 PCGS.** Crisply struck with a layer of translucent, milky toning over the obverse. The fields display watery reflectivity, and contact marks or hairlines are absent. A lovely Gem from the first year of Mercury dime proof coinage. (#5071)

613 **1936 PR65 NGC.** A gleaming, brilliant representative from the first of only seven proof Mercury dime issues. This exquisitely struck, carefully preserved Gem is one of just 4,130 specimens issued. (#5071)

614 **1936 PR65 NGC.** This is a beautifully brilliant proof Mercury dime with astonishingly reflective fields that appear to be made of glass. Expertly preserved and carefully kept from harm for the past 71 years. (#5071)

Premium Gem Proof 1936 Mercury Dime

615 **1936 PR66 PCGS.** A Premium Gem proof, this splendid dime is sharply detailed with deep mirrors on both sides. The surfaces have subdued silver color with hints of pale gold toning. The Mint stopped producing proof coins in 1916, just before the start of Mercury dime coinage, thus the 1936 is the first proof in the series. *From The Vanek Collection.* (#5071)

616 **1937 PR66 PCGS.** This intricately struck and low mintage Premium Gem has light milk-gray toning with a few russet freckles on the rims and Liberty's neck. Encapsulated in an old green label holder. (#5072)

Sharp 1937 Dime, PR68

617 **1937 PR68 NGC.** David Lange (2005) writes of 1937 proof dimes that "Their survival rate in gem condition seems to be higher as a percentage of total mintage." NGC/PCGS census/population data do indeed indicate a plentiful supply of this issue through the Premium Gem level. The numbers drop off in PR67, and the lofty grade of PR68 is rare. Wisps of iridescent cobalt-blue, lavender, and olive-tan visit both sides of this exquisitely struck specimen. Impeccably preserved surfaces do not deny the grade designation. Census: 24 in 68, 0 finer (5/07). (#5072)

Brilliant 1937 Dime, PR68

618 **1937 PR68 NGC.** This PR68 specimen exhibits the typical brilliance on both the fields and motifs. David Lange (2005) notes that these proofs suffer from: " ... over polishing of the die with a resultant loss of low relief elements. This includes: " ... the bridge of Liberty's nose, the leaves of the wreath and the dangling end of the leather thong that secures the fasces." These and all other design elements are fully intact and sharp on the present example. As expected, both sides exhibit near-pristine surfaces. Census: 25 in 68, 0 finer (6/07). (#5072)

Superlative 1939 Mercury Dime, PR68

619 **1939 PR68 NGC.** At the lofty PR68 grade, this piece is tied for the finest certified by either NGC or PCGS. The surfaces are fully mirrored with a hint of iridescent blue toning on the obverse. All details are boldly defined, and the devices show a faint trace of contrast, although clearly not sufficient for a Cameo designation. Census: 52 in 68, 0 finer (6/07). (#5074)

620 **1940 PR67 PCGS.** An impeccable coin, this piece has amazing proof surfaces with reflective devices and brightly mirrored fields. Both sides are fully brilliant with white-silver color. Although not particularly rare at this grade level, PCGS has only certified 18 finer pieces (6/07). (#5075)

Enticing 1940 Dime, PR68

621 **1940 PR68 NGC.** The devices on both sides offer needle-sharp detail, and the fields gleam beneath thin champagne-gray patina. Deeper gold and ruby patina graces the upper obverse rim as well. A lovely representative of this short-lived proof series. NGC has graded just one numerically finer specimen, and PCGS acknowledges none (5/07). (#5075)

ROOSEVELT DIMES

622 **1946-D MS68 ★ Full Torch NGC.** The Full Torch designation is the Roosevelt dime equivalent to the Full Band designation in the Mercury dime series. This superlative piece is fully struck with frosty silver luster shining through pastel blue, green, gold, and lilac toning. Census: 2 in 68★, 0 finer (6/07). (#85083)

623 **1947-S Over Mintmark MS66 PCGS.** FS-501, formerly FS-013. Sans Serif S. The *Cherrypickers' Guide* considers this to be an S over D variety, and so does CONECA. Medium golden-tan and aquamarine toning enriches this lustrous and boldly struck Premium Gem. (#5087)

624 **1950-S/D MS66 PCGS.** FS-501, formerly FS-014.5. This unmarked Premium Gem has faint olive toning and minor peripheral incompleteness of strike. CONECA and the Cherrypickers Guide disagree where this variety is an S over an inverted S or an S over D. Either way, it is a dramatic variety that carries a significant premium. (#5096)

PROOF ROOSEVELT DIMES

625 **1950 to 1964 PR67 PCGS.** This lot includes all 15 different Philadelphia Mint proof Roosevelt dimes. Each piece is separately certified by PCGS as PR67 in an early second generation green label holder. The 1956, 1961, and 1962 dimes are certified as PR67 Cameo. The pieces range from brilliant to moderately toned, most are lightly toned. (Total: 15 coins) (#5225)

626 **1983 No S PR69 Deep Cameo PCGS.** Virtually pristine surfaces exhibit "white-on-black" contrast. Essentially untoned, with all of the design features well impressed. Population: 62 in 69 Deep Cameo, 0 finer (6/07). (#95265)

TWENTY CENT PIECES

627 **1875 MS62 NGC.** Autumn-brown and sea-green blend throughout this well struck and typically abraded first-year type coin. From a low mintage of 36,910 pieces. (#5296)

Choice Mint State 1875-CC Twenty Cent

628 **1875-CC MS64 NGC.** This is an important opportunity, as the 1875-CC 20-cent piece is seldom found with such a strong strike. Typically, examples have the top portion of the left facing wing entirely flat without a single feather visible. However, on this example the details are nearly complete. Both sides have subdued mint frost with subliminal champagne toning. (#5297)

629 **1875-S MS61 PCGS.** MPD-001, Breen-3875. The mintmark is repunched, and a misplaced digit lurks in the dentils beneath the 7 in the date. A lustrous cream-gray type coin with peripheral apple-green toning. Certified in a first generation holder. (#5298)

630 **1875-S MS63 PCGS.** A well struck and frosty Select example of this popular type issue, easily the most available twenty cent piece. Lightly marked overall with hints of ruby, gold, and powder-blue color over each side. *From The Vanek Collection.* (#5298)

631 **1875-S MS63 PCGS.** Apple-green and autumn-brown alternate across this satiny and carefully preserved Seated type coin. The stars near the head are soft, but the overall strike is crisp. (#5298)

Crisply Struck 1875-S Twenty Cent, MS66, FS-302

632 **1875-S MS66 PCGS.** FS-302. The mintmark is nicely repunched, and the top of an apparent 5 is present in the denticles beneath the 7 in the date. Just a hint or two of barely discernible light orange color is noted on this highly lustrous and undisturbed Premium Gem. Crisply struck, beautiful, and worthy of a high quality silver type set. Population: 57 in 66, 4 finer (6/07). (#5298)

633 **1876 MS63 PCGS.** This white twenty cent piece displays sharply struck, lightly frosted devices. A few minute handing marks in the fields define the grade. From a paltry mintage of less than 15,000 pieces. (#5299)

Important MS65 1876 Twenty Cent Piece

634 **1876 MS65 NGC.** Second year of issue and a low mintage issue with only 14,750 circulation strikes. The striking details are fully defined on each side, including the head of Liberty, the upper left ridge of the eagle's wing, and the eagle's talons. The soft, frosted mint luster has an overlay of rose-gray in the centers with sea-green around the margins. An important Gem twenty cent piece. Census: 35 in 65, 20 finer (6/07). (#5299)

PROOF TWENTY CENT PIECES

635 **1875 PR62 NGC.** The design motifs on both sides of this proof are sharply detailed. Light hairlines and other blemishes are visible in the fields, limiting the grade. The devices have some remaining luster to provide light cameo contrast, although it does not qualify for such a designation. This is the first year of issue for the denomination, with proofs continuing through 1878. (#5303)

1876 Twenty Cent Piece, PR68
One of the Finest Known in the Series

636 **1876 PR68 NGC.** The twenty cent piece, or "double disme," was a short-lived coin that was primarily produced as another outlet for Comstock silver. The 1876 was the second year of production and only two other years, 1877 and 1878, were struck in a limited production run in proof format only. As one would expect, the surfaces of this piece are nearly perfect. Both sides are brilliant. The fields show the reflectivity seen on proofs, but what is unexpected is the significant overlay of mint frost on the devices. This results in a cameo contrast that has curiously been overlooked by NGC. When searching for pedigree identifiers, the only one we could find is a tiny milling mark in the left obverse field between star 4 and Liberty's arm. Only two other pieces have been so graded by NGC and, of course, none are finer (5/07). (#5304)

Brilliant Cameo PR64 1876 Twenty Cent

637 **1876 PR64 Cameo NGC.** Although more than a million twenty cent pieces were struck in the first year of the series, 1875, mintages fell dramatically the following year. San Francisco omitted the denomination, and Philadelphia and Carson City combined reached 25,000 pieces only with the help of the 1,260 P-mint proofs. Of course, most of the CC-mint production was melted prior to its circulation. This untoned stone-gray specimen has impressive white-on-black contrast and an exacting strike. Census: 13 in 64 Cameo, 31 finer (5/07). (#85304)

Cameo Proof 1876 Twenty Cent, PR66

638 **1876 PR66 Cameo NGC.** The twenty cent piece, or double dime as it was sometimes called, was a creation of Congressmen from the silver producing states, sponsored by Senator John Percival Jones of Nevada. It proved to be unpopular due to its size and design, both nearly identical to the quarter dollar. An entirely different design might have helped, although the more recent Susan B. Anthony and Sacagawea dollar coinages show that even a different design was not sufficient to promote circulation.

An amazing proof, this Premium Gem has gorgeous gold, sea-green, and iridescent toning, with sky blue on the reverse. The devices on both sides are sharp and intricately defined. Census: 11 in 66 Cameo, 2 finer (6/07). (#85304)

Sharply Delineated 1877 Twenty Cent, PR60 Details

639 1877—Cleaned—ANACS. PR60 Details. A well executed strike translates into crisp definition on the design elements of this proof-only twenty cent piece. Essentially brilliant surfaces reveal fine hairlines, and just hints of barely discernible light gold color occur around some of the devices. A few minuscule indentations, most likely mint made, are noted in the obverse fields. (#5305)

Challenging PR64 Cameo 1877 Twenty Cent

640 1877 PR64 Cameo PCGS. This untoned proof-only near-Gem has icy devices and glittering fields. The strike is unimprovable throughout. Carefully preserved and attractive. The lowest mintage issue of this scarce proof type. A scant 350 proofs were struck. Population: 13 in 64 Cameo, 7 finer (5/07). (#85305)

Choice Cameo Proof 1878 Twenty Cent

641 1878 PR64 Cameo PCGS. Honey-gold and plum-red cling to the borders, while the fields are ivory-gray. A well struck specimen with good eye appeal. The 1878 Trade dollar was also a proof-only issue. Both types were designed by William Barber, and share the same eagle motif. A stingy 600 proofs were struck. Population: 13 in 64 Cameo, 7 finer (5/07). (#85306)

End of Session One

Senator John P. Jones
Sponsor of the legislation that authorized the twenty cent piece.

LIBERTY

1796

SESSION TWO

Live, Internet, and Mail Bid Signature Auction #442
Thursday, July 12, 2007, 6:30 PM ET, Lots 642-1805
West Palm Beach, Florida

A 15% Buyer's Premium ($9 minimum) Will Be Added To All Lots

Visit HA.com to view full-color images and bid.

EARLY QUARTERS

Sharply Detailed 1796 B-1 Quarter

642 **1796—Cleaned—ANACS. AU58 Details.** Low 6. B-1, R.5. The ANACS holder also notes that this piece has adjustment marks, and they are found across much of the reverse. Two varieties of 1796 are known, and they are easily distinguished by the position of the 6, either high and touching the drapery, or low, about centered between the bust and border. The Low 6 variety is considered R.5 today, with about 45 to 60 examples known. Earlier, Robert Hilt believed that about 25 pieces had survived, and Walter Breen presented a roster of 17 coins that grade XF or finer in his revision of the Browning reference.

This is the first year of issue for the denomination, and it is also a one year type coin. The Draped Bust obverse was the work of Robert Scot and John Smith Gardner, after designs by Gilbert Stuart. The Small Eagle reverse design was used on various denominations for a brief period of time in the 1790s, but it was quickly replaced by the Large or Heraldic Eagle design that continued through much of the first decade of the 19th century.

In addition to the adjustment marks, this piece has light hairlines and numerous tiny surface marks on both sides. The fields are satiny and reflective, almost prooflike in appearance. This example has been cleaned and now has a bright silver appearance with no toning. It is sharply struck with excellent detail on both sides. The eagle's head is flat, but it is completely outlined. The impression is well centered, with full and wide dentilation around the entire circumference on both sides, including an outer rim around parts of the border. (#5310)

Rare 1804 Quarter, AG3, B-1

643 **1804 AG3 PCGS.** B-1, R.4. Two varieties are known. The B-1 variety is confirmed by the 4 in the date farther from the bust, and the upper left star that points to almost the bottom of the L in LIBERTY. Medium gray fields highlight lighter colored motifs. The date, LIBERTY, and the left-side stars are clear. A few right-side stars and the lower reverse legends are worn nearly smooth. A rare date that is pleasing for the grade, and displaying just honest wear. (#5312)

VG8 Sharpness 1804 Quarter B-1

644 **1804—Scratched—ANACS. VG8 Details.** B-1, R.4. Breen Die State I without cracks or clashes. A few thin marks are present in the field near the profile, and the reverse border has a faint pinscratch near 5 o'clock. The pearl-gray devices contrast slightly with the dove-gray fields. (#5312)

B-1 1804 Quarter VG10 Details

645 **1804—Plugged, Tooled—ANACS. VG10 Details.** B-1, R.4. Breen Die State II with clash marks above the bosom and the right (facing) wing. Apparently a fairly large hole was present near 12 o'clock. This has been plugged, and the upper obverse is re-engraved with some skill. No attempt has been made to re-engrave the large circular plug on the lower reverse. Both sides have been whizzed, and the obverse rim has a small ding at 2:30. A rare low mintage date. (#5312)

646 **1805—Cleaned—ANACS. VG8 Details.** B-5, R.5. This very scarce variety was unknown to Browning. A minutely granular pearl-gray quarter with pleasing definition on the horizontal shield lines. The tops of UNI are slightly weak, but the remainder of the peripheral stars and letters are clear. (#5313)

647 **1805—Cleaned—ANACS. XF45 Details.** B-3, R.1. Although the surfaces have light hairlines, this piece exhibits pleasing peripheral gold and blue toning on both sides. The reverse has light die cracks through the tops of some letters, along with prominent clash marks from the drapery. (#5313)

648 **1806/5 VF25 ANACS.** B-1, R.2. Breen Die State II. The overdate variety is associated with only one reverse. This attractive example displays considerable detail despite moderate wear, and the subtly luminous surfaces exhibit rich olive and midnight-blue patina. (#5315)

649 **1806 Good 6 ANACS.** B-5, R.5. Breen Die state is between I and II with a faint crack from the left corner of the Y. Incorrectly designated by ANACS as B-7, which has a star *beneath* the beak instead of immediately left. This slate-gray example has bold definition for the Good 6 grade, since the peripheral stars and legends are distant from the rim and some shield detail is present. Generally smooth with only a couple of minor pinscratches. (#5314)

650 **1806 Fine 15 ANACS.** B-9, R.1. Breen Die State VI. The bisecting vertical obverse die crack provides easy attribution. A light charcoal-gray representative that lacks relevant marks. About half of E PLURIBUS UNUM is clear. The stars above the eagle are softly struck, as they are opposite Liberty's high relief shoulder. (#5314)

651 **1806 XF40 ANACS.** B-9, R.1. Breen Die State IV with vertical die crack through the 1 in the date. Rich lilac and ocean-blue toning embraces this suitably defined Draped Bust quarter. The right obverse has a few minor marks beneath the patina. (#5314)

652 **1806—Scratched, Cleaned—ANACS. AU50 Details.** B-3, R.1. Breen Die State III with rim die breaks above LIBE. This Draped Bust quarter has little actual wear, since luster fills the wings and borders. Overly bright, and lavishly toned sea-green, gold, and orange. The hair near Liberty's ear has two thin marks, and the portrait has additional faint abrasions. The centers are indifferently struck. (#5314)

653 **1807—Cleaned—ANACS. VF30 Details.** B-1a, R.3. This late die state has lapped dies with some weakened or missing details on both sides. The surfaces are pewter gray with faint hairlines and a few other insignificant abrasions. (#5316)

BUST QUARTERS

Impressive Choice 1818/5 B-1 Quarter

654 **1818/5 MS64 NGC.** B-1, R.2. Breen Die State V, with die crack from rim through period to the center talon of the right (facing) claw. The overdate feature is undesignated on the NGC holder. Dusky apple-green and ivory-gray compete for territory across this satiny and refreshingly mark-free near-Gem. The strike is bold save for softness on the eagle's head and opposite on the drapery clasp. (#5323)

655 **1818 Good 4 ANACS.** B-9, R.4. Breen Die State II with heavy die clash of the arrows and 25 C above Liberty's cap. The base of the date and the edges of stars 8 and 9 approach the rim, but LIBERTY is bold, and the tail feathers have partial definition. (#5322)

656 **1818—Scratched, Whizzed—ANACS. XF40 Details.** B-5, R.5. Both sides are uniformly bright and minutely granular. Several thin and relatively light pinscratches are clustered above the bust truncation. A difficult die marriage. (#5322)

657 **1818—Cleaned—ANACS. AU50 Details.** B-3, R.2. Breen Die State I with bold clashmarks near the scroll and the eagle's lower body. Misattributed by ANACS as B-2, which has perfect feet on the 1s in the date and a die crack above the cap. The slate-gray surfaces are hairlined and slightly subdued, but the stars and plumage are well defined. (#5322)

658 **1818—Cleaned—ANACS. AU50 Details.** B-5, R.5. The fields display faint vertical hairlines, but the golden-brown toning near the rims is attractive, and substantial luster remains. The usual die state with a crack through the D in UNITED and a minor die break in the denticles near the M in AMERICA. (#5322)

659 **1818 AU53 NGC.** B-8, R.3. The dove-gray fields are bounded by golden-brown luster. A richly detailed example without mentionable abrasions. A reverse die crack at 7 o'clock reaches the eagle's left (facing) leg. (#5322)

Near-Mint B-2 1819 Large 9 Quarter

660 **1819 Large 9 AU58 NGC.** B-2, R.3. Breen Die State IV with a crack between the 18 in the date. Apple-green and orange-gold toning cannot conceal the shimmering luster throughout the devices and margins. Liberty's chin and drapery display faint wear. Pleasing despite a minor mark near star 4. (#5326)

661 **1820 Large 0 XF40 ANACS.** B-2, R.2. Primarily cobalt-blue, with infrequent tan-gold patina on the devices. A glossy example with moderate wear on the cheek, cap, and curls. (#5329)

662 **1821 VF35 PCGS.** B-3, R.2. Breen Die State II. The die crack between star 12 and the portrait is heavy. Slate-gray and almond-gold with gunmetal-blue highpoints. A pleasing, problem-free example. (#5331)

663 **1821—Cleaned, Scratched—ANACS. AU55 Details.** B-4, R.3. The right obverse field is lightly hairlined, and a minor pinscratch on the left reverse field is parallel with the nearby wing. The pearl-gray surfaces are subdued. A great many collectors would overlook these deficiencies, and concentrate on the extensive mint luster and boldly detailed devices. (#5331)

View color images of virtually every lot and place bids at HA.com

Very Rare VF20 Details 1823/2 Quarter

1824/2 Quarter, VF35 B-1

665 **1824/2 VF35 NGC.** B-1, R.3. The only dies for this better date Bust quarter issue. While this is an overdate variety, this example does not clearly show the underdigit. Light golden-gray patina bathes both sides, and the design elements reveal nice detail. Scrutiny with a glass shows no significant marks or spots. (#5335)

664 **1823/2—Plugged, Graffiti—ANACS. VF20 Details.** B-1, R.6. Aside from the essentially uncollectible 1827, the 1823/2 is the unchallenged key date of the Capped Bust quarter series. The lowest arrowhead is missing its lower left corner, and the upper arrow shaft is broken. Both of these mint-made features are diagnostic for the rare 1823/2. This hairlined example is plugged and whizzed above Liberty's cap and opposite near the denomination. A light cursive L is noted on the field beneath the eagle's beak, and a pair of short vertical lines are entered near the right border of the eagle's neck. Deep ocean-blue toning embraces the borders, while the centers are light chestnut-gray. (#5334)

Mint Engraver William Kneass, 1824-1835

Patinated 1825/4/3 Quarter AU58

666 **1825/4/3 AU58 NGC.** B-3, R.3. Die State IV with minor rim die breaks near stars 4 and 5. Sea-green, plum-red, and tan toning invigorates this boldly defined near-Mint Bust half. Clusters of faint marks are noted on the obverse field, but they can only be seen with a loupe. Census: 15 in 58, 38 finer (5/07). (#5336)

667 **1831 Large Letters AU58 PCGS.** B-6, R.3. Well struck with just a touch of softness on a couple of the obverse stars. The untoned silver-gray surfaces retain considerable luster. A few wispy field marks and hairlines define the grade, in the absence of noticeable highpoint wear. This example is housed in a first-generation holder from PCGS. Population: 3 in 58, 20 finer (6/07). (#5349)

Choice Mint State 1833 B-1 Quarter

668 **1833 MS64 PCGS.** B-1, R.2. Only two die varieties are known for the 1833 quarters, and they are easily distinguished by a quick glance at the lower reverse. Browning-1 has a period following 25 C and B-2 doesn't. Both sides of this piece are characterized by considerable die rust. This Choice Mint State piece has satiny luster beneath heather and iridescent toning. The surfaces are smooth and essentially mark-free, while the devices are boldly detailed. (#5352)

669 **1834 AU50 NGC.** B-4, R.1. Breen Die State II. Luster illuminates the devices and borders of this cream-gray and aqua-blue representative. Well struck aside from the star centers, and there are no remotely mentionable marks. (#5353)

670 **1834—Cleaned—ANACS. MS60 Details.** B-1, R.1. Breen Die State IV with a die crack to the cap from 1 o'clock. Powder-blue and orange-red toning embraces this lightly cleaned and satiny Bust type coin. Well struck and attractive. (#5353)

PROOF BUST QUARTERS

Impressive Proof 1827/3 Restrike Quarter

671 **1827/3 Restrike PR66 NGC.** B-2, High R.6. Square Base 2 in 25C. Two varieties of the celebrated 1827 quarter exist, known as Original and Restrike pieces, and they are quickly distinguished by the base of the 2 in 25C, curved or curled on the Originals, and squared on the Restrikes.

The 1827 Restrike quarters are known from two distinct die states, called Period One and Period Two in the Eliasberg catalog. Perhaps these could be labeled with three different classifications like the 1804 dollars. The 1804 Original dollars are now called Class I, the unique Restrike over the Swiss thaler is called Class II, and the later 1804 Restrike dollars are called Class III. Similarly, the 1827 Original quarters could be called Class I, the Period One Restrikes could be called Class II, and the Period Two Restrikes could be called Class III. Naturally, collectors of these coins may resist such a nomenclature, as it means that three coins are required for a complete set.

Like all 1827 Restrike quarters, Class II and Class III, this piece has a die crack through the right side of U in UNITED, from the border to the ring. The Class II coins, a.k.a. the Period One Restrikes, have little die rust and are struck over Draped Bust quarters. The Eliasberg specimen, the example offered by Bowers and Merena in their 1992 Somerset sale, and possibly one other piece are members of this category. It is believed that these coins were struck in the late 1850s. In his 1992 revision of the Browning reference, Walter Breen identified 14 pieces, including four examples of this Class, and 10 examples of the Class III state.

The remaining examples including this piece, perhaps as many as a dozen specimens, along with the copper strikes, belong to Class III, the Period Two Restrikes. These pieces are immediately recognized by their heavy die rust on both sides. This piece is sharp enough in strike and quality that it also shows extremely heavy die polishing lines on both sides, obviously an attempt to minimize the appearance of the die rust. These later Restrikes were struck at an unknown date, probably many years after the early Restrikes.

This is the fifth appearance of an 1827 quarter (all Class III) in one of our auctions since 1993, and it represents the third distinct example we have handled. The surfaces are toned steel-gray with strong underlying elements of rose, blue, and sea-green. The surfaces display the characteristic raised bumps produced when rusted dies were used to produce this restrike. The strike is razor-sharp and a few tiny hairlines are visible but these are well concealed by the toning and are obviously so minor from the grade given that they pose no threat to the technical grade of the coin.

Ex: Heritage (7/1997), lot 6234. (#5374)

Proof B-7 1835 Quarter

672 **1835—Graffiti—ANACS. PR60 Details.** B-7, R.2, R.7 as a proof. The absence of a period after the denomination confirms the variety. As expected of a rare proof striking, the devices and denticles are razor-sharp. The moderately mirrored fields are lightly hairlined, small faint initials E and M bookend the portrait, and a small X is entered on the neck below the ear. Honey-gold, lilac, and blue-green toning adds to the beauty of this very rare and desirable specimen. (#5383)

SEATED QUARTERS

Important 1839 Open Claws Quarter, AU55

673 **1839 No Drapery AU55 NGC.** Breen-3936, Briggs-1A. This is the Open Claws reverse that is described as "presently very rare" by Breen in his *Complete Encyclopedia*. Larry Briggs notes that this variety is scarcer than the Closed Claws reverse. Although we do not have further data on the rarity of this variety, it is certainly an important opportunity for the specialist.

This piece is also an example of the late die state with a horizontal bisecting crack across the eagle, from the T in UNITED to the R in AMERICA. The central obverse and reverse have pale heather toning surrounded by peripheral sea-green toning. The surfaces are lightly marked as expected for the grade. (#5392)

674 **1840-O No Drapery AU55 ANACS.** Briggs 1-A. The mintmark is bold and entered left relative to the other No Drapery marriage, Briggs 2-B. The 8 in the date is lightly repunched. Autumn-brown and aqua-blue borders frame the dusky gray centers. Nicely struck and partially lustrous. (#5393)

675 **1840 MS62 NGC.** This is the first year of issue for the modified obverse design with the addition of drapery at Liberty's elbow. It is quite rare in Mint State grades, especially above MS60. This piece is sharply detailed with satiny silver luster, light peripheral gold toning, and minor surface marks consistent with the grade. Census: 3 in 62, 3 finer (6/07). (#5397)

676 **1841-O Doubled Die Obverse MS61 NGC.** FS-001. Liberty's shield is widely die doubled, as are stars 1 to 3 and 9 to 12. A satiny representative with walnut-brown and steel-gray toning. The strike is somewhat soft on the eagle's left (facing) leg and on Liberty's lower curls. Undoubtedly rare in Mint State. FS-001 NGC Census: 2 in 61, 4 finer (6/07). (#5400)

677 **1842-O Small Date—Cleaned—ANACS. Fine Details, Net VG8.** Briggs-1A, R.5, the only Small Date dies. The rare 1842-O Small Date is encountered far less often than its plentiful Large Date counterpart. The cobalt-blue and pearl-gray surfaces are faintly porous. BERT in LIBERTY is bold. The upper reverse has a small scratch. *Ex: Dr. Richard Tavernetti Collection (Heritage, 5/03), lot 6118.* (#5403)

678 **1843-O—Cleaned—ANACS. AU55 Details.** Small O. A slightly glossy New Orleans quarter with dappled honey-gold and mauve toning. Slight wear is noted on Liberty's highpoints, but considerable luster is present. (#5405)

679 **1845 MS62 NGC.** Breen-3961. Repunched 5 over Smaller 5. This piece has a die crack extending through the base of the date to the left border. Additional die cracks can be seen around much of the obverse. Most of the obverse and reverse surfaces on this satiny Mint State piece are brilliant, with traces of pale gold and lilac toning along the obverse border. (#5408)

680 **1849 MS63 NGC.** Briggs 2-A. Stars 10 to 13 show heavy recutting, and the reverse is of the "Compass Point" variety, having a circular incomplete area within the first set of vertical lines at horizontal line juncture. The 1849 is rare in Uncirculated, for which Larry Briggs (1981) assigns an R.5 rarity rating. Golden-tan patina shows blushes of lavender. Generally well struck, with nice luster and minimal marks. Census: 6 in 63, 6 finer (6/07). (#5413)

681 **1850 MS61 PCGS.** Breen-3979. Part of Extra 1 in Border. Breen describes this variety as "Extremely Rare." Although it may not be quite so rare, there is no doubt that full Mint State examples are especially important.

Slate-gray and cobalt-blue patination dominates each side. The design elements are well struck, and the somewhat muted surfaces reveal just a few minute marks. (#5415)

682 **1853 No Arrows Cleaned—ANACS. Fine 12 Details.** The 53 in the date is repunched, as always for this low mintage issue. Only 44,200 pieces were struck prior to the addition of arrows and rays to the design. Cloudy from hairlines, but smooth aside from a pair of light marks on the obverse shield. (#5421)

683 **1854-O Huge O AG3 ANACS.** The Huge O variety is unmistakable, one of the most dramatic varieties in the entire series. Walter Breen explains: "This mintmark differs from all others in the series, being both larger and grossly thicker throughout, and fairly crude in shape ... Most likely this die was received at New Orleans without mintmark, and the O added by hand." This piece is extensively worn with a few typical surface marks, but the mintmark is clear and boldly visible. (#5434)

684 **1854-O Huge O—Cleaned—ANACS. Fine 15 Details.** It may be a stretch to compare the Huge O with a Yap stone, but the thick, crude mintmark was probably entered by hand onto the working reverse die. This lightly hairlined golden-gray Arrows example has a fully legible LIBERTY. (#5434)

Gem 1855 Arrows Quarter
A Rare and Important Type Coin

685 **1855 Arrows MS65 PCGS.** It remains a numismatic mystery why newly appointed Mint Director Col. James Ross Snowden decided to continue to use arrows at both sides of the date for 1854 and 1855 quarters, but not incorporate the reverse ray design as found on quarters dated 1853. The result of his decision was a two-year type coin in the Seated quarter series of which representatives are common in circulated grades, but exceptionally challenging to locate in Gem Mint State. This piece has lovely, soft mint frost and each side shows varying degrees of golden-russet toning with a significant arc of blue at the margin. Fully struck, and free from any of the troublesome abrasions seen on lower-grade coins. Population: 4 in 65, 2 finer (6/07). (#5435)

686 **1856 MS64 PCGS.** Lustrous and satiny, with tan, gold, and orange toning near the peripheries, and untoned centers. Several faint grease streaks (as struck) extend across the lower reverse. A pair of wispy pinscratches are noted in the upper right obverse field. Encapsulated in a first-generation PCGS holder. Population: 37 in 64, 20 finer (4/07). (#5438)

687 **1857 MS64 NGC.** A delightful example of the date, with both sides displaying frosty luster and brilliant silver surfaces. It appears to be a late die state with flowlined fields, especially on the obverse. On the reverse, the lowest crossbar extends through the shield border to the left, and both lines of the first vertical stripe cross several horizontal crossbars, line 2 extending to the top of the shield. (#5442)

688 **1857-S—Scratched, Cleaned—ANACS. AU50 Details.** A minutely granular and slightly subdued slate-gray and chestnut-tan example of this early and low mintage S-mint quarter. A few faint hair-thin marks near the 18 in the date provide a minor distraction. (#5444)

689 **1858 MS64 NGC.** A strongly lustrous representative of this post-weight-adjustment issue, well-defined in the centers with a touch of weakness at the right stars. Delicate tan-gold patina graces both sides. (#5445)

Attractive 1858 Gem Quarter

690 **1858 MS65 PCGS.** Faint gold toning visits this highly lustrous and lightly abraded Gem. Sharply struck save for minor softness on the eagle's upper left shield border. Frosty motifs exhibit nice contrast with partially prooflike fields that exhibit light die polish lines. An attractive No Motto type coin that is certified in a green label holder. Population: 31 in 65, 10 finer (5/07). (#5445)

Lustrous MS66 1858 Quarter

691 **1858 MS66 PCGS.** Although the 1858 quarter is considered common in terms of extant examples in all grades, high-end pieces are irrefutably challenging to locate. The public's motivation to hoard silver coinage diminished following a reduction in the silver content of minor denominations, commencing with the issues of 1853, and coinage of this era circulated freely. The finish on this piece is uncommonly lustrous for a coin from the 1850s. Mostly brilliant, a few streaks of grease (as made) are seen on the lower obverse and there is a bit of light brown color on the reverse. Fully struck. The coin in this lot is one of only 10 certified by PCGS as Premium Gem, with none finer (6/07). (#5445)

692 **1858-S—Cleaned—ANACS. XF Details, Net VF30.** Crisply detailed, but glossy and hairlined. The reverse rim has a minor ding at 4 o'clock. Just 121,000 pieces were struck. (#5447)

693 **1859-O AU58 NGC.** Bright with some luster in the fields and we note specks of gold forming in the fields. A scarcer date so close to mint state. This is a rare date that is seldom found in higher grades. Census: 8 in 58, 12 finer (6/07). (#5449)

694 **1861-S XF40 ANACS.** Medium honey-gray toning embraces this lightly abraded rare date Seated quarter. LIBERTY is bold, and traces of luster emerge when the coin is rotated beneath a light. Only 96,000 pieces were struck, and most survivors are well circulated or impaired.
Ex: St. Louis Central States Signature (Heritage, 5/05), lot 6864. (#5455)

695 **1862-S—Cleaned—ANACS. AU50 Details.** Light tan and ivory-gray toning. A partly lustrous example with subdued fields and a few faint marks near the eagle's head. Just 67,000 pieces were struck, and only a handful of Mint State examples are known. (#5457)

Lightly Toned 1864-S Quarter, VF35

696 **1864-S VF35 ANACS.** Light golden-gray patination runs over both sides of this high-end VF S-mint quarter, and is accented with Cabot-blue. Good, uniform definition is apparent on the design features. A few minor circulation marks scattered about do not detract. This rare date, with a mintage of 20,000 pieces, is in great demand. Census: 4 in 35, 17 finer (6/07). (#5460)

697 **1866-S—Environmental Damage—ANACS. Fine 12 Details.** A primarily slate-gray example with ebony patina along the obverse border, and charcoal toning throughout most of the reverse field. LIBERTY is clear, and the few marks are relatively inconspicuous, but both sides are minutely granular. Just 28,000 pieces were struck for this first-year Motto issue. (#5469)

698 **1867-S—Corroded, Cleaned—ANACS. VF30 Details.** A hairlined representative with minor ebony verdigris along portions of the reverse border. LIBERTY is bold. A faint, thin streak crosses the upper half of the obverse shield. Just 48,000 pieces were issued. (#5471)

699 **1868-S AU50 ANACS.** This issue is usually found in low grades with extensive wear. The present AU example is an attractive coin. Both sides have excellent pearl luster with some golden-brown toning. (#5473)

700 **1870 MS62 ICG.** This piece has satiny silver luster with full mint brilliance. All of the design features on each side are boldly struck. The fields are reflective, providing light contrast. Business strikes of this date are quite rare in Mint State grades. (#5476)

Series-Key 1870-CC Quarter, VF25

701 **1870-CC VF25 PCGS.** A single set of dies were employed to produce the 1870-CC Seated quarter. The minuscule mintage of 8,340 pieces is the second lowest in the entire series behind the 1873-CC. However, the 1873-CC is considered non-collectible as most of the mintage was melted shortly after striking and today only 5 examples are known to exist. As such, the 1873-CC is unobtainable by most collectors, and by default the 1870-CC the most challenging regular issue in the Seated quarter series. Breen relates in his *Complete Encyclopedia*: "CC-mint coins 1870-73 are of great rarity in all grades, because issues were deliberately kept limited for political reasons by official policy emanating from the Philadelphia Mint - which limitation was in turn urged as reason for abolishing the Carson City branch!" For collectors today, the limited production of 1870-CC quarters presents a problem. Unfortunately, that difficulty is exacerbated by the fact that few coins of this issue were saved and all examples known today are well-circulated, save for a solitary MS64 graded by NGC, which is the Eliasberg specimen. This piece shows deep gray-olive toning over both sides with the highpoints only slightly lighter in hue. Even wear on each side, there are a few shallow field marks to the right of Liberty. Population: 4 in VF25, 22 finer (6/07). (#5477)

702 **1871 MS63 NGC.** An elusive date in all Mint State grades, and a condition rarity at this numeric level, as the population data indicates. This example is sharply struck with satiny, reflective silver luster on both sides. The outer borders exhibit a trace of pale gold toning. Census: 4 in 63, 9 finer (6/07). (#5478)

703 **1875 MS64 NGC.** Breen-4072. Type One Reverse. Described as a rare variety by Breen. A frosty and lustrous piece with pleasing pearl surfaces that are accented by pale gold toning. Excellent eye appeal is evident on this near-Gem. (#5498)

704 **1875-S MS64 PCGS.** Breen-4075. Type One Reverse. A highly lustrous and lightly toned Seated Quarter with a razor-sharp strike and impressive surfaces. The peripheries have numerous spindly die cracks, as made. Although not a low mintage issue, the 1875-S is quite scarce in XF and better grades, and decidedly rare as a near-Gem. Population: 17 in 64, 8 finer (6/07). (#5500)

705 **1875-S MS64 PCGS.** Breen-4077. Type Two Reverse. Medium S Mintmark. This is a rare variety according to Breen, and the present examples is doubly desirable for the late die state, with extremely heavy die cracks nearly encircling the reverse. A lovely near-Gem specimen, the fields are reflective, beneath splendid gold and iridescent toning. (#5500)

706 **1876 MS64 NGC.** Type Two Reverse. Well struck and carefully preserved, this near-Gem displays pleasing dove-gray toning over the centers, and lovely olive-orange peripheral patina on both sides. Spindly die cracks encircle the obverse and reverse, along the outer devices. Surface marks are minimal for the grade. (#5501)

707 **1876-CC MS63 NGC.** Breen-4091. Type Two Reverse. Large or Tall CC Mintmark. This is an impressive example with fully prooflike fields and light cameo contrast shining through gold, lilac, and blue toning. (#5502)

708 **1876-CC MS64 NGC.** Type Two Reverse. A lustrous and solidly struck piece from the legendary Carson City Mint Orange-gold and sea-green toning graces the fields and devices. Housed in a pre-hologram NGC holder. Census: 46 in 64, 26 finer (5/07). (#5502)

709 **1877 MS65 NGC.** Although a common date, Gems are elusive. This piece has full mint brilliance with intense white frost. All of the design elements on both sides are fully detailed. (#5504)

Outstanding 1877 Quarter, MS66

710 **1877 MS66 NGC.** Type Two Reverse. Production of Quarter dollars in all the mints peaked in 1876 and 1877. Almost 11 million pieces were struck in Philadelphia in 1877. This issue is also known for its exceptional luster and high quality, the combination of which makes it a perfect coin for type purposes. As expected, this piece has outstanding mint luster, distinctly frosted in nature, and colorfully toned throughout. A mixture of deep crimson and sea-green colors amply decorate each side. Just a few minor ticks are noted in the obverse field that are nearly obscured by the toning. Census: 43 in 66, 33 finer (6/07). (#5504)

Frosty Superb Gem 1877 Quarter

711 **1877 MS67 NGC.** Type Two Reverse. This is a gorgeous Superb Gem whose richly frosted surfaces are complemented with light silver-gray patina enhanced with antique-gold at the rims. Pinpoint striking definition is noted throughout, and the virtually pristine features are smooth from rim to rim. An exceptional representative of both the issue and the type. Population: 27 in 67, 6 finer (5/07). (#5504)

712 **1877-CC MS63 NGC.** Plum-red toning endows this thoroughly lustrous and precisely struck Carson City quarter. The reverse is well preserved, while the obverse field has only a few faint grazes. Encapsulated in a prior generation holder. (#5505)

713 **1877-CC MS65 PCGS.** Rich jade-green and caramel-gold embrace this lustrous Gem. Smooth except for a few small marks on the raised arm. A conditionally rare example of this popular Carson City quarter. Population: 26 in 65, 16 finer (5/07). (#5505)

714 **1877-CC MS65 NGC.** This is the normally seen variety with the mintmark tall and closely spaced. The '77-CC quarter is popular with collectors as its high mintage and relative availability keep it modestly priced. This piece is fully lustrous and sharply struck with bright silver surfaces and a faint trace of gold toning at the borders. (#5505)

715 **1877-S MS64 PCGS.** With a mintage of nearly 9 million pieces, the 1877-S is one of the most available Seated quarters in the series (Larry Briggs, 1991). Pleasing luster glows under a coat of medium intensity golden-gray patina imbued with light blue accents. Some light vertical toning streaks are noted on the obverse. Well preserved throughout. Population: 76 in 64, 35 finer (6/07). (#5506)

716 **1877-S MS64 PCGS.** A decisively struck and satiny olive-gray Seated type coin with impressively smooth surfaces. Type Two reverse, as always for the '77-S. (#5506)

717 **1877-S MS64 PCGS.** This well preserved near-Gem displays variegated pastel olive-gold toning. Meticulously struck and attractive. (#5506)

718 **1878 MS64 PCGS.** Both sides are originally toned in mottled sea-green and turquoise shades that appear chiefly near the border on the obverse. The 1878 is a scarce Seated Quarter issue despite a mintage of 2.2 million pieces, most of which were probably melted to provide silver bullion for Morgan dollar production. Population: 19 in 64, 14 finer (6/07). (#5508)

719 **1878-CC MS63 PCGS.** Partially prooflike fields set off mildly frosted, well struck motifs. Light gold centers yield to splashes of cobalt-blue and lavender at the borders. An interesting as-struck (die line?) extends from Liberty's knee to the right (left facing) arm. Population: 35 in 63, 66 finer (6/07). (#5509)

720 **1879 MS64 PCGS.** At first glance, this piece looks just like the many surviving proofs, although closer examination reveals weakness of strike and other characteristics that prevent attribution as a proof. The head and upper obverse stars are mostly flat, while the remaining parts of the obverse and all of the reverse are boldly defined. Traces of gold toning are visible over pearl luster. (#5511)

721 **1879 MS65 NGC.** The Seated Liberty has light gold color, while the reverse is fully brilliant. A boldly struck and rather prooflike Gem that has a well preserved reverse. A scarce issue, as only 13,700 pieces were struck. (#5511)

Lustrous 1888 Premium Gem Quarter

722 **1888 MS66 PCGS.** The 1888 quarter was struck to the tune of 10,000 circulation strikes. Larry Briggs (1991) writes that this issue is: "Very scarce and underrated as a date." Both sides display the typical frosty luster that characterizes these coins. A well executed strike brings out sharp detail on the design features, except for minor softness in some of the star centers, and well preserved surfaces possess a silver-gray color imbued with hints of light tan. Population: 39 in 66, 8 finer (5/07). (#5520)

723 **1890 MS64 PCGS.** Hints of gold toning are evident over the sharply detailed devices of this near-Gem. Both sides are fully brilliant with frosty silver luster. (#5523)

724 **1891 MS64 NGC.** Splashes of golden-brown, apple-green, and steel-blue envelop this unmarked and satiny near-Gem. Boldly struck aside from the uppermost stars. Lightly clashed above the date and beneath WE. (#5524)

725 **1891 MS64 NGC.** Glowing luster exudes from well preserved surfaces lightly toned in gold-tan. A well executed strike brings out excellent definition in the design elements. This is an important attribute of this near-Gem example, because this issue is usually poorly struck! (Larry Briggs, 1991). (#5524)

726 **1891 MS64 NGC.** A Choice Mint State piece, this quarter has frosty white-silver surfaces with brilliant luster and only a faint trace of toning. The final year of issue, this date is relatively common in most grades. (#5524)

727 **1891 MS65 NGC.** Nearly 4 million examples of this date were coined at the end of the series, but Gems are elusive just the same. Both sides of this frosty and lustrous piece have full brilliance. Census: 52 in 65, 35 finer (6/07). (#5524)

728 **1891-O—Cleaned—ANACS. XF Details, Net VF35.** A bold but subdued cream-gray representative with wispy marks on the lower right obverse field and near the eagle's wings. The only Motto O-mint issue. The mintage is 68,000 pieces, although the 2008 *Guide Book* incorrectly reports it as 6,800 pieces.
From The Empire State Collection (Heritage, 6/05), lot 633. (#5525)

PROOF SEATED QUARTERS

729 **1858—Artificial Toning—NCS. Proof.** The 1858 quarter proof mintage is given as 80 pieces by Larry Briggs (1991), but as 300 coins by the 2008 *Guide Book*. Cobalt-blue and lavender coloration bathes glossy surfaces of this specimen. Exquisitely struck, with no significant marks. (#5554)

730 **1864 PR63 PCGS.** This wartime Select proof displays powerful reflectivity and a hint of champagne patina at the rims. Sharply struck with scattered hairlines and a few points of contact in the fields. (#5560)

Resplendent 1867 Quarter, PR65

731 **1867 PR65 NGC.** We present in this lot a resplendent proof quarter. Iridescent cobalt-blue, lavender, and golden-brown patination bathes both obverse and reverse, and frosted motifs stand amidst reflective fields, particularly on the obverse. An impressive strike resulted in crisp definition on the design features, further enhancing the coin's superlative eye appeal. Some inoffensive handling marks on the obverse preclude an even higher grade. Census: 23 in 65, 14 finer (6/07). (#5566)

732 **1867 PR64 Cameo NGC.** Cobalt-blue, magenta, lavender, and golden-tan patination runs over both sides of this lovely near-Gem. Both sides exhibit outstanding Cameo contrast and razor-sharp devices. A few trivial handling marks define the grade. Census: 8 in 64 Cameo, 11 finer (6/07). (#85566)

733 **1874 Arrows PR61 ANACS.** Penetratingly struck and unabraded with nice cameo contrast on the reverse. Mottled mauve and brown patina affects the obverse field reflectivity. Arrows Motto quarters were struck only in 1873 and 1874, with a combined proof mintage of only 1,240 pieces. (#5575)

734 **1879 PR64 ICG.** Type Two Reverse. Sharply struck with nicely reflective fields and some pastel orange-gold toning that appears along the lower obverse and over most of the reverse. This date is a low mintage proof issue (1,100 pieces), which is made even more desirable due to the rarity of business strikes. (#5580)

735 **1879 PR64 NGC.** Type Two Reverse. Colorfully toned with deep, variegated, multicolored iridescent hues. Sharply defined throughout with good reflectivity showing under the color. (#5580)

736 **1880 PR64 PCGS.** Type Two Reverse. This near-Gem proof quarter is layered in dense coloration across both sides, with amber, purple-rose, and electric-blue shades on the obverse and deeper plum and cobalt-blue iridescence on the reverse. Well struck with a few wispy marks on the obverse that limit the grade. (#5581)

737 **1882 PR63 ANACS.** Bright surfaces reveal brushes of golden-brown toning, especially around the margins. The design features are exquisitely struck up, further adding to the coin's eye appeal. Some wispy hairlines are apparent in the fields. (#5583)

738 **1882 PR63 Cameo ANACS.** This later Seated proof quarter is flashy and deeply reflective with distinct contrast and only a trace of silver-gray patina in the obverse fields. Decisively struck with an especially pleasing cameo effect on the lightly hairlined reverse. (#85583)

Colorful Superb Gem Proof 1883 Quarter

739 **1883 PR67 NGC.** A pinpoint-sharp Superb Gem with delightful ocean-blue and apricot toning. A small mint-made strike-through on the reverse touches one of the olive leaves. Because of heavy silver dollar production, quarters were struck in only limited numbers between 1879 and 1890, except for an anomalous large mintage at San Francisco in 1888. (#5584)

740 **1884 PR63 NGC.** A dense layer of charcoal-violet and electric-blue toning lies over the surfaces of this well struck proof quarter. The devices are more lightly toned, allowing a mild cameo effect to occur on each side. Free of handling marks, the piece exhibits a few trivial hairlines on the obverse. One of just 875 proofs produced in this low mintage year for Seated quarter production.
From The Vanek Collection. (#5585)

741 **1884 PR65 NGC.** Aquamarine and plum-mauve adorn this exquisitely struck Gem. Careful examination beneath a loupe locates only minimal hairlines on the left obverse field. A mere 875 proofs were produced, along with just 8,000 business strikes. (#5585)

742 **1885 PR64 NGC.** The 1885 quarter saw a mintage of 930 proofs. Deep magenta bathes both sides of this near-Gem, and is accented with whispers of cobalt-blue and violet. A sharp strike brings up all of the design features, and close examination reveals no significant marks. (#5586)

743 **1885 PR64 PCGS.** The design elements are generally sharp, except for the top of Liberty's head and some of the obverse stars. A dense layer of charcoal-green toning covers the reverse, while the obverse shows a mixture of variegated colors. A popular, low total mintage date. (#5586)

744 **1885 PR65 Cameo NGC.** This splendid Gem exhibits brilliant silver surfaces with tending toward pale ice blue. Both sides have deeply mirrored fields to frame the lustrous silvery-white devices. Although the last two stars are a trifle flat, the remaining details on both sides are fully defined. While they are not rare in proof, the quarter dollars of the 1880s are rarities in Mint State grades, thus the proof coins are subject to extra demand. Census: 17 in 65 Cameo, 19 finer (6/07). (#85586)

745 **1886 PR63 NGC.** Ex: Richmond Collection. Hints of forest-green, tan, and ruby patina grace the margins of this attractive Select piece, one that displays subtle contrast on both sides. The strongly reflective fields display minor hairlines. (#5587)

Lovely Premium Gem Proof 1886 Quarter

746 **1886 PR66 NGC.** The fields are glassy and deeply reflective, while the frosted devices betray hints of golden color. The resultant cameo effect is noteworthy on the obverse, if subdued by milky color in the fields on the reverse. A lovely Premium Gem proof that is distraction-free. Census: 22 in 66, 17 finer (5/07).
From The Vanek Collection. (#5587)

747 **1887 PR64 NGC.** A pleasing near-Gem proof quarter that displays soft violet on the obverse, and dappled violet and cobalt-blue on the reverse. Well struck, frosted design elements appear to float amidst reflective, watery fields. Well preserved throughout. (#5588)

748 **1889 PR64 PCGS.** Rich yellow-orange and tan toning with a touch of green graces the obverse of this near-Gem, while the reverse offers attractive blue-green patina. Strongly reflective at the thinnest areas of toning. (#5590)

Flashy Cameo PR66 1889 Seated Quarter

749 **1889 PR66 Cameo PCGS.** Since the frosty devices imparted by freshly prepared proof dies diminish quickly with use, the majority of coins of a proof issue will have a non-contrasted appearance, as opposed to a cameo effect. The current coin illustrates this point well: PCGS has graded a total of 184 1889 quarters as proof, yet only 30 have earned the Cameo designation and a scant five coins have been certified as Deep Cameo (6/07). This is an exceptionally attractive coin that brilliant on each side, defect-free, and starkly contrasted. (#85590)

BARBER QUARTERS

750 **1892 MS62 NGC.** Type Two Reverse. Although this piece does not carry a lofty numerical grade, the strike and toning are finer than many Gems. Both sides are fully defined, with excellent frosty luster beneath gold, green, lilac, and iridescent toning, deeper on the reverse. (#5601)

751 **1892 MS66 PCGS.** Type One Reverse. Sea-green and cherry-red toning enriches this lustrous and splendidly preserved Premium Gem. The strike is sharp aside from the fletchings and nearby right (facing) claw. (#5601)

Outstanding 1892 Quarter, MS67

752 **1892 MS67 PCGS.** Type One Reverse. This lovely Superb Gem quarter displays fantastic luster radiating from well preserved surfaces that have a satiny finish. Whispers of cobalt-blue and lavender concentrate at the obverse borders, while the same colors run over the entire reverse, where they are joined by traces of light gold. A solid strike emboldens the design features, including the upper right corner of the shield, which is sometimes weak. A simply outstanding first-year-of-issue! Population: 19 in 67, 2 finer (6/07). (#5601)

Near-Gem RPM 1892-S Quarter

753 **1892-S MS64 PCGS.** FS-501. Type One Reverse. The mintmark is sharply repunched southeast. A satiny and well struck near-Gem with impressively clean surfaces. Casual collectors are said to set aside pieces from the first year of issue, but the 1892-S is an exception, since it is very scarce in Mint State. Population: 15 in 64, 15 finer (5/07). (#5603)

Lovely Gem 1895-O Quarter Dollar

754 **1895-O MS65 NGC.** Most examples of Barber coinage are elusive in Gem or better grades, and the same holds true for pieces from New Orleans. The categories converge on this delectable Gem, which displays lovely amethyst, plum, and orange colors over subtly lustrous surfaces. Well-defined with a single horizontal flaw of note on the cheek. Census: 10 in 65, 7 finer (5/07). (#5611)

Key Date 1901-S Quarter, Fair 2

755 **1901-S Fair 2 PCGS.** On its own, the obverse grades Good, since the date, IN GOD WE TRUST, and the obverse stars are all distinct. UNITED STATES OF is worn smooth, but AMERICA, QUARTER, and DOLLAR range from one-third to two-thirds legible. The mintmark is filled but fully outlined. The key to the Barber quarter series. (#5630)

756 **1902 MS65 NGC.** Mottled jade-green, rose, and honey shades compete for territory throughout this lustrous and exactingly struck Gem. Pristine aside from minor contact above the hair ribbon. Census: 21 in 65, 7 finer (5/07). (#5631)

757 **1904 MS65 PCGS.** Apple-green, rose-red, and olive-gold toning envelops this intricately struck Gem. Both sides are splendidly smooth. Surprisingly rare in such quality, despite a mintage of close to 9.6 million pieces. Population: 13 in 65, 8 finer (4/07). (#5637)

758 **1904-O MS64 PCGS.** Waves of olive and sea-green toning grace the lustrous surfaces, and the devices are well-defined save for softness at the upper right corner of the shield and the eagle's claw. A diagonal planchet streak traverses Liberty's cheek and ear. A pleasing example of this 20th century New Orleans issue. Population: 17 in 64, 29 finer (5/07). (#5638)

759 **1906-O MS65 PCGS.** Sharply struck with bright satin luster and untoned silver-gray surfaces. The reverse appears pristine, and the obverse has a few nearly imperceptible hairlines. Population: 33 in 65, 23 finer (6/07). (#5644)

760 **1907-S MS64 PCGS.** Hints of tan-gold color visit highly lustrous surfaces that exhibit well defined motifs. A few grade-defining marks are noted on Liberty's cheek and neck. Population: 13 in 64, 17 finer (6/07). (#5648)

Originally Toned, Lustrous MS65 1909-D Quarter

761 **1909-D MS65 PCGS.** Both sides are draped in medium gray toning that yields to flashes of attractive reddish-orange color at the borders. Very well struck save for a couple of incomplete stars on the right side of the obverse. While struck in comparatively large numbers, very few Gem or better examples survive of this fourth year Denver issue. Population: 22 in 65, 16 finer (6/07). (#5654)

Captivating 1911-S Quarter, MS66

762 **1911-S MS66 PCGS.** San Francisco delivered just under a million quarters for this later Barber issue, one that seems slightly underappreciated by generalists and specialists alike. This attractive, well-defined example has a touch of golden toning on each side, a few tiny spots of deeper color, and large expanses of silver-white. Two small reed marks on Liberty's cap are the only grade-defining flaws; what appears to be a wispy abrasion on the cheek is a strike-through, possibly of thread. Population: 28 in 66, 4 finer (5/07). (#5661)

Impressive 1911-S Quarter, MS67

763 **1911-S MS67 NGC.** Intense luster radiates from both sides of this lovely Superb Gem. A melange of pastel gold, gray, yellow, and lime-green runs over the obverse, while the reverse takes on a deeper greenish-gray hue. Sharply struck on all of the design features, with well cared for surfaces. Census: 7 in 67, 1 finer (6/07). (#5661)

Scarce 1913 Gem Quarter

764 **1913 MS65 PCGS.** David Lawrence (1994), writing about the 1913 quarter (484,000-piece mintage), says the issue is: "Very scarce because of its low mintage, but saved to some extent." The PCGS/NGC population/census data certainly indicate the scarcity of this date in the better grades of Mint State; PCGS and NGC have seen fewer than 30 examples in MS65 and finer. Sparkling luster exudes from silver surfaces that have a thin coat of light tan-gold color, and the design elements exhibit good definition, except for the usual softness in the upper right corner of the shield. A few minor luster grazes are located on the obverse. Population: 13 in 65, 6 finer (6/07). (#5664)

765 **1913-S Good 6 PCGS.** The peripheral legends and stars are all distinct from the rim, and the majority of the reverse denticles are apparent. About half of LIBERTY and E PLURIBUS UNUM are legible. A collectible cream-gray example of this low mintage key date. (#5666)

766 **1913-S Good 6 PCGS.** Delicate rose-violet patina graces the surfaces of this heavily circulated key-date quarter, one of just 40,000 examples struck for the issue. Minimally marked with the letters L and Y still visible on Liberty's headband. (#5666)

767 **1915-D MS64 PCGS.** Straw-gold and slate-gray embrace this precisely struck Choice silver type coin. Lustrous and attractively preserved. (#5671)

768 **1915-D MS66 NGC.** Ice-blue, emerald-green, russet, and a few dashes of scarlet surround the margins with lighter colored centers. Only a few minute marks are detected on the portrait. Fully struck and attractively preserved with uncommon eye appeal. Census: 10 in 66, 4 finer (5/07). (#5671)

769 **1915-S MS66 NGC.** Lustrous and brilliant with a crisp strike and clean fields. The 1915-S is the final S-mint Barber quarter, and one would expect it to be somewhat plentiful, similar to the 1916-D. But the '15-S is scarce in all Mint State grades, and decidedly rare as a Premium Gem. Census: 8 in 66, 1 finer (5/07). (#5672)

770 **1916 MS65 PCGS.** Well struck and highly lustrous, with untoned surfaces that are pristine on the reverse and only show a few trivial marks on the obverse. A fine Gem example from the final year of the Barber quarter series. Population: 38 in 65, 23 finer (4/07). (#5673)

771 **1916-D MS65 PCGS.** Lustrous surfaces display dappled olive-green, tan-gold, violet, and russet patination, along with well struck design elements. A couple of trivial handling marks do not disturb. A very pleasing D-mint specimen. (#5674)

PROOF BARBER QUARTERS

Incredible 1896 Quarter, PR68 Deep Cameo

772 **1896 PR68 Deep Cameo PCGS.** Various styles of proofs have come and gone throughout American numismatic history, and the frosted proof is no exception. Prior to the contemporary era of frosted proofs, the technique reached its zenith in the mid-1890s, a fact acknowledged by many who write about the most famous proof issue of the time, the 1895 Morgan dollar. The finest examples of other issues confirm that opinion, specimens such as the piece offered here.

The mirrors have seemingly limitless reflectivity, and the surfaces remain essentially untoned. The decisively struck devices exhibit rich frost with only a few minuscule breaks at the lower neck. As carefully preserved as one could expect for a century-old coin, this example has remarkable and enduring visual appeal. A wonderful choice for the discerning collector. Population: 2 in 68 Deep Cameo, 0 finer (4/07). (#95682)

773 **1897 PR64 PCGS.** Navy-blue and tobacco-brown endow this flashy and precisely struck Choice proof type coin. A mere 731 proofs were struck. (#5683)

774 **1898 PR65 PCGS.** Apple-green, rose-red, and gold endow this needle-sharp Gem. Even prolonged inspection fails to find any hairlines or planchet imperfections. A stingy 735 proofs were produced. (#5684)

Fantastic 1898 Quarter PR67 Ultra Cameo

775 **1898 PR67 Ultra Cameo NGC.** The 1898 quarter comes with a mintage of 735 proofs. NGC and PCGS have certified several hundred pieces, and given the Ultra Cameo label to about 65 coins. The Superb Gem Ultra Cameo presented here exhibits fantastic field-motif contrast, and sees just a hint of barely discernible color. Exquisitely struck, and near-pristine surfaces. A small lint mark is located to the right of the lips. (#95684)

Impressive 1901 Barber Quarter PR66

776 **1901 PR66 NGC.** A scant 813 pieces comprised the mintage of this Barber quarter proof issue. Sharply struck with deep antique-gold toning and well preserved surfaces that are free of troublesome hairlines or distracting contact marks. Some wispy die lines are noted on Liberty's neck. Census: 28 in 66, 37 finer (5/07). *From The Vanek Collection.* (#5687)

777 **1902 PR64 NGC.** All of the design elements are crisply defined, and the fields show substantial reflectivity. A small mark resides between QUARTER and DOLLAR on the lower reverse. Each side of the piece exhibits a pleasing layer of olive toning, mediated by accents of blue and plum color. A "lucky" issue of 777 pieces. *From The Vanek Collection.* (#5688)

778 **1903 PR64 NGC.** Well struck and untoned, with watery fields and mildly frosted devices. Neither side reveals any evidence of coin-to-coin contact or mishandling, but a few wispy hairlines are noted in the obverse fields. A mere 755 pieces were produced. *From The Vanek Collection.* (#5689)

779 **1906 PR64 PCGS.** Both sides show razor-sharp detailing on all of the design motifs, including broad square rims with fully outlined dentils. There are no troublesome hairlines or contact marks on either side. Deep purple and golden-brown peripheral toning occurs on the obverse, while the reverse displays equally deep plum, lilac, and cobalt-blue coloration. (#5692)

780 **1909 PR65 NGC.** The 1909 proof quarter comes with a mintage of 650 pieces. The Gem specimen in this lot displays splotches of cobalt-blue, golden-brown, and lavender toning, and exquisitely struck design elements. Both sides are well preserved. (#5695)

Wonderful 1912 Quarter, PR66 Cameo

781 **1912 PR66 Cameo PCGS.** Though revised Mint processes for producing proof coins reduced the number of specimens with cameo contrast, a few still left the Mint each year. This borderline black-and-white example has lovely frost on the devices and just a trace of golden color at the margins. Deeply reflective and delightful with carefully preserved surfaces. (#85698)

Starkly Contrasted Cameo 1912 Barber Quarter, PR67

782 **1912 PR67 Cameo NGC.** An exceptionally attractive proof striking of this popular, late date in the Barber quarter series. Just the slightest overlay of rose toning can be seen on the obverse, and the reverse is essentially brilliant. The cameo contrast is stark on each side with thick, frosted devices set against the illimitable depth of mirrored reflectivity in the fields. Census: 5 in 67, 2 finer (5/07). (#85698)

783 **1913 PR65 Cameo PCGS.** This faintly toned and unabraded Gem has noticeable contrast between the intricately struck devices and the mirrored fields. A mere 613 proofs were struck. Population: 2 in 65 Cameo, 6 finer (5/07). (#85699)

784 **1915 PR64 PCGS.** Fully struck devices are seen on both sides of this appealing near-Gem proof. Plum and gold toning appear in a somewhat dappled fashion, limiting the reflectivity of the fields. Only 450 pieces were struck in this final year of issue; the second-lowest proof mintage of the entire series. Population: 33 in 64, 29 finer (6/07). (#5701)

STANDING LIBERTY QUARTERS

Attractive Choice VG 1916 Quarter

785 **1916 VG10 PCGS.** Despite the lower grade of this key date quarter, most of the date not only shows, but is relatively strong, particularly in the lower and middle portions of each digit. The surfaces yield a uniform, light silver-gray color, and are remarkably clean for a coin that has seen moderate to heavy circulation. All letters of IN GOD WE TRUST show, albeit weakly. The collector seeking a 1916 example for her/his Standing Liberty quarter set cannot go wrong on this lovely specimen. (#5704)

Key Date 1916 Quarter, Fine 15 Details

786 **1916—Cleaned—ANACS. Fine 15 Details** This key date to the Standing Liberty quarter series displays semi-bright surfaces visited by whispers of crimson, light green, and yellow-gold patination, somewhat more so on the obverse. The date is clear, though the top parts of the 916 exhibit the usual softness. Under magnification, we note some fine hairlines, slightly more noticeable on the reverse. This piece will fit nicely into a mid-grade Standing Liberty quarter collection, despite the light cleaning. (#5704)

787 **1917 Type One MS65 PCGS.** This short-lived type coin has booming luster and light autumn-gold toning. Liberty's head is incompletely defined, but the strike is otherwise precise. (#5706)

788 **1917 Type One MS66 Full Head NGC.** A trace of gold toning visits the peripheries of this amazing, attentively struck piece. Both sides have frosty silver luster and pristine surfaces, save for a slight luster graze on the obverse. Only 53 finer examples have been certified by NGC (6/07) (#5707)

789 **1917 Type Two MS65 Full Head NGC.** Boldly struck with full details on Liberty's head and shield rivets. Pleasing satin luster shimmers across both sides. The creamy alabaster coloration yields to speckled russet patina near the obverse periphery. Surface blemishes are nearly nonexistent. (#5715)

MS66 Full Head Type Two 1917-S Quarter

790 **1917-S Type Two MS66 Full Head PCGS.** This lovely Premium Gem is a beautiful example of this early mintmarked issue. The strike is impressive for a Standing Liberty Quarter, irrespective of date. We call special attention to Liberty's head, the inner shield, the gown lines, and, on the reverse, the eagle's breast feathers. Scintillating mint frost overlays both sides. Only the lightest overlay of golden iridescence is noted as the surfaces rotate under the light. Encased in a green label PCGS holder. Population: 10 in 66 Full Head, 7 finer (5/07). (#5719)

791 **1918-S MS64 PCGS.** Orange-gold, powder-blue, and lime enrich this lustrous and unmarked near-Gem. The top of the head is slightly soft, but the strike is decent for this early branch mint issue. The dies are clashed near Liberty's legs and opposite on AMERICA. (#5724)

792 **1918-S MS66 NGC.** A remarkably unabraded branch mint quarter with vivacious luster and infrequent glimpses of apricot toning. The date is well struck, while the head and waist are typically defined. (#5724)

793 **1918-S MS63 Full Head NGC.** A charming Select branch mint quarter from the early years of the Standing Liberty type. Lustrous and lightly toned with a bold date and a few weak shield rivets near the waist. (#5725)

Scarce 1918/7-S Standing Liberty Quarter VF30

794 **1918/7-S VF30 PCGS.** A pleasingly natural appearance greets the viewer of this piece. Both sides exhibit smooth surfaces with few blemishes and attractive dove-gray coloration. A few pinscratches are noted in the reverse fields. According to J.H. Cline, this variety was discovered in 1937, but did not appear in the Standard Catalog of coins until 1942. (#5726)

795 **1920 MS66 NGC.** A stone-white and highly lustrous Premium Gem with an immaculate obverse and a clean reverse. The centers are well struck, while the borders are occasionally slightly soft. (#5734)

796 **1921 MS66 PCGS.** A gleaming and carefully preserved example of this mid-date Type Two issue, well-defined overall with distinct rivets. Delicate golden patina graces the fields, while the remainder is silver-gray. Population: 14 in 66, 0 finer (4/07). (#5740)

Marvelous 1921 Gem Full Head Quarter

797 **1921 MS65 Full Head PCGS.** Nearly 2 million pieces were struck of this tough-date quarter. J.H. Cline (2007) speculates that: "There seem to be two types for this date and mintmark. Type I: struck before die modification. Most of these are weak overall. Type II: Outstanding. Full, sharp heads with sharp full lines in the shield. These coins are deeply struck ... . They nearly always have sharp lines in the gown, olive branch leaves, and berries with sharp shield lines, both vertical and horizontal." This Full Head Gem example is Type Two, displaying as it does excellent design delineation. Potent luster embraces both sides, and well preserved surfaces reveal traces of light tan-gold color. A simply marvelous Standing Liberty quarter. Population: 43 in 65 full Head, 19 finer (5/07). (#5741)

Elusive MS66 Full Head 1923 Standing Liberty

798 **1923 MS66 Full Head PCGS.** The 1923 is readily obtained if strike is unimportant, but those who wish Full Head pieces will find the issue surprisingly elusive. The present lustrous Premium Gem features caramel-gold and ivory toning. The obverse has minor incompleteness near 12 o'clock, but the strike is generally sharp. (#5743)

799 **1923-S VF30 ANACS.** Both sides of this moderately circulated piece have light pewter color with traces of champagne toning and splashes of deeper gold. (#5744)

800 **1923-S—Corroded—ANACS. AU53 Details.** The obverse is problem-free aside from an inconspicuous pinscratch on the shield. The reverse is granular from environmental exposure. A well detailed example of this little-saved low mintage issue. (#5744)

Key-Date 1923-S Quarter, MS64 Full Head

801 **1923-S MS64 Full Head NGC.** The 1923-S is an important key date in the Standing Liberty quarter series. MS65 Full Head examples are scarce (J.H. Cline, 2007), and even near-Gem Full Heads, such as the piece in the current lot, are tough to locate. Whispers of copper-gold color are scattered about, concentrating at the borders, and dazzling luster exudes from both sides. An attentive strike transcends Liberty's Full Head to brings out sharp definition in the other design elements, including the chain mail, the inner shield, and all but two of the rivets. Close scrutiny reveals no significant marks. (#5745)

802 **1926 MS64 Full Head PCGS.** A solidly struck representative from the first year of issue with the date in a protected exergue. Delicate peach and gold patina graces the obverse, while the reverse displays lighter champagne color. (#5755)

Adorable Superb Gem 1927 Quarter

803 **1927 MS67 NGC.** Pastel ice-blue and honey-gold tints enrich this lustrous and unabraded Superb Gem. Liberty's cheek is incomplete, but the strike is sharp on the date and the eagle's breast. A nearly imperceptible fingerprint is noted at 9 o'clock on the reverse. Census: 2 in 67, 0 finer (6/07). (#5760)

Charming MS66 Full Head 1927-D Quarter

804 **1927-D MS66 Full Head PCGS.** Only 976,000 pieces were produced of the 1927-D, and full head examples are very scarce, regardless of grade. Premium Gems with complete head definition are decidedly rare. The surfaces on this piece display soft, frosted mint luster and there is just a bit of golden iridescence on each side. The obverse is particularly well preserved. Population: 13 in 66, 0 finer (5/07). (#5763)

Attractive MS67 Full Head 1928 Quarter

805 **1928 MS67 Full Head NGC.** Faint streaks of honey color overlay the pastel rose and sky-blue surfaces of this highly lustrous Superb Gem. The strike is precise aside from the usual pair of shield rivets near the waist. A splendidly preserved representative of this conditionally elusive issue. Population: 5 in 67, 2 finer (3/04). (#5767)

806 **1929-S MS67 NGC.** Standing Liberty quarter specialist J.H. Cline (2007) writes that: "The 1929-S, as most S mints, were average or poor strikes. Full Heads are an exception and certainly not the rule." The Superb Gem in this lot is somewhat better struck than most. Liberty's chain mail and the inner shield are relatively sharp, and the head displays good (though not full) detail. Two or three of the lower rivets are weak. Dapples of reddish-tan visit highly lustrous surfaces that are devoid of mentionable marks. Census: 22 in 67, 0 finer (5/07). (#5776)

Incredible 1929-S Quarter, MS67 Full Head

807 **1929-S MS67 Full Head PCGS.** A gorgeous piece, frosty with a small patch of striking brilliance to the left of OF on the reverse. Essentially untoned with powerful detail overall and only two weak rivets on the shield, features that appear soft on even the sharpest examples. Carefully preserved with remarkable eye appeal.

Noted Standing Liberty quarter specialist Jay Cline points out that San Francisco issues for the series have, on average, worse strikes than their Philadelphia counterparts. In his fourth edition of *Standing Liberty Quarters* (2007), he estimates that approximately 5% of 1929-S pieces come with enough detail for a Full Head, and between the grade distribution and strike, a boldly impressed Full Head Superb Gem such as the present coin is a rare bird, which the PCGS *Population Report* corroborates. Population: 8 in 67 Full Head, 0 finer (5/07). (#5777)

808 **1930 MS66 PCGS.** An outstanding Standing Liberty quarter and very close to Full Head status. Thus, this piece would make an excellent type coin representative for the savvy collector who wants quality at a reasonable price. The surfaces are bright and exhibit the intense mint frost that is commonly seen on Standing quarters. A lovely coin. (#5778)

809 **1930 MS66 Full Head PCGS.** This is a splendid example of the final-year issue, with crisply defined motifs and lustrous, untoned, silver-white surfaces. A couple of tiny nicks are detected on each side, but only with the aid of a magnifier. (#5779)

810 **1930-S MS66 NGC.** Deep fire-red, apple-green, and plum-mauve patina embraces this lustrous and well preserved Premium Gem. An original prize for the connoisseur of colorfully toned coinage. Housed in an early, pre-hologram NGC holder. (#5780)

WASHINGTON QUARTERS

811 **1932-D MS62 PCGS.** Orange and dove-gray compete for territory across the obverse, while the reverse has lighter cream and straw-gold shadings. This well struck and satiny key date quarter is clean for the grade despite a minor reed mark above the cheekbone. A great example of this first-year key. (#5791)

Key-Date 1932-D Quarter, MS63

812 **1932-D MS63 PCGS.** The mintage figure for the 1932-D quarter is 436,800 pieces, higher than that of the 1932-S (408,000 coins). This disparity notwithstanding, David Bowers writes in his *Guidebook of Washington and State Quarters* that: " ... in grades of MS63 or better the 1932-D is at least 5 to 10 times rarer than the 1932-S." Light champagne color adheres to the lustrous surfaces of this Select '32-D specimen, and the design elements are well impressed. A few trivial marks define the grade. (#5791)

Pleasing Key-Date 1932-D Near-Gem Quarter

813 **1932-D MS64 PCGS.** David Bowers (2006) notes: "When the 1932-D was minted and distributed, no effort was made to handle the coins gently. As a result, most pieces saved in Mint State in 1932 and surviving to the present day are apt to be in MS60 to MS62 grades." We present in this lot a rather pleasing MS64 specimen that reveals just a few minor grade-defining marks on each side. Speckles of russet make occasional visits to highly lustrous surfaces, and a relatively sharp strike brings out good design definition. This key-date example will make a splendid addition to a high-grade Washington quarter set. (#5791)

Toned MS65 1932-D Quarter
The Key to the Washington Quarter Series

814 **1932-D MS65 PCGS.** Original silver-gray surfaces intermingle with blushes of golden-brown and apple-green toning. Satin luster is unbroken throughout both sides, and contact is minimal; a small mark on the upper left area of the eagle's breast is mentioned solely for pedigree purposes. The strike is bold, not only on the highpoints of the devices, but also across the legends near the rim. In short, this is a remarkable example of this coveted first-year issue, the unchallenged key to the series in Gem condition. Since NGC and PCGS combined have certified only one piece finer, the present coin represents the finest realistically obtainable quality, and would provide the cornerstone of a standout collection of the series. Population: 63 in 65, 1 finer (6/07). (#5791)

815 **1932-S MS63 NGC.** Straw-gold and steel-blue toning confirms the originality of this pleasing piece. The 1932-S is one of the two key dates to the series, and lustrous examples are under strong demand from set collectors. Certified in a prior generation holder. (#5792)

816 **1932-S MS63 NGC.** This key date quarter possesses booming luster and blushes of light gold toning. The strike is precise, and the few marks present are surprisingly minor. At the time of issue, many believed the Washington quarter was a one-year circulating commemorative. (#5792)

817 **1932-S MS63 PCGS.** Ice-blue and apricot toning endows this lustrous and precisely struck key date quarter. The left obverse has a few wispy grazes, but the eye appeal is impressive for the third party grade. Encapsulated in a green label holder. (#5792)

818 **1932-S MS64 PCGS.** Well struck with intense luster and light russet and lemon-gold toning on the upper and right portions of the obverse. A couple of superficial luster grazes are observed, also on the obverse. A solid near-Gem example of this important key date. (#5792)

819 **1932-S MS64 PCGS.** Freckles of tan patina grace the gunmetal-gray surfaces of this key-date piece, which has subtle, slightly satiny luster and pleasing detail. Along with its D-mint counterpart, the 1932-S ranks among the most valuable Washington quarters. (#5792)

820 **1932-S MS64 PCGS.** This key branch-mint piece has pleasing detail and areas of rose and orange-tan toning at the periphery. Choice and satiny with generous visual appeal for this first-year issue. (#5792)

821 **1932-S MS64 PCGS.** An impressive Choice Mint State piece, this '32-S quarter has frosty silver luster and sharp design motifs. Both sides are awash with pale lilac-gold toning. (#5792)

822 **1934-D Medium Motto MS66 PCGS.** The obverse is pearl-gray with dashes of russet. Rich lemon-gold patina graces the reverse. Lustrous, exactingly struck, and well preserved. (#5796)

823 **1934-D Medium Motto MS66 PCGS.** Charcoal and hazy tan-golden colors frame the steel-gray obverse portrait, while the reverse features a more even steel-silver appearance. The obverse is undisturbed, and only a wispy mark on the eagle's right (facing) leg denies a finer grade. Early Denver Mint issues of this popular series are invariably scarce and under collector demand in lofty Mint State grades. Population: 72 in 66, 3 finer (5/07). (#5796)

824 **1935-D MS66 PCGS.** Pearl-gray and honey-gold ensure the originality of this lustrous and generally smooth branch mint quarter. The devices are well struck, although the final letters in AMERICA are incompletely brought up. (#5798)

825 **1935-D MS66 PCGS.** Whispers of attractive olive-green toning exhibit gold-orange and crimson accents, and rest over brightly lustrous surfaces. The design elements are well brought up. Great overall eye appeal is typical for the issue. PCGS has only certified 12 finer examples (6/07). (#5798)

826 **1935-S MS67 NGC.** A well struck and satiny Superb Gem representative of this early S-mint Washington quarter. Gold-tinged overall with zones of haze evident in the fields on each side. NGC has graded no numerically finer pieces (5/07). (#5799)

827 **1936-D MS63 PCGS.** Sharply struck and satiny with infrequent hints of rose and gold patina. The 1936-D is a conditional rarity, much scarcer in Mint State than the lower mintage 1936-S. (#5801)

Lustrous 1936-S Superb Gem Quarter

828 **1936-S MS67 PCGS.** The 1936-S is tough in the lofty grade of MS67, as the population data below indicate. A medley of forest-green, lavender, orange, and yellow-gold toning covers most of the obverse, and delicately clings to the reverse margins. Both sides are awash in potent luster, and the design elements are well struck throughout. There are no mentionable marks to report. Population: 20 in 67, 0 finer (6/07). (#5802)

829 **1943-S Doubled Die Obverse MS64 PCGS.** FS-101. Strongly lustrous and Choice with pleasing detail overall, though the strongly doubled date is slightly soft. Essentially untoned aside from a streak of steel-gray color at Washington's hair. Listed on page 169 of the 2008 Guide Book. Population: 45 in 64, 19 finer (4/07). (#5823)

830 **1944 MS67 PCGS.** The 1944 quarter is an important condition rarity in Superb Gem, with no examples certified in any higher grades by PCGS. This piece has satiny silver luster with traces of peripheral toning. Population: 52 in 67, 0 finer (6/07). (#5824)

831 **1944-S MS67 PCGS.** Knob S mintmark. Potent luster and faint olive color are hallmarks of this beautifully preserved Superb Gem. The major devices are well struck, while the borders show moderate incompleteness. Population: 56 in 67, 2 finer (5/07).
Ex: Jack Canniff Collection (Heritage, 6/04), lot 8324, which realized $720. (#5826)

Gem 1950-S/D Quarter, FS-601

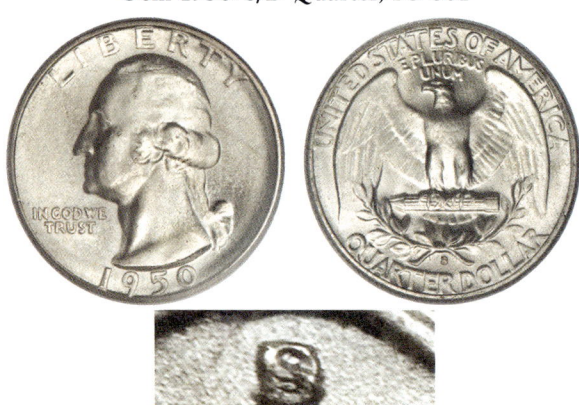

832 **1950-S/D MS65 PCGS.** FS-601, formerly FS-022. Well struck with substantial mint frost on both sides and a rich, lustrous sheen. The overmintmark feature is obvious under low magnification, and the smooth surfaces reveal just a few tiny marks. Population: 45 in 65, 35 finer (6/07). (#5845)

833 **1964-D MS67 PCGS.** The 1964-D quarter is readily obtainable in Mint State grades, though MS67 and finer coins are elusive, as the PCGS population data below indicate. Impeccably preserved surfaces of this Superb Gem are essentially untoned and radiantly lustrous. A sharp strike results in strong definition on the design features. Population: 28 in 67, 0 finer (4/07). (#5877)

834 **1964-D MS67 NGC.** The final year for regular-issue silver Washington quarters. This example is boldly struck with vibrant luster and crescents of rich, variegated coloration on both sides. Census: 55 in 67, 0 finer (6/07). (#5877)

PROOF WASHINGTON QUARTERS

835 **1936 PR63 PCGS.** This intricately struck Select specimen offers traces of ice-blue and apricot toning. Careful examination beneath a loupe and a strong light reveals nearly imperceptible obverse hairline patches near 2 and 9 o'clock. Certified in a first generation holder. (#5975)

836 **1936 PR64 NGC.** Fully struck with glassy fields and mere traces of mottled patina near the borders. Proof coinage was resumed in 1936 after a twenty-year respite.
From The Vanek Collection. (#5975)

Brilliant 1937 Quarter, PR67

837 **1937 PR67 PCGS.** In his *Guide Book of Washington and State Quarters*, David Bowers writes of the 1937 that: "Proofs of this year are the second scarcest date from 1936 to the present." This sharply struck specimen displays brilliant, well preserved surfaces. Some light die polish lines show up under magnification. Population: 79 in 67, 2 finer (4/07). (#5976)

838 **1941 PR68 NGC.** Powerful detail and a chromelike gleam beneath hazy patina enhance the eye appeal of this carefully preserved specimen, a delightful representative from this early proof Washington quarter issue. Gold-gray patina covers the centers, while the peripheries have deep amber and magenta toning. Census: 24 in 68, 0 finer (5/07). (#5980)

839 **1941 PR68 NGC.** An immaculate proof Washington quarter. Very few have been so graded by either of the major services. Don't expect contrast, but the fields and devices will definitely dazzle the viewer of this impressive coin. Brilliant. Census: 27 in 68, 0 finer (6/07). (#5980)

840 **1942 PR67 NGC.** The untoned centers of this marvelous Superb Gem quarter are surrounded by attractive bands of peripheral toning, in shades of maroon, gold, and green. Well struck and carefully preserved, save for a single handling mark near the top of Washington's head below E in LIBERTY. (#5981)

STATEHOOD QUARTERS

841 **2004-D Wisconsin Extra Leaf Low MS67 NGC.** FS-2004D-5902. Fully struck and highly lustrous, with a few wispy planchet flaws and bright, untoned surfaces. Soon after the release of the Wisconsin Statehood quarters, examples of this variety were discovered in Arizona and Texas, along with examples of the similar High Leaf variety. Both varieties are destined to become key dates in the immensely popular Statehood quarter series. (#814033)

842 **2004-D Wisconsin Quarter Three-Coin Set MS65 NGC.** The set includes: 2004-D Wisconsin MS65 NGC, 2004-D Wisconsin Extra Leaf High MS65 NGC, and a 2004-D Wisconsin Extra Leaf Low MS65 NGC. Each piece is essentially untoned with a pleasing appearance. An interesting three-coin set that allows for side-by-side comparison of the two enigmatic varieties with a typical example. Housed in a three-coin large-format NGC holder. (#914033)

843 **2004-D Wisconsin Quarter Three-Coin Set MS65 NGC.** The set includes: 2004-D Wisconsin MS65 NGC, 2004-D Wisconsin Extra Leaf High MS65 NGC, and a 2004-D Wisconsin Extra Leaf Low MS65 NGC. Each coin is a strongly lustrous and brilliant Gem. An interesting three-coin set, housed in a single NGC holder, that contains both of the popular and controversial varieties that appeared on Washington quarters. (#914033)

844 **2004-D Wisconsin Quarter Three-Coin Set MS65 NGC.** The set includes: 2004-D Wisconsin MS65 NGC, 2004-D Wisconsin Extra Leaf High MS65 NGC, and a 2004-D Wisconsin Extra Leaf Low MS65 NGC. Each piece has bold definition and powerful luster with little patina and few marks. An illustrative grouping that is housed in a custom NGC holder. (#914033)

845 **2004-D Wisconsin Extra Leaf High MS67 NGC.** FS-2004D-5901. Crisply struck with coruscant luster and brilliant surfaces that show just a few scattered "chatter" marks, which fail to limit the assigned grade. Certain to become a key date in the Statehood quarter series, along with the Low Leaf variety from the same issue. (#914033)

846 **2004-D Wisconsin Extra Leaf High MS67 NGC.** FS-2004D-5901. Fully struck and untoned, with intense luster and a few small surface blemishes. This type created a sensation when the Wisconsin Statehood quarters were released, and this error was quickly identified by sharp-eyed numismatists, along with a similar Low Leaf variety. (#914033)

EARLY HALF DOLLARS

847 **1795 2 Leaves—Reverse Re-engraved—ANACS. Fine 12 Details.** O-102, R.5. Thorough evaluation finally locates a series of faint lines on the eagle's wings, but this ivory-gray and russet example is otherwise surprisingly unabraded. The reverse has minor verdigris and translucent debris. (#6052)

848 **1795 2 Leaves Fine 12 PCGS.** O-107a, R.5. The reverse is bisected by a bold crack between 2:30 and 8:30. The obverse has a cherry-red, gold, and sky-blue margin and a lilac-gray portrait. Powder-blue, lavender, and lemon shades embrace the reverse. A few faint hairlines, but surprisingly unabraded overall. (#6052)

849 **1795 3 Leaves VG10 NGC.** O-111, High R.4. A popular Overton variety for two different reasons: the date is widely repunched south, and the reverse has three leaves beneath each wing. As usual, a prominent die break crosses the left (facing) wing and affects the STA in STATES. Dusky steel-gray toning drapes this nicely detailed and unblemished collector coin. (#6053)

1801 Half Dollar, XF40, O-101

850 **1801 XF40 ICG.** O-101, R.3. One of just two die varieties for the year, from a paltry mintage of 30,289 pieces. This variety shows a number of small to large die lumps on the reverse, especially between ER of AMERICA, at the left base of N in AMERICA, and at the arrow points. Splashes of light golden-tan patination are accented by whispers of sky-blue at the borders. Generally well defined, though parts of the shield are soft. The surfaces are quite clean for a circulated coin. (#6064)

851 **1802 Fine 15 PCGS.** O-101, R.3. A golden-gray piece with pleasing definition on Liberty's curls. About half of E PLURIBUS UNUM is present. The obverse has horizontal hairlines, and a thin mark is noted beneath the chin. (#6065)

Scarce and Popular 1802 Half Dollar, XF45
A Single-Die Year

852 **1802 XF45 ICG.** O-101, R.3. The entire mintage of 29,890 pieces struck for the year was completed with only on pair of dies. The reverse die was also previously used for the single-die 1801 issue. Seldom seen in mint condition, according to the Overton reference, and in fact, the vast majority of known examples are VF or less. This piece has light gray patina and noticeably traces of mint luster are seen around the devices on each side. Well struck, there are a few minor marks present but none that warrant individual mention. (#6065)

853 **1805 VF35 PCGS.** O-111, R.2. Medium gold and lilac toning embraces this slightly glossy Choice VF Bust half. Luster shimmers from the recesses of Liberty's hair and the eagle's shield. (#6069)

854 **1806 Knobbed 6, Small Stars VF30 NGC.** O-107, High R.4. This pearl-gray Draped Bust half is richly detailed for the VF30 level. E PLURIBUS UNUM is bold, and Liberty's tresses behind the ear and above the shoulder are impressively defined. Each side has a few tiny rim nicks, most noticeable on the reverse near 6 o'clock. (#6075)

855 **1807 Draped Bust VF20 PCGS.** O-105, R.1. A die lump between the final S of STATES and O of OF on the upper reverse is indicative of this final-year Draped Bust Overton variety. A pleasantly smooth pearl-gray piece that has hints of charcoal toning in protected areas. Certified in a first generation holder. (#6079)

856 **1807 Draped Bust XF45 PCGS.** O-105, R.1. Apple-green, rose-red, and gold toning dominates this partially lustrous final-year Draped Bust half. Struck from clashed and cracked dies, but not yet the scarce O-105a, which has a descending crack through STAT. (#6079)

857 **1807 Draped Bust XF45 PCGS.** O-105, R.1. Copious luster connects the obverse stars and fills the words in the reverse legends. Light honey-gold toning visits the obverse margin. The devices are typically struck, but the presence of luster within the wingtips and peripheral curls confirms the grade. (#6079)

BUST HALF DOLLARS

Choice AU 1807 50 Over 20 Capped Bust Half, O-112

858 **1807 Large Stars, 50 Over 20 AU55 NGC.** O-112, R.1. This is the popular variety with portions of a 2 visible beneath the 5 in the denomination. Apparently a mint worker thought he was working on a quarter before realizing the error. Deep gray toning fades to charcoal near the peripheries of the obverse, while the reverse displays multicolored hues over medium ivory-silver toning. (#6086)

Eye Appealing 1807 Fifty Cent
Large Stars, 50 Over 20
AU55, O-112

859 **1807 Large Stars, 50 Over 20 AU55 PCGS.** O-112, R.1. The 5 in the denomination is punched over a 2, with the curve of the 2 showing clearly to the upper left of the 5. O-112 has both serifs at the base of the 1 in the date. This is a lovely Choice AU specimen that displays ample luster in the recessed areas, and whose light gray surfaces are accented in cobalt-blue, lavender, and golden-brown around the borders. Excellent design detail adds to the coin's overall eye appeal, as does the fact that the surfaces are quite clean. A solitary mark between star 2 and the chin might serve as a pedigree marker. Housed in a green-label holder. Population: 26 in 55, 38 finer (6/07). (#6086)

AU 1807 Capped Bust Half, O-114

860 **1807 Capped Bust, Large Stars AU50 PCGS.** O-114, R.3. Die lumps beneath the downstroke of the 7 in the date confirm the variety. Incorrectly designated by PCGS as the Small Stars variety, which is O-113. The stars are well struck, while the RIB in PLURIBUS and the 50 in the denomination are softly brought up. Lustrous for the grade, although a thin vertical mark is noted near the profile, and a cluster of inconspicuous marks is present on the field beneath the cap. Struck from clashed dies. (#6088)

861 **1809 III Edge AU58 PCGS.** O-103, R.1. A satiny khaki-gold and pearl-gray near-Mint example with impressively smooth surfaces. Well struck on the stars and legends, while the eagle's head is a bit soft. Encapsulated in a green label holder. (#6094)

862 **1810 AU58 PCGS.** O-103, R.2. Deep gunmetal-gray and golden-brown toning envelops this satiny and well struck near-Mint Bust half. Pleasant smooth and boldly struck. Certified in an old green label holder. (#6095)

863 **1811 Small 8 AU58 NGC.** O-111, R.1. Dappled golden-brown and dove-gray embrace this satiny Borderline Uncirculated example. Original and lightly abraded with imposing eye appeal. (#6097)

864 **1811/10 AU50 NGC.** O-101, R.1. Ocean-blue and olive toning invigorates the borders. The fields and devices are golden-gray. The reverse rim is nicked at 10:30, but there are no other remotely relevant marks, and the portrait shows only moderate wear. (#6099)

865 **1812 AU58 PCGS.** O-105a, R.2. Gunmetal-blue and apricot shadings endow this smooth and satiny near-Mint Bust half. A worthy candidate for the date collector. Struck from multiply clashed dies. (#6100)

866 **1813 Over UNI AU50 NGC.** O-101, R.2. Autumn-gold and ice-blue peripheral toning frames the stone-white centers. Substantial luster bathes design recesses. A faint V-shaped mark is noted on the cheek. A popular *Guide Book* engraving blunder. Census: 4 in 50, 29 finer (5/07). (#6104)

867 **1814 AU58 NGC.** O-107, R.2. Multiple layers of clash marks provide for ready attribution. This lustrous Bust half has light to medium tan patina. An absence of identifying marks ensures the eye appeal. (#6105)

868 **1814 AU58 PCGS.** O-109, R.2. A well struck piece with comprehensive luster and only a hint of wear on the curl above the ear. Unabraded, although minor russet verdigris is present near Liberty's eye. Struck from heavily clashed dies. Certified in a first generation holder. (#6105)

Overton-109 1814 Half MS62

869 **1814 MS62 PCGS.** O-109, R.2. Walnut-brown and gunmetal-gray alternate across this lustrous example. The toning deepens slightly across the reverse border. Surprisingly smooth aside from a tick on the cheekbone. The reverse is well preserved. Struck from strongly clashed dies, and housed in a first generation holder. (#6105)

870 **1818/7 Large 8 AU53 NGC.** O-101, R.1. Intermingled blue, lilac, and gold toning. A decent strike that shows boldness in most areas except along the upper borders of the eagle's wings. Both surfaces display complete milling. The variety is one of the most distinctive of the year. In addition to the overdate feature, a gap in the dentils beneath the C in the denomination, makes the reverse easy to identify.
Ex: Jules Reiver Collection (Heritage, 1/06), lot 22762, which realized $747.50. (#6115)

871 **1821 AU55 NGC.** O-106, R.1. Dove-gray, lime, and almond-gold shades are illuminated by the partial cartwheel luster. Generally smooth, although minor marks are present on the chin and on the field above the eagle's neck. In an older generation holder. (#6128)

872 **1821 AU55 NGC.** O-103, R.2. Ocean-blue, sun-gold, and peach toning enlivens this partly lustrous and problem-free Choice AU 1821 half. Crisply struck, attractive, and housed in a prior generation holder. (#6128)

873 **1821 AU58 NGC.** O-105a, R.1. Dramatically toned gold, aquamarine, velvet-blue, and plum-red. A thin horizontal mark near star 2 is well concealed. Slight wear on the cap, drapery, and hair decides the grade. (#6128)

874 **1822 MS62 NGC.** O-104, R.3. Russet-brown, sea-green, and rose toning consumes the obverse and encompasses the reverse border. A few small ticks on Liberty's neck, but generally unabraded for the grade. Certified in an older generation holder. (#6129)

875 **1823—Scratched—ANACS. AU58 Details.** O-110, R.2. This Overton marriage evolves into the O-110a "Ugly 3," but the present piece has a perfect 3, and is instead identified by a die lump near the upper left border of vertical stripe 2. A dull pinscratch is located beneath each scroll end, but there is ample tawny-gold luster and the strike is consistent. (#6131)

876 **1824/1 AU50 NGC.** O-101a, R.2. Powder-blue and golden-brown bands endow the margins of this unmarked and slightly subdued overdate Bust half. Certified in an older generation holder. (#6139)

877 **1824 AU58 PCGS.** O-108, R.2. Rich cream-gray and cobalt-blue alternate across this satiny and unmarked representative. The RI in PLURIBUS is softly brought up, but the overall strike is good. (#6137)

878 **1827/6 AU58 NGC.** O-102, R.1. There are 49 known die marriages for the 1827, but the obvious curve of the underdigit 6 reduces the possibilities to just three varieties. The small break after the final A in AMERICA isolates O-102. This well struck example has smooth fields and rich olive-brown toning. Inconsequential contact is limited to the shield and cheek. (#6147)

879 **1827 Square Base 2 AU55 PCGS.** O-113a, R.4. 1827 was a productive year for Overton marriages, but O-113a is readily identified by the curved die crack from 6 o'clock to Liberty's cap. Lustrous for the grade with unblemished surfaces and occasional peripheral russet, plum, and navy-blue patina. The right-side stars are soft. Encapsulated in an old green label holder. (#6144)

880 **1827 Square Base 2 MS62 NGC.** O-135, R.3. The variety is attributed by the A in STATES being slightly higher at the base than the first T, but well below the second T. Lustrous surfaces are untoned and exhibit sharply struck design features. A handful of small contact marks are noted on the obverse. (#6144)

881 **1828 Curl Base 2, No Knob MS61 ANACS.** O-101, R.1. A small tine protrudes from the left side of Liberty's drapery, and on the reverse, the upper region of the F in OF is filled. This well struck and luminous piece has bands of golden-brown, orange, violet, and teal patina at the margins and silver-gray color at the centers. Light to moderate abrasions and a spot of deep patina affect the cheek. *From The Vanek Collection.* (#6148)

882 **1829/7 AU58 NGC.** O-101a, R.1. The reverse die is lapped, and the eagle's tail feathers and arrow shafts are missing design detail. A satiny and sharply struck tan-gray example that has a surprisingly unabraded appearance. Certified in a prior generation holder. (#6155)

883 1830 Small 0 AU58 PCGS. O-117, R.2. Golden-brown and forest-green toning adorns this satiny representative. Liberty's cheekbone and the curls beneath the cap show slight friction, but both sides are surprisingly unabraded. Crisply struck and attractive. Encapsulated in a first generation holder. (#6156)

884 1830 Small 0 MS62 NGC. O-113, R.2. The 1 in the date is slightly higher than 830. Peripheral die cracks on the upper reverse aid identification. Lustrous and essentially untoned, with few marks and a frosty sheen over each side. Highly appealing. (#6156)

Choice O-111 1831 Half

885 1831 MS64 PCGS. O-111, R.1. Luster dominates the fields and devices of this nearly untoned Choice Bust half. The fields are remarkably smooth, and only faint contact on Liberty's neck precludes an even finer grade. Well struck throughout the portrait and eagle, while the stars and the LUR in PLURIBUS are softly impressed. (#6159)

Lushly Toned O-112 1831 Half MS65

886 1831 MS65 NGC. O-112, R.3. Blended apple-green and orange-red enrich this lustrous Gem. The fields are unabraded, and only a faint vertical line above the jaw precludes a finer grade. The major devices are sharply struck, although a couple of stars and the TE in STATES lack complete definition. (#6159)

887 1832 Small Letters AU58 PCGS. O-102, R.1. A tine from the eagle's right wingtip and a die line through Liberty's lips confirm the Overton variety. Light mauve and sea-green toning endows this lustrous near-Mint half. The upper stars and the right claws are incompletely brought up, and clusters of wispy marks are noted beneath each scroll end. Encased in an old green label holder. (#6160)

888 1832 Small Letters MS62 PCGS. O-110, R.1. The small tine that protrudes from the top of Liberty's cap is the most obvious die marker, while the softness at the A of STATES on the reverse is typical for the variety. Well struck otherwise with soft luster beneath delicate rose and gold patina that graces each side. (#6160)

Near-Gem O-115 1832 Bust Half

889 1832 Small Letters MS64 PCGS. O-115, R.1. Dusky chestnut-gold and pearl-gray toning cannot deny the satin luster. Abrasions are unimportant and difficult to locate. The major devices are boldly struck, although the left-side stars and the PLU in PLURIBUS are indifferently brought up. A charming and original Bust type coin. (#6160)

890 1833 MS62 PCGS. O-102, R.1. Blazing luster brightens this impressive and nearly unabraded Bust half. Honey-gold borders encompass the untoned fields and devices. Well struck on the stars, although the horizontal shield lines are somewhat soft. Housed in a green label holder. (#6163)

Beautiful Gem 1833 Capped Bust Half, O-103

891 1833 MS65 NGC. O-103, R.2. Star 1 is recut, Liberty's profile is doubled, and all four digits in the date have been recut. The 5 on the lower reverse has a stubby, triangular top. This is a beautiful Gem example with even shimmering luster that highlights sky-blue, rose-gray, gold, and aquamarine coloration. The design features are crisply struck, except for the horizontal crossbars of the eagle's shield. Both sides of the piece are well preserved and free of distractions. Census: 27 in 65, 8 finer (6/07). (#6163)

892 1834 Large Date, Large Letters MS63 PCGS. O-102, R.1. The 3 in the date is broadly recut, while the 8 and 4 show less obvious recutting. Some bulging is noticeable in the left obverse field. Lustrous and originally toned, with sea-green, coral, and gold noted. An interesting planchet lamination (as struck) occurs between obverse stars 8 and 9. There are no obvious abrasions to report, on either side of this conditionally scarce example. (#6164)

893 1834 Large Date, Small Letters AU58 PCGS. O-108, R.2. Dusky tan, aquamarine, and gunmetal-gray toning blankets this partly lustrous and lightly abraded Borderline Uncirculated half. The star centers are soft, but the legends and major devices are crisp. (#6165)

894 1835 MS62 PCGS. O-107, R.1. Deep olive-brown, sea-green, and orange-gold embrace this satiny and lightly abraded Capped Bust half. The RI in PLURIBUS is softly defined, but the major devices are generally crisp. (#6168)

895 **1835 MS62 NGC.** O-106, R.1. Golden-brown, dove-gray, and powder-blue embrace this satiny and lightly abraded Bust half. O-106 is identified by the recut stand on the 5 in the date, and a tiny tine from the left border of the eagle's neck. Certified in a prior generation holder. (#6168)

REEDED EDGE HALF DOLLARS

Bold VF 1836 Reeded Edge Half

896 **1836 Reeded Edge VF30 PCGS.** The low business strike mintage of 1,200 pieces for the 1836 Reeded Edge has long fascinated collectors. Perhaps as many as 400 examples have survived, primarily in VF to AU grades. This attractively detailed first year type coin displays subdued powder-blue and tan-gold surfaces. A thin, faint mark is noted above the eagle's head. Encapsulated in an old green label holder. (#6175)

Richly Toned MS65 1837 Reeded Edge Half

897 **1837 MS65 NGC.** JR-24a. On the obverse, a heavy line extends from the rim through the right part of star 7, and there is a spike to the right from the curl over the left side of the L of LIBERTY. The reverse shows a fine line from the top of the U in UNITED slightly down to the right through N. The 1837 is one of only two issues of Christian Gobrecht's Reeded Edge, 50 CENTS Reverse half dollar. The scarcity of the low mintage (1,200 pieces) 1836 explains the desirability of the 1837 among high quality type collectors.

In 1836, the use of the "new" steam coining press necessitated a design change from John Reich's Capped Bust design to a somewhat similar design by Christian Gobrecht. The obsolete lettered edge was replaced by a reeded edge in 1836; however, as previously stated, only a limited number were struck. General production began the next year with more than 3.6 million 1837 examples coined (50 CENTS on the reverse), and these have become the most available date for this two-year type. Few survivors possess the appeal of this richly toned representative. Deep copper-rose and charcoal-gray toning overlays each side with sea-green patination interspersed. Boldly struck in all areas, this is an exceptionally smooth example with only a couple of almost invisible marks on Liberty's cheek. Census: 36 in 65, 12 finer (6/07). (#6176)

898 **1838 AU53 PCGS.** Light wear appears on the highpoints of this richly toned half, which has deep violet-gray and rose-pink color over each side. The well-defined devices display few marks on this early close-collar coin. (#6177)

Choice Mint State 1838 Half Dollar

899 **1838 MS64 PCGS.** This is an impressive Choice Mint State example of the Capped Bust type with the edge reeded, coined only from the end of 1836 to the beginning of 1839. This type actually has two minor design variations. The 1836 and 1837 pieces have the denomination 50 CENTS, while the 1838 and 1839 pieces have the denomination HALF DOL. An impressive gold toned example, this piece has frosty mint luster beneath the toning, with peripheral blue and lilac accents. It is sharply struck and most attractive. Population: 31 in 64, 8 finer (6/07). (#6177)

SEATED HALF DOLLARS

900 **1845-O—Cleaned—ANACS. VF20 Details.** FS-301, formerly FS-001.5. WB-104. The date is widely repunched east, with the outer right curve of an errant 5 plainly visible. Autumn-brown and sea-green embrace the obverse, while the reverse has deep powder-blue fields. A few minor rim nicks are present, and a faint scratch on the right obverse field is subdued by a cleaning. (#6249)

Lustrous 1846 Half Dollar, Medium Date, MS64, WB-102

901 **1846 Medium Date MS64 NGC.** WB-102, Medium Date, Errant 6. This variety was once regarded as an 1846/5 overdate: the Wiley-Bugert reference (1993) considers it to be a crudely repunched date. The authors note that: "The head die is paired with two tail dies, the second of which is easily identified by a large hole near the top of the first set of vertical stripes in the shield." This near-Gem example displays that characteristic, and its bright lustrous surfaces exhibit just a hint of incipient light tan color. All of the design features are well brought up. A few minor handling marks limit the grade. Census: 10 in 64, 7 finer (5/07). (#6251)

Lovely Near-Gem 1849 Half Dollar

902 **1849 MS64 PCGS.** A delightful piece, struck in the same year that the famed California Gold Rush would upset the tenuous balance between the value of gold and silver. This shining example has swirling luster and elements of golden patina in the obverse fields. Boldly defined, particularly on the reverse, with fewer marks than one might expect for the grade. Population: 10 in 64, 0 finer (4/07). (#6262)

903 **1852—Repaired, Cleaned—ANACS. VF30 Details.** Well detailed with all of the letters in LIBERTY clear and full. An irregular pattern of steel-gray and purple-violet coloration covers each side. A repair has occurred above Liberty's left (facing) shoulder and above HA on the reverse, probably where a hole in the coin was plugged. The piece has a subdued appearance from harsh cleaning. Only 77,130 halves were produced this year, and a great many of those were melted. As a result, examples are scarce in all grades. (#6268)

904 **1852 XF45 ANACS.** Luster shimmers from recessed areas of this silver-white, straw-gold, and ocean-blue example. Only 77,130 pieces were struck, since the bullion content exceeded face value due to an influx of California-mined gold. (#6268)

905 **1855/54 Arrows AU55 ANACS.** FS-301, formerly FS-005. WB-102. The crossbar of the underdigit 4 is unmistakable. This *Guide Book* variety is popular in all grades, and is very scarce in AU. Liberty's knees and cheek exhibit wear, but luster fills the borders and devices. (#6282)

906 **1855-O Arrows Shipwreck Effect NGC.** Ex: *S.S. Republic*. We believe this coin has XF details. The stone-white surfaces are granular from 140 years of exposure to saltwater. Some luster remains in design recesses. This lot is accompanied by a presentation box, booklet, DVD, and certificate of authenticity from Odyssey Marine Exploration, Inc.
From The Vanek Collection.(#6283)

Frosted MS64 1855-O Arrows Half

907 **1855-O Arrows MS64 PCGS.** The mintage of 3.6 million pieces for the 1855-O is not particularly impressive. However, PCGS has only certified 59 pieces in MS64 with 21 finer (5/07). What is immediately obvious about this coin is the frosted mint luster. O-mint silver coins are often seen with subdued, satiny luster. The mint frost is generally brilliant with no obvious color on either side. Somewhat irregularly struck on each side. An important coin for the Seated half specialist. (#6283)

908 **1861 MS63 PCGS.** This well struck Civil War half is attractively toned orange-gold, along with narrow blue-green bands near the rim. Less abraded than expected, although thorough study locates a few nearly imperceptible obverse hairlines. (#6302)

909 **1861-O Shipwreck Effect NGC.** Variety W-09. No details grade is designated by NGC, but we believe the coin has Mint State sharpness. The luster is diminished, and the white surfaces are slightly granular, particularly above UNITED STATES. This lot is accompanied by a presentation box, booklet, DVD, and certificate of authenticity from Odyssey Marine Exploration, Inc.
From The Vanek Collection. (#6303)

910 **1866-S No Motto—Cleaned—ANACS. VF20 Details.** This stone-gray rare date quarter is subdued and mildly granular from a chemical cleaning. The reverse rim has a moderate mark near 10 o'clock. Only 60,000 pieces were struck. (#6315)

Historic 1870-CC Seated Half AU50 Details

911 **1870-CC—Corroded—ANACS. AU50 Details.** In its first year of operation, the Carson City Mint struck three silver denominations: the quarter, half dollar, and dollar. The 1870-CC has a mintage more than double that of the quarter and dollar combined, but the survival rate was remarkably low, particularly when compared with the 1870-CC silver dollar. Apparently, no one, not even local Mint officials or workers, appreciated the significance of the issue sufficiently to set examples aside. As of (5/07), NGC and PCGS have each certified only one piece as Mint State, both as MS62. In terms of sharpness, the present lot is close to Mint State, but the slate-gray surfaces are subdued and granular. The fields have only a few minor marks. (#6328)

Elusive 1871-CC Half Dollar, XF40

912 **1871-CC XF40 PCGS.** The 1871-CC half dollar is quite scarce overall. Randy Wiley and Bill Bugert (1993) assign an R.5 rarity rating in XF condition. Medium golden-gray toning accented with lavender and sky-blue bathes both sides of the XF40 specimen in this lot. Good definition is noted on all of the design elements, and the surfaces are refreshingly clean for a coin that saw some circulation. Population: 11 in 40, 29 finer (6/07). (#6331)

Popular 1873-CC Arrows Half, XF45

913 **1873-CC Arrows XF45 PCGS.** WB-103. Large Mintmark. As with all the large arrows varieties of this date, the 3 has an open style. While nowhere as scarce as its No Arrows counterpart, the With Arrows halves are popular as it is from the two-year Arrows type and also because of its association with the historic Carson City mint. Small but noticeable traces of mint luster can be made out around the devices. Each side is lightly and evenly toned. Softly struck on the obverse, as are all 1870-1874-CC halves. (#6344)

Impressive 1875-S Half Dollar, MS65

914 **1875-S MS65 NGC.** Pastel golden-tan patination is occasionally joined by blushes of powder-blue, all of which rests upon radiantly lustrous surfaces. A powerful strike brings out crisp definition in the design features, further enhancing the eye appeal. a few minute obverse marks preclude an even higher grade. A highly impressive '75-S Gem! Census: 33 in 65, 9 finer (6/07). (#6351)

Gem 1876 Seated Half

915 1876 MS65 NGC. Type One Reverse with a split berry above the H in HALF. Cherry-red patina deepens toward the rims. This lustrous Gem is well struck save for minor weakness on the eagle's left (facing) ankle. A beautifully preserved and exceptionally attractive representative of this popular 19th century silver type. (#6352)

Lustrous Near-Gem 1877-CC Half Dollar

916 1877-CC MS64 PCGS. Type Two Reverse. Though the minor coins of Carson City are not so well known as its silver dollars or its gold pieces, examples such as the present piece have their own allure. Modestly reflective, strongly lustrous surfaces shine beneath rich, dappled tan, gray, and gold-orange color. The strike is sharp, and the overall eye appeal is undeniable. Population: 41 in 64, 21 finer (4/07). (#6356)

Beautiful MS64 1877-CC Half Dollar

917 1877-CC MS64 PCGS. Type Two Reverse. A lovely near-Gem, the lustrous surfaces are lightly toned on the obverse and more richly colored on the reverse. Both sides show varying shades of rose, violet, and pastel blue patina over each side. Nicely struck with intermittent dark spots and minimal marks. (#6356)

Magnificent MS67 ★ 1882 Seated Half

918 1882 MS67 ★ NGC. A precisely struck Superb Gem of this low mintage date. Lightly toned and semi-prooflike with remarkable preservation. Proofs and business strikes combined for only 5,500 pieces, since the mints were devoted to Morgan dollar production. NGC has awarded a Star designation to only three business strike 1882 half dollars, two of which grade MS67 with none finer (6/07). (#6364)

Semi-Prooflike MS66 1884 Seated Half

919 1884 MS66 PCGS. WB-102. Recut 4. A business strike-only die pairing, and one of only two, the other being the rare variant with the top of an errant 8 in the denticles beneath the 8 and 4. Most likely one of the first coins from the business strike dies (of which only 5,275 pieces were struck), the fields show significant brightness and reflectivity. The devices are also heavily frosted. Fully struck throughout. An exemplary 1884 half. Population: 14 in 66, 4 finer (6/07). (#6366)

920 1889 MS60 Prooflike ANACS. Solidly struck with moderate reflectivity evident in the lightly toned fields. Areas of gold, rose, and plum color grace the margins of this piece, which has fewer marks than the MS60 grade might suggest. Housed in a pre-Amos Press ANACS holder. (#6371)

Pleasing 1889 Premium Gem Half Dollar

921 1889 MS66 NGC. The 1889 half dollar comes with a sparse mintage of 12,000 pieces. The low-production rates for the 1880s half dollars is alluded to by Randy Wiley and Bill Bugert (1993): "The low mintages are no doubt due to the implementation of the Bland-Allison Act of 1878 which required mints to purchase vast amounts of silver bullion and produce large quantities of silver (Morgan) dollars." This Premium Gem displays pleasing satiny luster, and just the faintest hint of tan-gold color visible under high magnification. Exquisitely struck, with no mentionable marks. Census: 9 in 66, 0 finer (6/07). (#6371)

PROOF SEATED HALF DOLLARS

Colorful Gem Proof 1862 Seated Half

922 **1862 PR65 PCGS.** Splendid cherry-red, gold, apple-green, cream-gray, and silver-white toning embraces this intricately struck Gem. A Civil War date with a proof mintage of only 550 pieces. Desirable in such consummate quality. Encapsulated in a green label holder. Population: 15 in 65, 3 finer (4/07).
From The Vanek Collection. (#6416)

Elusive 1862 Half Dollar PR65 Cameo

923 **1862 PR65 Cameo NGC.** NGC and PCGS combined have certified nearly 300 1862 proofs, that saw a mintage of 550 pieces. Only 35 examples have been assigned the Cameo designation. Exquisitely struck, lightly frosted devices stand out amidst deeply mirrored fields. Cobalt-blue and lavender peripheral toning flanks essentially color-free centers. There are no significant marks to report. Census: 4 in 65 Cameo, 3 finer (6/07). (#86416)

Beautiful Cameo Gem 1866 Motto Half

924 **1866 Motto PR65 Cameo PCGS.** Ex: Stokely Collection. Golden-brown, champagne-rose, and ocean-blue toning endows this intricately struck Gem. Gorgeously smooth fields and icy devices combine for exemplary eye appeal. Any collector would be proud to display such a colorful and high quality specimen. The first Motto issue, and scarce due to a mintage of just 725 proofs. PCGS has certified just 15 pieces as Cameo. Population: 1 in 65 Cameo, 1 finer (5/07). *Ex: Stephen Stokely #1 PCGS Registry Set of Proof Seated Half Dollars (Heritage, 8/06), lot 3375, which realized $9,775.* (#86424)

925 **1868 PR63 PCGS.** Golden-brown and rose-red toning deepens along the peripheries. Light mint-made roller marks cross the eagle's neck. A mere 600 proofs were struck. Encased in a green label holder. Population: 47 in 63, 45 finer (4/07).
From The Vanek Collection. (#6426)

926 **1871 PR63 Cameo ANACS.** Sharply struck except for the eagle's left (facing) ankle. The brilliant centers are framed by milk-gray toning. A mere 960 proofs were struck. (#86429)

Gem Cameo Proof 1874 Arrows Half Dollar

927 **1874 Arrows PR65 Cameo NGC.** An amazing example of the short-lived With Arrows design type that was only struck for part of 1873 and all of 1874. The arrows are left and right of the date, and signify a slight reduction in the standard weight for the issue, in accordance with the Coinage Act of February 12, 1873.

This legislation was known as the "Crime of 73" in some circles. Although slight, the weight reduction was intended to bring the value of silver coins in line with prevailing market prices. It resulted in countless earlier coins being melted by hoarders for their bullion content, further diminishing the availability of silver coins in commerce at a time when such coins were already scarcely seen.

This proof has exceptional eye appeal created by intense contrast between the lustrous devices and deeply mirrored fields. All of the designs are fully detailed, and the surfaces are brilliant with no toning. The obverse qualifies as ultra cameo, while the reverse has less contrast. (#86435)

928 **1878 PR63 Cameo PCGS.** Type Two Reverse. A fair number of the 800 proof half dollars minted in 1878 have apparently survived the ravages of time, as evidenced by the relatively large number graded by PCGS and NGC. The two services have seen considerably fewer Cameo pieces, however. This Select Cameo example displays a thin coat of champagne-gold color, and exhibits pronounced field-motif contrast at virtually all angles. Moreover, sharp definition occurs on all of the design elements. A few minor handling marks define the grade. Population: 8 in 63 Cameo, 16 finer (4/07). (#86439)

929 **1878 PR64 Cameo NGC.** Type Two Reverse. This is a sharply detailed champagne proof with a crescent of deep blue and iridescent toning that extends clockwise from 4 o'clock to 10 o'clock, covering about 30% of the surface. The reverse has a few hints of lilac. (#86439)

930 **1879 PR63 NGC.** Type One Reverse. Only 1,100 proofs were struck out of a total proof and business strike production of 5,900 pieces. There are dappled russet and sky-blue colors on each side. A few faint hairlines are noted on the obverse, limiting the grade.
From The Vanek Collection. (#6440)

931 **1879 PR64 PCGS.** Type One Reverse. Only two varieties are listed for the 1879, one for proofs and one for circulation strikes. The popularity of this date comes from its low total mintage, the first year in a decade-long string of low mintage issues. This piece has nicely reflective fields that radiate strongly beneath the overlay of russet and blue toning. (#6440)

Low Mintage 1880 Half Dollar, PR66

932 **1880 PR66 NGC.** Type Two Reverse. The 1880 is one of the popular issues that is positioned at the beginning of this low-mintage decade (the low mintages actually began in 1879). Only 1,355 proofs were struck out of a total mintage of 11,555 pieces, the remainder of which are 8,400 circulation strikes. This is an attractive coin that displays light gray and rose patina over each side. The colors are enhanced by bright, flashy mirrors in the fields. As one would expect, there are no obvious contact marks on either side. Census: 22 in 66, 9 finer (5/07). (#6441)

933 **1884 PR63 NGC.** The fields display watery reflectivity beneath the rich charcoal-rose toning. The borders are a deep electric-blue and provide a strong two-toned accent on each side. A pleasing Select proof example of this popular, low total mintage issue.
From The Vanek Collection. (#6445)

Splendid, Attractively Toned 1885 Half Dollar PR65 Cameo

934 **1885 PR65 Cameo PCGS.** Bright, watery fields characterize this solid Gem proof example. Light golden toning is gently draped over both sides with cobalt-blue accents around the margins. Always of interest as a low total-mintage date with only 930 proofs and 5,200 circulation strikes produced. Population: 13 in 65, 1 finer (6/07). (#86446)

Conditionally Scarce 1886 Seated Half PR65

935 1886 PR65 NGC. This piece displays noteworthy cameo contrast on the obverse which only diminishes slightly on the reverse. The design motifs are as crisply detailed as expected, for a proof specimen. Free of grade-limiting hairlines or contact remnants; a lovely Gem proof. A conditionally scarce issue at this level, which is under added market pressure due to the scant number of business strikes produced. Census: 23 in 65, 27 finer (5/07). *From The Vanek Collection.* (#6447)

Exceptional PR66 1886 Half Dollar

936 1886 PR66 NGC. One of only 886 proofs struck in this low total mintage year. This is an absolutely splendid half dollar. The fields are deeply mirrored and the obverse has a large swath of golden-brown and blue toning that gives a strong accent against the brilliance seen elsewhere on that side. The reverse is completely brilliant. While not listed on the NGC insert, there is a noticeable amount of mint frost over the devices which provides a moderate contrast. Census: 20 in 66, 7 finer (5/07). (#6447)

Medium Toned 1889 Half Dollar, PR65

937 1889 PR65 NGC. The 1889 had a mintage of 711 proofs, of which about 300 have been certified by NGC and PCGS. The Gem in this lot displays medium intensity magenta, violet, and cobalt-blue patination. The design elements were the recipients of an impressive strike, with no areas revealing hints of weakness. There are no significant marks to report. Census: 25 in 65, 26 finer (6/07). (#6450)

938 1890 PR64 Cameo PCGS. A lovely near-Gem representative from the penultimate proof Seated half dollar issue. Strongly reflective with distinct contrast despite deep rose and amethyst patina at the margins. Minor hairlines in the fields preclude a finer grade. Population: 10 in 64 Cameo, 9 finer (4/07). (#86451)

BARBER HALF DOLLARS

939 1892 MS63 PCGS. This first-year-of-issue Barber half had a mintage of just under 1 million business strikes. Speckles of tan-gold patination run over the lustrous surfaces of this Select specimen, and the design elements exhibit sharp detail. Handling marks on Liberty's cheek and neck preclude a higher grade. (#6461)

940 1892 MS63 PCGS. A splendid first year of issue coin, this lovely half dollar has full luster beneath gray-gold and pale blue toning on each side. It is sharply detailed with bold design elements. (#6461)

941 1895-S MS63 NGC. Sharply struck overall, the mint luster radiates through layers of gray and golden toning that cover both sides. A lovely, essentially problem-free Barber half. Census: 17 in 63, 21 finer (6/07). (#6473)

942 1897-S—Cleaned—ANACS. AU58 Details. Light silver surfaces are accented by traces of peripheral gold toning on both sides of this piece. It is a scarce date that is desirable in all quality levels. (#6479)

Brilliant 1898-O Half MS65

943 1898-O MS65 NGC. As is often the case with New Orleans Barber coinage, the 1898-O is easily secured in AG through VG, but is surprisingly difficult to locate any finer. Mint State examples are rare, and the appearance of a Gem provides a major opportunity for the specialist. This brilliant piece has vibrant luster, and is nearly immaculate aside from faint slide marks on the cheek. The right shield corner and fletchings show incompleteness characteristic of the issue. (#6481)

Choice 1903-S Barber Half

944 1903-S MS64 PCGS. A virtually brilliant and thoroughly lustrous near-Gem with imposing eye appeal. Crisply struck with minor incompleteness on the right shield corner and fletchings. The fields are pristine, and the devices have just a couple tiny abrasions that keep this from a higher grade. Rare in Mint State despite a plentiful production. Population: 19 in 64, 12 finer (6/07). (#6497)

945 1907-D MS63 NGC. A lovely example from the second year of operation for Denver, solidly struck with zones of gold, rose, and sea-green color across both sides. A handful of wispy abrasions on the cheek preclude a finer grade. (#6509)

946 1910-S MS63 PCGS. David Lawrence (1991) writes that the 1910-S half dollar is "common in low grades, but surprisingly tough in AU55 and above." The Select specimen offered in this lot exhibits pleasing luster that issues from untoned surfaces. Sharp definition is apparent on the design elements. Light obverse handling marks limit the grade. Population: 4 in 63, 38 finer (4/07). (#6520)

Conditionally Rare 1910-S Barber Half MS66

947 **1910-S MS66 PCGS.** Highly lustrous and fully struck with remarkably clean surfaces that appear to be essentially untoned, despite a faint degree of speckled patina on the obverse. This issue had a fairly high mintage of nearly two million pieces, but only a tiny fraction of that number survive at the Premium Gem level of preservation. Population: 11 in 66, 4 finer (6/07). (#6520)

Lustrous MS66 1912-D Half Dollar
Ex: Eliasberg

948 **1912-D MS66 NGC.** Ex: Eliasberg. The 1912-D half dollar, with a mintage of 2,300,800 pieces, is one of the most, if not *the* most, common date in the Barber half dollar series. The "common" descriptor ends with the MS64 grade classification; MS65 coins are scarce, Premium Gems are rare, and finer examples are nearly unobtainable. This MS66 coin displays glowing luster from silver-gray surfaces that are peppered with speckles of olive-tan, especially on the obverse. The design elements are well impressed throughout. Census: 5 in 66, 0 finer (6/07). Ex: Eliasberg Collection (Bowers and Merena, 5/97), lot 2127. (#6525)

949 **1914—Cleaned—ANACS. AU58 Details.** Both sides of this piece have bright silver color with considerable remaining luster, as well as light hairlines from improper cleaning. This is a scarce date, considered to be one of the key issues in the Barber half dollar series. (#6530)

950 **1914-S MS61 ANACS.** Tinges of gold and ice-blue grace the strongly lustrous, subtly reflective surfaces of this later-date Barber half, a low-mintage issue along with the 1914-P. Well struck with a number of wispy marks present in the fields. (#6531)

951 **1914-S MS64 PCGS.** A well-defined Choice example that displays attractive luster and wisps of delicate golden patina over each side. The higher-mintage of two half dollar issues for this year, though the 1914-S had an original mintage of less than a million coins. Population: 28 in 64, 16 finer (4/07). (#6531)

PROOF BARBER HALF DOLLARS

952 **1893 PR64 PCGS.** Dappled golden-brown and lime dominate this nicely struck and moderately mirrored near-Gem. A mere 792 pieces were struck, many fewer than during the first year of issue. Population: 53 in 64, 52 finer (6/07). (#6540)

Unimprovable PR68 1895 Barber Half Dollar

953 **1895 PR68 NGC.** The 880-piece mintage of 1895 proofs is the fourth highest for the Barber half series, and a relatively large number have been certified by NGC and PCGS. This PR68 specimen displays electric-blue and lavender toning around the obverse periphery, and unevenly throughout the reverse. Sharply impressed design features are mildly frosted, and yield good contrast with deeply mirrored fields. The surfaces are unimprovable. Census: 12 in 68, 0 finer (6/07). (#6542)

954 **1896 PR64 NGC.** Splashes of cherry-red, ocean-blue, and apricot adorn the borders of this beautiful and razor-sharp near-Gem. Only 762 proofs were struck. Certified in an early pre-hologram NGC holder. (#6543)

CUTTING PRESSES.

Stellar 1897 Barber Half, PR68 ★ Cameo

955 1897 PR68 ★ Cameo NGC. NGC has certified three examples of this 731-piece issue as PR68 ★ Cameo (5/07), and interestingly, Heritage has offered all three. May 2003 saw our first specimen, a stunning blast-white coin, and the delicately toned Eliasberg/Hagun example sold in January 2005. The delectable piece offered here completes the triumvirate.

Both sides exhibit decisively struck, richly frosted devices. Aside from a small wisp of milky color to the right of Liberty's lips, the obverse is essentially untoned, as is the reverse. The surfaces are practically flawless, as demanded of the grade, and the overall eye appeal is beyond reproach. A stunning and worthy piece that showcases the vivid contrast found on the finest Cameo coins of the late 19th century. (#86544)

Outstanding 1898 Half Dollar, PR64 Cameo

956 1898 PR64 Cameo PCGS. The 1898 half dollar comes with a proof mintage of 735 pieces. Walter Breen writes of this issue that: "It is now very seldom that one is offered that has *not* been cleaned." PCGS and NGC data indicate that nearly 400 specimens have been certified by the two services; approximately 100 have been assigned the Cameo designation. The near-Gem Cameo offered in this lot is essentially untoned, and the frosty, crisply defined motifs establish excellent contrast with the deeply mirrored fields. Faint hairlines in the fields, visible only under high magnification, preclude full Gem status. Outstanding overall eye appeal. Population: 21 in 64 Cameo, 17 finer (5/07). (#86545)

Dazzling PR65 ★ Cameo 1898 Half Dollar

957 1898 PR65 ★ Cameo NGC. An outstanding Barber half of any date. This exceptional proof does indeed have extra eye appeal for the grade, as indicated by the star designation. The fields show unfathomable depth of reflectivity, and the devices have considerable mint frost that, when combined with the mirrored surfaces, produce a strong cameo effect. Brilliant on both obverse and reverse. (#86545)

Impeccable Premium Gem Proof 1898 Barber Half

958 1898 PR66 Cameo PCGS. Razor-sharp striking details and impeccable surface preservation are among the attributes of this conditionally scarce Premium Gem. Heavily frosted devices and highly reflective fields produce noteworthy cameo contrast on both sides. Light golden toning is seen near the peripheries. A lovely proof coin from a well produced issue in the Barber half dollar series. Population: 7 in 66 Cameo, 3 finer (4/07). (#86545)

959 1901 PR64 PCGS. Decisively struck with a measure of contrast on the deeply reflective reverse. Areas of moderate pewter-gray haze cover parts of the modestly hairlined obverse fields. A pleasing Choice example of this turn-of-the-century Barber issue. (#6548)

960 **1902 PR63 PCGS.** This Select proof has several important characteristics. First, it has excellent eye appeal with peripheral gold, lilac, and blue color. Second, it has sharp design motifs. Third, it has light cameo contrast. This last trait is especially important as the Mint was discouraging production of Cameo proofs in the early 20th century. (#6549)

961 **1902 PR63 NGC.** Well defined and essentially brilliant, with little contrast between the fields and devices. Nice, watery reflectivity is observed on each side, and there are no contact marks to limit the grade.
From The Vanek Collection. (#6549)

Pleasing Near-Gem Proof 1903 Barber Half

962 **1903 PR64 NGC.** A sharply struck and pleasing near-Gem that is essentially untoned over both sides. The cheek has only the faintest of slide marks, while the reverse is seemingly pristine. Struck in the no-contrast method employed for only a couple of years (1902-1903). 755 pieces were produced, a moderate proof mintage for the type.
From The Vanek Collection. (#6550)

963 **1907 PR62 NGC.** Sea-green and orange-red borders frame the silver-gray centers. The strike is a bit soft near the right shield corner, although the fletchings and claws are sharp. Attractive for the grade. A scant 575 proofs were struck. (#6554)

Stellar 1909 Half, PR68

964 **1909 PR68 PCGS.** A number of proof Superb Gem Barber pieces survive today, many of which hail from a small hoard of original proof sets released into the marketplace after the advent of certified grading. While it is impossible to state with certainty whether the present piece comes from that hoard, the stunning quality and visual appeal of the coin attest to decades of careful preservation.

This lovely example displays a vivid blend of cobalt-blue, lavender, and yellow-gold patina. All of the design elements are crisp, and they present a surprising level of contrast at the proper angle to the light. The specimen's impeccably preserved surfaces reveal no mentionable marks. Population: 6 in 68, 0 finer (5/07). (#6556)

Conditionally Scarce 1911 Barber Half PR66

965 **1911 PR66 NGC.** This is a marvelous Premium Gem proof Barber half dollar that will delight the connoisseur of original toning. Speckled reddish-brown and green patina covers both sides. The design elements are fully struck and the glassy fields are highly reflective. An immaculately preserved example of this conditionally scarce item. Census: 26 in 66, 18 finer (6/07). (#6558)

Splendid 1911 Half Dollar, PR66

966 **1911 PR66 NGC.** David Lawrence (1991), in discussing the 1911 proof half dollar, comments that "though the 543 proofs made is the third lowest for the series, a fairly high percentage have been certified making them readily available." Lawrence's contention holds through the near-Gem level, but PR65 coins are scarce, and finer specimens are rare. The current Premium Gem displays some field-motif contrast when the coin is tilted under a light source. Light gold and lavender toning gravitates to the margins, and a solid strike brings out sharp definition on the mildly frosted design features. Some unobtrusive handling marks on Liberty's cheek do not detract from the overall eye appeal. (#6558)

967 **1912 PR64 PCGS.** Sharply struck, as befits a proof, with just a touch of cloudiness over both sides from long-term storage. Even more faint are the tiny russet toning specks (not carbon) on the obverse. Contact marks are not evident, but faint, grade-limiting hairlines are noted in the fields. Just 700 proof half dollars were struck in 1912. (#6559)

Gem Proof 1914 Barber Half Dollar

968 **1914 PR65 PCGS.** All of the design elements are sharply struck. The fields are highly reflective beneath layers of milky patina. The obverse shows a combination of lilac, amber, and pale green coloration, while the reverse displays tan and sea-green toning. Hairlines and contact marks are nonexistent. Population: 23 in 65, 25 finer (6/07). (#6561)

WALKING LIBERTY HALF DOLLARS

Consignment Michigan: A Complete 1916 To 1933 Set Of Walking Liberty Half Dollars

969 **1916 MS62 PCGS.** A luminous representative from the first year of issue for this well-received Weinman design, well-defined with a clearly separated thumb on the branch hand. The obverse displays scattered russet-orange patina, while the reverse is largely silver-gray. (#6566)

970 **1916-D MS62 PCGS.** The shining surfaces of this first-year branch mint half offer pleasing luster and predominantly silver-gray color, though the obverse fields have a hint of gold. Well struck with only a handful of wispy, yet grade-defining abrasions. (#6567)

971 **1916-S MS62 PCGS.** Satiny and pleasing with above-average detail and splashes of russet patina at the upper obverse margins. Light abrasions appear on the figure of Liberty, including one near the branch hand. (#6568)

972 **1917 MS62 PCGS.** Unlike the Denver and San Francisco issues, the Philadelphia 1917 Walking Liberty half has just one variety, since there was no mintmark to change locations. Solidly struck with slightly hazy gold-green patina over lustrous surfaces. (#6569)

973 **1917-D Obverse MS63 PCGS.** A well-defined example of the short-lived Obverse Mintmark variety, lightly toned blue-gray overall with deeper violet color present at the rims. This Select piece has a few light abrasions on Liberty's lower skirt. (#6570)

974 **1917-D Reverse MS62 PCGS.** Hazy gold-gray patina graces the luminous surfaces of this unworn and pleasing piece. A single spot of deeper color appears just above Liberty's front foot. Despite having a higher mintage than its Obverse Mintmark counterpart, this issue has a mintage of under 2 million pieces. (#6571)

Lovely 1917-S Obverse Half, MS63

975 **1917-S Obverse MS63 PCGS.** San Francisco struck fewer than a million halves in 1917 before the mintmark changed positions from the obverse to the reverse. On this piece, while Liberty's branch hand shows only partial detail, the eagle exhibits unusual sharpness, though it also has a point of weakness on the inside of the leg. A frosty Select example from this lower-mintage issue, one that displays just a touch of color in the fields. (#6572)

976 **1917-S Reverse MS63 PCGS.** In 1917, the position of the mintmark on the Walking Liberty half changed from below IN GOD WE TRUST on the obverse to a place to the left of the rock on the reverse. Well struck with light golden patina on the obverse. (#6573)

977 **1918 MS62 PCGS.** An attractive example that offers strong luster and a degree of detail on the often-weak branch hand. Small streaks of hazy patina appear in the fields, and a splash of similar color appears over the center of the obverse. (#6574)

Captivating Select 1918-D Half

978 **1918-D MS63 PCGS.** A satiny example from the lowest-mintage circulating half for the year, well struck overall with a delineated thumb. The obverse is predominantly silver-gray, though the peach patina that appears at the upper obverse also occupies much of the reverse. A pleasing representative, housed in a holder with a light green label. (#6575)

979 **1918-S MS62 PCGS.** The outer regions have strong luster, though the lightly toned centers are more luminous than lustrous. Well struck with areas of hazy orange and cream patina that form a fingerprint pattern on the lower skirt. (#6576)

Beautiful Select 1919 Walker Half

980 1919 MS63 PCGS. Though its D-mint counterpart overshadows this issue in Mint State grades, the 1919 half is challenging in its own right. Light gold-gray patina graces much of this shimmering P-mint piece, while dappled blue-gray toning appears at the upper obverse periphery. A delightful Select example from this early issue, housed in a green label holder. (#6577)

Elusive 1919-D Half Dollar, MS63

981 1919-D MS63 PCGS. There is little doubt that the 1919-D half dollar is the rarest date in the entire Walking Liberty half dollar series in Mint State grades. It is also one of the most poorly struck issues in the entire series, and perhaps this accounts for its Mint State rarity. Even a brief period in circulation, not enough to actually exhibit any wear on fully struck pieces, could give a poorly struck coin the appearance of considerable wear.

This piece, in a green-label holder, exhibits considerable strike weakness at the center on each side, and also at Liberty's head. Both sides are fully lustrous with light champagne toning that deepens slightly near the borders. (#6578)

Delightful Select 1919-S Half

982 1919-S MS63 PCGS. Though the 1919-S was the highest-mintage issue for the year, in Mint State grades, the 1919-S half is more elusive than its P-mint counterpart. This strongly lustrous example has pleasing peripheral detail and modest definition on the highpoints. The thin, milky patina that covers most of both sides deepens in color and thickness at the word DOLLAR on the reverse. (#6579)

983 1920 MS62 PCGS. An attractive example of this post-Great War issue, well-defined with surfaces that gleam beneath scattered, hazy powder-blue and gold-gray patina. A single abrasion of note crosses Liberty's forward leg. (#6580)

Choice 1920-D Walking Liberty Half

984 1920-D MS64 PCGS. Well struck with lovely luster and solid definition on Liberty's branch hand, though Liberty's head shows softness. A few small spots of cloudy patina near the rims are nearly invisible at first glance. A well-preserved example of this lowest-mintage Walker half issue for the year, housed in a green label holder. (#6581)

Luminous 1920-S Half, MS63

985 1920-S MS63 PCGS. The satiny, lively surfaces of this attractive Select example display few marks for the grade. Light gold-gray patina graces the fields, while the rims have small specks of russet color. Despite a comparatively generous mintage of over 4.6 million pieces, only a small fraction survive in Mint State grades. (#6582)

986 1921 MS62 PCGS. The slightly satiny surfaces of this delectable 1921 dollar exhibit a touch of golden patina in the fields, with slightly brighter canary-yellow color near the rims. Though a handful of abrasions affect the figure of Liberty, the overall appearance suggests a finer grade. Interesting clash marks appear around the eagle's beak as well. An elusive issue, with a mintage of just 246,000 pieces. (#6583)

Attractive 1921-D Half, MS63

Important 1921-S Walker, MS63

987 **1921-D MS63 PCGS.** The 1921-D Walker is an important part of a complete set of these coins, and this piece is an attractive example that is housed in a PCGS green-label holder. Although a few light surface marks are present on each side, they are consistent with the grade. This piece is sharply struck with a fully visible thumb at the center of the obverse. The surfaces have bright silver luster with traces of heather toning.

According to Mint records, the mintage was 208,000 coins. However, Walter Breen discussed additional records of the Denver Mint that indicate two die pairs were used to strike 165,000 coins from one, and 92,672 coins from the other. These figures imply that there were 49,672 of these coins that were never distributed, almost certainly later melted and recoined. (#6584)

988 **1921-S MS63 PCGS.** In Mint State grades, there are four key issues to a complete set of Walking Liberty half dollars. In addition to this piece, the other keys are the 1919-D, the 1921, and the 1921-D. Inside the upper loop of the S mintmark can be seen a die chip that nearly fills this space. This is reminiscent of a similar die chip found on 1909-S VDB cents, a characteristic that is used to authenticate those coins.

This piece, certified in a green-label PCGS holder, has pleasing pearl color with frosty mint luster on both sides. Typical for many issues from the San Francisco Mint, it is somewhat weakly defined on Liberty's head, and also at the center of the obverse and reverse. Population: 28 in 63, 62 finer (6/07). (#6585)

Shining Select 1923-S Half

989 1923-S MS63 PCGS. A visually appealing example that has a blend of cloud-gray and pale orange patina in the obverse fields, while the reverse is largely untoned. The devices are well struck, with above-average definition on the head. The surfaces have few marks overall, though a small dig is noted to the right of Liberty's branch arm. This issue of under 2.2 million pieces came after a one-year hiatus, and no Mint would strike halves for circulation until 1927, when San Francisco reprised the denomination. (#6586)

990 1927-S MS62 PCGS. A flashy example of this Roaring Twenties issue with above-average peripheral detail, though the central highpoints are soft. Dots of milky patina appear over the right obverse and reverse. (#6587)

991 1928-S MS62 PCGS. Delicate peach and blue patina graces both sides of this lustrous and pleasing half. The surfaces have few marks for the grade, though the devices exhibit significant softness, particularly on Liberty's head and hand. (#6588)

992 1929-D MS63 PCGS. An attractive Select example from the first D-mint Walker half issue struck since 1921. Well-defined with powerful luster and a patch of milky haze in the upper right obverse field, and appealing despite light abrasions on the devices. (#6589)

993 1929-S MS63 PCGS. Unusually well-defined for this branch mint issue, the higher-mintage issue of two for the year despite a total production of just over 1.9 million pieces. Strongly lustrous with a thin coat of opaque, intermittent over the fields. A line of reed marks connecting the T and Y of LIBERTY accounts for the grade. (#6590)

994 1933-S MS62 PCGS. The 1933-S was the first half dollar issue in four years, and with under 2 million examples produced, it was the last issue before 1934 provided a turning point for the series with its higher-mintage issues. The strongly lustrous obverse of this solidly struck piece is largely untoned, though a large portion of the upper reverse has gold-orange patina. (#6591)

ADDITIONAL WALKING LIBERTY HALF DOLLARS

995 1916 MS64 PCGS. A satiny and crisply struck near-Gem with delightfully original silver-white and russet-brown toning. The reverse is well preserved. A low mintage first-year issue. (#6566)

996 1916 MS65 PCGS. Snow-white and highly lustrous, the surfaces of this first-year Walker are clean enough that many will see the potential of an even higher grade. Sharply defined, especially strong for an early Walker. (#6566)

Premium Gem 1916 Walking Liberty

997 1916 MS66 PCGS. Other than the 1921, the 1916 has the lowest mintage of any Philadelphia issue in the series. This lustrous cream-gray and caramel-gold Premium Gem has a penetrating strike, and is immaculate aside from an unimportant vertical mark on the eagle's leg. Encapsulated in an old green label holder. Population: 67 in 66, 4 finer (4/07).
From The Vanek Collection. (#6566)

Finest Certified 1916 Half Dollar, MS68

998 1916 MS68 NGC. The 1916 half dollar, with its 608,000-piece mintage, was saved in relatively large numbers, as is typical for most first-year-of-issue coins. NGC/PCGS census/population figures reflect this, showing nearly 2,000 Mint State pieces certified by the two services. The date is readily available through near-Gem, and even Gem and Premium Gem specimens are obtainable with patience and searching. MS67 pieces are rare, and a mere solitary coin (the example in this lot) has been certified in the lofty grade of MS68.

Gorgeous satiny surfaces display potent luster and are nearly untoned, save for barely discernible wisps of light tan and ice-blue. A powerful strike emboldens the design features, including virtually full definition in Liberty's left hand and the adjacent branches. As is typical with all issues through 1921, Liberty's gown lines are weak. Bruce Fox (1993) attributes this to the "... lack of engraving details on the working dies and/or weaker than needed striking force on the presses dialed in to preserve the dies." Both sides are impeccably preserved. The Walking Liberty half aficionado will not want to miss out on this unbelievable coin!
From The Vanek Collection. (#6566)

999 1916-D MS64 PCGS. A lustrous, sharply impressed, and nearly untoned first-year near-Gem whose pleasantly unperturbed surfaces approach a finer grade. (#6567)

1000 1916-D MS64 PCGS. This near-Gem has its mintmark on the obverse, which held true for the Walking Liberty half only in 1916 and part of 1917. This subtly lustrous example displays pleasing detail overall, including a degree of definition on the branch hand. Deep rose and violet patina at the margins surrounds cloud-gray centers. (#6567)

1001 1916-D MS64 PCGS. This lovely first-year example is close to Gem quality. Liberty's head and thumb are sharply struck, and the eagle is crisply defined as well. Surface blemishes are nearly nonexistent, and it may be that the slight degree of speckled patina and a few dark specks on the upper reverse have limited the grade. (#6567)

1002 **1916-D MS64 PCGS.** Variegated tan, apple-green, and lilac colors enrich this lustrous and reasonably struck near-Gem. A strike-thru (as made) on the field beneath Liberty's branch is not conspicuous.
From The Vanek Collection. (#6567)

1003 **1916-D MS64 PCGS.** The highest-mintage of three issues for this first year of the Walking Liberty design, though production barely surpassed a million pieces. This surprisingly well-defined Choice example has pleasing definition on the branch hand and eagle. Soft luster shines beneath a spread of gold, lavender, aqua, and sunset-orange colors. (#6567)

1004 **1916-D MS64 PCGS.** Well struck and satiny, with a layer of speckled russet, rose, and khaki-green patina across each side. Surface marks are minimal, but the coin's luster is a bit too subdued for a higher grade assessment. (#6567)

Important Semi-Key Date 1916-S Walker MS64

1005 **1916-S MS64 PCGS.** The surfaces exhibit intense satiny luster and are untoned except for a few faint whispers of color on the obverse. A few tiny nicks on the obverse are only noticeable with the aid of magnification; the reverse seems blemish-free. A semi-key first year date, and easily the scarcest of the three 1916 Walking Liberty issues.
From The Vanek Collection. (#6568)

Remarkably Smooth 1916-S Walker MS66

1006 **1916-S MS66 NGC.** A lustrous Premium Gem with golden toning deepening slightly at the obverse periphery and over most of the reverse. The matte-like, satin surfaces are nearly void of post-striking impairments. The strike, while not 100% full, is exceptional for this scarce first-year issue. The combination of first year of issue and obverse mintmark makes this date one of the most popular 20th century coins. The mintage is also among the lowest of the series. Only the 1921 and 1921-D keys and the hoarded 1938-D have lesser productions. Only two pieces have been certified finer by NGC and PCGS combined. Census: 11 in 66, 1 finer (5/07). (#6568)

1007 **1917 MS65 PCGS.** Light chestnut-gold toning visits this lustrous and sharply struck example. Well preserved aside from a few faint grazes above the motto. Certified in a green label holder.
From The Vanek Collection. (#6569)

Exceptional 1917 Premium Gem Half Dollar

1008 **1917 MS66 PCGS.** A mix of olive-green, lilac, and yellow-gold patination runs over the obverse of this Premium Gem, while the largely untoned central reverse is flanked by vivid multicolored toning. An attentive strike results in sharp definition on the design features, and highly lustrous surfaces do not exhibit the heavy abrasions typical for this issue. Population: 68 in 66, 2 finer (4/07). (#6569)

1009 **1917-D Obverse MS63 PCGS.** Lustrous and boldly struck with a faint golden cast and a slight degree of speckled russet patina near the borders. A brief type with the mintmark on the obverse that was only produced in 1916 and for part of 1917. (#6570)

1010 **1917-D Reverse MS62 NGC.** Satiny and boldly struck, with light layers of speckled toning near the peripheries, and nicely preserved surfaces. Surface marks are virtually nonexistent. A pleasing example of this early issue that may be a bit too lackluster for a higher grade. *From The Vanek Collection.* (#6571)

Lovely Reverse Mintmark 1917-S Half, MS64

1011 **1917-S Reverse MS64 PCGS.** Following an anomalous two-year stint on the obverse, the mintmark on Walking Liberty halves moved to the reverse, as was traditional for minor silver coinage for the time. This well struck piece displays lemon-gold patina overall with hints of pink and blue-gray color. Soft, pleasing luster peeks out beneath the toning. An attractive example of this early issue, one uncommonly seen in this grade. (#6573)

1012 **1918 MS64 NGC.** Essentially untoned (except for a few russet specks on the right side of the reverse), with a bold satiny sheen across both sides. Liberty's skirt lines are smooth, but the remaining design elements are nicely defined. A few minor obverse marks limit the grade. *From The Vanek Collection.* (#6574)

Lustrous MS65 1918 Walking Liberty Half

1013 **1918 MS65 NGC.** One of the more available issues among early Walkers, this is an attractive example that shows a strong strike on each side. The surfaces display thick mint frost that swirls around the obverse and reverse and is unimpeded by any noticeable abrasions. Census: 75 in 65, 7 finer (6/07). (#6574)

1014 **1918-D AU58 NGC.** Although designated as AU58, this unabraded half dollar has essentially full cartwheel luster, and there is only a whisper of friction on the eagle's breast feathers. Liberty's waist is typically brought up. (#6575)

1015 **1918-D—Damaged—ANACS. AU58 Details.** Four tiny depressions on the obverse figure seem to account for the designation that this piece is damaged, although we disagree that such a harsh description was necessary. The surfaces have light gold toning with frosty luster. The strike is a little blunt at the centers, and traces of highpoint wear are evident. (#6575)

Scarce Select Mint State 1918-D Half Dollar

1016 **1918-D MS63 NGC.** This is a lovely, satiny example with attractive light toning and nicely preserved surfaces. Just two to three minor marks are noted near the center of each side. The striking detail is typically soft on Liberty's head, branch hand, and skirt lines, as well as on the eagle's right (facing) leg. This issue is scarce at the Select Mint State level, and becomes increasingly elusive any finer. (#6575)

Toned Near-Gem 1918-S Walker

1017 **1918-S MS64 PCGS.** This satiny near-Gem has full silver luster beneath a blend of mustard-yellow and golden-brown toning that covers most of the obverse and reverse surfaces. Although some of the skirt lines are weak, it is actually a better than average strike that is sharp enough to exhibit a fully outlined thumb at the center of the obverse. (#6576)

Delightful Near-Mint 1919-D Half

1018 1919-D AU58 NGC. This lower-mintage branch mint issue was largely unappreciated at the time of its release, and as a consequence, higher-grade examples are elusive today. This still-lustrous silver-gray example displays just a touch of friction on the softly struck highpoints, and the fields are clean overall. Highly appealing and a more affordable alternative to a Mint State example. (#6578)

1019 1920 MS63 PCGS. Softly struck over the centers, as usual, this Select Mint State representative also reveals satin luster and cream-gray surfaces that display speckled olive-russet patina, mainly near the peripheries. A small milling mark in the right obverse field is the only minor distraction. (#6580)

1020 1920 MS64 NGC. Softly struck in the centers, with a beautiful satiny glow and even pearl-gray coloration. This lovely near-Gem shows a few minute marks and tiny russet specks on each side. *From The Vanek Collection.* (#6580)

1021 1921-D—Rims Damaged—ANACS. Fine 15 Details. The obverse rim has dings at 7:30 and 10:30, and the reverse rim has two small bruises at 3:30. The 1921-D is the lowest mintage issue of the widely collected series. (#6584)

1022 1921-D—Cleaned—ANACS. XF40 Details. Primarily cream-gray, but ice-blue and orange hues are present near the rims. Slightly cloudy from a mild cleaning. Liberty retains a majority of her skirt lines. The lowest mintage Walking Liberty issue. (#6584)

Low-Mintage 1921-D Fifty Cents, MS64

1023 1921-D MS64 PCGS. The 1921-D half dollar has the lowest mintage of the Walking Liberty series (208,000 pieces), and as might be expected, is scarce in all grades. Paul Green, in an August 21, 2001 *Numismatic News* article, explains this low mintage: "In 1921 all denominations experienced lower-than-average mintages because the Mint was working day and night to create silver dollars. The half dollar of 1921 probably suffered as much in terms of production as any denomination. You could make a strong case that 1921 half-dollar production from all three facilities was really a token amount."

Both sides of the near-Gem in this lot are awash in intense luster, and display barely discernible tan-gray color under magnification. The strike is typical for the issue, revealing weak definition in the centers, and fairly strong delineation in Liberty's lower gown lines. A few minute obverse marks define the grade. Population: 77 in 64, 33 finer (6/07). (#6584)

Choice Mint State 1921-S Walker

1024 **1921-S MS64 PCGS.** Although President Theodore Roosevelt was no longer in office, the Treasury Department conducted a coinage design competition in response to his desire for all new coinage designs, the same desire that resulted in the Lincoln cent, the Indian gold coins, and the Saint-Gaudens double eagle. Adolph A. Weinman submitted the winning designs for the Mercury dime and the Walking Liberty half dollar, and both designs made their first appearance in 1916.

A condition rarity in the series, the '21-S Walker is elusive in grades better than Fine. Examples that qualify as Mint State are highly desirable, and seldom seen, either in auctions or on bourse floors. The Heritage archives show more than 300 examples of this date offered in all grades, with just 50 of those in MS60 or finer condition, and only 15 pieces better than this example. In his *Complete Encyclopedia*, Walter Breen implied by his comments that only about 20 Mint State examples are known when he said: "Possibly all UNC survivors are from a single roll, mostly weak strikes." While it is evident today that there are more than 20 such pieces, the number of survivors clearly does not exceed the demand for such coins.

This example displays satiny silver luster that is created by microscopic die polish lines in the fields, imparting a reflective appearance. The surfaces are fully brilliant white, save for a trace of gold color on each side. The motifs are relatively sharp, with weakness located at Liberty's head, left hand at the center, and the upper skirt lines. Most of the reverse detail is boldly defined, including all of the breast feathers. Population: 45 in 64, 17 finer (6/07). (#6585)

Choice 1928-S Walking Liberty, Ex: Childs

1025 1928-S MS64 PCGS. Ex: Childs. Autumn-brown, forest-green, and rose-red adorn the borders of this lustrous near-Gem. The strike is usual for the issue, but the surfaces are well preserved with only a few trivial grazes above the motto. The Childs Collection is best known for its possession of the finest certified 1804 dollar, the Sultan of Muscat specimen.
Ex: Walter H. Childs Collection (Bowers and Merena, 8/99), lot 428.
From The Vanek Collection. (#6588)

1026 1929-D MS64 PCGS. The design features are uncommonly well executed, for this relatively low mintage branch mint issue. Both sides are untoned, and display pleasing satin luster. Other than a few tiny chatter marks, in the right obverse field, the surfaces are nearly pristine.
From The Vanek Collection. (#6589)

1027 1929-S MS64 PCGS. This well struck and softly lustrous example exhibits a pleasing appearance overall. Hints of ruby and gold patina appear at the margins, while the fields have a thin layer of soft silver-gray patina overall. A pleasing piece from this Great Depression year. (#6590)

1028 1929-S MS64 NGC. Essentially untoned, save for a few russet specks, with fine satin luster and typical striking definition for the issue which is somewhat weak over the centers. A couple of small milling marks are noted on each side. A conditionally elusive S-mint issue.
From The Vanek Collection. (#6590)

1029 1933-S MS64 PCGS. Opinions differ regarding the start of the so-called "short set" of Walkers. Some believe that 1933-S is the first issue of the abbreviated set, while others begin the series at 1934. This near-Gem has frosty silver luster with sharp details and splashes of light to dark gold toning. (#6591)

Conditionally Scarce Gem 1933-S Walker

1030 1933-S MS65 PCGS. The intensely lustrous surfaces of this Gem example are mostly untoned, but several russet toning streaks occur on the left side of the obverse. The striking details are excellent, and include crisp definition on Liberty's head and branch hand, as well as on the eagle's right (facing) leg. A conditionally scarce, low mintage issue at the current grade level.
From The Vanek Collection. (#6591)

1031 1934 MS66 PCGS. The main drawing card of this superior coin is its thick, swirling mint luster. Both sides are covered with pale golden-olive patina that adds even more to the visual appeal. Strongly struck on the hand of Liberty and skirt lines. (#6592)

1032 1934 MS67 PCGS. This intricately struck and lustrous Superb Gem displays lavish forest-green and khaki-gold patina. Exemplary aside from a wispy graze on the sun. As of (5/07), PCGS has certified only seven pieces finer. (#6592)

1033 1934 MS67 NGC. This solidly struck Superb Gem's swirling luster shines through rich reddish-orange, sun-gold, and steel-gray patina. The 1934 issue was the first non-commemorative half dollar issue struck at Philadelphia since 1921.
From The Vanek Collection. (#6592)

1034 1934 MS67 NGC. This remarkable example displays a full strike on the obverse, and only the eagle's right (facing) leg reveals faint weakness on the reverse (a virtually universal characteristic of business strikes). The pale silver-gray coloration over each side is enhanced by peach-gold, mint-green, and rose peripheral toning. Rarely seen in such an impressive state of preservation.
From The Vanek Collection. (#6592)

1035 1934-D MS66 PCGS. Lightly toned with highly lustrous underlying surfaces. Well struck throughout, save for Liberty's head, a few contact marks are scattered over each side. (#6593)

1036 1934-D MS66 NGC. Crisp striking details, shimmering luster, and outstanding surface preservation are all attributes of this lovely Premium Gem Walker. Much finer than the average example of this Depression-era branch mint issue. Census: 32 in 66, 1 finer (5/07).
From The Vanek Collection. (#6593)

Attractive Gem 1934-S Walking Liberty Half

1037 1934-S MS65 PCGS. A light coating of original, speckled patina covers both sides of this satiny Gem. Well struck and lustrous, the piece displays a couple of minor marks in the right obverse field, while the reverse seems blemish-free. The scarcest of the later dates in the Walking Liberty series, and in considerable demand by collectors of the "short set." (#6594)

1934-S Walking Liberty MS65

1038 1934-S MS65 PCGS. A brilliant example of this popular Depression-era issue. The strike is good for an S-mint Walker, despite some softness on Liberty's cheek and her branch hand. Thorough evaluation locates a shiny graze concealed within the wing, but the sun is pristine. (#6594)

Enticing Premium Gem 1934-S Half Dollar

1039 **1934-S MS66 PCGS.** This Depression-era San Francisco issue is the most elusive circulation-strike half dollar for the year in Mint State grades. The piece offered here has strong luster and a strong strike overall, with noteworthy detail evident on the branch hand. Subtle iridescent patina appears over the well-preserved fields. PCGS has certified just five coins finer (5/07). (#6594)

1040 **1935-D MS65 PCGS.** The Walking Liberty series is known for many issues that exhibit substandard strikes, and the 1935-D is one of the most egregious offenders, with many surviving examples displaying practically zero definition on the branch hand and Liberty's head. This luminous and satiny Gem, silver-gray with small splashes of bronze patina, exhibits separation on the thumb and cap, though this issue's other trouble spot, the eagle's right leg, shows only modest detail. Appealing and important. (#6596)

1041 **1935-D MS65 NGC.** A lovely satin finish over each side accents the pleasing alabaster surfaces of this Gem example. Typical striking softness occurs on Liberty's head and branch hand, but the piece is well preserved and free of all but the most minuscule marks. NGC has graded just six pieces finer, as of (5/07).
From The Vanek Collection. (#6596)

Tied for Finest 1935-D Half, MS66

1042 **1935-D MS66 PCGS.** This lovely Premium Gem is tied for the finest certified by either NGC or PCGS. It has frosty luster with full mint brilliance that is only interrupted by light peripheral gold and iridescent toning on each side. It is sharply detailed, except for weakness at Liberty's head and thumb, typical for this issue. Population: 77 in 66, 0 finer (6/07). (#6596)

Lovely Gem 1935-S Walking Liberty

1043 **1935-S MS65 PCGS.** Dashes of lemon and apricot toning visit the upper left reverse, and blushes of light tan grace the right obverse and the left half of the eagle. Crisply struck aside from the branch hand and upper skirt lines. Lustrous, well preserved, and encased in a green label holder. (#6597)

Important 1935-S Walking Half Dollar, MS66

1044 **1935-S MS66 NGC.** This is an important opportunity for the advanced collector, as Premium Gems only appear in auctions irregularly, and finer pieces are, for all practical purposes, nonexistent. This piece is a splendid example, with sharp details, frosty white-silver luster, and minimal surface marks. Census: 38 in 66, 3 finer (6/07). (#6597)

1045 **1936-D MS66 PCGS.** Sharply, but not quite fully struck, each side displays thick mint frost and light golden-russet toning. A nice, high-end '36-D half. (#6599)

Superb Gem 1936-D Walking Liberty

1046 **1936-D MS67 NGC.** An essentially brilliant Superb Gem whose scintillating luster sweeps the impeccably smooth surfaces. The strike is crisp, and the eye appeal is irrefutable. Despite the hardships of the Great Depression, a number of '36-D Walkers were set aside, but only a minuscule portion of these merit an MS67 grade. Census: 22 in 67, 0 finer (6/07). (#6599)

1047 **1936-S MS65 PCGS.** Well-defined and eminently pleasing with strong luster. Splashes of golden patina appear in the carefully preserved obverse fields. A great representative of this Depression-era S-mint issue.
From The Vanek Collection. (#6600)

1048 **1937 MS67 PCGS.** This flashy Superb Gem displays strong detail overall and powerful luster with a thin layer of intermittent golden patina over both sides. Despite the Walking Liberty design's popularity, it would last just another decade in its first incarnation. PCGS has graded two coins finer (5/07).
From The Vanek Collection. (#6601)

1049 **1937-D MS66 PCGS.** Satiny and boldly struck, with ivory-silver surfaces that are virtually unabraded. Reddish-brown specks are noted across the reverse. A popular, lower-mintage issue. (#6602)

1050 **1937-D MS66 PCGS.** With a mintage of under 1.7 million pieces, Denver had the lowest production of half dollars for the year. This well struck and frosty Premium Gem offers outstanding visual appeal. A few touches of peach color grace the fields, but the surfaces are untoned otherwise.
From The Vanek Collection. (#6602)

Jewel-Like 1937-D Half, MS68

1051 1937-D MS68 NGC. Breathtaking toning, above-average detail, and seemingly flawless surfaces converge on this singular representative, one of under 1.7 million pieces struck. Both sides exhibit vivid, loosely concentric bands of lemon-gold, aqua, rouge, and orange around a soft rose center. The softly shimmering, satiny surfaces display only the tiniest of flaws, even under magnification. The zones of highest relief display above-average definition for this often-weak issue, with a degree of detail evident on Liberty's branch hand.

The 1937-D ranks as one of the most challenging later Walking Liberty issues, and this Depression-era beauty in practically unheard-of condition deserves a place in the finest collection. The *only* MS68 example certified by either NGC or PCGS (5/07). (#6602)

1052 1937-S MS65 PCGS. This pretty S-mint Gem exhibits strong luster and delicate champagne and powder-blue patina over each side. Well struck with few of the tiny flaws one might expect on a coin in this grade.
From The Vanek Collection. (#6603)

1053 1937-S MS66 PCGS. Powerful luster and above-average definition characterize this pleasing Premium Gem. Subtle iridescent patina graces the shining and carefully preserved surfaces. A great example of this San Francisco issue, which had a mintage of just over 2 million pieces.
From The Vanek Collection. (#6603)

Solidly Struck 1938 Superb Gem Half Dollar

1054 1938 MS67 NGC. Shimmering luster adorns both sides of this untoned Superb Gem Walker, and a solid strike emboldens the design elements, including excellent definition in Liberty's gown lines, head, hand, and associated branches. Both faces are virtually pristine. Available through MS65, but quite elusive any finer. Census: 22 in 67, 0 finer (6/07). (#6604)

Superb Gem 1938 Walking Liberty

1055 1938 MS67 NGC. From the higher-mintage of the two issues for the year comes this lovely P-mint product, crisply struck with elegant golden patina over the shining fields. Highly appealing. Neither NGC nor PCGS has graded a numerically finer representative (5/07).
From The Vanek Collection. (#6604)

1056 1938-D MS64 PCGS. This strongly lustrous and essentially untoned piece offers strong visual appeal. Well struck with few marks on the devices, though the fields show a handful of abrasions. A lovely piece from this momentous year. (#6605)

1057 1938-D MS65 PCGS. Apple-green and golden-brown borders surround the untoned centers. Lustrous and splendidly smooth with pleasing head and skirt line definition. (#6605)

1058 1938-D MS66 PCGS. This is a lovely Premium Gem with untoned surfaces that have a pleasing satiny sheen across each side. A bit weak over the centers, as usual, but with acceptable definition overall. The key date among later Walking Liberty halves, the '38-D has an impressively low mintage, less than half of any other issue minted after 1921. (#6605)

1059 1938-D MS66 PCGS. Liberty's head is well struck, and the thumb is separated from the rest of the branch hand. The smooth and satiny surfaces are ice-blue and pale apricot. A popular low mintage issue. Housed in a green label holder.
From The Vanek Collection. (#6605)

Exceptional 1938-D Walking Liberty Half MS67

1060 **1938-D MS67 NGC.** A brilliant Superb Gem with no evidence of toning on either side. This is an exceptional example with satiny white luster created by extensive die polish in the fields on each side. Although not a full strike, the design definition is far finer than usual. This piece is tied as one of the finest examples certified by either NGC or PCGS. Census: 18 in 67, 0 finer (5/07). (#6605)

Impressive 1939 Walking Liberty Half MS68

1061 **1939 MS68 NGC.** This conditionally unimprovable example gains a tremendous amount of eye appeal from the multicolored pastel iridescence that appears over each side of the coin. The striking details are essentially full on Liberty's head and branch hand, and the eagle's right (facing) leg only shows a tiny bit of weakness. The lustrous, satiny surfaces are virtually pristine. A beautiful and technically impressive Superb Gem. Census: 16 in 68, 0 finer (5/07).
From The Vanek Collection. (#6606)

1062 **1939-S MS67 NGC.** This Superb Gem Walker lives up to its grade in every respect, even when closely inspected with the aid of a magnifier. Fully struck with a beautiful satiny sheen over each side, and untoned silver-alabaster surfaces that seem pristine. Census: 70 in 67, 0 finer (6/07). (#6608)

1063 **1940 MS67 NGC.** Tobacco-brown and green-gold patina embraces the peripheries, while the centers are only lightly toned. Crisply struck, thoroughly lustrous, and exceptionally free from marks. (#6609)

Immaculate 1940 Half Dollar, MS68

1064 **1940 MS68 PCGS.** The 1940 half is a common date with a mintage of over 9 million pieces. Indeed, PCGS and NGC have certified a few thousand examples through MS66. The population drops in MS67, and the two services have seen only about 30 MS68 coins. Dazzling luster radiates from the light tan and ice-blue surfaces of this MS68 piece. A solid strike manifests itself in sharp definition on the gown lines and Liberty's left (right facing) hand. Immaculate preservation shows on both sides. Population: 19 in 68, 0 finer (6/07). (#6609)

Colorful MS68 1940 Walking Liberty

1065 **1940 MS68 PCGS.** Effusive khaki-gold, lime-green, and salmon-pink patina embraces this highly lustrous and nearly pristine Superb Gem. Only the forefinger of the branch hand and the top of the E in LIBERTY lack needle-sharp definition. An unimprovable example worthy of the finest Registry holding. Population: 19 in 68, 0 finer (5/07). (#6609)

1066 **1940-S MS66 PCGS.** Aside from the usual lack of definition on Liberty's hand, this lustrous example has worthy detail. Blue, violet, and gold patina graces both sides. PCGS has certified just three coins finer (4/07). (#6610)

1067 **1940-S MS66 PCGS.** Lime and ice-blue tints grace this lustrous and virtually unabraded Premium Gem. The strike is above average for the mint, although the branch hand is blunt. Housed in an old green label holder. (#6610)

1068 **1940-S MS66 PCGS.** Despite evidence of weakness at the center of the obverse, this frosty Premium Gem is much sharper than usually encountered for the date. Both sides have full mint brilliance with exceptional surfaces. Fall in love with this lady. (#6610)

1069 **1940-S MS66 PCGS.** The frosty surfaces of this short-set S-mint half display a single patch of brilliance above the eagle's head. Well-defined and largely untoned with a single mark on the branch hand that precludes an even finer grade. PCGS has certified just three Superb Gems (5/07).
From The Vanek Collection. (#6610)

Conditionally Unsurpassed 1940-S Walker MS67

1070 **1940-S MS67 NGC.** Walking Liberty specialists should be thrilled by this beautiful Superb Gem, which exhibits a much higher than average degree of technical merit and eye appeal for the issue. Boldly struck, if just a tad weak on Liberty's branch hand, the piece has a lovely frosty sheen over untoned silver-white surfaces. The well preserved surfaces are nearly pristine. Census: 6 in 67, 0 finer at either service (6/07). (#6610)

1071 **1941 MS67 NGC.** Brilliant and fully struck with dazzling mint luster. An excellent high grade type coin. (#6611)

1072 **1941 MS67 ★ NGC.** A remarkable common date Walker, exhibiting dazzling, lightly toned surfaces that display pinpoint striking detail and an almost total absence of marks. NGC acknowledges the exceptional visual appeal of the piece by granting it the coveted "Star" designation. Census: 16 in 67 ★, 3 in 68 ★(6/07). (#6611)

1073 **1941-S MS65 PCGS.** This well struck short-set Gem displays pleasing luster and minimal patina. Only a handful of marks appear on the obverse devices, and the fields are clean for the grade. A lovely later San Francisco half.
From The Vanek Collection. (#6613)

1074 **1941-S MS65 NGC.** Well-defined on Liberty's cap and the peripheral elements, though the usual softness is noted on the branch hand and the eagle's forward leg. A hint of gold patina graces the strongly lustrous obverse. With a production of fewer than 8.1 million coins, the 1941-S is one of the lower-mintage short-set issues.
From The Vanek Collection. (#6613)

1075 **1942 MS67 NGC.** Surprisingly crisp detail characterizes this shining short-set Superb Gem. Powerful luster and faint wisps of champagne color only enhance the overall visual appeal. (#6614)

Beautiful 1942-S Fifty Cent, MS67

1076 **1942-S MS67 NGC.** It is easy to see why this coin was graded at MS67, on the basis of sheer eye appeal alone. Close examination of the piece also confirms its remarkable technical quality. The design elements are powerfully brought up on both sides, including relatively strong (though not quite full) definition on Liberty's hand and thumb. The lustrous surfaces have been carefully preserved, as evidenced by their lack of significant blemishes. Perhaps the most noteworthy attribute, however, is the rich, variegated cobalt-blue, golden-tan, and lavender peripheral toning that adorns the obverse and increases the visual allure. Census: 5 in 67, 0 finer (6/07). (#6617)

1077 **1943 MS67 NGC.** An amazing Superb Gem, this lovely piece has frosty luster with intense silver brilliance. It is sharply struck and presents exceptional aesthetic appeal. Only four finer examples have been certified by NGC (6/07). (#6618)

1078 **1943-D MS67 NGC.** FS-101, formerly FS-010.5. IN GOD WE TRUST is die doubled, as often seen on this issue. A lustrous and magnificently preserved Superb Gem with medium olive-gold and pearl-gray toning. The upper obverse border has a blush of sea-green and golden-brown. (#6619)

1079 **1943-S MS65 NGC.** This shining Gem of World War II vintage has delicate ice-blue and champagne patina over much of the surfaces. Well struck with a single spot of deeper color to the left of IN GOD WE TRUST.
From The Vanek Collection. (#6620)

1080 **1944-S MS66 PCGS.** The upper serif of the mintmark is repunched. Faint tan toning visits this lustrous and beautifully preserved Premium Gem. The strike is reasonable for an S-mint World War II Walker.
From The Vanek Collection. (#6623)

1081 **1944-S MS66 PCGS.** Large S. Lavishly patinated in caramel-gold, aqua-blue, and gunmetal-gray. A well preserved Premium Gem with a sharply struck head and pleasing skirt definition. The branch hand is soft, as usual for the issue. (#6623)

Finest Certified 1945-D Walking Liberty Half, MS68

1082 **1945-D MS68 NGC.** The finest example of this issue certified at either service, and as such destined to keenly interest Registry Set collectors. Even, light golden toning covers each side with strong underlying mint luster. As one would expect, there are no obvious abrasions on either side. Fully struck also, this is an immaculate type coin. (#6625)

1083 **1946 Doubled Die Reverse MS63 PCGS.** FS-801. The eagle's plumage and PLURIBUS are dramatically die doubled. Light gold patina denies full brilliance, but this is a lustrous and lightly abraded example of this elusive *Guide Book* variety. Population: 20 in 63, 39 finer (4/07).
From The Vanek Collection. (#6632)

1084 **1946-D MS67 NGC.** In the years immediately following World War II, demand for coinage fell, and fewer than 2.2 million pieces were struck for this D-mint issue. An elegant blend of sun-gold and violet patina graces the shimmering surfaces of the well struck Superb Gem offered here. Neither NGC nor PCGS has certified a numerically finer example (5/07).
From The Vanek Collection. (#6628)

1085 **1946-D MS67 NGC.** Frosty luster is accented by wisps of champagne toning over brilliant white surfaces. This sharply struck piece is tied for the finest certified by either NGC or PCGS. Census: 85 in 67, 0 finer (6/07). (#6628)

PROOF WALKING LIBERTY HALF DOLLARS

Sharp 1936 Fifty Cents, PR64

1086 1936 PR64 PCGS. Bruce Fox (1993) writes of the 1936 proof halves: "All proofs of 1936 were made with the second hub, featuring large stars and incised gown details at Liberty's neck. Finishes are brilliant and lack frosted devices." The near-Gem specimen in this lot fits the profile presented by Fox in that the design elements are razor sharp throughout, not just the gown lines. Slight field-motif contrast is noted, somewhat more on the obverse. Hints of milky color are visible under magnification, and close inspection reveals no significant marks.
From The Vanek Collection. (#6636)

Shining Gem Proof 1936 Half

1087 1936 PR65 PCGS. Though the renaissance of American proof coinage in 1936 would be brief, it was welcomed, and the program's production grew steadily until its cancellation in 1942. This crisply struck and gleaming example hails from the first-year issue, which consisted of just 3,901 specimens. Essentially untoned and free of significant distractions. (#6636)

Charming PR66 1936 Walking Liberty

1088 1936 PR66 PCGS. A satiny Premium Gem of this coveted first-year proof Walking Liberty half. Golden-russet patina hugs the borders, while the devices and fields are ivory-gray. The strike is razor-sharp, and the preservation is exceptional. Only 3,901 pieces were struck, the lowest mintage of the type. (#6636)

1089 1937 PR65 NGC. This Gem proof has slight cameo contrast, although not sufficient to receive such a designation. The surfaces are faintly toned on both sides, with deeper peripheral hues. (#6637)

1090 1937 PR65 PCGS. This stone-white Gem is unabraded and possesses a powerful strike. The devices offer hints of frost, although overall contrast is minimal. The second lowest mintage among the proof Walker dates. (#6637)

1091 1937 PR66 NGC. The 1937 is an overlooked early proof with an impressively low mintage. This deeply mirrored piece has brilliant surfaces except for a thin ring of golden over the denticles. Heavy die polishing on the obverse is evident from the attenuated rays on that side.
From The Vanek Collection. (#6637)

1092 1937 PR66 PCGS. A barely discernible veil of powder-blue and beige patina rests on impeccably preserved, bright surfaces. The motifs are crisply struck throughout on this second-year proof Walking Liberty half. (#6637)

1093 1937 PR66 PCGS. This attractive Premium Gem proof displays deeply mirrored fields that yield mild contrast with the motifs, especially when the coin is tilted slightly under a light source. Sharp delineation shows on the design features, befitting a proof strike, and the well preserved surfaces are nearly untoned, save for a wisp or two of barely discernible orange-gold color. (#6637)

1094 1937 PR67 NGC. A layer of milky reddish-tan patina decorates the obverse. The reverse only shows a hint of color. An exquisitely preserved Superb Gem proof Walker. (#6637)

1095 1937 PR67 PCGS. Though orders for proofs of 1937 represented a significant jump from the totals of the previous year, the half dollar deliveries amounted to just 5,728 specimens. This boldly defined and flashy piece displays thin, hazy olive patina in the fields. PCGS has graded just nine coins finer (5/07). (#6637)

Conditionally Unsurpassed 1937 Walker PR68

1096 **1937 PR68 NGC.** Fully struck and seemingly pristine, with some milky blue-green and antique-gold peripheral toning that surrounds creamy, untoned centers. Very appealing and with essentially unimprovable quality; a great Superb Gem example of this later Walking Liberty half dollar issue. Census: 17 in 68, 0 finer at either service (5/07).
From The Vanek Collection. (#6637)

1097 **1938 PR65 PCGS.** A boldly impressed and gleaming Gem example from the third of seven proof Walking Liberty half issues, silver-gray with light haze that is most evident on the obverse. One of just 8,152 examples struck.
From The Vanek Collection. (#6638)

1098 **1938 PR66 PCGS.** An exacting strike emboldens the design elements. In this regard, this new hub year features more incised detail in the drapery (Walter Breen, 1977; Bruce Fox, 1993). Lightly frosted central devices exhibit mild contrast with highly reflective fields, and both sides are free of color and mentionable marks. (#6638)

1099 **1938 PR67 PCGS.** This Superb Gem proof has notable visual appeal with fully brilliant silver surfaces on each side. Strongly mirrored with a surprising degree of contrast, though not enough for a Cameo designation. PCGS has certified just 10 pieces finer (5/07). (#6638)

1100 **1939 PR66 PCGS.** This needle-sharp Premium Gem appears fully brilliant at first glance, but delicate russet freckles cling to the reverse periphery. The immaculate fields are impressively mirrored, and the devices exhibit noticeable frost. (#6639)

1101 **1939 PR66 PCGS.** The otherwise brilliant surfaces show a slight degree of haze in the right obverse field. The depth of mirrored reflectivity is such that the light frost on the devices provides a modest cameo effect on both sides.
From The Vanek Collection. (#6639)

1102 **1939 PR66 NGC.** Pale, hazy patina is seen over each side, but it does not impair the strong flash from the deeply mirrored fields. An immaculate type coin.
From The Vanek Collection. (#6639)

1103 **1939 PR66 PCGS.** The untoned obverse yields to a few traces of speckled golden-orange color visible under magnification on the reverse. Impressively struck, and nearly pristine surfaces. From a mintage of 8,808 proofs. (#6639)

1104 **1939 PR67 NGC.** Fully struck and immaculately preserved, this brilliant proof exhibits deeply reflective, inky-black fields and slightly frosted devices that produce a mild cameo-like effect on both sides. (#6639)

1105 **1939 PR67 NGC.** A lightly toned and pinpoint-sharp Superb Gem. The mintage is lower than the three proof issues from the 1940s. Housed in a prior generation holder. (#6639)

1106 **1939 PR67 PCGS.** A brilliant and exquisitely struck Superb Gem with gorgeous surfaces. This lovely, carefully preserved specimen hails from the fourth of seven proof Walking Liberty issues, the last to have a mintage under 10,000 pieces. (#6639)

Attractive 1939 Half Dollar, PR68

1107 **1939 PR68 NGC.** 1939 proof half dollars, with a mintage of 8,808 pieces, are quite plentiful, right through the PR67 level. The certified population drops precipitously in PR68. A thin coat of pastel multicolored toning bathes both sides of this sharply impressed specimen. Close inspection reveals no marks worthy of note. Census: 70 in 68, 1 finer (5/07). (#6639)

1108 **1940 PR65 PCGS.** Delicate gold-gray patina graces the shining surfaces of this boldly impressed Gem, an eminently pleasing piece. Though many Walking Liberty pieces are ill-defined on the branch hand, many proofs show the area in detail, allowing for an otherwise seldom-available insight into the beauty of the design.
From The Vanek Collection. (#6640)

1109 **1940 PR66 NGC.** The design elements exhibit razor-sharp definition, and both sides of the coin are pristine. The highly reflective fields show deep pools of watery reflectivity, and slight frosting on the silver-gray devices. (#6640)

1110 **1940 PR66 NGC.** Well struck with watery fields and only slight cloudiness to keep them from being fully reflective. A few specks of apricot patina are noted on each side. Free of hairlines and contact marks. (#6640)

1111 **1940 PR66 PCGS.** Brilliant surfaces are impeccably preserved on both sides, and exhibit exceptionally well struck design elements. Walter Breen (1977) noted that this issue underwent "excessive lapping or polishing of the dies." This resulted in a weak AW monogram, a partially open D in GOD, and a short tail in the R of TRUST, all of which characterize the Premium Gem in this lot. (#6640)

1112 **1940 PR66 PCGS.** In their short time of production, the brilliant proofs of 1936-1942 only increased in popularity, and in 1940, all denominations had five-figure mintages. This moderately reflective silver-gray Gem offers crisp detail and strong visual appeal. The surfaces have an uncommonly clean appearance. (#6640)

1113 **1940 PR67 PCGS.** Deeply mirrored fields on each side, with a little imagination one can see a bit of contrast, especially on the reverse. Slightly speckled golden patina is seen on both obverse and reverse. An impressive proof striking. (#6640)

1114 **1940 PR67 PCGS.** This crisply struck and virtually untoned Superb Gem has a deeply reflective obverse and seemingly bottomless mirrors on the reverse. A well-preserved specimen and a wonderful representative of this all-too-short proof series. (#6640)

1115 **1940 PR67 PCGS.** The surfaces sparkle with intense brilliance and the fields are deeply reflective on each side. A Superb and essentially perfect proof Walking Liberty half. (#6640)

1116 **1941 PR66 PCGS.** The AW monogram is present. An essentially brilliant and razor-sharp Premium Gem. The dies are moderately rotated, and an interesting lintmark (as made) resides near the monogram. (#6641)

1117 **1941 PR66 PCGS.** A powerful strike brings out excellent delineation in the design elements, and bright surfaces exhibit just the slightest hint of incipient gold patina. Walter Breen (1977) notes that many specimens lack the "AW" monogram (this includes the present example). He states: "... they are all from the same working die which has been much repolished or lapped, probably to obliterate clash marks. An earlier state shows weak AW." Housed in a green-label holder. (#6641)

1118 **1941 PR67 PCGS.** No AW. Impressively struck on all of the devices and letters, with watery fields and milky beige peripheral patina on both sides. A carefully preserved and beautifully pristine Superb Gem, housed in an old green label holder. (#6641)

1119 **1942 PR66 PCGS.** Crisply struck with powerful reflectivity and just a faint touch of haze at the margins. Practically distraction-free to the unaided eye, as expected of the grade. A lovely example from the final year of issue. (#6642)

1120 **1942 PR66 PCGS.** Boldly impressed with strong reflectivity and a hint of milky patina in the fields. A delightful brilliant proof from the last of seven such issues for the Walking Liberty half dollar series. (#6642)

1121 **1942 PR66 PCGS.** An excellent strike, as befits a Premium Gem proof. Each side displays light milky color, with some light multicolored patina on the reverse. Well preserved throughout. (#6642)

1122 **1942 PR66 NGC.** Sharply struck and crisply detailed, as expected for a proof specimen. Both sides exhibit a thin layer of milky patina, which is not unattractive. An excellent Premium Gem example of the final proof issue in the Walking Liberty half dollar series. (#6642)

1123 **1942 PR66 PCGS.** Sharply struck with strong reflectivity and a touch of cream-colored patina on either side of the figure of Liberty. The fields are exceptionally clean overall, though a single tiny point of contact appears between the rays of the sun. (#6642)

1124 **1942 PR67 NGC.** The wartime exigencies that banished nickel from the nickels and brought steel to the cents closed the door on proof coinage as well, and the specimens from 1942 would be the last for several series. This gleaming and sharply struck Superb Gem has cloud-gray and gold patina with a crescent of plum and rose patina at the left obverse and reverse.
From The Vanek Collection. (#6642)

1125 **1942 PR67 PCGS.** This appealing Superb Gem proof is essentially untoned with stellar luster and lovely silver-blue surfaces. A decisively struck example from the final proof Walking Liberty half dollar issue. (#6642)

1126 **1942 PR67 PCGS.** Brilliant surfaces exhibit impressively struck design features, and close examination reveals both faces to be devoid of significant marks. All in all, a splendid Superb Gem proof. Bruce Fox, in his *Complete Guide to Walking Liberty Half Dollars*, writes of the 1942 half dollar: "I believe all nice proof issues are presently undervalued." (#6642)

Amazing PR68 1942 Walking Liberty Half

1127 **1942 PR68 NGC.** Brilliant on each side. The surfaces are virtually unblemished, as one would expect from the grade. The fields also show illimitable depth of reflectivity. While NGC lists four pieces in PR69, it is hard to imagine how a coin could have more visual appeal than this amazing proof. (#6642)

FRANKLIN HALF DOLLARS

Nearly Complete Set of Mint State Franklin Halves, Choice to Gem

1128 **Set of 35 Business Strike Franklin Halves MS64 to MS65 NGC.** This extensive set of circulation-strike Franklin half dollars, complete save for a second 1954 example where the 1954-D should be, can be enjoyed as is or used as the base for an even finer collection. The set includes: **1948 MS65**, softly lustrous beneath gold-rose patina and a splash of gray; **1948-D MS65**, gold-gray and violet color with deeper russet color on the reverse; **1949 MS65**, dappled gunmetal and cream-gray patina; **1949-D MS64**, champagne-toned with slate-gray at the reverse margins; **1949-S MS65**, vivid orange and blue-violet color overall; **1950 MS65**, subtle iridescent patina with sage color at the right periphery on both sides; **1950-D MS64**, soft shell-pink and gold toning over the fields; **1951 MS65**, dappled violet, tan, and silver-gray patina; **1951-D MS65**, mustard-gold toning overall with small areas of silver-gray; **1951-S MS65**, satiny with tiny, scattered spots of claret patina; **1952 MS65**, interlaced orange and gray patina on the obverse with a largely cloud-gray reverse; **1952-D MS65**, soft mustard-gold patina over softly lustrous surfaces; **1952-S MS65**, gold, pink, and gray color with deeper toning at the rims; **1953 MS65**, rich orange color at the peripheries with lighter silver-gray centers; **1953-D MS65**, dappled reddish-orange patina overall with concentrated color at the left obverse; **1953-S MS65**, amber-olive obverse peripheral toning with a brilliant center and reverse; **1954 MS65**, scattered gold-orange color on the obverse that covers most of the reverse; **1954 MS65**, splashes of gold patina in the centers with blue-gray color near the rims; **1954-S MS65**, elegant peach and champagne patina over both sides; **1955 MS65**, muted orange toning on the obverse with blue-gray elements on the reverse; **1956 MS65**, frosty with dots of milky patina over parts of each side; **1957 MS65**, dusky gray overall with zones of russet at the upper obverse and blue-gray on the reverse; **1957-D MS65**, soft denim-blue color with a hint of peach below the portrait; **1958 MS65**, orange and mustard colors around soft silver-gray centers; **1958-D MS65**, reddish-orange and silver-gray on the obverse with areas of claret and blue on each side; **1959 MS65**, dappled green-gold and brilliance on the obverse with more even coloration on the reverse; **1959-D MS65**, softly lustrous with a touch of champagne patina; **1960 MS65**, mostly brilliant with a few small spots of reddish patina; **1960-D MS64**, appealing for the grade with gold, peach, and gray patina over luminous surfaces; **1961 MS65**, strongly lustrous with subtle golden iridescence and traces of deeper patina at the rims; **1961-D MS65**, delicate pastel-yellow toning overall with orange color at the margins; **1962 MS65**, strongly lustrous beneath an appealing blend of yellow-gold and green-gray toning; **1962-D MS65**, soft peach and gold patina over much of each side; **1963 MS65**, flashy with thin streaks of intermittent slate-gray color; and an **1963-D MS65**, luminous beneath hazy cream-colored patina with a touch of faint green color. (Total: 35 coins)

1129 **1949-S MS65 Full Bell Lines Prooflike NGC.** A fascinating Gem that displays crisp overall detail and surfaces that exhibit distinct reflectivity. Speckles of blue-violet patina appear at the margins, and the fields exhibit strong die polishing lines visible to the unaided eye. Formerly assigned the same grade by ANACS; insert and inner holder accompany lot. (#86655)

Splendid 1950 Half Dollar, MS67 Full Bell Lines

1130 **1950 MS67 Full Bell Lines PCGS.** As PCGS/NGC population/census data show, the 1950 Franklin half is difficult to locate with Full Bell Lines in the lofty grade of MS67; a total of five such specimens have been certified to date, and none finer. The example in this lot displays radiantly lustrous surfaces with whispers of delicate golden-brown and yellow-green patina that is most obvious at the rim areas. A sharp, uniform strike leaves not only incised detail on the bell lines, but the bell lettering is legible as well. Close examination with a glass reveals impeccably preserved surfaces. A couple of trivial marks to the right of the ear, and another in the lower hair, are mentioned solely for identification purposes. Population: 3 in 67 Full Bell Lines, 0 finer (5/07). (#86656)

Patinated MS66 Full Bell Lines 1950-D Half

1131 **1950-D MS66 Full Bell Lines PCGS.** Beautifully toned olive-green, apricot, and slate. Cartwheel luster blasts through the iridescent patina. The strike is penetrating, and aside from minor marks near the bell crack, the surfaces are essentially pristine. (#86657)

1132 **1952 MS66 Full Bell Lines PCGS.** This sharply struck Premium Gem has attractive lilac, gold, and sea-green toning on both sides. Population: 210 in 66, 6 finer (6/07). (#86661)

1133 **1952-S MS65 Full Bell Lines PCGS.** A pleasing S-mint piece with noteworthy detail overall, particularly on the all-important bell. The satiny obverse displays largely silver-gray color with traces of rose-gold at the margins, while the reverse has rich russet patina with a small area of dappled cloud-gray in the center. PCGS has graded only 25 finer Full Bell Lines pieces (4/07). (#86663)

1134 **1954 MS66 Full Bell Lines PCGS.** Dappled forest-green, gold, and ruby patina graces both sides of this strongly lustrous piece. Well-defined and carefully preserved for this mid-date issue, though a mark at the left lip of the bell precludes a Superb Gem designation. Tied for the finest Full Bell Lines example graded by either NGC or PCGS (5/07). (#86667)

PROOF FRANKLIN HALF DOLLARS

Conditionally Scarce 1952 Franklin Half PR67 Cameo

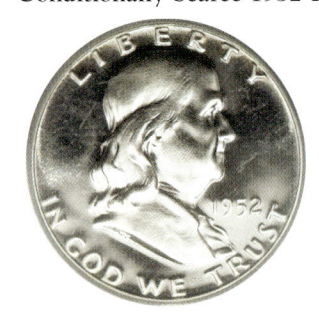

1135 **1952 PR67 Cameo PCGS.** Fully struck with jet-black fields, nicely frosted devices, and intense cameo contrast on both sides. Distraction-free with faint die lines on the central devices. A scarce early proof issue in the Franklin half dollar series. Population: 22 in 67 Cameo, 1 finer (4/07). (#86693)

1136 **1956 Type One PR67 Cameo PCGS.** The rarer Type One reverse displays four feather tips to the left of the eagle's perch, while the far more common Type Two coin has better relief and shows three feather tips. White-on-black surfaces show when the coin is viewed from a direct angle. Untoned and impeccably preserved. Population: 34 in 67 Cameo, 20 finer (4/07). (#86686)

1137 **1956 Type Two PR69 Ultra Cameo NGC.** This gleaming, practically perfect representative has deeply reflective surfaces that are practically devoid of toning. The devices have thick frost overall, though two patches of brilliance are present, one at Franklin's temple and the other on his lower curls. Virtually all of the proofs coined in 1956 are of the Type Two variety, which features a redefined eagle, among other features. Census: 8 in 69 Ultra Cameo, 0 finer (5/07). (#96697)

1138 **1961 PR68 Deep Cameo PCGS.** Visually unimprovable, the 1961 makes a perfect type coin. It is a well-produced later date in the Franklin series, and high grade cameo coins are among the more available dates in the series. Still, few are known in this grade. Brilliant throughout, each side shows stark white-on-black cameo contrast with illimitable depth of mirrored reflectivity in the fields. Population: 73 in 68, 0 finer (6/07). (#96702)

EARLY DOLLARS

Fine 15 Details 1795 B-5 Flowing Hair Dollar

1139 **1795 Flowing Hair, Three Leaves—Repaired, Cleaned—ANACS. Fine 15 Details.** B-5, BB-27, R.1. Bowers-Borckardt Die State II. Orange-gold and sea-green dominate the borders of this thickly hairlined Flowing Hair type coin. The right obverse field likely conceals a well-done repair. Collector demand for early silver type coins has risen substantially over the past ten years. (#6852)

Better B-7 1795 Flowing Hair Dollar VF30

1140 **1795 Flowing Hair, Three Leaves VF30 PCGS.** B-7, BB-18, R.3. Bowers-Borckardt Die State I. A scarce variety relative to B-5, the usual Three Leaves marriage. Liberty's hair and the eagle's plumage are well defined for the grade, and retain glimpses of luster. A few thin marks are noted on the portrait. Housed in an old green label holder. (#6852)

Choice VF 1795 Flowing Hair Dollar, B-5

1141 **1795 Flowing Hair, Three Leaves VF35 NGC.** B-5, BB-27, R.1. Die State III. The bar behind the upper trailing hair curl waves a red flag to specialists for prompt attribution. Light dove-gray and olive hues embrace this nicely detailed example. A few faint slide marks are detected near Liberty's jaw, and the upper left reverse rim has inconsequential blemishes, but the general appearance is surprisingly unmarked for the grade. Struck for only two years, the 1795 Flowing Hair is requisite to early silver type sets, since the 1794 exceeds the budgets of most collectors. (#6852)

Choice XF 1795 Flowing Hair Dollar, B-5

1142 **1795 Flowing Hair, Three Leaves XF45 PCGS.** B-5, BB-27, R.1. Bowers-Borckardt Die State II. Navy-blue, plum-red, and orange-gold toning surrounds the cream-gray obverse field and portrait. The reverse field is caramel-gold, while the border is navy-blue and cherry-red. This familiar variety is promptly identified by the thin "bar" behind the upper curl. The fields are relatively smooth, although the Flowing Hair bust has a few thin marks, including a horizontal abrasion located beneath the ear. Since Flowing Hair dollars were struck for only two years during George Washington's second term, survivors with some remaining luster are under formidable collector demand. (#6852)

Desirable AU B-5, BB-27 1795 Flowing Hair Dollar

1143 1795 Flowing Hair, Three Leaves AU50 NGC. B-5, BB-27, R.1. Bowers-Borckardt Die State II with a crack from left stem end to the rim. Early dollar specialists know to look for a thin raised line or "bar" behind the upper neck curl of Liberty. This bar is diagnostic for Bolender-5, the most available among the Flowing Hair varieties. Survivors in all grades are coveted for their status as the first silver dollar type coin. Most B-5 dollars are in XF or lower grades, but the present AU representative has plentiful glowing luster about the design elements, and a few feathers on the eagle's neck and back leg are visible. The generally smooth dove-gray surfaces exhibit delicate rose and lime tints once rotated beneath a light. (#6852)

Important AU53 1795 Flowing Hair Dollar, B-5

1144 1795 Flowing Hair, Three Leaves AU53 NGC. B-5, BB-27, R.1. Bowers-Borckardt Die State III. A splendidly detailed representative that appears deep steel-gray when viewed directly, but transforms into golden-brown, olive, and cobalt-blue once rotated beneath a light. The strike is precise aside from moderate softness at the centers. Faint mint-made adjustment marks are noted along the obverse denticles, and a group of more visible adjustment marks are present near Liberty's ear. For pedigree purposes, there are thin marks close to star 8 and above the bust tip. The reverse is remarkably void of abrasions. A desirable example of this initial and briefly produced large silver type. (#6852)

AU Details 1795 Flowing Hair Dollar
B-7, BB-18, Mint-Made Plug

1145 **1795 Flowing Hair, Silver Plug—Improperly Cleaned—NCS. AU Details.** B-7, BB-18, R.3. Bowers-Borckardt Die State I with two small die flaws beneath the left ribbon end. Mint-made silver plugs are known on several varieties of Flowing Hair dollars. A small central hole was made in the planchet, and the plug added, presumably to bring the weight of the planchet within standards. The strike effaced most evidence of the plug, identifiable as a small oval gray area on the eagle's breast and a slightly glossy corresponding area beneath Liberty's ear.

This is a cream-gray and tan-gold example that has substantial definition within the eagle's plumage. The eagle's breast has moderate wear, as do the curls near Liberty's ear. Subdued by a subtle cleaning, but there are no mentionable marks, and luster glints from design recesses. (#6854)

XF 1795 Centered B-15 Draped Bust Dollar

1146 **1795 Draped Bust, Centered XF40 PCGS.** B-15, BB-52, R.2. Bowers-Borckardt Die State III with a triangular die break in Liberty's hair near the ribbon. The surfaces have pale heather color at the centers, attractively framed by deeper steel toning at the borders. A generally smooth Draped Bust dollar with a couple of thin marks on each side of the jaw and a small spot near the upper right portion of the wreath. Housed in an old green label holder. (#6858)

AU Centered Bust 1795 Draped Dollar, B-15

1147 **1795 Draped Bust, Centered AU50 NGC.** B-15, BB-52, R.2. Bowers-Borckardt Die State IV, noted for its "jagged, vertically oriented lump" within Liberty's hair near the ribbon. B-14 and B-15 are the only two 1795 Draped Bust die varieties, and are historically significant as the first dies of the design type, which dominated the silver and copper denominations until John Reich's 1807 arrival. B-14 and B-15 receive separate entries in the *Guide Book* because the obverse device punch for the B-14 was entered too far to the left. The Bust device was correctly centered for B-15, the scarcer of the two marriages.

This partly lustrous example has medium golden-brown and aqua toning. The eagle retains some breast feathers, and the stars have distinctive centers. The obverse has a couple of insignificant adjustment marks, as made, and moderate marks are noted on the back of the neck and above the D in UNITED. (6858)

AU Details B-14 1795 Draped Bust Dollar

1148 1795 Draped Bust, Off Center—Scratched—ANACS. AU50 Details. B-14, BB-51, R.2. Deep dove-gray toning cannot conceal the glowing luster that outlines design elements. A richly detailed first-year Draped Bust dollar with substantial feather definition on the eagle's breast. A thin back-and-forth scratch along the lower reverse border is sufficiently distant from the focal points that some observers may miss it altogether. A pair of faint clashmarks are noted above the wreath, which contradicts Bowers' comment in his 1993 Silver Dollar Encyclopedia, "Die State I. Perfect dies. The only state known." (#96858)

1149 1796 Small Date, Large Letters—Obverse Graffiti—NCS. Fine Details. B-4, BB-61, R.3. Bowers-Borckardt Die State I. This slate-gray and sky-blue piece has an intersection trio of pinscratches on the right obverse field, and a horizontal pinscratch on the neck. The obverse has a minor ding at 2 o'clock, and the piece shows evidence of a cleaning. Still a nicely detailed example of this scarce date. (#6860)

First Philadelphia Mint building, circa 1903

Elusive Choice XF B-4 1796 Dollar

1150 1796 Small Date, Large Letters XF45 PCGS. B-4, BB-61, R.3. Bowers-Borckardt Die State I with a largely intact forehead curl. Golden-brown, cobalt-blue, and plum-mauve embrace this attractively defined Small Eagle dollar. The eagle's belly and legs display wear, but luster emerges from Liberty's hair, the wreath, and the stars and letters. The reverse is surprisingly devoid of abrasions, and the obverse field has only a limited number of small marks. According to Bowers in his 1993 Silver Dollar Encyclopedia, only 22 to 42 examples of the BB-61 variety are in AU50 and higher grades. Population: 31 in 45, 15 finer (6/07). (#6860)

XF45 Sharpness B-5 1796 Dollar

1151 **1796 Large Date, Small Letters—Cleaned—ANACS. XF45 Details.** B-5, BB-65, R.2. The die lump from the I in AMERICA is relatively large, but has yet to reach the letter C. This lilac, olive-green, and steel-blue example is slightly glossy, and has a trace of translucent residue on the reverse at 9:30. Only two marks are remotely worthy of mention, an obverse rim nick at 8 o'clock and a faint, thin mark on the reverse at 5 o'clock. A collectible example of the eagerly pursued Draped Bust, Small Eagle type. (#6861)

Popular XF 1797 9x7 Stars Dollar, B-1

1152 **1797 9x7 Stars, Large Letters XF40 PCGS.** B-1, BB-73, R.3. Bowers-Borckardt Die State IV to V. Warm gunmetal gray toning with delicate blue, violet, and golden-brown iridescent highlights. Both the obverse and reverse show excellent centering and full dentilation. U.S. coins with 16 obverse stars were produced for only a brief period of time at the Mint. The 16th star commemorates the admission of Tennessee as the 16th state to the Union. In 1798, the Mint returned to its custom of using only 13 obverse stars, perhaps because it was realized that as new states were added to the Union, the plethora of new stars would start to crowd out the other design elements. Excellent quality for the grade.
Ex: Thomas Wolfe Collection, Part One (Heritage, 9/05), lot 3655, which realized $8,050. (#6863)

Choice XF 10x6 Stars B-3 1797 Dollar

1153 **1797 10x6 Stars XF45 PCGS.** B-3, BB-71, R.2. Bowers-Borckardt Die State III with lapped right edges on the palm branch leaves. Deep forest-green, powder-blue, and gunmetal-gray toning drapes this relatively unabraded early dollar. Liberty's cheek and shoulder display wear, but the eagle possesses partial breast feathers. (#6865)

Pleasing 1797 10x6 Stars, Large Letters Dollar, XF45, B-3, BB-71

1154 **1797 10x6 Stars, Large Letters XF45 NGC.** B-3, BB-71, R.2. The is the only variety of the three known for the 1797 date that has 10 stars before LIBERTY and six after. Die State III, obverse and reverse die relapped. On obverse, highest wave of hair is incomplete, and stars 9 and 10 have the innermost points shortened; on the reverse, the right edges of some of the palm leaves are removed. Medium gray patination is joined by whispers of cobalt-blue, lavender, and gold at the peripheries. The design elements exhibit sharp detail, and are well centered on the planchet. A few light adjustment marks are noted in the lower left reverse quadrant, as are some small reverse rim bruises. Overall, a pleasing Choice XF early dollar. (#6865)

1155 **1798 Small Eagle, 15 Stars Good 6 PCGS.** B-2, BB-81, R.3. Bowers-Borckardt Die State II. All obverse design elements are clearly outlined, as is most of the wreath. The lower half of the eagle is indistinct. Deep steel-gray fields with lighter devices. The central reverse displays wispy marks. (#6868)

1156 **1798 Large Eagle—Cleaned—ANACS. VF20 Details.** B-27, BB-113, R.2. Bowers-Borckardt Die State II. Most letters in E PLURIBUS UNUM are at least partly legible. Two-toned slate-gray and lavender-brown. The obverse fields are cloudy, and the reverse has areas of minor granularity. The obverse rim has a small nick at 10 o'clock. (#6873)

1798 Large Eagle Dollar VF30, B-24

1157 **1798 Large Eagle VF30 NGC.** B-24, BB-124, R.2. Die State III. The first two stars at lower left point to the center of the denticles, and the reverse shows the well-known Blundered Stars pattern, in which the stars are placed too high. This is a well struck, honestly worn example showing light-gray to violet coloration and just a few small blemishes. An attractive example for the grade. (#6873)

B-28 1798 Heraldic Eagle Dollar AU50

1158 **1798 Large Eagle AU50 NGC.** B-28, BB-118, R.3. Bowers-Borckardt Die State I with a "perfect" reverse die. The reverse is misaligned toward 3 o'clock, while the obverse is well centered. Pockets of bright luster illuminate the wings and Liberty's hair. The borders are also partly lustrous. The light chestnut-gray toning is generally consistent, but deepens slightly on Liberty's cheek. A few of the stars above the eagle's head are soft, and thin obverse marks are noted beneath the ear, to the right of the 8, and beneath the bust truncation. (#6873)

XF B-6 1798 Five Stripes Dollar

1159 **1798 Large Eagle, Five Stripes, 10 Arrows XF40 PCGS.** B-6, BB-96, R.3. Bowers-Borckardt Die State IV. A die crack is present above the I in AMERICA, but the two sticks without arrowheads remain visible. This lightly toned example has occasional glimpses of tan toning on the devices. Luster emerges from the eagle's wings and the reverse legends. The strike is slightly soft near the eagle's head, but there are no remotely mentionable marks.
From The Vanek Collection. (#6874)

Choice XF B-23 1798 Wide Date Dollar

1160 **1798 Large Eagle, Wide Date XF45 NGC.** B-23, BB-105, R.3. Bowers-Borckardt Die State III with a lapped obverse die affecting the first two stars and the curl beneath the E in LIBERTY. Moderate walnut-brown toning cedes to gunmetal-gray on the cheek. Glints of luster brighten protected areas of the design, and the strike is bold on the shield and E PLURIBUS UNUM. Careful inspection cannot locate any remotely mentionable marks. (#6877)

1161 **1799 7x6 Stars VG8 PCGS.** B-9, BB-161, R.1. Bowers-Borckardt Die State II-III. The "Apostrophe" variety with a die break after the second S in STATES. The pearl-gray centers are framed by ebony-gray. Worn near the eagle's head, although all reverse stars are at least faintly visible. (#6878)

Bold VF 1799 7x6 Stars Dollar, B-10

1162 **1799 7x6 Stars VF35 PCGS.** B-10, BB-163, R.2. Bowers-Borckardt Die State IV, which Bowers called a "rare die state," adding, "The die could not have survived long beyond this point." Primarily pearl-gray, with glimpses of deeper steel-gray near the rims. Free from mentionable marks, and a charming representative of the terminal die state. (#6878)

B-8 1799 7x6 Stars Dollar XF40

1163 **1799 7x6 Stars XF40 ICG.** B-8, BB-165, R.3. Bowers-Borckardt Die State I. The right base and upright of the N in UNITED is repunched on this distinctive variety. Powder-blue and pearl-gray with glimpses of tan-gold luster in protected areas. The slightly glossy surfaces are generally smooth aside from a few faint vertical marks on the field near the profile. (#6878)

Choice XF Details 1799 Dollar, B-8

1164 **1799 7x6 Stars—Cleaned—ANACS. XF45 Details.** B-8, BB-165, R.3. Bowers-Borckardt Die State I-II. Light gold toning visits this predominantly ice-blue 1799 dollar. Cloudy from faint hairlines, but delightfully detailed, particularly on the wings and hair. E PLURIBUS UNUM is clear, and the shield lines are bold. The rims are problem-free, although a cluster of tiny marks is noted on each side of Liberty's jaw. (#6878)

Lightly Toned 1799 7x6 Stars
Choice AU Dollar, B-11, BB-161

1165 **1799 7x6 Stars AU55 NGC.** B-11, BB-161, R.3. A "No Berries" variety, and further distinguished by a broken U in UNITED and a die crack past the D in UNITED. On the obverse, the base of the I in LIBERTY is slightly below the adjacent B. While the obverse die had been relapped (David Bowers, 1993), heavy clash marks ("waves" from the reverse clouds) eventually reappeared, and are visible on the current example. Delicate cobalt-blue, golden-brown, and lavender patination visits bright surfaces that exhibit well defined design features. Vertical adjustment marks crossing Liberty's portrait co-exist with some unobtrusive circulation marks. (#6878)

1166 **1799 Irregular Date, 15 Stars Reverse—Corroded, Cleaned—ANACS. Fine 12 Details.** B-4, BB-153, R.4. Bowers-Borckardt Die State II. A slate-gray silver dollar with several dashes of charcoal-gray, mostly near the borders. The upper obverse has two faintly granular streaks. Softly struck near the eagle's head, but there are no distracting marks. (#6879)

Distinctive 1799 B-23 Dollar, 8x5 Stars Obverse

1167 **1799 8x5 Stars—Cleaned—ANACS. VF30 Details.** B-23, BB-159, R.4. This is an important and unusual *Guide Book* variety with the obverse stars arranged eight left and five right. It is the only early dollar variety with such a distinctive layout. The surfaces have pewter-gray color with lighter devices and deeper borders. (#6881)

Choice AU 1799/8 15 Stars Reverse Dollar

1168 **1799/8 15 Stars Reverse AU55 NGC.** B-3, BB-141, R.3. Bowers-Borckardt Die State III. The well known blundered die variety with 15 reverse stars. The engraver tried to hide his mistake by greatly enlarging the first and final clouds, yet two telltale points of an errant star emerge from each base of the oversized clouds. Pale aqua-blue luster dominates all but the open fields of this lightly toned overdate dollar. A hint of wear is present on Liberty's cheek and shoulder, and on the eagle's head and breast. Refreshingly unabraded, and a desirable example of this distinctive variety. (#6883)

XF Details 1799/8 13 Stars Reverse Dollar

1169 **1799/8 13 Stars Reverse—Scratched, Cleaned—ANACS. XF40 Details.** B-2, BB-143, R.4. Bowers-Borckardt Die State II. Dusky gunmetal-gray and cobalt-blue toning envelops this nicely defined overdate Bust dollar. A couple of relatively inconspicuous pinscratches near the arrowheads and the M in UNUM appear unworthy of the "Scratched" designation. The reverse field above the eagle is somewhat cloudy, and the obverse is minutely granular. (#6884)

Choice XF 1800 Silver Dollar, B-16

1170 **1800 XF45 ANACS.** B-16, BB-187, R.2. A Choice XF example of this relatively common variety. The surfaces are toned in a combination of olive, golden-brown, and medium-gray. The strike is typically weak, especially on the reverse, and the coin shows mostly minor handling marks, although a moderate abrasion is noted from the obverse rim out to between stars 4 and 5. This is a late die state, with an arcing die crack up through the last 0 of 1800, just touching Liberty's chin and extending to the tenth star. (#6887)

XF45 Details 1800 Dollar
Difficult B-5, BB-189 Variety

1171 **1800—Graffiti, Cleaned—ANACS. XF45 Details.** B-5, BB-189, R.5. Bowers-Borckardt Die State I. Die lump above right foot of the R in LIBERTY. The letter D is crudely pinscratched onto the left obverse field beneath the ribbon. Only mildly cleaned, and nicely toned with golden-brown and forest-green peripheral shades. Luster fills design recesses. A small nick is noted on the reverse rim at 4 o'clock. (#6887)

Choice AU 1800 "B-18a" Silver Dollar

1172 **1800 AU55 NGC.** B-13, 18, BB-193, R.4. Die State IV, a.k.a. B-18a. Rich grayish-gold and heather patina cover both sides of this splendid dollar. The surfaces are smooth and lustrous with only trivial marks on either side. Due to the dramatic difference in appearance, Bolender (who copied Haseltine) assigned different variety numbers to the early and late die states of this variety. Early die states, without clash marks on either side, were known as B-13, while those with moderate to heavy clash marks and other die failures were known as B-18. Today, we recognize these as die states of a single obverse and reverse combination.
From The Vanek Collection. (#6887)

1800 Wide Date, Low 8 Dollar AU53

1173 **1800 Wide Date, Low 8 AU53 PCGS.** B-10, BB-190, R.3. Bowers-Borckardt Die State VI with a crack between the arrows and left (facing) wing, and two parallel cracks through the ME in AMERICA. A pearl-gray example that has bright luster across the eagle's wingtips and other peripheral elements. A small edge defect is noted at 11 o'clock on the reverse, and faint thin marks are present beneath UNUM. (#6888)

AU 1800 12 Arrows Dollar, B-17

1174 **1800 12 Arrows AU50 NGC.** B-17, BB-196, R.1. Bowers-Borckardt Die State IV, which features a die crack from obverse star 6 to the ribbon. B-17 has only 12 arrows, a die engraving error that causes the variety to receive a separate *Guide Book* listing. Gold, aquamarine, and rose toning frames the medium gray centers. Luster glimmers from the devices and peripheries. Inconspicuous marks are present on the field near the eagle's head, but the overall appearance is unblemished. (#6890)

10 Arrows B-15 1800 Dollar VF25

1175 **1800 10 Arrows VF25 PCGS.** B-15, BB-195, R.3. The Bowers silver dollar encyclopedia lists only a single "perfect dies" state, but the present lot displays clashmarks from the bust truncation near OF, as does the Bowers plate coin for the variety. This early dollar is surprisingly sharp for the VF25 grade, particularly on the eagle's plumage and on E PLURIBUS UNUM, which is nearly fully visible. Thin marks are noted above the bust tip and near the eighth cloud. (#6891)

1176 **1801—Repaired, Improperly Cleaned—NCS. VF Details.** B-2, BB-212, R.3. Bowers-Borckardt Die State II with double "collar" clashmark above the cleavage. The obverse field is extensively smoothed, and the surfaces are whizzed, hairlined, and glossy. Nonetheless, this pale green-gold piece is sharply defined, particularly on the heraldic eagle. (#6893)

XF 1801 Dollar, B-3, BB-213

1177 **1801 XF40 ANACS.** B-3, BB-213, R.3. Bowers-Borckardt Die State III. Deep sea-green and rose-red toning envelops this moderately abraded XF Draped Bust dollar. Liberty's cheek and drapery exhibit wear, but rotation beneath a light confirms traces of luster within the devices and legends. (#6893)

XF45 Details 1801 Dollar, B-4

1178 **1801—Cleaned—ANACS. XF45 Details.** B-4, BB-214, R.4. Technically Die State III, although the die crack mentioned in Die State II is absent. An evenly struck and partly lustrous but dipped and hairlined example. Slightly granular on the hair above the ribbon, as made. The reverse rim has a few tiny nicks, and the portrait has a couple of thin marks. A bold representative of this popular, early, and large silver type. (#6893)

1179 **1802 Narrow Date—Cleaned—ANACS. VF20 Details.** B-6, BB-241, R.1. Bowers-Borckardt Die State III. A hairlined pearl-gray Bust dollar without heavy marks. Most of E PLURIBUS UNUM is legible, and the eagle's wings and tail exhibit partial plumage. (#6895)

1180 **1802 Narrow Date—Damaged, Cleaned—ANACS. VF30 Details.** B-6, BB-241, R.1. Rotation beneath a light reveals glimpses of luster within protected areas. The cream-gray and chestnut-tan fields are hairlined, and the portrait has three small gouges. The reverse rim has several dings, particularly at 2, 7, and 9 o'clock. (#6895)

1181 **1802/1 Wide Date VF30 ANACS.** B-9, BB-235, R.5. Die State III. The original Bolender silver dollar reference was published in 1950, and this variety was discovered by Bolender a short time later. In fact, it was actually discovered during production of the original edition of his reference, with a description included in the text, but it was not illustrated as the plates had already been sent to press. Many more examples have been discovered since the first notice, with about 50 specimens known today. This piece is an attractive light silver-gray example with smooth surfaces and a small reverse rim bruise at 5:30. *Ex: John Haugh Collection (Ira & Larry Goldberg, 2/02), lot 1185.* (#6899)

GOBRECHT DOLLARS

1836 Original Gobrecht Dollar, Fine 15 Details

1182 **1836 Name on Base, Judd-60 Original, Pollock-65, R.1—Repaired, Cleaned—ANACS. Fine 15 Details.** Silver. Plain Edge. Die Alignment I (Liberty's head opposite DO). One of 400 pieces struck in early December 1836. All these coins were struck with a proof finish, even though they were intended for circulation. There is no trace of the die scratch on the reverse, which would identifies late December strikings. The fields have been smoothed and each side is notably hairlined. However, the cleaning must have occurred quite a few years ago as the surfaces have since taken on a light gray patina with deeper accents around the devices and margins. (#11225)

1836 Gobrecht Dollar, March 1837 Issue, PR55

1183 **1836 Name on Base, Judd-60 Original, Pollock-65, R.1, PR55 ANACS.** Silver. Plain Edge. Die Alignment IV (medallic turn, center of Liberty's head opposite right side of F in OF). Sometimes called Second Original strikings, these coins were struck in March 1837, even though they are dated 1836. Struck as circulating proofs, as were all Gobrecht dollars. There were 600 March strikings, and as has been often told, the coins began in Die Alignment II (medal alignment, Liberty's head opposite the DO in DOLLAR). Apparently, the reverse die was loose and during the production run slowly rotated from the eagle in the "onward and upward" position to level (as in this case with the Die Alignment IV coins).

This is a lightly handled proof whose fields retain almost all of the original reflectivity. Well detailed throughout, with just the slightest bit of highpoint friction. Close examination shows a few widely scattered field marks, but the only mentionable abrasions are a couple of short, shallow digs in the obverse field near the rim at 3 o'clock. Light gray patina covers most of each side except the peripheries, which show lovely iridescence. (#11225)

1836 Gobrecht Dollar, Issue of 1837, VF Details

1184 **1836 Judd-60 Original—Repaired—NCS. Proof, VF Details.** Silver. Plain Edge. Die Alignment IV (medallic alignment with the head of Liberty opposite OF). This is from the third striking period: March 1837. The first and second periods are from early and late December 1836. While we have conveniently labeled this as a Die Alignment IV piece, the eagle is not technically flying level when given a medallic turn. This is because these March 1837 pieces started out in Die Alignment II (eagle flying upward) and the reverse die was apparently loose, making successive strikes lower and lower. This piece is technically an intermediate die alignment coin, but very close to Die Alignment IV.

The surfaces are light gray overall with a number of small marks and shallow scratches, as one would expect from a VF coin. The repair mentioned on the NCS insert is in the upper right obverse field. (#11226)

SEATED DOLLARS

1185 **1840 AU55 PCGS.** A well struck, briefly circulated example of this early business-strike Gobrecht dollar issue. Splashes of ruby and golden-brown patina appear at the margins, surrounding a silver-gray base that displays faint hints of blue and gold. (#6926)

1186 **1841 AU55 NGC.** Well struck with light wear evident on the highpoints. The surfaces are modestly marked overall, and the still-lustrous fields display colorful bands of aqua, midnight-blue, magenta, and gold-orange color. A pleasing representative of this early Seated dollar. (#6927)

1187 **1841 AU58 NGC.** Despite its availability in worn grades, examples of the 1841 dollar are elusive in or near Mint State condition. This steel-gray piece shows only a touch of friction on the highpoints. A bit softly struck on the highpoints of the devices, and a single curving mark is noted across Liberty's midsection. (#6927)

1188 **1842 MS60 PCGS.** All No Motto Seated dollars are scarce in Mint State, particularly if they lack a New Orleans mintmark. This well struck example is lustrous and exhibits a lemon-gold reverse rim. Typically abraded, and an interesting strike-through is noted at 1:30 on the reverse. (#6928)

Toned 1843 Select Dollar

1189 **1843 MS63 PCGS.** The 1843 dollar, with a mintage of 165,100 business strikes, is common in circulated grades, but is tougher to acquire in Mint State, especially the higher levels of Uncirculated. Medium gray toning is imbued with wisps of cobalt-blue, and a well executed strike sharpens the design features of this MS63 specimen. A few minor handling marks limit the grade. Population: 11 in 63, 4 finer (6/07). (#6929)

Pleasing MS63 1843 Silver Dollar

1190 **1843 MS63 PCGS.** A lustrous and lightly toned piece with impressively bagmark-free fields. Although No Motto Seated dollars are collectible in MS60 to MS62 grades, these are usually 1859-O and 1860-O, and have reduced eye appeal from heavy marks. In comparison, the present lot has superior eye appeal. Certified in a first generation holder. Population: 11 in 63, 4 finer (5/07). (#6929)

Borderline Uncirculated 1855 Silver Dollar

1191 **1855 AU58 ANACS.** Dappled orange-gold, lime, and powder-blue toning embraces this bagmark-free rare date dollar. Both sides display faint hairlines, but luster shimmers across the devices. The strike is good, with slight softness on the eagle's neck. A mere 26,000 pieces were struck, and few were set aside. (#6943)

1192 **1856—Rim Damaged, Cleaned—ANACS. XF40 Details.** This scarce date No Motto dollar has a cloudy appearance from a cleaning, and a trace of corrosion between the arm and star 4 has a cluster of pinscratches. Small rim nicks are present on the reverse at 12, 5, and 7 o'clock. (#6944)

1193 **1859 AU55 NGC.** This is a scarce date in comparison to the 1859-O hoard issue. The surfaces are faintly hairlined, with mottled gold, heather, and steel toning. (#6946)

1194 **1864—Cleaned—ANACS. Unc. Details, Net AU55.** Rose-gold and gunmetal-blue envelop this sharply struck and partly lustrous piece. Hairlines are present, but are faint given the ANACS notation. Only 30,700 pieces were struck for this elusive Civil War issue. (#6954)

Lustrous MS64 1871 Seated Dollar

1195 **1871 MS64 PCGS.** The 1871 and the 1872 are type coins in the With Motto series, primarily because of their relatively large mintages. However, even though more than a million Seated dollars were struck in 1871 only 67 pieces have been certified by PCGS and NGC in MS64. This is a lovely coin with cartwheel luster and the semi-prooflike fields that are often seen on Seated dollars. Fully struck in all areas. The surfaces generally present as brilliant but there is just the slightest hint of color present when closely examined. (#6966)

Originally Toned 1872 Silver Dollar MS62

1196 **1872 MS62 NGC.** Dappled autumn-brown and forest-green toning endows the margins, while the remainder of this satiny Seated dollar is pearl-gray. Crisply struck aside from several right-side stars. Minor field marks are less obtrusive than expected of the grade. IN GOD WE TRUST is lightly die doubled. Most of this issue was presumably exported for trade in the Orient. Census: 23 in 62, 40 finer (5/07). (#6968)

PROOF SEATED DOLLARS

Deeply Reflective PR64 1861 Seated Dollar

1197 **1861 PR64 PCGS.** Fully struck with deeply watery fields and golden toning on the devices. Mottled cobalt-blue, purple, and lilac iridescence occurs near the periphery. A few faint hairlines seemingly prevent the Gem grade assessment. A lovely, deeply mirrored No Motto type coin. Population: 22 in 64, 7 finer (6/07). (#7004)

Toned 1862 PR63 Dollar

1198 1862 PR63 NGC. Medium intensity gray, cobalt-blue, and red-orange patination covers both faces of this Select proof, and excellent detail stands out on the design features. Close scrutiny with a glass reveals no unsightly marks. Proof dollars of 1862 are especially desired today because of the low business strike mintage of just 11,540 pieces. (#7005)

Colorfully Toned 1864 Dollar, PR64

1199 1864 PR64 NGC. The 1864 is more available than one might imagine of a year in which only 470 proofs were officially produced. This is an exceptionally attractive coin that shows strong reflectivity from the fields through the layers of rose-gray toning in the center of each side and sea-green peripheral coloration. Census: 57 in 64, 29 finer (6/07). (#7007)

Patinated Choice Proof 1867 Seated Dollar

1200 1867 PR64 PCGS. Electric-blue, apricot, rose, and plum-mauve patina envelops this intricately struck Choice Motto proof. The holder is a bit scuffy, but the coin itself has pleasing preservation. A mere 625 proofs were struck, and most of the 46,900 business strikes were exported and eventually melted. Population: 67 in 64, 18 finer (5/07). (#7015)

Elusive PR62 1868 Seated Dollar

1201 1868 PR62 PCGS. This precisely struck specimen has milk-gray and pale gold toning. Much nicer than customary for the PR62 level, since the fields have only the faintest hairlines. The 1 in the date is lightly repunched, and STATES OF is minutely die doubled toward the rim. Only 600 proofs were struck. Certified in a green label holder.
From The Vanek Collection. (#7016)

Impressive 1869 Seated Dollar, PR66

1202 1869 PR66 NGC. This deeply toned Premium Gem proof has lovely lilac and steel-blue toning on both sides, more vivid on the reverse. The surfaces of this beauty are spectacular, without hairlines or other blemishes of any note.

While the original 600 coin proof mintage for this date certainly seems sufficient to supply collector demand today, with more than half that number certified, this issue remains a rarity in Gem or finer quality. For example, Heritage has sold exactly one piece better than PR65 during the past four years. Census: 11 in 66, 6 finer (6/07). (#7017)

Alluring PR64 Cameo 1871 Seated Dollar

1203 1871 PR64 Cameo NGC. The ice-white devices provide obvious contrast with the mirrored fields. The rims have a hint of gold toning, but the fields and motifs are brilliant. The strike is penetrating, even on the eagle's left (facing) ankle. Just 960 proofs were struck. Census: 5 in 64 Cameo, 5 finer (6/07). (#87019)

1204 1872 PR61 ANACS. Decisively struck with a largely untoned center surrounded by deep blue-violet patina edged with orange on the obverse. The reflective reverse has similar color over the entirety of that side. Scattered contact and hairlines in the fields define the grade. Just 950 specimens were struck for this penultimate proof Seated dollar issue. (#7020)

Lightly Toned 1872 Dollar, PR62

1205 1872 PR62 PCGS. Of the 950-piece mintage of 1872 proof Seated Liberty dollars, David Bowers (1993) says: " ... some Proofs probably remained unsold (from their inclusion in minor and silver Proof sets) at the end of the year and were melted in 1873." Whisper of light tan-gold color rest upon this PR62 specimen. Some field-motif contrast is noted, and all of the design features are exquisitely struck. Some inoffensive hairlines limit the grade. (#7020)

Choice Proof 1873 Seated Dollar

1206 1873 PR64 PCGS. Powder-blue and gunmetal-gray toning enriches this sharply struck and original near-Gem. The standard silver dollar was abolished in 1873 in favor of the Trade dollar, although the tables were turned in 1878. Only 600 proofs were struck. Housed in a first generation holder. Population: 35 in 64, 15 finer (5/07). (#7021)

TRADE DOLLARS

1207 1873 MS62 PCGS. Dusky walnut-brown and sea-green embrace this lightly abraded example. All 1873-dated Trade dollars are scarce in Uncirculated grades, regardless of mint of origin. Population: 28 in 62, 59 finer (4/07). (#7031)

1208 1873-S AU58 NGC. Considerable luster rests on light golden-gray surfaces, and excellent definition stands out on the design features, except for the usual softness in portions of Liberty's hair. Some prooflike characteristics are noted, especially on the reverse. It is thought that most of the 703,000-piece mintage was shipped to the Orient, helping to account for the difficulty in acquiring this date. (#7033)

MS62 Chop Mark 1875-CC Trade Dollar

1209 1875-CC Chop Mark MS62 PCGS. Type One Reverse. A solitary chop mark is deeply entered over the center of the olive branch, and causes a rough texture opposite near Liberty's upper right (facing) arm. The piece is slightly wavy, as a result of the chop mark, but no abrasions are worthy of mention. Both sides exhibit unbroken cartwheel luster. A few faint roller marks cross Liberty's cheek. (#87038)

Enticing Choice 1875-S Trade Dollar

1210 1875-S MS64 PCGS. Type One Reverse. With a mintage figure that approached 4.5 million pieces, the 1875-S had the highest mintage of any Trade dollar to that time, and Mint State pieces are available today. Still, near-Gem representatives can be elusive. This strongly lustrous example is subtly gold-tinged overall with a touch of deeper color at the beginning of AMERICA on the reverse. Well-defined overall, though a touch of softness is noted at Liberty's head and the eagle's right (facing) claw. (#7039)

Richly Toned and Lustrous MS64 1876 Trade Dollar Rare Type One Obverse, Type Two Reverse

1211 1876 MS64 PCGS. Type One obverse, Type Two reverse. The transitional variety that is seldom seen in any grade. This die combination is estimated to make up not more than 10% of all surviving 1876 Trade dollars. This piece is a remarkable example with heavy gold and steel toning over frosty silver luster. Fully struck on both obverse and reverse. (#7041)

Impressive Choice 1876 Trade Dollar

1212 1876 MS64 NGC. Type One Obverse and Reverse. A lustrous Gem with uncommonly clean fields for a Trade dollar. Only a few minute marks on the upper right obverse field decide the grade. The strike is bold, with only minor incompleteness on the right (facing) claw and breast. Faint gold toning here and there denies full brilliance. A lower mintage date relative to its S-mint counterpart, yet it trades as a type coin. (#7041)

1213 1877 MS63 PCGS. Original toning across both sides varies from light-gray to aqua to pastel orange. The coin displays excellent luster for a Trade dollar. The striking details are also better than average for the type, with the only noticeable weakness appearing on Liberty's head and on the eagle's right (facing) talons. Small abrasions on Liberty's neck and just to the left of her knee limit the grade of this appealing example. Population: 50 in 63, 64 finer (4/07). (#7044)

Richly Toned 1877 Trade Dollar, MS64

1214 1877 MS64 PCGS. Rich sea-green and golden-brown toning embraces this shimmering Trade dollar. Well struck despite the usual minor blending of detail on the right (facing) claw, but most importantly the head detail is well defined for an 1877. Moderate marks are noted above the extended arm and the arrow shafts. Population: 60 in 64, 4 finer (5/07). (#7044)

Pleasing 1877-CC Select Trade Dollar

1215 1877-CC MS63 PCGS. The 1877-CC Trade dollar, with a mintage of 534,000 pieces, is scarce in all grades, and quite rare in Mint State. David Bowers (1993), writing of this issue, cites a quote by John Willem, a pioneer researcher in the Trade dollar field: "Its relative rarity is due to the fact that all but 3,000 of the Carson City trade dollars were minted in June, July, and August of that year, and all of these coins were destined for shipment abroad. The 3,000 minted in December probably remained in the United States ... ." The current Select specimen displays pleasing luster and hints of light tan color at the margins. A well executed strike brings out great definition in the design elements. A few minor marks and luster grazes preclude a higher grade. Population: 25 in 63, 8 finer (6/07). (#7045)

1216 1878-CC XF40 NGC. From the final year of production for the Trade dollar, this piece garners extra cachet for its Carson City connection. Light to moderate wear is present on the highpoints of this well struck piece, and those areas have light cream color that contrasts with the deep gold-gray patina of the fields. (#7047)

Key 1878-CC Trade Dollar AU58 Details

1217 1878-CC—Cleaned—ANACS. AU58 Details. This key date Carson City Trade dollar has rose-pink, straw-gold, and powder-blue toning. The surfaces are glossy and exhibit numerous tiny marks and carbon flecks. Nonetheless, there is only slight highpoint wear on Liberty's hair and the eagle's claws. The 2008 Guide Book suggests that much of the mintage of 97,000 pieces was melted prior to release. (#7047)

1218 1878-S MS63 NGC. Though this issue's mintage of over 4 million pieces came on the heels of the year of highest production for Trade dollars, 1879 and every date afterward saw proof-only production. This Select example has thin washes of gold and violet patina over shining surfaces. Well struck with only shallow abrasions. (#7048)

Choice Mint State 1878-S Trade Dollar

1219 **1878-S MS64 PCGS.** This is an attractive Choice Mint State example of the final common date issue among trade dollars. This was the year that the Philadelphia Mint switched to proof only trade dollars, and the production at Carson City was limited. Only the 1878-S was produced in large numbers. This example has deep gold and steel toning intermingled across both the obverse and reverse. It is fully lustrous and has excellent eye appeal. Population: 66 in 64, 33 finer (6/07). (#7048)

PROOF TRADE DOLLARS

Choice Proof 1875 Trade Dollar

1220 **1875 PR64 PCGS.** Type Two Reverse. Medium golden-brown toning endows this flashy and carefully preserved near-Gem. Well struck in the centers with some softness near the borders. As a business strike, the 1875 is the scarcest Philadelphia issue, and proofs are also elusive, since just 700 pieces were struck. (#7055)

Gem Proof 1876 Trade Dollar
Scarce Type Two Obverse

1221 **1876 PR65 PCGS.** Type Two Obverse and Reverse. Our auction records suggest that less than one in three proof 1876 Trade dollars has a Type Two obverse, identified by the lower scroll end, which points down rather than to the left. Proofs were sold at the Mint booth at the Philadelphia Centennial Exposition, contributing to an above average proof mintage of 1,150 pieces. The present mark-free specimen has dusky aquamarine and rose-gray toning. Well struck save for the right (facing) claw. (#7056)

Conditionally Elusive 1878 Trade Dollar PR64

1222 **1878 PR64 NGC.** Impressively struck on all of the design elements, this piece has deep violet toning in the fields with silver-gray color on the frosted devices, creating a mild cameo contrast on each side. A few wispy pinscratches limit the grade. Difficult to locate in Choice Proof condition, despite a respectable mintage of 900 pieces. *From The Vanek Collection.* (#7058)

1223 **1879 PR62 NGC.** Fully struck with watery, dark fields and lightly frosted devices. A pinscratch on the upper right obverse, from the rim to the back of Liberty's head, and a few wispy field hairlines limit the grade. First of the proof-only issues at the end of the Trade dollar series.
From The Vanek Collection. (#7059)

Stunning Gem Proof 1879 Trade Dollar

1224 **1879 PR65 PCGS.** Beginning with 1879, only Philadelphia produced Trade dollars and exclusively in proof format. This gold-toned specimen offers deeply reflective fields with light haze at the margins. The devices are boldly impressed, and the eagle displays a degree of frost, which contributes to the reverse's distinct cameo effect. Population: 35 in 65, 29 finer (4/07). (#7059)

Sharp 1879 Trade Dollar PR65

1225 **1879 PR65 NGC.** The 1879 Trade dollar had a proof-only mintage of 1,541 pieces. David Bowers (1993) writes: "Most specimens were saved, but with varying degrees of care. Examples are readily available, for a price … ." Faint magenta and cobalt-blue patina runs over the obverse, while the same color pattern takes on slightly deeper hues on the reverse. The design elements are well impressed throughout. A couple of minor planchet flaws are visible at about 3 o'clock at the obverse border. Census: 40 in 65, 47 finer (6/07). (#7059)

Lovely 1880 Trade Dollar PR64 Cameo

1226 **1880 PR64 Cameo NGC.** This high mintage date has many survivors, but only a fraction of those have earned the Cameo designation from one of the major grading services. The frosted devices appear to stand out in sharp relief over the watery fields, resulting in a remarkably strong cameo effect on both sides. All of the design elements are fully struck and crisply outlined. A patch of curly die lines are noticeable near the date. A few tiny hairlines in the fields prevent a higher grade.
From The Vanek Collection. (#87060)

Stunning 1880 PR66 Cameo Trade Dollar

1227 **1880 PR66 Cameo NGC.** The 1880 Trade dollar was struck in proof finish only, and has the highest mintage of all proofs in the series. In his *Silver Dollars and Trade Dollars of the United States*, David Bowers writes that: "Most ... still exist, perhaps 1,300 to 1,700 of the 1,987 coined." NGC and PCGS have certified several hundred examples, but have assigned the Cameo designation to far fewer specimens.

The Premium Gem Cameo in this lot displays reddish-gold patina at the rims, leaving the central areas completely color free. The field-motif contrast is stunning, and assumes a white-on-black appearance when the coin is observed from an overhead angle. A powerful strike manifests itself in sharp delineation on the design elements, and close scrutiny reveals no significant contact marks. Census: 27 in 66 Cameo, 19 finer (5/07).
From The Vanek Collection. (#87060)

1228 **1882 PR62 NGC.** This piece has deeply mottled blue, gray, and golden-rose coloration over each side. Richly toned with strong detail, though the fields have scattered hairlines and minor contact. A pleasing example of this proof-only issue. (#7062)

Noteworthy 1882 Trade Dollar PR64 Deep Cameo

1229 **1882 PR64 Deep Cameo PCGS.** The proof-only 1882 Trade dollar had the fourth-highest proof mintage in the series, at 1,097 pieces, and is a relatively common date overall. With the Cameo designation, it becomes scarce, and it is scarcer still in Deep Cameo Condition. This near-Gem is fully struck, with intense white-on-black contrast noted on both sides. The inky-black fields display particularly noteworthy depths of reflectivity. A few wispy hairlines limit the grade. Population: 5 in 64 Deep Cameo, 9 finer (6/07). (#97062)

Conditionally Scarce 1883 Trade Dollar PR64 Cameo

1230 **1883 PR64 Cameo PCGS.** This dark-mirrored example displays frosted devices and exquisite cameo contrast on both sides. Razor-sharp striking details are noted on every design element, including the dentils. Only minor cloudiness and a few stray hairlines limit the grade. The last collectible issue of the Trade Dollar type, and scarce in Cameo condition. Population: 20 in 64 Cameo, 19 finer (5/07).
From The Vanek Collection. (#87063)

MORGAN DOLLARS

1231 **1878 8TF MS65 .** VAM-14.2. This pinpoint-sharp Gem has infrequent wisps of golden toning, but the unmarked surfaces are close to brilliant. A splendid example of the briefly produced introductory design subtype.
From The Reuben Reinstein Collection. (#7072)

High Grade, Flashy MS66 1878 Dollar, 8TF

1232 **1878 8TF MS66 NGC.** VAM-21. A boldly struck Premium Gem, nearly fully struck although the wreath bow has a hint of softness on the highpoints. Warm lilac-gold hugs the borders and frames the brilliant centers. The well preserved obverse is virtually pristine, and the reverse is nearly as clean. Both sides are lightly die doubled, most prominently on the N in ONE. Certified in an old-style NGC holder. Population: 28 in 66, 2 finer (6/07). (#7072)

1233 **1878 7/8TF Strong MS65 PCGS.** VAM-37. This faintly toned and lustrous first-year Morgan dollar has four bold tailfeather fragments beneath the prominent seven tailfeathers. The strike is crisp, and the few faint grazes are of little concern.
From The Reuben Reinstein Collection. (#7078)

Lustrous 1878 7TF Reverse of 1878 Dollar, MS66

1234 **1878 7TF Reverse of 1878 MS66 NGC.** The 1878 Reverse of 1878 dollar displays parallel arrow feathers, and flatness, or concaveness, on the eagle's breast. This color-free Premium Gem possesses great luster and design element delineation. Some inoffensive luster grazes are within the parameters of the grade designation. Census: 22 in 66, 0 finer (6/07).
From The Reuben Reinstein Collection. (#7074)

Beautiful Gem 1878 Dollar, Seven Tail Feathers, Reverse of 1879

1235 **1878 7TF Reverse of 1879 MS65 PCGS.** The Reverse of 1879, or Third Reverse, is distinguished by the slanted upper feather of the fletchings. This Gem displays just a hint of lemon-gold patina in the fields, and the otherwise untoned surfaces display strong luster. The devices are crisply struck with just a touch of frost on the highpoints. Highly elusive any finer, with just six such coins graded by PCGS (5/07). (#7076)

Splendid 1878 7TF Dollar, Reverse of 1879, MS66

1236 **1878 7TF Reverse of 1879 MS66 NGC.** The 1878 7 Tail Feathers dollar with the Reverse of 1879 is distinguished by a convex breast on the eagle (versus the flat, or concave breast on the Reverse of 1878), and by the slanting top arrow feather. In the Second Edition (2005) of his *A Guide Book of Morgan Dollars: A Complete History and Price Guide*, David Bowers estimates the circulation strike mintage of the Reverse of 1879 variety to be 1,500,000 pieces, compared to an estimate of 7,850,000 coins for the Reverse of 1878 variety, which logically helps to account for the greater scarcity of the former issue.

Potent luster enlivens both obverse and reverse of this Premium Gem specimen, and a well executed strike has left its mark in the form of sharply defined motifs, including the hair above Liberty's ear and the eagle's breast feathers. A few minor, unobtrusive marks prevent this lovely piece from attaining MS67. Census: 12 in 66, 0 finer (6/07).
From The Reuben Reinstein Collection. (#7076)

Choice Cameo DMPL 1878 Third Reverse Dollar

1237 **1878 7TF Reverse of 1879 MS64 Cameo Deep Mirror Prooflike ANACS.** The proof 1878 Third Reverse Morgan dollar is extremely rare, but the present lot provides an affordable alternative. The fields are flashy and reflective with only moderate cartwheel, and all devices are deeply frosted. Golden-gray toning is limited to Liberty's cheek and neck. Sharply struck and carefully preserved. (#97077)

1238 **1878-CC MS65 PCGS.** The design features of this first-year representative are sharply rendered, and pleasing mint frost gleams across the snow-white surfaces. A few superficial marks are noted on Liberty's face and neck, as well as in the left obverse field. (#7080)

1239 **1878-CC MS65 PCGS.** Delicate almond-gold toning visits this lustrous and carefully preserved Gem. The strike is unimprovable except on the lower reverse denticles. (#7080)

1240 **1878-CC MS65 NGC.** A frosty and delightful Gem from the first of many issues that would make the Carson City silver dollar a numismatic icon. Though practically brilliant at first glance, modest haze appears in the fields, which also exhibit subtle ice-blue iridescence.
From The Silver Fox Collection. (#7080)

Frosted White MS66 1878-CC Dollar

1241 **1878-CC MS66 NGC.** When one considers that more than 2.2 million pieces were struck of this issue, it is remarkable that so few are extant today in MS66 condition. NGC has only certified only seven coins finer (6/07). Fully and intricately detailed, the surfaces are bone-white with excellent luster characteristics. Very few abrasions are noted on either side of this impressive CC dollar.
From The Reuben Reinstein Collection. (#7080)

1242 **1878-CC MS65 Prooflike PCGS.** This borderline Deep Mirror Prooflike piece has fully brilliant mirrored surfaces with outstanding cameo contrast. The surfaces have a few tiny marks, but are virtually pristine. Only 12 finer prooflike examples have been certified by PCGS (6/07). (#7081)

1243 **1878-CC MS63 Deep Prooflike NGC.** Not only does this piece have deeply mirrored fields, but it also has excellent contrast between the fields and devices. The surfaces have light marks that are reflected in the fields, appearing more severe than they really are. (#97081)

1244 **1878-CC MS64 Deep Mirror Prooflike NGC.** Lavender and sea-green encompass the borders, while the mirrored fields are untoned. Well struck except for the claws and the base of the wreath. The reverse is well preserved. Encapsulated in a prior generation holder. (#97081)

1245 **1878-S MS66 PCGS.** This splendidly preserved Second Reverse silver dollar has only a trace of gold toning. The strike is exquisite, and the eye appeal is unassailable. (#7082)

1246 **1878-S MS66 PCGS.** A lovely Premium Gem example with even, frosty surfaces and just a few faint luster marks that detract little from the ample eye appeal. Struck during the very first year of the Morgan dollar series. (#7082)

1247 **1878-S MS66 PCGS.** Speckled green and russet patina decorates the obverse and reverse peripheries. Lustrous and well struck without distractions on either side. From the Short Nock reverse hub. (#7082)

1248 **1878-S MS66 PCGS.** This always-popular first-year issue has the usual full strike and thickly frosted surfaces. Both sides show a light overlay of light gray patina. (#7082)

1249 **1878-S MS66 NGC.** Bright cartwheel luster is seen on each side of this brilliant, snow-white Premium Gem dollar. All of the design motifs are sharply struck, including the often-difficult central details. A few small marks prevent an even finer grade assessment. (#7082)

Dazzling MS67 1878-S Morgan Dollar

1250 **1878-S MS67 NGC.** Numerous examples of the 1878-S were set aside at the time of issue, and such coins are often used for type purposes. This is a wonderful coin that is brilliant throughout, and it shows the usual bright, frosted mint luster. Fully struck, as always. The fields are semi-reflective and the coin has a modest, two-toned white-on-black appearance. Census: 29 in 67, 0 finer (6/07).
From The Reuben Reinstein Collection. (#7082)

1251 **1879 MS65 PCGS.** This piece is sharply detailed and highly lustrous with excellent eye appeal. Although not rare at this grade level, it is elusive in higher grades, with just 75 better examples certified by PCGS. (#7084)

1252 **1879 MS65 PCGS.** Honey-gold toning is limited to the rims of this lustrous and well preserved Gem. The centers are typically brought up. Liberty's profile is lightly die doubled. (#7084)

Flashy Premium Gem 1879 Morgan Dollar

1253 **1879 MS66 NGC.** This flashy Premium Gem dollar is essentially white and untoned, with cartwheel luster in the fields and a bright, clean overall appearance. There is a touch of softness on the hair detail just above Liberty's ear, but the other design elements are boldly struck. The 1879 Morgan dollar is surprisingly challenging in higher Mint State grades. Census: 44 in 66, 4 finer (6/07).
From The Reuben Reinstein Collection. (#7084)

1254 **1879-CC VF30 ANACS.** A key Carson City dollar with a clear mintmark and original cream-gray toning. Protected areas feature darker russet patina. The absence of significant marks confirms the collector quality. (#7086)

1255 **1879-CC XF45 ANACS.** Light champagne-gold surfaces display traces of luster in the protected areas of this Choice XF specimen. Devoid of significant marks, with relatively sharp design detail. Really quite a pleasing example of this scarce Carson City issue. (#7086)

1256 **1879-CC AU50 ANACS.** Clear CC. Deep steel-gray and caramel-gold toning embraces this moderately circulated and undipped better date CC-mint dollar. Collectors in search of a problem-free example of this want list perennial need look no further. (#7086)

Desirable 1879-CC Dollar, MS60

1257 **1879-CC MS60 NGC.** Whispers of light tan-gold color hug the rims of this Carson City issue, framing the color-free centers. The design elements are generally well impressed, though minor softness is apparent in the hair over Liberty's ear. Minute marks and luster grazes are scattered over lustrous surfaces. Actually, a nice coin for the grade designation. David Bowers (2006) writes: "In any grade, the 1879-CC is highly desired, and stands 2nd only to the 1889-CC in terms of rarity among Carson City issues." (#7086)

Popular Select 1879-CC Dollar

1258 **1879-CC MS63 PCGS.** Clear CC mintmark. Honey-gold and salmon-pink patina visits the borders, while the fields and devices are virtually untoned. Nicely struck and lustrous with an unabraded reverse and a few faint grazes on the cheek. Among the keys to a Carson City Morgan dollar collection. (#7086)

Well Struck 1879-CC Near-Gem Dollar

1259 **1879-CC MS64 PCGS.** From a mintage of 756,000 pieces, of which hundreds of thousands were probably melted under the 1918 Pittman Act (David Bowers, 2006). Essentially untoned surfaces display a fair amount of field-motif contras, and a well executed strike leaves strong definition on the design elements. Minute obverse marks limit the grade. (#7086)

Wonderful 1879-CC Dollar, MS65

1260 **1879-CC MS65 NGC.** David Bowers, in his *Silver Dollars and Trade Dollars of the United Sates*, states that: "After closing of the Carson City Mint, quantities of 1879-CC dollars were shipped in two directions for storage: westward to vaults in the San Francisco Mint, and eastward to Washington, D.C. In 1942-1943, several bags of 1879-CC dollars were paid out at face value in San Francisco. Apparently, the quantity was never large at that location.

The '79-CC offered in this lot displays frosty motifs that sit in mild contrast to partially prooflike fields. A well executed strike brings crisp definition to the design features, adding immensely to the coin's overall eye appeal. Both faces are color free, and were it not for some minuscule obverse marks, this coin would have graded at an even higher level. Census: 40 in 65, 0 finer (6/07).
From The Reuben Reinstein Collection. (#7086)

Snappy Prooflike MS64 1879-CC Dollar

1261 **1879-CC MS64 Prooflike PCGS.** Normal Mintmark. The semi-key 1879-CC dollar is an especially desirable coin with prooflike fields. And at the MS64 level, this is the final grade this date and mintmark can be located with any regularity. When the coins certified in MS64 Prooflike are combined from the two major services, the total is only 96 pieces. But more importantly, for the collector of high grade Morgans a mere 11 pieces have been certified in MS65, and none are finer (6/07).

This is a lovely, well-preserved '79-CC dollar. The centers are sharply struck, and the surfaces overall are minimally abraded with small abrasions scattered across the obverse but virtually none on the reverse. Brilliant throughout, the fields are nicely reflective and well-balanced from side-to-side. The devices are noticeably frosted and present a strong contrast on both obverse and reverse. An important coin for the Carson City collector. Population: 52 in 64, 6 finer (6/07). (#7087)

1262 **1879-CC Capped Die XF45 ANACS.** VAM-3. A Top 100 Variety. The well known VAM with tiny die chips around the mintmark. In this grade, the difference in appearance between the Normal and Capped mintmark varieties is minimal. A cream-gray example without any obtrusive marks. A die break fills the G in GOD. (#7088)

Mint State Capped Die 1879-CC Dollar

1263 **1879-CC Capped Die MS61 ANACS.** VAM-3. A Top 100 Variety. The "Capped Die" variety, noted for its cluster of die chips near the mintmark, constitutes a minority of the '79-CC issue. A Mint State VAM-3 is costly, but this has more to do with the scarcity of the '79-CC, which is more difficult to locate than the lower mintage '81-CC and '85-CC. This satiny and reasonably struck key date dollar is typically abraded and displays mottled golden-brown and steel-blue patina. (#7088)

Select Capped Die 1879-CC Dollar

1264 **1879-CC Capped Die MS63 ANACS.** VAM-3. A Top 100 Variety. The curious "Capped Die" variety, actually a Medium over Small CC mintmark. The tiny die chips within the mintmark area repelled collectors until recent decades, when the cause of such things was better understood. A lustrous almond-gold representative with pleasing surfaces. The centers are typically struck and display faint roller marks, as made. (#7088)

Lustrous 1879-CC Capped Die Dollar, MS64

1265 **1879-CC Capped Die MS64 PCGS.** VAM-3. A Top 100 Variety. This variety illustrates die chipping around the "Medium CC" mint mark, resulting from mint personnel's attempt to tool away an underlying "Small CC." This so-called "Capped Die" is the scarcer of the two. Glowing luster exudes from silver-gray surfaces that are tinted with light tan on the reverse. Generally well struck on the design elements, and possessing just a few minor obverse marks. Housed in a green-label holder. (#7088)

Brilliant Gem 1879-O Dollar

1266 **1879-O MS65 NGC.** A great many 1879-O dollars were released into circulation at the time of issue. Undoubtedly, much of this widespread circulation was from pent-up demand for coinage, as the 1879-O dollar was the first silver dollar struck in the New Orleans mint since 1860. This is an especially attractive example that shows thick, satiny mint luster with virtually none of the abrasions that are normally associated with this issue. Brilliant and sharply struck.
From The Reuben Reinstein Collection. (#7090)

1267 **1879-S MS66 PCGS.** Gorgeous aqua-blue patina dominates each side of this highly lustrous Premium Gem example. Varying shades of deep crimson and gold are also seen on each side. A wonderful second-year piece for the toning enthusiast. (#7092)

1268 **1879-S MS66 NGC.** Deep amber-gold toning dominates this lustrous Premium Gem, although the margins offer sea-green and navy-blue iridescence. Well struck and beautifully preserved. (#7092)

Lushly Patinated 1879-S Dollar MS67

1269 **1879-S MS67 NGC.** An amazing Superb Gem with dramatically toned obverse and reverse surfaces over satiny luster. Both sides have crimson, cobalt, and iridescent toning, with additional gold color on the reverse. The strike is intricate, as usual for the well made '79-S. (#7092)

1270 **1879-S MS67 ★ NGC.** This beautiful stone-white Superb Gem has semi-prooflike fields and an intricate strike. An exceptional silver type coin. A small planchet flaw (as produced) is present above star 10. (#7092)

1271 **1879-S MS67 PCGS.** Part of the allure of this Superb coin are the clean, bright, lustrous surfaces. The other part is the long arc of rainbow iridescence on the right side of the obverse. Exceptional quality and visual appeal. (#7092)

1272 **1879-S MS67★ NGC.** The obverse is rather prooflike, which no doubt inspired the Star designation from NGC. The reverse is merely semi-prooflike. A brilliant and beautiful Superb Gem that has the penetrating strike usual for the '79-S. The mintmark is slightly repunched. (#7092)

1273 **1879-S MS67 PCGS.** A flashy Superb Gem with intense luster and a needle-sharp strike, including excellent definition in the hair strands over Liberty's ear and on the eagle's breast feathers. The magnificently preserved devices of this untoned example are lightly frosted, and contrast nicely with partially prooflike fields. This example carries the Reverse of 1879, distinguished by the slanting top arrow feather. (#7092)

1274 **1879-S MS68 ICG.** Both the strike and luster quality are as exquisite as one would expect for an early date Morgan from the California branch mint. It is in the areas of surface preservation and eye appeal that this coin deviates from the norm. Swirls of multicolored bag toning alternate on the upper obverse. The sole imperfection is a faint fingerprint fragment on the reverse at 11:30. (#7092)

Exceptional Semi-Prooflike MS68 1879-S Dollar

1275 **1879-S MS68 NGC.** Early S-mint dollars are often used for type coins, and for good reason. They are undoubtedly the best-produced dollars in the entire series, and because so many were set aside they are also occasionally available in high grades. This is an exceptionally attractive coin that has nearly perfect surfaces. The fields have a confirmed reflectivity, perhaps not enough to warrant a Prooflike designation, but definitely enough to provide a black backdrop for the frosted devices. Fully struck, of course. Census: 101 in 68, 0 finer (6/07).
From The Reuben Reinstein Collection. (#7092)

1276 **1879-S MS67 ★ Prooflike NGC.** The obverse reflectivity is exceptional, though the reverse is "merely" Prooflike. Slightly hazy with strong detail on the portrait, which has a blush of rose. Fully struck and exceptionally well preserved. (#7093)

1277 **1879-S Reverse of 1878 MS64 PCGS.** Booming cartwheel luster and brilliant, snow-white surfaces are the hallmarks of this instantly appealing near-Gem. Well struck with a few scuff marks on Liberty's cheek and in the left obverse field that preclude a higher grade designation. (#7094)

1278 **1879-S Reverse of 1878 MS64 PCGS.** A near-Gem example of the scarce variety with the old reverse die, this piece has frosty silver luster with excellent surfaces. (#7094)

Scarce MS65 1879-S Reverse of 1878 Dollar

1279 **1879-S Reverse of 1878 MS65 NGC.** Top 100. A large number of Reverse of 1878 dollars were found in the Redfield hoard. While this greatly increased the availability of this variant, it also increased awareness of it and consequently also increased demand by even more collectors. Today, the Flat Breast 1879-S is an established variety in the Morgan series, and it is well known that high grade examples are very scarce. This Gem is fully struck and the surfaces are mostly brilliant with just the faintest hint of golden present on the denticles on the right side of the obverse. The reverse is fully prooflike.
From The Reuben Reinstein Collection. (#7094)

1280 **1880 MS65 PCGS.** A sharply struck, all-white example of this all-too-often heavily abraded early P-mint Morgan dollar. Soft frosted mint luster. (#7096)

Seldom Seen Gem 1880 Morgan Dollar, MS66

1281 **1880 MS66 PCGS.** More than 12 million 1880 silver dollars were struck under the provisions of the Bland-Allison Act of 1878. Many were dropped into circulation at the time of issue, and a sizeable number must have also been melted under the Pittman Act of 1918. As a result, in spite of the large mintage, Gem 1880 dollars have been a well-known condition rarity for decades. This is a brilliant coin that has smooth mint frost over each side and a clean cheek on Liberty's face. Fully struck in all areas. Population: 75 in 66, 0 finer (6/07).
From The Reuben Reinstein Collection. (#7096)

1282 **1880-CC MS65 PCGS.** VAM-3. A dash lurks beneath the second 8 in the date, and both Cs in the mintmark are filled by die chips. An impressive array of colors are displayed on the obverse of this vibrantly lustrous Gem. The design elements are boldly struck and surface marks are not excessive. (#7100)

1283 **1880-CC MS65 PCGS.** This Gem Morgan displays the Reverse of 1879, indicated by the slanted top arrow feather. Hints of light tan patina visit lustrous surfaces that exhibit well struck design elements, except for softness in the hair at Liberty's ear. A few minute marks are consistent with the grade designation. (#7100)

1284 **1880-CC MS65 PCGS.** Brilliant throughout, the mint luster is thick and frosted as one would expect from a CC dollar. What is unexpected is how clean each side is. Sharply struck also. (#7100)

1285 **1880-CC MS65 PCGS.** This virtually brilliant Gem has pleasing luster and a splendidly smooth reverse. The slight softness of strike in the centers is typical for the popular Carson City issue. (#7100)

Exceptional 1880-CC Dollar, MS66 Reverse of 1879

1286 **1880-CC MS66 NGC.** This 1880-CC Morgan dollar displays a slanted top arrow feather, meaning that it is the Reverse of 1879 variety. While this variety is more plentiful than the 1880-CC with a parallel top arrow feather (Reverse of 1878), many surviving specimens are extensively bagmarked, making it difficult to locate an example with good eye appeal. The Premium Gem coin in this lot fits the bill. Its radiantly lustrous surfaces are refreshingly clean and smooth. Whispers of incipient light tan-gold color are slightly more noticeable on the reverse. The design elements are generally well impressed, save for the usually seen softness in the hair strands at Liberty's ear.
From The Silver Fox Collection. (#7100)

1287 **1880-CC MS65 Prooflike PCGS.** The moderately reflective, slightly hazy fields contrast with decisively struck devices that exhibit rich frost. The portrait displays a touch of pink color, while the eagle's right (facing) wing has a band of tan-gray. A lovely Carson City dollar. (#7101)

1288 **1880-CC MS65 Prooflike PCGS.** Whispers of lavender, golden-brown, and cobalt-blue make themselves known around portions of the margins on this Gem Prooflike dollar. Lightly frosted, adequately struck motifs stand out against the backdrop of the reflective fields. A few small abrasions on Liberty's portrait prevent an even higher grade. (#7101)

Thickly Frosted MS66 1880-CC Dollar, 8 Over High 7

1289 **1880-CC 8 Over High 7 MS66 PCGS.** According to Van Allen and Mallis all 1880-CC dollars started out as overdates: "Normal dies without overdates do not exist." It is just a matter of how much of the underdigit(s) are visible. This coin was apparently struck from an 187- die, as none of the final digit is visible. Predictably scarce in high grades, only 59 pieces have been so graded by PCGS with five finer (6/07). The fields are bright and semi-prooflike with thick mint frost over the devices. Sharply defined, there are no mentionable marks on this lovely overdate CC dollar.
From The Reuben Reinstein Collection. (#7102)

1290 **1880-CC 8 Over High 7 MS63 Prooflike PCGS.** VAM-5. A Top 100 Variety. A flashy Carson City overdate dollar whose faint gold toning has no effect on the field reflectivity. A few minor marks are noted beneath Liberty's eye, but the reverse is well preserved. (#7103)

1291 **1880-CC 8 Over High 7 MS64 Prooflike PCGS.** VAM-5. A Top 100 Variety. A flashy and essentially brilliant example of this popular Carson City overdate. The reverse has a cameo appearance. Well preserved and attractive. Population: 24 in 64 Prooflike, 7 finer (4/07). (#7103)

1292 **1880-CC 8 Over Low 7 MS65 PCGS.** VAM-6. A Top 100 Variety. Lightly toned and lustrous with a semi-prooflike obverse. The centers display faint mint-made roller marks, but the fields are remarkably clean. (#7104)

MS64 Deep Mirror 1880-CC 8 Over 7 Dollar

1293 **1880-CC 8 Over Low 7 MS64 Deep Mirror Prooflike PCGS.** VAM-6. A Top 100 Variety. The remarkably reflective fields are essentially brilliant, although hints of gold patina adorn the borders. The devices are moderately frosted, contributing further to the eye appeal. Nicely struck and carefully preserved. Population: 13 in 64 Deep Mirror Prooflike, 6 finer (6/07). (#97105)

1294 **1880/79-CC Reverse of 1878 MS64 PCGS.** VAM-4. A Top 100 Variety. Sea-green and rose-red margins ensure the eye appeal of this lustrous and attentively struck Choice Carson City dollar. The reverse is remarkably free from marks. (#7108)

1295 **1880/79-CC Reverse of 1878 MS64 PCGS.** Although not especially rare, the overdate variety from the old reverse hub is clearly more elusive than those from normal dies. This piece is a pleasing near-Gem with mostly brilliant silver surfaces that are only interrupted by a brief crescent of gold at the upper obverse. (#7108)

1296 **1880/79-CC Reverse of 1878 MS64 ANACS.** VAM-4. A Top 100 Variety. A band of light peach toning adorns the lower reverse margin. Well struck and highly lustrous with impressively unabraded fields and only minor grazes on the portrait. (#7108)

MS66 1880/79-CC Second Reverse Dollar

1297 **1880/79-CC Reverse of 1878 MS66 PCGS.** VAM-4. A Top 100 Variety. The most obvious overdate in the Morgan dollar series, and one of only two 1880-dated VAMs that uses a Second Reverse die from 1878. This lustrous high grade dollar has clean fields and delicate tan-gold toning. Sharply struck for an '80-CC dollar, which are often seen with mushy centers and roller marks. (#7108)

Overdate 1880-CC Dollar, MS66
An Absolute and Condition Rarity

1298 **1880/79-CC Reverse of 1878 MS66 PCGS.** Probably no more than 10% to 20% of 1880-CC dollars survive with recognizable underdigits beneath the 80. On this coin, the 79 is especially strong. As such, this is both an absolute as well as a condition rarity among early Morgan dollars. As with all Carson City dollars, the surfaces are thickly frosted. As the mint luster swirls around each side, there are no obvious or detracting abrasions. Sharply struck also. Population: 48 in 66, 0 finer (6/07).
From The Reuben Reinstein Collection. (#7108)

1299 **1880/79-CC Reverse of 1878 MS64 Prooflike PCGS.** VAM-4. A Top 100 Variety. This prominent CC-mint overdate variety is also noteworthy for its use of an obsolete reverse die. The VAM-4 appeared in quantity within the GSA hoard, but Prooflikes are very scarce. The depth of field reflectivity approaches a DMPL designation. A well struck and lightly toned example with good white-on-black contrast. Population: 28 in 64 Prooflike, 7 finer (6/07). (#7109)

1300 **1880-O MS64 PCGS.** Medium Oval O. The dramatic powder-blue, peach, and lilac obverse toning has an end-of-roll pattern. The reverse is nearly brilliant. A sharply struck near-Gem with clean fields and a solitary mark near the mouth. (#7114)

1301 **1880-O MS64 NGC.** Micro O. Honey-gold, orange, and powder-blue toning graces the peripheries of this lustrous near-Gem. Sharply struck and lustrous with few marks. Certified in a prior generation holder. (#7114)

1302 **1880-O MS64 PCGS.** Micro O. Potent luster sweeps this brilliant and crisply struck near-Gem. Neither side displays any distracting marks. Difficult to find any finer. (#7114)

1303 **1880-O MS64 NGC.** Soft, pleasing luster enhances the visual appeal of surfaces that display wisps of cotton-colored patina in the fields. A crisply struck, minimally marked example of this early O-mint Morgan dollar issue.
From The Vanek Collection. (#7114)

1304 **1880/79-O MS64 PCGS.** VAM-4. A Top 100 Variety. Micro O. The overdate feature is undesignated on the PCGS holder. A lustrous chestnut-gold near-Gem that has a sharp strike and smooth fields. (#7116)

1305 **1880-S MS66 Obverse Ultra Deep Mirror ANACS.** The obverse offers immense reflectivity and richly frosted devices, while the reverse, though flashy, has more typical luster. A highly appealing representative like many of its counterparts, untoned in the centers with zones of claret and tan color at the margins. (#7118)

1306 **1880-S MS67 NGC.** Medium S. A solidly struck and flashy Superb Gem example of this popular type issue. Aside from a splash of orange color above the eagle's left (facing) wingtip, the carefully preserved surfaces are essentially untoned. (#7118)

1307 **1880-S MS67 NGC.** Large S. A clean-cheeked Superb Gem with dazzling cartwheel effect in the fields aided by peripheral splashes of orange and rose-red toning. (#7118)

Glorious 1880-S Dollar MS68

1308 **1880-S MS68 PCGS.** Large S. This sharply struck Superb Gem has beautiful powder-blue and golden-brown bands along the left borders. The reverse is prooflike, while the obverse exhibits blazing cartwheel sheen. Careful perusal with a loupe locates only minuscule contact. Certified in a green label holder.
From The Vanek Collection. (#7118)

Desirable MS68 ★ 1880-S Dollar

1309 **1880-S MS68 ★ NGC.** Medium S. The obverse is prooflike with a frosted portrait, characteristics that doubtlessly compelled the Star designation from NGC. The reverse has normal cartwheel luster. Virtually brilliant, crisply struck, and gorgeously preserved. The 1880-S ranks among the most available Morgan dollars, particularly in higher Mint State grades. Nonetheless, exceptional Superb Gems will always be under enormous demand as a superior representative of the type. (#7118)

Conditionally Scarce 1880-S Morgan Dollar MS68

1310 **1880-S MS68 NGC.** The 1880-S Morgan dollar is one of the most common early issues in the immensely popular series, and examples are easy to obtain at grade levels all the way through MS67! Only at MS68 does this date finally become scarce. The current offering is a truly beautiful coin that appears to have been saved very early from either circulation or long-term bag storage, as unlikely as that seems. The piece comes about as close to being pristine as possible for a business strike silver dollar. Fully struck with a layer of light cloudiness over the fields and wonderfully clean devices. A great Superb Gem from the San Francisco Mint.
From The Reuben Reinstein Collection. (#7118)

1311 **1880-S MS67 Prooflike NGC.** Medium S. A flashy Superb Gem whose field reflectivity approaches that of a Deep Mirror example. The devices are moderately frosty, and there is only a hint of gold patina. (#7119)

Dazzling MS68 Prooflike 1880-S Dollar

1312 **1880-S MS68 Prooflike NGC.** Medium S. This exquisitely struck Superb Gem is nearly bereft of toning and has only inconsequential contact. The fields offer dazzling, flashy luster. Those who desire the finest quality Morgan dollar for a silver type set need look no further. (#7119)

1313 **1880-S MS65 Deep Mirror Prooflike PCGS.** The large S mintmark leans left. This impressive Gem has frosty devices and glassy fields. The white-on-black contrast is particularly strong on the reverse. Brilliant aside from a few pinpoint ebony flecks. Certified in a first generation holder. (#97119)

1314 **1881 MS65 PCGS.** The soft, frosted mint luster is free from any troubling marks on either side. This sharply struck coin is high-end for the grade with a remarkably clean cheek on Liberty. (#7124)

1315 **1881 MS65 PCGS.** Faint gold toning enriches this lustrous and meticulously struck Gem. Free from consequential contact, and a worthy addition to a quality collection. Housed in a first generation holder. (#7124)

Colorfully Toned 1881 Morgan MS66

1316 **1881 MS66 NGC.** Dusky orange-gold centers are bounded by sea-green and plum-mauve patina. This lustrous Premium Gem has a good strike and clean fields. Careful evaluation locates a couple of faint grazes on the cheek, made inconspicuous by the lavish and attractive toning. (#7124)

Brilliant, Lustrous MS66 1881 Morgan Dollar

1317 **1881 MS66 PCGS.** While a common dollar in circulated grades, the 1881 is rarely encountered in MS66 condition. This is a brilliant example that has unusually flashy surfaces. The fields have a confirmed glimmer of semi-reflectivity, and the devices are notably frosted. Fully struck, the central motifs are free from the abrasions that often accompany this issue. Population: 57 in 66, 2 finer (6/07).
From The Reuben Reinstein Collection. (#7124)

1318 **1881-CC MS65 PCGS.** The design elements are well executed throughout, with no troublesome weakness evident above Liberty's ear or on the eagle's breast feathers. Intense mint frost produces a beautifully effulgent sheen across the snow-white surfaces. A few minor marks and luster grazes are too insignificant to prevent the Gem grade assessment. (#7126)

1319 **1881-CC MS65 PCGS.** Pronounced "flash" stands out on this popular, low mintage Gem Carson City dollar. Untoned surfaces exhibit partially prooflike fields and well struck design elements, including nice definition in the hair at Liberty's ear and on the eagle's breast feathers. A couple of small toning spots are noted on the reverse, and a few minor marks scattered about do not detract. Housed in a green-label holder. (#7126)

1320 **1881-CC MS65 PCGS.** A frosty and strongly lustrous Gem example of this popular Carson City issue. Streaks of peach and violet patina grace the obverse margins, while the reverse has only a hint of such color on the rims. (#7126)

1321 **1881-CC MS65 PCGS.** Bright and brilliant, with intense mint frost and snow-white surfaces. Boldly struck with a few minor, scattered marks on each side. A dazzling Gem, housed in a first-generation PCGS holder. (#7126)

1322 **1881-CC MS65 PCGS.** Light almond-gold toning graces this lustrous and boldly struck low mintage Carson City dollar. Only infrequent obverse luster grazes deny a higher grade. Housed in an old green label holder. (#7126)

1323 **1881-CC MS65 ANACS.** VAM-2. Light lemon-gold toning visits the peripheries of this precisely struck Gem. The reverse is nearly immaculate, and the portrait has only trivial contact. The sweet spot of the cheek is pristine. (#7126)

1324 **1881-CC MS66 PCGS.** This is a visually alluring example from the Carson City Mint. Intense mint frost cascades over each side, and the surfaces are essentially untoned and brilliant, save for faint hints of peripheral patina. Expertly preserved with few marks, the most noticeable of which resides on the eagle's breast. (#7126)

1325 **1881-CC MS66 PCGS.** Brilliant-white with intense mint frost and just a hint of golden peripheral color on each side. A beautiful Premium Gem example of this Carson City issue.
From The Vanek Collection. (#7126)

1326 **1881-CC MS66 PCGS.** VAM-2. Golden-brown, rose-red, and forest-green freckles hug the peripheries of this well struck and clean-cheeked Carson City dollar. Die fill within the upper loop of the second 8 is reminiscent of the VAM-6 "8 Over Low 7" 1880-CC overdate. (#7126)

1327 **1881-CC MS66 NGC.** Flashy fields, powerful cartwheel luster, and richly frosted devices converge on this delightful Carson City dollar. A hint of tan color at the right obverse rim offsets the brilliance found on the rest of the coin. A pleasing piece that has the appearance of a high-end dollar from the GSA sales.
From The Silver Fox Collection. (#7126)

1328 **1881-CC MS66 NGC.** VAM-2. Well struck and impressively smooth with only a whisper of chestnut toning on the devices. A lovely Premium Gem of this perpetually popular low mintage CC-mint issue.
From The Reuben Reinstein Collection. (#7126)

1329 **1881-CC MS64 Deep Mirror Prooflike PCGS.** The design elements are crisply defined and richly frosted, and the fields exhibit majestically deep reflectivity. Dramatic white-on-black contrast is the result, on both obverse and reverse. A few shallow marks on Liberty's cheek limit the grade. (#97127)

Highly Attractive 1881-CC Dollar MS65 Deep Mirror Prooflike

1330 **1881-CC MS65 Deep Mirror Prooflike PCGS.** Exquisitely struck, strongly frosted design elements reveal outstanding contrast with deeply mirrored fields. Just a few minor luster grazes on the cheek prevent an even higher grade. The 1881-CC is a low-mintage issue of 296,000 pieces. David Bowers (2006) contends that it: " ... is easy to find today in Mint State condition due to the dispersal of former Treasury holdings." (#97127)

1331 **1881-O MS65 PCGS.** An intricately struck Gem with faint gold toning and pleasing preservation. Conditionally scarce despite a plentiful mintage. PCGS has certified a mere 11 pieces in higher grades (5/07).
From The Reuben Reinstein Collection. (#7128)

1332 **1881-S MS66 NGC.** This outstanding piece displays the captivating toning, incredible detail, and breathtaking luster that characterize the most beautiful examples of this issue. Bands of lemon-gold, peach, teal, and violet toning grace the obverse, while the reverse has similar colors at the left and right margins.
From The Vanek Collection. (#7130)

1333 **1881-S MS67 NGC.** Sharply struck with only the tiniest of surface marks and bright, glassy, semi-reflective fields. An attractive crescent of aquamarine and reddish-tan patina along the upper obverse is matched by another arc of the same color scheme along the lower reverse periphery. (#7130)

1334 **1881-S MS67 NGC.** Boldly struck with powerful luster, two qualities that grace many examples of this popular type issue. The surfaces appear brilliant at first glance, though a touch of reddish-gold patina appears at the margins. (#7130)

1335 **1881-S MS67 NGC.** An essentially untoned example of this ever-popular early Morgan dollar issue, solidly struck with vibrant luster. Carefully preserved with a tiny streak of reddish-toning noted at the eagle's left (facing) wingtip. (#7130)

1336 **1881-S MS67 NGC.** This crisply struck and practically untoned type piece has powerful luster and a delightful overall appearance. Only a hint of haze appears in the fields surrounding the portrait. (#7130)

1337 **1881-S MS67 PCGS.** Outstanding eye appeal, the heavily basined dies show the usual semi-prooflike finish in the fields. Fully struck. While mostly brilliant, there is just a hint of pale golden color around the margins. (#7130)

1338 **1881-S MS67 PCGS.** An exactingly struck and thoroughly lustrous Superb Gem. A superior candidate for a silver type set. Exceptionally free from marks, and encapsulated in a small-sized first generation holder.
From The Reuben Reinstein Collection. (#7130)

Remarkable 1881-S Morgan Dollar MS68

1339 **1881-S MS68 NGC.** The 1881-S Morgan dollar is known to many numismatists as one of the most common issues in the entire series. Even Gems number in the tens of thousands. At the MS68 grade level, however, only around 210 pieces have been certified, through the combined efforts of NGC and PCGS. The current offering is a visually stunning piece that is fully struck and nearly pristine, with intense cartwheel luster on both sides. The eye appeal of this magnificent coin is increased by bright rainbow iridescence along the lower obverse periphery. (#7130)

1340 **1881-S MS67 Prooflike PCGS.** Crisply struck and flashy with blatantly reflective fields. The devices have a degree of frost, and are both sides are brilliant save for an obverse ebony speck at 7 o'clock. Population: 63 in 67 Prooflike, 1 finer (5/07). (#7131)

1341 **1882 MS65 PCGS.** A powerful strike leaves exquisite definition on the design elements, including the hair over Liberty's ear and the eagle's breast feathers. Highly lustrous silver-gray surfaces are visited by occasional wisps of barely discernible light tan. A few minor marks do not disturb. (#7132)

1342 **1882 MS66 NGC.** Sharply struck with shimmering luster and surfaces that are essentially untoned on the obverse, while showing a slight degree of tan color on the reverse. Other than a few tiny nicks and spots, both sides of the piece are remarkably well preserved.
From The Reuben Reinstein Collection. (#7132)

1343 **1882-CC MS66 PCGS.** Well struck with snow-white surfaces that exhibit intense mint frost and dazzling cartwheel splendor over both sides. Liberty's cheek is clean and the eagle's breast is pristine. A minimally marked, beautifully preserved Carson City dollar. (#7134)

1344 **1882-CC MS66 NGC.** Light golden toning endows this lustrous and unblemished high grade CC-mint dollar. Slight softness at the centers has no effect on the eye appeal. Struck from boldly clashed dies. (#7134)

1345 **1882-CC MS66 PCGS.** This lightly toned and unblemished CC-mint type coin has only minor incompleteness of detail on the hair above the ear and on the eagle's breast. (#7134)

1346 **1882-CC MS66 PCGS.** Radiant luster issues from both faces of this gorgeous Premium Gem, and a well executed strike left razor-sharp definition on the design features. Untoned surfaces are well preserved. (#7134)

1347 **1882-CC MS66 NGC.** Intense mint frost flashes over each side of this brilliant-white Premium Gem. Well struck with minimal marks. An attractive example of this relatively available Carson City issue.
From The Vanek Collection. (#7134)

1348 **1882-CC MS66 NGC.** Solidly struck with vibrant luster and a few small areas of milky haze in the fields. This attractive Premium Gem, from an issue that made up a significant proportion of the GSA dollars, has a few dots of deep crimson patina, two near the date and one on the tip of the eagle's right (facing) wing.
From The Silver Fox Collection. (#7134)

Visually Appealing 1882-CC Dollar, MS67

1349 **1882-CC MS67 NGC.** A common Carson City type coin but rarely encountered in Superb condition. The CC dollars that did survive after initial minting and distribution were generally roughly handled over the decades. As a result, abrasions are the usual traveling companion on most of the dollars from this popular Western mint. This particular coin is as clean as an early S-mint in high grade but, of course, the luster characteristics are different. The surfaces here are velvety smooth and thick with luster. Most of each side is brilliant with just the lightest arc of golden color at the bottom of the obverse. Sharply struck. Census: 41 in 67, 0 finer (6/07).
From The Reuben Reinstein Collection. (#7134)

1350 **1882-CC MS64 Deep Mirror Prooflike PCGS.** Sharply struck with frosted devices and deeply reflective, jet-black fields. Slightly scuffy on Liberty's cheek, and in the left obverse field. An attractive black and white near-Gem from the Carson City Mint. (#97135)

1351 **1882-O MS64 PCGS.** Glowing luster emanates from both sides of this attractive near-Gem. The reverse displays just a whisper of gold color in the upper portions, while the obverse is bathed with iridescent hues of cobalt-blue, lavender, golden-tan, and apple-green. The strike is above average for the issue. A few minor marks on each side define the grade. (#7136)

1352 **1882-O MS65 NGC.** Boldly struck overall, if slightly weak above the ear and on the eagle's breast feathers. The surfaces are lustrous and essentially untoned. A couple of faint pinscratches on the cheek and in the left obverse field are too slight to limit the grade. (#7136)

1353 **1882-O MS65 PCGS.** Virtually untoned with swirling satiny luster and well struck devices with excellent definition in the centers. The cheek and obverse fields are unusually clean and nearly abrasion-free. (#7136)

1354 **1882-O MS65 PCGS,** well struck and faintly toned with booming luster and outstanding preservation; and a **1900 MS65 PCGS,** crisply struck and untoned, lustrous, a clean obverse, housed in an old green label holder. (Total: 2 coins)
From The Reuben Reinstein Collection. (#7136)

Gem Mint State 1882-O/S Silver Dollar

1355 1882-O/S MS65 PCGS. VAM-4. A Top 100 Variety. Designated "Strong" by PCGS, referring to the sharpness of the overmintmark feature. Several O/S varieties are known, and Breen commented: "Those with less of the S visible at O command smaller premiums or will price as preceding," referring to the normal 1882-O variety. In 2005, Dave Bowers wrote: Be sure to buy one with the overmintmark distinct under a good 4x glass."

Bowers (1993) speculates that hundreds of thousands of the 6 million Silver Dollars produced at the New Orleans Mint in 1882 are of the O/S variety. Since this variety is plentiful in circulated grades, this estimate seems reasonable. Uncirculated examples are another matter entirely, and Bowers states: "The 1882-O/S is very scarce in lower Mint State grades, scarcest in MS64, and very rare in MS65." In 2005, he estimated a field population of 4,300 to 7,500 Mint State examples still exist today, commenting that the original mintage and distribution of this issue are not known.

PCGS has only seen this single example above MS64, and NGC reports just 11 (resubmissions?) coins in MS65 and none finer (6/07). This is a lovely, satin textured Gem with no toning and few abrasions. The strike is a trifle soft on the hair over Liberty's ear, but the overall definition is well above average by the standards of the New Orleans Mint. An important bidding opportunity for the Morgan Dollar specialist. (#7138)

1356 **1882-S MS67 NGC.** Pristine surfaces and brilliant throughout with blazing mint luster. A large number of '82-S dollars were set aside, and they were almost all well-made coins. (#7140)

1357 **1882-S MS67 PCGS.** This exactingly struck Superb Gem has booming luster and a hint of tan-gray toning. Exceptionally clean, as expected from the grade. Encapsulated in an old green label holder.
From The Vanek Collection. (#7140)

1358 **1882-S MS67 NGC.** Sea-green dominates the reverse, although the border offers glimpses of fire-red and gold. The obverse is mostly brilliant, but slender bands of golden-brown and powder-blue hug the lower left border. A well struck example with a smooth cheek and minor contact on the eagle's breast.
From The Reuben Reinstein Collection. (#7140)

1359 **1883 MS66 NGC.** Well-defined with lovely luster and a hint of steel-gray patina in the fields. This pleasing early P-mint piece displays a die crack through the lower part of the date.
From The Vanek Collection. (#7142)

1360 **1883 MS67 NGC.** The brilliant, snow-white surfaces display intense mint frost and glittering cartwheel effects in the fields. Sharply struck and remarkably well preserved. A gorgeous and conditionally scarce Superb Gem. Census: 94 in 67, 2 finer (6/07).
From The Reuben Reinstein Collection. (#7142)

1361 **1883-CC MS66 PCGS.** This Premium Gem features intense mint frost over the brilliant obverse and the lightly toned reverse. Crisply struck, minimally abraded, and highly attractive. (#7144)

1362 **1883-CC MS66 NGC.** This alluring Premium Gem is virtually untoned, with a lovely satiny sheen and a noticeable paucity of marks on both sides. A reddish-copper toning fleck covers obverse star 12. A popular and readily available Carson City issue. (#7144)

1363 **1883-CC MS66 PCGS.** Smooth, silky mint frost covers each side of this uncharacteristically clean CC dollar. Just a bit softly struck over Liberty's ear. A wonderful type coin. (#7144)

1364 **1883-CC MS66 PCGS.** Amazingly vibrant layers of crimson, gold, and green iridescence cover the entire obverse of this exquisitely preserved dollar. The reverse is mostly white, save for mere hints of lilac and gold coloration. Well struck and nearly blemish-free. (#7144)

1365 **1883-CC MS66 NGC.** A flashy and slightly frosty representative of this Carson City Morgan dollar issue, crisply struck with russet-peach patina restricted to the rims and essentially untoned surfaces elsewhere. One of slightly over 1.2 million examples coined.
From The Vanek Collection. (#7144)

1366 **1883-CC MS66 PCGS.** Pumpkin-gold toning graces the left obverse border of this otherwise brilliant Carson City Morgan. Boldly struck and thoroughly lustrous. (#7144)

Brilliant MS67 1883-CC Dollar

1367 **1883-CC MS67 NGC.** Untoned with a flashy, satiny appearance. The striking details are needle sharp over the frosty central devices. While a common Carson City dollar in mint condition, as the grade rises to the Superb level the population thins out dramatically. Census: 88 in 67, 0 finer (6/07).
From The Reuben Reinstein Collection. (#7144)

Beautiful 1883-CC Dollar
MS67 Prooflike

1368 **1883-CC MS67 Prooflike PCGS.** The 1883-CC dollar, with a mintage of 1,204,000 coins, includes a large number of prooflike examples. Indeed, PCGS and NGC have seen close to 4,000 prooflike specimens! Prooflike 1883-CCs are obviously common, except in the lofty Superb Gem level of preservation. The two services have certified fewer than 10 MS67 Prooflike pieces, and none finer. Iridescent golden-brown, lavender, and cobalt-blue patina occupy the obverse of this Superb Gem, while the reverse remains mostly untoned. Exquisite strike definition heightens the coin's eye appeal, as do the impeccably preserved surfaces. Additionally, both sides yield considerable field-motif contrast. Census: 2 in 67 Prooflike, 0 finer (6/07). (#7145)

1369 **1883-CC MS65 Deep Mirror Prooflike PCGS.** Beneath intermittent crimson-charcoal and silver-gray patina, exceptional reflectivity shines through. An exactingly struck and attractive Gem example of this Carson City issue, one popularized through the GSA sales. (#97145)

1370 **1883-CC MS65 Deep Mirror Prooflike NGC.** A stunning white-on-black cameo dollar. While the 1883-CC is often used as a type coin, Deep Mirror Prooflike pieces are much less available for such a purpose. Fully struck and brilliant. (#97145)

Lovely MS66 Deep Mirror Prooflike 1883-CC Dollar

1371 **1883-CC MS66 Deep Mirror Prooflike NGC.** The 1883-CC is one of the most frequently encountered CC dollars, but examples in MS66 combined with Deep Mirror Prooflike fields are infrequently found and they are objects of great beauty. This is a mostly brilliant coin with a couple of gray streaks of color on the reverse. Fully struck. The surfaces are clean (as would be expected) with rich mint frost set against the deeply reflective fields. Census: 35 in 66, 4 finer (6/07).
From The Silver Fox Collection. (#97145)

Rare Superb Gem 1883-O Morgan Dollar

1372 **1883-O MS67 NGC.** Untoned and intensely lustrous, with marvelously clean surfaces, this is a conditionally rare Superb Gem example of this New Orleans Mint issue. Dave Bowers (1993) estimated that several million Mint State examples had been dispersed from long-term storage, many of those in the great releases of 1962-1964. Out of those millions, however, only a tiny fraction have achieved this lofty grade level. Census: 26 in 67, 0 finer at either service (6/07). *From The Reuben Reinstein Collection.* (#7146)

1373 **1883-S MS62 PCGS.** The original autumn-gold and pearl-gray toning is moderately deeper on the reverse. Lustrous and exactingly struck with a clean reverse and a cluster of small marks on the lower cheek. (#7148)

1374 **1883-S MS62 PCGS.** The 1883-S is conditionally rare in Mint State. This lustrous example is suitably struck and has a clean reverse. The cheek displays scattered contact. Certified in a green label holder. (#7148)

1375 **1883-S MS62 PCGS.** Light peach-gold toning clings to the peripheries of this flashy and attentively struck better date dollar. The fields are unexpectedly clean, and even the cheek has only moderate grazes. (#7148)

1376 **1883-S MS62 ANACS.** A brilliant and fully lustrous piece with its share of minor obverse marks. Well struck, as is customary of the San Francisco Mint from this era. Conditionally rare in Mint State. (#7148)

1377 **1883-S MS62 NGC.** A well-defined example that has modestly reflective fields and powerful luster. A degree of haze is present in the fields of this lightly abraded S-mint piece, from an issue far less available than those of two or three years before. (#7148)

1378 **1883-S MS62 ANACS.** A brilliant and flashy representative of this conditionally rare issue. Well struck and lightly toned with a relatively clean reverse and only moderate marks on the portrait. (#7148)

1379 **1883-S MS63 PCGS.** This conditionally scarce silver dollar has dazzling luster and a good strike. Light tan toning confirms the originality. Scattered small marks are appropriate for the grade. (#7148)

1380 **1883-S MS63 NGC.** Booming luster and a decisive strike proclaim the eye appeal of this essentially brilliant better date dollar. Liberty's cheek has minor marks, while the fields are well preserved. (#7148)

Lustrous Choice 1883-S Dollar

1381 **1883-S MS64 PCGS.** While the San Francisco issues between 1878 and 1882 are commonplace, the 1883-S and 1884-S are surprisingly scarce in Mint State despite mintages in the millions. This is a beautiful near-Gem with peripheral gold and plum-red obverse toning. The reverse is nearly brilliant. Lustrous and minimally abraded with a good strike. (#7148)

Dazzling Choice 1883-S Dollar

1382 **1883-S MS64 PCGS.** A sharp strike with brilliant silver luster and attractive eye appeal. From a mintage of over 6 million coins, this issue is common in all circulated grades, but it becomes scarce in MS60 or higher. Choice quality specimens, such as the example we are offering here, are scarce, and Gems are rare. *Ex: The Chicago-Ark Collection (Heritage, 8/06), lot 2653, which realized $4,600.*
From The Reuben Reinstein Collection. (#7148)

Impressive 1883-S Gem Dollar

1383 1883-S MS65 NGC. The 1883-S dollar comes with a mintage of 6,250,000 pieces. David Bowers, in his book, *A Complete History and Price Guide*, writes that: "The distribution of the 1883-S began in large quantity soon after the mintage, with the result that examples in all grades were available to numismatists generations ago. However, by the 1940s the issue was viewed as scarce. In the 1950s some bags were released, but probably just a few. At least part of a bag found its way to Nevada investor LaVere Redfield. I am not aware of any quantities in the 1962-1964 Treasury release."

Dazzling luster exudes from both sides of this Gem. Untoned surfaces exhibit well impressed design features, including sharp definition in the hair at Liberty's ear and on the eagle's breast feathers. The few unobtrusive marks scattered about do not distract, and are certainly within the parameters of the MS65 grade designation. Census: 15 in 65, 3 finer (6/07).
From The Reuben Reinstein Collection. (#7148)

1384 1884 MS66 PCGS. This meticulously struck and thoroughly lustrous Premium Gem displays only a whisper of gold toning. The reverse is nearly immaculate, and only a thin mark on the ear determines the grade. (#7150)

Highly Lustrous MS67 1884 Dollar

1385 1884 MS67 NGC. A narrow ribbon of golden-tan toning hugs the right and lower obverse rim, while arcs of original cobalt-blue, lavender, and golden-tan are positioned along the right reverse border. The remaining areas are brilliant. Well preserved surfaces exhibit cartwheel luster and exquisitely defined motifs. Census: 31 in 67, 2 finer (5/07). (#7150)

Brilliant Superb Gem 1884 Dollar

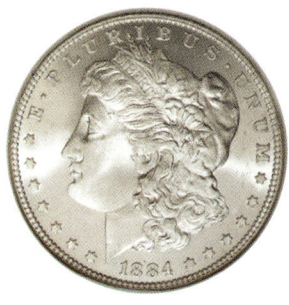

1386 1884 MS67 NGC. One of the more available P-mint dollars with more than 14 million pieces struck. Of course, most of the survivors (of which there are many) are in lower grades, and few qualify at the MS67 level. This is a marvelous coin that has thick mint luster and is brilliant throughout. Well struck. Census: 31 in 67, 2 finer (6/07).
From The Reuben Reinstein Collection. (#7150)

1387 1884-CC MS66 PCGS. Glowing luster radiates from the satiny surfaces of this Premium Gem Carson City issue. Nicely struck, including in the centers, areas that often exhibit weakness. Well preserved surfaces reveal no mark worthy of individual mention. (#7152)

1388 1884-CC MS66 PCGS. Exceptionally thick mint frost covers both sides of this impressive CC type coin. Both obverse and reverse are almost devoid of abrasions or luster grazes, and the striking definition is full. (#7152)

1389 1884-CC MS66 PCGS. Sharply struck with hints of ice-blue patina and occasional rose accents in the fields. A gleaming and carefully preserved Old West artifact struck at the legendary Carson City Mint.
From The Vanek Collection. (#7152)

1390 1884-CC MS66 PCGS. The crisply struck devices exhibit wonderful frost on this Carson City dollar, from an issue made famous by the GSA sales. Delicate touches of gold and claret color at the margins give this Premium Gem an elegant aura. (#7152)

Smooth MS67 1884-CC Dollar

1391 **1884-CC MS67 NGC.** Most of the 1.1 million-piece mintage survived in Uncirculated grades, and the last were finally distributed as part of the GSA holdings in the late 1970s. This is a fully struck example that shows none of the often-seen prooflike finish. Rather, the coin has even, thick mint frost over each side. Brilliant, the surfaces are nearly free from post-striking impairments of any size. Census: 75 in 67, 0 finer (6/07).
From The Reuben Reinstein Collection. (#7152)

1392 **1884-CC MS65 Deep Mirror Prooflike PCGS.** The devices are thickly frosted, and the fields are prominently mirrored. A white-on-black Carson City dollar with immense eye appeal. Crisply struck and clean overall with a small patch of thin marks above the arrowheads. (#97153)

Deep Mirror Prooflike 1884-CC Dollar MS66

1393 **1884-CC MS66 Deep Mirror Prooflike NGC.** VAM-7. A remarkable DMPL Carson City dollar. The devices are thickly frosted, and exhibit unimprovable white-on-black contrast with the glassy fields. The strike is precise, although the eagle displays minor mint-made granularity from a rusted or improperly prepared reverse die. The 18 in the date is recut. (#97153)

Impressive 1884-CC Morgan, MS66 Deep Prooflike

1394 **1884-CC MS66 Deep Mirror Prooflike NGC.** An amazing specimen, this piece will surely be a treat for the connoisseur. Both sides have exceptional mint brilliance with bright silver surfaces. The fields are fully and deeply mirrored, and they contrast nicely with the frosty and lustrous devices. A few minor marks are evident on each side, but they are not significant. Census: 38 in 66 Deep Prooflike, 3 finer (6/07). (#97153)

Impressive, Alluring Superb Gem 1884-O Dollar

1395 **1884-O MS67 NGC.** The New Orleans Mint produced only silver dollars in 1884, and 9.7 million coins flowed from the presses of the southern facility that year. Unfortunately, many of those pieces were softly defined on the central highpoints. Although a tad weak on the hair detail just above Liberty's ear, this untoned Superb Gem possesses nearly unsurpassable technical quality for the issue. An dynamic cartwheel sheen flashes over both sides, and there are no bagmarks that are worthy of individual mention.
From The Vanek Collection. (#7154)

Brilliant 1884-O MS67 Dollar

1396 **1884-O MS67 NGC.** The 1884-O dollar, with a mintage of 9.73 million pieces, is easy to obtain in Mint State, as the census/population data indicate. NGC and PCGS have certified tens of thousands of Uncirculated examples through MS65. Premium Gems are a bit tougher to locate, and MS67 coins can be elusive. Pleasing luster radiates from this Superb Gem, and untoned, well preserved surfaces reflect an attentive strike. Census: 73 in 67, 0 finer (6/07).
From The Reuben Reinstein Collection. (#7154)

Frosty Superb Gem 1884-O Dollar

1397 **1884-O MS67 NGC.** Both sides of this impressive piece have frosty silver luster with no trace of toning, save for the slightest crescent of pale gold along part of the reverse border. The design motifs are boldly rendered, and the overall eye appeal is excellent. Census: 73 in 67, 0 finer (6/07). (#7154)

Bold Superb Gem 1884-O Dollar

1398 1884-O MS67 NGC. Although the hair over Liberty's ear is typically weak, all other design features on both sides are boldly defined. The frosty white-silver surfaces are fully brilliant and highly lustrous. This is an excellent example of the date, qualifying in a tie for the finest certified by NGC. Census: 73 in 67, 0 finer (6/07). (#7154)

1399 1884-S AU58 ANACS. Since the cartwheel luster is complete, only a whisper of steel-gray on the central devices confirms a brief encounter with circulation. The borders offer light gold patina, and the obverse field is somewhat abraded. (#7156)

1400 1884-S AU58 ANACS. Well struck and free of toning, with prooflike fields and lightly frosted devices. Traces of highpoint wear and numerous small abrasions define the grade of this near-Mint example. (#7156)

Brilliant MS61 1884-S Dollar

1401 1884-S MS61 NGC. One of the great rarities in the Morgan series in mint condition. This piece is brilliant throughout with bright, semi-prooflike fields. The centers are well, but not fully struck. Numerous small abrasions are peppered over each side, thus accounting for the grade, but none are worthy of individual mention.
From The Silver Fox Collection. (#7156)

Distinguished 1884-S Dollar, MS61 Deep Mirror Prooflike

1402 1884-S MS61 Deep Mirror Prooflike NGC. As late as 2005, in his *Guide Book of Morgan Silver Dollars*, Q. David Bowers described this issue as "unknown" in Deep Mirror Prooflike, going so far as to describe such a coin as "a Holy Grail in the Morgan series." Yet the facts of numismatics are susceptible to change, and new discoveries can render decades of common wisdom obsolete. Far from being "merely" Prooflike, this coin has powerful, flashy mirrors that unquestionably merit the Deep Mirror Prooflike designation, and the piece stands alone as the **only** Deep Mirror Prooflike representative ever graded by either NGC or PCGS (5/07).

The 1884-S, while an available issue in circulated grades, becomes distinctly elusive in any Mint State grade. Unlike the famous S-mint issues from a few years before, the vast majority of 1884-S dollars saw considerable circulation, leaving only a handful of unworn survivors. With Mint or near-Mint condition as an inflexible prerequisite for Prooflike status, it is little wonder that few such pieces survive today, and that the survival of a Deep Mirror Prooflike coin would seem impossible.

The surfaces of this distinctive coin exhibit powerful mirrors despite minor haze, and while the piece has little contrast (as Wayne Miller described Prooflike representatives of the issue in 1982), the fields offer reflectivity even at arm's length. The devices have crisp detail overall, with just a touch of the usual weakness present at the hair over Liberty's ear. While the dollar displays a number of scattered abrasions that justify the grade, including a number in the fields and on the lower right cheek, these flaws have surprisingly little impact on the overall eye appeal. A noteworthy example that should appeal to even the most discerning collector of the series. (#97157)

1403 **1885 MS67 NGC.** As pointed out by Bowers, in his silver dollar *Encyclopedia*, this issue is very common and exists by the hundreds of thousands in lower grades of Mint State preservation. At the Superb Gem level, however, the issue suddenly becomes scarce. This example is well struck and untoned, with dynamic cartwheel luster and very clean surfaces. Attractive and technically impressive.
From The Vanek Collection. (#7158)

1404 **1885 MS67 PCGS.** Ex: Jackson Hole. As with most of the readily available Morgan issues, the 1885 comes in varying degrees of quality, but this exquisitely preserved Superb Gem has eye appeal in spades, with vibrant luster and boldly defined devices that display just a hint of rose patina. PCGS has graded only one coin finer (6/07). (#7158)

1405 **1885 MS67 NGC.** Fully struck with lavish luster and untoned silver surfaces. Impressively preserved and free of all but the most inconsequential of nicks and luster grazes.
From The Reuben Reinstein Collection. (#7158)

1406 **1885-CC MS65 PCGS.** A shining and solidly struck Gem example of this low-mintage, yet plentiful Carson City issue. The devices display a touch of frost, and aside from a few areas of haze on the portrait and over the lower reverse field, the surfaces are untoned. (#7160)

1407 **1885-CC MS65 PCGS.** Warm orange-gold and cooler blue-green patina graces the obverse, while the reverse has similar colors at the margins. Sharply struck with delightful luster and light frost on the reverse highpoints. Though this issue's mintage consists of just 228,000 pieces, the vast majority of them survive in high grades. (#7160)

1408 **1885-CC MS65 PCGS.** Streaks of walnut-brown toning invigorate the margins, but the centers are essentially brilliant. A boldly struck and clean-cheeked Gem of this low mintage Carson City favorite. (#7160)

1409 **1885-CC MS65 NGC.** A lovely, high grade coin that has swirling mint luster that is contrasted against flashy, semi-prooflike fields. Sharply struck. The obverse is brilliant while the reverse displays an accent of pale golden patina. (#7160)

1410 **1885-CC MS65 PCGS.** This virtually brilliant Gem has prominent luster and an assertive strike. Liberty's cheek is clean, and the same can be said about the fields. A widely collected low mintage CC-mint issue. (#7160)

1411 **1885-CC MS65 NGC.** A sharply struck and splendidly lustrous Gem that has a nearly unabraded reverse and only a few faint grazes on the cheek and neck. The 1885-CC enjoys the status as the lowest mintage CC-mint Morgan dollar. (#7160)

1412 **1885-CC MS66 PCGS.** Despite a mintage of only 228,000 pieces, Mint State representatives of this popular Carson City issue are readily available. Zones of pale yellow and ice-blue color grace the shining surfaces of this Premium Gem, decisively struck with strong eye appeal. (#7160)

1413 **1885-CC MS66 NGC.** A brilliant and highly lustrous example of this popular, low mintage CC dollar. Sharply struck and problem-free. (#7160)

1414 **1885-CC MS66 PCGS.** This is a rather spectacular example of the admittedly common 1885-CC Morgan dollar. Sharply struck and highly lustrous, with a beautiful frosty sheen, the stone-white surfaces are completely untoned. Surface marks are positively minimal for the grade.
From The Vanek Collection. (#7160)

1415 **1885-CC MS66 NGC.** Despite a modest mintage of only 228,000 pieces, the 1885-CC dollar remains available in higher Mint State grades due to the storage of most examples in government vaults. Vibrant luster and a trace of reddish patina characterize this lovely, sharply struck Gem.
From The Silver Fox Collection. (#7160)

Lustrous MS67 1885-CC Dollar

1416 **1885-CC MS67 NGC.** VAM-4. A Hot 50 Variety. The dash beneath the second 8 is said to be the most prominent of the Morgan dollar series. This intricately struck Superb Gem is essentially brilliant, although examination with a glass reveals a few otherwise imperceptible peripheral fingerprint traces. Abrasions are virtually absent, as expected of the MS67 grade. A popular low mintage CC-mint issue. (#7160)

Intensely Lustrous MS67 1885-CC Dollar

1417 **1885-CC MS67 NGC.** The low mintage of the 1885-CC will always be a lure for collectors, but truth be told, this issue is many times rarer in circulated grades than in mint condition. Not so in Superb condition, though. This is an immaculate coin that shows bright, swirling cartwheel luster. Brilliant, except for a razor-thin accent of golden color over the denticles. Census: 47 in 67, 5 finer (6/07).
From The Reuben Reinstein Collection. (#7160)

Conditionally Scarce 1885-CC MS66 Prooflike

1418 **1885-CC MS66 Prooflike NGC.** This brilliant silver dollar is one of the more attractive examples that we have examined recently, from the 1885 Carson City issue. Q. David Bowers has noted that Prooflikes are available for this date, but mostly in lower Uncirculated grades. This piece is frosty, radiant, and beautiful. Census: 20 in 66 Prooflike, 3 finer (6/07). (#7161)

1419 **1885-CC MS63 Deep Mirror Prooflike PCGS.** The fields offer imposing reflectivity, and the devices are thickly frosted. This crisply struck and low mintage CC-mint dollar has a well preserved reverse and the expected moderate marks on the cheek. Housed in a green label holder. (#97161)

1420 **1885-CC MS64 Deep Mirror Prooflike PCGS.** Choice and boldly impressed with deep reflectivity and excellent contrast. The heavily frosted devices have few marks for the grade, though the fields are lightly abraded. A wonderful example of this low-mintage, yet available issue. Housed in a green label holder. (#97161)

Outstanding 1885-CC Dollar
MS65 Deep Mirror Prooflike

1421 **1885-CC MS65 Deep Mirror Prooflike PCGS.** David Bowers (2005) writes that: "The 1885-CC exists by the hundreds of thousands of pieces, as more than half of the original mintage (228,000 pieces) survived and was distributed in the late 20th century." The surviving specimen in this lot is a gorgeous Gem with deep mirror fields that establish outstanding contrast with frosted, sharply struck design elements. Essentially untoned, except for a few speckles of milky-tan color scattered about. There are no significant contact marks to report. (#97161)

1422 **1885-O MS65 ★ NGC.** A spectacular arc across the right obverse exhibits ruby-red, lemon, powder-blue, and apple-green. This lustrous Gem is otherwise untoned, and is well struck save for a shallow strike-through on the eagle's belly. (#7162)

1423 **1885-O MS67 NGC.** A lustrous and essentially brilliant high grade example with undeniable eye appeal. The strike is decidedly above average for a New Orleans dollar from this decade. (#7162)

1424 **1885-O MS67 PCGS.** A frosty and essentially untoned New Orleans Superb Gem, untoned save for thin bands of aqua, gold, magenta, and blue-green at the lower left obverse. A delightful example of this early issue, more elusive in the highest grades than its mintage of over 9.1 million pieces might suggest. Tied for the finest certified by PCGS (5/07). (#7162)

1425 **1885-O MS67 NGC.** The 1885-O is the most common of all Morgan dollar issues from the New Orleans Mint, and there are literally millions of them that survive in Uncirculated condition, according to Q. David Bowers (1993). At the Superb Gem level, however, the numbers are relatively few, with just over 500 pieces so graded by NGC and PCGS combined. This example is well struck, untoned, and nearly pristine. It also emits a lovely, effulgent sheen that further increases the overall eye appeal of the piece.
From The Vanek Collection. (#7162)

1426 **1885-O MS67 NGC.** Traces of tan patina grace this sharply struck and highly lustrous Superb Gem. A well preserved example of this collectible New Orleans issue. NGC has certified only 9 pieces in higher grades (6/07).
From The Reuben Reinstein Collection. (#7162)

1427 **1885-O MS67 NGC.** Crisply detailed with shimmering mint frost over both sides and mostly-white surfaces that display bands of gold near the right side borders. Other than a faint graze in the upper left obverse field, and a few trivial marks and spots, the Superb surfaces are remarkably clean. (#7162)

1428 **1885-O MS67 NGC.** Intense frosty mint luster radiates from the bright, snow-white surfaces of this Superb Morgan dollar. The design elements are well struck, except for a flat area just above Liberty's ear. Surface marks are nearly nonexistent. (#7162)

1429 **1885-S MS64 PCGS.** With a mintage of just under 1.5 million pieces, the 1885-S does not rank among the keys to the series, though examples are more elusive than those of a number of other issues. Both sides of this crisply defined silver-gray example reveal a degree of reflectivity in the modestly marked fields. (#7164)

1430 **1885-S MS65 NGC.** VAM-2. The 5 in the date is lightly recut at the peak. This is a highly lustrous Gem with an occasional wisp of faint tan patina in localized areas. Well preserved, with just a couple of minor luster grazes on Liberty's cheek. NGC has certified a mere 12 pieces finer (6/07).
From The Reuben Reinstein Collection. (#7164)

MS66 1885-S Dollar With Flashy Fields

1431 **1885-S MS66 NGC.** This is a fully brilliant and sharply struck Gem example without any evidence of toning on either side. It has bright silver surfaces with frosty devices and satiny fields, creating an attractive cameo effect, despite not qualifying as prooflike. In spite of the numerous '85-S dollars in the Redfield Hoard, MS66 coins (by today's standards) were virtually non-existent. It would be interesting to know the pedigree of this coin. (#7164)

Extremely Scarce Premium Gem 1885-S Morgan Dollar

1432 **1885-S MS66 ICG.** This is a frosty and well made Premium Gem that presents untoned surfaces with dazzling cartwheel luster in the fields. Just a few wispy luster breaks are noted on each side of the coin. This issue is exceedingly scarce at the MS66 grade level, where just 37 pieces have been certified by the two major services (5/07).
From The Vanek Collection. (#7164)

1433 **1885-S MS64 Prooflike NGC.** Boldly struck, frosty, and brilliant, this snow-white near-Gem displays flashy, prooflike fields and nicely frosted central devices. Several blemishes on Liberty's face prevent a higher grade designation.
From The Vanek Collection. (#7165)

1434 **1886 MS67 NGC.** This exquisite Superb Gem has thin crescents of teal and peach at the left obverse and a hazy zone of similar colors at the right reverse. Untoned otherwise with pleasing detail and swirling luster, which combine for uncommonly strong visual appeal. NGC has certified just eight numerically finer pieces (5/07).
From The Vanek Collection. (#7166)

1435 **1886 MS67 NGC.** This boldly struck Superb Gem has an unabraded cheek and an untoned appearance. Scintillating luster ensures a lofty grade. Each side has only a whisper of tan toning.
From The Reuben Reinstein Collection. (#7166)

1436 **1886 MS67 NGC.** One of the most notoriously common dates in the series, the 1886 Morgan dollar becomes more elusive at the Superb Gem grade level. This marvelously preserved example is fully struck and essentially untoned, with only the tiniest of imperfections noted on either side. (#7166)

1437 **1886 MS67 NGC.** Fully struck and brilliant, this silvery-white Morgan dollar displays a flashy cartwheel sheen across each side, and only faint marks that prevent perfection. One of the most common silver dollar issues and one of the most popular for type purposes. (#7166)

1438 **1886 MS67 NGC.** This is a beautifully clean and lustrous Morgan dollar, from a high-mintage issue that is relatively easy to obtain, even at the current lofty grade level. Untoned and bright-white with crisply struck devices and near-pristine surfaces. A faint beige toning streak on Liberty's jaw fails to limit the grade of this lovely Superb Gem. (#7166)

1439 **1886-O MS61 ANACS.** This piece exhibits a typically indifferent strike along with relatively unimpressive luster. The satiny pearl-gray surfaces reveal a few scattered toning specks and some small marks. The '86-O is a scarce issue in Mint State, despite its high original mintage of more than 10 million pieces. (#7168)

1440 **1886-O MS62 PCGS.** Golden-brown and lavender embrace the obverse. The reverse is nearly untoned. The strike is above average for this conditionally rare issue. A pair of marks beneath the eye require mention, but the piece is otherwise smooth. (#7168)

1441 **1886-O MS62 PCGS.** This satiny silver-gray Morgan dollar has peripheral butter-gold toning. The profile has a few small marks, and the eagle's claws and the hair above the ear are slightly soft. The mintmark is lightly repunched south. A conditionally rare O-mint issue. (#7168)

1442 **1886-O MS62 PCGS.** A brilliant, satiny, and lightly abraded example of this challenging New Orleans issue. The centers are incomplete, but sharper than often seen. The 1886-O is notoriously scarce in Mint State. Certified in a green label holder. (#7168)

1443 **1886-O MS62 ANACS.** VAM-1A. A Top 100 Variety. The "E Reverse" variety with a prominent E (from LIBERTY) clashed beneath the tail feathers. The "two clashes" subvariety of VAM-1A. This desirable VAM is considered rare in Mint State. Lightly toned and satiny with surprisingly smooth surfaces. (#7168)

1444 **1886-S MS64 PCGS.** VAM-2. A Top 100 Variety. Faint caramel-gold toning visits this highly lustrous better date near-Gem. The centers show some blending of detail, but the overall strike is good. The obverse field is well preserved, while the portrait displays minor marks. The mintmark serifs are repunched. (#7170)

1445 **1886-S MS65 NGC.** Strongly lustrous with a bit of flash and above-average detail for this issue. The essentially untoned surfaces of this S-mint Gem have few marks for the grade.
From The Silver Fox Collection. (#7170)

Exceptional MS66 1886-S Dollar

1446 **1886-S MS66 NGC.** Always considered a better date, the only sizeable release of the '86-S was from the Redfield hoard. Those coins are widely dispersed now, and most were in lower Uncirculated condition. On this piece, the grade and visual appeal is not only derived from the paucity of abrasions that normally are seen on this issue, but also from the heavily basined dies. This is especially evident on the obverse, as seen from the concavity of the fields, and the pronounced die striations on the lower part of that side. Sharply struck throughout. Census: 14 in 66, 2 finer (6/07).
From The Reuben Reinstein Collection. (#7170)

1447 **1887 MS67 NGC.** This beautiful silver type coin has dazzling luster and relentlessly smooth surfaces. The strike is crisp, and the peripheral orange-gold patina contributes further to the eye appeal. (#7172)

1448 **1887 MS67 NGC.** Aside from a light scattering of haze in the reverse fields, the shining surfaces are essentially untoned. A solidly struck example of this Philadelphia issue, from a series that had picked up an assortment of colorful monikers during its decade of existence.
From The Vanek Collection. (#7172)

1449 **1887 MS67 NGC.** The striking details are crisp, if not quite full, and the mostly untoned surfaces display lovely, creamy luster. Surface marks are minimal, as they should be on a Superb Gem.
From The Reuben Reinstein Collection. (#7172)

1450 **1887/6 MS64 PCGS.** VAM-2. A Top 100 Variety. This untoned and lustrous overdated Morgan dollar retains a hint of granularity on the reverse, as struck on an improperly prepared planchet. The few faint obverse grazes are inconsequential for the grade. Certified in a green label holder. (#7174)

Scarce Gem Overdate 1887/6 Dollar

1451 **1887/6 MS65 PCGS.** Bright and satiny, the surfaces of this piece are unusually clean for this normally troublesome issue. Examination with a loupe reveals the distinct lunule of a previously punched 6 at the bottom of the 7. According to Bowers, slightly less than one half percent of the mintage of the 1887 shows this underdigit. Population: 100 in 65, 4 finer (6/07).
From The Reuben Reinstein Collection. (#7174)

Prooflike Gem 1887/6 Morgan

1452 **1887/6 MS65 Prooflike PCGS.** VAM-2. A Top 100 Variety. The curve of the base of the underdigit 6 is evident on each side of the base of the 7. The fields are flashy and smooth, and the devices are also impressively smooth. Sun-gold patina adorns the obverse but is confined to the lower margin on the reverse. Portions of the obverse are mildly granular, as struck. (#7175)

1453 **1887-O MS64 PCGS.** A lightly toned near-Gem that has refreshingly clean obverse field and a remarkably smooth reverse. The hair above the ear and the eagle's claws are slightly soft, as usual for the issue. (#7176)

Satiny MS65 1887-O Dollar
End-of-the-Roll Obverse Toning

1454 **1887-O MS65 PCGS.** With a mintage in excess of 11 million pieces, it is not surprising that the 1887-O is common in the lower grades of Uncirculated. But poor luster and weak strikes thin out the ranks and surprisingly few Gems are known today. This is certainly a pleasing example. The obverse has end-of-the-roll toning, and the surfaces are uncommonly lustrous with a pronounced satin-like finish. Clean on each side, the striking details are somewhat soft in the centers. (#7176)

Clean, Brilliant 1887-O Dollar, MS65

1455 **1887-O MS65 PCGS.** Long considered a common date in the Morgan series, the 1887-O is now recognized as an important condition rarity in MS65 and better grades. This is a lovely coin with superior luster characteristics. Each side has thick, satiny mint luster and there is no trace of toning. Remarkably clean for an '87-O, the only negative aspect of this piece is the usually seen softness of strike in the centers.
From The Reuben Reinstein Collection. (#7176)

1456 **1887-S MS64 PCGS.** Well struck and essentially untoned, save for scattered tan specks on each side, with bright satiny luster that approaches semi-prooflikeness in the fields. A few light marks are consistent with the assigned grade. Faint roller marks (as struck) travel across Liberty's ear and jaw. (#7180)

Bright, Lustrous MS65 1887-S Dollar

1457 **1887-S MS65 NGC.** While many 1887-S dollars were released into circulation in the 19th century, a considerable number of the 1.7 million minted were also set aside and not released until the 1930s. This is a brilliant coin that is fully struck in the centers. Bright mint luster races around each side of this attractive Gem.
From The Silver Fox Collection. (#7180)

Sparkling MS65 1887-S Morgan Dollar

1458 **1887-S MS65 PCGS.** The 1887-S is a better date among the Redfield holdings. Of the bags in his hoard, most were in lower Uncirculated grades. Few Gems are known of this issue, and we are pleased to have two in this sale. This fully struck Gem has bright, satiny mint luster that races around the surfaces as it is rotated beneath a light. As one would expect from an MS65, there are no singularly mentionable or detracting marks on either side.
From The Reuben Reinstein Collection. (#7180)

Highly Lustrous 1888 Dollar, MS67

1459 **1888 MS67 NGC.** Highly lustrous surfaces see a sliver of medium intensity golden-tan and cobalt-blue toning at the lower left obverse margins, and whispers of light gold color at the upper left reverse rim area. The design features exhibit sharp definition for an issue that sometimes can be weakly struck. Impeccably preserved surfaces occur on both sides. Census: 35 in 67, 1 finer (6/07). (#7182)

Appealing 1888 Superb Gem Dollar

1460 **1888 MS67 NGC.** Bright luster exudes from the untoned surfaces of this lovely Superb Gem Morgan, and a well executed strike manifests itself in crisp definition on the design features, further enhancing the coin's outstanding eye appeal. Near-pristine surfaces are the rule on both obverse and reverse. Large quantities of this issue were released by the Treasury Department between 1955 and 1964 (David Bowers, 2006). Census: 35 in 67, 1 finer (6/07).
From The Reuben Reinstein Collection. (#7182)

1461 **1888-O MS66 NGC.** This well struck and strongly lustrous O-mint dollar has only a hint of golden patina and ample visual appeal. NGC has certified just one coin finer, while PCGS has assigned no examples a higher grade (5/07).
From The Silver Fox Collection. (#7184)

1462 **1888-O MS66 PCGS.** A lustrous Premium Gem with light and original pearl-gray and caramel-gold toning. Crisply struck and beautifully preserved with exemplary eye appeal.
From The Reuben Reinstein Collection. (#7184)

1463 **1888-S MS64 PCGS.** Dappled layers of mauve, turquoise, and russet patina adorn the lustrous surfaces that display well impressed design elements. A few grade-limiting marks are seen on Liberty's cheek and neck. (#7186)

1464 **1888-S MS64 PCGS.** Dusky straw-gold and gunmetal-blue patina cannot impede the comprehensive cartwheel luster. The reverse is well preserved, and the left obverse is only lightly abraded. A lower mintage date. (#7186)

1465 **1888-S MS64 PCGS.** Gentle tan-gold toning visits this thoroughly lustrous near-Gem. The fields are beautifully smooth, and the cheek has only minor contact. The mintmark is repunched within the upper loop. A lower mintage date, certified in a green label holder. (#7186)

Radiant 1888-S Dollar, MS66

1466 **1888-S MS66 NGC.** The radiantly lustrous surfaces of this Premium Gem exhibit wisps of beige and ice-blue on portions of the central devices. Well struck for the most part, indeed above average for the issue about which David Bowers (2006) says: "While many if not most San Francisco Morgan dollars are sharply struck, the 1888-S is an exception." A few minor luster grazes do not distract. Census: 12 in 66, 1 finer (6/07).
From The Reuben Reinstein Collection. (#7186)

1467 **1888-S MS64 Prooflike NGC.** The fields are highly reflective on both sides of this brilliant Morgan dollar. The design elements are sharply struck throughout, and there are only small, scattered marks to prevent a higher grade assessment. Census: 53 in 64 Prooflike, 6 finer (5/07).
From The Vanek Collection. (#7187)

1468 **1889 MS66 PCGS.** Liberty's ear is lightly die doubled. A Hot 50 variety, and probably VAM-16, since the right-side stars are also lightly die doubled. Lustrous and well struck with magnificently smooth surfaces. Liberty's cheek is particularly close to pristine. Nearly unobtainable any finer. (#7188)

1469 **1889 MS66 PCGS.** A magnificently preserved Premium Gem that has a good strike and nearly untoned surfaces. PCGS has certified only five pieces in higher grades (5/07). (#7188)

1470 **1889 MS66 NGC.** Lustrous and crisply struck, with good definition over the centers and untoned stone-white surfaces with flashy fields. There are a few wispy surface marks that are not excessive for the grade. This issue had the highest mintage of any business strike Morgan dollar except for the vast numbers produced in 1921. Census: 99 in 66, 2 finer (6/07).
From The Reuben Reinstein Collection. (#7188)

1471 **1889-CC Fine 12 PCGS.** A mix of steel-gray and slate colors characterizes this key-date coin, one that doubtless spent a number of years in circulation. Pleasing detail for the grade with light, scattered marks as expected. (#7190)

1472 **1889-CC Fine 15 PCGS.** A significantly worn, yet pleasing example of this famous Carson City dollar issue, steel-gray and subtly luminous with gold and blue overtones. One of just 350,000 pieces struck. (#7190)

1473 **1889-CC Fine 15 ANACS.** A slate-gray key date Carson City dollar with glimpses of charcoal patina within design crevices. Design detail remains evident within the hair and plumage. Problem-free for the grade. (#7190)

1474 **1889-CC—Rims Filed, Scratched—ANACS. VF20 Details.** A thin vertical scratch descends from the corner of Liberty's eye, and the reverse rim is filed near 10 o'clock. Less apparent rim filing is present at 4:30 and 10:30 on the obverse, and at 7:30 on the reverse. A small reverse rim bump at 3 o'clock has been left alone. Considerable device detail remains.
From The Vanek Collection. (#7190)

1475 **1889-CC—Tooled, Cleaned—ANACS. VF20 Details.** This key date Carson City dollar is slate-gray from a chemical cleaning. Liberty's hair and the eagle's wings are crudely re-engraved with thin scratches. (#7190)

1476 **1889-CC—Damaged—ANACS. VF20 Details.** This slate-gray Carson City key date dollar has brief radial scratches at 1, 5, and 7 o'clock on the obverse, and at 11 and 1 o'clock on the reverse. Ample wing and hair detail remains. (#7190)

1477 **1889-CC VF25 NGC.** Unlike its lower-mintage 1885-CC counterpart, the 1889-CC dollars faced heavy circulation, and VF examples such as the present piece are available to collectors. The silver-gray surfaces of this moderately worn example have a touch of tan at the margins and light, scattered abrasions. (#7190)

1478 **1889-CC—Cleaned—ANACS. VF30 Details.** A moderately worn, lightly hairlined example that displays a handful of abrasions on the cheek. The fields have predominantly deep rose-violet color, while the devices have gold-gray color of varying intensity. A desirable example of this Carson City key, one of just 350,000 pieces struck. (#7190)

1479 **1889-CC VF30 PCGS.** Though a number of earlier Carson City dollar issues had lower mintages, most such pieces never saw circulation, while many 1889-CC dollars served in the channels of commerce. This moderately worn piece has a touch of lemon-gold patina in the cloud-gray fields, which retain tiny remnants of luster. Highly appealing. (#7190)

Key Date 1889-CC Morgan Dollar VF35

1480 **1889-CC VF35 ANACS.** This key date dollar has a pleasing, natural appearance with mostly medium-gray color and faint golden-tan peripheral accents. There are a few small abrasions on each side, and several scrapes are noted near the peripheries. Only 350,000 pieces were minted, and the '89-CC is easily the scarcest of all Carson City dollars. (#7190)

Difficult XF 1889-CC Dollar

1481 **1889-CC XF40 PCGS.** A predominantly pearl-gray example of this famous Carson City rarity. The eagle's wings display most of their initial definition. Minor dark russet buildup is noted near protected design elements, and a few faint marks are apparent beneath the date and near IN GOD WE TRUST. (#7190)

AU Details 1889-CC Morgan Dollar

1482 **1889-CC—Rims Filed—ANACS. AU Details, Net XF40.** This key date Carson City dollar has delicate gold toning and only slight wear on the hair above the ear. Luster dominates all but the open fields. The obverse and reverse rims are filed throughout, aside from a portion of the upper reverse rim. Both sides are lightly hairlined. (#7190)

1889-CC Silver Dollar AU Details

1483 **1889-CC—Rim Damaged, Scratched—ANACS. AU Details, Net XF45.** Bright luster fills the borders and devices of this lightly toned and briefly circulated rare date Carson City dollar. At first glance, the piece appears problem-free, aside from a hair-thin pinscratch east of the arrowheads. Close examination locates a concealed scratch on the forehead, and the rims have uneven width, particularly beneath the date. (#7190)

AU53 Sharpness 1889-CC Morgan

1484 **1889-CC—Cleaned—ANACS. AU53 Details.** Only a single 1889-CC dollar appeared within the vast GSA hoard. This fact, when combined with a low mintage of 350,000 pieces, ensures its key date status. This well struck example has only slight wear above the ear and on the eagle's breast. Both sides are hairlined, and the cheekbone has a couple of thin marks. (#7190)

1889-CC Silver Dollar, AU53 Details

1485 **1889-CC—Cleaned—ANACS. AU53 Details.** Both sides of this piece have pale golden toning over light silver surfaces. Light hairlines on each side attest to the cleaning that took place at an unspecified time. The fields still retain traces of luster and prooflike reflectivity. The '89-CC is a key to the Morgan dollar series and the rarest issue from the Carson City Mint. (#7190)

Desirable 1889-CC Morgan Dollar, AU55

1486 **1889-CC AU55 NGC.** This is the key Carson City issue in the Morgan dollar series, always in demand regardless of its grade. This example has a sharp strike with nearly full luster and only slight wear on the highest design points. The fields are fully prooflike, although the brief period of circulation has diminished the contrasting appearance. (#7190)

Key Date 1889-CC Morgan Dollar MS60

1487 **1889-CC MS60 NGC.** According to Q. David Bowers (1993): "Nearly all 1889-CC dollars are well struck with excellent definition of details." The current offering is no exception, as crisp definition appears over each side, including the hair detail just above Liberty's ear and the eagle's breast feathers. The piece displays excellent cartwheel luster indicative of a Mint State coin, and the shining silver-white surfaces are untoned. What appears to be a faint grease streak rests beneath US in PLURIBUS. A few minor nicks and blemishes occur on each side, but a moderate milling mark on Liberty's jaw area is the most obvious grade-limiter. The 1889-CC is, of course, the scarcest of all Carson City silver dollars, and an important key date in the Morgan dollar series. (#7190)

1488 **1889-O MS64 PCGS.** Light golden-gray toning drapes the obverse, while the reverse is essentially brilliant. A lustrous near-Gem with fewer marks than usual, although a hair-thin vertical mark crosses the ear. The centers are a bit soft, as nearly always for the '89-O. (#7192)

Condition Scarcity 1889-O Gem Dollar

1489 **1889-O MS65 PCGS.** Silver-gray surfaces display pleasing luster, and reveal just a few unobtrusive luster grazes. Lightly struck at the centers, as is typical for this issue (David Bowers, 2005). The 1889-O, with a mintage approaching 12 million pieces, is relatively plentiful in lower Mint State grades, but becomes elusive at the Gem level. *From The Reuben Reinstein Collection.* (#7192)

1490 **1889-S MS65 ICG.** This razor-sharp better date dollar has potent luster and refreshingly clean fields. Inconspicuous marks are present beneath the date and on the tip of the nose. (#7194)

Gorgeous 1889-S Dollar, MS66

1491 **1889-S MS66 NGC.** Sparkling luster abounds on this gorgeous Premium Gem dollar, and a well executed strike left its imprint on the design elements, including good definition on the hair at Liberty's ear and on the eagle's breast feathers. Color-free surfaces reveal no marks that are worthy of individual mention. Readily available in the lower grades of Mint State, but tough in MS66 and above. Census: 24 in 66, 0 finer (6/07). *From The Reuben Reinstein Collection.* (#7194)

1492 **1890 MS64 NGC.** A well struck and pleasing Choice piece, lightly toned gold-gray overall with small streaks of thicker color at the margins. Only minor, scattered marks appear on the lustrous surfaces. Elusive any finer. (#7196)

1493 **1890 MS65 PCGS.** Aquamarine, cherry-red, and yellow-gold enrich this lustrous and refreshingly unabraded Gem. The hair above the ear and the eagle's breast are slightly incomplete. Given its mintage of 16.8 million pieces, the 1890 is surprisingly rare above the MS65 level. (#7196)

1494 **1890 MS65 PCGS.** Lustrous and nearly brilliant with a good strike and delightfully unabraded surfaces. The 1890 has a mintage, but is confoundingly difficult to locate with exemplary quality. PCGS has certified only two pieces above the MS65 level (5/07). (#7196)

1495 **1890 MS65 NGC.** The 1890 Morgan dollar is surprisingly scarce at the Gem level of preservation, and more than ten times as many pieces have been graded at MS64 than at MS65, by NGC and PCGS combined. This snow-white example is bright, well struck, and nicely preserved, with just a few trivial surface blemishes. *From The Reuben Reinstein Collection.* (#7196)

Deep Mirror Prooflike 1890 Silver Dollar, MS64

1496 **1890 MS64 Deep Mirror Prooflike PCGS.** At first glance, this gorgeous Mint State piece looks like a proof, due to the extremely deep mirrors on each side. The devices are lustrous with moderate mint frost. This date is not particularly known for prooflike coins, thus this example will provide an excellent opportunity for the advanced collector. Population: 65 in 64, 6 finer (6/07). (#97197)

Captivating 1890-CC 'Tail Bar' Dollar, MS62

1497 **1890-CC Tail Bar MS62 PCGS.** VAM-4. A Top 100 Variety. The famous Tail Bar variety displays a die gouge that runs from the left side of the eagle's tailfeathers down to the wreath. As one of the most visible of the Top 100 Varieties and a Carson City variant, the Tail Bar has enduring popularity. This lightly abraded example displays strong luster beneath a thin layer of silver-gray patina and above-average detail. The highpoints of the reverse yield a touch of frost. (#87198)

Lustrous MS62 1890-CC 'Tail Bar' Dollar

1498 **1890-CC Tail Bar MS62 PCGS.** Ex: Carson City Collection. Original dusky gray patina on the obverse shows an arc of golden toning on the left rim. The reverse is completely brilliant. Sharply struck. A number of small to medium-sized abrasions on each side account for the grade. A popular and easy-to-identify variety (actually an error). (#87198)

Collectible 'Tail Bar' 1890-CC Morgan, MS62

1499 **1890-CC Tail Bar MS62 PCGS.** Ex: Carson City Collection. VAM-4. A Top 100 Variety. A lustrous, crisply struck, and virtually brilliant example of this popular and easily recognized Carson City variety. Wispy grazes on the cheek deny a higher grade, but the reverse is generally well preserved. (#87198)

Fascinating Select 1890-CC 'Tail Bar' Dollar

1500 **1890-CC Tail Bar MS63 PCGS.** VAM-4. A Top 100 Variety. A bold, straight line of relief links the eagle's tailfeathers and the lower wreath on this distinctive die variety. The coin offered here displays strong luster and just a hint of ice-blue patina in the fields. Solidly struck with a comparatively clean reverse, though a number of small abrasions on the obverse restrict the grade. (#87198)

Brilliant MS63 1890-CC 'Tail Bar' Dollar

1501 **1890-CC Tail Bar MS63 PCGS.** Ex: Carson City Collection. A second and even finer example of the Tail Bar variant from this collection. This is an attractive MS63 coin that shows bright mint luster and no traces of toning on either side. Sharply defined in the centers. There are only small, individually insignificant abrasions on the obverse and reverse. (#87198)

Select 1890-CC 'Tail Bar' Dollar

1502 1890-CC Tail Bar MS63 PCGS. VAM-4. A Top 100 Variety. FS-004, formerly FS-007. The famous "Tail Bar" variety, named for a broad die scratch (as made) near the left border of the tail feathers. This lustrous and lightly toned Carson City dollar has a clean reverse and a moderately abraded obverse. Certified in a circa-1994 oversized PCGS Prestige holder.
From The Vanek Collection. (#87198)

MS65 'Tail Bar' 1890-CC Dollar Single-Finest PCGS-Certified

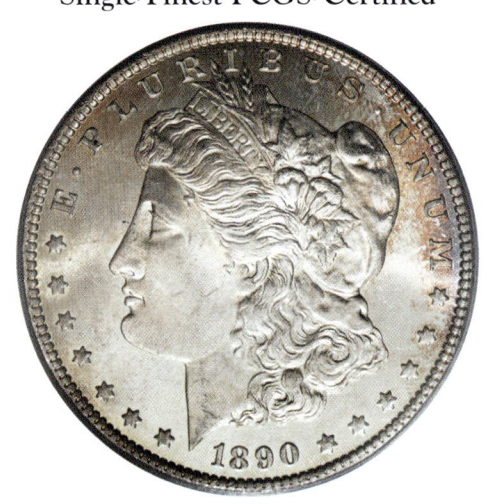

1503 1890-CC Tail Bar MS65 PCGS. VAM-4. A Top 100 Variety. Here it is, the single finest PCGS-certified 1890-CC Tailbar dollar. NGC has also certified only one example as MS65, as of (6/07). Of course, a few pieces may lurk within undesignated third party holders, but the significance of the present opportunity cannot be overemphasized. The Tail Bar variety is a well known "naked eye" variety, immediately confirmed by the presence of a broad die line beneath the left edge of the tailfeathers.

This lustrous Gem has orange-red and lemon peripheral shadings. The strike is precise, and the fields are gorgeously smooth. Only a couple of inconspicuous portrait grazes determine the grade. Population: 1 in 65, 0 finer (6/07). (#87198)

1504 1890-CC MS63 PCGS. Incipient light-tan color makes occasional visits to highly lustrous surfaces that exhibit well impressed design features. A handful of minute marks prevent a higher grade. (#7198)

1505 1890-CC MS63 PCGS. The reverse is well preserved, and the obverse is also attractive for the MS63 level. Sharply struck for this better Carson City date. Each side has only a whisper of gold toning. (#7198)

1506 1890-CC MS63 PCGS. Ex: Carson City Collection. Vivacious luster sweeps the impressively clean fields. A nicely struck example of this better Carson City issue. The reverse rim has minor marks near 2 o'clock. (#7198)

1507 1890-CC MS63 PCGS. Ex: Carson City Collection. Lightly toned and lustrous with smooth fields and only faint grazes on the cheek. A small spot is noted between the TE in STATES. (#7198)

1508 1890-CC MS63 NGC. A crisply struck Select representative from the waning years of the Carson City Mint, strongly lustrous with a hint of frost on the highpoints. Light, scattered abrasions affect each side, and a patch of roller marks appears on the chin. (#7198)

1509 1890-CC MS63 NGC. An attractive Carson City dollar in Select Mint State condition. Essentially untoned, with dynamic cartwheel luster in the fields, and a well preserved reverse. The obverse shows a few grade-limiting marks, mainly on Liberty's face and in the upper left obverse field. (#7198)

1510 1890-CC MS64 PCGS. A flashy, lightly toned, and sharply struck representative of this scarcer Carson City issue. The fields are well preserved, and even the portrait has only a few faint grazes. (#7198)

1511 1890-CC MS64 PCGS. Despite a mintage of over 2.3 million pieces, the 1890-CC is not so available in Mint State grades as some earlier issues with much lower production figures. This sharply struck Choice piece has powerful luster, though splashes of chalk-white and cloud-gray color appear on the natural silvery surfaces. Small, scattered abrasions are present as well. (#7198)

1512 1890-CC MS64 PCGS. A well executed strike brings out sharp detail on the design elements, including the hair over Liberty's ear and the eagle's breast feathers. Both sides are awash in dazzling luster, each displaying barely discernible wisps of light tan on portions of the central devices. A scattering of minute marks define the grade. (#7198)

1513 1890-CC MS64 PCGS. The highly lustrous surfaces take on deep splashes of cobalt-blue, golden-brown, and lavender toning on the obverse, while the reverse shows golden-tan at portions of the borders. Generally well struck, save for minor softness in the hair at Liberty's ear. A few minute and concealed marks on the cheek define the grade. (#7198)

1514 1890-CC MS64 PCGS. Ex: Carson City Collection. Light golden-brown toning graces this lustrous and crisply struck near-Gem. Pleasing aside from a solitary contact mark on the back of the jaw. (#7198)

1515 1890-CC MS64 PCGS. Ex: Carson City Collection. This decisively struck example offers pleasing frost on the devices and delightful luster in the fields. Aside from a touch of cloud-gray haze at the margins, the surfaces are otherwise untoned. Despite a mintage of over 2.3 million pieces, the 1890-CC dollar is less available in Mint State grades than a number of earlier Carson City issues. (#7198)

1516 1890-CC MS64 PCGS. Ex: Carson City Collection. Bag quantities of the 1890-CC were paid out by the Treasury Department from the 1930s through the 1950s. However, by the time of the GSA distributions in the 1970s only 3,949 examples remained. This is a brilliant piece that is not quite fully struck in the centers. Lightly abraded on the obverse, the reverse is notably free of marks. (#7198)

1517 1890-CC MS64 PCGS. Ex: Carson City Collection. VAM-12. The "Line in Eye" VAM, which also has a repunched mintmark. This well struck and lightly toned near-Gem provides potent luster and has a refreshingly mark-free reverse. The few faint grazes on the portrait are appropriate for the grade. (#7198)

1518 1890-CC MS64 PCGS. Ex: Carson City Collection. A brilliant, flashy, intensely lustrous near-Gem from this later Carson City issue. Well struck and nicely preserved, with a few grade-limiting marks that are relatively minor for the grade. (#7198)

1519 **1890-CC MS64 PCGS.** The obverse is bright and untoned, with cartwheel luster in the fields. The reverse displays prooflike fields and an opaque layer of blue-gray toning that yields to coral color on the eagle, and speckled russet patina in the fields. Well struck and minimally marked for the grade. (#7198)

1520 **1890-CC MS64 PCGS.** Light golden-brown toning denies full brilliance. A smooth and lustrous Carson City dollar with moderate striking incompleteness in the centers. The base of the 9 in the date is repunched. Encapsulated in a green label holder. (#7198)

Gem 1890-CC Dollar With Cartwheel Luster

1521 **1890-CC MS65 NGC.** While always available for a price in less-than-Gem grades, the 1890-CC is seldom located in Gem condition. This piece has especially pronounced mint luster that rolls around each side as the coin is slowly tilted beneath a light. Fully struck over the ear of Liberty and the eagle's breast. The surfaces are remarkably clean for an 1890-CC. Census: 56 in 65, 2 finer (6/07).
From The Silver Fox Collection. (#7198)

Sharply Struck 1890-CC Gem Dollar

1522 **1890-CC MS65 NGC.** A solid strike brings about sharp definition on the design features, including the hair strands above Liberty's ear and the eagle's breast feathers. Radiantly lustrous surfaces display hints of incipient light tan-gold color at the peripheries under magnification. A couple of trivial luster grazes are located on the obverse. David Bowers (2006) estimates that over 1 million of the 2.3 million mintage was melted under the 1918 Pittman Act. Census: 56 in 65, 2 finer (6/07).
From The Reuben Reinstein Collection. (#7198)

1523 **1890-CC MS64 Prooflike PCGS.** The depth of reflectivity is startling in the fields of this Prooflike near-Gem dollar. Crisply struck with bold design details on each side. Small surface marks are not inconsistent with the assigned grade level. Population: 68 in 64 Prooflike, 10 finer (4/07). (#7199)

1524 **1890-CC MS62 Deep Mirror Prooflike NGC.** Brilliant and deeply mirrored on each side, as are many '90-CC dollars. This is a fully struck example that shows a number of small abrasions on each side. (#97199)

1525 **1890-CC MS63 Deep Mirror Prooflike PCGS.** VAM-3. Strong doubling is evident on the lower 9 and 0 in the date. This Select piece's powerful mirrors shine through scattered cloud-gray haze. Crisply struck with modest contrast and light, well-distributed abrasions that account for the grade. (#97199)

1526 **1890-CC MS63 Deep Mirror Prooflike PCGS.** A flashy better-date Carson City dollar with an attentive strike and a well preserved reverse. Traces of gold toning prevent full brilliance. Housed in a green label holder. (#97199)

1527 **1890-O MS65 PCGS.** Ample luster illuminates the essentially untoned surfaces, which reveal a splash of gold color near the reverse center. Generally well struck, even if slightly weak above the ear and on the eagle's breast feathers. A lovely, minimally abraded Gem. (#7200)

1528 **1890-O MS65 PCGS.** The reverse is practically pristine, while the obverse of this expertly struck Gem has only faint contact. A flashy and desirable representative of this high mintage but conditionally elusive issue.
From The Reuben Reinstein Collection. (#7200)

1529 **1890-O MS65 Prooflike NGC.** This remarkable Gem has a razor-sharp strike, which is uncharacteristic of New Orleans issues from the era. The fields are exceptionally reflective, even for a prooflike silver dollar. The cheek is clean and has only a whisper of gold toning. Census: 11 in 65 Prooflike, 1 finer (6/07). (#7201)

1530 **1890-S MS65 PCGS.** An attractive ring of iridescent peripheral toning frames the frosty luster of the devices. This is a lovely Gem with excellent eye appeal. (#7202)

Vibrant 1890-S Dollar, MS66

1531 **1890-S MS66 PCGS.** Ex: Cajun Collection. Vibrant luster radiates from both sides of this Premium Gem, and the usually seen sharp strike characteristic of this issue brings out strong definition on all of the design features. While appearing color-free at first glance, close inspection displays faint hints of light tan color at the margins. A few minute marks and luster grazes do not disturb.
From The Reuben Reinstein Collection. (#7202)

1532 **1891 MS64 PCGS.** Speckled toning blankets the obverse, and the reverse displays golden-tan and turquoise iridescence near the periphery. Well struck with vibrant luster and few marks. A pleasing Morgan dollar for the grade. (#7204)

1533 **1891 MS64 PCGS.** The surfaces of this near-Gem exhibit vibrant luster and boldly struck, frosty-white devices that have escaped noteworthy coin-to-coin contact. Quite scarce in this attractive, well preserved state. A luster graze in the upper left obverse field and a couple of minor abrasions on the eagle's lower abdomen preclude a higher grade. (#7204)

Satiny MS65 1891 Morgan Dollar

1534 **1891 MS65 NGC.** One of the unsung condition rarities for many years, the 1891 is now recognized as one of the most challenging P-mint Morgans in Gem condition. The surfaces on this high quality example are satiny-white, show excellent sharpness in the centers, and no mentionable marks. Census: 65 in 65, 2 finer (6/07).
From The Reuben Reinstein Collection. (#7204)

1535 **1891-CC MS63 NGC.** Lightly abraded overall with hints of frost on the highpoints. A touch of peach color complements the silver-white of the surfaces. One of slightly over 1.6 million pieces struck for this later Carson City issue. (#7206)

1536 **1891-CC MS63 PCGS.** The flashy surfaces display booming cartwheel luster and sharply struck design motifs. Mild scuffiness on Liberty's face and neck, and in the left obverse field, define the grade of this Select Mint State example. (#7206)

1537 **1891-CC MS63 PCGS.** Intensely lustrous surfaces display golden-tan patination on the obverse that is accented with a sliver of cobalt-blue and lavender at the upper margin. The reverse is untoned except for whispers of cobalt-blue and lavender that gravitate to the borders. Sharply struck, save for the obverse center. A few minute marks are scattered about the obverse. (#7206)

1538 **1891-CC MS63 PCGS.** Radiant luster exudes from the untoned surfaces of this Select Carson City Morgan, and a sharp strike imparts good definition to the motifs. A few light contact marks and luster grazes define the grade. This coin possesses great technical quality and aesthetic appeal for the grade designation. (#7206)

1539 **1891-CC MS63 PCGS.** VAM-3. A Top 100 Variety. Undesignated as the "Spitting Eagle" VAM, but the die lump near the beak confirms the attribution. Plum-red margins frame brilliant centers. Crisply struck and attractive. (#7206)

1540 **1891-CC MS63 PCGS.** A highly lustrous and largely untoned example from the waning years of the Carson City Mint, Select and solidly struck with light abrasions overall. A hint of cream-colored patina appears in an arc above the eagle. (#7206)

1541 **1891-CC MS63 PCGS.** VAM-3. A Top 100 Variety. Faint cherry-red toning clings to the peripheries. This lustrous Carson City dollar has a clean reverse and only minor obverse grazes. (#7206)

1542 **1891-CC MS63 ANACS.** VAM-3. A Top 100 Variety. The popular "Spitting Eagle" variety, named for a die chip beneath the eagle's beak. Each side has a mere whisper of gold toning. Cleaner than expected for the grade despite occasional faint grazes. (#7206)

1543 **1891-CC MS64 PCGS.** A captivating combination of pink and peach patina drapes much of this Choice dollar. A well-defined example of this later Carson City dollar that might have qualified for a Gem grade if not for an abrasion on the eagle's breast. (#7206)

1544 **1891-CC MS64 PCGS.** VAM-3. A Top 100 Variety. This nicely struck CC-mint silver dollar is close to brilliant and provides effusive luster. Minor contact near the mouth is suitable for the grade. (#7206)

1545 **1891-CC MS64 PCGS.** VAM-6. STATES OF AMERICA and TRUST are lightly die doubled. This attentively struck Carson City dollar has sweeping luster and faint olive toning. The reverse is well preserved. (#7206)

1546 **1891-CC MS64 NGC.** The shimmering snow-white surfaces display intense mint frost and uniformly well struck design elements. Carefully preserved and minimally marked for the grade. A conservatively graded near-Gem from the Carson City Mint. (#7206)

1547 **1891-CC MS64 PCGS.** VAM-3. A Top 100 Variety. Booming luster sweeps this carefully preserved Carson City dollar. The centers display minor incompleteness, but the overall strike is good. Encased in a green label holder. (#7206)

Gem 1891-CC Morgan Dollar

1548 **1891-CC MS65 ANACS.** Freckles of peach-gold patina cling to the borders of this lustrous and suitably struck Gem. Considerably nicer than the typical '91-CC, which grades MS63 and has a scuffy cheek. On the present piece, the sweet spot of the cheek is well preserved. (#7206)

Silky Gem Uncirculated 1891-CC Dollar

1549 **1891-CC MS65 NGC.** While not an absolute rarity, the 1891-CC is certainly a much scarcer date than the common CCs from the 1880s, and it is almost as difficult in Gem condition as the 1890-CC. This is an especially attractive dollar that has smooth, silky mint luster and is brilliant throughout. Fully struck. There are no mentionable or detracting abrasions on either side of this lovely Gem.
From The Silver Fox Collection. (#7206)

Lightly Toned 1891-CC Dollar, MS65

1550 **1891-CC MS65 PCGS.** Pastel powder-blue and beige patination graces the highly lustrous surfaces of this Carson City Gem, and a powerful strike emboldens the design elements, including the hair strands at Liberty's ear and the eagle's breast feathers. The surfaces on both sides are quite well preserved. David Bowers (2005) says that: "The 1891-CC is a 'must have' coin because it is from Carson city and is usually available in Uncirculated grade. However, although the mintage figure is generous for a CC dollar (1,618,000 pieces), today the coin is not in the 'common' class."
From The Reuben Reinstein Collection. (#7206)

1551 **1891-O MS64 PCGS.** A rich allotment of electric-blue and reddish-golden-brown peripheral toning appears on each side of this highly lustrous near-Gem. Typically struck and a trifle weak over the centers, with a well preserved reverse and a few grade-limiting blemishes on the obverse. (#7208)

1552 **1891-O MS64 PCGS.** This nearly stone-white near-Gem possesses blazing luster and smooth surfaces. The strike is a crisp for this often mushy New Orleans issue. Encapsulated in an old green label holder. (#7208)

1553 **1891-S MS65 NGC.** A flashy '91-S dollar that was struck from heavily basined dies, resulting in concave fields that are bright and nearly Prooflike. Brilliant and fully struck. (#7210)

Outstanding 1891-S Dollar, MS67

1554 **1891-S MS67 NGC.** Mint State 1891-S dollars, sporting a mintage of 5,296,000 pieces, are readily available through the near-Gem grade level, as attested to by the several thousand coins that have been seen through this condition by NGC and PCGS. Even MS65 examples are obtainable with a little patience and searching. Premium Gems are quite scarce, and MS67 specimens are rare.

Coruscating luster adorns both sides of this Superb Gem, and whispers of barely discernible incipient olive-green color shows up under magnification. A solid strike emboldens the design features, including delineation in the hair strands over Liberty's ear and on the eagle's breast feathers. Well preserved surfaces yield a satiny finish, and reveal no marks worthy of individual mention. A simply outstanding Morgan! Census: 2 in 67, 0 finer (6/07).
From The Reuben Reinstein Collection. (#7210)

1555 **1891-S MS64 Deep Mirror Prooflike NGC.** Well struck with intense reflectivity in the fields and an effulgent, dazzling sheen across both sides. Trace amounts of milky patina are located mainly near the peripheries; otherwise the piece is untoned. A small scrape in the left reverse field prevents the Gem assessment, but does little to inhibit the visual splendor of this deeply prooflike example. Census: 37 in 64 Deep Mirror Prooflike, 5 finer (5/07).
From The Vanek Collection. (#97211)

1556 **1892 MS64 PCGS.** The Philadelphia Mint produced fewer and fewer silver dollars as the early 1890s progressed, culminating in the famous "missing" mintage of 1895. In 1892, the total was slightly over 1 million pieces, coins such as this richly toned near-Gem. Well struck with strong luster beneath muted peach and plum colors. An abrasion is noted on the eagle's breast. (#7212)

1557 **1892 MS64 PCGS.** Golden-brown margins surround the untoned fields and devices. The reverse is well preserved, and this suitably struck low mintage dollar has only faint obverse grazes. Housed in an old green label holder. (#7212)

1558 **1892 MS64 PCGS.** Typically struck with thick satiny luster and minimal marks, particularly on the reverse. Several pinscratches and a few minor luster grazes occur in the left obverse field and on Liberty's face. An attractive and essentially untoned example of this relatively low-mintage date. (#7212)

Alluring Gem 1892 Morgan Dollar

1559 **1892 MS65 PCGS.** This creamy-white Gem has instant eye appeal and no shortage of technical merit. Dynamic luster produces an effulgent sheen across both sides, and the striking details are more than adequate, even if typically weak on some of the central highpoints. A few minor marks preclude an even finer grade assessment. (#7212)

Lustrous 1892 Gem Dollar

1560 **1892 MS65 PCGS.** David Bowers (2005) writes of 1892 Mint State dollars that: "Most are in lower grade ranges, MS60 to 62, and poorly struck. Really choice MS64 and gem MS65 or finer coins are very hard to find." The current Gem displays great luster and adequately struck design elements, though softness is visible in the centers. Occasional wisps of gold-tan color occur at the margins. A few minute marks are within the confines of the grade designation.
From The Reuben Reinstein Collection. (#7212)

1561 **1892-CC AU53 ANACS.** An untoned and lightly abraded CC-mint dollar that boasts a band of bright luster across the borders. Faint friction on the eagle's breast and above the ear confirms brief circulation. (#7214)

1562 **1892-CC—Cleaned—ANACS. MS60 Details.** This scarce date Carson City dollar has shades of orange-red along the borders. The strike is intricate, and both sides are nearly void of bagmarks. Careful inspection with a loupe reveals numerous faint hairlines. (#7214)

1563 **1892-CC MS61 ANACS.** Golden-brown and powder-blue endow the upper right obverse margin, and glimpses of tan-gold are noticeable elsewhere. This lustrous Carson City dollar has a typical strike and clean fields, but the lower cheek is shiny from a graze. (#7214)

1564 **1892-CC MS62 PCGS.** Honey-gold, cherry-red, and blue-green visit the peripheries, but this mildly prooflike Carson City dollar has untoned fields and devices. Less abraded than expected for the MS62 level. (#7214)

1565 **1892-CC MS63 PCGS.** The 2 in the date shows a thick die chip, as made. This flashy Carson City dollar is frosty and untoned, with bright white surfaces that display sharply struck design elements and only mild obverse scuffiness that limits the grade. (#7214)

1566 **1892-CC MS63 PCGS.** Dusty rose, pink, and peach patina saturates the obverse of this Select piece, while the reverse has just a touch of color at the right rim. Well-defined with strong luster and few marks for the grade. A lovely example from the penultimate year of operation for the Carson City Mint. (#7214)

1567 **1892-CC MS63 PCGS.** This lightly toned better date Carson City dollar has pleasing luster and a well preserved reverse. Wispy grazes on the cheek combine to limit the grade. The strike is good with some softness on the claws and centers. (#7214)

Popular 1892-CC Near-Gem Dollar

1568 **1892-CC MS64 PCGS.** David Bowers (2005) notes of the 1892-CC dollar: "Year in and year out this coin has been in great demand. MS63 and MS64 offer excellent acquisition possibilities ... ." The near-Gem offered in this lot displays glowing luster emanating from untoned surfaces. Fairly sharp definition is visible on the design elements, and just a few minor obverse marks limit the grade. Housed in a green-label holder. (#7214)

Attractive 1892-CC Dollar, MS65

1569 **1892-CC MS65 NGC.** This lovely Carson City Gem exhibits a sharp strike throughout the design features, including the hair over Liberty's ear and the eagle's breast feathers. Hints of light tan color visit both sides, being slightly more evident on the reverse. The fields display some prooflike characteristics, and establish mild contrast with the motifs. A few minor obverse marks prevent an even higher grade.
From The Silver Fox Collection. (#7214)

Exceptional 1892-CC Dollar, MS65

1570 **1892-CC MS65 PCGS.** The intensely lustrous surfaces of this Carson City Gem reveal whispers of golden-tan color around the margins, and on portions of the central devices. An attentive strike left impressive definition on the design features, including the hair at Liberty's ear and the eagle's breast feathers. This relatively well preserved specimen is exceptional, in that most Mint State examples of this issue are heavily bagmarked (David Bowers, 2006).
From The Reuben Reinstein Collection. (#7214)

1571 **1892-O MS64 PCGS.** Much better struck than most '92-O dollars. This piece shows strong, satiny mint luster and only a couple of central abrasions that keep it from an MS65 grade. (#7216)

1572 **1892-O MS64 PCGS.** A gently toned and thoroughly lustrous O-mint dollar with the expected minor blending of detail at the centers. Difficult to locate in finer grades. Certified in a green label holder. (#7216)

Attractive 1892-O Gem Dollar

1573 **1892-O MS65 NGC.** Orange-gold patination encircles the peripheries of this Gem O-mint representative, being somewhat more intense on the obverse. The strike is above average for this notoriously poorly struck issue; some definition is apparent in the eagle's breast feathers, though the hair at Liberty's ear is soft. The surfaces possess nice luster and are quite well preserved for the grade.
From The Reuben Reinstein Collection. (#7216)

Important MS64 Deep Mirror 1892-O Dollar

1574 **1892-O MS64 Deep Mirror Prooflike NGC.** The 1892-O is very rare as either Prooflike or Deep Mirror Prooflike. NGC has certified only 10 pieces as Prooflike, three in AU grades, and only seven pieces as Deep Mirror Prooflike, two of which grade AU58. NGC has yet to grade any pieces MS65 or finer as Prooflike or Deep Mirror Prooflike. Sharply struck for a New Orleans dollar from this era, and the flashy fields display light milk-gray and gold toning. There are surprisingly few marks. Housed in a prior generation holder. Census: 2 in 64 DMPL, 0 finer (5/07). (#97217)

1575 **1892-S—Cleaned—ANACS. XF45 Details.** A cloudy but richly detailed rare date silver dollar with subdued, distributed obverse marks. Mildly granular near the I in PLURIBUS. (#7218)

1576 **1892-S AU50 PCGS.** This rare date silver dollar is only faintly toned and retains ample bright luster throughout the stars, legends, and devices. Marks are minimal given its limited journey in circulation. (#7218)

1577 **1892-S AU50 PCGS.** Although VF pieces are available, the 1892-S is among the most difficult issues in the series to locate in AU and finer grades. This untoned representative has few marks for the grade, and displays traces of luminous luster within the devices and legends. Housed in a green label holder. (#7218)

Elusive Choice AU 1892-S Dollar

1578 **1892-S AU55 PCGS.** Light gold toning clings to the margins. Bands of bright luster connect peripheral elements, and luster also bathes the eagle and Liberty's hair. Moderate wear at the centers is consistent with the grade. The reverse has a tiny rim nick at 6:30, but this key date dollar otherwise has surprisingly few marks. (#7218)

1579 **1893 MS62 PCGS.** Powder-blue and peach patina embraces the borders of this shimmering and nicely struck example. Cleaner than customary for an MS62. The 1893 ranks among the lowest mintage Philadelphia issues. (#7220)

1580 **1893 MS62 PCGS.** This low mintage silver dollar has a good strike and unbroken luster. Faint grazes on the left obverse decide the grade. Liberty's profile is lightly die doubled. (#7220)

1581 **1893 MS63 ANACS.** This low mintage Morgan dollar has unencumbered luster and only a hint of gold toning. Crisply struck, and void of relevant marks. (#7220)

1582 **1893 MS63 PCGS.** A lustrous, well struck example of this low mintage issue that displays a few too many abrasions to be assigned a higher grade. The untoned, silver-white surfaces display flashy cartwheel effects in the fields. A good choice for date purposes, since the other mintmarked issues of 1893 are scarcer and more expensive. (#7220)

1583 **1893 MS63 ANACS.** The borders offer pale peach patina, and the lustrous fields are essentially brilliant. This nicely struck and low mintage dollar has well preserved fields, although the lower cheek has moderate marks. The familiar VAM with a die doubled profile and light recutting atop the 3 in the date. (#7220)

1584 **1893 MS64 PCGS.** This beautiful near-Gem possesses light khaki-gold toning, and is unusually free from marks for the grade. Liberty's chin is lightly die doubled, and the peak of the 3 is repunched. (#7220)

1585 **1893 MS64 PCGS.** This nicely struck Choice Morgan dollar has a hint of golden toning near the obverse rim. The fields and eagle are remarkably unabraded, and the portrait has only a few faint grazes. The peak of the 3 is repunched, as usual for this low mintage date. (#7220)

1586 **1893 MS64 PCGS.** This low mintage Morgan dollar provides vivacious luster and a bold strike. The centers have a hint of golden toning. Well preserved despite minor grazes on the left obverse. In a green label holder. (#7220)

1587 **1893 MS64 ANACS.** Hints of rose patina grace the rims, but the lustrous fields and devices are untoned. The hair above the ear is soft, but the strike is generally sharp. A strike-through is noted near the base of the cap. Liberty's profile is lightly die doubled, and the peak of the 3 is recut. (#7220)

Sharply Defined 1893 Gem Dollar

1588 **1893 MS65 NGC.** Highly lustrous surfaces display faint traces of light tan color on this Gem dollar. The design elements are better defined than often seen on the issue, including good definition in the hair over Liberty's ear and on the eagle's breast feathers. A few minor marks do not disturb. In Mint State, 1893 dollars are elusive in comparison to the demand for them (David Bowers, 2005).
From The Silver Fox Collection. (#7220)

Remarkable 1893 Dollar, MS65

1589 **1893 MS65 NGC.** The 1893 dollar comes from a mintage of 378,000, and according to David Bowers (2005): "In Mint State, the dollars of 1893 are elusive in comparison to the demand for them." This untoned Gem displays pleasing frosty luster and well impressed design features. Remarkably well preserved for the grade designation, though some trivial marks are noted on the upper reverse.
From The Reuben Reinstein Collection. (#7220)

1590 **1893-CC—Scratched, Rim Filed—ANACS. Fine 12 Details.** A relatively small obverse scratch at 9:30 is of little concern. The reverse rim is dinged and lightly filed at 10:30. An affordable example of this semi-key CC-mint issue. (#7222)

1591 **1893-CC—Cleaned—ANACS. XF40 Details.** This untoned key date Carson City dollar has received a chemical cleaning, but luster glistens from recessed areas, and the designs display much of their initial detail. (#7222)

1592 **1893-CC XF45 PCGS.** Light autumn-brown toning visits the borders of this richly detailed rare-date CC-mint dollar. The centers show only moderate wear, and luster glimmers from selected areas. Thin marks are noted on the reverse rim at 6 and 7 o'clock. (#7222)

Key Date 1893-CC Dollar MS61

1593 1893-CC MS61 PCGS. This bright, highly lustrous example is softly struck over the centers, especially on the obverse. The untoned silver surfaces are nicely preserved on the reverse, but are moderately abraded on the obverse, where heavy bagmarks are noted on Liberty's face and neck, and in the adjoining field area. This was the final year of coin production at the Carson City Mint, and Uncirculated survivors are always in great demand. (#7222)

Flashy 1893-CC Dollar MS62

1594 1893-CC MS62 PCGS. This semi-prooflike Carson City dollar has flashy luster and rich golden-brown toning near the rims. The strike is typical, but the reverse is clean, as is the obverse field. A moderate mark on the cheek limits the grade more than the eye appeal. A scarce date excluded from the vast 1970s GSA dispersal. (#7222)

Sharply Struck 1893-CC Dollar, MS62

1595 1893-CC MS62 PCGS. David Bowers, in his 2004 *A Guide Book of Morgan Silver Dollars*, writes of the 1893-CC, the last of the Carson City dollars, that "Mint State 1893-CC dollars are well known for being extensively bagmarked, some actually appearing quite abused. Accordingly, the majority of Mint State pieces are in lower MS grades." Bright, untoned surfaces on this MS62 specimen display sharply impressed design elements, and lack the heavy abrasions that usually plague the issue. We mention some relatively unobtrusive luster grazes and hairlines on the obverse. Housed in a green-label holder. (#7222)

Lightly Toned 1893-CC Dollar, MS62

1596 1893-CC MS62 ANACS. This MS62 1893-CC dollar exhibits prooflike tendencies, slightly more so on the reverse, with mild overall field-motif contrast. Splashes of cobalt-blue and gray-mauve occupy the obverse, while the reverse is essentially untoned. A few light marks are scattered about, but certainly not of the number or severity typically occurring on most Mint State examples. The usual strike softness is noted in the centers. (#7222)

Exceptional Select 1893-CC Dollar

1597 1893-CC MS63 PCGS. Pleasing luster envelops both sides of this Select Carson City issue, and each is essentially untoned. A much better-than-average strike makes itself known on the design features, including sharp definition in the hair over Liberty's ear and the eagle's breast feathers. A few minute obverse marks limit the grade, but in reality, this specimen reveals fewer marks than usually seen on this issue. (#7222)

Immaculate 1893-CC Dollar, MS65
A Historic and Numismatically Significant Issue

1598 **1893-CC MS65 NGC.** Anyone who has ever been to Carson City, Nevada, has probably walked or driven past the old mint. For coin collectors the little stone building is nostalgic, a place that lures our imaginations back to a time of simplicity in the American West. Most of the public, of course, has no idea that this place on the main street, just a few blocks from the seat of state government and within "jingling" noise distance of the casinos, once poured out a river of beautiful, bright, brand-new coins, mostly silver coins, made from ore taken from mines not far away.

The Comstock Lode created Nevada's first millionaires, out of ordinary men. At first they had no market for their product. The Bland-Allison Act of 1878 was a political boondoggle of its time, a favoritism of American brand, born to use up the tons of silver that eventually shored up the wealth of the Treasury, but in 1878 was a godsend to nobody but the silver miners. A dozen years after the Morgan dollar was born, millions sat unused in government vaults as backing for the increasing volume of paper currency "certificates" in circulation.

In 1890, the Bland-Allison Act was repealed. The Sherman Act replaced it on July 14 of that year. In his masterful study *Fractional Money*, Neil Carothers explains that "Under the new provisions the Treasury was to buy 4,500,000 ounces of silver per month, to be paid for with Treasury notes that were to be legal tender. The notes were to be redeemable in gold coin or in silver dollars coined from the bullion purchased." This act, in fact, bolstered government support for Nevada's silver miners, providing a use for their product. Some 5.8 million silver dollars were minted every month beginning in 1890, yet most of the Treasury notes were redeemed in gold.

The government's vaults soon bulged with gleaming new silver dollars. "In 1893," Carothers notes, "a series of adverse economic developments brought disaster to the Treasury." Its store of gold was being rapidly diminished, while silver was accumulating. "This operation, which would eventually destroy the solvency of the government, was merely the process by which the excessive issues of silver dollars and paper money were displacing gold ... " which was being exported to Europe.

In 1890 the Sherman Act was repealed. "As a net result of the laws of 1878 and 1890 the country acquired approximately 570,000,000 silver dollars," Carothers states. Politicians argued the merits of gold versus silver. Silver dollars circulated mainly in the west and south. When the Carson City Mint was closed in 1893, the nation was awash in silver dollars, gleaming new coins not quite worth their intrinsic value. It was the end of an era at Carson City, and an alluring rarity was born.

Even if the 1893-CC silver dollar was not a low mintage issue with a low survival rate, it would still be popular as the final year of issue, just as the 1893-CC double eagle is of interest to collectors. This is one of the few Gems known. The brilliant surfaces gleam with mint luster and show a hint of semi-reflectivity in the fields. Fully struck throughout. There are no noticeable abrasions on either side of this immaculate coin. Only 14 pieces have been so graded by the two major certification services, seven at each, and none are finer (6/07).
From The Reuben Reinstein Collection. (#7222)

1599 **1893-O AU50 PCGS.** A briefly circulated example of this difficult low mintage New Orleans issue. Luster surrounds the borders and devices, and there are no distracting marks. (#7224)

1600 **1893-O AU53 PCGS.** The 1893-O is the lowest mintage New Orleans Morgan dollar, and is considered the second scarcest, after the 1895-O. This example has peripheral golden-brown toning, and the centers exhibit only slight wear. Luster dominates protected areas. (#7224)

1601 **1893-O AU58 NGC.** Luster dominates except on Liberty's cheek. There are a few moderate marks near the date, but the reverse is nearly unabraded. The lowest mintage O-mint Morgan dollar. (#7224)

1602 **1893-O AU58 ANACS.** The cartwheel luster is slightly subdued and the centers have a touch of gunmetal-gray, two indications that this better date dollar has experienced momentary wear. Lightly toned with surprisingly few marks. The lowest mintage New Orleans Morgan issue. (#7224)

New Orleans Mint

Conditionally Rare 1893-O Dollar, MS64

1603 **1893-O MS64 NGC.** Typical of most New Orleans Mint dollars, this piece has slight weakness in the centers, over Liberty's ear on the obverse, and the eagle's breast on the reverse. Aside from the usual weakness, this is an exceptional and highly attractive near-Gem specimen with amazing brilliant silver surfaces and slightly prooflike fields. The '93-O Morgan is one of the great condition rarities in the series, common enough in circulated grades and available in lower Mint State levels, but extremely rare in grades finer than MS63. Census: 29 in 64, 3 finer (6/07).
From The Reuben Reinstein Collection. (#7224)

Exceptional MS65 1893-O Dollar
One of the Finest Examples Known

Exceptional MS65 1893-O Dollar
One of the Finest Examples Known

1604 **1893-O MS65 NGC.** Ten obverse dies were shipped to the New Orleans mint in 1893 but no new reverse dies shipped. The reverse dies used for this issue were leftover from previous years. Altogether only five varieties are known of this very scarce issue, struck from three obverse dies and two old reverse dies. No more were apparently needed to produce the paltry mintage of only 300,000 coins, but the usage of leftover reverse dies may go a long way toward explaining why the striking details are less than sterling on the majority of 1893-O dollars.

On this particular piece the striking definition is somewhat weak both on the eagle's breast as well as on Liberty's hair over the ear. However, there is no doubt about the outstanding quality of this Morgan rarity. Unlike the dull luster seen on many examples, the surfaces on this piece are bright with the semi-prooflike sheen that is sometimes encountered. This is significant as it adds more eye appeal to the coin, and as Wayne Miller pointed out "Semi-prooflike specimens ... are often more attractive than fully prooflike pieces." The reason for this is that often times when a fully prooflike 1893-O is located it is heavily abraded. On this coin there are no distinctive marks on either side, just a few shallow luster breaks on the obverse.

The 1893-O has always been on the radar screen of New Orleans collectors as the scant output of 300,000 pieces was the lowest in the entire series of O-mint dollars. Beginning in the late 1950s, when silver dollar collecting began to gain widespread popularity, it began to be noticed that no bags of this issue were available and what few rolls were available brought a substantial premium. Today it is recognized that the '93-O is scarce in all grades and very rare in the better grades of Mint State. It is extremely rare in Gem condition and this is one of only three Gems we have handled in the past ten years. NGC has only certified one other piece as a Gem with one finer (6/07), while PCGS has graded nine pieces as MS65 with none finer (6/07).
From The Reuben Reinstein Collection. (#7224)

Fine 12 Details 1893-S Morgan

1605 **1893-S—Scratched, Cleaned—ANACS. Fine 12 Details.** This snow-white key date dollar is overly bright from a dip, and a few criss-cross pinscratches are present on the eagle. The eagle's wings and tail display substantial plumage for the Fine 12 details grade. Even the beginning Morgan dollar collector can quote the population for the '93-S, only 100,000 pieces. (#7226)

Choice Fine Key 1893-S Morgan

1606 **1893-S Fine 15 PCGS.** The battleship-gray fields transform into chestnut-gold when the piece is rotated beneath a light. Ice-blue portions of the devices correspond to the device highpoints. A tiny dig on the field above the eagle's head will identify this key date representative. (#7226)

VF Details Key 1893-S Dollar

1607 **1893-S—Rim Damaged—ANACS. VF Details. Net Fine 15.** The reverse rim is bruised at 6 o'clock, and a minor pinscratch is noted near the M in UNUM. Light gold and sky-blue toning helps recover the eye appeal. The eagle's wings and tailfeathers retain much plumage detail. A collectible example of this coveted series key. (#7226)

Remarkable 1893-S VF20 Dollar

1608 **1893-S VF20 PCGS.** The key-date 1893-S is highly desired in all grades. We offer here a super VF20 specimen that displays attractive medium gray patination. Moreover, there are no mentionable contact marks on this piece; indeed, the surfaces are remarkably clean for a silver dollar that has seen moderate circulation. Relatively sharp and uniform detail is visible on the design elements. This coin will be an excellent addition to a mid-grade Morgan dollar set. (#7226)

Key-Date 1893-S Dollar, VF20 Details

1609 **1893-S—Cleaned—ANACS. VF20 Details.** Light gray patination adheres to semi-bright surfaces that reveal some fine hairlines under high magnification, and the design elements display fairly good detail. A few circulation marks and pinscratches are noted, especially on the obverse. The minor flaws occurring on this key-date representative should not dissuade the collector attempting to complete a mid-grade collection of Morgan dollars. (#7226)

Desirable Key Date 1893-S Morgan Dollar VF20

1610 **1893-S VF20 NGC.** Unquestionably authentic and undoubtedly original, this example is about as attractive as possible, for the grade. It is evenly worn and displays appealing aquamarine and gold patina near the obverse and reverse peripheries. Severe abrasions are not found on either side of the piece. One of the chief key dates in the Morgan dollar series, along with its predecessor (the '92-S); an example of the '93-S is a welcome addition to any numismatic auction. (#7226)

Key Date 1893-S Morgan Dollar XF40

1611 **1893-S XF40 ANACS.** An original example of this rare key date Morgan dollar, clearly showing all authentication characteristics. Light greenish-gray toning covers both sides, with golden colored patina in the recesses and around the devices. A pleasing coin with just a couple of non-distracting marks. (#7226)

Pleasing 1893-S Choice XF Dollar

1612 **1893-S XF45 PCGS.** Writing about the 1893-S dollar in his *Guide Book of Morgan Silver Dollars* (2005), David Bowers says: " The majority of known pieces, into the thousands, are in the single grade category of Very Fine. Most such pieces circulated in the American West, and for an appropriate but apparently restricted time, to bring them to this grade."

We offer the opportunity here for the Morgan dollar specialist, or even for non-specialists who want to acquire key-date coins, to obtain a pleasing Choice XF example. Traces of luster reside in the protected areas of the silver-gray surfaces that exhibit occasional wisps of gold-tan color, and the design features are nicely detailed. A few minuscule marks on the cheek are not out of context for a large, heavy silver coin that saw limited circulation. This piece will fit comfortably in a high-grade Morgan dollar date/mintmark set. (#7226)

XF45 Details 1893-S Morgan

1613 **1893-S—Scratched, Cleaned—ANACS. XF45 Details.** Steel-gray and caramel-gold are prevalent, although a brief band of blue-green is noted near 2 o'clock on the reverse. A dull vertical scratch on the cheekbone provides the only mentionable mark. Subdued by a chemical cleaning, but above average for this rare issue, since luster illuminates recessed design areas. (#7226)

Lightly Circulated 1893-S Dollar, XF45

1614 **1893-S XF45 ANACS.** This wonderful Choice XF example has light wear limited to the high points of the design. The surfaces have faint hairlines that are not unusual, although this piece does not qualify as a cleaned example. It has not received any improper treatment through the years.

The 1893-S is the classic rarity in the Morgan dollar series, with its limited availability (especially in higher grades) explained by the combination of low mintage and immediate circulation of nearly the entire mintage. There have not been any major hoards of this date located over the years, although every now and then, a modern day Virgil Brand will sell off a roll or two that have been pulled out of numismatic circulation over several decades. These types of offerings do not increase the known population as a true hoard does, but rather they merely redistribute the existing population. (#7226)

1615 **1894—Re-engraved, Cleaned—ANACS. VF20 Details.** Golden-brown and navy-blue visit the borders. Liberty's hair and the eagle's wings are tooled with thin scratches to simulate design detail. Glossy from a moderate cleaning. The lowest mintage Philly date aside from the proof-only 1895. (#7228)

1616 **1894 VF25 ANACS.** A pearl-gray representative of this low mintage Philadelphia issue. Design crevices have minor dark buildup, a confirmation of its originality. A thin subdued mark above the jaw is hardly worthy of mention. (#7228)

1617 **1894 XF40 PCGS.** Satiny and toned in shades of dove-gray, with glimmers of luster near the peripheral devices, this high-end XF example displays virtually complete definition over most of the design elements, and typical wear shows on the obverse and reverse highpoints. (#7228)

1618 **1894—Cleaned—ANACS. XF45 Details.** This key date Morgan dollar is pearl-gray with rose and sea-green overtones. Richly detailed, but the surfaces are cloudy from a chemical cleaning. Liberty's jaw and the field beneath the left (facing) wing are moderately abraded. (#7228)

Challenging AU 1894 Morgan

1619 **1894 AU50 PCGS.** Luster beckons from the eagle's plumage, Liberty's hair, and the stars and legends. A briefly circulated pearl-gray example of this key date silver dollar. An inconspicuous shallow abrasion is noted on the cheekbone. Only the 1893-S and 1895 have lower mintages. (#7228)

Low Mintage 1894 Silver Dollar AU50

1620 **1894 AU50 PCGS.** Only the 1893-S has a lower mintage than the 1894, if the proof-only 1895 is excluded. This partly lustrous key date dollar is close to brilliant and has a hint of wear above the ear and on the eagle's breast. (#7228)

1621 **1894—Graffiti, Whizzed—ANACS. AU50 Details.** This key date dollar is granular and hairlined from whizzing, and the eagle's breast has a few criss-cross fine lines from an idle hour long ago. Still a sharp example of this low mintage issue. The borders are toned light to medium gold. (#7228)

Almost Uncirculated 1894 Dollar

1622 **1894 AU53 PCGS.** A scarce and always sought-after date in the Morgan series, and an issue that is generally not located finer than AU. This is a brilliant coin with light friction over the highpoints. A couple of small marks on the cheek of Liberty are all that detract from the overall appearance of this piece. (#7228)

Mint State Sharpness 1894 Morgan

1623 **1894—Environmental Damage, Cleaned—ANACS. Unc. Details, Net AU55.** This crisply struck stone-white key date dollar displays no evidence of wear, and the cartwheel luster is subdued but unbroken. Overdipped, but remarkably free from abrasions. Only the famous 1893-S and 1895 issues have lower mintages than the 1894. (#7228)

1624 **1894—Scratched, Cleaned—ANACS. AU58 Details.** This untoned rare date dollar has only a hint of wear on the centers of the devices, but the luster is diminished by an improper dip. Marks are minimal aside from a thin diagonal scratch beneath the center of the cheek. (#7228)

Desirable Near-Mint 1894 Dollar

1625 **1894 AU58 PCGS.** The cartwheel luster is unencumbered, and shimmers across Liberty's cheek. Only the experienced eye can detect traces of friction on the eagle and portrait, and undoubtedly this piece would have been cataloged as Uncirculated in the years prior to certification. A pearl-gray key date dollar with smooth surfaces despite a few tiny marks above the eagle. (#7228)

Sharply Struck 1894 Dollar, MS61

1626 **1894 MS61 PCGS.** This key date Morgan has one of the lowest mintages in the series (110,000 circulation strikes). Examples are elusive in all grades, and Mint State coins are mostly in the lower ranges (David Bowers, 2004). This MS61 specimen exhibits whispers of golden-brown color, along with an attentive strike that leaves sharp definition on the design features, including the hair at Liberty's ear and the eagle's breast feathers. Contact marks and luster grazes are noted on the cheek and in the left obverse field. This piece reposes in a green-label holder. (#7228)

Important 1894 Morgan Dollar, MS65

1627 **1894 MS65 PCGS.** With a mintage of just 110,000 coins, this issue is the first Morgan dollar rarity from the Philadelphia Mint, along with the proof-only 1895, and the conditionally rare 1901. While a few bags of 1894 Morgan dollars turned up during the middle of the 20th century, it does not appear that this date was part of the Treasury release that took place from 1962 to 1964.

Mint State examples of this date are generally found at the lowest levels, and true Gems are extremely rare. The combined Mint State populations of NGC and PCGS show that just over 1,700 examples of this date have been certified in MS60 or higher grades, but only 28 of those pieces have been graded MS65 or better.

Wayne Miller provides information about the distribution of this issue in The Morgan and Peace Dollar Textbook: "Since the 1894-P was minted in fewer quantities than any other business strike dollar except for the 1893-S, it is scarce in all grades. However, it is not as rare in uncirculated condition as might be expected. Because of its low mintage many pieces were undoubtedly set aside from the first days of issue. A solid bag of uncirculated 1894-P dollars surfaces in Great Falls, Montana in the early 1960s. These coins were widely dispersed, and account for a considerable percentage of the BU 1894-P dollars now in existence."

This Gem is housed in a green-label PCGS holder, and it exhibits frosty silver luster with a few tiny specks or splashes of gold toning limited to the obverse. Both sides are sharply detailed, including the hair over Liberty's ear and the eagle's breast feathers. The surfaces are particularly pleasing, with only a few tiny luster grazes on each side. Population: 21 in 65, 3 finer (6/07).
From The Reuben Reinstein Collection. (#7228)

1628 **1894-O MS62 PCGS.** The pale orange patina that graces the obverse margins appears as deeper color over much of the reverse. Well struck with above-average, pleasing luster, though scattered abrasions affect Liberty's cheek and nose. (#7230)

1629 **1894-O MS62 PCGS.** Lustrous and close to brilliant with a typical O-mint strike at the centers. There are fewer marks than expected of the grade. The fields are particularly clean. In a green label holder. (#7230)

Select Mint State 1894-O Morgan Dollar

1630 **1894-O MS63 PCGS.** Generally well struck, except for the slight weakness above Liberty's ear and on the eagle's breast feathers. This conditionally scarce example displays untoned stone-white surfaces that are intensely lustrous. The reverse is nearly blemish-free, while the obverse shows a number of trivial marks on Liberty's cheek, as well as in the left obverse field. (#7230)

1631 **1894-S MS62 PCGS.** The peripheral russet-brown toning is attractive, and the potent luster gives the initial impression of a finer grade. The reverse is well preserved, while the cheek and neck exhibit delicate slide marks. (#7232)

1632 **1894-S MS62 PCGS.** A lustrous and virtually untoned better date dollar. The cheek is unexpectedly clean for the MS62 level, and the field marks are also minor. (#7232)

1633 **1894-S MS63 PCGS.** Well struck with excellent definition noted on the hair detail above Liberty's ear and on the eagle's breast feathers. The brilliant white surfaces are highly lustrous. A small charcoal-brown spot rests on Liberty's jawline, and a typical number of scuffy marks are seen for the grade. (#7232)

1634 **1894-S MS63 PCGS.** An impressive Select better date silver dollar with sweeping luster and delicate tan patina. Crisply struck and worthy of a look. Housed in a prior generation holder. (#7232)

1635 **1894-S MS63 ANACS.** Dazzling luster and light cherry-red toning ensure the originality of this meticulously struck better date Morgan dollar. The reverse is well preserved, and the portrait has only minor grazes. (#7232)

1636 **1894-S MS64 PCGS.** In Select and finer grades, the 1894-S is the most available of the three silver dollar issues for that year, though attractive examples can be elusive. This near-Gem has strong luster and notable detail overall. Lightly gold-toned in the fields with a few spots of opaque chalk-white color on the obverse.
From The Vanek Collection. (#7232)

1637 **1894-S MS64 PCGS.** Dazzling luster and a hint of peripheral rose toning confirm the originality of this nicely struck near-Gem. The reverse is especially smooth. Housed in a green label holder. (#7232)

Bright 1894-S Gem Dollar

1638 **1894-S MS65 NGC.** The 1894-S is a readily available issue through near-Gem, whereas MS65 and finer coins are rare. The Gem being offered in this lot displays bright luster, and just a whisper of barely discernible color under magnification, primarily on the obverse. A sharp strike brings out the design features, except for minor softness at the obverse center. A higher grade is precluded by light obverse luster grazes. Census: 39 in 65, 8 finer (6/07).
From The Silver Fox Collection. (#7232)

Dazzling Gem 1894-S Morgan Dollar

1639 **1894-S MS65 PCGS.** This Gem is one of the flashiest 1894-S dollars that we have examined in recent years. The surfaces are essentially brilliant, and the cartwheel luster in the fields is simply sensational. Striking detail is generally good except over the centers, where horizontal roller marks (as made) are noteworthy on both sides. A few wispy marks prevent an even loftier grade designation.
From The Reuben Reinstein Collection. (#7232)

1640 **1895-O AU50 PCGS.** An untoned key date New Orleans dollar with glimpses of bright luster throughout the borders and devices. Light highpoint friction is consistent with the grade. (#7236)

1641 **1895-O AU50 PCGS.** Despite a higher mintage, the 1895-O Morgan dollar is more elusive in all grades than its S-mint counterpart. This modestly circulated example displays slightly streaky violet, aqua, and orange patina over each side. Well-defined with plenty of original luster in the fields. (#7236)

1642 **1895-O—Cleaned—ANACS. AU50 Details.** Dashes of orange patina cling to the borders. Luster emerges from the hair, wings, and legends. Subdued by a cleaning, but still a suitable example of this key New Orleans dollar. (#7236)

1643 **1895-O AU53 NGC.** Golden-brown and sky-blue toning enriches the borders of this partly lustrous key date New Orleans Morgan. Impressively unmarked, and attractive despite its brief circulation. (#7236)

1644 **1895-O AU53 ANACS.** Luster fills the peripheries and devices. A momentarily circulated example of this key New Orleans issue. The reverse rim has a minor ding at 5:30, and a thin mark journeys from the bridge of the nose to a stop in the legend. (#7236)

1645 **1895-O AU55 PCGS.** Soft cloud-gray patina graces the subtly lustrous surfaces of this lightly worn O-mint dollar, one that displays an unusually sharp strike at the hair above the ear. Highly appealing despite light, scattered abrasions and a desirable example of this key issue. (#7236)

Challenging Near-Mint 1895-O Morgan

1646 **1895-O AU58 PCGS.** Very lightly worn, free of most mentionable marks, and with lots of original mint luster. A scarce coin in this grade and certainly much more affordable than the costly Mint State examples. The key date of New Orleans portion of the series. Worth a close look. (#7236)

Attractive 1895-O Morgan Dollar, AU58

1647 **1895-O AU58 PCGS.** One of the semi-key dates in the Morgan dollar series, in a condition far above the usually encountered VG or Fine. This example has a nice strike, light even wear, and scattered trivial marks. It also retains a high degree of mint luster for the grade. Bright, untoned, and attractive. (#7236)

1648 **1895-S XF45 ANACS.** Dusky gunmetal-gray, powder-blue, and autumn-brown toning envelops this splendidly detailed low mintage Morgan dollar. The fields are smooth, and the portrait has only minor contact concealed by the patina. (#7238)

Scarce Choice AU 1895-S Dollar

1649 **1895-S AU55 PCGS.** This Choice AU semi-key dollar has extensive luster which manages to penetrate the open fields. An untoned piece with only a whisper of friction above Liberty's ear. Unimportant marks are present near the arrowheads, but the remainder of the surfaces are surprisingly smooth. (#7238)

Borderline Uncirculated 1895-S Morgan

1650 **1895-S AU58 PCGS.** At first glance, this better date silver dollar appears to be Mint State, since the cartwheel luster is unencumbered and the strike is crisp. Inspection with a loupe locates traces of wear at the centers, although this piece would likely have been cataloged as Uncirculated in appearances prior to the advent of PCGS. Golden-brown toning enriches the borders. Lovely and lightly abraded. (#7238)

Original Near-Mint 1895-S Morgan

1651 **1895-S AU58 NGC.** An original near-Mint rare date dollar with only minor friction on the eagle's breast and the hair above the ear. Luster dominates the borders, eagle, and wreath, and fills Liberty's hair. The 1895-S has a mintage of only 400,000 pieces, and unlike the similarly-produced 1899, few Mint State examples emerged from Treasury holdings. (#7238)

Well Struck 1895-S Dollar, MS62

1652 **1895-S MS62 PCGS.** 1895-S Mint State coins are usually heavily bagmarked. Indeed, David Bowers (2006) writes that: " ... the booby prize for bagmarking should go to the 1895-S or the 1893-CC; it's probably a tossup." The MS62 specimen in this lot displays lustrous surfaces that are quite well preserved on the reverse; a milling mark on Liberty's cheek (a focal area) is likely all that precludes a higher grade on this coin. The design elements are well impressed, and the surfaces nearly untoned, save for a couple hints of color on the obverse. Housed in a green label holder. (#7238)

1895-S Morgan Dollar MS62

1653 **1895-S MS62 ANACS.** A small area in the hair detail just above Liberty's ear is softly defined and flat, but the remaining design elements are boldly struck. There is a light coating of milky color over each side that yields to gold and coral accents near the periphery. A slightly scuffy appearance on the obverse limits the grade. (#7238)

Impressive MS63 1895-S Dollar

1654 **1895-S MS63 PCGS.** A satiny Select silver dollar whose surprisingly smooth surfaces offer faint gold toning. Light roller marks here and there are strictly of mint origin. The 1895-S is the key to a *date* set of Morgan dollars, since the 1895 is proof-only and the 1895-O is even scarcer than the 1895-S, despite a slightly higher mintage. (#7238)

Exceptionally Attractive MS64 1895-S Dollar

1655 **1895-S MS64 PCGS.** One of the most sought-after issues in the Morgan series, the 1895-S is scarce in all grades. This satiny near-Gem has excellent eye appeal created by a combination of brilliant silver surfaces and traces of russet toning along the lower obverse border. A few scattered marks on the reverse prevent an even higher grade. The reverse fields are nearly prooflike. Sharply struck. (#7238)

Uncommon Superb Gem 1896 Morgan Dollar

1656 **1896 MS67 NGC.** The 1896-P may be a common date, but there is nothing "common" about this example. Basically untoned, except for faint golden peripheral color, with thick, satiny luster and a creamy-smooth portrait of Liberty that boasts a pristine cheek. Trivial field marks are noted on the obverse, but the overall eye appeal of this Superb Gem dollar is simply outstanding. Census: 42 in 67, 0 finer (6/07).
From The Reuben Reinstein Collection. (#7240)

1657 **1896 MS65 Deep Mirror Prooflike PCGS.** The flashy fields are exceptionally free from marks, and luster grazes are limited to the cheekbone and jaw. The 1896 has a high mintage, but DMPLs constitute only a tiny percentage of survivors. Certified in a green label holder. (#97241)

1658 **1896-O MS60 PCGS.** Though 1896-O dollars are not particularly difficult to acquire even in AU grades, Mint State examples of this issue prove elusive. This minimally toned example is well struck and displays above-average luster. A number of wispy abrasions on the portrait confirm the grade. In a green label holder. (#7242)

Lustrous MS63 1896-O Dollar

1659 **1896-O MS63 PCGS.** The 1896-O has triple trouble: strike, luster, and abrasions. The strike is often "below average, insipid and unattractive," to quote Bowers, and the luster is "typically dull and lifeless." The present coin is a happy exception, and a coin seldom seen in so fine a grade. The luster has considerable flash, and the strike is far above average. A few light abrasions are noted, mostly away from the prime focal areas, that determine the grade, but this is an exceptional Morgan dollar that bears serious consideration. PCGS has graded only 26 pieces finer (6/07). (#7242)

Spectacular 1896-O Morgan Silver Dollar, MS65

1660 **1896-O MS65 NGC.** While not particularly rare in circulated grades, the 1896-O dollar is elusive in all Mint State grades, and a major rarity in Gem quality. In *The Morgan and Peace Dollar Textbook,* Wayne Miller wrote: "No other Morgan dollar is as consistently deficient in luster, strike, and degree of surface abrasions as the 1896-O. A fully struck piece is rare; an 1896-O with minimum bagmarks is even more unusual. In the author's opinion, the 1896-O is the rarest of all Morgan dollars in truly Gem condition."

In 1896, the New Orleans Mint coined 4,900,000 silver dollars, following several years of lean production. This mintage is only a little over 300,000 fewer silver dollars than had been struck in New Orleans during the previous four years combined. It is almost certainly the case that those four years of limited production created this condition rarity as nearly all of these pieces were actually placed in circulation in 1896.

This issue provides an excellent illustration of the often confusing relationship between rarity and mintage. With a production of nearly 5 million coins, the '96-O has a substantial mintage for Morgan dollar issue. There are nearly 50 different issues that have a lower mintage, including such issues as 1884-CC, 1897, 1898-O, and 1904-O, just to name a few, and none of these dates come even close to the rarity of the '96-O in high grade. In the Morgan dollar series, rarity is not based on mintage, but on survival. For many dates, substantial portions of the mintage were placed in storage at the Treasury for several decades, until they were released in the 1960s, or even into the 1970s for some of the Carson City issues. Dates that were placed in storage are now the common dates in the series. Other dates, such as the 1896-O, that were released into circulation, are now the rarities or condition rarities of the series. In a few instances, such as the 1893-S, the rarity is explained by a combination of low mintage and release into circulation, and these are the dates that are keys to the series in all grades. The 1889-CC is another example.

The condition rarity status of this date is similar to the 1901 silver dollar. Both are essentially common in circulated grades, but rare in Mint State grades, and when such pieces are found, they are usually at the lowest numerical levels. However, proof examples of 1901 are available to collectors, but not so for the 96-O. Dave Bowers writes: "Those who are edged out of buying a Gem Mint State 1901 can wink twice and buy a proof quickly, but the collector seeking an 1896-O has no such fallback possibility."

Van Allen and Mallis describe 18 different varieties, mostly minor date recutting of limited interest. This specimen appears to be an example of VAM-2, with the O mintmark tilted slightly to the left.

The population of this date is limited, with just three MS65 pieces certified by NGC and none finer. For comparison, PCGS has graded one MS65 and two MS66. Therefore, the combined population of 1896-O silver dollars in Gem quality totals just six pieces, and this assumes that none of these represent resubmissions.

Most examples of this issue are weakly struck with fairly dull luster, according to Van Allen and Mallis. They suggest that prooflike examples are extremely rare, and those that exist have little contrast. This atypical Gem specimen, with full mint brilliance and light gold toning, is bluntly struck over the ear as always seen. However, the rest of the detail is better than average for the date. All of the remaining hair strands are sharply defined. The reverse has full feather detail in the wings, and even the breast feathers are clearly delineated. Both sides have satiny silver luster that is exceptionally bright. The reverse is reflective with light contrast between the field and devices. With only the slightest grazes visible on the obverse, and none on the reverse, this Gem '96-O dollar presents a high degree of aesthetic appeal for the connoisseur.
From The Reuben Reinstein Collection. (#7242)

1661 **1896-S AU53 PCGS.** Plum-mauve and sea-green augment the eye appeal of this briefly circulated semi-key Morgan dollar. Substantial luster emerges from recessed areas. (#7244)

1662 **1896-S MS61 ANACS.** This satiny better date Morgan dollar has autumn-brown and cream-gray toning. Abrasions are minor for the designated grade, and the highpoints show no indication of friction. (#7244)

MS62 1896-S/S Dollar With Obverse Strike-Through

1663 **1896-S/S—Obverse Struck Through—MS62 ANACS.** VAM-5. A Hot 50 Variety. The mintmark is widely repunched northeast. Perhaps even more interesting, a thin rod-shaped strike-through crosses the obverse field between the N in UNUM and the 6 in the date. Despite a mintage of 5 million pieces, the 1896-S is rare in quality Mint State grades. (#7244)

Lightly Toned 1896-S Select Dollar

1664 **1896-S MS63 PCGS.** Wisps of light tan patination make occasional visits to the lustrous surfaces of this S-mint Morgan dollar. We note some prooflike tendencies, especially on the reverse, where die polish lines reside in the fields. The strike is better than average for the issue, though softness occurs in the hair over Liberty's ear. A few minute marks preclude a higher grade. (#7244)

Deeply Toned 1896-S Dollar, MS63

1665 **1896-S MS63 NGC.** Both sides of this scarcity are fully lustrous with frosty surfaces. The obverse is entirely toned in deep steel, emerald, gold, and lilac. The reverse has similar toning around the entire coin, limited to the extreme border, plus an hourglass pattern of additional toning to the left and below. The surfaces have light marks that are consistent with the grade. (#7244)

Pleasing 1896-S Morgan Dollar MS64

1666 **1896-S MS64 NGC.** According to Wayne Miller, the 1896-S Morgan dollar is very scarce in Uncirculated condition, despite a high mintage of 5,000,000 pieces. This near-Gem example is well struck and lustrous, with smoky plum-gray toning in the fields and light golden accents at the peripheries. A couple of small milling marks on Liberty's portrait limit the grade.
From The Silver Fox Collection. (#7244)

1667 **1897 MS66 NGC.** With a mintage of slightly over 2.8 million pieces, Philadelphia produced the fewest silver dollars of the three mints in 1897. Airy yellow-orange color graces the peripheral zones, while the strongly lustrous centers have hints of steel-gray patina. Crisply struck with strong luster beneath the toning. (#7246)

1668 **1897 MS66 NGC.** A crisply defined, shining Premium Gem from the late 19th century. The majority of the surfaces remain untoned, though the reverse has light haze that is most evident at the word DOLLAR, which has a faint green appearance.
From The Silver Fox Collection. (#7246)

Conditionally Rare 1897 Morgan Dollar MS67

1669 **1897 MS67 NGC.** Well struck with a light coating of silver-white patina over both sides and impeccably preserved surfaces. Two or three tiny contact marks are noted on the lower parts of the eagle. Both Wayne Miller and Dave Bowers have called the 1897 Morgan dollar a common date, but they were obviously not referring to MS67 coins. A mere 25 pieces have been certified at this grade level, by NGC and PCGS combined, with none finer (6/07).
From The Reuben Reinstein Collection. (#7246)

1670 **1897-O MS61 PCGS.** Strongly lustrous with above-average detail on the devices. The surfaces are untoned save for a few points of deep russet color at the upper reverse rim. Scattered abrasions, including a number on the portrait, account for the grade for this later O-mint Morgan dollar. In a green label holder. (#7248)

1671 **1897-O MS61 NGC.** Generally well struck, except for slight weakness above Liberty's ear, with unabated luster and surfaces that seem minimally abraded, for the MS61 grade level. The obverse displays pale violet-red toning, while the reverse has a pale golden-silver cast. (#7248)

1672 **1897-O MS62 PCGS.** A satiny and nearly untoned better date dollar that has surprisingly smooth surfaces for the designated grade. The centers are slightly softly defined, as generally seen. (#7248)

1673 **1897-O MS62 ANACS.** Like the '96-O, the '97-O has a prodigious mintage, yet is scarce in Mint State and a major rarity in MS65 and better grades. This example has good luster and clean surfaces. A rim nick at 7:30 is barely worthy of mention. (#7248)

Select 1897-O Dollar, MS63

1674 **1897-O MS63 PCGS.** Ex: Cajun Collection. An excellent strike, considering it is a late New Orleans Mint dollar. There is good detail to the breast feathers, and a reasonable amount of the detail above the ear is also present. The fields are silver-white, and show abundant cartwheel luster for this often lackluster issue. (#7248)

1675 **1897-S MS66 NGC.** A brilliant and magnificently unmarked Premium Gem with good luster and a precise strike. The '97-S is among the more available later date S-mint Morgans, but examples with the present eye appeal are scarce.
From The Reuben Reinstein Collection. (#7250)

1676 **1898 MS66 PCGS.** The cheek shows a trace of almond-gold, but most collectors would regard this lustrous Morgan dollar as brilliant. Nicely struck, lustrous, and clean despite a thin mark above the eagle's head. (#7252)

Sharp 1898 Dollar, MS67

1677 **1898 MS67 NGC.** The 1898 Morgan dollar, having a mintage of close to 6 million pieces, is plentiful through MS65, as NGC and PCGS have graded several thousand coins through that grade level. The certified population drops somewhat in Premium Gem, and decreases precipitously at the MS67 level. Untoned surfaces on this Superb Gem possess dazzling luster, and are impeccably preserved. A well executed strike brings out sharp definition in the design elements. Census: 11 in 67, 0 finer (6/07).
From The Reuben Reinstein Collection. (#7252)

1678 **1898-O MS67 NGC.** Thoroughly lustrous with a crisp strike. Devoid of both toning and marks, with a freshness that exceeds many New Orleans dollars in peer grades. PCGS and NGC have each certified only one example in higher grades (6/07).
From The Reuben Reinstein Collection. (#7254)

1679 **1898-S MS61 ANACS.** A lustrous and untoned S-mint dollar kept from a higher grade by a patch of faint slide marks on the cheek. (#7256)

1680 **1898-S MS64 PCGS.** Well struck and strongly lustrous with an essentially untoned obverse that yields to lovely magenta, orange, pink, and pale blue-gray colors on the reverse. An attractive example of an issue that becomes elusive any finer. Certified in an old green label holder. (#7256)

1681 **1898-S MS64 PCGS.** This flashy, nicely struck near-Gem has autumn-red toning around the rims. Surface marks are minimal for the grade. An upper-end example of this later date S-mint, housed in a green label PCGS holder. (#7256)

1682 **1898-S MS65 NGC.** VAM-4. The mintmark is nicely repunched. This lustrous near-Gem has light honey-gold patina and delightfully smooth surfaces. The strike is precise with the exception of the area near Liberty's ear, which displays a few faint mint-made roller marks.
From The Silver Fox Collection. (#7256)

Lustrous 1898-S Dollar, MS66

1683 **1898-S MS66 PCGS.** Wisps of gold-tan color around the margins show up under high magnification, and pleasing luster emanates from well cared for surfaces. An attentive strike resulted in relatively strong definition on the design features, though characteristic minor softness is apparent in the hair over Liberty's ear. Population: 58 in 66, 2 finer (6/07).
From The Reuben Reinstein Collection. (#7256)

Flashy 1898-S Dollar, MS64 Deep Mirror Prooflike

1684 **1898-S MS64 Deep Mirror Prooflike PCGS.** The solidly defined devices of this near-Gem are a pleasing complement to the seemingly fathomless mirrors of the fields, an unusual feature for this issue. Aside from a touch of haze in the reverse fields, the surfaces are essentially untoned. A handful of small abrasions appear on the cheek, as does a patch of roller marks. Population: 26 in 64, 7 finer (4/07). (#97257)

1685 **1899 MS65 PCGS.** Virtually untoned, with lustrous silver-gray surfaces and a couple of dark reddish-brown spots near the rim on each side of the coin. A well struck and distraction-free Gem example of this popular issue that had a low mintage of 330,000 pieces. (#7258)

1686 **1899 MS65 PCGS.** Crisply struck and lustrous with pleasing preservation. Brilliant aside from a small darkly toned planchet flaw on the reverse rim at 10:30. A popular low mintage issue. (#7258)

Vibrant 1899 Premium Gem Dollar

1687 **1899 MS66 NGC.** The 1899 dollar is a popular semi-scarce date with a low-mintage figure of 330,000 business strikes. The Premium Gem in this lot displays vibrant luster and is essentially untoned. Nice detail is present on the design elements, including good definition in most of Liberty's hair strands and on the eagle's breast feathers. A minor luster graze or two on the obverse does not detract. Census: 60 in 66, 2 finer (6/07).
From The Reuben Reinstein Collection. (#7258)

1688 **1899 MS65 Prooflike PCGS.** Golden-brown and apple-green freckles enrich the borders of this attractively preserved, satiny, and crisply struck Gem. A popular low mintage date. Certified in an old green label holder. Population: 68 in 65 Prooflike, 7 finer (5/07). (#7259)

1689 **1899-O MS67 NGC.** The New Orleans Mint was the only facility in a former Confederate state to re-open after the Civil War, though by the time this dollar was struck in 1899, New Orleans would have only a decade of production left. This flashy and largely brilliant piece, well-defined save for the highpoints of the obverse, has a touch of amber toning at the margins.
From The Silver Fox Collection. (#7260)

1690 **1899-O MS67 NGC.** This is a beautifully preserved dollar from the New Orleans Mint that exhibits an effulgent satiny sheen over the untoned silver-white surfaces. A peripheral die crack and a few wispy field marks are noted on the reverse, but the obverse is virtually pristine. Census: 79 in 67, 0 finer (6/07).
From The Reuben Reinstein Collection. (#7260)

1691 **1899-S MS64 PCGS.** Golden-brown, ruby-red, and apple-green congregate across the borders of this lustrous and suitably struck near-Gem. Clean for the grade, and elusive any finer. (#7262)

1692 **1899-S MS65 PCGS.** Pleasing luster emanates from untoned surfaces, and an attentive strike brings out good definition on the motifs, save for minor softness in the hair at Liberty's ear. A few minor obverse marks are consistent with the grade designation. (#7262)

Sharply Struck 1899-S Dollar, MS66

1693 **1899-S MS66 NGC.** Both sides of this Premium Gem S-mint Morgan are awash in dazzling luster. Sharp strike definition complements this attribute, as does the smooth satiny finish. We note just a few minor marks on the obverse. The 1899-S is of medium scarcity (David Bowers, 2005). Census: 21 in 66, 1 finer (6/07).
From The Reuben Reinstein Collection. (#7262)

1694 **1900-O MS66 PCGS.** As with all 1900-O dollars, this piece displays lovely satin-like luster. What is unusual, though, are how clean the surfaces are. Sharply struck also. (#7266)

Elusive Superb Gem 1900-O Morgan Dollar

1695 **1900-O MS67 NGC.** Well struck throughout, with Superb surfaces that are untoned and nearly pristine. A faint grease streak (as made) along Liberty's jawline does not affect the technical grade of the piece, and does minimal harm to the overall eye appeal of this conditionally elusive New Orleans Mint product. Census: 54 in 67, 0 finer at either service (6/07).
From The Reuben Reinstein Collection. (#7266)

1696 **1900-O MS66 Prooflike PCGS.** Creamy luster and highly reflective fields make this Premium Gem an attractive representative of the issue. The piece also reveals sharply struck design elements and minimally marked surfaces. Numerous die lines are evident on each side, a common feature of this turn-of-the-century New Orleans Mint production. Population: 21 in 66 Prooflike, 0 finer in Prooflike at either service (4/07).
From The Vanek Collection. (#7267)

1697 **1900-O/CC MS64 NGC.** VAM-10A. A Top 100 Variety. The N in IN is die clashed near Liberty's neck, characteristic of this seldom-encountered VAM. VAM-8 and VAM-11 are the two most common O/CC VAMs. A lustrous and nearly untoned near-Gem with smooth surfaces and minor incompleteness of strike in the centers. (#7268)

1698 **1900-O/CC MS64 PCGS.** VAM-8. A Top 100 Variety. This crisply struck, lustrous, and essentially brilliant near-Gem has remarkably clean fields. Only a solitary light vertical graze above the jaw prevents a much higher grade. (#7268)

1699 **1900-O/CC MS64 PCGS.** VAM-8. A Top 100 Variety. A well-defined example of this noteworthy overmintmark variety, not as clear as VAM-7, but still dramatic. Essentially untoned with only light flaws on the portrait. (#7268)

1700 **1900-O/CC MS64 PCGS.** VAM-12. A Top 100 Variety. The most obvious of the overmintmark VAMs, with the curves of the Carson City mintmark visible on each side the prominent New Orleans mintmark. Lightly toned, lustrous, and well preserved. In a green label holder. (#7268)

Well Struck 1900-O/CC Dollar MS65, VAM-12

1701 **1900-O/CC MS65 PCGS.** VAM-12. A Top 100 Variety. This variety features the most prominent remnants of the underlying Carson City mintmark, along with light die cracks at the point of Liberty's bust, and the top of the cap. Sharply struck, with bright luster, and hints of light color on the central reverse. A few minor obverse marks are within the confines of the grade designation. (#7268)

High Grade (MS66) 1900-O/CC Dollar

1702 **1900-O/CC MS66 PCGS.** VAM-11. A Top 100 Variety. According to Breen, several reverse working dies were found during the removal of furnishings from the Carson City Assay Office, which was previously the Carson City Mint. The dies were shipped to the Philadelphia Mint where they were modified for production of 1900 O-mint Morgan dollars. Variety specialists now believe that no fewer than seven reverse dies were overmintmarked for the 1900-O production, all of which show remnants of the original CC mintmark. While relatively easy to locate in lower grades, the O/CC is quite a challenge in the better Mint State grades. This is a brilliant coin that exhibits dazzling, satiny mint luster. Fully struck in the centers, and free from any annoying abrasions. Population: 76 in 66, 2 finer (6/07).
From The Reuben Reinstein Collection. (#7268)

1703 **1900-S MS65 NGC.** A shining Gem representative of this late 19th century issue, well-defined save for the hair above Liberty's ear. The surfaces are largely untoned save for a hint of khaki patina at the margins. In a prior generation holder.
From The Silver Fox Collection. (#7270)

Sleek MS66 1900-S Morgan Dollar

1704 **1900-S MS66 NGC.** Brilliant throughout and white with smooth, satiny luster and nicely impressed devices. Virtually unfazed by marks, as one would expect from an MS66, the overall appearance is outstanding for this popular S-mint issue. Only two pieces have been certified finer by NGC and PCGS combined (6/07).
From The Reuben Reinstein Collection. (#7270)

Prooflike Gem 1900-S Morgan

1705 **1900-S MS65 Prooflike PCGS.** A virtually brilliant Gem that boasts a remarkably clean cheek. The obverse field is also well preserved. The 1900-S is a better date to begin with, especially as a Gem, and is very scarce with Prooflike fields. Encapsulated in an old green label holder. Population: 24 in 65 Prooflike, 6 finer (5/07). (#7271)

1706 **1901 AU58 PCGS.** The 1901 is a famous conditional rarity, plentiful in VF but elusive in Mint State. This example has satin cartwheel luster and dusky dove-gray, forest-green, and golden-brown toning. Distributed small marks on the face are of little concern. (#7272)

1707 **1901 AU58 PCGS.** A touch of friction blends with minor weakness on the highpoints of this near-Mint example. Wisps of golden patina grace surfaces that retain nearly all of their original luster. A pleasing example of this turn-of-the-century issue, one that has a deserved reputation as elusive in higher grades. (#7272)

1708 **1901 AU58 NGC.** Admittedly, the highpoints of the hair have a mere whisper of friction, but many collectors would regard this Morgan dollar as Mint State. Cartwheel luster is unbroken, although slightly diminished on Liberty's cheek. Lightly toned and conditionally rare. (#7272)

1709 **1901 AU58 NGC.** This lightly toned Morgan dollar has a mere whisper of friction at the centers. Mint luster is essentially complete. Along with the 1884-S and the 1892-S, the 1901 is one of the few issues in the series with more pieces certified as AU58 than in all Mint State grades combined. (#7272)

1710 **1901—Obverse Damage—NCS. Unc Details.** The lustrous and nearly untoned surfaces display a near-vertical scrape that traverses Liberty's cheek and neck. A famous conditional rarity. (#7272)

Conditional Rarity 1901 Morgan MS61

1711 **1901 MS61 NGC.** Despite a mintage of nearly 7 million pieces, the 1901 is scarce in any Mint State grade. Perhaps the issue contributed to the 1918 Pittman Act melt, which removed more than 270 million silver dollars from the Treasury vaults. This lustrous representative has peripheral plum-red and jade-green toning. Small marks here and there are consistent with the grade. Certified in a prior generation holder. (#7272)

Lustrous MS62 1901 Morgan Dollar

1712 **1901 MS62 PCGS.** Only two years separate the 1899 from the 1901, yet the low mintage 1899 is plentiful in Mint State, while the high mintage 1901 is rare in Uncirculated grades. Such inconsistencies are frequent within the Morgan dollar series, since the status of an issue depended on its distribution pattern as much as its original mintage. The present example is lustrous and friction-free, and has only a hint of toning. Minor marks on the left obverse are unimportant for the grade. (#7272)

Lightly Toned 1901 Dollar, MS62

1713 **1901 MS62 ANACS.** David Bowers (2006) says of the 1901 dollar: "Exceedingly rare in Mint State. Even an MS63 is a major rarity." Hints of light tan color visit the lustrous surfaces of this MS62 specimen, a bit more evident on the reverse. The design elements are somewhat better struck than usually seen on this typically poorly defined issue, though some softness is still visible in the hair at Liberty's ear. (#7272)

1714 **1901-O MS66 PCGS.** The 1901-O is often selected for date sets, since it is available in Mint State relative to the 1901 and 1901-S. But the 1901-O becomes scarce in MS66, and PCGS has graded only three pieces finer (5/07). Lightly toned and lustrous with minor mint-made granularity on the obverse center. (#7274)

1715 **1901-O MS66 NGC.** New Orleans was the only Mint to close permanently during the 20th century, and as that century dawned, the facility still produced silver dollars such as the present coin. Well struck with strong detail and minimal color.
From The Silver Fox Collection. (#7274)

Superb Gem 1901-O Morgan, MS67

1716 **1901-O MS67 NGC.** Although this date is not as common as some other New Orleans issue, it is common enough that any collector can own a nice Mint State example with little difficulty. However, Superb Gem pieces are extremely rare, with just 14 pieces certified by NGC and PCGS combined.
This specimen is highly lustrous with frosty silver surfaces on both sides. The brilliant white color is enhanced by the faintest champagne toning imaginable. It is a pristine example that is entirely free of surface marks. all of the design details are boldly detailed. Census: 11 in 67, 0 finer (6/07).
From The Reuben Reinstein Collection. (#7274)

1717 **1901-S MS64 PCGS.** A bit weakly struck over the centers, but highly lustrous and additionally enhanced in its overall appearance by lavender toning near the peripheries. A nicely preserved silver dollar with relatively few marks for the grade. A difficult San Francisco Mint issue at all Mint State grade levels. (#7276)

1718 **1901-S MS64 PCGS.** This well struck near-Gem has vivacious luster and gentle caramel-gold toning. S-mint Morgans from this decade are elusive, and the 1901-S is no exception. (#7276)

1719 **1901-S MS64 PCGS.** Choice with strong, delightful luster and excellent eye appeal. A touch of softness on the highpoints and light, scattered marks deny a finer grade. This early 20th century piece is housed in a green label holder. (#7276)

1720 **1901-S MS64 NGC.** A well struck piece coined in San Francisco, from an issue that preceded that Mint's moment of greatest glory by just five years. The slightly satiny surfaces have soft, pleasing clover-green patina, and the overall visual appeal is tantalizingly close to that of a Gem. (#7276)

1721 **1901-S MS64 ANACS.** The peripheries are toned light golden-brown and lilac, while the fields and devices are nearly brilliant. This impressively smooth scarce date dollar has the preservation of a higher grade, but the centers are incompletely brought up. (#7276)

Lustrous 1901-S Gem Dollar

1722 **1901-S MS65 PCGS.** Pastel ice-blue and mauve color rests over highly lustrous surfaces, joined on the reverse by occasional speckles of olive-green. A sharp strike brings up good definition on the design elements, including the eagle's breast. A few minor marks are scattered about each side, none of which are worthy of individual mention.
From The Reuben Reinstein Collection. (#7276)

1723 **1902 MS66 NGC.** This untoned, lustrous, and carefully preserved Premium Gem has a good strike and undeniable eye appeal. (#7278)

1724 **1902 MS66 NGC.** A satiny and virtually brilliant Premium Gem with pleasing preservation and a decisive strike. The 1902 is plentiful in MS63 to MS65 grades, but is surprisingly scarce any finer. NGC has certified only eight coins finer than the present MS66 (5/07). (#7278)

1725 **1902 MS66 PCGS.** This beautiful silver-white Premium Gem has a needle-sharp strike, and both sides are refreshingly free from contact. Unlike the 1901, the 1902 is collectible in quality Mint State, but just 18 pieces have been certified finer by PCGS (4/07). (#7278)

1726 **1902 MS66 NGC.** An untoned and semi-prooflike example of this conditionally rare Philadelphia issue. The cheek and fields are refreshingly void of bagmarks, and the strike is full. (#7278)

1727 **1902 MS66 PCGS.** Faint chestnut toning visits this suitably struck and unmarked Premium Gem. Flagrant luster confirms the originality. PCGS and NGC combined have certified a mere 26 pieces finer (5/07). (#7278)

1728 **1902 MS66 NGC.** Powerful luster and above-average detail characterize this attractive Premium Gem. A touch of blue-tinged haze floats over fields that take on a pleasing cloud-gray color. A great example from the waning years of the design's original run.
From The Silver Fox Collection. (#7278)

Exceptional 1902 Dollar, MS67

1729 **1902 MS67 NGC.** The 1902 Superb Gem dollar that we offer in the current lot features well struck design elements for an issue that David Bowers says: "Striking is apt to be indifferent or downright poor." In addition, both sides exude vibrant luster, and just the slightest hint of light gold color at the peripheries. Both faces are immaculately preserved. Census: 8 in 67, 0 finer (6/07).
From The Reuben Reinstein Collection. (#7278)

Superb Gem 1902-O Morgan

1730 **1902-O MS67 NGC.** An exquisite strike and impressively clean surfaces ensure the high grade of this shimmering and virtually brilliant Superb Gem. Morgan dollars with such formidable quality are typically S-mints struck between 1878 and 1882. New Orleans issued large quantities of silver dollars, and many have survived in Mint State, but those that compare with the quality of the present coin are few and far between. Census: 19 in 67, 0 finer (6/07). (#7280)

Sharp 1902-O Superb Gem Dollar

1731 **1902-O MS67 NGC.** In discussing the 1902-O dollar, David Bowers (2005) cites Wayne Miller who wrote in 1982 that the issue is: "Typically among the poorest struck of the late New Orleans dollars. Most are flatly struck with horrible luster." Not so the Superb Gem we present in this lot! Essentially untoned surfaces yield dazzling luster and sharply struck design elements. While minor softness is noted in the hair at Liberty's ear, the eagle's breast feathers are well brought up. There are no mentionable marks to report. Census: 19 in 67, 0 finer (6/07).
From The Reuben Reinstein Collection. (#7280)

1732 **1902-S—Scratched, Cleaned—ANACS. AU58 Details.** A hairlined and dipped white example with a hint of golden retoning on the upper obverse margin. Although designated as "Scratched" by ANACS, the only remotely mentionable mark is relatively unimportant, and on the neck above the bust tip. (#7282)

1733 **1902-S MS64 PCGS.** Light caramel-gold toning endows this lustrous better date dollar. The centers are incompletely brought up and exhibit faint roller marks, as made. The reverse is well preserved. (#7282)

1734 **1902-S MS64 PCGS.** Dove-gray and khaki-gold illuminate this satiny and clean-cheeked near-Gem. Minor grazes on Liberty's chin and a few pinpoint flecks on the eagle's body decide the grade. (#7282)

1735 **1902-S MS64 PCGS.** Captivating luster and pleasing overall detail characterize this later San Francisco piece, which has a thin layer of iridescent patina over the obverse. Faint abrasions on the cheek and the eagle's breast confirm the grade. Encased in a green label holder. (#7282)

1736 **1902-S MS64 ANACS.** Delicate orange-red patina endows the margins of this crisply struck and lustrous near-Gem. Faint marks near the cheek and mouth deny an even higher grade. The 1902-S is difficult to locate in quality Mint State, like all S-mint Morgans from that decade. (#7282)

Rare Premium Gem 1902-S Morgan Dollar

1737 **1902-S MS66 NGC.** Brilliant and highly lustrous, with a clean cheek and no blemishes on the eagle's breast area. As is frequently the case for many Morgan dollars, of any date, there is a trace of weakness on the hair detail just above Liberty's ear. All of the other design elements are well struck and crisply outlined, however. A rare Premium Gem example of this San Francisco Mint issue. Census: 8 in 66, 0 finer (6/07).
From The Reuben Reinstein Collection. (#7282)

Outstanding MS67 1903 Morgan Dollar

1738 **1903 MS67 NGC.** An exceptionally attractive example of this uncommon-in-high-grade Morgan dollar. Frequently encountered in lower grades, only 77 coins have been certified as MS67 by NGC with one finer (6/07). Fully and intricately detailed throughout, the brilliant surfaces display rich, satiny mint luster and, of course, lack any meaningful abrasions. An opportunity for the Morgan dollar collector. (#7284)

Well Impressed 1903 Dollar, MS67

1739 **1903 MS67 NGC.** This Superb Gem 1903 Morgan possesses radiant luster, and was subjected to a powerful strike, as excellent definition is apparent on the motifs. Brilliant surfaces reveal no significant marks, further adding to the coin's great eye appeal. Census: 77 in 67, 1 finer (6/07).
From The Reuben Reinstein Collection. (#7284)

1740 **1903 MS65 Prooflike NGC.** Delicate bands of apricot patina cling to the lower reverse and upper right obverse. This penetratingly struck Gem has moderately flashy luster and a clean cheek. Census: 32 in 65, 4 finer (5/07). (#7285)

1741 **1903-O MS66 PCGS.** The soft, satin-like surfaces are virtually unblemished by coin-to-coin contact. The strike is sharp, and there is lovely golden-russet peripheral toning on the obverse. As an issue, the 1903-O is one of continuing interest and fascination for numismatists because of this date's status as a key date until the release of several bags in 1962. (#7286)

1742 **1903-O MS66 PCGS.** From the third of just four 20th century O-mint issues comes this carefully preserved and well struck piece. Strongly lustrous with soft silver-gray surfaces and splashes of peach color at the peripheries. (#7286)

1743 **1903-O MS66 NGC.** The penultimate silver dollar issue struck at New Orleans, as the denomination temporarily vanished in 1904 and by the time production resumed in 1921, that Mint was no more. This flashy Premium Gem offers strong detail and just a trace of milky patina. NGC has certified 34 Superb Gems (5/07).
From The Silver Fox Collection. (#7286)

1744 **1903-O MS66 NGC.** Well struck and essentially brilliant with vibrant luster and exceptional eye appeal. The 1903-O is famous for its former status as a great rarity, which ended with the release of Treasury bags circa 1962. (#7286)

Nicely Detailed 1903-O Dollar, MS67

1745 **1903-O MS67 NGC.** The 1903-O had a mintage of 4.450 million pieces, but David Bowers (2006) estimates that 4 million were melted under the terms of the 1918 Pittman Act. This Superb Gem displays excellent design definition, including that on the strands of Liberty's hair and the feathers on the eagle's breast. Close examination exhibits wisps of faint tan-gold color at the margins. Census: 34 in 67, 0 finer (6/07).
From The Reuben Reinstein Collection. (#7286)

1746 **1903-O MS63 Deep Mirror Prooflike PCGS.** The 1903-O is no longer considered a great rarity, as it was in 1962 before the release of a Treasury hoard. But prooflike pieces are very scarce, and DMPL examples are rare. This sharply struck and brilliant example has flashy fields, and is clean aside from a subtle graze on the chin. Population: 16 in 63 DMPL, 42 finer (4/07). (#97287)

1747 **1903-S—Cleaned—ANACS. XF40 Details.** Slightly glossy from a past cleaning, but partly retoned autumn-brown. Glimpses of luster outline design elements. (#7288)

1748 **1903-S AU55 ANACS.** Light tawny-gold, plum-red, and cobalt-blue emerge across portions of the perimeters. Luster brightens the devices and margins. A small mark on the eagle's breast, but the cheek has minimal contact. (#7288)

Select Uncirculated 1903-S Morgan Dollar

1749 **1903-S MS63 NGC.** An affordable example of this scarce, late date dollar. Fully struck, the surfaces are a bit lackluster (thus explaining the grade) and there is a light ring of golden color around the margins. A light scrape is noted in the right obverse field, this being the only mark worthy of mention on the coin. (#7288)

High End 1903-S Morgan Dollar MS63

1750 **1903-S MS63 NGC.** Crisply detailed and highly lustrous, this Select Mint State dollar is also untoned, except for a few russet-orange specks on each side that are only evident with the aid of a magnifier. Only a handful of scattered, trivial marks are encountered on obverse and reverse alike, leading us to believe that this piece has been conservatively graded by NGC. (#7288)

Magnificent 1903-S Dollar, MS66

1751 **1903-S MS66 PCGS.** The 1903-S is a rare issue in the Morgan dollar series, and Mint State coins are desirable at all levels of preservation. The elusiveness of this date in Mint State is perhaps summed up best by David Bowers in his *Silver Dollars and Trade Dollars of the United States*: "This is an important, key issue. I have never handled a quantity of them, and few other dealers have either."
Potent luster exudes from both sides of this magnificent Premium Gem, and the usually seen solid strike brings out excellent definition on the design features. Untoned surfaces are remarkably well preserved, enhancing the coin's outstanding eye appeal. Population: 34 in 66, 3 finer (6/07). (#7288)

Exceptional 1904 Dollar, MS65

1752 1904 MS65 NGC. The 1904 dollar has a reputation for being less than well produced. David Bowers (2005) says of this issue: "Most coins seen today are poorly to indifferently struck and with poor luster—all in all, rather sorry looking." The Gem in this lot exhibits dazzling luster and is generally well struck, with only minor softness in the centers. Untoned surfaces are quite well preserved.
From The Silver Fox Collection. (#7290)

Elusive Premium Gem 1904 Morgan Dollar

1753 1904 MS66 NGC. Well struck, highly lustrous, and untoned, this Premium Gem is well preserved, as can be expected from the lofty grade designation. A shallow mark on Liberty's jaw is too faint to limit the grade. According to Bowers' *Silver Dollar Encyclopedia*, "In full MS-65, sharply struck, the 1904 is among the most elusive dollars in the Morgan series." The current example is just such a dollar, except that its grade is MS66! Census: 5 in 66, 0 finer (6/07).
From The Reuben Reinstein Collection. (#7290)

Conditionally Scarce 1904-O Morgan Dollar MS67

1754 1904-O MS67 NGC. The 1904-O Morgan dollar went from being one of the rarest issues in the entire series, in Mint State, to becoming one of the most common, after the Philadelphia Mint released more than a million Uncirculated pieces from long-term storage in 1962. At the Superb Gem level of preservation, however, the '04-O remains elusive. This example is intensely lustrous, with semi-reflective fields and brilliant silver-white surfaces. Well struck except for typical weakness over the centers, this lovely dollar coin is minimally marked on both sides; a testament to its restful preservation in a mint bag for many decades. Census: 69 in 67, 0 finer at either service (6/07).
From The Reuben Reinstein Collection. (#7292)

Prooflike Superb Gem 1904-O Morgan

1755 1904-O MS67 Prooflike NGC. This flashy Superb Gem has a whisper of gold toning on Liberty's cheek, although many observers would consider the piece as brilliant. The strike is exacting, and the preservation is exceptional. No 1904-O dollars have been certified in MS68 or finer grades by either NGC or PCGS. Census: 2 in 67 Prooflike, 0 finer (6/07). (#7293)

1756 1904-S AU58 ANACS. Light pumpkin-gold patina invigorates the margins of this lustrous and attractive slider. Evidence of highpoint wear is scant, and since marks are inconsequential, the eye appeal is superior for the grade. (#7294)

Lustrous 1904-S Dollar MS62

1757 1904-S MS62 PCGS. Orange-gold freckles visit the rims, but this lustrous and crisply struck silver dollar is otherwise untoned. A thin mark on the eagle's body and a few wispy slide marks on the cheek decide the grade. S-mint silver dollars from this era must have been primarily paid out rather than held as Treasury reserves, since they are scarce in Mint State. Certified in a green label holder. (#7294)

Brilliant MS63 1904-S Dollar

1758 1904-S MS63 PCGS. A brilliant example of this scarce, later date, post-1900 Morgan dollar. Well struck with a few minor abrasions on the obverse, the reverse is virtually free from marks. Exceptionally lustrous with a hard, satiny sheen over both obverse and reverse. Generally not located in higher grades. (#7294)

Elusive Select 1904-S Dollar

1759 **1904-S MS63 PCGS.** Attractive freckles of golden-brown and rose endow the peripheries of this lustrous example. The centers are slightly soft, but the reverse is well preserved. An abrasion is noted above the bust tip. The 1904-S is a much better date, scarce even in circulated grades. (#7294)

Better Date 1904-S Dollar, MS64

1760 **1904-S MS64 PCGS.** Effulgent cartwheel luster graces the surfaces of this high-end and in-demand near-Gem Morgan dollar. The brilliant, nearly untoned, silver-white surfaces display just a few hints of light gold-tan color, and are superbly appealing, despite a few stray marks that prevent a Gem rating. David Bowers (2005) writes: "The 1904-S dollar is one of the key issues in the series, and in comparison to the demand for them, Mint State pieces are elusive." (#7294)

Conditionally Rare 1904-S Dollar MS65 Prooflike

1761 **1904-S MS65 Prooflike NGC.** Solidly struck with shallow-mirrored fields that achieve a mild contrast with the central devices. Die striations help to promote the illusion of prooflike reflectivity on both sides. Slight cloudiness and a few minor marks preclude an even finer grade assessment; but this Gem is one of a mere five coins to be certified as MS65 Prooflike, by NGC, with none finer (6/07).
From The Reuben Reinstein Collection. (#7295)

1762 **1921 MS66 NGC.** Gleaming mint frost covers each side of this brilliant Premium Gem. Fully struck and carefully preserved, the piece only shows an occasional minor surface blemish. Surprisingly rare any finer, with just 15 examples certified at higher grades by NGC (5/07). (#7296)

1763 **1921 MS66 PCGS.** Sharply struck with dazzling mint luster. The surfaces are brilliant and lack the abrasions normally encountered on this common, high mintage issue. (#7296)

1764 **1921 MS66 PCGS.** Almond-gold toning drapes this lustrous and carefully preserved final-year Morgan dollar. Occasional portions of the wreath lack absolute detail, but the centers provide exceptional definition. (#7296)

1765 **1921 MS66 NGC.** This issue is not scarce at the current grade level, but a 1921 Morgan at any grade level is unlikely to match the eye appeal of this lustrous Premium Gem. The mint frost is intense, the striking details are crisp, and the surfaces are well preserved. Perhaps its most noteworthy attribute, however, is the lovely peripheral toning that adorns each side, and significantly increases the coin's overall visual allure. (#7296)

1766 **1921 MS66 NGC.** Well struck with exuberant cartwheel luster and pale creamy-gold coloration across both sides. Two or three trivial field marks on the obverse, and a tiny milling mark on the eagle's lower abdomen, are all that preclude an even loftier grade assessment for this impressive Premium Gem dollar.
From The Reuben Reinstein Collection. (#7296)

Dynamic 1921 Dollar MS66 Prooflike

1767 **1921 MS66 Prooflike NGC.** Fully struck with an undeniably flashy appearance, as the snow-white surfaces reveal dynamic reflectivity in the fields and considerable mint frost over both sides. A few milky spots are noted, but surface blemishes are minimal, as expected for a Premium Gem. Census: 3 in 66 Prooflike, 1 finer (5/07).
From The Vanek Collection. (#7297)

1768 **1921-D MS66 NGC.** The first silver dollar issue struck at Denver, the 1921-D Morgan dollar had a production of over 20 million pieces, though finding anything finer than a Gem can prove time-consuming. This boldly struck, slightly hazy example displays a number of die cracks at the reverse periphery. Predominantly frosty, though a few vertical streaks of brilliance are noted behind the eagle. NGC has certified just six coins finer (5/07).
From The Silver Fox Collection. (#7298)

1769 **1921-D MS66 PCGS.** A lightly toned example with clean fields and a splendidly smooth reverse. Liberty's cheek and the lower portion of the wreath lack a complete strike. The sole Denver Mint issue.
From The Reuben Reinstein Collection. (#7298)

1770 **1921-S MS65 PCGS.** A lustrous and faintly toned final-year Morgan dollar with the usual incompleteness of strike at the centers and on the lower portion of the wreath. A high mintage issue, but difficult to find well preserved. (#7300)

1771 **1921-S MS65 PCGS.** Better struck than the usual '21-S dollar, with only softness limited to small portions of the wreath and claws. A lustrous and unabraded Premium Gem with a few pinpoint ebony freckles. (#7300)

1772 **1921-S MS65 NGC.** Despite the strong mintages for the Morgan dollar issues of 1921, Gem S-mint pieces are elusive, partly due to striking problems. This example offers swirling luster and few post-strike marks, though the champagne-tinged portrait displays a number of tiny planchet marks on the unstruck cheek and temple and the eagle's breast. (#7300)

1773 **1921-S MS65 NGC.** A brilliant and beautifully preserved Gem that possesses sweeping cartwheel luster. Slightly soft in the centers and on the lower left portion of the wreath, but the strike is sharper than usual for this hastily produced issue. (#7300)

Brilliant 1921-S Morgan Dollar, MS66

1774 1921-S MS66 NGC. The untoned surfaces of this Premium Gem S-mint yield glowing luster, and possess a somewhat orange-peel effect in the fields. This issue traditionally comes weakly struck. In fact, David Bowers (2006) writes that the strike is: "Poor; about as poor as a Morgan dollar can be." The design definition on the obverse of this example is actually well brought up; sharp detail shows in most of Liberty's hair. The reverse exhibits softness on some of the lower wreath. A couple of trivial luster grazes do not disturb. Census: 43 in 66, 1 finer (6/07).
From The Reuben Reinstein Collection. (#7300)

PROOF MORGAN DOLLARS

1775 1879 PR63 NGC. Fully struck with a layer of creamy toning over both sides and well preserved surfaces free of bothersome contact marks or hairlines. Mint records indicate that 1,100 pieces were produced, but Breen and others believe that the number minted was actually lower than that.
From The Vanek Collection. (#7314)

Choice Proof 1879 Morgan Dollar

1776 1879 PR64 NGC. Generally sharply struck, although the hair just above Liberty's ear shows some incompleteness of detail. The fields are watery and deeply reflective and the devices are mildly frosted. A small splash of milky red-brown color is noted along the reverse border, near NIT. Some wispy hairlines in the obverse fields limit the grade.
From The Vanek Collection. (#7314)

Wonderful 1879 Morgan Dollar, PR68 Cameo

1777 1879 PR68 Cameo NGC. Records indicate a mintage of 1,100 proof Morgan dollars for 1879, a smaller figure than the number of proof Trade dollars for that year, though much larger than the meager production of proof gold dollars. The specimen offered here ranks among the finest survivors of this second-year issue. The steel-gray fields have strong reflectivity with only one minor, isolated spot of haze to the right of the arrowheads. A splash of cherry-red at the E in ONE adds a touch of color. The devices have solid detail overall, though the hair above the ear is a trifle weak as always, and light, even frost contributes to this coin's distinct contrast. Both sides are carefully preserved, with only two unimportant contact marks in the upper reverse fields. NGC has graded just three pieces as PR68 Cameo, while PCGS acknowledges just one, with no finer Cameo examples certified by either service (5/07). (#87314)

Pleasing 1880 Morgan Dollar, PR64

1778 1880 PR64 PCGS. According to David Bowers (2005), the 1,355-piece proof mintage of 1880 Morgan dollars was: " ... a figure caused by the carry-along factor from those who were speculating in Proof Trade dollars this year. Today, many Proofs of this date are cleaned." The lovely near-Gem specimen offered here exhibits considerable field-device contrast, especially when the coin is tilted under a light source. Faint blue and gold-tan color rests over both faces, and an impressive strike brings out great definition in the elements. No significant marks are apparent. Liberty's cheek, neck, forehead, and temple are amazingly clean! A very pleasing coin overall. (#7315)

1779 1881 PR63 NGC. Needle-sharp definition and intense reflectivity are the most obvious characteristics of this Select Proof. The lightly hairlined fields display a thin veil of cloud-gray patina, and a trio of reed marks are noted on the neck.
From The Vanek Collection. (#7316)

Outstanding 1882 Dollar, PR64 Cameo

1780 1882 PR64 Cameo PCGS. This near-Gem Cameo displays pronounced field-motif contrast irrespective of the angle from which the coin is observed, and untoned surfaces exhibit well impressed design features, further enhancing the coin's outstanding eye appeal. Some unobtrusive handling marks define the grade. Population: 19 in 64 Cameo, 12 finer (4/07). (#87317)

Near-Gem Proof 1883 Trade Dollar

1781 1883 PR64 NGC. Sharply struck with mildly frosted devices and nearly full cameo contrast on both sides. A slight degree of milkiness in the fields seems to preclude both the PR65 grade and the Cameo designation. Still an attractive specimen from this proof-only issue.
From The Vanek Collection. (#7318)

1782 1884 PR63 NGC. Elegant plum and amethyst patina graces the deeply reflective fields, while the lightly frosted devices exhibit comparatively lighter color. This sharply struck, lightly hairlined Select proof is one of just 875 specimens distributed.
From The Vanek Collection. (#7319)

Brilliant PR65 1884 Morgan Dollar

1783 1884 PR65 NGC. Brilliant throughout, the fields display deep reflectivity and the devices are lightly frosted, which renders a moderate cameo contrast on each side. Pinpoint striking details are seen in the center of each side. The 1884 is one of the more available and best-produced proof Morgan dollars, and it is often used as a proof type coin. Census: 31 in 65, 20 finer (6/07). (#7319)

1784 1885—Cleaned—ANACS. PR60 Details. Rotation beneath a light reveals chestnut-gold toning. The fields are hairlined, but the devices are well struck and exhibit mild contrast with the mirrored fields. Just 930 proofs were struck. (#7320)

Lightly Toned Near-Gem Proof 1886 Morgan Dollar

1785 1886 PR64 NGC. Fully struck and lightly toned, with a combination of gold and pale green tinting, especially along the rims and in the fields. Faint hairlines limit the grade, in the absence of contact marks or striking deficiencies. According to Bowers: "886 Proofs were minted, most of which remain today. High level, unimpaired, uncleaned coins are rare."
From The Vanek Collection. (#7321)

Near-Gem Proof 1887 Morgan Dollar

1786 1887 PR64 NGC. The peak of the 7 in the date is lightly repunched to the north. The watery fields are deeply reflective, and the striking details seem virtually unimprovable. Lightly toned with accents of pale green and gold. The mildly frosted devices allow an appreciable degree of field-to-device contrast on both sides. Free of contact marks and only faintly hairlined.
From The Vanek Collection. (#7322)

Conditionally Scarce 1888 Morgan PR66 Cameo

1787 **1888 PR66 Cameo NGC.** Breen-5600, "Very rare." The 18 in the date is recut. This specimen also displays an unusual area of planchet roughness which is noticeable on the hair detail just above and below Liberty's ear, as well as on the ear itself. Otherwise, the piece shows suitable proof sharpness on the remaining design elements, along with frosted devices and reflective fields that show trace amounts of cloudiness on both sides. Census: 10 in 66 Cameo, 4 finer (5/07).
From The Vanek Collection. (#87323)

1788 **1889 PR62 PCGS.** A pinpoint-sharp proof Morgan with smooth pearl-gray fields. The eagle's wings and Liberty's hair are lightly frosted. A few trivial slide marks on the cheek account for the conservative grade. A stingy 811 proofs were struck. Encapsulated in a green label holder.
From The Vanek Collection. (#7324)

Scarce Select Proof 1890 Morgan

1789 **1890 PR63 NGC.** Glimpses of orange, forest-green, and navy-blue patina enrich the rims of this exactingly struck Select proof Morgan. The left obverse field has a few trivial hairlines, and the upper reverse field is slightly hazy. A mere 590 proofs were struck, the lowest mintage of the series aside from the three proof 1878 tailfeather varieties. The devices are thickly frosted. Certified in a prior generation holder. (#7325)

Attractive PR64 1891 Morgan Dollar

1790 **1891 PR64 PCGS.** Grayish-gold and amber-tinged surfaces are lustrous, with few mentionable distractions save for a single straight-line contact mark through the earlobe and lower curls of Liberty. The strike on the obverse center is a bit on the soft side, as usually seen on this date. The fields are deeply mirrored and there is significant contrast present because of the mint frost that covers the devices. An appealing and affordable near-Gem. (#7326)

Superlative 1891 Dollar, PR68

1791 **1891 PR68 NGC.** This piece should be designated Cameo due to the full contrast that is visible on each side. However, most of the obverse and all of the reverse are thickly toned in steel, heather, lilac, and sea-green, and this toning prevents such a designation. The obverse has a small circular area near the center that is brilliant white. It is an excellent example for the advanced collector assembling a set of proof Morgans, the collector putting together an 1891 proof set, or the collector of high quality type coins.

NGC has certified five 1891 dollars at the PR68 level, two without any designation, two others as Cameo (one is a PR68★ Cameo), and one as Ultra Cameo. No examples have been called PR69 (6/07). (#7326)

Choice Cameo Proof 1892 Dollar

1792 1892 PR64 Cameo PCGS. An untoned specimen with frosty motifs and nicely mirrored fields. Crisply struck aside from the usual softness above the ear. Because of the introduction of the Barber dime, quarter, and half, proof mintages of the Morgan dollar rose from 650 pieces in 1891 to 1,245 pieces in 1892. Nonetheless, the proof 1892 is scarce, particularly with seamless cameo contrast. Population: 14 in 64 Cameo, 12 finer (5/07). (#87327)

Scarce and Important Gem Proof 1894 Dollar

1793 1894 PR65 PCGS. Of the two known varieties of proofs from this year, this piece is struck from the dies that have the date to the left, the 9 is heavy and closed, and die file marks slant down to the right between the back of the eagle's neck and wing. Always of interest to advanced collectors as high grade 1894 business strikes are so scarce. This is a lightly toned Gem that has bright, highly reflective fields on each side. A nearly defect-free proof with strong visual appeal. (#7329)

Deep Cameo 1894 Morgan, PR63

1794 1894 PR63 Deep Cameo PCGS. Proof examples of this issue are closely related to those of 1901. Both dates are rarities in business strike, although for different reasons. The 1894 is rare because it was a low mintage issue, while the 1901 is conditionally rare because most of the mintage was placed in circulation. The common characteristic is that collectors who desire an attractive piece can choose a proof. This example has amazing contrast beneath light champagne toning. (#97329)

PR64 Ultra Cameo 1894 Dollar

1795 1894 PR64 Ultra Cameo NGC. The devices offer deep, consistent frost, and the mirrored fields ensure impressive cameo contrast. The strike is razor-sharp aside from the few strands of hair directly above the ear. Only 972 proofs were struck, and the 1894 business strike is the rarest Philadelphia issue aside from the unproven 1895. Census: 2 in 64 Ultra Cameo, 4 finer (6/07). (#97329)

Richly Toned PR63 1895 Morgan Dollar

1796 **1895 PR63 ANACS.** This coin was created toward the end of a shining era in American history. The Civil War of the 1860s was a gloomy memory. The era of Reconstruction, 1865-1877, had been fraught with criminality as con artists known as Carpet Baggers sought to enrich themselves as the nation recovered from war, and the Indian Wars in the west caught the public's attention. The 1880s was called the Gilded Age by none other than Mark Twain himself. It was the decade of the robber barons, when the pursuit of wealth trumped the recent, gloomy, warring past. As coin collectors all know, silver mines in Nevada underscored this pursuit of wealth, for a vast fortune was regularly being taken from the earth and added to Treasury vaults via the Bland-Allison Act of 1878, which gave the value of one dollar to about 80 cents worth of silver. It supported western mining and was controversial in its day, yet the irony is that, over time, as fiat money (paper currency) suffered from the ravages of inflation, this very commodity became a precious asset, both for individuals and for the nation and its government.

Any silver dollar of this date is a "key date" and highly desirable. Millions of collectors may seek to own one, but the truth is that few ever will. Its rarity is undeniable, but what of its place in time? The 1895 Morgan silver dollar is even more alluring once given its historical setting. Baseball Hall of Famer Babe Ruth was born in this year, and so was boxing champion Jack Dempsey. The first U.S. Open golf championship was held in 1895, and for the first time ever a professional football game was played in this same year-in Latrobe, Pennsylvania. Little more than a hundred years ago, sports in America were mostly amateur affairs. Nostalgia beckons to many collectors. It forms the essence of why they collect. The United States in 1895 had not yet become a major international nation. That distinction lay ahead. It came after a terrible war was fought, in Europe, by many boys and young men born in this year. America would never be able to recapture the innocence that lulled the land in 1895.

This 1895 dollar is a symbol of that late 19th century era. It is deeply toned on each side and this depth of color does much to conceal the underlying hairlines that account for the PR63 grade. Other than the brightness from cleaning, there are no nicks or scratches that need to be mentioned. (#7330)

Lovely Cameo PR65 1895 Dollar

1797 1895 PR65 Cameo NGC. For silver dollar enthusiasts, the year 1895 has always been magical, and a myth was born about a hundred years ago when Morgan dollars of this date, without mintmarks and therefore made at Philadelphia, were occasionally listed in auctions and dealer sales lists as slightly circulated pieces. Such coins continued to appear on the numismatic scene for the first seven decades, approximately, of the 20th century. The Red Book continues to list this year's mintage as 12,880. Proofs made for collectors account for the 880 coins, a fairly normal number, but what of the 12,000 figure? It is an official U.S. Mint account of silver dollars struck. Evidently it was a clerical error, possibly pertaining to 1894 dollars struck at the end of the year, possibly just an errant figure entered into mint production logs, or it is remotely possible that 12,000 Morgan dollars were minted for commerce but that they were melted. Many ideas have been published. Whatever the truth may be, the myth of this date existing as business strikes has been carried forth into our own time.

However, long before there were grading services, long before there were data bases for PCGS and NGC or other grading companies, and long before today's more scientific and systematic examination of rare coins, a darkly toned or impaired proof might well have been confused with a business strike, and listed in an auction or dealer list as, say, About Uncirculated. The term itself perpetuated the myth. Third-party grading services have now been in existence for several decades, and PCGS with its data base is more than 20 years old. Close-up photography, including digital imaging, has brought an added dimension to coin examination that was not possible when the myth of the business strike 1895 silver dollar was born. No silver dollar of this date from Philadelphia has yet been discovered to be other than of proof manufacture. Thus, the coin often called the "King of Silver Dollars" has a total possible population of just 880 pieces, certainly among the smallest number among coins of this, one of the most popular of all series of U.S. coins. It is a date so sought after by collectors that even major auctions sometimes do not offer a single coin. The majority of the 880 coins struck are always "off the market."

This piece also will surely be "off the market" soon. A solid Gem proof, the surfaces are nearly defect-free. The fields show the deep reflectivity one would expect from a well-produced proof, and the devices have a significant amount of mint frost which yields a noticeable cameo contrast on each side. Both obverse and reverse are evenly draped with light golden-brown toning. Certainly one of the most attractive 1895 dollars we have seen in some time.
From The Reuben Reinstein Collection. (#87330)

Exceptional PR67 Cameo 1896 Morgan Dollar

1798 1896 PR67 Cameo PCGS. Of the 27 proof Morgan dollar issues (1878 through 1904), only eight dates have a lower mintage than the 1896, of which 762 pieces were struck for collectors. Even the heralded 1895 proof Morgan dollar saw a higher production. The combined total of 1896 dated proofs graded at NGC and PCGS is 521 coins (6/07), which is indicative of a high survival rate for this issue. However, that total includes all proof dollars, regardless of the quality of manufacture and/or post-mint impairments. As specialists of this series know, many proofs were mishandled through poor storage choices and improper cleaning. The current coin resides in the upper echelon of all extant examples, as established by the current PCGS population of two in 67 Cameo with none finer (6/07). The PCGS Population Report has changed little in recent years for the 1896 proof Morgan dollar and it is unlikely that any new examples will be graded at this lofty level or higher, barring a chance upgrade of one of the few PR66 examples.

As expected, this proof is almost perfectly preserved. The fields are deeply mirrored and the devices display heavy mint frost which gives the coin a stark cameo contrast on each side. Both obverse and reverse have an overlay of pale rose-gray patina. Exceptional quality. (#87331)

Extraordinary PR68 ★ Ultra Cameo 1896 Dollar

1799 **1896 PR68 ★ Ultra Cameo NGC.** After several years of sparse P-mint emissions, the Morgan dollar came roaring back in 1896, to the tune of nearly 10 million business strikes, along with about 5 million pieces each in New Orleans and San Francisco. The proof mintage was typical for the era, at 762 specimens. The 20 million examples of the 1896 Morgan dollar joined the hundreds of millions of earlier Morgan dollars in Treasury vaults, unwanted by the public, unneeded in commerce, undesired by the government, yet mandated by the inflexible terms of the Bland-Allison Act of 1878, a sop to the Western mining interests and domestic banks that had grown considerably in power in the intervening years since the "Crime of '73."

The year 1896 was notable for another event in the life of the Morgan dollar (or the Bland dollar, as it was almost universally called throughout its lifetime). 1896 was the year that Miss Anna Williams, the model for the head of Liberty on the coin, married her husband. Mint Director Henry Richard Linderman, who was of the opinion that U.S. coinage designs were unacceptable, offered designer George T. Morgan, an Englishman and former student of A.B. Wyon, a job as assistant engraver at the Philadelphia Mint in 1876, although both Mint Chief Engraver William Barber and his son Charles strongly—and unsurprisingly—resisted the appointment. Morgan came to America that same year and was enlisted to design a new silver dollar. His friends directed him toward the classic beauty of Miss Williams, and when he first approached her, like most proper ladies of the time, she immediately turned him down. *Her* friends interceded, however, and she relented, agreeing to pose. Apparently Miss Williams "kept her looks" well, as she married nearly 20 years later, in 1896.

The year 1896 was also an especially kind one for Morgan dollar proofs, and for this particular specimen as well. While only a couple of dozen proofs have been certified as fine as this piece at NGC, that service has certified four 1896 dollars in PR68 ★ Ultra Cameo, including the present example, and only one PR69 ★ coin (6/07). The coin is brilliant silver-white, without detectable patina, and stunning silver-on-black, deeply contrasting surfaces. Perusal even under a loupe reveals only surface minutiae unworthy of singular mention. Simply a phenomenal and phenomenally attractive piece. (#97331)

Attractive 1899 Morgan Dollar PR64

1800 **1899 PR64 NGC.** Fully struck with lovely russet and gold peripheral toning, and mild cameo contrast; with lightly frosted devices atop watery fields. Free of all but the faintest hairlines in the fields, and a couple of wispy slide marks below Liberty's eye. An interesting patch of die lines reside near Liberty's jawline, and onto her neck.
From The Vanek Collection. (#7334)

Choice Proof 1901 Morgan Dollar

1801 **1901 PR64 NGC.** A trace of gold toning is present on this crisply struck specimen. Liberty's nose has a scratch. ONE DOLLAR is lightly die doubled, as usual for proofs of this date, and a diagnostic to distinguish them from the rare Mint State business strikes. Only 813 proofs were struck.
From The Vanek Collection. (#7336)

Magnificent PR66 Cameo 1901 Dollar

1802 **1901 PR66 Cameo PCGS.** Light honey toning embraces the borders of this sharply struck and magnificently preserved Premium Gem. Frosty devices confirm the Cameo designation. ONE DOLLAR is lightly die doubled, not to be confused with the rare VAM-3 *Guide Book* variety. A scant 813 proofs were struck, and examples are coveted due to the scarcity of Uncirculated business strikes. Population: 7 in 66 Cameo, 0 finer (5/07). (#87336)

1803 **1902 PR62 NGC.** A pleasing example of this 20th century Morgan dollar proof, gold-toned with small patches of milky patina in the fields. Scattered hairlines appear on the surfaces, and a thin contact mark appears just to the right of Liberty's lips.
From The Vanek Collection. (#7337)

1804 **1903 PR62 PCGS.** Razor-sharp design elements reflect a well executed strike, and just a wisp or two of light color visits the rim areas. David Bowers (2005), writing about the 1903 proof Morgans, says: "The portraits and certain recessed parts of the die were polished—what student of the series Michael Fuljenz calls 'the chrome look'." The grade is apparently defined by a few minor obverse wispy handling marks visible under magnification. Perhaps conservatively graded? Housed in a green-label holder. (#7338)

Alluring 1903 Morgan Dollar PR64

1805 **1903 PR64 NGC.** American collectors have grown accustomed to Cameo coins as the preferred style of proof coinage. Some issues, however, produced without frosted devices (such as the 1903 Morgan dollar) manage to convey a pleasing appearance without showing field-to-device contrast. This is such a specimen. The design motifs are sharply struck, and both sides are free of contact marks and hairlines. Some cloudiness in the fields and a small spot near obverse star 12 are noted as possible grade-limiting factors.
From The Vanek Collection. (#7338)

End of Session Two

SESSION THREE

Live, Internet, and Mail Bid Signature Auction #442
Friday, July 13, 2007, 1:00 PM ET, Lots 1806-2230
West Palm Beach, Florida

A 15% Buyer's Premium ($9 minimum) Will Be Added To All Lots

Visit HA.com to view full-color images and bid.

PEACE DOLLARS

1806 **1921 MS64 PCGS.** A dove-gray near-Gem with faint lime overtones. Crisply struck for the date, and the cheek is splendidly smooth. Liberty's profile is strike doubled. (#7356)

1807 **1921 MS64 PCGS.** Splashes of autumn-brown toning are particularly prominent across the reverse. A satiny and impressively preserved near-Gem denied an even finer grade by a faint graze on the cheekbone. (#7356)

1808 **1921 MS64 PCGS.** Essentially untoned surfaces yield dazzling luster, and the design features benefited from a well executed strike, except for minor weakness in the hair at Liberty's ear. Some minute marks define the grade. (#7356)

1809 **1921 MS64 PCGS.** Essentially untoned surfaces yield pleasing luster. The design elements are well struck, save for minor softness in the center areas. A few minor marks limit the grade. Faint die polish lines are visible in the obverse fields. (#7356)

1810 **1921 MS64 PCGS.** Pleasing golden-gray patina rests on the highly lustrous surfaces of this near-Gem first-year-of-issue Peace dollar. Generally well struck. A few light marks are noted on the reverse. (#7356)

1811 **1921 MS64 NGC.** Radiantly lustrous surfaces are essentially untoned, and devoid of significant marks. Typical strike weakness is noted in the centers. (#7356)

1812 **1921 MS64 PCGS.** Glowing luster resides on minimally abraded surfaces that exhibit delicate golden-gray patina. The usually seen weakness is apparent in the centers of both obverse and reverse. (#7356)

1813 **1921 MS64 PCGS.** Speckles of cobalt-blue, gold-tan, and lavender patina concentrate around the borders of this near-Gem specimen, and the design elements are for the most part well defined, save for softness in the hair at Liberty's ear. A few minute marks scattered about the lustrous surfaces define the grade. (#7356)

1814 **1921 MS64 NGC.** A pleasing Choice example of this first-year high-relief issue, well struck with strong, attractive luster. Light, scattered marks, particularly one visible on the chin, bar the way to a finer grade. (#7356)

1815 **1921 MS64 PCGS.** Luster dominates this faintly toned introductory year Peace dollar. A good strike for the issue, with only minor incompleteness on the centers and the date. A few ticks on the cheek are consistent with the grade. Housed in a green label holder. (#7356)

1816 **1921 MS65 PCGS.** Potent luster exudes from silver-gray surfaces tinged with hints of light tan, and a typical strike leaves minor weakness in the centers. A few minute obverse marks are noted. (#7356)

1817 **1921 MS65 PCGS.** Light autumn-gold patina enriches this lustrous Gem. The reverse is well preserved, and the obverse has only faint central grazes. The strike is incomplete on the hair over the ear, as nearly always for this high relief date. (#7356)

1818 **1921 MS65 NGC.** A delightfully toned Gem representative of this early Peace dollar, strongly lustrous beneath thin gold patina with pleasing definition aside from the typically soft highpoints. Carefully preserved with plenty of eye appeal. (#7356)

1819 **1921 MS65 PCGS.** Dashes of honey-gold patina adorn this lustrous and crisply struck high relief Peace dollar. The reverse is particularly unblemished. Popular as a single-year, low mintage subtype. Certified in a green label holder. (#7356)

1820 **1921 MS65 PCGS.** A lovely gold-tinged Gem that displays pleasing luster and the usual softness at the highpoints. Marks are few and far between, which reaffirms the grade of this delightful first-year piece. (#7356)

1821 **1921 MS65 NGC.** The light gold toning deepens slightly across the centers. Lustrous and sharply struck with well preserved fields and a couple of faint marks on the portrait. A desirable Gem of this low mintage, high relief date. (#7356)

Lustrous 1921 Premium Gem Dollar

1822 **1921 MS66 PCGS.** Dusky apricot-gold patina rests on highly lustrous, well preserved surfaces. The centers are not fully developed, as is usual for this high relief issue, but the remaining design elements have sharp definition. An important issue, not only for its low mintage of just over 1 million pieces, but as the first year of the type. It is the only collectible date that has high relief, which some regard as a separate type. (#7356)

Brilliant 1921 High Relief Peace Dollar, MS66

1823 **1921 MS66 PCGS.** Ex: Troy Wiseman Collection. A wonderfully well-preserved example of the High Relief variety. Attractive luster radiates from each side. Though the hair on Liberty's brow shows slight striking weakness, this is typical, and the grade does not unduly suffer for it. PCGS has only certified six finer examples (4/07). (#7356)

Radiant 1921 Gem Peace Dollar, VAM-3, Top 50 Variety

1824 **1921 VAM-3, Line Through L, Top 50, MS65 PCGS.** A ray runs over the bottom crossbar of the first L in DOLLAR, and there are myriad parallel die polish lines in the recesses of the lower reverse. Radiantly lustrous surfaces display a thin veneer of gold-tan color, and we note sharply defined devices, save for the near-always weak centers. The few minor marks scattered about are within the parameters of the grade designation. A very interesting VAM variety. (#133734)

Surprisingly Rare MS67 1922 Dollar

1825 **1922 MS67 NGC.** The reverse is dusky chestnut-gray with a peripheral arc of sea-green and ruby toning. The obverse is light pearl-gray aside from a trace of golden-russet near the rim. A well preserved Peace dollar that benefits from a good strike and dazzling luster. As common as the 1922 is, it unexpectedly emerges as a rarity in the MS67 grade. Census: 10 in 67, 0 finer (6/07). (#7357)

1826 **1922 MS64 PCGS.** VAM-1F. A Top 50 Variety. The Field Break variety, which displays a prominent die break in the reverse field just to the right of the eagle. This crisply struck and frosty Choice example has a thin veil of gold and rose patina over each side. Small, scattered abrasions are of little consequence. Population: 1 in 64, 0 finer (4/07). (#133736)

1827 **1922 MS63 PCGS.** VAM-2A. A Top 50 Variety. The "Earring" variety, distinguished by a prominent die break that crosses Liberty's lower hair, roughly where her ear would be. This well struck piece has elements of champagne and rouge patina over softly lustrous silver-blue surfaces. Population: 3 in 63, 2 finer (4/07). (#133737)

1828 **1922 MS65 PCGS.** VAM-2E. A Top 50 Variety. A pair of die breaks sets apart the "Wing Break" variety. One crosses the truncation of the bust, while the other is a small, yet prominent worm-shaped flaw at the upper edge of the eagle's wing. A touch of rose color appears in the fields, and small patches of wine-colored patina appear at the B of LIBERTY and the E of ONE, but the shimmering surfaces are untoned otherwise. An abrasion is noted just above the eagle's legs. Population: 1 in 65, 0 finer (4/07). (#133739)

1829 **1922 MS63 PCGS.** VAM-4. A Top 50 Variety. The lower right design elements of the obverse show considerable doubling. Select and lightly abraded overall with crisp detail, attractive luster, and splashes of milky patina in the obverse fields. Population: 2 in 63, 3 finer (4/07). (#133741)

1830 **1922 MS64 PCGS.** VAM-5. A Top 50 Variety. One of the few tripled die varieties known for the series, most easily visible on the leaves of the olive branch (hence "Tripled Leaves") and the eagle's talons. This well struck and softly lustrous example has areas of hazy olive patina most noticeable at the upper reverse. Population: 2 in 64, 0 finer (4/07). (#133742)

1831 **1922 MS64 PCGS.** VAM-5A. A Top 50 Variety. The dramatic "Scar Cheek" or "Scarface" variety, which combines a dramatic die break on Liberty's cheek with the "Tripled Leaves" reverse. Strongly lustrous with splashes of rose-violet patina evident on the obverse, though the well-defined reverse is largely untoned. (#133743)

1832 **1922 MS63 PCGS.** VAM-7. A Top 50 Variety. The eagle's right wing exhibits distinct doubling. This lightly abraded Select example displays a blend of brick-red, orange, and silver-blue patina on the obverse with similar, softer colors on the subtly lustrous, well-defined reverse. (#133745)

1833 **1922 MS62 ANACS.** VAM-12A, A Top 50 Variety. A large die break below Liberty's nose results in the "Moustache" nickname for this scarce variety. Deep layers of brown, green, and blue patina cover both sides of this well struck, vibrantly lustrous near-Gem. A few scattered blemishes and a fingerprint fragment, in the right obverse field, prevent a higher grade designation. (#133747)

1834 **1922 MS64 PCGS.** VAM-12A. A Top 50 Variety. The popular Moustache obverse is combined with a doubled die reverse on the VAM-12A. An extensive die break affects much of Liberty's upper lip, while the eagle's talons and the nearby rays show doubling. Well-defined and strongly lustrous with little patina aside from a zone of carmine-orange near the eagle's tail feathers and lower wing. Population: 5 in 64, 1 finer (4/07). (#133747)

1835 **1922-D MS66 PCGS.** Faint ice-blue and chestnut toning graces this satiny and unmarked Premium Gem. Worthy of the highest quality Peace dollar Registry Set. As of (5/07), PCGS has certified only three pieces finer. (#7358)

1836 **1922-D MS66 NGC.** Both sides of this satiny piece have brilliant luster and sharp design features. Few examples can qualify for the Premium Gem grade level, and seldom are nicer quality pieces located. NGC has only certified seven pieces finer than this. (#7358)

1837 **1922-D VAM-3, MS63 PCGS.** A Top 50 Variety. The "Doubled Leaves" variety displays strong doubling on many of the lower reverse elements, though the olive branch exhibits the effect prominently. Crisply struck and essentially untoned with powerful luster and a swooping die crack that traverses the lower obverse. (#133748)

Select 1922-D Dollar, Scarce VAM-4, Top 50 Variety

1838 **1922-D VAM-4, Doubled Motto, Top 50, MS63 PCGS.** Attributed by doubling on the bottom edges of the crossbar and the base of the first T in TRUST, and the top inside and base of the left upright of the R. This variety is apparently scarcer than originally thought, as few specimens have been uncovered. Lustrous silver-gray surfaces exhibit sharply defined motifs, and the minute marks scattered about just barely preclude the next highest grade. (#133749)

1839 **1922-D MS63 PCGS.** VAM-7. A Top 50 Variety. Though the tripling on the olive branch on the reverse is the most important feature of this "Tripled Reverse" variety, a die line between the 9 and the first 2 in the date is an important diagnostic. Well-defined and frosty with a hint of golden patina over each side. (#133750)

1840 **1922-S MS65 PCGS.** Lustrous and untoned with an above average strike and a remarkably clean cheek. The 1922-S has an inordinately large mintage, but in the present quality it is uncommon. PCGS has certified only six pieces finer. (#7359)

1841 **1922-S MS65 PCGS.** Well struck with soft, frosted mint luster and lovely smoky-gray toning. Minimally marked, as expected for the grade. 1922-S Peace dollars are relatively scarce at the Gem Mint State level of preservation, considering that almost 17.5 million pieces were originally produced. (#7359)

1842 **1923 MS65 NGC.** VAM-1-'O', Top 50. "The Bar Wing" variety. A die bar extends near the upper right (facing) tip of the eagle's wing. A die break from the bottom of E in ONE diagonally crosses the eagle's wing. Fabulously intense mint frost shines over both sides of this lovely Gem Peace dollar. The surfaces exhibit a faint golden pallor over each side. Boldly struck and nicely preserved, with few marks. (#7360)

Stunning 1923 Dollar, MS67

1843 **1923 MS67 NGC.** Deep, frosty luster covers surfaces on the verge of perfection. Barely discernible light champagne and ice-blue color envelops both sides of this stunning Superb Gem. While considered common in lower grades (NGC and PCGS have graded tens of thousands through MS66), the 1923 Dollar is anything *but* common in MS67. Census: 42 in 67, 0 finer (6/07). (#7360)

1844 **1923 MS65 PCGS.** VAM-1A. A Top 50 Variety. The "Whisker Jaw" variety, which has a substantial die break at the center of Liberty's jaw. Strongly lustrous with pleasing detail and small areas of deeper color against gold-tinged surfaces. Population: 6 in 65, 0 finer (4/07). (#133752)

1845 **1923 MS66 NGC.** VAM-1A, Top 50. A prominent die break is visible at the juncture of Liberty's jaw and neck on this so-called "Whisker Jaw" variety. This Premium Gem example displays highly lustrous, silvery-gray surfaces that are imbued with deep mint frost on both sides. Strong definition is noted on the design elements, and surface marks are nearly nonexistent. (#133752)

Lustrous MS64 1923 Dollar, Scarce VAM-1C, Top 50 Variety

1846 **1923 VAM-1C, Tail on O, Top 50, MS64 PCGS.** This is one of the scarcest and most desirable of the Top 50 VAM varieties in the Peace dollar series. A die break from the bottom of the O in DOLLAR extends into the field below DO, resembling a backward Q. Pale olive-gold color bathes lustrous surfaces that exhibit sharply struck design elements. A few minor marks prevent Gem status. A pleasing high-end MS64! (#133754)

1847 **1923 MS63 PCGS.** VAM-1D. A Top 50 Variety. The "Whisker Cheek" variety has a prominent die break in the center of Liberty's cheek and ranks as one of the most striking Peace dollar variants. Lightly abraded overall and well struck with dusky olive-gold and steel-gray color over lustrous surfaces. Population: 8 in 63, 3 finer (4/07). (#133755)

1848 **1923 VAM-1E, Broken Wing, MS62 PCGS.** A Top 50 Variety. Several droplet-shaped die breaks lie in a roughly vertical line across the eagle's wing on the "Broken Wing" variety. Subtly lustrous with soft rose-gray patina over much of the surfaces and light to moderate abrasions that define the grade. Population: 1 in 62, 1 finer (4/07). (#133756)

Exemplary MS66 1923-D Peace Dollar

1849 **1923-D MS66 NGC.** Lightly toned olive-gold aside from a faint cream-gray area above the eagle's head. A lustrous Premium Gem with intricately struck devices and only slight blending of detail across the peripheral obverse legends. Well preserved and scarce in such quality. Census: 20 in 66, 0 finer (5/07). (#7361)

1850 **1923-D MS63 PCGS.** VAM-2. A Top 50 Variety. The doubling on this "Doubled Head" variety appears on most of the reverse design elements, though the effect is most prominent at its namesake location. Select and well struck with pleasing luster and a touch of rose-gold patina on the surfaces. Population: 2 in 63, 1 finer (4/07). (#133761)

1851 **1923-S MS64 PCGS.** Beautifully toned chestnut-gold, cherry-red, and electric-blue. The borders are particularly colorful. A lustrous and impressively unblemished near-Gem. The reverse field exhibits interesting clash marks. (#7362)

1852 **1923-S MS64 PCGS.** The snow-white surfaces are lustrous, and lack individually mentionable marks. The eagle's leg and the hair above the ear are typically defined. (#7362)

Gem 1923-S Silver Dollar

1853 **1923-S MS65 PCGS.** Nearly every San Francisco Mint Peace dollar is an important condition rarity in MS65 grade, and this date is certainly no exception. Both sides have pale yellow color with subtle hints of russet near the borders. Liberty's cheek and neck are splendidly smooth, and the strike is good with only unimportant incompleteness in the centers and on the motto. Population: 93 in 65, 3 finer (5/07). (#7362)

Frosty Gem 1923-S Peace Dollar, MS65

1854 **1923-S MS65 PCGS.** Few finer examples of this date have been certified by either NGC or PCGS. While examples of the 23-S are easy to locate in lower Mint State grades, those coins that exceed MS64 quality are elusive. This piece has a sharp strike with frosty silver luster. The slightest hints of pale gold toning add to its overall eye appeal. Population: 93 in 65, 3 finer (4/07). (#7362)

1855 **1924 MS66 PCGS.** This flashy Peace dollar displays white, matte-like surfaces and sharply struck design elements. A few minuscule marks occur on the eagle, but in general this is a well preserved specimen. PCGS has certified only 22 specimens higher (6/07). (#7363)

Outstanding MS67 1924 Peace Dollar

1856 **1924 MS67 NGC.** An exemplary Peace dollar that would make an excellent type coin. The surfaces are heavily frosted and brilliant on each side, and the strike is full in the centers. There must be abrasions on this piece somewhere, but examination with the unaided eye fails to reveal them. Few Peace dollars have attained Superb Gem status over the 21 years the two main grading services have been in operation. Census: 59 in 67, 0 finer (5/07). (#7363)

1857 **1924 MS64 PCGS.** VAM-5A. A Top 50 Variety. The "Broken Wing" variety for the year, with a prominent die crack that runs through most of the eagle's wing. Swirls of milky patina appear at the margins of this strongly lustrous, solidly struck near-Gem. Population: 8 in 64, 0 finer (4/07). (#133766)

1858 **1924 MS65 PCGS.** VAM-8A. A Top 50 Variety. A number of notable die cracks in Liberty's hair take on the appearance of strands in this "Extra Hair" variant. This slightly frosty, well-preserved Gem displays pleasing detail. Population: 3 in 65, 0 finer (4/07). (#133764)

1859 **1924-S MS64 PCGS.** The obverse has delightful golden-brown, ice-blue, and lime-green toning. The reverse has lighter streaks of sky-blue and olive-tan. Lustrous and suitably struck with pleasing preservation. (#7364)

1860 **1924-S MS64 PCGS.** Powerful luster and a splash of sun-gold patina across the centers distinguish this delectable near-Gem. Well-defined overall with few marks for the grade and excellent visual appeal. A great example of this lower-mintage San Francisco issue. Certified in a green label holder. (#7364)

1861 **1924-S MS64 NGC.** Original chestnut-gold and cream-gray toning enriches this lustrous and carefully preserved better-date near-Gem. Housed in a prior generation holder, which has a small chip on the lower right corner with no impact on the coin itself. (#7364)

Toned Gem 1924-S Peace Dollar

1862 **1924-S MS65 PCGS.** This is an outstanding Gem, noted for its attractive display of peripheral toning. Deep gold and lilac color only encroach slightly upon the design of the obverse. The reverse is entirely brilliant with no toning. It is a boldly struck piece with especially sharp details in the eagle. Population: 64 in 65, 5 finer (6/07). (#7364)

1863 **1924-S MS62 PCGS.** VAM-3. A Top 50 Variety. The only Top 50 variety for this low-mintage issue, the "Doubled Reverse" exhibits spread on the lower feather tips and the olive berries. Though this piece is lightly abraded overall with splashes of milky patina, the luster is strong, and the reverse has stronger detail than usual. Population: 1 in 62, 1 finer (4/07). (#133767)

1864 **1925 MS66 PCGS.** A brilliant and thoroughly lustrous Premium Gem. Well struck in the centers, and the peripheral elements are nearly as crisp. A beautifully preserved type coin. (#7365)

1865 **1925 MS66 PCGS.** This yellow-gold Premium Gem has a remarkably clean obverse, and the lustrous surfaces are well struck. A thin mark on the IT in UNITED is all that prevents an even finer grade. (#7365)

Scintillating 1925 Peace Dollar MS67

1866 **1925 MS67 NGC.** A thoroughly lustrous Superb Gem with well preserved fields and an assertive strike. The obverse border has a hint of tan patina, but the surfaces are otherwise brilliant. The obverse has a mattelike appearance, as delivered from a die long in use. Census: 36 in 67, 1 finer (5/07). (#7365)

1867 **1925 MS66 PCGS.** VAM-1A. A Top 50 Variety. The die gouge centered below the B in LIBERTY skips through the rays of Liberty's tiara, hence the "Tiara Die Gouge" nickname. This strongly lustrous Premium Gem is lightly gold-toned overall with streaks of milky patina evident at the margins. (#133768)

1868 **1925 MS65 PCGS.** VAM-3. A Top 50 Variety. The "Doubled Shoulder" variety has spread not just on the eagle's wing, but on the nearby ray and the olive branch as well. A lovely Gem example of this interesting variant, strongly lustrous with glints of gold and areas of milky color over each side. Population: 2 in 65, 0 finer (4/07). (#133769)

1869 **1925-S MS64 PCGS.** Well struck with unusually crisp detailing over the central devices. This is a lustrous and attractive silvery-gray example that displays die polish lines in the fields, and only faint cloudiness on either side. A few minor coin-to-coin marks limit the grade. (#7366)

1870 **1925-S MS64 PCGS.** This brilliant near-Gem exhibits potent luster, and the centers and eagle's leg are suitably struck. Minor grazes on the left obverse preclude a higher grade, but the eye appeal is undeniable. (#7366)

1871 **1925-S MS64 PCGS.** This cream-gray and olive-gold near-Gem has unencumbered luster and a hint of striking softness in the centers. The occasional faint grazes are customary for the grade. (#7366)

1872 **1925-S MS64 PCGS.** Bright and semi-prooflike, with speckled red-brown and forest-green peripheral patina and silver-gray centers. Clean for the MS64 grade level, and surprisingly rare any finer. (#7366)

1873 **1925-S MS64 PCGS.** Peach and sky-blue toning enriches this satiny and nicely struck better date silver dollar. Liberty's cheek and neck are impressively unabraded. Housed in a green label holder. (#7366)

1874 **1925-S MS64 PCGS.** VAM-2. A Top 50 Variety. This "Doubled Reverse" variety has prominent doubling on most of the central design elements. Well struck with subtle luster that peeks out from beneath rich, dappled plum and champagne patina. Population: 5 in 64, 0 finer (4/07). (#133771)

1875 1925-S MS64 PCGS. VAM-3. A Top 50 Variety. This "Doubled Wing" variety displays a distinct additional outline on the right side of the eagle. Well struck with powerful luster and an area of reddish-orange patina in the center of the obverse against otherwise untoned surfaces. Population: 5 in 64, 0 finer (4/07). (#133772)

Bright 1926 Premium Gem Dollar, VAM-2, Doubled Reverse

1876 1926 VAM-2, Doubled Reverse, Top 50 Variety, MS66 PCGS. Attributed by doubling on the olive leaves and stems, the eagle's back leg feathers, and the internal rays. The *Official Guide to the Top 50 Peace Dollar Varieties* (2002) states that "... this variety is not a major rarity. However, of the two hundred or so Peace dollar die varieties now cataloged by Van Allen/Mallis, only a handful can compare with the strength of the doubling on this reverse. Indeed, what the VAM 2 lacks in terms of rarity, it more than makes up in desirability." Bright luster adorns well preserved surfaces on this Premium Gem specimen. Hints of incipient gold color adhere to both sides, and a well executed strike emboldens the design elements. (#133773)

1877 1926-S MS65 PCGS. Dashes of autumn-gold overlie the lustrous pearl-gray fields and devices. A boldly struck and attractively preserved Gem. The portrait is especially free from marks. (#7369)

1878 1926-S MS65 PCGS. Light to medium autumn-gold toning graces this lustrous and crisply struck example. Nicely preserved, and a better date in quality Mint State. (#7369)

Delightful 1926-S Peace Dollar, MS66

1879 1926-S MS66 PCGS. This Premium Gem has satiny silver luster with ivory color and peripheral gold toning around part of the obverse. Both sides are creamy and smooth with pristine surfaces. The strike is excellent, although not completely full. Overall, this is a remarkable example that is seldom found any nicer. Population: 57 in 66, 2 finer (6/07). (#7369)

1880 1926-S VAM-4 Dot Variety, MS65 PCGS. A Top 50 Variety. The "Dot Variety," sometimes nicknamed the "Extra Berry" for its anomalous circular depression at the lower olive branch, is popular with collectors. This Gem example has waves of cloud-gray patina varied by splashes of wine color at the margins. Well-defined and pleasing. Population: 3 in 65, 0 finer (4/07). (#133774)

Impressive Gem 1927 Peace Dollar

1881 1927 MS65 PCGS. The bright silver surfaces are essentially untoned. Better struck than most examples of its type, this Gem displays essentially full detailing on Liberty's hair and on the eagle's back and leg feathers. Surface blemishes are relatively minor, especially for a Peace dollar. A popular low mintage issue of only 848,000 coins. (#7370)

1882 1927-D MS64 PCGS. A boldly struck and unmarked near-Gem with pleasing eye appeal for the grade. Medium olive and tan toning intermingles across the lustrous fields. Certified in a green label holder. (#7371)

1883 1927-D MS64 PCGS. VAM-2. A Top 50 Variety. Notching on the E in WE is the primary evidence for the "Doubled Motto" on this variety. The flashy, frosty surfaces display the wispy diagnostic die crack that extends from below the motto onto the base of Liberty's portrait on the obverse, where dappled milky patina is spread throughout. Modestly marked with only a few grazes. Population: 3 in 64, 2 finer (4/07). (#133777)

1884 1927-S MS64 PCGS. Delicate tan and cream-gray toning graces this satiny and unmarked near-Gem. Sharply struck except for the upright of the Y in LIBERTY. A low mintage date. (#7372)

1885 1927-S MS64 PCGS. Solidly struck with attractive luster. At first glance, the surfaces appear untoned, though closer inspection reveals thin, milky patina in the fields on each side. One of just 866,000 pieces coined. In a green label holder. (#7372)

1886 1927-S MS64 PCGS. VAM-3. A Top 50 Variety. "Doubled Leaves" are not the only attraction on the reverse, since the mintmark is repunched as well. A flashy and well struck near-Gem that displays areas of milky patina on the obverse and a touch of gold at the reverse margins. (#133778)

1887 1928—Cleaned—ANACS. MS60 Details. Light powder-blue and caramel-gold toning drapes this lustrous low mintage dollar. Well struck, and smooth aside from a thin diagonal mark on the cheek. Only lightly hairlined. (#7373)

1888 1928 MS62 PCGS. Well struck with shimmering luster and untoned, ivory-gray surfaces. Nicely preserved with just a few minor marks and a small purple alloy spot noted on the lower reverse, just above CE in PEACE. With the lowest mintage in the series, 1928 Peace dollars are an important key issue. (#7373)

1889 1928 MS64 PCGS. A lovely Choice Mint State specimen with frosty silver luster and faint champagne toning. The obverse has a few minor marks and tiny splashes of coppery toning while the reverse is pristine. (#7373)

1890 1928 MS64 PCGS. Lightly toned and lustrous with vibrant luster and a decent strike. Well preserved despite minor marks on the neck truncation. This low mintage date is an eternal collector favorite. (#7373)

1891 1928 MS64 NGC. A lovely Choice example of the lowest-mintage regular-issue Peace dollar issue, which has been popular since the year it was struck. The well-defined devices are largely untoned, though the fields have a trace of golden patina. Carefully preserved overall, though a line of faint reed marks on the cheek denies Gem status. (#7373)

1892 1928 MS64 PCGS. Golden-tan freckles dance over the highly lustrous surfaces of this gorgeous near-Gem. An impressive strike left relatively sharp detail on the motifs, including the strands in Liberty's hair and the juncture of the eagle's leg and wing. A few minor handling marks preclude an even higher grade. (#7373)

1893 **1928 MS64 PCGS.** Booming luster and an attentive strike confirm the quality of this lustrous example. Splendid aside from a pair of hair-thin marks above GOD. This low mintage Peace dollar is housed in a green label holder. (#7373)

1894 **1928 MS64 PCGS.** A lovely Choice representative of this famous low-mintage issue, well-defined with pleasing luster and champagne patina over each side. Scattered pinpoint marks and a more significant abrasion to the left of the eagle combine to limit the grade. (#7373)

1895 **1928 MS64 PCGS.** Light golden-brown toning enriches this highly lustrous and carefully preserved near-Gem. An attentively struck representative of this low mintage issue. (#7373)

1896 **1928 MS64 PCGS.** Well struck and highly lustrous, with deep layers of brownish-green toning over the obverse. The reverse shows some golden-brown peripheral patina, along with numerous small brown spots on the upper field area. A splash of vibrant sky-blue color is noted on the lower left reverse border, just below ONE. Surface marks are trivial, and few in number. One of the keys to the Peace dollar series. (#7373)

Low-Mintage 1928 Gem Dollar

1897 **1928 MS65 PCGS.** The low-mintage 1928 dollar (360,649 pieces) had the reputation of being a "cornerstone dollar" after the Treasury Department released only a few in the year of coinage, saying, according to David Bowers (1993): " ... that such were available for cornerstone-laying or other ceremonial purposes." This created the notion that the 1928 was exceedingly rare, but later large quantities were released. The Gem in this lot displays highly lustrous surfaces that yield sharply struck design elements. Well preserved surfaces are visited by occasional wisps of light tan. (#7373)

Sharp 1928 Dollar, MS65

1898 **1928 MS65 PCGS.** The 1928 has the lowest mintage (360,649 pieces) of the Peace dollar series (except for the 1922 High Relief). Dazzling luster adorns essentially untoned surfaces that possess a satiny finish, and a well executed strike imparts sharp definition on the design features. A few minor ticks on the motifs just barely prevent a higher grade. PCGS has seen only 11 pieces finer (5/07). (#7373)

1899 **1928-S MS64 PCGS.** This brilliant and lustrous better date near-Gem has a good strike and a smooth cheek. The neck and fields display light grazes. LIBERTY is strike doubled. (#7374)

1900 **1928-S MS64 PCGS.** Light golden-brown freckles enrich this lustrous better date Peace dollar. Liberty's cheek is exceptionally smooth, and the strike is crisp save for the mintmark. (#7374)

1901 **1928-S MS64 PCGS.** Lustrous with above-average striking detail. Light orange and aqua toning laps at the reverse rims, while bands of crimson, peach, and sky-blue surround the untoned center of the obverse. (#7374)

Well Struck 1928-S Dollar, MS65

1902 **1928-S MS65 PCGS.** David Bowers (1993) writes that: "Many bags of 1928-S dollars came on the market in the late 1930s and early 1940s. More bags were released in 1949 and 1950 ... . There was little numismatic interest in them, however, as Peace dollars were not a popular series and, in any event, the market was in a slump."

Dappled olive-green patination runs over the obverse of this Gem specimen, while the reverse is essentially color free. The surfaces are somewhat satiny, and release pleasing luster. While most examples of this date are poorly struck, this piece exhibits generally well defined design features, including in the usually weak center areas. A few minute reverse marks do not subtract from the coin's appeal. Population: 45 in 65, 1 finer (6/07). (#7374)

Exceptional 1928-S Gem Dollar

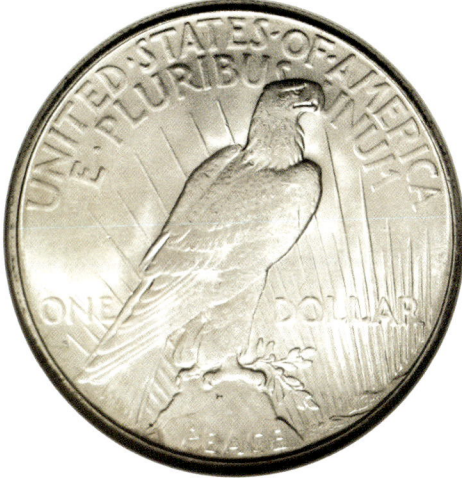

1903 **1928-S MS65 NGC.** Mint State 1928-S Peace dollars are seen with regularity on the market today, but most are in the lower grade levels of Uncirculated, as they are poorly struck and/or heavily bagmarked. NGC and PCGS have certified several thousand pieces through near-Gem, but full Gem coins are another story. Indeed, the two services have seen fewer than 90 MS65s, and a mere two examples finer!

Delicate pastel golden-tan color bathes intensely lustrous surfaces, and a well executed strike levees better-than-average definition on the motifs, including the normally weak centers. Close inspection under high magnification shows just a few minute marks, fewer perhaps than what might be expected for the grade. Census: 38 in 65, 1 finer (6/07). (#7374)

1904 **1928-S MS64 PCGS.** VAM-3. A Top 50 Variety. A later die state example of this popular "Doubled Motto" variety, with strong spread visible on the first T of TRUST. Modestly marked overall with gold, orange, and golden-brown colors at the margins and cloud-gray patina over the rest of this well struck and lustrous piece. Population: 6 in 64, 0 finer (4/07). (#133779)

1905 **1928-S MS64 PCGS.** VAM-3. A Top 50 Variety. The low mintmark, doubled motto VAM. Collectors neglected the 1928-S dollar at first, focusing on its P-mint counterpart. Today, in Choice and better grades, the branch mint pieces command higher prices. This well-defined piece exhibits pale gray patina over both sides. Minimally marked with strong luster beneath. Housed in a green label holder. (#133779)

1906 **1934 MS65 PCGS.** Wonderful satiny surfaces yield pleasing luster, and just a hint of occasional light color. A solid strike brings out sharp detail in the design elements. A few minor marks, especially on the reverse, preclude an even higher grade. The 1934 is readily available in Mint State. (#7375)

1907 **1934 MS65 PCGS.** A captivating Gem example of the last circulation-strike dollar issue to have a mintage of under 1 million pieces. Solidly struck with wonderful luster and only a few tiny marks on the subtly yellow-tinged silver-gray surfaces. (#7375)

1908 **1934-D MS64 PCGS.** Medium D. Highly lustrous and flashy, with an ivory-gray obverse and bright golden toning across the reverse. A few wispy marks and luster grazes are noted on each side. (#7376)

1909 **1934-D MS64 PCGS.** Micro D. This low mintage Denver Mint dollar has all-encompassing luster and a splendidly smooth appearance. Crisply struck except for the Y in LIBERTY. High-end for the grade. (#7376)

1910 **1934-D MS65 PCGS.** Micro D, the scarcer of the two mintmark size varieties. Medium golden-gray toning endows this precisely struck and lustrous Gem. A well preserved representative of the final collectible Denver issue. (#7376)

1911 **1934-D MS65 PCGS.** A rare Denver-Mint dollar in Gem. Speckles of gold-tan color run over lustrous surfaces. Sharply struck, and no significant marks. (#7376)

1912 **1934-D MS65 PCGS.** Medium D. Gentle tan toning graces this highly lustrous and well preserved Gem. Sharply struck save for the Y in LIBERTY. The lower obverse is lightly strike doubled. A lower mintage issue. (#7376)

1913 **1934-D MS65 PCGS.** VAM-3, A Top 50 Variety. A frosty Gem example of this strong obverse doubled die, most visible at GOD WE and distinguished from its VAM-4 counterpart by the filled Medium D mintmark on the reverse. Well-defined and essentially untoned with strong doubling visible on the motto and profile. A reed mark on the bridge of Liberty's nose is the only flaw of note. Population: 4 in 65, 2 finer (4/07). (#133780)

1914 **1934-S AU58 PCGS.** Golden-gray patination bathes both sides of this high-end AU dollar. Traces of luster reside in the recesses of this adequately struck specimen that is minimally abraded. (#7377)

Delightful 1934-S Peace Dollar, MS63

1915 **1934-S MS63 PCGS.** Close examination will reveal the slightest traces of gold toning on the obverse, with a fully brilliant and untoned reverse. This is an attractive example that is really quite acceptable for the grade. MS63 is a popular grade level for collectors of Mint State Peace dollars. (#7377)

Attractive, Key-Date 1934-S Dollar, MS65

1916 **1934-S MS65 PCGS.** The 1934-S is the key-date Peace dollar in Mint State. This was not always the case. For example, David Bowers writes that: " ... there was a time in the early 1940s when the 1925 Philadelphia dollar ... was priced higher, considered to be rarer, and was in greater demand than the 1934-S." The 1925-P is now considered to be among the most common Philadelphia dollars in Mint State. The '34-S Gem in this lot displays dazzling luster exuding from untoned surfaces, and sharply struck design elements. A few trivial marks apparently precluded an even higher grade. A minute, light toning spot on Liberty's neck is mentioned for complete accuracy. (#7377)

Key-Date 1934-S Dollar, MS64, VAM-3, Top 50 Variety

1917 **1934-S MS64 PCGS.** VAM-3, Doubled Tiara, Top 50 Variety. Doubling on the rays is visible to the right of the B and the E in LIBERTY. A scarce and desirable variety, in addition to being the key Peace dollar in Mint State. Dappled olive-green and lilac patination rests on dazzling luster, and sharp definition is noted on the design elements, including Liberty's hair strands. A few inoffensive marks account for the grade. (#133782)

1918 **1935-S MS65 PCGS.** Three rays beneath ONE. Faint tan toning visits the obverse center, but the remainder of this lustrous Gem is brilliant. Sharply struck and carefully preserved. (#7379)

1919 **1935-S MS65 PCGS.** Four rays below ONE. A strongly lustrous Gem representative, this piece has a hint of frost on the highpoints and a touch of hazy gold patina in the fields. One of fewer than 2 million pieces struck. Certified in a green label holder. (#7379)

PROOF EISENHOWER DOLLAR

Resplendent 1976-S Silver Bicentennial Dollar, PR70 Deep Cameo

1920 **1976-S Silver PR70 Deep Cameo PCGS.** A stunning white-on-black Bicentennial dollar. The obverse is completely untoned, while the reverse displays just the slightest hint of incipient gold color around the borders under magnification. An exquisite strike leaves crisp delineation on the design features, and close scrutiny reveals unimprovable surfaces. Population: 11 in 70 Deep Cameo (4/07). (#97436)

COMMEMORATIVE SILVER

1921 **1893 Isabella Quarter MS64 NGC.** A whisper of lemon patina clings to the rims of this highly lustrous and powerfully struck Choice quarter. Queen Isabella and Leif Ericson rank among the few foreign leaders to appear on silver commemorative types. (#9220)

1922 **1893 Isabella Quarter MS64 PCGS.** This Isabella quarter displays boldly struck design elements and original rose-gray toning that yields to intermingled red, gold and olive iridescence near the peripheries. Distracting surface blemishes are nonexistent. (#9220)

1923 **1893 Isabella Quarter MS64 PCGS.** A brilliant and boldly struck Choice Isabella whose clean fields and potent luster confirm its quality. The mintage of 24,214 pieces is only a fraction of the 1.55 million pieces coined for the 1893 Columbian half. (#9220)

1924 **1893 Isabella Quarter MS64 PCGS.** Dazzling luster illuminates this brilliant near-Gem. Well struck and impressively preserved. Encased in a first generation holder. (#9220)

1925 **1893 Isabella Quarter MS64 PCGS.** The Board of Lady Managers was meant as a feminist statement, though scholars have noted that the inclusion of Mrs. Potter Palmer, every bit the socialite, sabotaged its effectiveness. This lustrous and solidly struck example has a blend of rose, violet, blue, and silver-gray patina over each side. (#9220)

1926 **1893 Isabella Quarter MS64 PCGS.** Medium golden-brown toning embraces this lustrous and precisely struck near-Gem. A charming and original example of this Columbian Exposition issue. Housed in an old green label holder. (#9220)

1927 **1893 Isabella Quarter MS64 PCGS.** Deeply toned in rich shades of cobalt-blue, plum and golden-brown. Lustrous, well preserved surfaces and a bold strike make this a desirable example of our country's only commemorative quarter dollar. (#9220)

Important MS65 Isabella Quarter

1928 1893 Isabella Quarter MS65 PCGS. A rare and important early commemorative that is seldom located in Gem condition. The mostly brilliant surfaces are encircled by golden peripheral color on each side. Essentially abrasion-free, as one would expect from the grade, and sharply defined, which is not always the case. (#9220)

Gorgeous 1893 Gem Isabella Quarter

1929 1893 Isabella Quarter MS65 PCGS. Paul Green, in a December 24, 1996 *Numismatic News* article, wrote: "The Isabella quarter was part of the 1892 and 1893 effort to financially bail out the Columbian Exposition ... (that) ... was a costly undertaking ... ." Dazzling luster adorns this gorgeous Gem, and a well executed strike has resulted in strong definition on the design elements. Hints of light tan color visit well preserved surfaces.
From The Silver Fox Collection. (#9220)

Toned 1893 Isabella Quarter, MS66

1930 1893 Isabella Quarter MS66 PCGS. Deep steel-blue, sea-green, and lighter gold toning entirely cover the obverse and reverse surfaces of this splendid Premium Gem. While this commemorative quarter dollar is not particularly rare at this grade level, it is elusive any finer. PCGS has only certified 36 better examples (6/07). (#9220)

1931 1900 Lafayette Dollar MS60 ANACS. DuVall 1-B. Golden-brown and powder-blue toning drapes this satiny and crisply struck example. Washington's cheek has a few small marks likely present on the planchet prior to the strike. A couple of tiny dark hairs on Washington queue suggest subtle lacquer. (#9222)

1932 1900 Lafayette Dollar MS62 NGC. DuVall 1-B. Light silver-gray toning graces this lustrous and attractive example. Marks are minor for the MS62 level, despite a faded pinscratch above the right end of the statue base. (#9222)

1933 1900 Lafayette Dollar MS63 PCGS. DuVall 1-B. A satiny cream-gray representative of the sole pre-1983 silver dollar commemorative type. The fields are beautifully void of marks, as is the portrait of Lafayette. (#9222)

Interesting Choice 1900 Lafayette Dollar

1934 1900 Lafayette Dollar MS64 PCGS. DuVall 1-B. Though the silver dollar is a staple of the modern commemorative market, the classic commemorative series has just one issue, the Lafayette dollar, with a net mintage of just over 36,000 pieces. This strongly lustrous and well-defined example has hints of rose, pink, and gold patina at the margins against otherwise silver-gray surfaces. Light grazes and marks on Washington's cheek prevent a Gem designation. (#9222)

Lustrous MS64 1900 Lafayette Dollar

1935 1900 Lafayette Dollar MS64 PCGS. DuVall 1-B. This variety is attributable by the thin branch above the date, and the left-leaning A in DOLLAR. This is a particularly lustrous coin that is kept from a higher grade by the presence of a few barely perceptible marks on the face of Washington. Light golden-rose toning on the obverse and brilliant on the reverse. (#9222)

1900 Lafayette Dollar, MS65 And Lustrous

1936 1900 Lafayette Dollar MS65 PCGS. DuVall 2-C. The second S in STATES is broadly repunched on this variety. Delicate cream-silver surfaces exude dazzling luster, and an attentive strike emboldens the design elements. A few minuscule marks and toning spots on the obverse are mentioned for complete accuracy. Overall, quite a pleasing commemorative dollar.
From The Silver Fox Collection. (#9222)

1937 **1921 Alabama MS64 PCGS.** Frosty and lustrous silver surfaces are fully brilliant with tinges of peripheral iridescence on each side. (#9224)

1938 **1921 Alabama MS65 PCGS.** Satiny silver surfaces are essentially brilliant with faint champagne toning on the highpoints. Central design weakness is noted, as almost always found. (#9224)

1939 **1921 Alabama MS65 PCGS.** Well struck with swirling luster and a light coat of tawny patina over much of both sides. A pleasing example of this early Laura Gardin Fraser effort, which came at the start of an illustrious career in commemorative design.
From The Silver Fox Collection. (#9224)

1940 **1921 Alabama 2x2 MS64 PCGS.** Violet and gold peripheral accents enliven the central powder-blue and silver-gray colors of this near-Gem. A well-defined representative of this early Laura Gardin Fraser design with few marks overall. (#9225)

1941 **1921 Alabama 2x2 MS64 PCGS.** A sharply struck and satiny near-Gem with light olive and gunmetal-gray patina. The eagle is bisected by a faint vertical die crack, as made. (#9225)

1942 **1921 Alabama 2x2 MS65 PCGS.** The jugate busts on the Alabama commemoratives had a "then and now" theme with the two governors, a concept that would reappear on later issues such as the Sesquicentennial and Arkansas halves. This lustrous and well struck piece, one of the 6,006 examples of the 2x2 variety, has thin golden-rose patina over much of both sides. (#9225)

1943 **1921 Alabama 2x2 MS65 NGC.** This low-mintage variant, which amounted to just 6,006 pieces, was part of a trend for distributors to create multiple varieties with subtle differences to extract more revenue from collectors. The softly lustrous surfaces have a touch of tan-gold color on the obverse and a hint of olive on the opposite side.
From The Silver Fox Collection. (#9225)

Brilliant and Highly Lustrous MS66 Alabama 2x2

1944 **1921 Alabama 2x2 MS66 NGC.** Rarely found in MS66 condition, and as such an important coin for the commemorative collector. This piece has the usual bright, frosted mint luster. However, on this piece it seems even more bright and frosted as the surfaces are brilliant throughout. An exceptionally clean and problem-free example of this key commemorative issue. Census: 60 in 66, 1 finer (6/07). (#9225)

1945 **1936 Albany MS66 PCGS.** Reddish-orange patina of varying intensity drapes the periphery of this lustrous and well struck piece. A faint fingerprint comes between the colonists' heads on the obverse, but is the only minor detraction. (#9227)

1946 **1936 Albany MS67 NGC.** The reverse is tab-toned in original gold, russet, and pearl-gray colors, and the obverse displays variegated honey, russet, and battleship-gray toning. Outstanding quality for this lustrous and virtually immaculate Superb Gem. (#9227)

1947 **1937 Antietam MS64 PCGS.** Well struck with satin luster and carefully preserved surfaces. The silver-white obverse is essentially untoned, but the reverse displays deep plum coloration. Surface blemishes are minimal, and include one small milling mark on Robert E. Lee's jaw. (#9229)

1948 **1937 Antietam MS65 NGC.** This lustrous and impressively smooth Gem has faint olive toning with an occasional russet freckle near the margins. A popular Civil War type. (#9229)

1949 **1937 Antietam MS65 PCGS.** A well-defined, softly lustrous Gem representative of this 75th anniversary commemorative, a classic-era ancestor of the 1995 Civil War Battlefields three-coin set. The obverse has areas of mustard-gold toning, while the reverse displays dappled reddish-tan color at the margins.
From The Silver Fox Collection. (#9229)

1950 **1937 Antietam MS66 PCGS.** Decisively struck and slightly satiny with deep plum, claret, and reddish-orange colors at the margins. A well-defined example from one of the most notable Civil War commemorative issues of the classic era. (#9229)

1951 **1937 Antietam MS66 PCGS.** Subtle, slightly hazy gold and sky-blue patina graces the softly shimmering surfaces. The well-defined devices reflect careful preservation. A crisply struck piece meant to commemorate the diamond anniversary of the devastating battle. Housed in a green label holder. (#9229)

Original 1935 Arkansas Half, MS67

1952 **1935 Arkansas MS67 PCGS.** The Arkansas commemorative series is one of several designs that spanned a number of years from the 1920s to the 1950s. Each of these series offer examples from all three mints, in some instances incorporating low mintages that created instant rarities. This piece has rich mint luster and is overlaid by ivory color with peripheral burgundy toning. Population: 10 in 67, 0 finer (5/07). (#9233)

Superb Gem 1935-D Arkansas Half

1953 **1935-D Arkansas MS67 PCGS.** One of just 5,505 pieces struck for this first-year branch mint issue, this carefully preserved example displays subtle golden-tan patina at the margins and satiny silver-gray color in the centers. Better-defined than usual, particularly on the portraits, with uncharacteristically strong eye appeal. Tied for the finest certified by PCGS (5/07). (#9234)

1954 **1935 Arkansas PDS Set MS65 NGC and PCGS.** The set includes: **1935 MS65 PCGS,** peripheral cobalt-blue freckles, a good strike; **1935-D MS65 NGC,** nicely struck and lustrous with light autumn-brown toning; and a **1935-S MS65 PCGS,** orange-gold and forest-green adorn the margins, well struck, the reverse is nearly immaculate.
From The Silver Fox Collection. (Total: 3 coins) (#9236)

1955 **1936 Arkansas PDS Set MS65 NGC.** The set includes: **1936,** sharply struck and satiny with an especially clean reverse; **1936-D,** nicely struck, dove-gray toning, faint obverse grazes, the date and denomination are lightly die doubled; and a **1936-S,** well struck, lightly toned, the reverse is essentially pristine.
From The Silver Fox Collection. (Total: 3 coins) (#9240)

1956 **1937-D Arkansas MS66 PCGS.** Bright, radiantly surfaces are color free, and display sharply struck design elements. We mention a few light marks on the obverse portraits for complete accuracy. (#9242)

1957 **1937 Arkansas PDS Set MS65 PCGS.** Each coin is graded MS65. The set looks like it could have been together since the year of issue, but the PCGS numbers are not consecutive. Each is lightly to moderately toned with occasional deeper russet accents around the margins on the P and S coins. A clean, attractive, and lustrous set. (Total: 3 coins) (#9244)

1958 **1937 Arkansas PDS Set MS65 NGC and PCGS.** The set includes: **1937 MS65 NGC,** intricately struck, clean fields; **1937-D MS65 PCGS,** boldly struck, impeccably free from marks; and a **1937-S MS65 PCGS,** a good strike, the reverse is well preserved, in a green label holder.
From The Silver Fox Collection. (Total: 3 coins) (#9244)

1959 **1938 Arkansas PDS Set MS65 NGC and PCGS.** The set includes: **1938 MS65 NGC,** untoned and fully struck; **1938-D MS65 NGC,** brilliant, a good strike, only minor marks; and a **1938-S MS65 PCGS,** light tan-gray toning, boldly struck, a well preserved reverse.
From The Silver Fox Collection. (Total: 3 coins) (#9248)

Superb Gem 1939-D Arkansas Half
Only 2,104 Pieces Struck

1960 **1939-D Arkansas MS67 NGC.** A sliver of golden-tan, lavender, and light green toning clings to the reverse margins, framing the silver-gray center, while the obverse displays just whispers of light color around the periphery, along with occasional faint streaks of russet. The design elements are well impressed, and both sides have been well cared for. From a small mintage of 2,104 pieces. Census: 7 in 67, 0 finer (5/07). (#9250)

1961 **1939-S Arkansas MS65 PCGS.** A satiny Gem with medium olive, sky-blue, and caramel-gold toning. Well struck, and the reverse is splendidly preserved. Among the lowest mintage commemorative issues. (#9251)

1962 **1939-S Arkansas MS66 PCGS.** Well struck with satiny luster, appealing dove-gray color, and dappled apricot toning near the borders. Exquisitely preserved with no distractions. One of just 2,105 pieces minted for this issue as an era of American commemorative history limped to a close. PCGS has certified only four coins finer (5/07). (#9251)

1963 **1939 Arkansas PDS Set MS65 NGC and PCGS.** The set includes: **1939 MS65 NGC,** nearly untoned, meticulously struck, inconspicuous contact on the Indian's chin; **1939-D MS65 PCGS,** occasional golden-russet freckles, sharply struck and smooth; and a **1939-S MS65 NGC,** untoned and well struck with clean cheeks. A low mintage set.
From The Silver Fox Collection. (Total: 3 coins) (#9252)

1964 **1935 Boone PDS Set MS65 NGC and PCGS.** The set includes: **1935 MS65 NGC,** luminous beneath dusky mustard-gold patina; **1935-D MS65 PCGS,** strongly lustrous and slightly hazy with dashes of charcoal color on the obverse and a patch of purplish patina at the lower reverse; and a **1935-S MS65 NGC,** lightly gold-toned overall with a milky appearance.
From The Silver Fox Collection. (#9261)

1965 **1935/34-S Boone MS66 NGC.** Subdued luster is the result of pearl toning with traces of gold iridescence at the obverse border. The branch mint issues of the 1935/34 Boone half dollars are much scarcer than the Philadelphia Mint coins. (#9264)

1966 **1935/34 Boone PDS Set MS65 NGC.** The set includes: **1935/34 MS65 NGC,** strongly lustrous with a touch of golden patina; **1935/34-D MS65 PCGS,** dusky golden-tan toning with speckles of red at the upper obverse; and a **1935/34-S MS65 NGC,** satiny with subtle champagne color over the fields.
From The Silver Fox Collection. (Total: 3 coins) (#9265)

1967 **1935/34 Boone PDS Set MS65 to MS66 PCGS.** The set includes: **1935/34 MS65,** light chestnut-gold toning, a well preserved reverse; **1935/34-D MS66,** faintly toned and lustrous with a bold strike and exceptional preservation; and a **1935/34-S MS65,** delicate sun-gold toning, a nearly pristine reverse. (Total: 3 coins) (#9265)

1968 **1936 Boone MS67 NGC.** Original cream-gray, powder-blue, and apricot patina embraces this satiny and attractively preserved Boone commemorative. The reverse is virtually pristine. (#9266)

1969 **1936 Boone PDS Set MS65 NGC and PCGS.** The set includes: **1936 MS65 NGC,** essentially untoned with strong luster; **1936-D MS65 NGC,** frosty with a touch of golden patina; and a **1936-S MS65 PCGS,** powerful luster with speckles of slate-gray toning.
From The Silver Fox Collection. (Total: 3 coins) (#9269)

1970 **1937 Boone PDS Set MS65 NGC and PCGS.** The set includes: **1937 MS65 PCGS,** soft, hazy golden patina over each side; **1937-D MS65 NGC,** practically untoned and frosty; and a **1937-S MS65 PCGS,** strongly lustrous beneath milky patina that assumes tan color on the reverse.
From The Silver Fox Collection. (Total: 3 coins) (#9272)

1971 **1938 Boone PDS Set MS65 NGC and PCGS.** The set includes: **1938 MS65 PCGS,** frosty and brilliant aside from a faint dollop of gold at the top of Boone's musket; **1938-D MS65 NGC,** potent luster and light champagne toning overall; and a **1938-S MS65 NGC,** brick-red toning over the obverse margins with tan patina on the reverse.
From The Silver Fox Collection. (Total: 3 coins) (#9277)

1972 **1925-S California MS65 PCGS.** More than 75 years later, the California half remains one of the most emblematic commemoratives ever issued by the United States. This strongly lustrous, slightly hazy Gem displays rich amber-gold patina around the figures of the miner and bear. (#9281)

1973 **1925-S California MS65 NGC.** This silver-white Gem example has powerful luster and considerable eye appeal. The surfaces appear brilliant at first, though closer inspection reveals just a touch of color at the margins. Well-defined with few marks for the grade.
From The Silver Fox Collection. (#9281)

1974 **1936 Cincinnati PDS Set MS64 to MS65 NGC.** The set includes: **1936 MS64,** the reverse sports variegated forest-green and lilac toning; **1936-D MS64,** pastel cherry-red and lime-gold reverse patina; and a 1936-S MS65, dappled ruby-red, apple-green, and ivory-gray toning on the reverse. The key to the PDS sets, due to low mintages and a single-year type. (Total: 3 coins) (#9286)

1975 **1936 Cincinnati PDS Set MS65 NGC and PCGS.** The set includes: **1936 MS65 PCGS,** satiny with woodgrain-pattern tan and gray patina; **1936-D MS65 PCGS,** subtly gold-tinged with a spot of deep amber patina at the bottom of the obverse; and a **1936-S MS65 NGC,** powerful luster beneath gold-gray and wheat patina with patches of silver color.
From The Silver Fox Collection. (Total: 3 coins) (#9286)

1976 **1936 Columbia MS64 PCGS.** Boldly struck with pleasing satin luster and faint silver-green toning that yields to pale rose coloration near the center of the reverse. A few wispy marks limit the grade, but they are faint and undistracting. (#9291)

1977 **1936 Columbia MS67 PCGS.** Fully struck and well preserved, with bright satiny luster and light toning that yields to an area of dark, multicolored iridescence near 2 o'clock on the obverse rim, and near 5 o'clock on the reverse. Only 9,007 examples of this commemorative issue were struck, celebrating the sesquicentennial of South Carolina's capital city. Population: 52 in 67, 0 finer (6/07). (#9291)

1978 **1936 Columbia PDS Set MS65 PCGS.** The set includes: **1936 MS65 PCGS,** a satiny and lovely chestnut-gray Gem; **1936-D MS65 NGC,** refreshingly smooth, a few faint ebony streaks; and a **1936-S MS65 PCGS,** lightly toned and unabraded aside from a nick on the forehead.
From The Silver Fox Collection. (Total: 3 coins) (#9294)

1979 **1892 Columbian MS65 PCGS.** Orange, ruby-red, electric-blue, and pearl-gray blanket this lustrous and well preserved Gem. The 1892 Columbian is the first commemorative issue, and is elusive in quality Mint State, although it is plentiful between XF and MS63. (#9296)

1980 **1892 Columbian MS65 PCGS.** FS-301. The peak of the 2 is repunched. The nicest of the three repunched date varieties listed in the fourth edition, Volume 2 of the *Cherrypickers' Guide.* Rich golden-brown, powder-blue, and plum-red toning adorns this satiny and suitably struck Gem. (#9296)

1981 **1892 Columbian MS66 NGC.** Concentrically toned with lavender and reddish-orange in the center and blue-green at the periphery. Solidly struck with pleasing luster and clean surfaces. A delightful representative of the nation's first silver commemorative. (#9296)

1982 **1892 Columbian MS66 PCGS.** Although not designated as such by PCGS, this piece has fully prooflike surfaces beneath radiant multi-colored toning. Just nine finer examples have been certified by PCGS (6/07). (#9296)

Superb Gem 1893 Columbian Half Dollar

1983 **1893 Columbian MS67 NGC.** A Superb Gem, this piece ranks among the finest 1893 Columbian half dollars that still exist today, although NGC has certified two finer pieces. The central obverse has pale heather toning, framed by lovely lime-green, gold, and pale blue toning. The reverse is similar, but with deeper gold at the center, surrounded by blue and lilac toning. (#9297)

1984 **1935 Connecticut MS66 NGC.** Dappled autumn-gold toning enriches this lustrous and intricately struck tercentenary example. The fields are beautifully unabraded. (#9299)

1985 **1936 Elgin MS67 NGC.** Olive-gold toning graces the fields of this lustrous and impressively smooth Superb Gem. The strike is crisp, since only the hair above the ear lacks definitive detail. (#9303)

1986 **1936 Gettysburg MS65 PCGS.** Peripheral russet and lime-gold toning enriches this lustrous, expertly struck, and beautifully preserved Gem. The obverse has interesting retained laminations (as made) at 9 o'clock and on the left (facing) cap. Housed in a first generation, small-sized holder. (#9305)

1987 **1922 Grant no Star MS65 NGC.** One of 67,405 pieces struck of the No Star variety, the more available of two issues for the Grant half dollar. This subtly lustrous, practically untoned example has well-preserved surfaces overall.
From The Silver Fox Collection. (#9306)

1988 **1922 Grant no Star MS66 PCGS.** The vivid auburn-orange patina that graces the upper obverse periphery saturates most of the reverse, though the softly lustrous surfaces are untoned otherwise. A well struck example of the highest-mintage Grant commemorative across four varieties in two denominations. (#9306)

Attractive MS64 Grant With Star Half

1989 **1922 Grant with Star MS64 PCGS.** This low mintage rarity is necessary for a complete set of commemoratives. It has commanded a significant premium since first issued and today is one of the keys to the series. The swirling die polish lines are present, as always, and give the coin a brightness that few other commemorative halves possess. The obverse is covered in shades of rich rose and emerald-green colors, while the reverse is brilliant in the center with an arc of color on the left margin. A lovely, high grade example of this important half. (#9307)

Appealing Silver-White Grant With Star Half, MS64

1990 **1922 Grant with Star MS64 NGC.** According to Anthony Swiatek's *Commemorative Coins of the United States* (2001), the Grant with Star was the highest-priced of all U.S. silver commemorative halves in 1935, when a certain dentist decided to buy numerous Grant no Star pieces and incuse his own star! Fortunately, nearly all genuine examples show a clash mark around Grant's chin and just left of the G in GRANT, while the few examples produced before the dies clashed show a small raised pimple or lump of metal inside the star, just below the 9 o'clock location. This piece, aside from showing both genuine diagnostics, offers appealing silver-white surfaces with just a couple of small ticks on the portrait that preclude Gem consideration. (#9307)

Pleasing 1922 Grant With Star Commemorative Half, MS65

1991 **1922 Grant with Star MS65 NGC.** The 1922 Grant Memorial half dollars (and the gold dollars) issued to honor the centennial of Grant's birth were not all that well received by collectors and the non-collecting public upon their release. The 85-year-old coins today, however, especially the starred obverse half dollars, are highly sought by collectors. This Gem example with Star displays highly lustrous, essentially untoned surfaces that exhibit sharply struck design elements. Typically seen die polish lines are noted in the obverse fields, and mentionable blemishes are totally lacking.
From The Silver Fox Collection. (#9307)

Appealing 1928 Hawaiian Gem Half

1992 **1928 Hawaiian MS65 PCGS.** The 1928 Hawaiian half dollar is one of the keys of the 50-piece set of "traditional" U.S. commemorative halves from 1892 to 1954. This Gem representative is impressively struck, and possesses intense luster. Splashes of delicate champagne patina visit each side, being slightly more intense at the margins. Well preserved surfaces add to the pleasing eye appeal. Housed in a green-label holder.
From The Silver Fox Collection. (#9309)

Bank of Hawaii Hoard 1928 Half Dollar, MS66

1993 **1928 Hawaiian MS66 PCGS.** This is a distinctive example of the Hawaiian half dollar that is most likely from the Bank of Hawaii hoard that was dispersed in 1986. Both sides have the unusual mustard-yellow and iridescent toning that is often seen on the hoard coins. Population: 58 in 66, 1 finer (6/07). (#9309)

Premium Gem 1928 Hawaiian Half

1994 **1928 Hawaiian MS66 NGC.** Boldly struck and pleasantly lustrous, with light lemon-gold, silver-beige, and rose toning. This well preserved Hawaiian half dollar will likely complete an exemplary quality collection of classic silver commemoratives. Rare at this grade level, and nearly uncollectible any finer. Census: 60 in 66, 4 finer (5/07). (#9309)

1995 **1935 Hudson MS64 NGC.** Light honey, russet, and pearl-gray toning enrich this shimmering and attractively preserved near-Gem. A bold strike with only trivial incompleteness on Neptune and the upper left sail. A challenging type. (#9312)

1996 **1935 Hudson MS64 PCGS.** Typically struck with pleasing satiny luster and blended tan and rose coloration on the obverse. The silver-gray reverse is untoned except for a slight amount of speckled peripheral patina. Surface marks are not excessive for the grade. (#9312)

1997 **1935 Hudson MS65 PCGS.** Splotches of purple, golden-tan, and russet concentrate at the periphery of this Gem commemorative. Well preserved surfaces display strong luster and well impressed design elements. This coin marked the 150th anniversary of the founding of Hudson, New York, a small city on the east bank of the Hudson River, about 40 miles south of Albany. (#9312)

1998 **1935 Hudson MS65 NGC.** A flashy and practically brilliant example of this lower-mintage single-issue design, minimally marked on the obverse with only a handful of minor flaws on the ship. Slight softness is noted on Neptune and the flanking figures in the city coat of arms.
From The Silver Fox Collection. (#9312)

Tab-Toned 1935 Hudson, MS66

1999 **1935 Hudson MS66 NGC.** A tab-toned piece housed in an early generation holder. The medley of golden-gray, medium gray, lavender, and ice-blue toning visits lustrous surfaces that exhibit well struck design elements. Close scrutiny with a glass reveals no significant marks on either side. (#9312)

2000 **1924 Huguenot MS66 PCGS.** This lustrous and exactingly struck tercentenary commemorative is gently toned in sun-gold shades. Seldom encountered any finer. (#9314)

2001 **1924 Huguenot MS66 PCGS.** Rich olive and plum colors appear in a broad crescent along the right obverse of this lustrous piece, while the reverse has similar colors along the rim with ocean-blue and denim colors in the center. A well-defined and carefully preserved example of this commemorative, one that combined the political and religious aspects of the American colonies. (#9314)

2002 **1925 Lexington MS66 NGC.** A splendid Premium Gem, this piece has radiant silver luster with full mint brilliance. The fields are satiny with a hint of reflectivity. Only nine finer examples have been certified by NGC (6/07). (#9318)

2003 **1918 Lincoln MS66 NGC.** Green-gray patina graces most of both sides, while olive, yellow-green, and strawberry colors appear at the peripheries. Decisively struck with lovely luster and the clean appearance shared by the finest representatives of this first statehood centennial issue. (#9320)

2004 **1918 Lincoln MS66 PCGS.** Freckles of golden-brown and yellow-gold toning enrich this lustrous and exactingly struck half dollar. The reverse is pristine; the obverse has only inconspicuous contact. (#9320)

2005 **1918 Lincoln MS66 PCGS.** Freckled golden-russet and ocean-blue colors overlay ivory-gray patination. This lustrous and attentively struck example has well preserved surfaces that reveal just a few minor obverse marks. (#9320)

2006 **1918 Lincoln MS66 PCGS.** Exquisitely struck with satiny luster and irregular patches of speckled, multicolored patina near the obverse and reverse borders. A few trivial obverse handling marks do not detract from the status of this wonderful Premium Gem. The reverse seems pristine. (#9320)

2007 **1918 Lincoln MS67 NGC.** Both sides of this Superb Gem are essentially brilliant, with attractive gold and iridescent toning limited to the peripheries, encroaching only slightly upon the outer legends. Census: 69 in 67, 3 finer (6/07). (#9320)

Impeccable 1936 Long Island Half MS67

2008 **1936 Long Island MS67 NGC.** A lovely example with splashes of pastel gold and iridescent toning over lustrous light gray surfaces on both sides. Crisply struck, and immaculate aside from a solitary and inconspicuous vertical mark on the lower right sail. Census: 48 in 67, 2 finer (5/07). (#9322)

2009 **1934 Maryland MS66 PCGS.** This lustrous example has an attractive overlay of reddish-golden toning that deepens slightly at the borders. (#9328)

2010 **1934 Maryland MS66 NGC.** This Premium Gem displays a noticeably better-than-average strike for the issue, especially on the portrait of Cecil Calvert. Highly lustrous with attractive, speckled russet and dark-green patina near the peripheries. (#9328)

2011 **1921 Missouri MS64 NGC.** Crisply struck and lustrous, with lovely golden-brown coloration over both sides, and speckled amber-russet patina near some of the borders. A handful of tiny nicks in the left obverse field limit the grade of this near-Gem key date commemorative. (#9330)

2012 **1921 Missouri MS64 NGC.** Satin luster and light speckled patina are seen on both sides of this key date commemorative coin. Carefully preserved with minimal marks for the grade. (#9330)

2013 **1921 Missouri MS64 PCGS.** This is a frosty and highly lustrous near-Gem with brilliant, untoned surfaces. The design elements on both sides of this piece are uncharacteristically sharp. (#9330)

Lustrous 1921 Missouri 50 Cent, MS65

2014 **1921 Missouri MS65 NGC.** The Missouri half dollar was conspicuous as to the absence of certain design elements. Specifically, it did not include the words LIBERTY or IN GOD WE TRUST or E PLURIBUS UNUM. This prompted *Numismatic News* writer Paul Green to say: "As a silver half dollar, it should have had those phrases, but did not, causing some to refer to it as the 'lawbreaker' coin." Both sides of this Gem specimen are awash in luster, and display a thin veneer of light beige-gold color. A few minor obverse marks are well within the parameters of the grade designation, and the design features are well impressed.
From The Silver Fox Collection. (#9330)

2015 **1921 Missouri 2x4 MS63 NGC.** Freckles of russet and peach visit this primarily pearl-gray Missouri half. Crisply struck with good luster and no mentionable marks. The Missouri type is scarce, with or without the 2x4 in the field. (#9331)

2016 **1921 Missouri 2x4 MS64 PCGS.** The jade-green and russet-gold shadings are most prominent near the rims. A satiny and suitably struck near-Gem with minimal field contact. A difficult statehood type. (#9331)

Lightly Toned 1921 Missouri 2x4 Half Dollar, MS65

2017 **1921 Missouri 2x4 MS65 PCGS.** The 2★4 on the Missouri Centennial half dollar signifies that Missouri was the 24th star on the flag. In a March 1, 2005 article in *Numismatic News*, however, staff writer Paul Green says: "... the real reason was almost certainly sales, as those 5,000 were the first 5,000 made with the incuse addition." Delicate pastel ice-blue and lilac color rests on the highly lustrous surfaces of this MS65 specimen. The design definition is bold, and there are no bothersome marks to contend with.
From The Silver Fox Collection. (#9331)

2018 **1923-S Monroe MS64 PCGS.** A brilliant and lustrous near-Gem whose clean surfaces confirm the Choice designation. The strike is above average, although incomplete (as always) near the top of Adams' ear. (#9333)

2019 **1923-S Monroe MS64 PCGS.** Well struck with mottled gold and russet toning over much of the obverse, while the highly lustrous reverse has only a touch of peripheral patina. Light abrasions in the fields deny a Gem grade. Along with the Columbian and Stone Mountain halves, the Monroe was one of the commemoratives most often found in circulation during the Great Depression. (#9333)

2020 **1923-S Monroe MS64 PCGS.** A lustrous near-Gem example of this conditionally difficult commemorative type. Brilliant aside from a few tiny tan obverse freckles. Pleasing despite occasional nearly imperceptible obverse hairlines. (#9333)

Interesting Gem 1923-S Monroe Half

2021 **1923-S Monroe MS65 NGC.** For decades, the Monroe half has had a reputation as conditionally elusive in Gem and better grades. This MS65 example displays a touch of frostiness on beige-tinted surfaces. The definition is above-average, and the piece has notable visual appeal. An attractive example of this early branch mint commemorative half, originally minted in vast quantities. (#9333)

Brilliant Gem 1923-S Monroe Half

2022 **1923-S Monroe MS65 NGC.** Practically untoned with pleasing luster, though the discerning eye can identify a touch of ice-blue color in the obverse fields. Softly detailed as always on the dual portraits and the personified continents, though the former has slightly above-average detail. The clean surfaces contribute to this coin's surprisingly high visual appeal.
From The Silver Fox Collection. (#9333)

Attractive 1938 New Rochelle Commemorative, MS67

2023 **1938 New Rochelle MS67 NGC.** Dazzling luster radiates through the medium-intensity, iridescent multicolored toning that graces this Superb Gem New Rochelle commemorative. Impeccably preserved surfaces exhibit well defined motifs, further enhancing the coin's overall eye appeal. Struck to observe the founding of this downstate New York city by French Huguenots in the late 1600s. (#9335)

2024 **1938 New Rochelle MS66 Prooflike NGC.** This untoned silver commemorative has an immaculate obverse, and the reverse is only lightly abraded. The fields are flashy and lustrous. Census: 54 in 66 Prooflike, 14 finer (6/07). (#89335)

2025 **1936 Norfolk MS67 PCGS.** A stone-white Superb Gem with clean surfaces and vibrant cartwheel sheen. An unusually verbose commemorative type often available in quality condition. (#9337)

Outstanding 1936 Norfolk Half Dollar, MS68

2026 **1936 Norfolk MS68 PCGS.** Both sides of this Superb Norfolk commemorative are awash in outstanding luster, and exhibit whispers of pastel golden-brown and ice-blue toning in the center areas, yielding to deeper golden-brown and reddish-gold color at the peripheries. Sharp definition is noted on the intricate design features, and close inspection reveals no mentionable marks. On a historical note, Paul Gilkes, in a January 22, 2007 *Coin World* article, writes: "Depicted on the reverse is the Royal Mace, with the British crown on top, the only such scepter presented to an American city during the Colonial period." (#9337)

2027 **1926 Oregon MS67 NGC.** Solidly struck and well preserved, with highly lustrous surfaces that are essentially untoned, save for a faint golden pallor over both sides. A pleasing Superb Gem example of this first-year issue in the Oregon Trail commemorative series, which was to continue, with interruptions, through 1939. Census: 38 in 67, 4 finer (6/07). (#9340)

Superb Gem 1928 Oregon Trail Half Dollar

2028 **1928 Oregon MS67 PCGS.** To the naked eye, this 1928 Oregon is virtually flawless. Although slightly hazy when viewed head-on, this coin displays attractive colors when rotated under a light source. The obverse is mostly a light russet tone with a gentle blush of fluorescent green and violet coloration at the upper right periphery. The reverse is a lovely light copper color. Both sides are amply lustrous, as one would expect. The tag is of the old green label type. Population: 62 in 67, 0 finer (6/07). (#9342)

2029 **1933-D Oregon MS67 NGC.** Delicate pearl-gray, lime, and gold patina endows this shimmering and smooth Superb Gem. One of the few issues of any denomination struck at the Denver Mint in 1933, the trough year of the Great Depression. (#9343)

2030 **1936-S Oregon MS67 PCGS.** This issue of 5,006 pieces came a decade after the original Oregon Trail issues of 1926. This lustrous, carefully preserved piece is lightly gold-toned overall with small splashes of red-violet patina at the margins. PCGS has graded just four pieces finer (5/07). (#9346)

Near-Perfect MS68 1936-S Oregon Half

2031 **1936-S Oregon MS68 NGC.** This is a gorgeous Superb Gem with olive-gold color over satiny silver luster on both sides. Traces of peripheral rose, lilac, and iridescent toning can be seen near the borders. This low-mintage (5,006) issue is rather elusive in high grades. Census: 10 in 68, 0 finer (6/07). (#9346)

2032 **1937-D Oregon MS67 PCGS.** Russet and aqua freckles overlie the smooth pearl-gray surfaces of this lustrous Superb Gem. Well struck on the oxen, although the second T in STATES and the back of the wagon are incompletely brought up. (#9347)

2033 **1938-S Oregon MS67 PCGS.** This is a wonderful Superb Gem example of the Frasers' Oregon Trail commemorative design, with all of the complex details fully brought up. Satin luster highlights the smooth, immaculately preserved surfaces. A bit of iridescent peripheral toning increases the eye appeal of the piece. Population: 95 in 67, 9 finer (4/07). (#9350)

2034 **1938-S Oregon MS67 PCGS.** Golden-brown margins cede to olive-gray fields and devices. A well struck and nearly immaculate Superb Gem with good luster and excellent eye appeal. (#9350)

2035 **1938 Oregon PDS Set MS65 to MS66 PCGS.** The set includes: **1938 MS66,** peach and pearl-gray toning, well struck aside from ejection flatness on the oxen's back; **1938-D MS65,** light peripheral russet patina, satiny, minor incompleteness on the back of the wagon; and a **1938-S MS66,** decisively struck, an immaculate obverse, honey-gold and slate toning. (Total: 3 coins) (#9351)

2036 **1938 Oregon PDS Set MS65 NGC and PCGS.** The set includes: **1938 MS65 NGC,** luminous beneath soft pewter-gray patina with hints of gold; **1938-D MS65 PCGS,** essentially untoned with strong detail; and a **1938-S MS65 NGC,** brilliant with strong visual appeal.
From The Silver Fox Collection. (Total: 3 coins) (#9351)

2037 **1938 Oregon PDS Set MS66 NGC.** The set includes: **1938,** a satiny beautiful with light gold toning, well struck aside from the back of the ox; **1938-D,** magnificently preserved, nicely struck, gentle satin luster; and a **1938-S,** crisply struck and unabraded, delicate gold and ice-blue toning. (Total: 3 coins) (#9351)

2038 **1939 Oregon PDS Set MS65 to MS66 NGC.** The set includes: **1939 MS65,** boldly struck and untoned, well preserved; **1939-D MS65,** brilliant and crisply struck with satiny surfaces; and a **1939-S MS66,** intricately struck, light caramel-gold patina, nearly pristine.
From The Silver Fox Collection. (Total: 3 coins) (#9355)

Original, Matched Set of 1939 Oregon Trail Halves

2039 **1939 Oregon PDS Set PCGS.** The Philadelphia and Denver coins grade MS66 and the S-mint is MS65. A key issue in the Oregon Trail series with only 3,000 pieces struck. This is a lovely, matched set with consecutive PCGS numbers. Virtually brilliant with smooth, lustrous surfaces and remarkably clean. (Total: 3 coins) (#9355)

2040 **1915-S Panama-Pacific MS64 PCGS.** The charcoal-gray surfaces display specks of darker patina that are most noticeable near the borders. Well struck and carefully preserved, with a nearly complete absence of surface marks. (#9357)

2041 **1915-S Panama-Pacific MS64 PCGS.** Well struck and subtly lustrous beneath deep plum and rose patina. Minimally marked for the grade, though Liberty's lower arm displays a light abrasion. The Panama-Pacific half is one of several early commemoratives that splits design credit between Charles Barber and George Morgan. (#9357)

2042 **1915-S Panama-Pacific MS64 PCGS.** The rich blue-green, lapis, watermelon-red, and orange patina that covers the obverse margins is thinner and less extensive on the reverse. The centers of each side are untoned, and the devices have above-average detail. A lustrous example of this early silver commemorative, one that has surprisingly few marks for the grade. (#9357)

2043 **1915-S Panama-Pacific MS65 NGC.** Gunmetal-gray patina complements the deeper ebony color that appears at the rims. A sharply struck beauty that should appeal to the toning enthusiast, and a great example of the half dollar that revived the denomination for commemorative use. The mintmark is repunched north.
From The Silver Fox Collection. (#9357)

Premium Gem 1915-S Panama-Pacific Half

2044 **1915-S Panama-Pacific MS66 NGC.** An amazing example with brilliant satin luster that is mostly brilliant white, framed by a trace of champagne toning near the borders on each side. All design elements are sharply detailed and the surfaces are nearly perfect with only the slightest imperfections. Only 63 finer examples of the variety are currently holdered by NGC (6/07). (#9357)

2045 **1921 Pilgrim MS66 NGC.** Dusky rose, pewter-gray, and rust-russet colors cover most of each side, while hints of powder-blue grace the reverse margins. Subtly lustrous beneath the color with pleasing definition. The mintage of slightly over 20,000 pieces for the 1921 Pilgrim issue was a shadow of the production for the 1920 edition. (#9360)

2046 **1936 Rhode Island PDS Set MS65 NGC.** The set includes: **1936,** peach and lemon toning illuminates the borders, a reasonable strike; **1936-D,** well struck and smooth with the usual curious mint-made die rust, in a green label holder; and a **1936-S,** lightly toned, clean fields, a shiny mark on the anchor, in a green label holder.
From The Silver Fox Collection. (Total: 3 coins) (#9366)

2047 **1936 Rhode Island PDS Set MS65 PCGS.** The set includes: **1936,** mottled peach, forest-green, and sky-blue toning; **1936-D,** alternating dove-gray, orange, and jade-green patina; and a **1936-S,** blushes of apricot, lilac, and ice-blue endow this smooth and satiny Gem. (Total: 3 coins) (#9366)

Unbelievably Toned 1937 Roanoke Half Dollar, MS67

2048 **1937 Roanoke MS67 PCGS.** A melange of deep gold, sky-blue, crimson, lime-green, and forest-green patination adorns the radiantly lustrous surfaces of this Superb Gem commemorative, and an attentive strike brings forth exquisite delineation on all of the design features. Close examination reveals no significant marks on either side, though for complete accuracy we mention a couple of light grazes in the left obverse field that are completely concealed within the toning. Outstanding technical quality and aesthetic appeal. The connoisseur of toned coins will not want to miss out on this piece! (#9367)

2049 **1937 Roanoke MS67 NGC.** An attractive blend of olive and plum patina visits the strongly lustrous surfaces of this attentively struck Superb Gem. Carefully preserved and highly appealing. The event celebrated, the founding of Roanoke Colony, ended in one of the most puzzling mysteries of its era of adventure. Housed in an older generation holder. (#9367)

2050 **1937 Roanoke MS67 PCGS.** Amber-gold, light-green, and crimson iridescence covers the obverse, while the reverse displays similar color near the borders and a small splash of the same hue at the exact center, presumably from long-term residence in an original holder. Powerfully struck with delightful luster. A lovely piece that celebrates one of the earliest chapters in British colonial history. (#9367)

2051 **1935-S San Diego MS67 PCGS.** Attractively toned at the obverse margins with richer, more widespread gold-orange and powder-blue patina on the reverse. Well-defined and strongly lustrous with the immense eye appeal that characterizes the finest examples of this series, which consists of two different dates and two different mints. PCGS has graded just three coins finer (5/07). (#9371)

Intensely Lustrous MS67 1936-D San Diego Half

2052 **1936-D San Diego MS67 PCGS.** The San Diego halves are certainly among the most lustrous halves in the commemorative series. Each side of this piece shows pale pinkish color with deeper russet and sea-green patina around the margins. A nearly perfect example of this popular half. Population: 66 in 67, 0 finer (6/07). (#9372)

2053 **1926 Sesquicentennial MS64 PCGS.** A thin veneer of light tan-gold color covers lustrous surfaces that host well struck devices. Small, isolated spots of deep toning appear at the margins. A pleasing piece that falls just shy of the coveted Gem grade, largely due to a single mark on Coolidge's chin. (#9374)

2054 **1926 Sesquicentennial MS64 PCGS.** The prime focal areas are free of distracting marks, save for a single tick on Washington's cheek. The toning is a deep blend of plum-gray, yellow, green, and blue, irregularly scattered on both sides. Surprisingly appealing for the grade assigned, just one point shy of the Gem status so prized for this issue. (#9374)

Attractive Gem 1926 Sesquicentennial Half Dollar

2055 **1926 Sesquicentennial MS65 PCGS.** According to the *Encyclopedia of United States Silver and Gold Commemorative Coins* (Swiatek and Breen): "Survivors among the half dollars, as with many earlier issues, seldom qualify as choice. Many are bag marked; others were nicked, scratched or poorly cleaned, or otherwise mishandled by their non-numismatic owners." This Gem example suffers from none of these indignities. It is a well struck and nicely preserved Sesqui half dollar, with fine satiny luster and natural light toning on both sides. A die crack extends across the lower edge of the Liberty Bell. A very shallow abrasion appears higher on the Liberty Bell, just below ORDER OF THE, but the coin is otherwise unmarked. (#9374)

Lightly Toned 1926 Sesquicentennial Half Dollar, MS65

2056 **1926 Sesquicentennial MS65 NGC.** For the first time, the portrait of a president appeared on a coin struck during his own lifetime, with President Coolidge depicted with George Washington on the Sesquicentennial half dollar. This MS65 example displays warm golden-gray patina hovering over lustrous surfaces. All of the design features are well impressed, and just a few minute obverse marks preclude an even higher grade.
From The Silver Fox Collection. (#9374)

2057 **1935 Spanish Trail MS64 NGC.** A subtly lustrous Choice representative of this low-mintage single-issue design, well-defined overall with areas of steel-gray, sunset-orange, and violet patina. Modestly marked for the grade. (#9376)

2058 **1935 Spanish Trail MS65 PCGS.** Well struck with intense satin luster and smoky silver-gray toning enhanced by slight amounts of speckled russet patina near the reverse periphery. Nearly blemish-free, save for a few small marks on the reverse fields. A popular low mintage issue in the silver commemorative series. (#9376)

2059 **1935 Spanish Trail MS65 PCGS.** Light apricot and gold bands cling to the lower obverse margin, but this satiny Gem is generally faint honey-gray. A well struck example of this low mintage silver type. (#9376)

2060 **1935 Spanish Trail MS65 PCGS.** Delicate gold and lavender toning appears against the silver-gray surfaces, which have subtle, shimmering luster. Solidly struck with only a few stray marks. A faint planchet flaw is noted near 9 o'clock on the reverse rim. (#9376)

2061 **1935 Spanish Trail MS65 NGC.** Perhaps the least-known sculptor of any American commemorative, Edmund J. Senn was the unemployed artist L.W. Hoffecker hired to translate his simple drawings for the Spanish Trail half into three-dimensional models. Senn's lack of work at the time is the only detail supplied for him in most numismatic references. This luminous Gem is predominantly steel-gray with splashes of reddish-orange color. The solidly struck devices display few marks, as do the fields. *From The Silver Fox Collection.* (#9376)

2062 **1935 Spanish Trail MS66 PCGS.** In one of the more egregious incidents of the scandal-ridden history of commemoratives, the entire Spanish Trail mintage was delivered to a single dealer-speculator, L.W. Hoffecker. Subtly lustrous with delicate pastel blue and yellow colors over the carefully preserved surfaces. A single thin mark is noted below Alabama on the reverse. (#9376)

2063 **1935 Spanish Trail MS66 PCGS.** What stands out most on this lovely Premium Gem commemorative is the lack of numerous contact marks on its lustrous surfaces; the wide-open, exposed fields of this issue often show abrasions of all sorts. In addition, the design elements are sharply impressed, and hints of light tan-gold color are visible on both sides. (#9376)

2064 **1925 Stone Mountain MS67 PCGS.** Walnut-brown, olive-green, and plum-mauve hug the margins of this sharply struck and unabraded Superb Gem. Except for the Columbian half, the Stone Mountain is the most plentiful type within the classic commemorative series, yet examples with the present quality are seldom encountered. (#9378)

2065 **1935 Texas MS67 PCGS.** This lovely Superb Gem has an elegant appearance. The design features are fully struck, the luster is excellent, and a pleasing antique-gold cast has settled over both sides. This is augmented by steel-blue accents in the obverse fields. Surface marks are almost nonexistent. (#9382)

2066 **1935 Texas PDS Set MS65 PCGS.** The set includes: **1935,** light gold toning, beautifully smooth, well struck, housed in an old green label holder; **1935-D,** well struck and unabraded, a faint fingerprint fragment on the upper right obverse; and a **1935-S,** lime, rose, and gold hues grace this lustrous and beautiful Gem. *From The Silver Fox Collection.* (Total: 3 coins) (#9385)

2067 **1935 Texas PDS Set MS66 PCGS.** Each coin grades MS66. The set is uniform in appearance with light golden-brown toning and strong underlying mint luster. The coins are consecutively numbered, a strong indication that this was an original set when it was submitted. (Total: 3 coins) (#9385)

2068 **1936 Texas MS67 NGC.** One of three issues struck in the third of five years of production for the design, the 1936 Texas half had a net mintage of 8,911 pieces. This well-defined example has hazy gold-gray color over much of the piece and deeper color at the lower left reverse rim. NGC has certified only six higher-graded pieces (5/07). (#9386)

2069 **1936 Texas MS67 NGC.** Bright mint luster swirls around each side of this impressive type coin. Not a trace of color can be found on this immaculate piece. Fully struck and nearly perfect in terms of preservation of surfaces. (#9386)

Superlative 1936 Texas Half, MS68

2070 **1936 Texas MS68 NGC.** This issue, while not minted in substantial numbers, is known to come nice. In fact, the combined Gem or better populations of PCGS and NGC number well over 2,000 pieces. That aside, the example offered here is nothing short of astonishing quality for the issue. Both sides offer glowing, near-perfect surfaces with thin crescents of orange toning on each side. Census: 6 in 68, 0 finer (6/07). (#9386)

Exceptional 1936-D Texas Half, MS68

2071 **1936-D Texas MS68 PCGS.** Highly lustrous with frosty silver surfaces and hints of ice blue color. The obverse has additional small splashes of orange and amber toning on the upper part of that side. An impressive example of the issue, tied with several others as finest certified by PCGS. Population: 12 in 68, 0 finer (6/07). (#9387)

2072 **1936-S Texas MS67 NGC.** An essentially untoned Superb Gem that exhibits above-average detail, this 1936-S piece is one of 9,055 struck. Only a few tiny flaws appear to the unaided eye. Census: 55 in 67, 2 finer (5/07). (#9388)

2073 **1936 Texas PDS Set MS65 to MS66 NGC and PCGS.** The set includes: **1936 MS65 PCGS,** glimpses of walnut-brown toning across the reverse, precisely struck; **1936-D MS66 NGC,** well struck except for the Winged Victory's knee; and a **1936-S MS65 NGC,** light honey-gold toning, impeccably preserved, minor softness on the Winged Victory.
From The Silver Fox Collection. (Total: 3 coins) (#9389)

2074 **1937-S Texas MS66 Prooflike NGC.** This is a popular low mintage commemorative type that is rarely seen in Prooflike condition. In fact, just eight pieces have been certified as Prooflike by NGC, and the current example is highest-graded of those and the only one at MS66 (5/07). It is sharply struck and untoned, with some wispy die polish lines on the obverse and well preserved, blemish-free surfaces. (#89392)

2075 **1937 Texas PDS Set MS65 to MS66 NGC and PCGS.** The set includes: **1937 MS65 NGC,** dashes of golden toning, crisply struck and impeccably preserved; **1937-D MS66 PCGS,** pastel apricot and sky-gray patina, a few tiny marks; and a **1937-S MS65 NGC,** lightly toned and lustrous with an above average strike.
From The Silver Fox Collection. (Total: 3 coins) (#9393)

2076 **1937 Texas PDS Set MS65 PCGS.** The set includes: **1937,** blushes of gold and lime toning endow this boldly struck and lovely Gem; **1937-D,** unabraded, a few charcoal flecks, the knee is slightly soft; and a **1937-S,** untoned aside from a blush of golden-brown and sea-green along the upper reverse border. (Total: 3 coins) (#9393)

2077 **1938-D Texas MS66 NGC.** This beautifully preserved Premium Gem has an impressively sharp strike, even on the often mushy Winged Victory. Mostly white with a few pale tan freckles. The lowest mintage issue of the Texas type. (#9395)

2078 **1938-S Texas MS67 NGC.** Light, even gray toning covers each side with iridescent highlights around the margins. The underlying mint luster is bright and enlivens the overlay of color. An exceptionally pleasing Texas commemorative. Nearly perfect. (#9396)

2079 **1938 Texas PDS Set MS65 NGC.** The set includes: **1938,** light gold patina, satiny and only lightly abraded; **1938-D,** orange-russet shades visit the generally cream-gray fields and devices, a good strike; and a **1938-S,** pumpkin-gold hugs the borders, sharply struck and unmarked.
From The Silver Fox Collection. (Total: 3 coins) (#9397)

2080 **1925 Vancouver MS65 NGC.** A strongly lustrous example of this Laura Gardin Fraser effort, which came a year before her greatest artistic triumph with the Oregon Trail obverse design. Light yellow and orange toning at the peripheries heightens the brilliance of the centers. Well struck with great eye appeal.
From The Silver Fox Collection. (#9399)

2081 **1927 Vermont MS65 PCGS.** An impressive Gem whose light golden-brown surfaces are both smooth and lustrous. The strike is sharp, as usual for the type despite its uncommonly high relief. Encased in a green label holder. (#9401)

2082 **1927 Vermont MS65 PCGS.** Bands of powder-blue and gold patina grace the peripheral regions on this gorgeous Gem, a coin that celebrated the sesquicentennial of the Revolutionary War's Battle of Bennington. A well-defined example with pleasing luster and carefully preserved surfaces. (#9401)

2083 **1927 Vermont MS65 PCGS.** A well-defined example with excellent luster and pleasing patina. The surfaces are awash in golden toning on the obverse with elements of blue-green and specks of deeper color on the reverse. The Vermont half was authorized nearly two years before its production, as part of a bill that created two designs of 1925.
From The Silver Fox Collection. (#9401)

2084 **1927 Vermont MS66 PCGS.** Smooth, subtle luster shines beneath rich sea-green and cream patina. A few flecks of deeper color appear on Ira Allen's well-defined portrait, though the corresponding surfaces are practically mark-free. (#9401)

2085 **1927 Vermont MS66 PCGS.** A highly lustrous example that has russet and violet-gold patina, and a powerful strike emboldens the design elements of this very attractive Premium Gem. A couple of minuscule marks are well within the parameters of the grade. (#9401)

2086 **1946 Booker T. Washington MS67 NGC.** Fire-red, sea-green, and silver-white toning embraces this satiny and suitably struck high grade example. Impressive aesthetic quality from the initial year of the type. Census: 49 in 67, 0 finer (5/07). (#9404)

2087 **1946-S Booker T. Washington MS67 PCGS.** Finely speckled multicolored toning covers both sides with strong underlying mint luster. A rare issue in Superb condition. (#9406)

2088 **1946-S Booker T. Washington MS67 NGC.** Cherry-red, forest-green, and powder-blue toning enriches this lustrous and nicely impressed Superb Gem. Essentially void of post-strike contact. Census: 67 in 67, 4 finer (5/07). (#9406)

2089 **1946-S Booker T. Washington MS67 NGC.** Attractive fire-red, gold, and aquamarine envelop the unabraded fields. This lustrous Superb Gem has a good strike, although the texture of the planchet is sometimes visible on the portrait. (#9406)

2090 **1947 Booker T. Washington MS66 PCGS.** Subtle sky-blue and champagne shadings grace the luminous surfaces of this later classic commemorative. Well-defined with only a trace of the planchet roughness typically found on the cheek. PCGS has graded only two coins finer (5/07). (#9408)

2091 **1948-D Booker T. Washington MS66 PCGS.** This lustrous olive-gray Premium Gem has an unusually precise strike on the portrait of Booker T. Washington, and the fields are delightfully unabraded. Impressive quality for this low mintage issue. (#9413)

MS67 1948-D Booker T. Washington, None Finer

2092 **1948-D Booker T. Washington MS67 PCGS.** This Superb Gem coin is mostly silver-white, with just a dab of smoky gray patina at the obverse rim, while the reverse is largely untoned. The 1948-D had a typical emission for a mintmarked piece from this series of 8,005 pieces, but the present example is one of only five so graded at PCGS, with none finer at either service (6/07). (#9413)

2093 **1948-S Booker T. Washington MS66 PCGS.** Light almond-gold toning coats the fields and devices, while the borders exhibit subtle apple-green and plum-red freckles. A lustrous, sharply struck, and beautifully preserved Premium Gem. (#9414)

2094 **1949 Booker T. Washington MS67 PCGS.** A well struck example of this low-mintage later commemorative issue, well struck with few marks evident in the fields. Lightly toned gold-gray overall with a splash of violet-russet patina evident at the lower obverse rim. The usual planchet roughness is present on the portrait. (#9416)

2095 **1949 Booker T. Washington PDS Set MS66 NGC.** The set includes: **1949,** lightly toned and lustrous with minor planchet chatter on the cheek; **1949-D,** well preserved and brilliant with booming luster and a sharp strike; and a **1949-S,** stone-white, vibrant luster, well struck, a faint graze on the cheekbone. (Total: 3 coins) (#9419)

2096 **1950-S Booker T. Washington MS67 NGC.** Well struck and softly lustrous beneath thin gold and blue toning. This minimally marked representative is tied for the finest certified by either service. Census: 44 in 67, 0 finer (5/07). (#9422)

2097 **1951-D Booker T. Washington MS67 NGC.** The reverse has a streak of russet at the lower right, while the remainder of the piece is essentially untoned. Well struck and highly lustrous, this piece is tied with several others as finest certified by both NGC or PCGS (6/07). (#9425)

2098 **1951-D Booker T. Washington MS67 NGC.** While readily available in lower grades, a Superb Gem example of this issue is a condition rarity. This piece has sparkling luster and is largely untoned with no distractions of any note. One of just 7,004 pieces struck for this issue, one of the last for the design. Neither NGC nor PCGS has certified an MS68 or better coin (5/07). (#9425)

Pleasing 1951 Washington-Carver Half Dollar, MS66

2099 **1951 Washington-Carver MS66 PCGS.** This Premium Gem is attractively toned with a medley of light to medium apple-green, gold, olive, and violet coloration, and exhibits pleasing luster. All of the states on the reverse map depict clear boundaries and are devoid of mentionable marks, unusual features for the issue. The Washington-Carver coin is available through near-Gem, but scarce any finer. Population: 25 in 66, 0 finer (4/07). (#9430)

2100 **1951-S Washington-Carver MS66 PCGS.** Olive-green and rose toning alternate positions on the obverse and reverse of this lustrous, high grade coin. This piece is tied for the finest certified by PCGS (6/07). (#9432)

Intense Superb Gem 1952 Washington-Carver

2101 **1952 Washington-Carver MS67 NGC.** Despite the common date status, this is an elusive Superb Gem, one of just 12 similar examples certified by NGC, with none finer (6/07). The 1952 is undoubtedly the most plentiful of all Carver half dollars. Both sides are intensely and deeply toned with gold, lilac, sea-green, and steel toning. (#9434)

2102 **1936 Wisconsin MS67 PCGS.** The bright mint luster enlivens the light overlay of golden-olive toning on each side. Notably clean for this often heavily abraded commemorative. (#9447)

2103 **1936 Wisconsin MS67 PCGS.** Similar in brightness and overall appearance to the coin above, but with deeper rose-colored peripheries. Highly lustrous. (#9447)

2104 **1936 Wisconsin MS67 PCGS.** Subtle ice-blue and pale golden color is seen over each side of this lovely, high grade example. (#9447)

COMMEMORATIVE GOLD

2105 **1903 Louisiana Purchase/Jefferson AU58 NGC.** Although each side has a trace of wear, the pleasing orange-gold luster is virtually unbroken. Magnification reveals a few scattered hairlines and other minor marks. (#7443)

2106 **1903 Louisiana Purchase/Jefferson MS64 NGC.** An outstanding near-Gem, this piece has frosty and brilliant luster with delightful orange-gold color. Traces of coppery toning can be seen on the reverse. (#7443)

2107 **1903 Louisiana Purchase/Jefferson MS64 PCGS.** A moderately prooflike near-Gem that has an exquisite strike and a hint of orange-gold toning. A scarce gold commemorative type. Encased in a first generation holder. (#7443)

Reflective 1903 Jefferson Gold Dollar, MS66

2108 **1903 Louisiana Purchase/Jefferson MS66 PCGS.** Two varieties of the Louisiana Purchase Exposition gold dollars were created, one featuring a portrait of Thomas Jefferson who spear headed the Louisiana Purchase, and the other depicting William McKinley who was President at the time that the convention was first planned. A sharp strike and deep honey-gold color are the hallmarks of this reflective, nearly prooflike Premium Gem. Both sides have nearly perfect surfaces with radiant luster and exceptional aesthetic appeal. Only 67 finer examples of this commemorative gold dollar have been certified by PCGS (6/07). (#7443)

1903 Louisiana Purchase/Jefferson Gold Dollar MS66

2109 **1903 Louisiana Purchase/Jefferson MS66 PCGS.** This honey-gold Premium Gem provides potent luster, and the strike is precise except for the HA in PURCHASE, which is opposite the highpoint of Jefferson's shoulder. Trivial mint-made alloy spots are noted on at 5 o'clock on the obverse and at 10:30 on the reverse. Encapsulated in an old green label holder. (#7443)

2110 **1903 Louisiana Purchase/McKinley MS62 PCGS.** Highly attractive for the MS62 level, with lime borders and apricot centers. Well struck save for the reverse denticles between 5 and 8 o'clock. Certified in a green label holder. (#7444)

2111 **1903 Louisiana Purchase/McKinley MS64 PCGS.** Well struck with bright luster and appealing apricot-gold coloration. A mild orange-peel texture (as struck) is observed near the obverse and reverse peripheries. A die crack extends from the reverse rim near 9 o'clock along the left side of the second I in LOUISIANA. A carefully preserved near-Gem that is blemish-free. (#7444)

Exemplary MS66 1903 Louisiana Purchase/McKinley Dollar

2112 **1903 Louisiana Purchase/McKinley MS66 PCGS.** This predominantly yellow-gold Premium Gem nonetheless has infrequent dashes of golden-brown and steel-blue. The preservation is exemplary, and both sides demonstrate potent cartwheel luster. Well struck aside from the HA in PURCHASE, which is opposite the high-relief shoulder. Struck in equal quantities to the Louisiana Purchase-Jefferson gold dollar commemorative. (#7444)

Premium Gem 1903 McKinley Gold Dollar

2113 **1903 Louisiana Purchase/McKinley MS66 PCGS.** Both sides of this Premium Gem Louisiana Purchase/McKinley commemorative are awash in bright luster covered in yellow-gold patination that is imbued with tinges of light green and orange. The design features are well brought up throughout, and just a few inoffensive luster grazes preclude a higher grade. A short die crack is visible near the rim at 9 o'clock on the reverse. (#7444)

Frosty 1903 McKinley Gold Dollar, MS66

2114 **1903 Louisiana Purchase/McKinley MS66 PCGS.** This frosty Premium Gem has fully brilliant and lustrous yellow-gold surfaces with a halo of reflectivity around McKinley's portrait. Traces of orange accents are evident, mostly on the reverse. The surfaces are exceptional and virtually perfect. Only slight peripheral weakness keeps this from a higher grade. (#7444)

Lustrous 1903 McKinley Gold Dollar, MS66

2115 **1903 Louisiana Purchase/McKinley MS66 PCGS.** A sharp strike and brilliant yellow-gold luster characterize this frosty Premium Gem. Both sides have pristine, essentially unblemished surfaces that are free of spots. This is an exceptional piece that will please the fastidious collector or connoisseur. (#7444)

MS66 Louisiana Purchase/McKinley Gold Dollar

2116 **1903 Louisiana Purchase/McKinley MS66 PCGS.** Struck from slightly worn dies, each side shows evidence of metal flow around the margins and there is a die crack on the reverse at 2 o'clock. The rich mint luster is uninterrupted by the small marks that usually accompany these gold coins. An interesting, high grade McKinley gold dollar. (#7444)

Beautiful Superb Gem 1903 McKinley Dollar

2117 **1903 Louisiana Purchase/McKinley MS67 PCGS.** Dashes of peach endow this predominantly lime-green Superb Gem. Virtually mark-free, and the cartwheel luster is spectacular. The legends and devices are exquisitely struck, while the lower reverse dentils show some softness. President McKinley sanctioned the Louisiana Purchase Exposition, but it was his assassination in 1901 that led to his appearance on one of the two gold dollar types. (#7444)

2118 **1904 Lewis and Clark AU58 NGC.** The borders are lustrous, and the lightly abraded fields and portraits exhibit only a whisper of friction. The only two-headed commemorative type. (#7447)

Lovely Choice 1904 Lewis and Clark Dollar

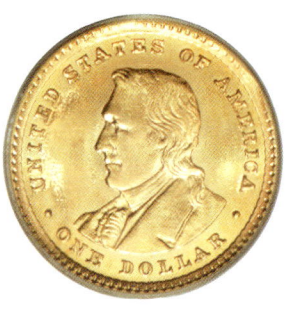

2119 **1904 Lewis and Clark MS64 PCGS.** The luster of this near-Gem representative is more vibrant than usual, particularly near the legends, which have uncommonly strong flash. The yellow-gold surfaces, varied by glints of orange, have few flaws of any note, and the overall detail on the portraits is pleasing. Significant die erosion noted at the margins suggests that the coin was minted late in the production run. (#7447)

2120 **1904 Lewis and Clark MS63 Prooflike NGC.** Mirrored fields confirm the NGC designation, and are unusual for this issue. A well struck piece with a few faint field hairlines only visible beneath a loupe. Census: 6 in 63 Prooflike, 3 finer (5/07).
From The Vanek Collection. (#77447)

2121 **1905 Lewis and Clark MS62 PCGS.** A well struck yellow-orange representative of this second-year issue, the first of only two instances where a gold commemorative design carried over to a second year. Light, scattered marks that appear on the lustrous surfaces account for the grade. (#7448)

2122 **1905 Lewis and Clark MS62 PCGS.** This issue is generally considered to be the scarcest of all commemorative gold dollars. It is a pleasing, sharply struck example with yellow-gold surfaces and mirrored fields. (#7448)

Gorgeous 1905 Lewis and Clark Select Gold Dollar

2123 **1905 Lewis and Clark MS63 PCGS.** Gorgeous orange-gold patination, imbued with faint hints of light green, lavender, and light blue, runs over highly lustrous surfaces. The strike is impressive, resulting in rather sharp definition on the design elements, including excellent definition in the hair strands on both portraits. Many examples have been cleaned or otherwise mishandled in some way, making original, undamaged pieces numismatic prizes. (#7448)

Lustrous and Sharp 1917 McKinley Dollar, MS66

2143 **1917 McKinley MS66 PCGS.** Attractive sea-green and rose toning increases the eye appeal of this lustrous and reasonably struck Premium Gem. Immaculate aside from a solitary, hair-thin mark on the left obverse field. Type collectors were satisfied with their 1916 McKinley dollars, which led to a lower net mintage for the 1917. (#7455)

2144 **1922 Grant no Star—Cleaned—ANACS. AU58 Details.** Rather attractive yellow-gold surfaces display traces of luster in the recesses of this Grant no Star gold dollar. The design elements are well defined, and aside from some light hairlines visible under magnification, both sides are devoid of significant marks. In a May 26, 1997 article in *Coin World*, Paul Gilkes wrote that: "While the 1922 Grant ... gold dollars ... were received less than enthusiastically by numismatists and the general public upon their release, the ... coins today ... are highly sought by collectors." (#7458)

2145 **1922 Grant no Star MS62 NGC.** Light yellow-gold with brilliant surfaces showing a hint of green patina. This is a pleasing example, sharply struck, and fully lustrous. (#7458)

Satiny Near-Gem 1922 Grant No Star Dollar

2146 **1922 Grant no Star MS64 PCGS.** The satiny surfaces of this near-Gem have exceptional luster with rich orange-gold color. Both sides are sharply detailed and fully brilliant. Two varieties of the Grant half dollars and gold dollars were coined, each denomination having Star and No Star variations. (#7458)

Gem No Star 1922 Grant Dollar

2147 **1922 Grant No Star MS65 PCGS.** Predominantly sun-gold, although a glimpse of sky-blue is seen on the obverse at 4 o'clock, and the reverse shows an occasional hint of lilac. The strike is penetrating except for the unavoidable incompleteness on the tree trunk near the window. Encapsulated in a green label holder. (#7458)

Wonderful Gem 1922 Grant No Star Dollar

2148 **1922 Grant no Star MS65 NGC.** This is a wonderful Gem with frosty yellow-gold luster that is accented by light orange toning on both sides. It is sharply defined with surfaces that have only the slightest marks or imperfections. Prominent die polishing lines in the obverse field are a common characteristic of the Grant gold dollars and the similarly designed half dollars. (#7458)

Vibrant 1922 Grant No Star Dollar, MS67

2149 **1922 Grant no Star MS67 PCGS.** Bowers (1991) mentions that nearly all of the original mintage of Grant gold dollars (both with and without star) still exists. Despite the availability of Choice and even Gem examples, for the No Star variety, MS67 coins, such as the one in this lot, remain elusive. The strongly lustrous surfaces exhibit rich peach-gold and mint-green patination and are impeccably preserved. Sharp definition is noted on the design elements. Tied for the finest certified by PCGS (5/07). (#7458)

Appealing Grant With Star Gold Dollar, MS66

2150 **1922 Grant with Star MS66 NGC.** The appealing surfaces are interestingly patinated in a lighter gold color than normally seen on these pieces, almost a silver-gold hue. Gorgeous luster sweeps both sides of this satiny piece, and singular abrasions are expectedly nil. The concept of stockkeeping units might not have existed at the time, but marketing was alive and well when the Grant with Star gold dollars and silver half dollars were created. (#7459)

1922 Grant With Star Gold Dollar, MS66 PCGS

2151 **1922 Grant with Star MS66 PCGS.** This Premium Gem is awash with blazing luster over orange-gold surfaces. Well struck and free of distractions, save for a couple of minor copper spots that are discernible only with the aid of magnification, this example is a delight to behold. Housed in an older generation PCGS holder. (#7459)

Alluring 1922 Grant With Star Gold Dollar MS67

2152 **1922 Grant with Star MS67 PCGS.** Careful examination of this highly lustrous example shows that the surfaces are virtually pristine on both sides. A faint mark between Grant's ear and collar is the only exception. The pleasing lime-gold coloration is imbued with accents of rose near the centers. The overall eye appeal of the piece is considerable. (#7459)

Splendid 1922 Grant With Star Gold Dollar, MS67

2153 **1922 Grant with Star MS67 PCGS.** Paul Gilkes, in a May 26, 1997 *Coin World* article, cites commemorative books by Anthony Swiatek and David Bowers, in saying that: " ... there appears to have been no special reason to place the star on the coin other than to appease the Grant Centenary Memorial Commission. It seems the Commission was hoping to reap additional profits to have a special mark on their coins like the Alabama and Missouri commemoratives ... ." The current Superb gem displays dazzling luster emanating from orange-gold surfaces that are immaculately preserved. A powerful strike brings out excellent definition on the motifs. (#7459)

2154 **1926 Sesquicentennial MS63 NGC.** Glowing luster emanates from the peach-gold surfaces of this Select two and a half dollar gold commemorative. An attentive strike bring out excellent definition on the design features, with no areas revealing hints of weakness. A couple of small milling marks above Liberty's right (left facing) shoulder apparently prevent a higher grade. These should not intimidate, as they do not detract from the coin's overall appeal. (#7466)

2155 **1926 Sesquicentennial MS64 PCGS.** Boldly struck and highly lustrous, with minimally disturbed surfaces that are fully brilliant. A pleasing near-Gem representative of this classic gold commemorative, struck to help celebrate the 150th anniversary of American independence. (#7466)

2156 **1926 Sesquicentennial MS64 PCGS.** Lustrous, as always, with no mentionable marks on either side. There is a curious feature on this piece that we have not noticed on other examples: The peripheral lettering was apparently punched into the die with too much force, creating an extra outline around each letter. (#7466)

2157 **1926 Sesquicentennial MS64 PCGS.** Boldly struck with shimmering luster and lovely uniform orange-gold color. A handful of obverse marks prevent a higher grade. From a mintage of 46,019 pieces. Liberty holds a scroll representing the Declaration of Independence, and the Philadelphia Independence Hall is depicted on the reverse. (#7466)

2158 **1926 Sesquicentennial MS64 PCGS.** This highly lustrous example displays shimmering luster and essentially untoned surfaces. A tiny mark is noted on Liberty's chin. Struck to commemorate the 150th anniversary of the United States. (#7466)

2159 **1926 Sesquicentennial MS64 PCGS.** Strongly lustrous peach-gold surfaces add to the eye appeal of this near-Gem. A couple of tiny marks are noted in the right reverse field, and a small dark-colored spot is seen to the left of the torch on the obverse. Challenging any finer. (#7466)

2160 **1926 Sesquicentennial MS64 PCGS.** The lustrous copper-gold surfaces are graced with hints of hazel-gray near the peripheries. Despite excellent eye appeal, this well struck example shows a few too many marks to reach the elusive Gem status. (#7466)

2161 **1926 Sesquicentennial MS64 PCGS.** A touch of orange enhances the shining yellow-gold surfaces of this appealing near-Gem. A well-defined example of this final gold classic commemorative issue, one that displays just a few too many marks for a finer grade. (#7466)

2162 **1926 Sesquicentennial MS64 PCGS.** This is a delightful representative of the commemorative quarter eagle produced in connection with the Sesquicentennial Celebration held in Philadelphia during the year. It has brilliant and frosty yellow-gold luster with exceptional surfaces for the grade. (#7466)

2163 **1926 Sesquicentennial MS64 NGC.** Both sides have excellent surfaces with only a few scattered marks that one would expect for the grade. This pleasing near-Gem specimen has frosty yellow-gold luster and sharp design definition. (#7466)

Flashy Gem Sesquicentennial Two and a Half

2164 **1926 Sesquicentennial MS65 PCGS.** Gem Sesquicentennials are a mainstay of the gold commemorative set, and in MS65 they are the highest-graded pieces readily obtainable by most collectors, as the certified population in MS66, the next grade level, decreases by an order of magnitude. The present Gem boasts flashy orange-gold surfaces tinged with hazel that are much better struck on the highpoints of this difficult low-relief design than usually seen. A nice coin for the grade and the type. (#7466)

MODERN ISSUES

2165 **1988-W Olympic Gold Five Dollar PR70 Deep Cameo PCGS.** A spectacular specimen that has a needle-sharp strike and unperturbed glassy fields. The 1988 Olympics were held in South Korea. Population: 28 in 70 (4/07). (#9671)

2166 **1993-W Bill of Rights Gold Five Dollar PR70 Deep Cameo PCGS.** This prominently mirrored representative has an intricate strike and a tiny tick above the A in LOYALTY. Scott R. Blazek designed the obverse, featuring Madison inspecting his remarkably influential document. Population: 27 in 70 (4/07). (#9673)

2167 **1991-1995-W World War II Gold Five Dollar MS70 PCGS.** A fully struck gold commemorative with subtle peripheral orange toning. The reverse design features Morse code for the letter V, signifying victory in the wars against Germany and Japan. (#9678)

2168 **1995-W Olympic/Torch Runner Gold Five Dollar MS70 PCGS.** The five dollar gold commemoratives of the 1996 Olympic games all have low mintages, particularly for the Uncirculated finish issues. This is a perfect straw-gold example with seamless satin surfaces. (#9732)

2169 **1995-W Olympic/Stadium Gold Five Dollar PR70 Deep Cameo PCGS.** Cherry-red and honey tints enrich the borders of this fully struck and pristine specimen. An undipped example of this attractive Olympic issue. Population: 27 in 70 (4/07). (#9735)

Near-Perfect 1997-W Jackie Robinson Five Dollar Gold, MS69

2170 **1997-W Jackie Robinson Gold Five Dollar MS69 PCGS.** This modern commemorative issue is notable for its tiny mintage of just 5,174 pieces. The example offered here displays rich orange-gold color with a blush of peach at the margins, though the centers are wheat-gold, which gives the boldly impressed coin a distinctive appearance. A tiny flaw to the left of the C in COURAGE on the reverse bars the way to a perfect grade. (#9759)

Unsurpassable Jackie Robinson Five Dollar Gold, PR70 Deep Cameo

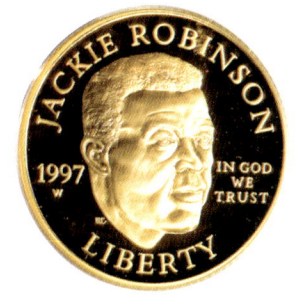

2171 **1997-W Jackie Robinson Gold Five Dollar PR70 Deep Cameo PCGS.** Like most issues, the Jackie Robinson five dollar gold design has a substantially higher mintage for the proof format compared with the standard finish. Still, the net production for proofs amounted to fewer than 25,000 pieces. This vibrant yellow-gold example has excellent contrast, particularly evident on the baseball-themed reverse, and the mirrors are fathomless. Technically perfect with stunning visual appeal. (#9760)

2172 **1997-W Franklin D. Roosevelt Gold Five Dollar PR70 Deep Cameo PCGS.** This low mintage issue features President Roosevelt in a oversized boating jacket. The 1933 date on the reverse refers to his inauguration, rather than the notorious gold recall of the same year. A pristine piece with rich peach-gold and mauve toning. Population: 20 in 70 (4/07). (#9749)

2173 **1999-W Washington Gold Five Dollar PR70 Deep Cameo PCGS.** Laura Gardin Fraser's designs for the 1932 Washington quarter were instead implemented decades later on the Washington death bicentennial half eagle. Radiant yellow-gold devices rise above the perfectly smooth, darkly mirrored fields. Population: 28 in 70 (4/07). (#99777)

2174 **1999-W Washington Gold Five Dollar PR70 Ultra Cameo NGC.** A technically perfect representative of this Laura Gardin Fraser design, a distinctive and unexpected last bow for a design created over six decades ago. The richly frosted devices offer bold contrast with the fathomless yellow-gold fields. (#99777)

2175 **2000-W Library of Congress Bimetallic Ten Dollars MS69 PCGS.** A virtually perfect example of the strikingly beautiful bimetallic Library of Congress gold piece. Both sides are fully brilliant with satin luster. (#9784)

Impeccable 2000-W Library of Congress Ten Dollar Piece, MS70

2176 **2000-W Library of Congress Bimetallic Ten Dollars MS70 PCGS.** A flawless representative of the nation's first and only bimetallic commemorative issue, also the first to incorporate platinum as a coinage metal. Precisely detailed with wonderful contrast between the butter-yellow outer ring of gold and the satiny surfaces of the inner ring of platinum. One of the most elusive modern commemoratives, with just 7,261 pieces struck. (#9784)

2177 **2000-W Library of Congress Bimetallic Ten Dollars PR70 Deep Cameo NGC.** A gleaming, flawless, and deeply reflective specimen of this distinctive commemorative, the nation's only bimetallic commemorative to date. Both the outer ring of gold and the inner ring of platinum show stellar contrast. (#99784)

2178 **2001-W Capitol Visitor's Center Half Eagle MS69 PCGS.** An essentially perfect example of this modern commemorative gold piece, struck in satiny yellow-gold. (#9792)

2179 **2001-W Capitol Visitor's Center Half Eagle MS70 PCGS.** The Capitol Visitor's Center program had little national appeal. The Uncirculated finish mintage of 6,761 pieces ranks among the lowest of any modern commemorative issue. Those who ordered are now glad they did, since prices have climbed in recent years. Silky luster sweeps the immaculate, fully struck surfaces. (#9792)

2180 **2001-W Capitol Visitor's Center Half Eagle PR70 Deep Cameo PCGS.** Deep proof fields with thick mint frost over the devices. A gorgeous example of this widely sought low mintage issue. Population: 43 in 70 (4/07). (#99792)

2181 **2002-P Olympics Silver Dollar PR70 Deep Cameo PCGS.** The vast expanses of mirror-finish silver surfaces show bottomless reflectivity, while the textured devices show rich, delightful frost. A crisply struck and perfect proof that offers impressive visual appeal. (#99798)

MODERN BULLION COINS

2182 **1986-S Silver Eagle PR70 Ultra Cameo NGC.** Brilliant save for an obverse glimpse of rose-red near 5 o'clock. A fully struck and gorgeously smooth specimen from the introductory year of the silver eagle. (#9802)

2183 **1992-W One-Ounce Gold Eagle PR70 Ultra Cameo NGC.** Unimprovable contrast exists between the yellow-gold devices and the deeply mirrored fields. Although the holder has a few hair-thin marks, the coin itself is flawless. (#9865)

2184 **10th Anniversary Set Proof Bullion Coins PR67 Cameo Uncertified.** All five pieces reside in the lovely red velvet presentation case and red cardboard box of mint issue with certificate of authenticity enclosed. The set includes: **1995-W One-Tenth Ounce Gold Eagle PR67 Cameo Uncertified; 1995-W One-Quarter Ounce Gold Eagle PR67 Cameo Uncertified; 1995-W One-Half Ounce Gold Eagle PR67 Cameo Uncertified; 1995-W One Ounce Gold Eagle PR67 Cameo Uncertified; and a 1995-W American Eagle Silver Dollar PR67 Deep Cameo Uncertified.** (Total: 5 coins) (#9887)

2185 **1995-W Silver Eagle PR69 Deep Cameo PCGS.** Outstanding white-on-black contrast ensures the exemplary eye appeal of this brilliant and flawless modern rarity. The 1995-W, with its paltry 30,125-piece mintage, remains the uncontested key to the silver American Eagle series. (#9887)

2186 **An Uncertified 1995-W 10th Anniversary American Eagle Proof Set.** This set includes the key 1995-W proof American Eagle in silver, as well as the tenth-ounce, quarter-ounce, half-ounce, and one-ounce proof gold eagles. All five pieces approach technical perfection.. The certificate of authenticity, maroon box, and presentation case of mint issue accompany the lot.. (#9887)

2187 **An Uncertified 1995-W 10th Anniversary American Eagle Proof Set.** This set contains the key date of the silver eagle series, the proof 1995-W. Also included are the tenth-ounce, quarter-ounce, half-ounce, and one-ounce proof gold eagles. All five pieces are practically immaculate, and grade PR69 Deep Cameo. The certificate of authenticity, maroon box, and presentation case of mint issue accompany. (Total: 5 coins) (#9887)

2188 **An Uncertified 1995-W 10th Anniversary American Eagle Proof Set.** The set with the famous 1995-W proof silver eagle. Also included are the tenth-ounce, quarter-ounce, half-ounce, and one-ounce proof gold eagles. The individual pieces are beautifully preserved, and grade PR69 Deep Cameo. The lightly handled maroon box and presentation case of issue accompany. The COA is included. (Total: 5 coins) (#9887)

2189 **2006-P Silver Eagle Reverse Proof PR70 PCGS.** A technically perfect and absolutely untoned representative of this distinctive silver American Eagle issue, powerfully defined with gleaming devices and finely granular fields. Striking and appealing. (#799977)

2190 **2006-P Silver Eagle Reverse Proof PR70 NGC.** An utterly unimprovable representative of this fascinating modern issue, vibrant and stunning with brilliant and boldly impressed devices and flawless frost on the fields. A desirable and distinguished American Eagle. (#799977)

2191 **Uncertified 2006 One-Ounce Gold Eagle Set.** This is a beautiful set of three one-ounce American Eagle gold coins. One of the pieces is in Mint State, one is a regular proof striking, and the third is a "reverse" proof—with the mirror-like polished finish applied to the devices rather than the fields. According to the US Mint's website: "Sales of the American Eagle 20th Anniversary Gold Coin Set quickly reached its product limit of 10,000 and the set is no longer available." All three coins are dated 2006 and bear the "W" mintmark of the West Point Mint. They are stored in a lovely black hard plastic box which itself resides in an attractive cardboard holder that is gold in color. (Total: 3 coins)

2192 **2006-W One Ounce Gold Eagle Reverse Proof PR69 PCGS.** An outstanding example of a "black-on-gold" appearance, with the boldly defined design features having a brilliant finish that contrasts with satiny fields. Virtually pristine surfaces are noted on both sides. (#89994)

COINS OF HAWAII

2193 **1883 Hawaii Quarter MS65 PCGS.** Mottled golden-brown and navy-blue endow this lustrous and intricately struck example. Neither side has any individually mentionable marks. (#10987)

Premium Gem 1883 Hawaiian Quarter

2194 **1883 Hawaii Quarter MS66 PCGS.** The Hawaiian quarter is more properly known as the "hapaha," the Hawaiian equivalent for the denomination. This piece is a wonderful Premium Gem with frosty silver luster and fully brilliant white surfaces, save for a thin crescent of pale gold toning along the lower reverse border. Population: 69 in 66, 9 finer (6/07). (#10987)

Splendid 1883 Hawaiian Quarter, MS66

2195 **1883 Hawaii Quarter MS66 PCGS.** This is an attractive Premium Gem with brilliant satin luster and full design features. The surfaces are pristine with few marks of any kind on either side. Although not the finest certified, it ranks high in the current population reports. Population: 69 in 66, 9 finer (6/07). (#10987)

2196 **1871 Hawaii Wailuku Token—Scratched—NCS. VF Details.** Medcalf 2TE-2, incorrectly designated as TE-1A by NCS. The strike favors HI, the starfish, and the date, but portions of the design are softly defined. Generally golden-brown with minor gray buildup in protected areas. The reverse field has numerous thin, faded marks. (#600503)

ERRORS

2197 **(1858) Small Letters Flying Eagle Cent—85% Off Center—AU58 PCGS.** Struck far off center toward 6 o'clock. The obverse displays the partial legend ATES O. The reverse shows the ribbon ends of the wreath. The small letters in TES confirm the date as 1858, since the 1856 and 1857 issues are from Large Letters hubs. The unstruck portion of the obverse has a small edge mark.
From The Vanek Collection.

Double Struck, Second Strike 85% Off Center 1899 Cent AU58

2198 **1899 Indian Cent—Double Struck, Second Strike 85% Off Center—AU58 NGC.** The second strike is off center toward 6 o'clock, and is located at 12 o'clock relative to the first strike. The first strike is normal, the second strike is uniface. Remarkably, the second strike has a nearly complete date. This chocolate-brown piece appears Mint State aside from faint wear on the wreath ribbon, but has minor build-up near design recesses, and the cheek is moderately abraded.

60% Off Center 1917-S Cent AU55

2199 **1917-S Lincoln Cent—60% Off Center—AU55 PCGS.** Struck widely off center toward 3 o'clock. The date and mintmark are fully intact, but LIBERTY and IN GOD WE are off the flan. This golden-brown mint error has a diagonal mark on the unstruck portion of the obverse, but the struck areas are pleasing.
From The Vanek Collection.

1998 Cent on a Struck 1998-P Dime MS66

2200 **1998 Lincoln Cent—Double Denomination, On Struck Dime—MS66 PCGS.** The 98 in the cent date is bold, as is the Philadelphia mintmark from the dime. The upper half of the dime date is clear, just enough to identify the date as 1998. Roosevelt looks down relative to the portrait of Lincoln. The flame of the torch is faintly apparent on the upper right corner of the memorial. Lustrous with light gold toning.
From The Vanek Collection.

Gem 1999-D Cent Struck on a 1999-D Dime

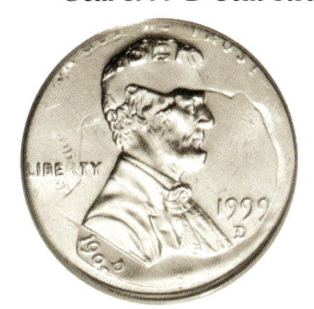

2201 **1999-D Lincoln Cent—Double Denomination, Overstruck on a 1999-D Dime—MS65 PCGS.** Both dates and mintmarks are bold. Roosevelt gazes north relative to the portrait of Lincoln. Well struck for the amount of metal present with a touch of lemon-gold color in the fields and small flecks of deeper color at the reverse rim.

10% Off Center MS66 1937 Buffalo Nickel

2202 **1937 Buffalo Nickel—10% Off Center—MS66 PCGS.** Moderately off center toward 11 o'clock, with a broad area of unstruck surface opposite near 5 o'clock. The strike is razor-sharp in the centers, since the collar die was not present to limit the approach of the obverse and reverse dies. The bison's tail is stretched due to collar-unrestrained metal flow. Lustrous and nearly untoned with a few inconsequential gray flecks.
From The Vanek Collection.

1977 Nickel on a Struck Cent MS65

2203 **1977 Jefferson Nickel—Struck on 1977 Cent—MS65 Red and Brown NGC.** A lustrous orange-red double denomination error. The NGC insert states the host cent is dated 1977, but there is no trace of the cent date. LIBERTY is prominent in the left obverse field, and Lincoln's profile is noticeable within Jefferson's hair. The panes of the Lincoln Memorial overlap Monticello, with the statue of Lincoln above the steps.

10% Off Center 1921 Mercury Dime AU55

2204 **1921 Mercury Dime—10% Off Center—AU55 PCGS.** Any off center Mercury dime would be of interest, but this is a 1921, a semikey with the lowest Philadelphia Mint emission. Certainly a stopper in an off-center date collection. Moderately off center toward 5 o'clock. The lower obverse has several thin marks, particularly near the rim. Struck from boldly clashed dies.
From The Vanek Collection.

2205 **2005-P Kennedy Half—Reverse Rim Burr at 1 O'clock—MS67 Satin Finish NGC.** The rim burr appears as a small piece of missing metal with the underlying copper exposed.

5% Off Center AU55 1921-S Morgan Dollar

2206 **1921-S Morgan Dollar—Struck 5% Off Center—AU55 PCGS.** Off center toward 6 o'clock, but the date is complete, as is the mintmark. A relatively broad area of unstruck surface is present near 12 o'clock. The devices show slight friction. The strike is unusually sharp for a '21-S, since the collar die was absent, allowing the obverse and reverse dies to further approach.
From The Vanek Collection.

Double Struck, 90% Off Center 1921-S Morgan AU58

2207 **1921-S Morgan Dollar—Double Struck, Second Strike 90% Off Center—AU58 PCGS.** The first strike was normal, but the piece failed to fully eject from the dies, and was struck a second time 90% off center toward 6 o'clock. The second strike is at 6 o'clock relative to the first strike, but the top of the date is apparent, and its status as a 1921-S is confirmed by the minute mintmark and spade-shaped eagle's breast. No additional planchet was fed in between the two strikes. A satiny cream-gray silver dollar with a typical strike and a mere whisper of highpoint friction.
From The Vanek Collection.

2208 **Undated Eisenhower Dollar Type One Planchet NGC.** 22.5 gm. The rims are not raised on this Type One planchet, since it never made a pass through the upset mill. Faint powder-blue, gold, and tan toning. One side of the planchet has several light to moderate pinscratches.

3% Off Center Choice AU 1912 Quarter Eagle

2209 **1912 Indian Quarter Eagle—Struck 3% Off Center—AU55 PCGS.** Moderately off center toward 11 o'clock, which takes portions of LIBERTY and DOLLARS off the flan. A radiant yellow-gold example with minimal wear and good eye appeal. Off center gold coins are rarely encountered, and are usually absent from off center type collections.
From The Vanek Collection.

2210 **1999-W Quarter-Ounce Gold Eagle—Struck With Unfinished Proof Dies—MS69 PCGS.** In 1999, the gold and platinum bullion coins were all struck at the West Point Mint, but the W mintmark was only supposed to appear on proofs. Yet a relatively small number of mintmarked tenth-ounce and quarter-ounce pieces emerged with satiny fields and unfrosted motifs, a Mint mix-up in die distribution probably caused by high Y2K demand. An essentially pristine honey-gold example.
From The Vanek Collection. (#99942)

MISCELLANEOUS

2211 **Uncertified Cent Planchet Strip.** Zinc cent planchet strip, 176 x 96 mm. There are 35 complete and 10 incomplete holes punched into the strip.

PROOF SETS

2212 **1950 Proof Set PR65 to PR67 Uncertified.** A nearly untoned and high grade example of this scarce, low mintage proof set. The set is contained within the cellophane wrappers and cardboard box of its initial issue. (Total: 10 coins)

2213 **1951 and 1952 Proof Sets PR65 to PR67 Uncertified.** Both sets are in the original cellophane wrappers and cardboard boxes of Mint issue. A lightly toned and beautifully preserved grouping. (Total: 2 sets)

MINT SETS

2214 **Uncertified 1947 Double Mint Set.** Most pieces grade MS64 to MS66, although the 1947-D halves and a 1947-D quarter are abraded. The coins remain within their mint-issued cardboard holders, and the silver coins are lightly to moderately toned. No 1947-S Walking Liberty halves were struck. (Total: 28 coins)

2215 **Uncertified 1952 Double Mint Set.** The coins grade between MS63 and MS66. The silver coins have various degrees of original and attractive toning. This set remains housed in the cardboard holders of Mint issue. (Total: 30 coins)

2216 **Uncertified Mint Set Lot with (3) 1954 Mint Sets and a 1957 Mint Set.** All are housed in the original government cardboard holders of issue. Many of the coins are colorfully toned from years of storage in the containers. The coins grade between MS61 and MS66, with the 1957 set particularly nice. Two mailing envelopes are included, postmarked May 2, 1955, and Feb. 6, 1958. (Total: 110 coins)

ADDITIONAL CERTIFIED COINS

2217 **1883 MS65 Paramount International (MS63),** a sharply struck and lustrous Select Mint State survivor with attractive peripheral toning on both sides; **1887 MS65 Paramount International (MS63),** great cartwheel luster with a brilliant reverse and lovely peripheral toning on the obverse; **1889 MS65 Paramount International (MS63),** well struck with bright satiny luster and relatively few surface marks; **1890 MS65 Paramount International (MS63),** well struck with intense mint luster and typical marks for the grade; and an **1891 MS65 Paramount International (MS63),** an attractive Select Mint State example without the Spitting Eagle. All five pieces are Ex: Redfield, and housed in red holders. (Total: 5 coins)

2218 **1892-CC MS65 Paramount International (MS63).** Ex: Redfield. A frosty Select representative of this later Carson City dollar issue, solidly struck with soft, attractive blue-gray and gold patina over the peripheries. The centers remain largely untoned on this lightly abraded piece. (#7214)

Shining 1893-CC Dollar, MS62

2219 **1893-CC MS65 Paramount International (MS62).** Ex: Redfield. Coinage at the Carson City Mint ceased abruptly in 1893, and that facility had struck just 677,000 dollars for the year before its shutdown. This sharply struck, highly lustrous example is a pleasing, unworn survivor. The obverse periphery has a band of golden-tan color, while the reverse is essentially brilliant. Light to moderate abrasions are present on the cheek, though the fields and reverse are comparatively clean. (#7222)

Toned Select 1896-S Morgan Dollar

2220 **1896-S MS65 Paramount International (MS63).** Ex: Redfield. A solidly struck example of this late 19th century S-mint issue, elusive in Mint State despite a mintage of 5 million pieces. The centers are essentially brilliant, while the margins have an appealing blend of violet and peach colors. Light, scattered abrasions on each side account for the grade. (#7244)

GSA DOLLARS

Elusive 1879-CC GSA Dollar MS63

2221 **1879-CC MS63 NGC.** A brilliant and semi-prooflike representative of this desirable Carson City issue. A good strike with only a hint of incompleteness in the centers. The fields are well preserved, and the cheek has only a few minor grazes unable to challenge the Select designation. The box and certificate of issue are included. The certificate is serial #79000085. (#7086)

2222 **1880-CC 8 Over High 7 MS65 NGC.** VAM-5. A Top 100 Variety. The overdate feature and VAM are undesignated on the NGC label. Well struck for an '80-CC, which often has soft central details. Honey-gold toning dominates the upper left obverse quadrant. This lustrous example has a smooth reverse and an unabraded obverse field. (#7102)

2223 **1883-CC MS66 NGC.** VAM-4. The date appears repunched. Pervasive luster sweeps the gorgeously smooth surfaces of this nicely struck Premium Gem. Both sides have only a whisper of almond-gold patina. (#7144)

2224 **1885-CC MS65 NGC.** Delicate tan toning invigorates this lustrous and assertively struck GSA dollar. The obverse field is well preserved, and the cheek has only minor marks. The lowest mintage Carson City Morgan. (#7160)

INGOTS

22-Ounce 1956 San Francisco Mint Silver Ingot

2225 1956 San Francisco Mint Silver Ingot. A silver slab of considerable size and heft. The top side has the oval imprint of the San Francisco Mint, followed by 1272 on the next line, then 22.78 OZS, and 999.75 FINE on the lowest line. Batch number (?) 164 is imprinted on the short lower side. The back side has the circular imprint of the mint and the date 1956. A number of gas bubbles have left depressions on each side, but more naturally are on the back side.

2226 Bitron Gold Ingot Uncertified. This small, modern ingot is stamped BITRON/CRIPPLE CREEK/.999 FINE/ 1.072 TR OZ.

2227 Bitron Gold Ingot Uncertified. Another small ingot of modern manufacture. This one is stamped on the top side: BITRON/CRIPPLE CREEK/.999 FINE/1.365 TR OZ. Bright yellow-gold color on this piece, as with all five of these.

2228 Bitron Gold Ingot Uncertified. A third small ingot from this modern Colorado gold producer. This one is stamped: BITRON/CRIPPLE CREEK/.999 FINE/1.219 TR OZ. Again, bright yellow-gold color overall, but here seen with a slight reddish cast in the recesses of the lettering.

2229 Bitron Gold Ingot Uncertified. A smooth, well cast ingot. The top side reads: BITRON/CRIPPLE CREEK/.999 FINE/ 1.616 TR OZ.

2230 Bitron Gold Ingot Uncertified. The largest ingot from this consignment of Bitron ingots. The top face reads: BITRON/CRIPPLE CREEK/.999 FINE/2.101 TR OZ.

End Of Session Three

SESSION FOUR

Live, Internet, and Mail Bid Signature Auction #442
Friday, July 13, 2007, 6:30 PM ET, Lots 2231-3362
West Palm Beach, Florida

A 15% Buyer's Premium ($9 minimum) Will Be Added To All Lots

Visit HA.com to view full-color images and bid.

PATTERNS

Choice Proof 1838 Half Dollar, Judd-72

2231 1838 Half Dollar, Judd-72, Pollock-75, R.5, PR64 PCGS. A large bust of Liberty faces left, with stars and the date at the margins. The reverse features an eagle with spread wings. For many decades, the obverse design was attributed to William Kneass, but Gobrecht was almost certainly the engraver, as the portrait bears close resemblance to his 1838 to 1840 issued gold designs. Struck in silver with a reeded edge and medal turn. Plum-red, electric-blue, and sea-green toning endows this nicely struck near-Gem. The left obverse has a few thin toning streaks, but marks are nearly absent. Housed in an old green label holder. Population: 6 in 64, 3 finer (5/07). (#11282)

Choice Judd-72 1838 Half Dollar

2232 1838 Half Dollar, Judd-72, Pollock-75, R.5, PR64 PCGS. Gobrecht's large head of Liberty faces left. On the reverse, a perched eagle with unfurled wings looks to its right. Struck in silver with a reeded edge. The reflective golden-brown fields are bounded by ruby-red and ocean-blue margins. A well preserved beauty with traces of striking incompleteness near the centers. Certified in an old green label holder. Population: 6 in 64, 3 finer (5/07). (#11282)

Beautiful Radiant Cap 1850 Three Cent Silver Pattern Silver Striking, Judd-125

2233 1850 Three Cent Silver, Judd-125 Original, Pollock-147, R.4, PR66 NGC. Similar in design to the famous Judd-67 gold dollar pattern from 1836; however, the date has been moved to the obverse below the cap, and the denomination within the palm frond is expressed with a large Roman numeral III. Struck in silver with a plain edge. This outstanding representative is by far the nicest we have handled. Bright, noticeably striated surfaces are essentially untoned through the centers while displaying occasional russet and charcoal peripheral accents. (#11536)

Undated (1851) Ring Cent Pattern, Judd-127 Original, MS65

2234 1851 One Cent, Judd-127 Original, Pollock-149, Low R.6, MS65 PCGS. This annular pattern curiously omits the date. The obverse features CENT at the top and ONE TENTH SILVER at the bottom, while the reverse depicts a laurel wreath and the legend UNITED STATES OF AMERICA. Struck in billon (10% silver, 90% copper) with medal turn and a plain edge. The fields are noticeably striated and each side has gray-silver color with russet accents around the devices. A lovely, problem-free example. (#11543)

Undated (1851) Ring Cent Pattern, PR65
Judd-127

2235 **1851 One Cent, Judd-127 Original, Pollock-149, Low R.6, PR65 PCGS.** Struck on a perforated annular planchet. The obverse has CENT above and ONE TENTH SILVER below. The reverse shows a wreath of laurel around the second, larger ring with the legend UNITED STATES OF AMERICA outside. Struck in billon with a plain edge. An early attempt at a small cent coin, these pieces were made in response to Congressman Sam F. Vinton of the House Ways and Means Committee's bill that was drafted in 1849. Light gray patina overall with occasional patches of deeper gray. (#11545)

1852 Seated Dollar in Copper, Silver Plated, Judd-134

2236 **1852 Dollar, Judd-134, Pollock-161, R.7, Proof, Plated, NCS.** Die trials striking of the restrike 1852 Seated Dollar, struck in copper with a reeded edge and then silver plated. This is an important coin due to the rarity of the 1852 date (1,100 originals produced) in the regular issue Seated Dollar series. All design elements are sharply defined, and the surfaces display a bright, untoned sheen that is somewhat glossy. There are scattered hairlines, most notably on the reverse, with some of the underlying copper in evidence over a few of the raised features on that side. The first example of this rare and significant die trials striking that we have offered. (#11571)

Judd-211 1858 Cent Pattern, PR63

2237 **1858 Indian Cent, Judd-211, Pollock-255, 262, R.4, PR63 PCGS.** The obverse of this popular pattern displays James Longacre's Indian Head motif that appears on the production cent of 1859. The reverse shows a thick oak wreath not unlike that which the Mint would mate with a shield for its 1860 cent production. Struck in copper-nickel with a plain edge. Struck from the dies with the date centered, and as such is the more frequently encountered of the two date variants of this pattern. This is a sharply defined example that has olive-brown surfaces and light haziness overall. (#11893)

Select Proof 1858 Indian Cent, Judd-213

2238 **1858 Indian Cent, Judd-213, Pollock-258, R.5, PR63 PCGS.** The obverse is similar to the Indian cent issued in 1859, but the bust tip is broad rather than narrow. The reverse is identical to the issued 1858 Low Leaves Flying Eagle cent. Struck in copper-nickel with a plain edge. A well struck specimen with mildly mirrored fields and consistent almond-gold toning. Attractive for the designated grade. (#11897)

2239 **1859 Half Dollar, Judd-245, Pollock-301, Low R.6—Cleaned—ANACS. PR60 Details.** The obverse features the "French Head" of Liberty facing right. A large eagle with a heraldic shield dominates the reverse. The eagle clutches a ribbon in its beak, and the claws grasp an olive branch and three long arrows. The "Perfect Ribbon" subvariety, which Pollock listed as R.7. Struck in silver with a reeded edge. A well struck, untoned, and hairlined specimen. (#11988)

Bronzed 1862 Ten Dollar Pattern, PR65 Brown
Judd-298, Low Date

2240 **1862 Ten Dollar, Judd-298, Pollock-357, Low R.6, PR65 Brown PCGS.** The obverse is identical to the regular issue ten dollar dies for 1862. The reverse is similar to the adopted design, with the addition of the motto GOD OUR TRUST set in the field above the eagle. Struck in copper with a reeded edge. This Gem specimen has a subtle reddish tinge in the recesses and rather shallow reflective qualities, as usual, as these pieces were bronzed. This Judd number was struck from two different obverse dies, this piece was produced from the Low Date obverse die. (#60448)

1863 Two Cent Pattern, Judd-312, PR65 Brown

2241 **1863 Two Cents, Judd-312, Pollock-377, R.4, PR65 Brown PCGS.** The obverse is similar to the regular issue obverse of 1864, with GOD OUR TRUST on the ribbon above the shield. The reverse shows the denomination 2 CENTS sharply curved in a wreath with the legend UNITED STATES OF AMERICA around. Struck in bronze with a plain edge. A fairly common pattern; the USPatterns.com website notes that examples vary in weight from 76 to 101 grains. Crisply defined on each side, the surfaces are deep brown with a hazy overlay of gray-blue patina. (#60467)

Judd-356 1864 Cent, PR64, 10% Tin Alloy

2242 **1864 One Cent, Judd-356, Pollock-426, Low R.6, PR64 PCGS.** Struck from the same dies as the No L proof cents. Composed of 90% copper and 10% tin, according to the ninth edition of the Judd reference, with a plain edge. The fields are deeply mirrored with lovely iridescent red, brown, and cobalt-blue color on each side. A light scrape is seen near the center of the reverse, and there are a couple of thread-like depressions on the cheek of the Indian, these being the only mentionable defects on this lovely pattern. (#60524)

1864 With Motto Half Dollar Pattern, Judd-391, PR63

2243 **1864 Half Dollar, Judd-391, Pollock-459, Low R.7, PR63 PCGS.** Transitional striking for the half dollar. The obverse has the usually seen obverse, while the reverse has the With Motto reverse as adopted in 1866. Struck in silver with a reeded edge. These pieces are actually restrikes made circa 1869 and into the early 1870s. They were offered with restrikes of other denominations in complete sets. This is a deeply mirrored proof that shows an unacknowledged cameo contrast on each side. Pale rose toning is seen over both obverse and reverse. (#60562)

Judd-413 1865 Three Cent Nickel in Copper, PR62 Red and Brown

2244 **1865 Three Cents, Judd-413, Pollock-484, R.5, PR62 Red and Brown PCGS.** From regular issue dies, but struck in copper with a plain edge. Presumably struck to demonstrate the new designs prior to large-scale production of the series. A well struck and attractive specimen with rose-red and olive-brown toning. A small strike-through (as made) is noted near the nose. Housed in a green label holder. (#70594)

Rare and Popular 1866 Washington Five Cent Pattern Judd-481, PR65 Example

2245 **1866 Five Cents, Judd-481, Pollock-571, Low R.7, PR65 PCGS.** Five cent pattern with the head of Washington facing right. The reverse has a fancy numeral 5 in the center that is surrounded by a laurel wreath and UNITED STATES OF AMERICA at the margin. Struck in nickel with a plain edge. Both sides of this nearly spot-free representative are cloaked in dusky tan-gold patina. Judd-481 is the only collectible variety of the GOD AND OUR COUNTRY Washington type. Judd-480 through Judd-485 and the double-headed Judd-521 through Judd-524 share the same obverse die, but all are prohibitively rare aside from Judd-481, which is merely very rare. (#60677)

PR64 1867 Seated Quarter in Copper, Judd-590

2246 **1867 Quarter Dollar, Judd-590, Pollock-654, High R.7, PR64 Brown PCGS.** Struck from regular issue dies with a reeded edge, but in copper alloy. The obverse is cherry-red with glimpses of cobalt-blue, while the reverse is rose-red, olive-gold, and ocean-blue. A fully struck and unmarked near-Gem with minor gray debris near the date. (#60802)

Gem Cameo Judd-605 1868 Cent Pattern

2247 1868 One Cent, Judd-605, Pollock-670, R.5, PR65 Cameo PCGS. Diminutive pattern cent with an obverse similar to the adopted three cent nickel design, and a reverse with a large Roman numeral I in the center surrounded by a wreath. Part of the 8 in the date is buried in Liberty's lowest curl. Struck in nickel with a plain edge. An extraordinarily well preserved example of this popular pattern. Even though there is a slightly granular texture on each side, this does not hinder the bright reflectivity seen in the fields. The devices are noticeably frosted and provide a strong cameo contrast. At first one perceives this piece to be brilliant, but close examination reveals the presence of light streaky gray patina over each side. (#60817)

1869 Standard Silver Dime, Judd-708, PR64

2248 1869 Standard Silver Ten Cents, Judd-708, Pollock-787, R.5, PR64 PCGS. Liberty faces right and wears a band ornamented with a star. IN GOD WE TRUST is placed on a banner beneath the bust. On the reverse, an undersized wreath crowds the 10/CENTS denomination. The reverse periphery displays STANDARD SILVER and the date. Struck in silver with a reeded edge. An attractive example of this fairly common Standard Silver pattern. Both sides are enveloped with deep blue toning that shows a significant amount of rose color in the centers. (#60933)

Very Rare 1870 Standard Silver Quarter, Judd-903

2249 1870 Standard Silver Quarter Dollar, Judd-903, Pollock-1018, High R.7—Improperly Cleaned—NCS. Proof. The bust of Liberty faces right on the obverse with UNITED STATES OF AMERICA around and the motto IN GOD WE TRUST on a scroll below. Liberty's hair is tied in a bun. On the reverse, the denomination 25 CENTS and date 1870 are in a wreath of cotton and corn with the inscription STANDARD above. Struck in copper with a plain edge. This boldly struck example is recolored salmon-pink and sea-green, but is nonetheless mark-free and attractive. (#61147)

R.8 Judd-1000 1870 Standard Silver Dollar PR64

2250 1870 Standard Silver Dollar, Judd-1000, Pollock-1132, R.8, PR64 PCGS. William Barber's Seated Liberty design, interesting for its depiction of the Liberty pole, which appears to pierce her arm. The reverse depicts an agricultural wreath. UNITED STATES OF AMERICA is omitted from both dies. Struck in aluminum with a reeded edge. A well struck near-Gem, smooth aside from a few trivial hairlines above the D in DOLLAR. The pastel lime and lilac toning adds to the eye appeal. Certified in an old green label holder. An extremely rare Judd variety, we can locate no other auction appearances since 1995. Population: 1 in 64, 1 finer (5/07). (#61247)

Gem 1871 Indian Princess Half Dime Pattern
Judd-1068
Ex: Harry Bass

2251 1871 Half Dime, Judd-1068, Pollock-1204, High R.7, PR66 PCGS. Liberty is seated facing left on the obverse. The date is below. She is wearing an Indian headdress and holding a liberty pole with her right hand. Her left hand rests on a globe inscribed LIBERTY. A circle of 13 stars surrounds her. The reverse design is the same as was used to coin regular-issue half dimes. Struck in silver with a reeded edge. About a half dozen silver strikings are known, and examples were also produced in copper and aluminum. Deeply mirrored, the fields on each side show pronounced die striations. Mottled gray-russet and blue toning is seen over each side. This is the finest certified by the two major services.
Ex: Stanley Kesselman; Bass I (Bowers and Merena, 5/99), lot 1079.
(#61327)

1871 Judd-1069 Indian Princess Half Dime
PR66 Brown

2252 1871 Half Dime, Judd-1069, Pollock-1205, Low R.7, PR66 Brown NGC. James Longacre's "Indian Princess" design features Liberty facing left, wearing an Indian headdress. Her right hand supports a pole topped by a Liberty Cap, and her left hand rests on a globe that is inscribed LIBERTY. Two flags behind Liberty are draped down behind the globe. The field has 13 stars around with the date below. The reverse is from the regular production half dime die that was first introduced in 1860. Struck in copper with a reeded edge. Probably around a half dozen are known in copper. The surfaces are covered with deep teal toning which is highlighted by the deeply reflective fields on each side. An immaculate pattern. (#61328)

Double Struck PR64 1871 Indian Princess Half, Judd-1108

2253 1871 Half Dollar, Judd-1108, Pollock-1244, High R.7, PR64 PCGS. Ex: HW Bass Jr. Collection. Longacre's Indian Princess design with 13 stars on the flag and none along the periphery, paired with a regular Seated half reverse die. Struck in silver with a reeded edge. Well struck and nearly brilliant with flashy mirrored fields. **The reverse is double struck with a clockwise spread of approximately five degrees.** The obverse shows no evidence of a double strike, and was apparently the anvil die. The reverse (hammer) die was apparently loose, and rotated between the two strikes customary for proof coinage. Population: 3 in 64, 1 finer (4/07).
Ex: Col. E.H.R. Green; James Kelly, 5/43; New Netherlands 61st Sale (6/70), lot 41; The Harry W. Bass, Jr. Collection, Part I (Bowers and Merena, 5/99), lot 1211.
From The Vanek Collection. (#61367)

PR64 Brown 1871 Indian Princess Dollar, Judd-1148

2254 1871 Dollar, Judd-1148, Pollock-1290, Low R.7, PR64 Brown PCGS. Longacre's Indian Princess design dominates the obverse. The periphery displays 13 stars, while the flag exhibits 22 stars. The pattern obverse is paired with a standard Motto Seated dollar reverse. Struck in copper with a plain edge. A beautiful, intricately struck near-Gem with rich fire-red, forest-green, olive, and electric-blue patina. A small V in the field near the profile provides an identifier. The target-shaped pattern over the central obverse is on the holder, and not the coin. Certified in a first generation holder.
Ex: Stack's, 5/98, lot 538, which realized $3,520.
From The Vanek Collection. (#61410)

Choice Proof 1873 Trade Dollar, Judd-1322

2255 1873 Trade Dollar, Judd-1322, Pollock-1465, R.4, PR64 PCGS. The obverse is similar to the issued Trade dollar, except the ground extends right virtually to the border at 4:30. The reverse features a smaller eagle than the issued design, and the eagle clutches the banner E PLURIBUS UNUM. Struck in silver with a reeded edge. Gentle rose-gold toning overlies the smooth surfaces. The strike is bold aside from the eagle's right (facing) claw. Housed in an old green label holder. (#61608)

2256 1875 Twenty Cents, Judd-1407, Pollock-1550, Low R.6—Damaged, Polished—ANACS. XF40 Details. The obverse closely resembles the issued twenty cent piece, but LIBERTY is incuse rather than in relief, and the date is smaller. The reverse eschews the usual eagle reverse in favor of a slender wreath and verbose legends, which define the denomination in two different ways. Struck in silver with a plain edge. A glossy slate-gray specimen with distributed small marks. The BE in LIBERTY are faint but legible, all other letters are bold. (#61714)

Red Gem 1878 Morgan Dollar in Copper, Judd-1551

2257 1878 Morgan Dollar, Judd-1551, Pollock-1728, High R.6, PR65 Red NGC. A Morgan dollar pattern distinguished from Judd-1550b by the base of the eagle's wings, which are notched on Judd-1551. There are three leaves on the olive branch, instead of nine as on Judd-1153. In his patterns reference, Pollock lists three subvarieties. Pollock-1728, R.7, has the bust tip centered between a star and the 1 in the date, and the R in PLURIBUS is separated from the wheat ear. Struck in copper with a reeded edge. A well struck Gem with consistent brick-red toning and exquisite preservation.
Ex: Lindesmith Collection (Bowers and Merena), lot 2035.
From The Vanek Collection. (#81912)

Barber's Rejected 1878 Dollar Design, Judd-1554, PR62

2258 1878 Dollar, Judd-1554, Pollock-1733, 1737, 1741, R.5, PR62 PCGS. The head of Liberty is large and faces left with IN GOD WE TRUST at the top and the date below, similar to the pattern fifty dollar gold pieces from 1877. The reverse has a spread-winged eagle with E PLURIBUS UNUM in Gothic lettering above. UNITED STATES OF AMERICA is at the top and ONE DOLLAR on the bottom rim. Struck in silver with a reeded edge. This design was believed to be Barber's rejected dollar design, as indicated in early auction catalogs that offered this pattern. Research in mint archives by Roger Burdette shows that at least 50 pieces were struck between December 1, 1877 and January 2, 1878. The surfaces of this piece are bright and deeply mirrored in the fields. Each side has a silver-gray center that is surrounded by sea-green and rose at the margin. (#61915)

2259 1878 Goloid Dollar, Judd-1557, Pollock-1749, Low R.6, PR55 PCGS. William Barber's bust of Liberty faces left. She wears a cap with cereal grains, and her hair is bound with a ribbon. The reverse has a circle of 38 stars along with statutory legends and a description of alloy. Struck in goloid alloy (3.6% gold, 86.4% silver, 10.0% copper) with a reeded edge. No wear is readily evident, but the lightly toned surfaces are faintly hairlined and lack reflectivity. Housed in a green label holder. (#61919)

PR62 1878 Goloid Metric Dollar, Judd-1563

2260 1878 Goloid Metric Dollar, Judd-1563, Pollock-1754, Low R.6, PR62 PCGS. Liberty faces left and wears a cap with the legend LIBERTY in incuse letters. The reverse has the alloy composition and weight within a circle of 38 stars. Struck in goloid alloy with a reeded edge. This boldly struck and delicately toned specimen has a few faint hairlines. Encapsulated in a green label holder. (#61925)

Gem 1878 Morgan Dollar, Judd-1565

2261 1878 Morgan Dollar, Judd-1565, Pollock-1732, High R.7, PR65 Red and Brown PCGS. The obverse is very similar to the issued Morgan dollar, but the 18 in the date is repunched south, and the M initial is raised. The reverse die is that used for Judd-1554. A large eagle stands with raised head and outstretched wings. Both sides have the legend E PLURIBUS UNUM, neither side has IN GOD WE TRUST. Struck in copper with a reeded edge, the only Judd number for this muled die pair. Rich salmon-pink with glimpses of gunmetal-blue. The eagle is well struck, while occasional curls within the portrait lack absolute detail. Unabraded with minimal carbon, and housed in an old green label holder. PCGS and NGC combined have certified only three examples of this extremely rare pattern.
Ex: E. Maris Collection; Garrett Collection, Part II (Bowers and Ruddy, 3/80), lot 1053; Jascha Heifetz Collection (Superior, 10/89), lot 3323, which realized $17,050. (#71927)

Important Red Gem 1878 Morgan Dollar Pattern, Judd-1565

2262 1878 Morgan Dollar, Judd-1565, Pollock-1732, High R.7, PR65 Red PCGS. A regular Morgan dollar obverse die is muled with the pattern reverse die of Judd-1554. An eagle stands with raised head and extended, drooping wings. The eagle grasps an olive branch and three arrows within its claws. Statutory legends include E PLURIBUS UNUM in an unusual serif font. The Morgan dollar obverse is Type Two with a raised M initial and an unevenly divided ear. Both sides have the legend E PLURIBUS UNUM, neither side has IN GOD WE TRUST. This decisively struck Gem has rich orange and rose-red surfaces. Abrasions are absent, and the grade is only limited by an infrequent carbon fleck. Judd-1565 is extremely rare. PCGS has certified just three pieces in all grades, and NGC has yet to certify any. Encapsulated in an old green label holder. Population: 2 in 65 Red, 0 finer (4/07).

Ex: Bowers and Merena, 8/89, lot 4181; Dr. Thomas S. Chalkley Collection (Superior, 1/90), lot 2787; Auction '90 (Superior, 8/90), lot 1439; Bowers and Merena, 8/98, lot 2104; Superior, 5/99, lot 3211.
From The Vanek Collection. (#81927)

PR66 Red 1879 Morgan Half, Judd-1600

2263 1879 Morgan Half Dollar, Judd-1600, Pollock-1795, Low R.7, PR66 Red NGC. The obverse is reminiscent of the standard Morgan dollar, but the border arrangement of stars and E PLURIBUS UNUM differs. The reverse features a large perched eagle with unfurled wings. The eagle clutches three large arrows and an olive branch. IN GOD WE TRUST is widely spread around the eagle. Struck in copper with a reeded edge. This beautiful pattern is orange-red with occasional dashes of sky-blue and olive-gold. Both sides are remarkably smooth, and the strike is crisp overall despite slight softness in the centers. NGC and PCGS combined have certified only seven examples, and the present piece is tied with one other for the honor of finest certified (5/07).

Ex: Bowers and Merena, 8/98, lot 2096.
From The Vanek Collection. (#81978)

Red Gem 1879 Morgan Dollar Pattern, Judd-1612

2264 1879 Morgan Dollar, Judd-1612, Pollock-1808, Low R.7, PR65 Red PCGS. Ex: HW Bass Jr. A regular Morgan dollar obverse is paired with a pattern reverse featuring a large perched eagle with unfurled wings, clutching an olive branch and three arrows. Struck in copper with a reeded edge. A razor-sharp orange-red Gem with minor aqua-blue peripheral toning and splendid preservation. Population: 2 in 65 Red, 1 finer (4/07).
Ex: Brinton T. Schorer, 5/73; Harry W. Bass, Jr. Collection, Part One (Bowers and Merena, 5/99), lot 1291, which sold for $6,325.
From The Vanek Collection. (#81990)

2265 1879 Metric Dollar, Judd-1617, Pollock-1813, R.4, PR61 PCGS. Liberty wears a coronet with a border of pearls. The elaborate reverse presents a partial wreath of cotton and corn tied at the base, a ribbon, and DEO EST GLORIA on a tablet above. Among the final designs credited to Chief Engraver William Barber, who died in 1879 and was replaced by his son Charles. Struck in goloid alloy with a reeded edge. A lightly toned pearl-gray specimen with peripheral golden-brown freckles and a few wispy field hairlines. Encapsulated in a green label holder. (#61995)

2266 1879 Goloid Metric Dollar, Judd-1626, Pollock-1822, R.4, PR62 ANACS. William Barber's design for the Goloid Metric dollar with a capped head of Liberty on the obverse, paired with a reverse that carries verbose statutory as well as elemental inscriptions. A circle of stars about the central inscriptions breaks the otherwise continuous wording. Struck in goloid (5.46% gold, 84.54% silver, 10.00% copper) with a reeded edge. Golden-brown, ice-blue, and olive toning grace this well struck example. In an old ANA cache holder. (#62004)

PR62 1879 Goloid Metric Dollar in Silver, Judd-1627

2267 1879 Goloid Metric Dollar, Judd-1627, Pollock-1823, R.5, PR62 NGC. The obverse features a bust of Liberty by William Barber. She wears a large cap with cereal grains, and her curls are bound by a ribbon. The reverse displays eight separate legends that state the value, weight, and alloy. Struck in silver with a reeded edge. Scarcer than the usually seen Goloid alloy. Medium golden-brown and powder-blue patina graces this boldly struck example. A few faint slide marks on the portrait limit the grade but not the eye appeal.
From The Vanek Collection. (#62005)

Judd-1654 1880 Goloid Metric Dollar PR55

2268 1880 Goloid Metric Dollar, Judd-1654, Pollock-1854, Low R.7, PR55 PCGS. Liberty faces left with her hair braided into a coil at the back of the head. The reverse presents a circle of 38 stars enclosing a four-line description of alloy. Outside the circle are the legends DEO EST GLORIA and GOLOID METRIC DOLLAR. A briefly handled dove-gray metric dollar with a pair of moderate marks on the chin. Struck in goloid with a reeded edge. (#62039)

Red Gem 1881 Liberty Cent, Judd-1666

2269 1881 Liberty Head One Cent, Judd-1666, Pollock-1866, High R.6, PR65 Red NGC. Charles Barber's Liberty nickel portrait dominates the obverse, which features UNITED STATES OF AMERICA instead of stars. The wreath from the Liberty nickel provides the reverse motif. The denomination is expressed by a large Roman numeral. Struck in copper with a plain edge. A well struck and unabraded fire-red Gem, perfect except for a few pinpoint toning flecks. Census: 1 in 65 Red, 0 finer (5/07).
From The Vanek Collection. (#82062)

Transitional 1882 Liberty Nickel, Judd-1690, PR63

2270 1882 Liberty Head Five Cents, Judd-1690, Pollock-1892, R.5, PR63 PCGS. A transitional pattern nearly identical to the issued 1883 No Cents Liberty nickel. The bust is slightly different in location relative to the stars, and the wreath differs slightly in relation to the peripheral legend, features that are only apparent upon side-by-side comparison. The S in PLURIBUS is widely repunched. Struck in nickel with a plain edge. A couple of light scrapes on the figure of Liberty limit the grade. Light, hazy blue-gray patina covers each side with strong reflectivity in the fields. (#62095)

Transitional 1883 No Cents Nickel, Judd-1714, PR64

2271 **1883 Liberty Head Five Cents, Judd-1714, Pollock-1919, Low R.6, PR64 PCGS.** Similar to the No CENTS Liberty nickel regular issue of 1883, but LIBERTY is not present on the coronet. Instead, the legend is spread across the upper obverse margin. The stars are also smaller, and are arranged 6 x 7. Struck in nickel with a plain edge. Well mirrored for a nickel product, the devices show slight mint frost that gives the coin a moderate two-toned appearance. Pale gray patina over each side. Repunching is noticed on the 883 in the date, star 13, and the S in PLURIBUS. (#62131)

Superb Gem 1884 Annular Cent, Judd-1721

2272 **1884 One Cent, Judd-1721, Pollock-1929, R.5, PR67 PCGS.** The obverse is plain aside from the legends UNITED STATES OF AMERICA and 1884. The reverse displays ONE CENT, a small Federal shield, and two olive branches. Struck in nickel alloy with a plain edge on a perforated planchet. A gorgeous Superb Gem with delicate peach, lime, and powder-blue toning. Encapsulated in an old green label holder. (#62150)

Interesting 1896 Five Cent Pattern, Judd-1771, PR65 Allegedly Struck in Pure Nickel

2273 **1896 Five Cents, Judd-1771, Pollock-1986, Low R.6, PR65 PCGS.** The obverse depicts a shield with 13 stripes and a scroll inscribed LIBERTY that passes in front. Behind are two crossed poles, one bearing an eagle, the other a liberty cap. E PLURIBUS UNUM is above, 1896 is below. The reverse shows 5 CENTS within a curved olive sprig with UNITED STATES OF AMERICA around. The border is beaded on both sides. Struck in nickel with a plain edge. Allegedly these pieces are struck in pure nickel, but pure nickel is a difficult metal to strike coins from. Pieces are also known from this design struck in standard coin nickel and at least six variants of German silver. Moderately reflective, the striking details are sharply defined and there is no evidence of die breakage—two attributes one would look for on a pure nickel coin. Untoned with problem-free surfaces. (#62225)

GOLD DOLLARS

2274 **1849 Open Wreath MS63 PCGS.** Small Head, With L. This exactingly struck and lustrous first-year gold dollar is kept from a finer grade by a few faint obverse field grazes. The Open Wreath was only struck in 1849. (#7502)

2275 **1849 Open Wreath MS63 NGC.** Small Head, with L. Crisply struck with intense mint luster and gorgeous sunset-orange and lime-green toning over both sides. The design elements are boldly struck, and clash marks are absent. Small surface blemishes define the grade. (#7502)

2276 **1849 Closed Wreath MS62 PCGS.** Large Head, With L. At first glance, this lustrous khaki-gold representative appears worthy of an even finer grade, since there is a shortage of visible marks. Study beneath a loupe locates a single, hard-to-find abrasion between the NI in UNITED.
From The Vanek Collection. (#7503)

2277 **1849 Closed Wreath MS64 ICG.** Large Head, With L. This is an amazingly well preserved example of the first-year 1849 gold dollar. This is the so-called Closed Wreath, one of several distinct *Guide Book* varieties for the date. Lustrous and virtually blemish-free, with typically mushy details on DOLLAR and the date. (#7503)

Choice AU 1849-D Gold Dollar

2278 **1849-D AU55 PCGS.** Variety 1-A. The gold dollar was a new denomination in 1849, added to the Mint's lineup along with the double eagle, providing additional demand for the new gold being mined in California. Meanwhile, in Dahlonega, production of gold dollars began with a mintage of 21,588 coins, making this issue the most common of all Dahlonega gold dollars. This lustrous light yellow example has a trace of wear on the highpoints, appearing as deeper orange color. Despite a few minor imperfections, the surfaces are exceptional for the grade. (#7507)

2279 **1849-O MS60 NGC.** A basic Mint State piece, this is a pleasing example featuring an Open Wreath as always from New Orleans. Closed Wreath dies were shipped but not received in time. Sharply detailed and lustrous with a few faint hairlines and abrasions. (#7508)

2280 **1849-O MS62 NGC.** Fully lustrous and sharply detailed, this piece has light yellow-gold surfaces with hints of green coloration. (#7508)

2281 **1851 MS63 NGC.** Yellow-gold color with some greenish hues. Nice luster, sharp details, and minimally abraded surfaces. (#7513)

Well Struck 1851-C Gold Dollar, MS60

2282 **1851-C MS60 NGC.** Variety 5-E. The mintmark is lightly doubled on this variety, and slightly to the left of the bowknot. Excellent definition appears on the design elements, and lustrous surfaces yield canary-gold color that gives off a slight green cast. Small handling marks are scattered over both sides. This issue is moderately scarce in the lowest Mint State grades (Douglas Winter, 1998). (#7514)

2283 **1852 MS63 NGC.** Full luster with attractive orange-gold coloration. A few light ticks and grazes limit the grade. (#7517)

2284 **1852 MS64 PCGS.** Lustrous and boldly detailed, with only faint weakness on LLA and the right side of the wreath. A small mark on Liberty's cheek prevents a higher grade assessment, but this is still a pleasing coin for the grade. (#7517)

2285 **1852-D—Tooled, Cleaned—ANACS. AU Details, Net XF40.** Variety 4-F. Virtually Mint State in terms of sharpness, this rare-date Dahlonega gold dollar has an impressive strike and no apparent marks. The reverse has short radial die cracks at 2, 5, 7, and 11 o'clock. The curiously smooth fields are minutely granular. (#7519)

Rare 1852-D Gold Dollar, AU58

2286 **1852-D AU58 PCGS.** Variety 4-F, the only known pairing. The 1852-D gold dollar, with its 6,360-piece mintage, is scarce in all grades. It is most frequently seen in grades Extremely Fine to mid-About Uncirculated. Near-Mint and Uncirculated pieces are rare. Yellow-gold surfaces on this AU58 specimen retain a good amount of luster and are quite clean. All of the design elements are well brought up. (#7519)

2287 **1852-O MS62 NGC.** A dark greenish-yellow example of this scarcer date with sharp design elements throughout. In Mint State grades, this date is considered one of the top three rarities in the series of New Orleans gold dollars. Census: 39 in 62, 29 finer (6/07). (#7520)

Desirable Premium Gem 1853 Gold Dollar

2288 **1853 MS66 PCGS.** This vibrantly lustrous gold dollar displays lovely apricot-gold toning that seems imbued with underlying accents of lime-green. The design motifs are crisply and essentially fully struck on each side. Clash marks are absent, while spidery die cracks are noted near the obverse periphery. A couple of superficial pinscratches, near DOLLAR and the date on the reverse, preclude an even loftier grade assessment for this desirable Premium Gem. (#7521)

2289 **1853-O MS61 NGC.** Despite a few small scrapes on the reverse that limit the grade, this is a lovely Mint State example with frosty and brilliant yellow-gold luster. It is sharply struck from a late die state with extensive flowlines. (#7524)

2290 **1853-O MS62 NGC.** For the type collector, this is the easiest New Orleans gold dollar to obtain in any grade. A sharply detailed piece, with excellent green luster, the gold probably originating in California. (#7524)

2291 **1854 Type One MS63 PCGS.** This is a crisply detailed example with pleasing orange-gold color. Boldly defined throughout with a few incidental clashmarks. Certified in a green label holder. (#7525)

2292 **1854 Type One MS64 NGC.** Vibrant sunset-orange and butter-yellow colors enhance the visual appeal of this solidly struck Choice gold dollar. A lovely and well-preserved example of this final Type One issue. (#7525)

2293 **1854 Type Two AU58 NGC.** A satiny near-Mint example with lustrous orange-gold surfaces. A few insignificant blemishes are noted on each side of this important type coin. (#7531)

2294 **1854 Type Two AU58 NGC.** This near-Mint example has pale yellow color with splashes of pinkish-orange toning. Both sides have the usual minor imperfections that are expected for the grade. (#7531)

2295 **1854 Type Two AU58 NGC.** This is a well struck near-Mint example with typical clash marks on each side. DOLLAR and the date are both sharply and evenly struck. A handful of raised die lines occur just to the right of the large number 1 on the upper reverse. Lightly worn with a few faint pinscratches. (#7531)

2296 **1854 Type Two MS62 PCGS.** Sharply struck with less die clashing than usual, and just a few small, scattered abrasions and pinscratches that limit the grade. Noteworthy as a scarce Mint State example of this short-lived type, created in mid-1854 when the gold dollar was redesigned by James B. Longacre. (#7531)

2297 **1855 AU55 NGC.** This is an attractive Choice AU example with only slightly muted luster and a trace of wear on Liberty's crown and upper hair detail. Clash marks are noticeable on both sides, and a couple of vertical pinscratches are evident on the upper reverse field. Popular as a type coin; the Type II gold dollar was only produced from 1854 through 1856. (#7532)

2298 **1855 AU58 NGC.** This unblemished olive-gold Borderline Uncirculated Type Two dollar has bold definition on the portrait. The outer borders of the lower cotton leaves show minor incompleteness of strike. Lightly clashed inside the wreath, as usual for the issue. (#7532)

2299 **1855 AU58 NGC.** A highly lustrous near-Mint specimen, this lovely piece has full orange-gold brilliance with only a trace of wear on the design highpoints. Light clash marks are evident in the fields, especially on the reverse. (#7532)

2300 **1855 AU58 NGC.** Fiery red-orange and lime-green toning is the hallmark of this near-Mint gold dollar. Typically struck with wispy field marks and a trace of highpoint wear on the central devices. Clash marks are seen on the reverse, as usual.
From The Vanek Collection. (#7532)

2301 **1855 AU58 NGC.** Bright brassy-gold surfaces reveal considerable luster, and a well executed strike imparts good definition on the design elements, save for the usual softness on the top of the 8 in the date. the normal assortment of marks are noted. The reverse is clashmarked. (#7532)

Uncirculated 1855 Type Two Gold Dollar, In-Demand Type

2302 **1855 MS60 NGC.** The 1855 gold dollar, along with the 1854, is the most common of the various issues that constitute the short-lived Type Two design. This piece is a nice, strictly Uncirculated example of this difficult and in-demand gold type, one that shows a few signs of contact on each side, along with the prominent die clashing on both surfaces that is so omnipresent on these coins. But both the orange-gold color and the radiant luster confirm a nonetheless-appealing example. (#7532)

Well Struck 1855 Gold Dollar, MS62

2303 **1855 MS62 NGC.** Many 1855 gold dollars are weakly struck, especially the central portions of the reverse. The MS62 specimen presented in this lot is well defined over most of the design elements, save for a touch of softness in the top of the 8 in the date. Peach-gold lustrous surfaces reveal just a few minor luster grazes, as well as clash marks on each side. (#7532)

Enticing Choice 1855 Gold Dollar

2304 **1855 MS64 NGC.** Garrett and Guth (2006) note for this issue: "Many are seen softly struck, especially in the central portions of the reverse, and extensive die clashing is not unusual." The pattern holds true for this example, which displays shallow detail on the L's of DOLLAR and the 8 in the date, as well as much of an outline of Liberty's head within the wreath. A touch of die erosion on that side also hints at extended die use, the reason for this example's delightful luster. The attractive luster enhances the visual impact of the piece's warm orange-gold surfaces, which have hints of lemon-yellow and rose color. An attractive example of this noted type issue, one that displays beautifully with considerably above-average eye appeal for the obverse. NGC has graded 44 pieces as Gem or better (5/07). (#7532)

2305 **1857 MS64 PCGS.** This is an important opportunity for the advanced collector, as this date does not often appear on the market in higher Mint State grades. This piece is fully brilliant with satiny luster and reflective fields. Population: 32 in 64, 22 finer (6/07). (#7544)

Near-Mint 1858-D Gold Dollar

2306 **1858-D AU58 NGC.** Variety 10-M as always for this date. Only slight traces of wear is evident on this piece, with subdued greenish-gold luster on both sides. The surfaces exhibit a few hairlines, and some dark verdigris around the lettering and central motif on the obverse. (#7549)

2307 **1860 MS63 PCGS.** A lovely and original green-gold representative of this better date gold dollar. Much scarcer than the 1855, which trades for 10 times as much. Population: 14 in 63, 21 finer (4/07). (#7555)

Singular 1861 Gold Dollar, MS67

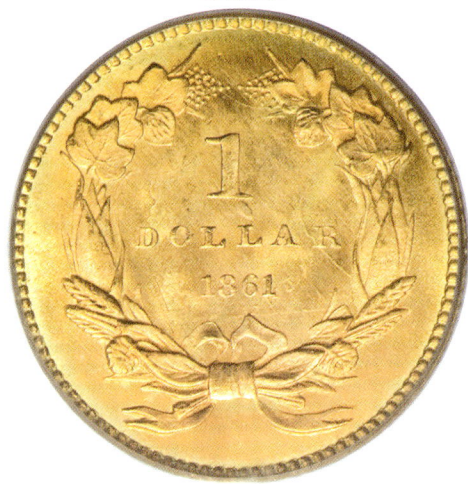

2308 **1861 MS67 PCGS.** The mintage for the 1861 gold dollar exceeded half a million pieces, the first issue to have such a high mintage since 1857. This generous production has made the 1861 popular with type collectors, and in lower Mint State grades, examples are common. Unlike the later issues of the 1880s, however, Gems are only occasionally available, and NGC and PCGS combined have certified just three coins in MS67, with the representative offered here the *only* such piece graded by the latter firm (5/07).

This sharply struck beauty has a breathtaking appearance. The obverse has vivid sun-gold color tempered by orange at the margins, while the reverse has vibrant butter-yellow color. Strong, though not flashy luster enhances the warm tones of the surfaces and emphasizes the near-perfect preservation of the piece. A wonderful, entrancing example of this Civil War issue. (#7558)

2309 **1867 MS63 PCGS.** This low mintage gold dollar is scarce in all grades, yet remains affordable. A smooth and suitably struck example. All letters in LIBERTY are legible beneath the date, the result of clashed dies. Population: 4 in 63, 18 finer (4/07). (#7566)

2310 **1870 MS63 PCGS.** This is a wonderful yellow-gold example with satiny and reflective luster on the obverse, frosty on the reverse. It is important at this grade level with only 38 finer pieces certified by PCGS (6/07). (#7569)

2311 **1871 MS61 NGC.** A lustrous and suitably struck yellow-gold representative. The fields are smooth, although faint, thin marks are noted beneath the date and on the cheek. Only 3,900 pieces were struck for this underappreciated date. (#7571)

2312 **1873 Open 3 MS64 PCGS.** A sharply detailed and fully brilliant example, this Choice Mint State piece has light yellow-gold luster on frosty surfaces. PCGS has certified a mere 40 finer pieces (6/07). (#7573)

2313 **1873 Open 3 MS64 PCGS.** Lustrous and well struck with light yellow-gold and salmon toning over both sides. A diagnostic die line extends vertically down Liberty's neck. The surfaces are minimally disturbed for the near-Gem grade level. (#7573)

2314 **1873 Open 3 MS62 Prooflike NGC.** An impressively mirrored and meticulously struck gold dollar that has imposing eye appeal for the assigned grade. A plentiful issue in Mint State, but certainly scarce with prooflike fields. Population: 6 in 62 Prooflike, 7 finer (5/07). *From The Vanek Collection.* (#77573)

2315 **1874 MS64 PCGS.** A lovely and lustrous Choice gold dollar with a refreshingly unmarked appearance. The knot of the bow and the 87 in the date are indistinct, but the remainder of the design is well struck. (#7575)

2316 **1874 MS64 PCGS.** A slightly frosty butter-yellow example that displays few flaws to the unaided eye. Light clash marks are noted within the wreath. With a mintage that approached 200,000 pieces, the 1874 is one of a handful of issues popular with type collectors. (#7575)

2317 **1874 MS64 PCGS.** Fresh, original luster is the defining characteristic of this captivating yellow-gold piece, one that hails from the highest-mintage issue of the 1870s. The strike and surface quality are pleasing as well. A lovely candidate for a type collection. (#7575)

Rare 1875 Gold Dollar, MS61 Prooflike

2318 **1875 MS61 Prooflike NGC.** Any 1875 gold coin except the double eagle is an instant magnet for enthusiasts of rare-date gold, since all other denominations were produced in minuscule quantities, totaling 1,120 business strikes for the gold dollar through the eagle. In the case of the gold dollar the mintage was a paltry 400 pieces, accompanied by 15 proofs, so it is little wonder that most of the circulation strikes are prooflike. This coin displays some light hairlines and field chatter on each side, but thick mint frost coats the devices, and the fields retain a superb amount of mirrored reflectivity. (#77576)

Wonderful MS67 Prooflike 1880 Gold Dollar

2319 **1880 MS67 Prooflike NGC.** Reflective fields and lightly frosted motifs confirm the Prooflike designation. This well struck Superb Gem is remarkably unabraded, and the surfaces are uniform aside from a faint tan toning streak near the chin. A mere 1,600 business strikes were issued. Census: 9 in 67 Prooflike, 1 finer (5/07). (#77581)

Colorful 1881 Gold Dollar, MS66

2320 **1881 MS66 PCGS.** Lovely prooflike surfaces enhance the variegated lilac and peach-gold coloration that is seen on each side, with the lilac color seen over the highpoints of the devices. A sharp, even strike is seen throughout, and there are no significant marks to report. A popular date from the 1880s, and one with a mintage of only 7,600 pieces. (#7582)

2321 **1881 MS63 Deep Mirror Prooflike NGC.** Breen-6102. The 88 in the date is recut. No doubt this prominently mirrored gold dollar has been offered in the past as a proof, particularly since the devices are frosty. A mere 7,620 pieces were struck. NGC has certified only two examples as Deep Mirror Prooflike, as of (5/07). (#77582)

2322 **1885 MS65 NGC.** A shining and attractive representative of this later gold dollar issue, well-defined with a touch of emerald-green against the prevailing butter-yellow color that characterizes the surfaces. This delightful Gem is one of just 11,100 pieces coined. (#7586)

2323 **1885 MS64 Prooflike NGC.** According to Garrett and Guth, this issue normally trades at only a small premium above type. They were probably not thinking of Prooflike examples, however, when making that observation. This example displays sensational reflectivity in the fields. The design elements are well struck and post-striking surface blemishes are nearly nonexistent, although some wispy roller marks (as struck) are noted on each side of the piece. Census: 5 in 64 Prooflike, 5 finer (6/07). (#77586)

2324 **1887 MS63 PCGS.** Bright and satiny with attractive coloration and nicely preserved surfaces. A few minute marks limit the grade. The mintage of 7,500 pieces was rather small, but most survivors seem to be in Mint State. (#7588)

Gorgeous Toned MS66 ★ 1889 Gold Dollar

2325 **1889 MS66 ★ NGC.** Despite the relatively low 28,950-piece business strike mintage, 1889 gold dollars are readily found in any grade. Jeff Garrett and Ron Guth (2006) point out that small hoards have turned up with regularity over the years. They also suggest that the date's high survival rate is probably due to its status as the last year of the type and the end of gold dollars in general.

Outstanding luster enlivens both sides, each of which displays rich reddish-gold, orange, and mint-green coloration on frosty surfaces. A powerful strike emboldens all of the design features, including virtually full delineation on the intricacies of the reverse wreath. An inoffensive handling mark or two precludes an even higher grade. The coin's overall eye appeal is breathtaking! (#7590)

2326 **1889 MS63 Prooflike NGC.** A distinctly reflective and flashy yellow-gold example from the final year of issue that offers strong detail on the devices. Light, scattered marks in the fields preclude a finer grade. Census: 2 in 63 Prooflike, 15 finer (5/07). (#77590)

Prooflike MS66 1889 Gold Dollar

2327 **1889 MS66 Prooflike NGC.** A flashy and beautifully smooth Premium Gem with meticulously struck devices and imposing eye appeal. The ribbon is die doubled, as always on business strikes of this popular final-year issue. The reverse border has a slender peripheral die crack, which suggests that the dies were removed from service and lapped, then restored before striking the present piece. Census: 2 in 66 Prooflike, 6 finer (5/07). (#77590)

PROOF GOLD DOLLARS

Attractive 1884 Gold Dollar PR64 Cameo

2328 **1884 PR64 Cameo ICG.** Breen-6107, Doubled Date. This relatively high mintage issue of 1,006 pieces has a surprisingly small number of survivors; only around 100 have been certified by NGC and PCGS, including possible resubmissions. This sparkling example has a frosty appearance, and noteworthy field-to-device contrast on both sides. The devices reveal pinpoint striking sharpness. A milky fingerprint fragment in the left obverse field limits the grade. *From The Vanek Collection.* (#87634)

Spectacular 1885 Gold Dollar, PR68 Cameo

2329 **1885 PR68 Cameo NGC.** Garrett and Guth (2006) write of the 1885 proof gold dollar: "A few truly superb examples of this date have been graded by the services, the finest being an NGC PF-68 coin." Though it is impossible to determine which coin the two writers had in mind, the phrase "truly superb" seems appropriate on viewing this delightful specimen. The fathomless mirrors appear jet-black from a distance, though closer inspection reveals vivid yellow-gold color with a hint of carrot color at the margins. The boldly impressed devices exhibit light frost as well, which contributes to the coin's striking contrast. A slight orange-peel effect on the obverse only confirms this coin's status as a proof, and while a handful of lint marks are present in the fields, their impact on the coin's visual appeal is trivial at worst. A breathtaking example, one practically at the pinnacle of preservation, a true rarity that emerges from the comparatively common status of the issue. Census: 2 in 68 Cameo, 0 finer (5/07). (#87635)

Flashy Cameo Gem Proof 1889 Gold Dollar

EARLY QUARTER EAGLES

Rare AU50 Details 1832 Quarter Eagle

2331 **1832—Repaired—ANACS. AU50 Details.** Breen-6135, BD-1, R.4. The only known dies, identified by the recut U in UNITED and a high 1 in the date. The present piece is carefully repaired on the open fields, and the portrait appears gently whizzed. Nonetheless, luster brightens the stars and legends, and the eagle's plumage is boldly defined. (#7672)

2330 **1889 PR65 Cameo PCGS.** 1889 is a watershed year in U.S. numismatics. Not only did the three cent nickel series terminate, but both the one dollar and three dollar gold series ended as well. In the case of the one dollar gold, the business strike mintage swelled to 28,950 coins in 1889, from mintages that were typically only in the four digits for much of the 1870s and 1880s. The proof mintage was also the largest by far in the entire series, at almost 1,800 coins. But time and attrition have considerably thinned the ranks of those survivors, and today a Gem 1889 proof dollar is a rare item indeed. PCGS has certified only 16 Gem coins within all contrast levels, with 13 finer.

The present example appears to border on a Deep Cameo designation. The coin hails from late in the proof mintage, as die polishing has effaced most of ERT in LIBERTY (Breen's *Proof Encyclopedia* notes that the obverse was reused from the 1888 proofs). While most of the devices are covered in thick mint frost and the fields are nicely reflective, a small mirrored area is noted below Liberty's ear and downward onto her neck. Tiny reverse die cracks are noted between each half of the wreath exterior and the denticles. None of those mostly microscopic mint-caused flaws, however, detract in any way from the significant flash and huge eye appeal of this lovely Gem Cameo proof, an ideal selection for a last-year type set. Population: 3 in 65 Cameo, 2 finer (6/07). (#87639)

Andrew Jackson, 7th President
(1829-1837)

CLASSIC QUARTER EAGLES

Lovely 1836 Head of '37 Quarter Eagle, MS64

2332 **1836 Block 8 MS64 PCGS.** Breen-6144. Head of 1837, Reverse with Olive Bud. This variety is relatively common, with a quite a number of Mint State examples known, including Choice and Gem specimens. The Head of 1837 is identified by the shape of the hair over the top left corner of the headband, sweeping back into the top curl that is below star 7. This head type is known with two different reverse dies, either with a small olive bud in the branch, or without. The type without a berry or bud in the branch is extremely rare, with only one Mint State piece known. This is a lovely Choice Mint State specimen with brilliant greenish-yellow gold that is enhanced by a trace of pale orange toning. The central obverse and reverse details are a little weak, but overall it is sharper than most. The surfaces are quite exceptional, with few marks of any consequence. (#97694)

2333 **1837 AU50 PCGS.** McCloskey-B, R.3. Lustrous for the grade with a few inconspicuous obverse pinscratches. Significantly scarcer than the earlier Philadelphia issues of the type, since only 45,080 pieces were struck. Housed in a green label holder.
From The Vanek Collection. (#7695)

2334 **1838 AU55 NGC.** This is a scarcer issue in the brief (1834-1839) Classic quarter eagle series. This example displays somewhat soft striking details, as usual, with light wear and some wispy hairlines in the fields. Just 47,030 pieces were struck. (#7696)

Well Defined 1838-C Two and a Half Dollar, AU53 Details

2335 **1838-C—Cleaned—ANACS. AU53 Details.** Variety 1-A, the only known die pairing. Douglas Winter (1998) indicates that the 1838-C is usually seen in Very Fine and Extremely Fine grades, and is rare in About Uncirculated and very rare in Mint State. Bright yellow-gold surfaces of this AU53 Details example display better-than-average definition on the design features. Fine hairlines are scattered over both sides, but this light cleaning should not dissuade prospective bidders. (#7697)

1839 Quarter Eagle, AU50

2336 **1839 AU50 NGC.** Breen-6148, R.3. The only known dies. Jeff Garrett and Ron Guth (2006) write that "all examples were struck from a defective punch, which, in the past, has been called an overdate (and sometimes certified as such)." Bright yellow-gold surfaces reveal hints of luster in the recessed areas, and exhibit relatively well defined motifs. A few minute marks do not significantly detract. (#7698)

Scarce 1839-C Quarter Eagle, AU53 Details
McCloskey-B, Breen-6149

2337 **1839-C—Cleaned—ANACS. AU53 Details.** McCloskey-B, Breen-6149, R.4. The mintmark is small and centered between the bust and the top of the 3 in the date. On the reverse, the tip of the branch extends to the right edge of the upright of the D. Bright yellow-gold surfaces retain traces of luster in the recesses, and reveal some light hairlines under magnification. Good definition is noted on the design features. A scarce coin in AU, and quite rare in Mint State. A rather nice piece, despite the light cleaning. (#7699)

Near-Mint State 1839-O Quarter Eagle With Obverse Mintmark and Medal Alignment

2338 **1839-O AU58 NGC.** Low Date, Close Fraction, Breen-61532, McCloskey-B, R.4. On the reverse the denomination features an abnormally large loop on the 2 that touches the fraction bar, with the numerator nearly so. This coin is popular as the one-year Obverse Mintmark subtype, as an example of New Orleans Mint gold from the debut year of that mint, and also because, as seen here, the issue is often found in perfect medallic alignment, rather than coin turn. This charming piece shows just a touch of light circulation on the still-lustrous green-gold surfaces. Although construction was completed in 1839 at the New Orleans Mint, a severe outbreak of yellow fever curtailed its operation from July 1 until November 30. (#7701)

LIBERTY QUARTER EAGLES

2339 **1840-O XF45 PCGS.** One of the rarest and most undervalued of all O-mint quarter eagles; very scarce in XF and better grades. This piece is softly struck, as always, and exhibits bright lime-green and yellow-gold coloration. It is typically worn for the grade, with mostly small surface marks. The '40-O had a mintage of 33,580 pieces, but it has been estimated that fewer than 100 examples still exist. (#7720)

2340 **1840-O XF45 NGC.** Softly struck, as usual, with smooth surfaces that are free of large marks, and evenly worn highpoints on both sides. The obverse displays a noticeable reddish tint in the fields. The '40-O is a scarce and underrated early O-mint quarter eagle, and is even more challenging than its small mintage of 33,580 pieces would suggest. (#7720)

Choice XF 1842-D Two and a Half

2341 **1842-D XF45 PCGS.** Variety 3-F. The 184 in the date is widely repunched south, diagnostic for this rare issue. Only 4,643 pieces were struck, and perhaps no more than 200 pieces have survived in all grades. This moderately abraded and slightly bright example has a bold strike across the stars and denticles, while the major devices display localized softness. Population: 12 in 45, 19 finer (5/07). (#7725)

1843-C Large Date Quarter Eagle, MS61

2342 **1843-C Large Date, Plain 4 MS61 NGC.** Variety 5-D. Bright yellow-gold surfaces exhibit a hint of greenish color. This piece is sharply struck and minimally abraded. The two varieties of this date are easily distinguished by the presence of a crosslet 4 on the Small Date and a plain 4 on the Large Date. The Large Date variety is easily the more common of the two, yet it is elusive in Mint State grades. Census: 7 in 61, 6 finer (6/07). (#7728)

2343 **1845-O—Scratched—ANACS. AU Details. Net XF40.** This partly lustrous and nicely struck quarter eagle appears impressive at first glance, but a cluster of brief pinscratches is present between star 12 and the portrait. The 18 in the date is repunched. A mere 4,000 pieces were struck, and relatively few were saved. (#7739)

2344 **1847 AU53 PCGS.** A lovely example with hints of pale green color on honey-gold surfaces. This piece is sharply detailed and exhibits satiny luster. This date is scarce in all grades. (#7744)

2345 **1847 AU58 Prooflike NGC.** Breen-6188, which he considered "very rare." The base of the 18 is boldly repunched. The reverse is shattered by lengthy radial cracks at 11 o'clock, 4 o'clock, and 6:30. These cracks intersect above the shield. But perhaps of greatest interest, both fields exhibit prooflike luster. The present lot is the **only** pre-1854 quarter eagle designated as Prooflike by NGC (6/07). Clean for the grade with minor softness of strike on the curls and plumage. (#77744)

Elusive 1848 Quarter Eagle, MS61

2346 **1848 MS61 NGC.** This is a popular date due to the existence of the 1848 CAL quarter eagles. However, it is the normal 1848 variety that is actually rarer in Mint State grades. Just 6,500 of these were struck, and nearly all survivors show evidence of circulation. Although the left facing leg is a trifle weak, all other details on both sides are nicely defined. The surfaces are brilliant and frosty with pleasing orange-gold luster. Census: 7 in 61, 8 finer (6/07). (#7748)

2347 **1849 AU50 NGC.** The devices are quite well struck, particularly the obverse, and moderate highpoint friction accounts for the grade, along with tiny scattered marks and a few wispy hairlines. A shallow pinscratch is noted in the right obverse field. A scarce, seldom encountered date in the Liberty Head quarter eagle series. (#7752)

2348 **1851 MS62 PCGS.** The gold coins of the early 1850s are generally quite plentiful, due to the gold discoveries in California. This piece, a lovely Mint State specimen, has brilliant green-gold luster with frosty surfaces. (#7759)

Near-Mint 1851-O Quarter Eagle

2349 **1851-O AU58 NGC.** This is a wonderful example of the date, exhibiting nearly full designs on both sides, with the exception of the left facing leg that is invariably weak. The surfaces are highly lustrous with only a trace of rub. Both sides have satiny green-gold with splashes of orange toning. (#7762)

2350 **1853 MS63 PCGS.** Quite frosty with just a touch of striking softness on the eagle's left (facing) leg. A few wispy marks are noted on each side. A popular early quarter eagle issue. (#7767)

Sharp 1854-D Quarter Eagle

2351 **1854-D—Repaired—NCS. AU Details.** Variety 17-M. This rare Dahlonega date has a low mintage of 1,760 pieces, and survivors in all grades are desirable. This piece has repairs between stars 3 and 4, near stars 9 and 12, and on the reverse field near the eagle's neck and right (facing) wing. A couple of inconspicuous pinscratches are noted close to the bust truncation. Glossy from a cleaning, but the strike is bold except for the eagle's extremities. (#7771)

2352 **1856 MS62 PCGS.** The strike is sharp save for minor weakness on the eagle's left (facing) leg. Smooth for the grade with good luster and green-gold toning. Housed in a green label holder. Population: 47 in 62, 53 finer (4/07).
From The Vanek Collection. (#7777)

Uncirculated 1856-S Two and a Half

2353 **1856-S MS60 NGC.** The 1856-S is noteworthy as the first collectible San Francisco issue of the denomination. The 1854-S is a spectacular rarity, and the denomination was passed over in 1855, probably since mint resources concentrated on double eagle production. Most '56-S survivors grade between XF and AU. This luminous and intricately struck example has a few wispy marks, but fewer than expected of the grade. Census: 7 in 60, 17 finer (6/07). (#7781)

Beautiful Choice 1856-S Quarter Eagle

2354 **1856-S MS64 PCGS.** While the San Francisco Mint produced numerous double eagles in its early years of operation, the smaller gold denominations suffered comparative neglect, and production was low. The famed 1854-S quarter eagle is the most dramatic illustration of this principle, and the 1856-S quarter eagle has an original mintage of only 72,100 pieces, many of which saw heavy circulation.

This carefully preserved survivor breaks the pattern. The shimmering, carefully preserved surfaces display lovely sun-gold color overall with subtle peach accents on the reverse. The largely mark-free devices have crisp detail, particularly on the needle-sharp obverse portrait, and only a handful of small marks in the fields preclude a Gem grade. A delightful representative that could find a home in the finest of sets. Population: 4 in 64, 3 finer (5/07). (#7781)

2355 **1858 MS61 NGC.** Generally well struck, if slightly soft on the hair detail just above Liberty's forehead and on the eagle's left (facing) leg. Pretty lime-green and peach toning adorns the satiny surfaces. A few tiny marks and somewhat weak luster restrict the grade. Census: 26 in 61, 31 finer (5/07). (#7786)

Old Hub 1859 Quarter Eagle, MS62

2356 1859 Old Reverse, Type One MS62 PCGS. The reverse hubs used to produced dies were modified in 1859, creating additional varieties for collectors in the transitional years of 1859 and 1860. The varieties are interchangeably labeled Type One and Type Two or Old Reverse and New Reverse. This Old Reverse piece is sharp and brilliant with frosty orange-gold luster and minimal abrasions. Population: 4 in 62, 7 finer (6/07). (#97788)

2357 1860-S AU55 NGC. From a mintage of 35,600 pieces, the 1860-S is a scarce issue. A lightly worn wheat-gold example that displays the usual striking weakness on the eagle's leg, and the surfaces contain considerable luster. Some circulation marks are noted on the obverse. (#7793)

Lustrous, Elusive AU 1862-S Quarter Eagle

2358 1862-S AU50 NGC. The paltry mintage of 8,000 pieces created a near-instant rarity, as the vast majority of the production apparently entered circulation, like so many S-mint gold coins of the era. Few Mint State pieces are known, and the typical survivor grades AU or so. This piece is typical in condition, but atypical in appeal. The strike is well executed at the peripheries, with minor weakness noted on the hair below Liberty's coronet and the eagle's left (facing) leg. Much luster radiates from the semi-prooflike fields. Census: 2 in 50, 32 finer (6/07). (#7798)

Conditionally Scarce 1867-S Quarter Eagle MS61

2359 1867-S MS61 PCGS. Bright luster dominates the devices and legends. The striking details are sharp in all areas except on LIBERTY and the eagle's left leg, as seen on almost all S-mint quarter eagles from this era. A few wispy marks are scattered over each side, but the surfaces are generally clean for an MS61 gold coin. Moderate clash marks outline the devices. Only 28,000 pieces were struck. Population: 3 in 61, 3 finer (4/07). (#7806)

2360 1868 AU58 PCGS. A precisely struck and pleasing Borderline Uncirculated example that has a smooth appearance and consistent straw-gold toning. A mere 3,600 pieces were struck for this challenging issue. (#7807)

2361 1869 AU55 NGC. The quarter eagle was not a workhorse denomination in the late 1860s, and Philadelphia struck just 4,300 such pieces in 1869. This briefly circulated survivor has pleasing detail and distinctive yellow-orange coloration. The reverse offers partial reflectivity, consistent with this issue's low mintage. (#7809)

Rarely Seen MS61 1869 Quarter Eagle

2362 1869 MS61 PCGS. The mintage of 4,320 pieces for the 1869 quarter eagle is enough to grab most people's attention. However, only a handful of Uncirculated coins have been graded with the finest at the MS63 level. This is an outstanding example, especially for the grade. The fields are brightly mirrored, as one would expect from such a limited production run. The devices are strongly defined on each side. A number of small abrasions are present, but are only discernible with a loupe, that define the grade. Population: 1 in 61, 6 finer (6/07). (#7809)

2363 1869-S AU55 NGC. The 1869-S quarter eagle's mintage greatly exceeded that of its P-mint counterpart, though the total amounted to just 29,500 pieces. Curiously, the S-mint issue has a greater value through all higher grades. This briefly circulated piece has ample remaining luster and rich orange-gold color. Well struck save for the centers, which have a degree of softness on the highpoints. (#7810)

2364 1870 AU55 NGC. A scarce low mintage issue, with only 4,555 pieces originally coined. Lightly worn with bright yellow-orange surfaces and moderate scattered abrasions. (#7811)

2365 1873 Closed 3 MS64 NGC. A lustrous orange-gold near-Gem with smooth surfaces and blatant eye appeal. The forehead curls and the eagle's left (facing) leg are typically struck. Census: 36 in 64, 3 finer (5/07). (#7818)

2366 1873-S AU58 NGC. Only 27,000 pieces were struck, so it comes as little surprise that the 1873-S is rare in Mint State. This bright mustard-gold example lacks detectable highpoint wear, but the fields flash instead of displaying cartwheel sheen. A clean piece with minor weakness of strike on the eagle's body. Census: 49 in 58, 25 finer (5/07). (#7820)

2367 1877 AU53 PCGS. Boldly struck with an interplay of lime-gold and reddish coloration over both sides. The surfaces display a noteworthy lack of abrasions. Faintly worn with a few wispy hairlines in the fields. Only 1,632 business strikes were produced. (#7826)

2368 1877 AU55 ANACS. A mere 1,632 quarter eagles were struck in 1877. One can only image what a double eagle with such a mintage would sell for in AU55, but the little-saved 1877 quarter eagle trades for substantially less, and has to be considered a bargain in U.S. numismatics. Lustrous and crisply struck with a couple of thin marks near the eagle's left (facing) wing. (#7826)

2369 1877-S MS61 NGC. This meticulously struck S-mint example has fewer marks than expected of the grade, and the borders display formidable cartwheel sheen. Scarce in Mint State compared with the post-Victorian dates. Census: 66 in 61, 65 finer (6/07). (#7827)

2370 1879 MS63 PCGS. Although this date carries little premium over common issues, it is scarce in higher Mint State grades. This piece has sharp details and excellent luster with frosty yellow-gold surfaces. (#7830)

2371 1880 AU58 NGC. A briefly circulated representative of this low-mintage issue, well-defined with considerable prooflike luster evident at the margins. The surfaces are largely yellow-gold with a subtle undercurrent of orange. Census: 34 in 58, 49 finer (5/07). (#7832)

Flashy Near-Gem 1882 Two and a Half

2372 1882 MS64 NGC. This pinpoint-sharp near-Gem has flashy fields and appears to merit a prooflike designation, although the prior generation NGC holder bears no such notation. A small bright mark is present between stars 3 and 4. A mere 4,000 pieces were struck, and since there was little if any contemporary collecting, Mint State examples are rare, more so than the costly 1882 three dollar.
From The Silver Fox Collection. (#7834)

2373 1886 MS62 PCGS. A flashy and unworn butter-yellow representative of this low-mintage issue, one of just 4,000 pieces struck. Solidly struck with a degree of reflectivity in the fields and scattered, grade-defining abrasions. Population: 13 in 62, 14 finer (4/07). (#7838)

2374 1887 MS61 NGC. This attentively struck and unblemished better date quarter eagle has good luster and excellent eye appeal. Only 6,160 business strikes were produced. (#7839)

Scarce Low Mintage 1890 Quarter Eagle MS66

2375 1890 MS66 NGC. Low mintage quarter eagles from the 1880s and 1890s combine both scarcity and collectibility, and it is surprising that relatively few numismatists collect this subset. Despite a tiny mintage of 8,720 pieces, the 1890 is obtainable and affordable in Mint State. Of course, the present flashy Premium Gem is much better than the usual 1890, since the semi-prooflike fields are nearly immaculate. The strike is also exquisite, and only a single shiny spot on the neck prevents an even finer grade. Attractive brass-gold color adorns both sides. Virtually unimprovable quality for this scarcer date. The die scratch in the mid-right side of the shield is present on some, if not all, examples (Jeff Garrett and Ron Guth, 2006). Census: 7 in 66, 1 finer (5/07). (#7842)

2376 1891 MS63 PCGS. A flashy peach-gold piece with clean surfaces and a penetrating strike. Prominently die doubled on AMERICA and other right-side design elements, as always on this underappreciated business strike issue. Only 10,960 pieces were struck. (#7843)

2377 1891 MS64 NGC. The right reverse has dramatic die doubling, characteristic of this low mintage date. Lustrous and intricately struck. This honey-gold and lime near-Gem appears worthy of a finer grade at first glance, although a loupe reveals a few nearly imperceptible obverse hairlines. Census: 29 in 64, 4 finer (5/07). (#7843)

2378 1898 MS64 NGC. An amazing example with loads of eye appeal, this satiny near-Gem is sharply struck and highly lustrous. (#7850)

2379 1898 MS64 Prooflike NGC. This flashy and meticulously struck near-Gem exhibits bright honey-gold color and surprisingly clean fields. Expect a conservative bid to be inadequate to obtain this impressive example. One of just 24,000 pieces struck. NGC has encapsulated only five 1898 Quarter Eagles as Prooflike. Census: 2 in 64 Prooflike, 0 finer (5/07).
From The Vanek Collection. (#77850)

Exuberant, Underrated Gem 1899 Quarter Eagle

2380 **1899 MS65 NGC.** Quarter eagle mintages from late in the Liberty Head series are surprisingly low, a fact sometimes forgotten in the face of the relative abundance of half eagles from the same timeframe. In the case of the 1899 quarter eagle, for example, no more than 27,200 business strikes plus 150 proofs were produced, and yet it trades like an ordinary type coin. This Gem example offers exuberant luster over sharply struck antique-gold surfaces. A thin circular scrape, visible only at a certain angle, likely limits a potentially finer grade. Census: 46 in 65, 37 finer (6/07). (#7851)

Delightful 1899 Quarter Eagle, MS66

2381 **1899 MS66 PCGS.** The 27,200 pieces struck for this turn-of-the-century issue would be the last mintage for a circulating issue to be so low. This carefully preserved and delightful orange-gold example is one of the finest surviving representatives. The strongly lustrous and carefully preserved orange-gold surfaces host sharply struck devices with soft peach overtones. Population: 16 in 66, 4 finer (5/07). (#7851)

2382 **1902 MS64 PCGS.** Outstanding luster issues from well preserved peach-gold surfaces. Excellent definition reaches across all of the design features. (#7854)

2383 **1903 MS64 PCGS.** This expertly struck and lustrous almond-gold near-Gem is impeccably preserved, and encased in a green label holder. (#7855)

Glorious Superb Gem 1903 Quarter Eagle

2384 **1903 MS67 PCGS.** A common coin, but one that is seldom encountered so fine. As of (6/07), PCGS has certified 46 pieces in MS67, with none finer. As befits a Superb Gem, the luster is deep and unbroken, and the strike is perhaps just a hair short of full, but barely so. Tinges of hazel in the recesses complement the more prominent glorious orange-gold patination. (#7855)

2385 **1905 MS65 PCGS.** A delightful Gem example of this early 20th century issue, well-defined with soft, swirling luster and carefully preserved surfaces. The fields display a blend of sun-gold and peach colors. (#7857)

Dazzling 1906 Quarter Eagle, MS67

2386 **1906 MS67 PCGS.** The vibrant honey-gold and lemon-gold surfaces retain the same flashy, powerful luster that they had a century ago, and the decisively struck devices remain just as sharp. Carefully preserved and practically flawless to the unaided eye, this coin would make an excellent addition to a top-notch type set. NGC has graded just two coins finer, while PCGS notes just one (5/07). (#7858)

2387 **1907 MS64 PCGS.** Well struck with ample luster and pleasing coloration, this piece is unmarked and very close to Gem quality. Several specks of grayish verdigris adhere to some of the devices, and there is some purplish toning near the date. An attractive example of this final-year issue.
From The Vanek Collection. (#7859)

2388 **1907 MS64 NGC.** An impressive piece with excellent eye appeal created by frosty orange-gold luster and sharp design features. (#7859)

2389 **1907 MS64 PCGS.** The base of the 7 in the date is repunched. This sun-gold near-Gem has vibrant luster and a precise strike. A small gray spot is noted on the L in LIBERTY. (#7859)

PROOF LIBERTY QUARTER EAGLE

Choice Cameo Proof 1900 Two and a Half

2390 **1900 PR64 Cameo ANACS.** A razor-sharp near-Gem with flashy fields and frosty devices. A couple of faint hairlines are present beneath the wings, but these require a loupe and patience to observe. The base of the 1 in the date is lightly repunched. Only 205 proofs were struck. (#87926)

INDIAN QUARTER EAGLES

Glowing Gem 1908 Quarter Eagle

2391 1908 MS65 PCGS. Though a certain number of 1908 quarter eagles were saved for their novelty value, the negative initial public reaction limited that figure, and though examples through near-Gem are available for a price, Gems and better appear on the market with less frequency. This attractive example has a largely wheat-gold obverse and an orange-gold reverse. The devices are well-defined, and the fields have pleasing, shimmering luster. (#7939)

Shimmering Gem 1908 Two and Half

2392 1908 MS65 PCGS. Ice-blue and lilac tints visit this primarily apricot-gold Gem. Luster dominates the beautifully unperturbed fields and devices. The strike is exacting, even within the recesses of the headdress. When Bela Lyon Pratt's incused relief types were introduced, noted numismatist S.H. Chapman complained that the design was unhygienic, arguing that germs might lurk within the sunken elements. (#7939)

2393 1909 MS63 NGC. Well struck with soft satin luster and a pleasing display of light copper-golden toning over both sides. A high-end type coin with very clean surfaces for the grade. A small group of trivial abrasions in the upper right reverse field limit the grade. (#7940)

2394 1909 MS63 PCGS. This satiny and dusky green-gold example is clearly original, and has a surprisingly sharp strike within the headdress. The absence of remotely relevant marks further ensures the eye appeal. Housed in a first generation holder. (#7940)

2395 1911 MS64 PCGS. Well-defined overall with soft, satiny luster and distinctly above-average eye appeal. The vibrant, gleaming orange-gold surfaces exhibit only tiny, inoffensive marks. An attractive example of this higher-mintage Philadelphia issue, one that contrasts sharply with its Denver counterpart. (#7942)

2396 1911 MS64 NGC. The eye appeal of this Choice Uncirculated example is enhanced by a subtle interplay of lime and pastel peach hues over each side. The fine-grain surfaces exhibit pleasing satin luster and are surprisingly clean for the grade. A readily available issue that is much more affordable than its Denver Mint cousin. (#7942)

Coveted Near-Mint 1911-D Quarter Eagle

2397 1911-D AU58 PCGS. Of the 15 issues that comprise the Indian Head quarter eagle series, none is so celebrated as the low-mintage 1911-D. The briefly circulated example offered here displays a trace of friction on the well-defined devices and in the still-lustrous orange-gold fields. A few small copper spots are noted at the Indian's chin and throat. A pleasing example of this key date, one available for a fraction of the price a Mint State example would command. (#7943)

Key Date 1911-D Quarter Eagle AU58

2398 1911-D AU58 PCGS. This satiny example has the appearance of a Mint State piece at first glance. Only close examination reveals a trace of highpoint friction on the obverse, and a couple of shallow abrasions on the reverse. As noted by Garrett and Guth (2006): "The 1911-D Indian Head quarter eagle is the key to the series in all grades." (#7943)

Lustrous Near-Mint 1911-D Quarter Eagle

2399 1911-D AU58 NGC. Nearly full luster is exhibited on this near-Mint coin with pale yellow-gold surfaces. This is a highly collectible example of the key-date Indian quarter eagle. Examples at this grade level are always in demand, as they generally fit nicely in an otherwise Mint State set of these coins. (#7943)

Popular 1911-D Quarter Eagle Key, AU58

2400 1911-D AU58 NGC. The 1911-D Indian Head quarter eagle, half eagle, and eagle are all key coins within their respective series, and yet the Saint-Gaudens 1911-D double eagle is a fairly common issue with a considerable mintage. It is a puzzlement to the present cataloger why this should be so, but the best explanation appears to be that there was simply little *need* for the smaller denominations after several years of abundant emissions. This attractive near-Mint State specimen offers few visible signs of post-strike contact, just light rub on the lustrous orange-gold and hazel-tinged surfaces. (#7943)

Denver Mint

Key 1911-D Quarter Eagle, MS62

2401 1911-D MS62 PCGS. Denver was the only branch mint to produce quarter eagles of the Indian Head design, and it did so in only three years: 1911, 1914, and 1925. While the 1925-D quarter eagle ranks as one of the most available issues of the entire series, the 1911-D and 1914-D are far less common, and the 1911-D is the most prized and publicized quarter eagle of the entire series.

Like its higher-mintage counterparts, the 1911-D quarter eagle was not saved in quantity, and Mint State representatives are always in demand. This yellow-orange example has strong detail and pleasing, satiny luster. The surfaces have only wispy marks, though these are enough to limit the grade. A single claret-colored copper spot appears between 2 and 3 o'clock on the obverse, near the tips of the feathers on the Indian's headdress. (#7943)

Fascinating 1911-D Quarter Eagle, MS62

Important 1911-D Quarter Eagle, MS63

2402 1911-D MS62 PCGS. The Denver Mint made its first quarter eagles in 1911, the same year that it struck its first cents. While the facility churned out more than 12 million of the bronze pieces that year, it struck just 55,600 of the gold coins, which created a key issue that remains popular to this day.

The surfaces of this pleasing piece are predominantly yellow-gold with a touch of wheat color on the obverse and orange overtones on the reverse. The well-defined devices are primarily mark-free, though the reverse fields display a handful of abrasions, including one that extends from the back of the eagle's neck to the I in IN. This desirable example displays beautifully and would fit well in a date set with similarly graded pieces. (#7943)

2403 1911-D MS63 NGC. The combination of a bold strike, frosty yellow-gold luster, and pristine surfaces makes this example a highly desirable specimen of the elusive 1911-D Indian quarter eagle, considered the key to a complete set of these coins. This example has a bold mintmark, an important consideration when selecting an example.

The rarity of this issue is easily explained by the low mintage of just 55,680 coins, combined with the immediate release of these pieces into circulation. Few were saved by contemporary collectors.

A relatively high population, when compared to the mintage, is explained by the rarity of the date. In any series, higher values translate to higher submissions to the grading services. More importantly, higher values mean substantially higher resubmissions of coins that have already been certified. (#7943)

Appealing 1911-D Gem Quarter Eagle

2404 1911-D MS65 PCGS. The 1911-D is the key to the Indian Head quarter eagle series in all grades. It boasts the lowest mintage (55,680 pieces) of the series, few examples of which were apparently saved at the time of issue (Jeff Garrett and Ron Guth, *Encyclopedia of U.S. Gold Coins, 1795-1933*). PCGS/NGC population/census figures indicate that most survivors are in the Very Fine to mid-Uncirculated grade range. Gems are scarce, with approximately 80 MS65 examples having been seen by both services, several of which are likely resubmissions. Five Premium Gems have been reported, and none finer.

In a September 17, 1996 *Numismatic News* article entitled "Don't Overlook Indian Head Quarter Eagles," Paul Green writes of the 1911-D that:

> "It had not become any more common over the years. It always has, and always will be the key date in the Indian Head quarter eagle set. Its prices routinely run four or five times higher than the prices of common dates. None question that it is the key date to the set and worth the price."

The MS65 coin being offered in the present lot displays radiantly lustrous surfaces that yield a gorgeous peach-gold patination, accented with a few splashes of bluish-gray on the obverse. A powerful strike sharpens the design features, including bold delineation in the Indian's hair, headdress feathers, and the eagle's plumage. The mintmark is also strong. We can discern no significant marks, which is unusual for the type, considering the vulnerability of the exposed, raised fields. A hardly noticeable alloy spot is visible on each side. This lovely piece is encapsulated in a green-label holder. Population: 17 in 65, 3 finer (6/07). (#7943)

1911 Weak D Quarter Eagle, XF45

2405 1911-D Weak D XF45 ANACS. Magnification shows just the slightest outline of the D mintmark. Further confirmation that this is a Denver coin can be seen by the presence of the wire rim on the right side of the obverse. Light, even friction can be seen over the highpoints on both obverse and reverse. Rich orange-gold color, with no mentionable marks on either side. (#7954)

Choice 1912 Two and a Half

2406 1912 MS64 PCGS. This canary-gold Choice Indian quarter eagle is well struck aside from the customary minor blending of detail on the lower extremities of the headdress. Satiny luster shimmers across the unmarked surfaces. An attractive example of this popular and collectible gold type. (#7944)

2407 1913 MS63 PCGS. Despite a series-high mintage of 722,000 pieces, the 1913 is less available in Mint State grades than the issues of the 1920s. This well-defined, subtly lustrous example has a butter-yellow obverse and deeper sunset-orange color on the reverse. (#7945)

2408 1913 MS63 PCGS. Rich apricot-gold luster shows hints of light green, and a relatively sharp strike results in good detail on the design elements, save for minor softness on some of the plumage. A few light handling marks define the grade. (#7945)

2409 1914 MS61 NGC. A luminous caramel-gold representative with surprisingly few marks. The eagle's plumage is well struck. Only the 1911-D has a lower mintage. (#7946)

2410 1914 MS62 PCGS. The 1914 has the second lowest mintage of the type, and is considered a semi-key in Mint State. This crisply struck piece has clean fields and occasional glimpses of pale lime-green toning. (#7946)

2411 1914-D MS63 PCGS. This sharply detailed piece has a special look, with pale pinkish-gold luster at the centers, surrounded by deeper orange-gold at the borders, especially on the obverse. (#7947)

Lustrous, Sharply Struck MS64 1914-D Two and a Half

2412 1914-D MS64 PCGS. In addition to its recent recognition as a rarity in the Indian quarter eagle series, the 1914-D is also well known as a strike rarity. This particular coin, however, shows none of the softness usually seen, nor does it have the buckled appearance of many examples. The mint luster is bright and frosted with no obvious interruptions of post-striking impairments. This is a splendid Indian quarter eagle, regardless of the issue, and it is an especially noteworthy 1914-D. (#7947)

2413 1915 MS64 NGC. The 1915 quarter eagle is obtainable in all grades through MS64, but becomes a moderate challenge in MS65, and is rare any finer. This near-Gem possesses apricot-gold luster and sharply impressed design elements. A few minute handling marks account for the grade. (#7948)

2414 1915 MS64 NGC. Pale orange-gold surfaces exhibit frosty luster. The devices are boldly defined on both sides of this near-Gem. (#7948)

Exuberant Gem 1915 Quarter Eagle

2415 1915 MS65 PCGS. Garrett and Guth note of the 1915 quarter eagle that it is "roughly on par with the 1909 issue in Gem MS-65 condition, but decidedly scarcer than the common 1908 issue." This exuberant Gem boasts typically mattelike khaki-gold surfaces that show nary a distraction on either side. A single unbothersome tick on the Indian's cheek is perhaps all that kept this piece from the rarefied atmosphere above MS65. Population: 84 in 65, 3 finer (6/07). (#7948)

2416 1925-D MS63 PCGS. This satiny piece, in a green-label holder, has pleasing yellow-gold luster with light orange and pale blue patina. (#7949)

2417 1925-D MS64 PCGS. The first coinage for the denomination in a decade would be the last for Denver, as quarter eagles were struck in Philadelphia only from 1926 on. This well struck apricot-gold example has soft, shimmering luster and few marks on the obverse. (#7949)

2418 1925-D MS64 PCGS. Sharp design elements and brilliant mint frost are hallmarks of this lovely yellow-gold near-Gem. (#7949)

2419 1925-D MS64 PCGS. A lovely near-Gem, this piece has highly lustrous and frosty yellow-gold surfaces with sharp design elements. (#7949)

2420 1925-D MS64 PCGS. This is an impressive near-Gem with frosty and brilliant orange-gold luster. Both sides are fully and intricately detailed. (#7949)

2421 1925-D MS64 NGC. A frosty representative, this attractive piece has brilliant yellow-gold surfaces and full luster. Both sides are slightly weak at the center. (#7949)

2422 **1925-D MS64 PCGS.** Vibrant yellow-gold color with lemon accents is the most striking feature of this attractive near-Gem. A well struck example from the final quarter eagle issue struck at the Denver Mint. (#7949)

2423 **1925-D MS64 NGC.** Some blending of detail is noted on the lower headdress, but the strike is otherwise precise, and the softly glowing fields display only inconsequential marks. Struck from moderately rotated dies. (#7949)

2424 **1926 MS63 PCGS.** Copper-red toning in the fields is contrasted against bright lime-gold devices. Lustrous and crisply struck, with minimal marks for the grade. Encapsulated in a green label PCGS holder, probably more than 15 years ago. (#7950)

2425 **1926 MS63 PCGS.** A pleasing Mint State piece with excellent yellow-gold luster and frosty surfaces. This is a desirable piece with full design details. Faint reverse hairlines limit the grade. (#7950)

2426 **1926 MS63 NGC.** A gorgeous pink-gold example, this Select Mint State quarter eagle has a few scattered abrasions and streaks of darker toning on the reverse. (#7950)

2427 **1926 MS64 NGC.** A well struck Choice example that displays subtle luster and minor marks on the yellow-orange surfaces. Subtle violet accents appear in the hollows of this Roaring Twenties piece. (#7950)

2428 **1926 MS64 PCGS.** A slightly frosty representative of this late-date quarter eagle, lemon-gold on the obverse with an orange-gold reverse. Well-defined overall with just a few too many marks to qualify for a Gem grade. (#7950)

2429 **1926 MS64 PCGS.** An attractive example of this Roaring Twenties issue, well-defined overall with satiny yellow-orange surfaces. The obverse is largely mark-free, though a few wispy marks are noted to the right of the eagle's head. (#7950)

2430 **1926 MS64 PCGS.** This boldly struck apricot-gold near-Gem has only faint grazes across the gently shimmering fields and devices. The first Philadelphia issue in 11 years, with the long gap partly due to World War I. (#7950)

2431 **1926 MS64 PCGS.** An intricately struck representative with khaki-gold toning and impressively undisturbed fields. A minor luster graze above the mouth is all that precludes a higher grade. (#7950)

2432 **1926 MS64 PCGS.** An originally toned sea-green and peach-gold type coin that has vibrant luster and a sharp strike. A thin mark in front of the chin is of little concern. (#7950)

2433 **1927 MS63 NGC.** The satiny surfaces are bright and highly lustrous. The light wheat-gold and peach toning is quite attractive. Nearly blemish-free on the obverse, the piece shows a few wispy marks on the upper reverse field. At just 388,000 pieces, the mintage for this later Indian Head quarter eagle was rather modest. (#7951)

2434 **1927 MS64 PCGS.** This luminous pumpkin-gold near-Gem is refreshingly devoid of relevant contact. The eagle and arrows are exquisitely struck, and even the often indistinct headdress has only minor incompleteness. (#7951)

2435 **1927 MS64 PCGS.** Though its mintage is slightly lower than that of its fellows, this issue commands no premium that would dissuade type collectors. This satiny and well-defined piece has yellow-gold color on the carefully preserved obverse and mustard-gold on the reverse. (#7951)

2436 **1927 MS64 PCGS.** A highly lustrous and frosty near-Gem with exceptional eye appeal. This grade level provides a good combination of grade and price. (#7951)

2437 **1927 MS64 PCGS.** Highly lustrous light yellow surfaces are splashed with specks of coppery-orange toning on each side. A few insignificant surface marks keep it out of the Gem category. (#7951)

2438 **1928 MS64 PCGS.** This satiny sun-gold quarter eagle has delightfully smooth fields, and the devices are also impressively unabraded. A tiny carbon fleck on the Indian's neck is barely worthy of mention. (#7952)

2439 **1928 MS64 PCGS.** Rich brass-gold surfaces show especially pleasing mint luster. The design elements are strongly struck throughout. (#7952)

2440 **1928 MS64 PCGS.** A well struck piece that exhibits uncommonly strong luster and occasional emerald accents against the vivid yellow-orange that comprises the majority of the surfaces. A highly appealing representative of the penultimate quarter eagle issue. (#7952)

2441 **1929 MS63 NGC.** A frosty yellow-gold example with excellent design details. This is the final year of issue and the only common gold coin issued in 1929. (#7953)

THREE DOLLAR GOLD PIECES

2442 **1854 XF45 PCGS.** Yellow-gold and tan surfaces reveal occasional wisps of light green, and traces of luster in the protected areas. Sharp definition is noted on the design features, though smoothness in portions of Liberty's hair is associated with the typically incomplete strike in that area. Some light circulation marks over each side are not bothersome. Many pieces were probably saved in this first year of issue. (#7969)

2443 **1854 AU53 PCGS.** This colorful example is primarily lemon-gold, but has blushes of olive, ruby, and ice-blue. A smooth and lovely piece despite a trivial strike-through near the ER in AMERICA. Encased in a green label holder. (#7969)

2444 **1854—Lamination—AU53 ANACS.** A small lamination has peeled on the right obverse field near the ER in AMERICA, and a hair-thin retained lamination crosses the obverse between 3:30 and 9:30. Liberty's curls have slight wear, but considerable luster beckons from the wreath and borders. (#7969)

2445 **1854 AU55 PCGS.** First year of issue and always a popular date with collectors as such. The 1854 is also the only year of the Small Letters reverse in the three dollar gold series. This piece is remarkably well struck, with no weakness noted whatsoever on the reverse wreath. Mere traces of highpoint friction and scattered small field marks define the grade.
From The Vanek Collection. (#7969)

2446 **1854 AU55 ANACS.** The first year-of-issue for the three dollar gold piece. Ample luster adorns the yellow-gold surfaces of this Choice AU example, and a well executed strike brings up the design elements. A few trivial marks are noted on each side. (#7969)

2447 **1854 AU58 PCGS.** An initial impression of this first-year piece is that it is Mint State, with nearly all of the ebullient luster still intact, but examination with a loupe confirms light wear on the highpoints of the hair and cheek. Nonetheless, the lovely canary-yellow coloration and a relative absence of surface impairments make this piece high-end in its appeal. A nice type coin for a first-year set. (#7969)

2448 **1854 AU58 NGC.** A briefly circulated example of this first-year issue that displays just a touch of friction on the highest parts of the devices. Well struck with considerable remaining luster in the sun-gold fields. (#7969)

2449 **1854 AU58 NGC.** This first year of issue coin has light yellow color with frosty luster and only a trace of wear on the design highpoints. (#7969)

Popular 1854 Three Dollar Type, MS61

2450 **1854 MS61 NGC.** Although the 1854, 1874, and 1878 three dollar gold are the most widely collected for type purposes due to their relatively plentiful mintages, the 1854 is the most abundant of the three in terms of its original emission, at 138,618 business strikes plus a smattering of proofs. Today the 1854 is the second most abundant in Mint State, superseded by the 1878. The 1854 still edges out the 1878 in being one of the always-popular first-year issues of a new type, and it is technically a one-year subtype, with the Small Letters reverse. This piece displays deep, mellow orange-gold patina, with some claims to a finer grade in terms of good eye appeal and a relative absence of distracting abrasions. (#7969)

Visually Impressive 1854 Three Dollar Gold MS64

2451 **1854 MS64 PCGS.** The first-year of issue 1854 three dollar piece, like many other first year coins, was undoubtedly saved in large numbers. Roughly 5,000 or so examples have been certified by NGC and PCGS in all grades, but with a concentration in About Uncirculated and the lower levels of Mint State. Near-Gems, the condition of the coin in this lot, can be acquired with a little patience and searching, but higher grade specimens are elusive. Both sides are awash in blazing luster and highly attractive orange-gold and mint-green patination. The design features are sharply impressed, except that portions of Liberty's hair are a tad soft. Some light handling marks, including a few faint hairlines, prevent the attainment of a higher grade. (#7969)

2452 **1854-O—Rim Damaged, Cleaned—ANACS. XF40 Details.** Each side has one or two small mint-made strike-throughs. Glossy and somewhat bright with minor edge crimping at 5 o'clock on the reverse. The sole O-mint issue of the denomination. (#7971)

Popular 1854-O Three Dollar, Choice XF

2453 **1854-O XF45 PCGS.** A perennially popular type coin, the 1854-O has numerous attributes in its favor: It is a one-year subtype along with the 1854 P- and D-mint issues because of the small-size ONE DOLLAR denomination; it is, of course, a mintmarked piece from the first year of the three dollar series; and it is the only O-mint issue of the entire three dollar coinage. The present piece shows considerable luster remaining on the yellow-orange surfaces, which show a bit of light field chatter but no singular distractions. The central strike is a bit soft on the 85 of the date, as often seen. (#7971)

First-Year 1854-O Three Dollar Gold, AU53

2454 **1854-O AU53 NGC.** The 1854-O three dollar gold is a popular (and essential) coin for collectors attempting to assemble a complete mintmarked set of this series. While there are numerous alternatives available for the P- and S-mint issues, for the Dahlonega and New Orleans coins, only the respective 1854 pieces will suffice. This example offers light yellow-gold surfaces with few visible distractions and good luster, although a few light ticks and scrapes appear under a loupe, attesting to a short spate in circulation. (#7971)

2455 **1855 AU55 NGC.** Slight wear on Liberty's hair and forehead confirms the Choice AU designation, but luster is plentiful except across the open fields. The right obverse has a couple of traces of struck-in grease. (#7972)

2456 **1855 AU58 NGC.** Boldly detailed with nice yellow-gold color, substantial luster for the grade, and only slight indications of highpoint wear. An appealing coin with minimal damage from circulation.
From The Vanek Collection. (#7972)

Lustrous 1856 Three Dollar, MS62

2457 1856 MS62 NGC. Among regular issue gold coins, this denomination is the rarest overall. The 1856 three is relatively plentiful in circulated grades, but it is hard to locate in Mint State. The average certified grade is just 54.3, according to Jeff Garrett and Ron Guth, and this is inflated by the rule that higher grade coins are more likely to be submitted and resubmitted. This piece is a splendid representative of the date and denomination with frosty yellow-gold luster and excellent surfaces. Some design weakness is evident on each side. (#7974)

1856-S Three Dollar Gold, AU55

2458 1856-S AU55 NGC. Medium S. If the unique 1870-S is excluded, the San Francisco Mint struck three dollar gold pieces for only four years, from 1855 to 1857 and again in 1860. The 1856-S is the most available of the four dates, but since only 34,500 pieces were struck, survivors are scarce. The present nearly unabraded example has a band of bright luster across the obverse legends, and luster also illuminates the wreath, date, and denomination. (#7975)

Condition Scarcity 1857 Three Dollar, MS62

2459 1857 MS62 PCGS. One of the more available of the early dates in the three dollar series, the 1857 is usually found well circulated and strict Mint State coins are quite scarce. This MS62 piece displays some orange-golden color and faint die striations that are usually seen on high grade pieces of this issue. The strike is somewhat soft on the upper hair curls and bow knot. Minor obverse handling marks are noted. Population: 19 in 62, 15 finer (6/07). (#7976)

2460 1859 AU55 PCGS. Hints of subtle luster grace the margins of this lightly circulated mustard-gold example. A well struck and minimally marked piece, one of just 15,500 coins minted. (#7979)

2461 1859 AU55 NGC. The present AU55 piece boasts canary-yellow centers that deepen to auburn at the obverse rims and the protected areas on the reverse. Singular distractions are nil, and a goodly portion of the original mint luster is expectedly still present. (#7979)

2462 1860 XF45 ANACS. Orange luster brightens the legends of this moderately circulated example. A faded, thin, diagonal mark is noted near the LL in DOLLARS. A scant 7,036 pieces were struck. (#7980)

Choice AU 1860 Three Dollar

2463 1860 AU55 ANACS. The mintage of just 7,036 pieces means that this date is scarce in all grades. Like most examples of this date, this piece is sharply struck and exhibits frosty green-gold luster. Hints of orange toning are visible on the reverse. A few faint hairlines and other tiny blemishes are visible on each side. (#7980)

Choice XF 1860-S Three Dollar

2464 1860-S XF45 NGC. An attractive Choice XF example, this piece exhibits satiny luster in the protected areas on each side. The surfaces are light yellow with hints of pink overtones. Just four officially produced three dollar gold coins came from the San Francisco Mint (the 1870-S issue is not considered here), including this issue and 1855-S, 1856-S, and 1857-S. Total production for all four dates was only about 62,000 coins, including a mintage of 7,000 pieces in 1860. (#7981)

2465 1862—Scratched—ANACS. AU58 Details. Substantial orange-gold luster bathes protected areas. A few light horizontal pinscratches surround DOLLARS and the date. This Civil War date has a mintage of just 5,750 pieces, and the survival rate is lower than the low mintage issues that close the series. (#7983)

2466 1863—Cleaned—ANACS. XF45 Details. This Civil War date has a tiny mintage of 5,000 pieces. The yellow-gold fields are glossy from hairlines, but there is only one noticeable mark, beneath the D in DOLLARS. Struck from boldly clashed dies. (#7984)

Difficult AU53 1866 Three Dollar

2467 **1866 AU53 PCGS.** The highpoints have a hint of wear, but luster dominates the legends, wreath, and crown. Thorough inspection locates no remotely mentionable marks. A mere 4,000 business strikes were coined, and it is likely that less than 10% of the mintage has survived. Housed in a green label holder. (#7987)

2468 **1872 XF45 PCGS.** The 1872 had a low mintage of only 2,000 business strikes. This piece shows noticeable semi-prooflikeness in the fields, a usual feature of this issue. There are no distracting blemishes, but wispy hairlines are noted on each side. Not quite as scarce as the mintage might indicate, but still a desirable coin at this grade level. (#7994)

Low Mintage Choice AU 1872 Three Dollar

2469 **1872 AU55 PCGS.** The 1872 has a low mintage of 2,000 pieces, and those were saved in small numbers. PCGS has certified only 27 pieces in Mint State, or about one per year of its operations, assuming that at least a few represent resubmissions. This orange-gold example has slight wear on the cheek and hair, but the surfaces are unperturbed aside from a rose-red spot on the wreath near 9 o'clock. Housed in a green label holder. Population: 19 in 55, 60 finer (4/07). (#7994)

Choice AU 1872 Three Dollar

2470 **1872 AU55 NGC.** Prooflike luster fills the legends of this handsome, lightly handled representative. A solitary thin mark near the CA in AMERICA is mentioned as a pedigree identifier. A scant 2,000 pieces were struck, and problem-free examples with light circulation are seldom seen. Encased in an early generation holder. (#7994)

Important 1872 Three, AU58

2471 **1872 AU58 NGC.** Just shy of Mint State, this piece has nearly full yellow-gold luster with traces of orange toning. The fields show a hint of mirrored surface, suggesting that this piece was prooflike when it was struck. Despite a mintage of just 2,000 coins, this issue is generally available in XF and AU grades, but Mint State coins are seldom seen. Census: 55 in 58, 28 finer (6/07). (#7994)

2472 **1874 AU55 NGC.** An ideal Choice AU type coin, slightly scarcer than the most common dates and free from remotely mentionable marks. Pockets of orange luster outline the legends and devices. (#7998)

2473 **1874 AU55 ANACS.** This issue ranks among the three highest mintage dates of the denomination, a common coin for type collectors. Both sides are satiny and slightly reflective with green-gold coloration. (#7998)

2474 **1874 AU58 NGC.** Though 1874 was a fruitful year for business strikes, 41,800 pieces in total, the following two years saw proof-only issues. This strongly lustrous wheat-gold example has pleasing detail and just a touch of friction on the highpoints. Highly appealing. (#7998)

2475 **1874 AU58 PCGS.** The satin luster is nearly complete, and only a hint of friction on the design's high points separate this lovely piece from Mint State. Well struck except for the bow on the wreath, and free of individually noticeable surface marks. (#7998)

Flashy 1874 Three Dollar Gold MS62

2476 **1874 MS62 PCGS.** This is a flashy, frosty Mint State example that boasts pleasing greenish honey-gold coloration and uniformly crisp striking details. Wispy marks, located mainly in the fields, limit the assigned grade of the piece. One of the three most commonly encountered dates in the series, the 1874 is often used for three dollar gold type purposes. (#7998)

2477 **1878 AU55 PCGS.** The grade is discounted slightly due to a few faint hairlines on each side. Only the slightest wear visits the highpoints. Both sides have nearly full satin luster with light yellow color. (#8000)

Richly Colored MS64 1878 Three Dollar

2478 **1878 MS64 PCGS.** The 1878 is the most frequently encountered three dollar and is most commonly used for type purposes. For the collector who wants something extra, this piece has rich, original rose and lilac patina interspersed over each side. As usual, the mint luster is thick and frosted and on this piece further enhances the lovely colors. Lightly abraded, as one would expect from an MS64. (#8000)

2479 **1879—Damaged—ANACS. AU55 Details.** This well struck example possesses considerable flashy luster, but close study locates a dig above the bust tip, and concealed mark on the forehead. The central reverse is slightly wavy. Only 3,000 pieces were struck. (#8001)

2480 **1879 AU55 NGC.** Apricot-gold and mint-green coloration adheres to minimally abrades surfaces. Traces of luster reside in the recessed areas, and the design elements are well defined. From a mintage of 3,000 business strikes. (#8001)

Near-Mint 1881 Three Dollar Gold

2481 **1881 AU58 PCGS.** In 1881, Philadelphia produced just 500 business strikes, the third-lowest quantity coined behind the non-collectible 1870-S and the 1873 Close 3 restrikes. This well-defined orange-gold example displays a generous amount of partially prooflike luster, while the highpoints of devices reveal just a hint of friction. Population: 16 in 58, 25 finer (6/07). (#8003)

Choice AU 1882 Three Dollar

2482 **1882 AU55 ANACS.** Only 1,500 business strikes were issued for this difficult three dollar issue. This example has slight friction on the forehead and the left border of the hair, but luster fills the plumes, wreath, and legends. The 2 is widely repunched north, as usually seen. (#8004)

Well Struck 1882 Three Dollar, MS62 Prooflike

2483 **1882 MS62 Prooflike NGC.** The low-mintage 1882 three dollar piece (1,500 circulation strikes) has a fairly high Mint State survival rate. Few of them are Prooflike, however. Indeed, NGC has seen just 12 such coins, including the MS62 example in this lot. Peach-gold surfaces yield strong motif-field contrast, along with sharply defined devices. Inoffensive handling marks in the fields define the grade. Circulation strikes are differentiated from proofs by a repunched 2 in the date, with the remnants of an earlier 2 above and in the center of the final 2 (David Bowers, 2005).
From The Vanek Collection. (#78004)

Well Defined 1888 Three Dollar, MS61

2484 **1888 MS61 PCGS.** The net distribution of 1888 three dollar gold coins may have been less than the 5,000 business strikes minted, per a comment by numismatist S.H. Chapman: "Of the later years of the $3, large numbers were remelted at the Philadelphia Mint." A sharp strike emboldens the design features of this lustrous apricot-gold MS61 example. A small linear mark on Liberty's jaw and wispy handling marks in the fields preclude a higher grade. Housed in a green-label holder.
From The Vanek Collection. (#8010)

Desirable 1888 Three Dollar MS66

2485 1888 MS66 PCGS. The 1888 is one of many issues within the three dollar series with enticingly low mintages. Only 5,000 pieces were struck, which, if put into perspective, is only 5% of the mintage of the 1893-S dollar. It is true that the 1888 circulated little, since survivors are more often found in Mint State than in worn condition. It is also true that the majority of the issue has likely been melted, since the combined NGC and PCGS population is less than 1,000 pieces, which undoubtedly includes a large number of resubmissions over the past 20 years. The MS62 to MS64 grades account for a sizeable portion of Uncirculated 1888 examples. Gems are scarce, and Premium Gems are rare. Speculators often gravitate toward the 1888 because of its low mintage, which is only about 6% of the 1878 type coin. Yet the 1888 trades for only a small premium above type prices. Shrewd gold type collectors often select the 1888, since it provides greater value than the "common" 1878.

This splendid representative possesses rich apricot toning that is deepest across the open fields. The strike is penetrating, even on the plumes of the headdress and the knot of the bow, which are sometimes mushy on this denomination. As one would expect from the MS66 grade, Liberty's cheek is refreshingly unabraded, and the obverse field is also clean. On the reverse, contact is minimal aside from a couple of minor grazes relegated to the periphery near 9 o'clock. UNITED is strongly die doubled, a diagnostic for business strikes of the date. This lustrous Premium Gem would make a suitable contribution to a high grade gold type set, and would also set a lofty standard for a date collection of the series. Population: 26 in 66, 2 finer (4/07). (#8010)

Attractive 1889 Three Dollar, MS63

2486 1889 MS63 PCGS. Both sides of this piece have satiny yellow-gold luster with hints of field reflectivity. The surfaces have numerous tiny abrasions, but none that individually stand out. It is sharply detailed, although not fully struck. This issue, the final date of the denomination, was only produced to the extent of 2,300 coins, although the survival rate was high and Mint State pieces are only considered slightly better than common today. (#8011)

Oliver C. Bosbyshell
Superintendent of the Philadelphia Mint
1889-1894

EARLY HALF EAGLES

Well Defined 1795 Small Eagle Five Dollar
AU Details, BD-3

2487 **1795 Small Eagle—Obverse Damage, Improperly Cleaned—NCS. AU Details.** Breen-6412, BD-3, High R.3. Star 11 overlies the Y of LIBERTY and joins star 12, the only 1795 obverse with this feature. On the reverse, a leaf touches the bottom of U in UNITED, another touches the right bottom of the left foot of N and extends past the center of N, and the wreath has four berries, two each side, inside and out.

Yellow-gold surfaces retain traces of luster in the recesses, and display splashes of apricot and red. Sharp definition is noted on the well centered design elements, and the dentilation is complete and strong on both sides. A small scalloped mark (hardly noticeable at first glance) was punched into Liberty's shoulder and the field below, causing a nearly imperceptible bulge in the corresponding area of the reverse, and some fine hairlines are visible under magnification. These flaws are really not all that bad, and should not intimidate the prospective bidder. (#8066)

Lustrous 1806 BD-2 Half Eagle
XF45 Details

2488 **1806 Pointed Top 6, 8x5 Stars—Damaged, Cleaned—ANACS. XF45 Details.** Breen-6447, BD-2, R.5. Both sides of this piece have bright green-gold color with extensively abraded surfaces. The central obverse and reverse show considerable weakness, the result of heavy adjustment marks at the center of the reverse. Despite the issues, this coin retains considerable luster and eye appeal. (#8090)

Elias Boudinot, Mint Director
1795-1805

Gorgeous 1807 Bust Left Five Dollar, MS65, BD-8

2489 **1807 Bust Left MS65 PCGS.** Breen-6453, BD-8, R.2. The reported mintage of this first-year-of issue Capped Bust to Left design type was 51,605 pieces. Jeff Garrett and Ron Guth, discussing the 1807 Capped Bust Left in their *Encyclopedia of U.S. Gold Coins, 1795-1933*, write that "circulated examples are easily obtained across all grade levels, and even Mint State examples can be found with ease. The usual Mint State grade falls at MS62 or MS63; gems are very rare." In this regard, we note that PCGS and NGC combined have certified, to date, only 13 MS65 and finer 1807 Bust Left examples.

This issue consists of two varieties, BD-7 and BD-8, each having the same obverse but different reverses. On the BD-8 die marriage, the more common of the two varieties, the bottom tip of the arrow feather points to the tip of the flag in the 5, the O(F) is centered over the N of UNUM, and the upper middle leaf is near the U of UNITED.

Apricot-gold color imbued with wisps of mint-green enriches both sides of this gorgeous Gem, each of which displays glowing luster. A powerful strike manifests itself in uniformly crisp definition on the nicely centered design elements, and the dentilation is complete and strong, save for minor softness in the upper left reverse quadrant. A few light adjustment marks at the upper left and upper right reverse border serve as pedigree markers to help identify this particular example, as does a faint, completely inoffensive linear mark that extends diagonally from the lower point of star 8 to below the cap.

A simply outstanding specimen that is worthy of the finest collection, and as such is expected to elicit spirited bidding. Population: 5 in 65, 2 finer (4/07). (#8101)

Sharply Struck 1808 Five Dollar, MS61, BD-4

2490 **1808 MS61 PCGS.** Wide 5 D, Breen-6457, BD-4, High R.3. This variety is confirmed by the non-overdate with the date centered between the dentils and the bust, a widely spaced 5 D, centering of the A in STATES over the U of PLURIBUS, and the A near the wing.

Apricot-gold surfaces display hints of light tan, with the most potent luster residing in the areas around, and in the interstices of, the motifs. An attentive strike brings out sharp definition on the well centered design elements. Clash marks are noted on both sides, and a reverse crack travels from the middle of the left (right facing) wing through RICA and D to the field below the right (left facing) wing. Overall, a sharp early half eagle. (#8102)

CLASSIC HALF EAGLES

2491 **1834 Plain 4—Cleaned—ANACS. XF45 Details.** First Head, Breen-6501, McCloskey 3-B, R.2. The devices are bold and lustrous, but this first-year Classic five is a bit bright, and the upper reverse field is abraded. (#8171)

2492 **1834 Plain 4 AU53 NGC.** First Head, Breen-6501, McCloskey 1-A, R.3. Well struck for the type, and wear is limited to friction on the eyebrow and curl highpoints. Clean, aside from a diagonal mark on the cheek. (#8171)

2493 **1834 Plain 4 AU53 ANACS.** First Head, Breen-6501, McCloskey 3-A, R.3. The portrait highpoints exhibit slight wear, but ample luster illuminates the hair, eagle, and peripheral elements. The occasional minor marks are fewer than expected of the grade. (#8171)

2494 **1834 Plain 4 AU55 NGC.** First Head, Breen-6501, McCloskey 3-B, R.2. This crisply struck half eagle has ample luster and unblemished surfaces. Cherry-red, orange, and lime tints adorn the margins. (#8171)

2495 **1834 Plain 4 AU55 NGC.** Second Head, Breen-6502, McCloskey 2-A, R.2. Golden-brown luster bathes protected areas of this lightly circulated and attractive Classic Head type coin. The strike shows minor blending on Liberty's forehead curls and on the eagle's shield. (#8171)

2496 **1834 Plain 4 AU55 PCGS.** Second Head, Breen-6502, McCloskey 2-B, R.3. Triple punched 4 in the date with the arrow feather on the reverse centered over the 5 in the denomination. The eagle does not have a tongue. This variety is considered scarcer than the common varieties. Both sides have pleasing surfaces with greenish-gold luster and traces of highpoint wear. (#8171)

Smooth 1834 Plain 4 Classic Five MS62

2497 **1834 Plain 4 MS62 PCGS.** Second Head, Breen-6502, McCloskey 2-A, R.2. A lovely lemon-gold Classic five dollar piece from the introductory year of the short-lived type. The reverse is impressively smooth, and the few minor obverse marks are relegated to the margins. The strike is good, with slight softness limited to the cheekbone curl and the left shield border. (#8171)

2498 **1835 XF40 NGC.** Second Head, Breen-6505, McCloskey 3-D, R.3. Luster emerges from Liberty's curls and the eagle's plumage and shield. A thin mark is found beneath the beak, but the subdued surfaces generally are only lightly abraded. (#8173)

2499 **1835—Cleaned—ANACS. AU58 Details.** First Head, Breen-6504, McCloskey 1-A, R.2. Light hairlines cross this well struck Classic five, but there are surprisingly few bagmarks. Luster dominates the devices and reverse legends. (#8173)

2500 **1836 XF45 PCGS.** Small Head, Large Date, Breen-6508, McCloskey 5-D, R.3. A moderately circulated Classic gold type coin. Glimpses of dirt within design recesses confirm the originality. A thin horizontal mark on the upper right reverse field is of only minor concern. (#8174)

2501 **1838 AU50 PCGS.** Large Arrows, Small 5, Breen-6514, McCloskey 1-A, R.2. This smooth yellow-gold representative has a precise strike and only moderate highpoint wear. Luster outlines design elements, and there are no obtrusive marks. (#8176)

2502 **1838 AU53 PCGS.** Large Arrows, Small 5, Breen-6514, McCloskey 1-A, R.2. A lovely representative from the final year of the short-lived type. Golden-brown luster outlines the richly defined design elements, and the slightly subdued fields are void of distracting marks. (#8176)

Radiant 1838-D Half Eagle, AU58

2503 **1838-D AU58 PCGS.** Variety 1-A, McCloskey 1-A, R.3. The year's production for this denomination, 20,583 pieces from a single set of dies, is the point of intersection for many Mint milestones, oft-mentioned but worth repeating: the first and only denomination coined in the initial year of operation for Dahlonega, the only Classic Head half eagles from that Mint, and the corresponding niche as the only half eagles from that Mint to have the mintmark on the obverse.

The yellow-orange surfaces of this piece display ample remaining luster and surprisingly few marks. The devices are well-defined, a trait shared by many high-grade examples, with only a touch of highpoint friction. Though this issue is available for a price in grades through lower About Uncirculated, a near-Mint representative is a condition rarity, and many concede that the certified population contains a number of resubmissions. Population: 21 in 58, 11 finer (4/07). (#8178)

LIBERTY HALF EAGLES

Condition Rarity AU53 1840-D Half Eagle, Variety 3-B

2504 **1840-D Tall D AU53 NGC.** Variety 3-B. Seldom seen better than Extremely Fine, the 1840-D is a first-year subtype, as the design was modified from the 1839 portrait, and the mintmark was placed on the reverse, where it would subsist until 1907. This variety is easily distinguished by the die defect touching star 13, which extends from the rim, and the Tall D on the reverse bears an opening that is more than "twice the width of its upright," as Winter says. Although Breen believed that Broad Mill (wide-diameter 22.5-mm coins) were struck, all of the later research indicates that only Narrow Mill pieces exist, with a 21.7-mm width.

Regardless of variety, the 1840-D as an issue is rare in AU or finer condition. The present specimen boasts a sharp obverse strike, with moderate reverse softness on the eagle's legs and neck, and the fletchings. Considerable luster and a relative paucity of singular abrasions complete the attractive package. Census: 5 in 53, 26 finer (6/07). (#8198)

Bright 1840-D Five Dollar, XF40 Variety 4-C, Small D

2505 **1840-D Small D XF40 NGC.** Variety 4-C. The Small Mintmark variety with diagnostic die crack extending above and below the D. The surfaces on both sides are bright yellow-gold, and reveal the normal amount of contact marks scattered about. Generally well defined, except for some weakness on the eagle's plumage. Rare any finer. (#8199)

2506 **1842-D Small Date—Obverse Rim Filed—NCS. XF Details.** Variety 8-E. The obverse rim is filed near 6 and 9 o'clock. This Dahlonega Mint half eagle has also been cleaned, but there are no mentionable marks. (#8210)

2507 **1844-D—Graffiti, Cleaned—ANACS. XF45 Details.** Variety 11-H. The initials DA are lightly entered on the left obverse field, and TC is faintly pinscratched onto the upper reverse field. This coin is subdued from a chemical cleaning, but noticeable luster remains, especially on the reverse. (#8221)

AU 1846-D Liberty Five

2508 **1846-D AU50 NGC.** Variety 16-K. The date is low, and the Dahlonega mintmark shows no sign of repunching. Luster brightens the stars, legends, and device crevices. The fields and portrait are generally smooth for an AU gold coin. The dies appear perfect except for minor clashing near Liberty's chin. (#8228)

2509 **1848-C XF45 PCGS.** Variety 11-E, the only known variety. Both sides have light abrasions with deep green-gold color at the centers, framed by rich lilac toning. (#8237)

1848-D Five Dollar, XF Details

2510 **1848-D—Cleaned—ANACS. XF45 Details.** Variety 15-J. Die State I. A scarcer D-mint five and seldom seen any finer than XF. This particular coin does not show the obverse die cracks seen on later states. The surfaces are cleaner than usually seen, with the only mentionable mark a shallow scratch in the field in front of the arrow tips. Bright from cleaning. Well defined. (#8238)

Elusive Choice AU 1848-D Five

2511 **1848-D AU55 PCGS.** Variety 18-M. This tan-gold Dahlonega five is generally sharp, with the exception of the eagle's neck and the curl below the ear. A smooth piece that retains glowing luster in selected areas. Radial die cracks are noted at 5 o'clock on the obverse and at 10:30 and 4:30 on the reverse. A further crack is present between 5 and 6 o'clock on the reverse, and the obverse is clashed above the chin and beneath the hair bun. Population: 14 in 55, 19 finer (5/07). (#8238)

2512 **1849/49 AU55 NGC.** Breen-6582. The 49 in the date is boldly repunched south. Orange and rose toning enhances this refreshingly unmarked No Motto five. Ample luster brightens recessed areas. The eagle's neck is typically struck. Census: 6 in 55, 10 finer (5/07). (#8240)

Pleasing, Sharp MS61 1850 Five, Rare in Mint State

2513 **1850 MS61 PCGS.** "Perhaps if wealthy collectors from the Philadelphia area were to pursue collecting the Philadelphia Mint issues, prices would finally reflect the true rarity of these scarce coins." So say gold pundits Jeff Garrett and Ron Guth in relation to this issue, to which they append that it is "very rare in Mint State..." This lovely and historic piece, from the antebellum mintage of 64,491 pieces, suggests at first glance the eye appeal of a finer grade, with brilliant luster radiating from the charming canary-yellow surfaces. Only under a loupe does one note the numerous small scrapes and two reeding marks on Liberty's chin. A well struck and pleasing example. Population: 2 in 61, 4 finer (6/07). (#8243)

2514 **1850-D XF40 NGC.** Variety 24-P. This pale green-gold Dahlonega five has noticeable glimpses of soft luster within protected areas. The strike is typical on Liberty's hair and the eagle's neck and fletchings. (#8245)

Charming Choice AU 1851-C Five

2515 **1851-C AU55 NGC.** Variety 16-G. This impressive Charlotte Mint five exhibits substantial glowing luster and is void of remotely mentionable marks. Well struck for a branch mint issue with only minor blending of detail on the eagle's neck and fletchings, and on the curl beneath Liberty's ear. Census: 21 in 55, 28 finer (5/07). *From The Vanek Collection.* (#8247)

Elusive Near-Mint State 1851-C Half Eagle

2516 **1851-C AU58 NGC.** Variety 16-G, characterized by what branch mint gold pundit Douglas Winter calls a "punch" on Liberty's earlobe that resembles an earring. The antique-gold surfaces of this piece show only light abrasions, along with a good, if less than full strike. Considerable luster remains, as expected, and the eye appeal is equally generous. A nice near-Mint State example of this elusive issue, seldom seen finer. Census: 17 in 58, 11 finer (6/07). (#8247)

AU 1851-D Half Eagle, Ex: Bass

2517 1851-D AU50 PCGS. Ex: Bass. Variety 26-O. Well struck and undipped with a pleasing band of luster across the left-side stars. The "Weak D" variety, although the upper half of the mintmark is unmistakable. Occasional glimpses of green debris are inconspicuous within design crevices.
Ex: Superior, 12/72, lot 1951; Harry W. Bass, Jr. Collection, Part II (Bowers and Merena, 10/99), lot 1028. (#8248)

2518 1852 AU58 NGC. Peach-gold toning graces this lightly abraded and partly lustrous No Motto five. A few stars are indifferently struck, but the devices are attractively defined. (#8250)

Desirable 1852-D Half Eagle, AU50

2519 1852-D AU50 NGC. Variety 27-U. This is an attractive light yellow-gold example that has somewhat blunt details especially evident on the obverse. A few minor abrasions are visible from a brief time in circulation. Considerable luster is still present in the protected areas around the devices on both sides. (#8252)

Desirable 1853-C Half Eagle, AU53

2520 1853-C AU53 PCGS. Variety 21-H. A lightly worn representative of this popular, comparatively available Charlotte issue, well-defined save for softness at the hair to the right of Liberty's eye and the eagle's claws. The softly lustrous yellow-orange surfaces have deeper color near the margins. Though the fields and devices display scattered abrasions, like many examples of later Charlotte gold, the overall effect is less distracting than on most pieces. Population: 14 in 53, 34 finer (5/07). (#8254)

AU55 Sharpness 1853-D Five

2521 1853-D Large D—Cleaned—ANACS. AU55 Details. Variety 29-T. This mildly bright Dahlonega representative is well struck save for star 4 and the fletchings. Close scrutiny with the aid of a loupe locates a faint pinscratch along the profile and faint marks near the date. The reverse has a minor rim bruise at 7 o'clock. (#8255)

Attractive Choice AU 1853-D Half Eagle

2522 1853-D Large D AU55 NGC. Variety 29-V. A suitable coin for a type or mintmark set to represent the Liberty Head half eagle, the 1853-D is the most widely encountered D-mint half eagle due to its generous mintage of nearly 90,000 examples. This piece displays the typically weak borders, with attractive, problem-free orange-gold surfaces otherwise. (#8255)

Nice AU58 1853-D Large D Five

2523 1853-D Large D AU58 NGC. Variety 29-T, with the left serifs of the D mintmark centered over the top left diagonal of the V in FIVE. This coin would be a superb example for type or date purposes, as much prooflikeness appears on each side, and even the normally weak borders are much better struck than typically seen on this issue. A nice near-Mint State specimen! Census: 85 in 58, 35 finer (6/07). (#8255)

Incredible 1853-D Half Eagle, Large D, MS62

2524 1853-D Large D MS62 PCGS. Variety 29-U. The satiny and softly shimmering surfaces of this marvelous Mint State representative exhibit warm yellow-orange color with a handful of delicate, deeper overtones. While the stars and other peripheral elements on the obverse are slightly weak, the centers are strong, and the overall eye appeal is noteworthy. The obverse has few marks for the grade, though the upper and right reverse fields show wispy abrasions.

This is an important example that would make an excellent addition to a date set or stand out as a marquee coin in a broader collection. Though the 1853-D half eagle is widely known as one of the most easily obtainable pieces of early branch mint gold, even this "available" issue becomes elusive in Mint State grades, and the population figures are doubtless influenced by resubmissions. Population: 9 in 62, 6 finer (5/07). (#8255)

2525 1854-O AU55 NGC. A sharply struck Choice AU O-mint five that is without mentionable marks. Infrequent freckles of russet cling to protected peripheral areas. Only 46,000 pieces were struck. Census: 23 in 55, 48 finer (6/07). (#8259)

2526 1854-O AU55 NGC. The 1854-O is one of the more available O-mint fives and the most frequently encountered from the 1850s. However, it is scarce above VF-XF and AU pieces are infrequently seen. This is a well, but not fully struck coin that shows almost no abrasions. The surfaces are devoid of any noticeable luster. (#8259)

Borderline Uncirculated 1855-D Five

2527 1855-D Large D AU58 NGC. Variety 32-AA. Once the San Francisco Mint reached full operation, mintages of half eagles at Dahlonega dwindled rapidly. Only 22,432 pieces were struck in 1855, a sizeable drop-off from the 89,678 pieces struck just two years before. Most certified survivors are in XF and AU grades, with only a handful of Mint State pieces known. This clean example has noticeable luster and smooth surfaces. Well struck near the borders with typical definition on the eagle's neck and the curl below the ear. Census: 17 in 58, 6 finer (5/07). (#8263)

2528 1856—Scratched—ANACS. AU55 Details. Liberty's hair has only a trace of friction, and the sun-gold surfaces are lustrous. Hair-thin marks are present on Liberty's neck curls, and an X is pinscratched on the field near the nose. (#8266)

2529 1856 MS60 NGC. This is a pleasing Uncirculated example that displays shimmering luster and attractive coloration. Numerous small marks define the grade, few of which are individually noticeable. A conditionally scarce issue in Mint State. Census: 5 in 60, 31 finer (6/07). (#8266)

Radiant 1856-C Half Eagle, AU55

2530 1856-C AU55 NGC. Variety 24-J. Surprisingly well-defined for this issue, with only slight weakness on the portrait and the eagle's neck. The wings and shield, among other features, display uncharacteristic sharpness. The reverse of this straw-gold example displays few marks, though the obverse exhibits scattered abrasions, including one of note just to the left of star 12. Just a touch of wear is present on the highpoints. (#8267)

2531 1856-O VF35 PCGS. The right-side stars and the left wing are sharp, and luster remains in selected areas. This slightly bright example is typically struck and lacks mentionable marks. Only 10,000 pieces were struck, even fewer than the more famous 1847-O. (#8269)

Near-Mint 1857-C Five Dollar

2532 **1857-C AU58 NGC.** Variety 25-J. Luster fills the margins of this lightly abraded Charlotte Mint five. A good strike for the Southern facility, with noticeable incompleteness only on the eagle's neck and fletchings. Just 31,360 pieces were struck. Census: 43 in 58, 19 finer (6/07). (#8272)

2533 **1857-O XF45 ANACS.** A scant 13,000 pieces were struck for this challenging New Orleans issue. This slightly bright example lacks objectionable marks, and the strike is good with only moderate blending within the hair and fletchings. (#8274)

2534 **1857-S AU50 NGC.** The 1857-S saw extensive use in the daily commerce of the California Gold Rush, and most survivors are well circulated (Jeff Garrett and Ron Guth, 2006). This bright brassy-gold example with traces of luster in the recesses is one of the few survivors in high grade. Excellent definition shows on the motifs, and both sides are minimally abraded. Census: 9 in 50, 56 finer (6/07). (#8275)

2535 **1858 AU53 NGC.** This is a low-mintage date, with a production of just 15,136 coins. Most survivors are well circulated and rather unattractive. This example is a pleasing exception with lustrous greenish-gold surfaces. (#8276)

Choice XF 1859-D Five Dollar

2536 **1859-D Medium D XF45 NGC.** Variety 36-CC. The usual Winter variety for this low mintage issue. A partly lustrous apricot-gold Dahlonega five that has only one mark of any consequence, a brief pinscratch beneath the jaw. The eagle's neck and Liberty's hair are typically brought up, but the remainder of the design is bold.
From The Vanek Collection. (#8282)

Low Mintage Choice AU 1859-D Five Dollar

2537 **1859-D Medium D AU55 NGC.** Variety 36-CC, as usually found on this low mintage issue, since the Large D (Variety 36-EE) is rare. But the issue as a whole is a low mintage one, with only 10,366 examples coined of both varieties. This example offers attractive orange-gold and reddish-gold surfaces that are only lightly abraded, with considerable prooflikeness remaining. The strike is somewhat soft on the central highpoints, as is typical for the issue. Census: 16 in 55, 45 finer (6/07). (#8282)

Choice AU 1859-D Large D Five

2538 **1859-D Large D AU55 NGC.** Variety 37-EE. The rare Large D variety, which apparently constituted a small portion of the 10,366 pieces struck. Breen was unaware of this variety. This older holder example has plentiful luster for the grade, and the radiant surfaces are unblemished. The major devices are typically struck, while peripheral elements are sharp. An opportunity for the knowledgeable Southern gold specialist.
From The Vanek Collection. (#98282)

Conditionally Rare 1863-S Half Eagle, AU58

2539 1863-S AU58 NGC. To give an idea of the conditional rarity of this coin, the Smithsonian Institution's sole example is an extensively circulated Very Fine example. In the early days of the San Francisco Mint, gold coinage was much in demand (in distinct preference to unassayed gold dust or nuggets, indivisible large gold bars, or the detested paper money that was unacceptable out West), and most newly minted pieces flowed into the channels of commerce with no delay. The 1863-S is no exception, and it is accordingly all but unknown in Mint State. In fact, PCGS has certified a single Uncirculated piece (an MS61), while NGC has never certified a Mint State example as of this writing.

The present AU58 piece—among the handful of finest-obtainable pieces—is thus cause for celebration and spirited bidding on the part of rare-date gold enthusiasts. The yellow-gold surfaces retain nearly all of their original exuberant luster, with a bold strike and only light abrasions on this briefly circulated specimen. Census: 23 in 58, 0 finer (6/07). (#8295)

Scarce AU53 1868-S Five

2540 1868-S AU53 PCGS. A scarce and often-overlooked S-mint in the With Motto series. Noticeable traces of mint luster are seen around the devices and there are only minimal abrasions visible on each side. A bit softly struck in the center of the obverse, as one would expect. Medium orange-gold color. (#8316)

2541 1873 Open 3 MS62 PCGS. A beautiful orange-red example of this low mintage and conditionally rare Philadelphia issue. The luster is a bit subdued, but the unmarked appearance ensures the eye appeal. Population: 15 in 62, 18 finer (5/07). (#8328)

2542 1874-CC Fine 15 NGC. This Choice Fine half eagle exhibits peach-gold surfaces that assume slightly deeper hues in the recessed areas. The design elements retain nice definition; all of the letters in LIBERTY are strong, as are most of the beads on the hair bun and the letters in the ribbon motto. Both sides show some circulation marks consistent with the grade level. Fortunately though, heavy abrasions do not riddle the surfaces, as is typical for most '74-CC fives (Douglas Winter, 2001). (#8334)

2543 1874-CC VF35 PCGS. The surfaces of this piece, housed in a green-label holder, are subdued with pale yellow color and hints of prooflike mirrors close to the devices. This issue is a relatively common one among Carson City gold of the decade. (#8334)

Well Struck 1875-CC Half Eagle Condition Rarity AU55

2544 1875-CC AU55 PCGS. As its 11,828-piece mintage might indicate, the 1875-CC half eagle is a rare issue in higher grades. Douglas Winter (2002) says: "This was clearly an issue that saw considerable circulation and most survivors grade Extremely Fine 40 or below. The 1875-CC becomes very scarce in Extremely Fine 45 and is rare in the lower About Uncirculated grades. This is a very rare coin in higher About Uncirculated grades ... " We would add that Mint State pieces are virtually unknown.

This Choice AU55 coin displays a fair amount of luster on peach-gold surfaces, and benefited from an exceptional strike, unusual for an issue that Winter calls: " ... one of the worst struck Carson City half eagles." A few minor obverse circulation marks are noted. (#8337)

Rare AU58 1876 Half Eagle, Centennial Souvenir

2545 1876 AU58 NGC. The rarity of the 1876 half eagle, with a mintage of only 1,432 business strikes plus 45 proofs, is overshadowed by the 1875 half eagle, one of the classic rarities in U.S. numismatics that was produced to the extent of only 200 circulation strikes plus 20 proofs. While the 1876 is rarely seen in any grade, according to Garrett and Guth, the authors reminds us that the date is one of the few With Motto early half eagles occasionally seen in Gem condition, perhaps owing to its status as a souvenir of the U.S. Centennial celebration.

This coin offers semiprooflike reflectivity over the distraction-free yellow-gold surfaces, and a decent strike save for light softness on the eagle's neck and feathers. As an indication of the rarity of this issue, both NGC and PCGS combined have certified only nine pieces in AU58, exceeded by 13 coins at both services and including the inevitable duplications (6/07). (#8339)

Scarce 1876-CC Five Dollar, XF45

2546 1876-CC XF45 NGC. The 1876-CC has the lowest mintage figure of any Carson City half eagle. According to Douglas Winter (2001): "It is a scarce coin in all grades and the majority of survivors fall into the Very Fine—Extremely Fine range." This Choice XF example exhibits reddish-gold patination and well defined motifs, save for the usual softness on the hair curl at the ear. We point out a few obverse minute contact marks. (#8340)

2547 1879-CC XF45 NGC. A pleasing Choice XF example of this comparatively available 1870s Carson City issue, well struck with lightly abraded butter-yellow surfaces that display a touch of emerald color. Lightly circulated with faint remnants of original luster at the reverse margins. (#8349)

2548 1879-S MS62 Prooflike NGC. Flashy luster endows this moderately abraded representative. A good strike with slight softness on the lovelock and the eagle's neck. The final branch mint issue of the type. Census: 2 in 62 Prooflike, 1 finer (6/07). (#78350)

2549 1880 MS64 NGC. A frosty near-Gem, this piece has lovely bright yellow-gold surfaces with olive peripheries and sharp design elements. Census: 89 in 64, 24 finer (6/07). (#8351)

2550 1880-CC XF45 NGC. Pockets of luminous luster outline the legends and stars of this yellow-gold Carson City five. Marks are insignificant, but the strike shows some softness on Liberty's hair and the eagle's neck and fletchings. (#8352)

2551 1880-CC—Cleaned—ANACS. AU53 Details. This scarce Carson City five is thickly hairlined but has only slight wear on the eyebrow and coronet tip. Well struck on the stars, while the eagle's neck and fletchings are typically brought up. (#8352)

2552 **1881/0 MS62 Prooflike ANACS.** Breen-6715. FS-301, formerly FS-005. Technically an 1881/1880 variety, since the 188 is clearly repunched. Well struck and flashy with distributed small field marks. Rare in Mint State, and (as of 5/07) none have been certified as Prooflike by NGC.
From The Vanek Collection. (#78355)

2553 **1881-S MS64 NGC.** This lovely half eagle has subdued mint frost on both sides with pink and olive-gold color. A condition rarity any finer, just 16 higher grade pieces have been certified by NGC (6/07). (#8357)

Conditionally Rare 1882 Half Eagle, MS65

2554 **1882 MS65 NGC.** A splendid Gem, this piece is an important condition rarity in the Liberty half eagle series, as shown by the population data. Just two finer pieces have been certified by NGC, and no finer examples have been examined by PCGS. Both sides are sharply detailed with rich and fully brilliant orange-gold luster. Census: 27 in 65, 2 finer (6/07).
From The Silver Fox Collection. (#8358)

2555 **1882-S MS64 NGC.** A sharply detailed and fully brilliant example, this piece has lovely honey-gold luster with subtle pink overtones. NGC has only certified 26 finer examples of this date (6/07). (#8360)

2556 **1883 MS64 NGC.** Both sides of this piece have intense satin luster with brilliant orange-gold surfaces. A few scattered surface marks keep it from a Gem grade level. Census: 19 in 64, 3 finer (6/07). (#8361)

2557 **1883-S MS63 PCGS.** A brilliant greenish-gold example with frosty luster. A single mark in the left obverse field is evident, but no other significant marks are visible on either side. This is an extremely important opportunity to acquire a difficult date. Population: 11 in 63, 3 finer (6/07). (#8363)

2558 **1883-S MS63 NGC.** An attractive example for the grade, a strongly lustrous piece with orange-gold color at the margins and lighter yellow-gold evident at the centers. Decisively struck with great eye appeal despite light, scattered abrasions. One of just 83,200 pieces coined. (#8363)

2559 **1884 MS62 NGC.** Somewhat subdued luster emanates from the lightly abraded surfaces of this 1884 five dollar. Generally well struck, with peach-gold patina. Increasingly rare in choice condition. Census: 45 in 62, 18 finer (6/07). (#8364)

2560 **1885-S MS63 PCGS.** A gorgeous orange-gold representative that boasts eye-catching luster and surprisingly unabraded surfaces. Certain to receive strong bids before the hammer finally falls. Encapsulated in a green label holder. (#8368)

2561 **1885-S MS64 NGC.** This boldly struck salmon-pink near-Gem has a beautifully smooth reverse, and the obverse is free from mentionable marks. A small strike-through, as made, is present on the second S in STATES. (#8368)

2562 **1886-S MS64 PCGS.** A frosty near-Gem with brilliant yellow surfaces and sharp design details. This condition rarity is exceeded by just six finer pieces certified by PCGS (6/07). (#8370)

2563 **1890-CC MS61 NGC.** This issue is only moderately difficult to locate in Mint State grades, although it has considerable demand from type collectors who seek Carson City Mint coins for their collections. A pleasing Mint State coin, the surfaces exhibit satiny green-gold luster with hints of rose toning along the borders. (#8376)

Scarce 1891-CC Five Dollar, MS64

2564 **1891-CC MS64 PCGS.** The 1892-CC five dollar, with its 208,000-piece mintage, is the most common Carson City half eagle. It is readily available though all AU grade grades, as well as the lower Mint State levels. It is moderately scarce in MS63, scarce in near-Gem, and extremely rare in Gem (Douglas Winter, 2001). A sharp strike emboldens the design elements of the MS64 coin in the current lot, and glowing luster issues from its peach-gold surfaces. Some minor handling marks define the grade. Population: 38 in 64, 1 finer (6/07). (#8378)

2565 **1892 MS63 PCGS.** Well struck and pleasingly lustrous, with lovely pink-rose and red-gold toning. The obverse is surprisingly smooth, and the reverse is also clean for the designated grade. (#8379)

Fully Struck MS66 1892 Half Eagle

2566 **1892 MS66 PCGS.** Undoubtedly one of the most impressive survivors from the plentiful mintage exceeding three-quarters of a million pieces, the present coin boasts a full strike atop its long list of cherished attributes. Others include a noteworthy paucity of singular abrasions, and delectable orange-gold surfaces on each side. Population: 25 in 66, 2 finer (6/07). (#8379)

2567 **1892-CC AU55 PCGS.** This Choice AU Carson City five has bright bands of peripheral luster, and the well struck devices display only traces of highpoint friction. The absence of consequential contact further ensures the quality for the grade. (#8380)

2568 **1893-CC MS61 NGC.** Lustrous with appealing peach and steel-green coloration and consistently bold striking details. A fair number of superficial marks define the grade of the piece. Final year of coinage at the Carson City Mint, and always a popular issue for type purposes. (#8384)

2569 **1893-O MS61 NGC.** This fully lustrous example will appeal to series specialists due to its low mintage and associated low population. This is a sharply detailed yellow-gold example with brilliant mint frost and splashes of orange toning. (#8385)

2570 **1895 MS64 NGC.** A straw-gold near-Gem that is well struck except for minor die bounce doubling along the right reverse border. Faint obverse field grazes are observed beneath a glass. (#8390)

2571 **1895 MS64 PCGS.** A meticulously struck canary-gold near-Gem with no more than the expected number of faint obverse grazes. The reverse is well preserved. PCGS has certified just 15 pieces finer (4/07). (#8390)

2572 **1895 MS64 NGC.** This pleasant near-Gem has light peach-gold toning and a precise strike. Examination beneath a loupe locates no relevant contact. The reverse legends are strike doubled. (#8390)

2573 **1897-S MS62 NGC.** The 1897-S is very tough to locate in the better grades of Mint State. Greenish-gold luster exudes from the lightly marked surfaces of this MS62 example. An attentive strike emboldens the design elements. Census: 19 in 62, 10 finer (6/07). (#8395)

2574 **1898 MS64 PCGS.** This crisply struck representative has pleasing luster and great overall visual appeal. Light, scattered marks are present on each side, and a copper spot appears just below the chin. A great example of this later Gobrecht issue. Population: 37 in 64, 4 finer (5/07). (#8396)

2575 **1899 MS64 PCGS.** This satiny and unperturbed turn-of-the-century gold coin has a penetrating strike and rich orange toning. A charming near-Gem certain to please its next owner. (#8398)

2576 **1900 MS64 PCGS.** This carefully preserved and sharply impressed near-Gem displays vibrant luster. The eye appeal is undeniable. A short set of Liberty half eagles, 1898 to 1908, can be completed in Choice Mint State with only one difficult date, the 1904-S. (#8400)

2577 **1900 MS64 PCGS.** A highly lustrous example of the date with frosty yellow-gold surfaces. PCGS has only certified 57 finer examples (6/07). (#8400)

2578 **1900 MS64 NGC.** Sharply detailed and highly lustrous, this near-Gem has brilliant mint frost. It is an attractive example that will please most collectors. (#8400)

2579 **1900 MS64 PCGS.** A Choice Mint State specimen, this issue is seldom encountered any finer, with just 57 better pieces certified by PCGS. Both sides have sharp details and frosty yellow luster. (#8400)

2580 **1901-S MS64 NGC.** This meticulously struck and thoroughly lustrous near-Gem has impressively clean fields and a smooth cheek. An affordable yet high quality example of this popular gold type. (#8404)

2581 **1901-S MS64 PCGS.** Booming lustrous and canary-gold toning combine with an intricate strike to confirm the eye appeal. The cheek is void of contact, although a brief thin mark is noted beneath TRUST. (#8404)

2582 **1903 MS64 NGC.** This precisely struck and lustrous near-Gem is pleasantly unperturbed by contact, and has imposing eye appeal for the grade. Although plentiful in MS61 to MS63, the 1903 is very scarce in MS64. Encased in an older generation holder. Census: 59 in 64, 29 finer (6/07). (#8407)

Lustrous Gem 1904 Half Eagle

2583 **1904 MS65 PCGS.** Pale lime-green enriches the peripheries, while the centers are straw-gold. The strike is pinpoint-sharp, and thorough evaluation beneath a loupe locates only infrequent and inconsequential contact. The 1904 is common in MS61 to MS63 grades, but becomes scarce at the MS65 level. Population: 46 in 65, 16 finer (5/07). (#8409)

2584 **1904-S MS63 PCGS.** Even with a mintage of 97,000 pieces, the 1904-S proves to be an elusive coin in all grades of Mint State. This is a charming piece that shows richly lustrous yellow-gold surfaces that are free of all but the tiniest abrasions. Definitely a nice example for the grade. Population: 11 in 63, 8 finer (4/07). (#8410)

Lovely 1905 Half Eagle, MS66

2585 **1905 MS66 PCGS.** Despite its rather high mintage of 302,308 pieces, the 1905 is a surprisingly scarce issue in the better grades of Mint State. PCGS has certified only seven pieces as Premium Gems, with none finer (6/07). This is a lovely coin that has orange-golden and green-golden mint luster with no singularly reportable abrasions. Well defined throughout. (#8411)

Potent Premium Gem 1906 Half Eagle

2586 **1906 MS66 PCGS.** Vivid sunset-orange color dominates the shining surfaces, while the centers have just a touch of lighter straw-gold. Sharply detailed with strong visual appeal. The Gobrecht design, which had appeared on the half eagle since 1839, was on its way out by 1906, with the Pratt design just two years away. Population: 16 in 66, 3 finer (4/07). (#8413)

2587 **1906-D MS63 Obverse Prooflike ANACS.** The obverse is prominently mirrored, and the reverse is moderately prooflike as well. Unusual mint-made die lines are present from the tip of the middle arrowhead to the rim between the AM in AMERICA. An interesting and high quality souvenir from the first year of Denver Mint coinage.
From The Vanek Collection. (#8414)

Sharp 1906-S Gem Five Dollar

2588 **1906-S MS65 PCGS.** Jeff Garrett and Ron Guth (2006) write that: "Although the 1906-S half eagle is not rare in most grades, it is certainly underpriced in the higher states of preservation." The Gem that we offer in this lot displays potent luster and vibrant peach-gold color, and a sharp strike brings out strong definition on the design elements. Some minute marks are noted on the cheek and neck and in the left obverse field. Population: 9 in 65, 5 finer (5/07). (#8415)

2589 **1907 MS63 PCGS.** Lustrous and exactingly struck with rich, original pumpkin-gold patina. The reverse is well preserved, while the left obverse has a few minor marks. Encapsulated in an old green label holder. (#8416)

2590 **1907-D MS64 NGC.** This near-Gem example displays nice yellow-rose coloration and shimmering luster. Well struck and carefully preserved, there are only trivial marks exhibited on either side. Liberty Head half eagles were only struck for two years at the Denver Mint. (#8417)

Gem 1908 Liberty Head Five, End of an Era

2591 **1908 MS65 NGC.** The 1908 Liberty Head half eagle occupies a singular niche in U.S. numismatics, as the only 1908-dated Liberty Head gold coinage and the end of the long era of the Christian Gobrecht design that began in 1838 with the eagle, 1839 with the half eagle, and 1840 with the quarter eagle. This attractive Gem offers sparkling luster over the yellow-gold, problem-free surfaces, with abundant eye appeal and a nearly full strike. NGC has certified 53 coins finer (6/07). (#8418)

INDIAN HALF EAGLES

2592 **1908 MS62 ANACS.** A satiny and sharply impressed half eagle with smooth, pale sun-gold surfaces. Unlike its ten dollar counterpart, the Indian half eagle was introduced with the motto IN GOD WE TRUST. (#8510)

2593 **1908 MS63 PCGS.** Light yellow-gold luster is evident on each side of this sharply defined example. Traces of dark verdigris can be seen within the recesses of the devices. (#8510)

2594 **1908 MS64 PCGS.** Rich honey-gold luster and satiny surfaces are evident on both sides of this attractive near-Gem. Hints of pinkish toning are visible within the design elements. Bela Lyon Pratt learned from the mistakes of President Roosevelt and Augustus Saint-Gaudens, since the new quarter eagle and half eagle designs bore the legend IN GOD WE TRUST. (#8510)

Near-Gem 1908 Half Eagle

2595 **1908 MS64 NGC.** This is an amazing near-Gem that possesses exceptional eye appeal with its frosty yellow-gold luster and extraordinarily sharp design elements. Bela Lyon Pratt's reverse is quite similar to the reverse of the Saint-Gaudens ten dollar piece, but the legends IN GOD WE TRUST and E PLURIBUS UNUM are switched in location. (#8510)

First-Year 1908 Indian Head Five, MS64

2596 **1908 MS64 NGC.** The premier issue of the Indian Head design of Yale-educated Bela Lyon Pratt, and as such a popular choice for a first-year-of-type set. This boldly struck orange-gold piece shows only a couple of thin marks before the Indian's face that likely limit a Gem grade. This high-end, lovely coin would make a nice accompaniment to the Gem Liberty Head 1908 half eagle in the present sale. (#8510)

Distraction-Free MS64 1908 Indian Head Five

2597 **1908 MS64 PCGS.** The plentiful mintage exceeding a half-million pieces, coupled with the eternal propensity of the collecting public to save first-year issues, means that today the 1908 Indian Head eagle is generally available for a price, up to and including MS65. This near-Gem piece offers attractive khaki-gold surfaces that show essentially no distractions. A nice piece for the grade, since the price about quadruples in MS65. (#8510)

Lustrous 1908-D Half Eagle, MS63

2598 **1908-D MS63 PCGS.** Peach-gold surfaces yield good luster, much more pleasing than is often seen on this issue. A well executed strike brings out sharp definition on the design elements, except for minor softness in the eagle's shoulder feathers. Minute marks on the Indian's cheek and on the raised, exposed surfaces account for the grade. (#8511)

Bold 1908-D Five Dollar MS63

2599 **1908-D MS63 NGC.** A subtly lustrous and well struck orange-gold representative of this first-year Denver issue. The lightly abraded upper reverse field exhibits hints of emerald-green. The mintmark location is opposite the arrows, unlike the 1908-D No Motto ten, which has the mintmark above the olive branch. (#8511)

Select 1908-D Indian Five

2600 **1908-D MS63 PCGS.** The attractive khaki-gold coloration is imbued with reddish accents. Satin luster highlights the well struck design elements. A few tiny marks limit the grade of this appealing Select Mint State half eagle. Although priced at similar levels as the 1908, the 1908-D is scarcer, probably due to its low mintage of 148,000 pieces. (#8511)

Elusive Choice 1908-D Indian Five

2601 **1908-D MS64 PCGS.** Original apple-green and orange-gold toning graces this satiny near-Gem. The obverse is refreshingly devoid of marks, and the reverse field has only scattered faint luster grazes. Although the 1908-D generally trades as a type coin, it is substantially scarcer than the 1909-D. PCGS has certified just eight pieces finer (5/07). (#8511)

2602 **1908-S MS61 NGC.** Unlike most of the S-Mint Indian eagles, this date ranks among the most common issues of the series, despite a mintage of just 82,000 coins. This piece has subtle pink toning around lemon-yellow color with matte-like brilliant yellow luster (#8512)

Low-Mintage 1908-S Five Dollar, MS63

2603 **1908-S MS63 NGC.** The 1908-S comes from a relatively small mintage of 82,000 pieces. The NGC/PCGS population data indicate that this issue is available from VF to Mint State, though not in particularly large numbers in each grade category. The MS63 coin in this lot exhibits lustrous apricot-gold surfaces. Sharp definition is visible on the design elements, though the eagle's shoulder reveals minor softness, which is typical for this issue. A few inoffensive marks define the grade. (#8512)

Lustrous Choice 1908-S Half Eagle

2604 **1908-S MS64 PCGS.** The 1908-S has a miserly mintage of 82,000 pieces. Only the key 1909-O and the semi-key 1911-D have lower productions. Since gold coins still circulated to a limited extent on the West Coast in 1908, PCGS has certified pieces in grades as low as VF25. These factors, as well as its early date, make the 1908-S scarce in any Mint State grade, more so than, for example, the 1911-D quarter eagle. This pumpkin-gold near-Gem has pleasing luster and a decisive strike. The reverse field has a few wispy abrasions, and a thin mark crosses the T in LIBERTY. (#8512)

2605 **1909 MS62 NGC.** Well struck with subtle, pleasing luster and bold sunset-orange color. A touch of rose graces the fields of the lightly abraded reverse. Overall, an interesting example of this early Pratt half eagle issue. (#8513)

2606 **1909 MS62 PCGS.** Lustrous and attractive, with pleasing honey-gold and lime toning. A few grade-limiting marks are noticeable on the reverse fields. (#8513)

2607 **1909 MS62 PCGS.** Orange and steel-gray colors endow this intricately struck Indian Head five. The fields have only inoffensive marks. Certified in an old green label holder. (#8513)

2608 **1909-D MS62 PCGS.** A well struck gold type coin with uncommon definition on the headdress feathers. The fields are minimally abraded, and the devices shimmer with luster. (#8514)

2609 **1909-D MS62 PCGS.** Satiny and nicely preserved with smooth, matte-like fields and sharply struck devices. Only trivial marks on the reverse limit the grade. This Indian Head half eagle issue is the one most often used for type purposes. (#8514)

2610 **1909-D MS62 PCGS.** A frosty light yellow-gold example with fully brilliant surfaces and sharp details. This is a plentiful date, the issue most often chosen for type sets. (#8514)

2611 **1909-D MS62 NGC.** This is the most common issue of the popular and widely collected Indian Head half eagle series. The appeal of this example derives from its rich, attractive coloration and satiny mint frost. A number of small marks in the reverse fields limit the grade. (#8514)

2612 **1909-D MS63 NGC.** Both sides of this Select half eagle are awash in luster, and yellow-gold surfaces exhibit sharply defined motifs, though minor softness is noted on the eagle's shoulder. Light contact marks, especially in the raised, exposed fields, preclude a higher grade. The 1909-D is a common date of the series, and available in most Mint State grades (Jeff Garrett and Ron Guth, 2006). (#8514)

2613 **1909-D MS63 NGC.** Bright luster adorns both sides of this '09-D five dollar, and a well executed strike brings out sharp definition on the design elements, including excellent detail on the Indian's bonnet feathers, and on the eagle's plumage. Peach-gold surfaces reveal a scattering of grade-defining marks.. (#8514)

2614 **1909-D MS63 PCGS.** This khaki-gold Select Indian five has an unmarked appearance, and the bold strike is confirmed by its exquisite headdress definition. The mintmark is distinct. The 1909-D has the highest mintage for the series, while its branch mint counterpart, the 1909-O, has the lowest production of the type. (#8514)

2615 **1909-D MS63 PCGS.** Glimpses of olive patina embrace selected areas of this shimmering and lightly abraded Select gold type coin. Precisely struck throughout, with the mintmark particularly distinct. (#8514)

2616 **1909-D MS63 PCGS.** Intense satin luster brightens the straw-gold surfaces of this nicely preserved Indian Head half eagle. A few wispy marks are seen in the reverse fields, but they seem minimal for the grade. (#8514)

2617 **1909-D MS63 PCGS.** The bold striking details are immediately noticeable on this coin, along with satin luster and appealing coloration. A few abrasions in the reverse fields restrict the grade, but the obverse seems blemish-free. (#8514)

2618 **1909-D MS63 PCGS.** This satiny gold type coin has refreshingly smooth surfaces, and the strike is pleasing, particularly on the mintmark, the branch, and the headdress. (#8514)

2619 **1909-D MS64 NGC.** A blend of antique-gold and orange color graces the glowing surfaces of this well struck example. Well-preserved overall with only a few wispy marks in the reverse fields and a single small abrasion on the cheek. In 1909, four mints produced half eagles, including the nascent Denver Mint and New Orleans in its final year of production. (#8514)

2620 **1909-D MS64 PCGS.** The 1909-D, with its 3,423,560-piece mintage, is among the most available dates of the Indian Head five dollar series. The current near-Gem displays brass-gold color and highly lustrous surfaces. Sharply struck with a few grade-defining marks on the reverse. (#8514)

2621 **1909-D MS64 PCGS.** This is a splendid near-Gem with excellent pinkish-orange luster. Both sides are sharply detailed with minimal surface marks. PCGS has only certified 85 finer examples of this issue (6/07). (#8514)

2622 **1909-D MS64 NGC.** A Choice Mint State example, this piece has frosty pink-gold luster with brilliant surfaces. While always available at this grade level, NGC has only certified 63 finer pieces (6/07). (#8514)

Key 1909-O Five, Only O-Mint Indian Head Gold Coin, AU53

2623 **1909-O AU53 NGC.** The last gold coin produced at the New Orleans Mint, and the only Indian Head gold coin made there, since the mint closed in 1909 after 70+ years of coinage operations—an event likely hastened by the beginning of coinage in Denver at a new Mint facility in 1906. The 1909-O is a low-mintage key to its series, one for which demand and prices have soared in recent years. The present coin offers lightly circulated yellow-gold surfaces with good eye appeal and no singular distractions. (#8515)

Low-Mintage 1909-O Five Dollar, AU58

2624 1909-O AU58 ANACS. The 1909-O half eagle has the lowest mintage of the Indian Head five dollar series, with 34,200 pieces. Very Fine and Extremely Fine examples are readily available, and About Uncirculated coins are fairly scarce. Mint State pieces are very scarce to rare (Douglas Winter, *Gold Coins of the New Orleans Mint, 1839-1909*).

Ample luster resides on this high-end AU example, and peach-gold color enriches both sides. A sharp, uniform strike leaves good definition on the design elements, though minor softness occurs on the eagle's shoulder. A few trivial marks are noted on the raised, exposed fields, especially the upper reverse, though none are worthy of individual mention. (#8515)

2625 1909-S MS60 NGC. The peach-gold surfaces of this unworn S-mint half eagle display soft, swirling luster and occasional green-gold accents. Well struck with a number of moderate abrasions visible in the fields, though the MS60 grade seems harsh for a piece that displays a measure of eye appeal. (#8516)

2626 1910 MS62 PCGS. A solid strike brings out nice definition on this 1910 five dollar, and lustrous surfaces exhibit warm peach-gold color. A few small contact marks scattered over each side limit the grade. Readily available in Mint State grades. (#8517)

2627 1910 MS62 PCGS. Hints of greenish color can be seen on both sides of this sharply detailed Mint State Indian half eagle. The surfaces are fully brilliant with frosty luster. (#8517)

2628 1910-S MS61 ANACS. Satiny and well struck with lustrous surfaces that display light khaki coloration, augmented by coppery-red accents on the higher points of the design. Surface marks are noticeable on both sides, but do not seem excessive for the grade. (#8519)

2629 1911 MS62 PCGS. One of the higher-mintage issues for the Indian Head half eagle design, with 915,000 pieces coined. This yellow-orange representative is well-defined overall and displays light, scattered abrasions over lustrous surfaces. (#8520)

2630 1911 MS62 NGC. Orange-gold surfaces yield average luster and above average definition on the headdress. We note a few minor marks on each side. (#8520)

2631 1911 MS62 PCGS. A lustrous example of this popular P-mint five dollar Indian. Lightly abraded overall, the only mark of note is located in the upper reverse field. (#8520)

Near-Gem 1911 Half Eagle

2632 1911 MS64 PCGS. The rich, satiny luster of this 1911 quarter eagle seems commensurate to a higher grade. However, close examination of the obverse reveals a thin scratch on the Indian's headdress. This minor flaw is perhaps the only distraction precluding this example from a Gem designation. PCGS has assigned higher grades to only 44 pieces. (#8520)

Pleasing 1911 Near-Gem Five Dollar

2633 1911 MS64 PCGS. Apricot-gold surfaces reveal traces of light green and tan, and possess somewhat subdued luster, which tends to be characteristic of the issue. A relatively strong strike brings up the design features, including most of the feathers in the headdress, an area that is usually weak on this date. A few minor handling marks define the grade. (#8520)

2634 1912 MS62 NGC. This unblemished almond-gold representative displays subtle cartwheel luster upon rotation beneath a light. A good strike with some blending of definition on the headdress. (#8523)

2635 1912 MS62 NGC. This honey-gold five dollar piece displays soft luster and well impressed design features. A handful of light abrasions is scattered over each side. An obtainable issue, from a mintage of 790,000 pieces. (#8523)

2636 1912 MS62 PCGS. While the surfaces are lightly abraded, this is an attractive example with full luster. Both sides have light yellow color with faint greenish tendencies. (#8523)

Rare 1912-S Indian Half Eagle, MS64

2637 1912-S MS64 PCGS. There are several scarce and rare dates in the Indian half eagle series, including this issue. Jeff Garrett and Ron Guth comment: "One of the classic rarities and most difficult issues to obtain in Mint State, the 1912-S issue has earned its reputation, which is quite a feat considering the number of rarities among the Indian Head half eagle series."

The present near-Gem specimen is a splendid exception to the usual rule, having excellent overall quality. Although the mintmark is a trifle weak, it is completely visible, and all other details on both sides are nicely defined. The surfaces have a few scattered marks that are expected for the grade. The luster is exceptional, with fully brilliant orange-gold frost. Population: 20 in 64, 1 finer (6/07). (#8524)

2638 1913 MS62 PCGS. The slightly flashy surfaces have vivid yellow-gold color tempered by orange accents. A solidly defined mid-date example with light, scattered abrasions that account for the grade. (#8525)

2639 1913 MS62 NGC. A frosty Mint State piece, both sides have dark patina on lustrous yellow surfaces. Not a particularly rare date through MS64, the 1913 is a rarity in Gem quality. (#8525)

Select 1913 Indian Five

2640 1913 MS63 NGC. Both sides of this Select Mint State piece exhibit attractive honey-gold color with frosty luster. Most of the design details are bold, although slight weakness is noted at the top of the headdress. This issue ranks among the common dates in the Indian half eagle series, although it is rare in higher Mint State grades. (#8525)

Lovely MS63 1913 Indian Five

2641 1913 MS63 PCGS. This lovely Indian half eagle has rich orange toning and unencumbered cartwheel sheen. The strike is precise throughout, and the smooth surfaces display no marks remotely worthy of discussion. Mint State gold type has lagged the market since the introduction of the Buffalo gold bullion coin, but the underlying demand for classic Indian gold designs remains strong. (#8525)

Sharp 1913 Half Eagle, MS64

2642 1913 MS64 PCGS. The 1913 Indian Head half eagle, like most Philadelphia Mint issues, is usually found with a good strike and eye-appealing luster (Jeff Garrett and Ron Guth, 2006). The near-Gem in this lot is no exception, as the design elements stand out, and attractive apricot-gold luster exudes from both sides. A handful of minuscule handling marks define the grade. (#8525)

High-End MS64 1913 Indian Head Five

2643 **1913 MS64 PCGS.** While the major services have certified several hundred examples of this date in Choice condition, Gem specimens thin out by an order of magnitude, although still somewhat available for a (much higher) price. The present near-Gem accordingly strikes a pleasing balance between condition and cost. The plus sign in the equation, however, is that it also appears high-end for the grade, with pleasing orange-gold coloration and a bold strike, seemingly barred from the Gem ranks only by a single tick on the Indian's cheek. PCGS has certified 49 pieces finer (6/07). (#8525)

2644 **1913-S MS60 ANACS.** This well-defined yellow-orange example exhibits no trace of wear and strong luster. Abrasions on the Indian's cheek and throat and in the fields account for the grade, though the overall appearance suggests that MS60 is an uncharitable assessment. (#8526)

Choice Mint State 1914 Half Eagle

2645 **1914 MS64 PCGS.** A lovely near-Gem, exhibiting brilliant yellow-gold color with hints of green. The design elements on both sides are boldly detailed. The surfaces have typical granular or matte surfaces that are often seen on this issue, but not usually encountered on any other dates struck in Philadelphia. Not particularly rare at this grade level, but only 22 finer examples have been certified by PCGS (6/07). (#8527)

Compelling MS64 1914 Indian Half Eagle

2646 **1914 MS64 NGC.** This piece is perhaps only one tiny tick on the Indian's cheek away from a finer grade, as the surfaces are relatively mark-free, and the headstrong luster is compelling in its radiance. The strike is well, if not fully executed, and the combination altogether pleasing. Seldom seen finer: NGC has certified only 15 pieces in higher grades (6/07). (#8527)

Lustrous 1914 Near-Gem Five Dollar

2647 **1914 MS64 PCGS.** The 1914 half eagle is available in all grades up to MS65, and is generally found with strong luster. A well executed strike results in sharp definition on the design elements of this near-Gem specimen, and pleasing luster emanates from rich peach-gold surfaces. Small marks in the raised, exposed reverse fields preclude a higher grade. (#8527)

Pleasing 1914-D Half Eagle, MS64

2648 **1914-D MS64 NGC.** Peach-gold surfaces are imbued with whispers of mint-green, and exude pleasing luster. The design features are sharply defined, having benefited from a well placed strike. Close examination reveals a few minor marks, primarily in the vulnerable, exposed fields that are raised on this design type. (#8528)

Lustrous 1914-D Near-Gem Five Dollar

2649 **1914-D MS64 NGC.** The 1914-D is available in most grades up to MS64, but the population falls dramatically at the MS65 level. Rich apricot-gold color adheres to the lustrous surfaces of the near-Gem in this lot, and an attentive strike brings up most of the detail in the design elements. A few minor handling marks define the grade. (#8528)

2650 **1914-S MS61 NGC.** Swirling pumpkin-orange and sun-gold colors converge on the subtly lustrous surfaces of this well-defined piece. Scattered light to moderate abrasions on each side restrict the grade. (#8529)

2651 **1915 MS62 PCGS.** The penultimate circulation-strike half eagle issue from Philadelphia, as no more would come from that mint until the final production run in 1929. The softly lustrous yellow-orange fields displays pleasing glints of wheat color. A solidly struck piece that displays a hint of frost on the well-defined devices and few marks for the grade. (#8530)

2652 **1915 MS62 NGC.** A green-gold Indian half eagle with pleasantly unperturbed fields and devices for the third party grade. Luster is particularly effusive within the devices. Always a popular gold type. (#8530)

2653 1915 MS62 PCGS. The 588,000 pieces delivered by Philadelphia in 1915 would be the last half eagles struck by that Mint for 14 years, as only San Francisco produced the denomination in 1916 and no sites made further examples until 1929. This solidly struck orange-gold example has soft, pleasing luster and scattered, grade-defining marks in the fields. (#8530)

2654 1915 MS63 NGC. Bright mint luster and sharply struck throughout. The surfaces have rich reddish-golden color, and there are remarkably few abrasions present for an MS63. One of the more readily obtainable P-mint five Indians. (#8530)

2655 1915-S AU58 PCGS. This issue's mintage of 164,000 pieces is less than one-third that of its P-mint counterpart. This well-defined, briefly circulated piece has a brassy appearance with just a touch of friction on the highpoints. (#8531)

Elusive 1915-S Half Eagle, MS62

2656 1915-S MS62 PCGS. The 164,000-piece 1915-S half eagle is elusive in all grades, especially so in Mint State, where about 270 coins in all grades of Uncirculated are reported by PCGS and NGC. Just 35 Select pieces have been seen, and fewer than 20 near-Gems. The finest certified 1915-S half eagle is a solitary NGC MS65! Honey-gold surfaces yield satiny luster on the MS62 piece for sale here, and sharp definition is apparent on the design elements. Several minute, but grade-defining marks are visible on both sides. Population: 64 in 62, 31 finer (6/07). (#8531)

2657 1916-S MS62 PCGS. After the 1916-S half eagle issue, 90 years would pass before San Francisco struck the denomination again. This well-defined piece has lightly abraded yellow-orange surfaces that display above-average luster. A few tiny copper spots are noted at the upper right reverse. (#8532)

Choice 1916-S Half Eagle

2658 1916-S MS64 PCGS. San Francisco was the only Mint to produce half eagles for the year, and no more would come until 1929, when Philadelphia struck the last circulating issue for the denomination. This shimmering near-Gem piece displays lovely yellow-gold color with a touch of orange at the left obverse and reverse. Solidly struck with pleasing luster and uncommon eye appeal. Population: 68 in 64, 11 finer (4/07). (#8532)

EARLY EAGLE

AU55 Details 1797 Ten Dollar

2659 1797 Large Eagle—Scratched, Cleaned—ANACS. AU55 Details. Breen-6834, Taraszka-8, BD-2, High R.4. The eagle has a lengthy, narrow neck on this scarce die variety. Careful rotation beneath a light reveals faint hairlines across both sides, and a hair-thin pinscratch crosses Liberty's neck. But the reverse has nearly full luster, and obverse luster fills the border and hair. A few faint adjustment marks are present on the right obverse field. (#8559)

LIBERTY EAGLES

2660 1842 Large Date AU53 PCGS. Plenty of design detail remains evident on each side of this AU example. The lime-green surfaces exhibit nice luster as well. Numerous small marks and a faint amount of friction determine the grade. Population: 6 in 53, 17 finer (6/07). (#8584)

2661 1842 Small Date AU53 PCGS. Lustrous and bright with enticing lime-green and peach coloration. Both sides of the coin reveal modest highpoint wear and numerous small to moderate abrasions and wispy hairlines. A little more available than its PCGS population numbers would seem to suggest. Population: 5 in 53, 9 finer (6/07). (#8585)

Choice AU 1842-O Ten

2662 1842-O AU55 NGC. Round O. The 1842-O is midway in rarity between the nearly uncollectible 1841-O and the relatively plentiful 1843-O. The 1842-O is scarce in all grades. Most certified examples are in XF and AU, and NGC has certified only three pieces as Mint State, one each between MS60 and MS62. This partly lustrous and crisply struck piece is slightly bright but lacks mentionable marks. Census: 19 in 55, 19 finer (5/07). (#8587)

2663 1845-O AU50 PCGS. Breen-6870. The date is obviously repunched south. A richly detailed and generally smooth example that has noticeable luster, particularly on the reverse. The top of the second shield stripe has a circular piece absent, as made and a cousin to the "Hole in Ear" varieties of certain large cents and half eagles from the 1840s. Population: 23 in 50, 21 finer (5/07). (#8593)

Interesting 1846/5-O Eagle, AU53

2664 1846/5-O AU53 NGC. The lump within the 6 in the date is traditionally regarded as an overdate, though most researches believe the cause is a defective logotype punch. This briefly circulated yellow-orange piece offers subtle luster at the margins and uncommonly strong detail, particularly in the centers. While both sides have scattered abrasions, these marks are well-distributed and do not interfere much with the visual appeal. An intriguing example that deserves closer inspection. (#8596)

2665 1848 AU53 NGC. Despite a substantial mintage for the No Motto type, the 1848 is surprisingly scarce, especially in AU or finer grades. This piece has considerable luster with medium yellow surfaces and splashes of pale orange toning. (#8599)

New Orleans Mint, 1838-1909

Green-Gold MS60 1850-O Ten Dollar

2666 1850-O MS60 NGC. The finest known 1850-O ten dollar is the Eliasberg coin, which currently resides in a PCGS MS65 holder. Beyond the Eliasberg specimen, high grade examples are rare in the every sense of the word and opportunities to acquire a true Mint State example of this date are far and few between. To illustrate this point, consider that as of (6/07), NGC has certified only three 1850-O eagles in MS60; there are none finer. Furthermore, PCGS has not graded a single Mint State example, other than the aforementioned MS65. Even the small hoard of 16 pieces salvaged from the *S.S. Republic* shipwreck failed to yield a single Uncirculated example, although a few AU58 coins were found. Thus, the 1850-O ten is a true condition rarity. The population summary provided by Garrett and Guth in their *Encyclopedia of U.S. Gold Coins* indicates an average grade of only 47.8 for the 225 coins graded by NGC and PCGS combined (2006). As such, the current coin provides a seldom-seen chance to obtain an 1850-O eagle that is almost certainly a Condition Census piece.

The green-gold surfaces retain significant portions of mint luster and there is a noticeable overlay of reddish patina on each side. A bit softly stuck, as one would expect from a New Orleans product. A few small to medium-sized field marks are located on each side, the most obvious being on the obverse. (#8605)

2667 1851-O AU55 NGC. Lustrous for the AU55 level, and careful inspection fails to find mentionable marks. A few high relief stars are soft, but the major devices are crisp. A shield ring rests atop the second stripe, as always for this popular New Orleans issue. (#8607)

2668 1851-O AU55 NGC. While the surfaces of this Choice Mint State piece are abraded, both sides have nearly full green-gold luster, typical of gold pieces from the early 1850s. The reverse has a small rim scraped over ED. (#8607)

2669 1851-O AU55 NGC. Luster beckons from the devices, stars, and legends. Each side has a couple of moderate field marks. As always for this issue, a shield ring is present atop the second vertical stripe. (#8607)

Scarce 1852-O Ten Dollar, AU53

2670 **1852-O AU53 NGC.** The 1852-O, with a mintage of 18,000 pieces, is scarce in About Uncirculated, and virtually unobtainable in Mint State (three pieces have been certified by NGC and PCGS). This yellow-gold AU53 example displays sharp definition and relatively few marks for a piece that saw some circulation. (#8609)

2671 **1853-O AU53 PCGS.** No shield ring is present atop the second stripe, as sometimes seen. The 53 in the date is lightly recut. A sharply struck piece with luminous honey-gold surfaces. Only 51,000 pieces were struck. Population: 19 in 53, 24 finer (4/07). (#8612)

2672 **1853-O AU53 PCGS.** The luster is ample for the grade, and the honey-tinged surfaces are unblemished. A scant 51,000 pieces were struck. The base of the 53 in the date is repunched, and a shield ring rests atop the second vertical stripe. Examples *without* the shield ring are also known, unlike the '51-O.
From The Silver Fox Collection. (#8612)

2673 **1854-O Large Date XF45 PCGS.** The '54-O Large Date and Small Date varieties are roughly equal in scarcity, and are given identical values in the 2008 Guide Book. The varieties are challenging, as they divide the low mintage of 52,500 pieces. This yellow-gold example has smooth, subdued surfaces and minor struck-in grease near the coronet and bun. Population: 10 in 45, 50 finer (6/07). (#98614)

2674 **1854-S AU50 PCGS.** An original orange-gold example of the first San Francisco ten dollar issue, which is collectible unlike its quarter eagle and half eagle counterparts. Well struck, and smooth aside from thin marks near the cheekbone. Certified in a green label holder.
From The Vanek Collection. (#8615)

2675 **1855-S VF20 PCGS.** The '54-S and '56-S are available by the standards of No Motto San Francisco eagles, but the '55-S is a rarity. Only 9,000 pieces were struck, since the Mint focused on double eagle production. Well defined for the VF20 grade, and luster remnants are present, particularly within the shield. Housed in an old green label holder. Population: 1 in 20, 47 finer (6/07). (#8618)

Borderline Uncirculated 1856-S Ten

2676 **1856-S AU58 NGC.** Medium S. Well struck and smooth with bountiful glowing peripheral luster. Except for the '54-S, the '56-S is the least rare of the pre-1879 San Francisco issues. But since only 68,000 pieces were struck, and since there was little contemporary interest in Gold Rush coinage, examples are scarce regardless of grade. The NGC Census undoubtedly includes a number of duplicate submissions, since only three NGC AU58 pieces have appeared in prior Heritage Signature auctions. Census: 43 in 58, 1 finer (6/07). (#8621)

2677 **1858-O XF45 PCGS.** Olive and apricot toning aids the eye appeal of this unblemished example. The major devices are crisply struck, although some of the stars are incomplete. A scant 20,000 pieces were struck for this scarce New Orleans issue. (#8626)

AU58 1858-O Eagle, Rare in Mint State

2678 **1858-O AU58 NGC.** Examples of this issue are seldom found in grades above AU or so, and Mint State pieces are exceedingly elusive. This near-Mint State specimen displays considerable semiprooflikeness over untroubled, pristine surfaces. In combination with the attractive greenish-gold coloration they create *eye appeal*, that most elusive and indefinable of all numismatic qualities. While both sides show numerous small abrasions in the fields, the only one that requires singular mention is a small, metal-moving scrape on the reverse under ED of UNITED, and none of them dampen one's enthusiasm for this lovely and conditionally rare piece. Census: 35 in 58, 6 finer (6/07). (#8626)

2679 **1862 VF30 PCGS.** 1862 marked the beginning of a long run of low mintage Liberty eagles, finally broken by the "high" mintage 1874. Few attempt to complete all of those rare dates, but the 1862 is under greater demand as it was struck during the Civil War. Sharp for the grade with some remaining luster and the usual distributed small marks. Certified in an old green label holder. Population: 4 in 30, 64 finer (6/07). (#8635)

Attractive 1874 Liberty Ten MS62

2680 **1874 MS62 NGC.** The smooth surfaces have the eye appeal of a slightly finer grade. A crisply struck example of this underappreciated issue. The open field luster is subdued. Only 53,140 pieces were struck, and Mint State examples are rare, since the series received little if any numismatic consideration until two decades later. Census: 11 in 62, 8 finer (5/07). (#8669)

2681 **1874-CC VF20 PCGS.** Pleasing apricot-gold patination with red accents enriches both sides of this '74-CC specimen. All of the design elements show good definition, and the surfaces are quite clean for a coin that saw moderate circulation. This issue is scarce in XF and rare in AU and Uncirculated. Housed in a green-label holder. (#8670)

2682 **1879 AU58 PCGS.** This is the "So-Called Overdate," Breen-6993. The "overdate," such as it is, is clearly visible; Breen called this a 9/8, but what exactly is under the 9 is open to debate. There is evidence of repunching in both the upper and lower portion of the 9, more so in the lower. The description in the Breen *Encyclopedia* states, "Part of the lower right loop of 8 within loop of 9." Prospective bidders may decide for themselves. The surfaces are well struck and bright, with full luster. Sufficient marks and highpoint wear exist to justify the grade. This example is housed in one of the PCGS "Premium" holders, which were discontinued some years ago. (#8683)

2683 **1880-CC AU53 NGC.** One of only 11,190 pieces produced, this coin is a problem-free AU survivor of this important CC-mint eagle issue. The 1880-CC is, along with the 1874-CC, the only readily obtainable pre-1890 eagle from the Carson City Mint. Minimally abraded for a circulated gold coin, the bright surfaces show ample remaining luster and bold striking definition. (#8688)

2684 **1881-CC XF45 PCGS.** A nicely struck and original honey-gold ten with unblemished fields and a thin mark on the jaw. A small quantity of 1881-CC tens have returned from foreign bank holdings in recent decades, but the issue remains scarce, since only 24,015 pieces were struck. Certified in a green label holder. (#8692)

1881-CC Ten Dollar, MS60

2685 **1881-CC MS60 NGC.** The 1881-CC is the most available Carson City ten dollar struck prior to 1890. This MS60 example displays peach-gold color and well struck design elements, except for the usually seen softness in the hair above Liberty's ear; this however is quite minor. Several light abrasions scattered about confine the most potent luster to the recesses. (#8692)

2686 **1882 MS63 PCGS.** This Select Mint State representative is a wonderful piece with highly lustrous yellow-gold surfaces that are enhanced by traces of pink and olive toning. A condition rarity, PCGS has only certified 27 finer pieces (6/07). (#8695)

2687 **1882 MS62 Prooflike NGC.** The reflective fields exhibit moderate marks consistent with the grade. A boldly struck example of an issue available in Mint State, but very scarce with prooflike surfaces. Census: 8 in 62 Prooflike, 1 finer (5/07).
From The Vanek Collection. (#78695)

2688 **1884-S MS62 PCGS.** A pleasing combination of honey-gold, apricot, and pastel rose coloration adorns the intensely lustrous surfaces of this conditionally scarce gold eagle. The fields are especially bright and flashy on this piece. Numerous small marks and a couple of moderate abrasions (on the obverse) define the grade. The '84-S is scarce at the MS62 level and rare in Select Mint State, where NGC and PCGS combined have certified only six examples, with none finer (4/07). (#8705)

Desirable MS63 1885 Liberty Eagle

2689 **1885 MS63 NGC.** A sharply struck example with brilliant yellow luster, this piece has satiny surfaces and reflective fields that exhibit only the usual minor bagmarks in the fields. This date is moderately scarce, with many survivors in the AU and lower Mint State grades, but in MS63 and higher quality, few pieces remain. Census: 23 in 63, 12 finer (5/07). (#8706)

2690 **1885-S MS62 PCGS.** Traces of pink toning are visible over honey-gold surfaces with fully brilliant mint frost on both sides. Minor surface marks on each side limit the grade of this piece. Just 47 finer examples have been certified by PCGS (6/07). (#8707)

2691 **1886 Prooflike MS62 NGC.** Flashy and richly toned, with glassy, prooflike fields and generally bold striking details. A few of the obverse stars lack complete definition, and numerous small abrasions are seen on each side. Census: 1 in 62 Prooflike, 0 finer (5/07). (#78708)

2692 **1886-S MS63 PCGS.** A satiny and attractive Liberty ten that boasts a sharp strike with fewer marks than is usual for the MS63 grade. The 1886-S is plentiful in abraded Mint State, but lustrous examples with eye appeal are scarce. (#8709)

2693 **1886-S MS63 NGC.** A lustrous lime and yellow-gold representative. Sharply struck, and although the fields are moderately abraded, the portrait is smooth for the grade. NGC has certified only nine pieces in higher grades (6/07). (#8709)

2694 **1888-S MS62 PCGS.** A sharply struck and lightly abraded pumpkin-gold representative of this conditionally challenging issue. Although a quantity of Mint State examples have returned from European bank holdings over the past few decades, neither NGC nor PCGS have certified any in grades above MS64. (#8714)

2695 **1888-S MS63 NGC.** The 1888-S ten dollar is relatively common through MS62. In MS63, its population drops significantly, and anything finer is virtually unobtainable. Apricot-gold surfaces reveal soft luster and wisps of light tan. Generally well struck, and with minute grade-defining marks. Census: 46 in 63, 5 finer (6/07). (#8714)

2696 **1889-S MS62 PCGS.** This boldly struck and lustrous ten has relatively clean fields, and gives the initial impression of a higher grade. A thin, light mark on the cheek is found upon further scrutiny. (#8716)

2697 **1889-S MS63 PCGS.** Sharply struck with flashy, effulgent luster and light yellow-gold, peach, and mint-green toning. A normal number of minor abrasions are noted for the grade. An elusive issue that is only occasionally seen in this grade and rarely any finer. (#8716)

2698 **1889-S MS63 NGC.** Impressive for the grade, since the lustrous peach-gold fields and devices lack the multiple moderate marks that often accompany the MS63 level. Sharply struck, and conditionally scarce. Census: 77 in 63, 4 finer (5/07). (#8716)

2699 **1890 MS60 ANACS.** A fully lustrous representative with moderate obverse marks and a surprisingly clean reverse. Only 57,980 pieces were struck, and although Uncirculated pieces are collectible, they are scarce, and the issue is nearly unobtainable above MS62. (#8717)

2700 **1890 MS62 PCGS.** Apricot-gold surfaces show the most potent luster in the interstices of, and the areas around, the design elements, all of which are well struck up. Light contact marks are scattered about. (#8717)

2701 **1890 MS61 Prooflike NGC.** 1890 was a low mintage year at Philadelphia, and only 57,980 eagles were struck. This pumpkin-gold example has flashy fields and a precise strike. A scratch beneath the branch stem determines the grade. Census: 1 in 61 Prooflike, 0 finer (5/07).
From The Vanek Collection. (#78717)

Impressive Condition Rarity, Select 1890-CC Ten

2702 **1890-CC MS63 NGC.** The 1891-CC is the usually encountered Mint State Carson City eagle. The 1890-CC is perhaps 10 times scarcer, and examples with full luster and without noticeable abrasions are rare. As of (5/07), NGC and PCGS combined have certified 20 pieces in MS63 with one finer, but those figures almost certainly include a number of duplicate submissions, since only a single MS63 has ever appeared in a Heritage auction, back in May 2003. (Heritage auctioned the sole certified MS64 for $80,500 in June 2006.) This well struck yellow-gold eagle has pleasing eye appeal for the MS63 level. A little-known fact about the 1890-CC is that IN GOD WE TRUST is die doubled toward the upper rim on all examples seen. That one reverse die was used comes as little surprise, given that only 17,500 pieces were struck. (#8718)

2703 **1891-CC MS62 PCGS.** Breen-7035, FS-501. The Carson City mintmark is clearly repunched west. A well struck and mildly prooflike example with the expected number of small marks. (#8720)

2704 **1891-CC MS62 Prooflike NGC.** The 1891-CC is plentiful by Carson City standards, but prooflike pieces are very scarce. This flashy and crisply impressed Liberty ten has a clean portrait and good eye appeal. Census: 9 in 62 Prooflike, 0 finer (5/07). (#78720)

2705 **1893 MS63 NGC.** This sharply struck and lustrous ten dollar piece lacks mentionable marks, and will serve as a quality representative of the gold type. (#8725)

2706 **1893 MS64 PCGS.** A sharply struck near-Gem with dynamic luster and a paucity of noticeable marks. As of (4/07), PCGS has certified only two pieces in finer grades. (#8725)

2707 **1893-S MS62 ANACS.** Olive-tinted borders frame the subtle peach interiors. This sharply struck and highly lustrous better date eagle has a pleasantly smooth reverse, and the obverse is also relatively unmarked, given its grade. (#8728)

2708 **1894 MS63 PCGS.** This is an appealing Select Uncirculated representative with light straw-gold and pastel rose coloration and shimmering luster. The design elements are sharply struck and the number of surface blemishes seems consistent with the assigned grade level. (#8729)

2709 **1894 MS64 PCGS.** The bold copper-red and steel-gray toning over each side is attractive and somewhat unusual, for the type. Well struck, except for a couple of the obverse stars, with shimmering luster and a few scattered marks that prevent a higher grade. This issue is scarce at the MS64 level, and PCGS has yet to certify a single Gem, as of (5/07). (#8729)

2710 **1894 MS64 NGC.** This Choice orange-gold type coin has sweeping luster and a bold strike. Distributed grazes are present, along with a mark on a portion of the first star.
From The Vanek Collection. (#8729)

2711 **1896 MS63 NGC.** The yellow-orange surfaces have rich luster and well-defined devices. The mintage is low for a later Philadelphia issue. Only 76,270 pieces were struck. (#8735)

2712 **1897 MS63 NGC.** Highly lustrous and well struck, with alluring peach-gold coloration. Numerous small marks are noted on each side, and there is a moderate abrasion that extends beneath RICA on the reverse. Not often seen any finer than this Select Mint State representative. (#8737)

2713 **1899 MS63 NGC.** A powerful strike emboldens the design elements on this Select ten dollar, and glowing luster radiates from honey-gold surfaces. Minute, inoffensive contact marks limit the grade. An excellent type coin. (#8742)

2714 **1899 MS64 NGC.** A canary-gold type coin that possesses a precise strike and vibrant cartwheel sweep. Faint luster grazes are largely confined to the obverse. (#8742)

2715 **1899 MS64 PCGS.** This crisply struck and original green-gold near-Gem possesses vibrant luster, and thorough evaluation locates only scattered wispy field grazes. (#8742)

2716 **1899 MS64 PCGS.** Shimmering luster and unusually light, straw-gold coloration are the most immediately noticeable characteristics of this attractive near-Gem. The surfaces are generally clean, but a few trivial marks on Liberty's cheek, and on the lower reverse field, prevent an even finer grade assessment. (#8742)

Conditionally Rare Choice 1899-S Ten

2717 **1899-S MS64 PCGS.** The mintage of the 1899-S is approximately two-thirds that of the 1899. But the difference in rarity at the MS64 level between the two issues is much more dramatic. PCGS and NGC combined have certified nearly 1,198 MS64 1899 eagles, but only a total of 23 MS64 1899-S eagles, with just eight pieces finer (5/07). The present near-Gem is well struck and has areas of prooflike luster along the reverse border. The portrait and the reverse are splendidly unabraded. (#8744)

2718 **1899-S MS62 Prooflike NGC.** This reflective yellow-gold eagle features a precise strike and moderately abraded fields. NGC has certified only five pieces as Prooflike. Census: 2 in 62 Prooflike, 0 finer (5/07). (#78744)

2719 **1901 MS63 PCGS.** Well struck and highly lustrous, with attractive coloration and surprisingly few surface blemishes for the grade. An easily available issue at the Select Mint State level that would serve admirably as a type coin. (#8747)

2720 **1901 MS64 NGC.** Well struck with visually enticing luster and delightful coloration. Surface marks are minimal on each side of this lovely type coin. (#8747)

2721 **1901 MS64 NGC.** This well struck sun-gold Liberty eagle has unencumbered luster and good eye appeal. Clean for the grade aside from an inconspicuous abrasion on Liberty's shoulder. (#8747)

2722 **1901 MS64 PCGS.** A lustrous and impressively preserved green-gold Choice Liberty ten with pleasing eye appeal for the designated grade. (#8747)

2723 **1901-O MS62 PCGS.** This lower mintage New Orleans eagle is well struck and lustrous. A few field marks are distributed, but the eye appeal is undeniable. Encapsulated in a green label holder. *From The Vanek Collection.* (#8748)

2724 **1901-S MS64 PCGS.** The 0 in the date is repunched south. This thoroughly lustrous Choice gold type coin is well struck and pleasing despite a hair-thin mark beneath the left (facing) claw. (#8749)

2725 **1901-S MS64 PCGS.** The deep orange-gold and lime toning is highlighted by intense cartwheel luster on both sides of this attractive type coin. The design elements are sharply struck, save for two or three of the obverse stars. A few trivial contact marks limit the grade. (#8749)

2726 **1901-S MS64 PCGS.** Olive-tined borders bound the pale peach centers. An original and satiny near-Gem whose smooth surfaces and sharply struck devices testify to its quality. (#8749)

2727 **1901-S MS64 PCGS.** This near-Gem is sharply defined with bright greenish-gold color and full mint frost. The '01-S is a common choice for type collections, with the advantage that a large population allows for careful selection. (#8749)

2728 **1901-S MS64 PCGS.** All of the design elements on both sides of this Choice Mint State piece are fully detailed, and the surfaces have frosty green-gold luster. (#8749)

2729 **1901-S MS64 NGC.** A delightful near-Gem, this sharply detailed piece has rich honey-gold luster framed by peripheral olive toning. Both sides have frosty mint surfaces. (#8749)

2730 **1901-S MS64 PCGS.** This satiny near-Gem is kept out of a higher grade level by the presence of a few faint hairlines on the obverse. A faint swirl of toning is visible in the left obverse field. (#8749)

Dynamic Superb Gem 1901-S Ten

2731 **1901-S MS67 NGC.** Breen-7075. The base of the first 1 is boldly repunched. Lighter recutting is visible on the base of the 9 and the top of the 0. The date was initially entered with an upward slant, then corrected. The reverse is also interesting for its strike doubling on UNITED STATES and the left (facing) wing. This doubling is mentioned in Breen's *Encyclopedia* under Breen-7074, but was caused by a loose reverse die rather than a doubled die, as Breen believed. Presumably, Breen relied upon second-hand information instead of verifying the variety with his own eyes.

This is a splendid gold type coin, well struck and highly lustrous. The obverse is remarkably smooth for a Liberty ten business strike, which are plentiful but generally found abraded. A graze above the TE in TEN is mentioned for pedigree purposes. As of (5/07), neither NGC nor PCGS has certified any examples finer. (#8749)

2732 **1902-S MS63 PCGS.** This exactingly struck Liberty ten exhibits unbroken cartwheel sheen. The obverse and right reverse have surprisingly few marks for the Select level, while the left reverse field has only minor abrasions. (#8751)

Select 1903-O Liberty Ten

2733 1903-O MS63 PCGS. This lustrous New Orleans ten has a penetrating strike and an impressively clean obverse. A small mint-made strike-through is noted near 6 o'clock on the reverse, and that side also has inconspicuous spots on the fletchings and near the C in AMERICA. The 1903-O is available in bagmarked Mint State, but becomes difficult to find at the MS63 level. Population: 73 in 63, 8 finer (5/07). (#8753)

2734 1903-S MS64 PCGS. This lovely straw-gold near-Gem has potent luster and a penetrating strike. Marks are few and inconsequential. Among 20th century issues, less often seen than the 1901, 1901-S, and 1907. (#8754)

Impressive Choice 1904 Ten Dollar

2735 1904 MS64 PCGS. A beautiful butter-gold near-Gem. Well struck save for the centers of a few stars, and the lustrous fields have only minimal contact. Although the 1904 is a Philadelphia issue struck during the tail end of the Liberty eagle's long run, it would be a mistake to regard it as anything other than very scarce at the MS64 level. Population: 30 in 64, 2 finer (5/07). (#8755)

2736 1904-O MS62 PCGS. A pleasing Mint State example of this 20th century New Orleans gold issue, well-defined with vibrant luster and pretty peach-gold color on the obverse that yields to vivid sun-gold on the reverse. The grade-defining marks are wispy, not the heavy abrasions often found on this issue. (#8756)

2737 1905 MS63 NGC. The striking impression is razor-sharp, with all of the details in Liberty's hair visible and every feather in the eagle well defined. Only obverse star 13 is a bit weakly struck. The lightly marked surfaces display a few grade-defining abrasions, including a noticeable scrape in the upper left obverse field. The satiny luster gives this piece nice eye appeal for the grade. (#8757)

2738 1905 MS63 PCGS. An intricately struck and lightly abraded example of this somewhat scarcer date. Original green-gold toning aids the eye appeal. (#8757)

2739 1905 MS63 NGC. The 1905 ten dollar is readily available in the lower grades of Mint State. MS63 pieces can be somewhat tougher to locate, and finer examples are scarce to rare. A sharp strike complements intensely lustrous, peach-gold surfaces on this Select example. Free of significant contact marks; a couple of spots are noted on the reverse. (#8757)

Gem 1906-D Liberty Ten

2740 1906-D MS65 NGC. The 06 in the date is lightly repunched, a different variety than Breen-7089. 1906 was the first year of coinage at the Denver Mint, and a small number of high grade eagles are known, perhaps set aside by a Mint official as the first of their kind. This highly lustrous Gem has a razor-sharp strike and an unabraded portrait. The reverse and the right obverse field are also splendidly smooth. Census: 19 in 65, 2 finer (5/07).
From The Vanek Collection. (#8760)

2741 1906-O MS62 NGC. This date was apparently not found to any great extent in European hoards, as Uncirculated examples are scarce (Jeff Garrett and Ron Guth, 2006). This MS62 specimen displays glowing luster emanating from orange-gold surfaces that yield sharply struck design elements. Census: 58 in 62, 42 finer (6/07). (#8761)

2742 1907 MS63 PCGS. This canary-gold type coin has vibrant luster and a precise strike. Minor marks are present, but none are distracting.
From The Vanek Collection. (#8763)

2743 1907 MS64 PCGS. A frosty near-Gem example of the final Liberty eagle, this piece has brilliant yellow luster and sharp design details. Although plentiful at this grade level, it is a rarity any finer with just nine better pieces certified by PCGS (6/07). (#8763)

Choice 1907-S Liberty Ten

2744 1907-S MS64 PCGS. The 1907-S is surprisingly scarce in Mint State, and becomes significantly rare in MS63 and higher grades. This is a beautiful near-Gem with smooth, lustrous surfaces and a penetrating strike. A small planchet flaw near star 7 is of little import. Population: 10 in 64, 2 finer (6/07). (#8765)

Gorgeous 1878 Ten Dollar, PR63
Trompeter Specimen

2745 **1878 PR63 PCGS.** Ex: Trompeter Collection. The 1878 proof ten dollar is part of Gobrecht's Coronet, Motto Above Eagle design type (1866-1907). Robert Loewinger, in his *Proof Gold Coinage of the United States*, writes: "This 'Motto Added' design was made by the Chief Mint Engraver, Longacre, and now included a scroll with the motto 'In God We Trust' on the reverse. The Reverend Watkinson, as a means of healing the scars of the Civil War, lobbied the Treasury Secretary, Salmon Chase, and the Congress to recognize God on the coins."

A mere 20 proof eagles were produced in 1878. In their *Encyclopedia of U.S. Gold Coins*, Jeff Garrett and Ron Guth said: " ... less than half the original mintage survives." In this regard, we note that PCGS and NGC combined have certified seven examples (6/07). Additionally, we list below a roster of five separate 1878 proof eagles. Eight other auction appearances between 1990 and 2005 are not included here, as we cannot be sure whether or not they are duplicates of those in the roster.

PR65. Garrett Collection (Stack's, 3/1976), lot 459; Auction '79 (Paramount, 7/1979), lot 338.
PR64 Deep Cameo. Smithsonian Institution.
PR64 PCGS. Stack's (6/1973); Harry W. Bass, Jr. (Bowers and Merena, 10/1999), lot 1561.
PR63. David S. Wilson (S.H. Chapman, 3/1907); Clapp Collection (1942); Eliasberg Collection (Bowers and Ruddy, 10/1982), lot 662.
PR63 PCGS. The present piece. Philip Straus Estate (Stack's, 5/1959), lot 2505; Stack's (1976 ANA Sale), lot 3101; Auction '80, lot 956; Ed Trompeter Collection (Superior, 3/1992), lot 218; Heritage (1/1999), lot 8240.

Rich apricot-gold color adorns both sides of the gorgeous Select proof, and a near gold-on-black appearance is seen when the coin is observed from a direct angle. Exquisite definition is visible on the design elements, though the hair curl at Liberty's ear is a tad soft. Some light hairlines visible under magnification are interspersed with die polish lines. A tiny alloy spot beneath star 9, and another under star 10 identify the coin. (#8818)

INDIAN EAGLES

Popular 1907 Wire Rim Ten, MS60 Details

2746 1907 Wire Rim—Scratched—ANACS. MS60 Details. The Wire Rim ten is generally acknowledged today to be a pattern issue. It was a first and unsuccessful effort to produce the Saint-Gaudens design for the new ten dollar gold coins. The coins were considered to have an indistinct appearance, and the design was soon changed to the even more unacceptable Rolled Rim variant. Finally, the Mint hit upon the regular issue that continued to the end of the design in 1933. This is a crisply struck coin with the usual bright yellow-gold surfaces. The singular distraction is a shallow scratch that extends from the obverse rim at 2:30 to almost 8 o'clock. (#8850)

Gorgeous 1907 No Periods Ten Dollar, MS64

2747 1907 No Periods MS64 PCGS. Rich apricot-gold patination tinged with mint-green and lilac envelops both sides of this radiantly lustrous near-Gem. A sharp strike brings out great definition on the design features, including most of the hair and bonnet feathers, areas that are usually weak on this issue. Close scrutiny reveals fewer marks than what might be expected for the grade designation. Housed in a green label holder.
From The Vanek Collection. (#8852)

Instantly Appealing MS64 1907 No Periods Ten

2748 1907 No Periods MS64 NGC. Never let it be said that coin collecting is an unemotional business. While a coin such as the present piece inspires an instant emotional response—"Oh, how wonderful, I need it, I want it"—a coin cataloger's job is to objectify that emotional response, translating it into quantifiable, understandable terms for potential bidders. The glorious luster is nearly unparalleled for the issue, and is the chief source of unqualified admiration. Frosty yellow-orange surfaces, with a dash of satiny velvet on the reverse, also contribute, and the couple of tiny ticks on the Indian's cheek fail to distract. Worth spirited—and emotional—bidding. (#8852)

Attractive 1907 No Periods Eagle, MS64

2749 1907 No Periods MS64 PCGS. The 1907 ten dollar No Periods, with a mintage of 239,406 pieces, is one of the most available of the Indian Head eagles. Mint engraver Charles Barber made some modifications to Saint-Gaudens' design, including removing the triangular stops or periods, reshaping the branch, and strengthening the feather ends (Jeff Garrett and Ron Guth, 2006). Variegated apricot-gold and mint-green patina resides on the highly lustrous surfaces of this near-Gem, and the design elements are well impressed. Some minute obverse marks define the grade. Housed in a green-label holder.
From The Silver Fox Collection. (#8852)

Two-Year Type Coin, 1908 No Motto Ten, MS64

2750 1908 No Motto MS64 NGC. Although the 1908 No Motto eagle has a much smaller mintage than the 1908-D No Motto—33,500 coins compared with 210,000—in the higher Mint State grades the 1908-D sells for considerably more, relegating the 1907 and 1908 issues to the status of two-year type coins. This example offers lush and lustrous yellow-gold patina with a tinge of mint-green at the rims on each side, along with generous eye appeal and relatively few signs of contact. Census: 49 in 64, 33 finer (6/07). (#8853)

2751 **1908-D No Motto MS61 NGC.** This lower mintage Indian ten has satiny luster and only minor marks on the devices. Straw-gold with infrequent gray hues. The N in UNUM appears to be lightly die doubled. (#8854)

2752 **1908-D No Motto MS62 NGC.** Jeff Garrett and Ron Guth (2006) write of the 1908-D No Motto eagle that: "Most of the original mintage did not survive in high grade." Soft luster resides on the peach-gold surfaces of this MS62 example. A few trivial obverse marks are noted. (#8854)

2753 **1908 Motto MS62 PCGS.** Soft luster emanates from the yellow-gold surfaces of this MS62 ten dollar, and the design elements display relatively sharp definition. A few scuffs and contact marks are noted on each side. (#8859)

2754 **1908 Motto MS63 NGC.** The bright satiny surface reveal fine-grained surface textures and nice olive-gold coloration. A few shallow marks define the grade. The first year of the With Motto Indian Head eagle type. (#8859)

2755 **1908-D Motto MS62 NGC.** Lustrous surfaces are somewhat fine grained, and exhibit sharply impressed design features, including good delineation on the Indian's hair. Peach-gold color enriches both sides, each of which reveals a few small contact marks. Census: 92 in 62, 48 finer (5/07). (#8860)

Elusive 1908-D Motto Eagle, MS63

2756 **1908-D Motto MS63 NGC.** Significantly more elusive and pricier in the higher Mint State grades despite a mintage considerably more generous than that of the 1908 No Motto, the 1908-D is nonetheless high on the want lists of many collectors. It is infrequently found in grades above MS63, so the current MS63 example represents a good balance of price and appearance. The radiant luster is this piece's chief attribute, although the surfaces are somewhat rough and pebbly-appearing. The few small ticks and scrapes are consistent with the Select grade, but much eye appeal remains. Census: 24 in 63, 24 finer (6/07). (#8860)

2757 **1908-S AU58 NGC.** A shimmering and subtly lustrous butter-gold example that displays minor friction on the highpoints and minor abrasions overall. A handful of tiny copper spots are noted at the rims. The 1908-S pieces are all of the With Motto variety and from the first issue of the design struck at San Francisco. (#8861)

Desirable and Scintillating 1908-S Eagle, MS64

2758 **1908-S MS64 NGC.** The 1908-S eagle is much more desirable and elusive in the higher Mint State grades than its P- or D-mint siblings, thus the present coin represents a significant offering in the present sale. This piece displays much that is desirable, including scintillating luster over distraction-free yellow-gold surfaces and premium appeal. Only a single light scrape before Liberty's face in the obverse left field appears to limit a potentially finer grade. Census: 15 in 64, 22 finer (6/07). (#8861)

2759 **1909-D MS62 PCGS.** Appealing khaki and rose coloration adorns the matte-like surfaces of this example; from a scarce issue in the Indian Head gold eagle series. The grade is defined partly by a small abrasion on Liberty's cheekbone, and a few wispy marks in the reverse fields. (#8863)

2760 **1910 MS62 PCGS.** Lustrous surfaces display peach-gold coloration and sharply struck devices. A few minor marks are not at all detracting. Both sides have a pleasing grainy finish. One of the more available dates in all grades. (#8865)

2761 **1910 MS63 NGC.** This attractive Indian Head eagle seems conservatively graded at the Select Mint State level. Satiny and carefully preserved, the matte-like surfaces display lovely, even coloration and a minimal number of trivial surface blemishes for the grade. (#8865)

2762 **1910 MS63 PCGS.** A lustrous and impeccably unabraded Select gold type coin with blended peach and olive toning. Evenly struck and undeniably attractive. (#8865)

Near-Gem 1910-D Indian Ten

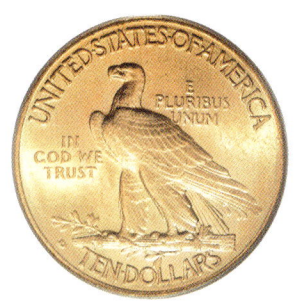

2763 **1910-D MS64 PCGS.** This lustrous gold type coin has light olive-green patina near the rims, while the centers offer peach iridescence. A faint graze is noted above the eyebrow, but the surfaces are generally well preserved. The obverse field, cheek, and neck are particularly smooth. The mintmark is bold, as is the design except for the rightmost portion of the branch. (#8866)

2764 **1911 MS62 NGC.** Lovely lime-gold and rose toning adorns the glittering, lustrous surfaces. The fine-grained surfaces show a handful of minor abrasions on the reverse that prevent a higher grade. (#8868)

2765 **1911 MS63 PCGS.** This shining Select representative has appealing wheat-gold color on the obverse with slightly richer yellow-gold evident on the reverse. Well-defined with small, scattered abrasions evident on each side. This issue's production of over 500,000 pieces dwarfs that of its branch-mint cousins. (#8868)

2766 **1911 MS63 NGC.** Radiantly lustrous surfaces exhibit sharply struck motifs and pretty peach-gold coloration. The grade is defined by a few minor marks. (#8868)

Attractive 1911 Ten Dollar, MS64

2767 **1911 MS64 NGC.** Rich and attractive orange-gold surfaces create exceptional eye appeal for this sharply struck near-Gem specimen. A few trivial surface marks have prevented a higher grade. The 1911 eagle is considered one of the common issues in the Indian series, but it is still elusive in Gem condition, and Choice pieces are in strong demand. This piece displays great technical quality and eye appeal. (#8868)

Highly Lustrous Near-Gem 1911 Ten Dollar

2768 **1911 MS64 PCGS.** Highly lustrous peach-gold surfaces yield a greenish cast, and have a fine pebbly appearance, a characteristic often seen on this issue. Sharp definition prevails on the design features, and both sides are devoid of mentionable marks. This coin possesses tremendous eye appeal for the grade. Encapsulated in a green-label holder.
From The Vanek Collection. (#8868)

2769 **1912 MS63 PCGS.** This honey-gold representative has relatively few marks, and the cartwheel sheen is comprehensive. In 1912, the Denver Mint passed on the eagle denomination, the first such occurrence since its operations began in 1906. (#8871)

Vibrant 1912 Eagle, MS66

2770 **1912 MS66 PCGS.** The 1912 eagle, with a mintage of just over 400,000 pieces, has a reputation as one of the more available issues in the Saint-Gaudens series. While not present in such quantities as the 1926 or 1932, Garrett and Guth (2006) state that enough "were coined and saved to satisfy collector demand." While this holds true even for Gems, anything finer is a condition rarity.

The surfaces of this immensely appealing Premium Gem are yellow-orange with a touch of peach at the upper right obverse. Aside from a touch of softness at the hair below the headband, the minimally marked devices have strong detail, and the glowing fields have a slightly satiny appearance. One of just nine pieces so graded by PCGS, with just two finer across both major services (5/07). (#8871)

2771 **1913 MS63 PCGS.** Excellent luster radiates from this Select ten dollar. Gorgeous apricot-gold color is imbued with hints of light green. Kept from a higher grade by a handful of minor marks. (#8873)

2772 **1913 MS64 NGC.** Strong, satiny luster and rich butter-yellow and orange color are the most eye-catching features of this Saint-Gaudens eagle. The surfaces of this well-defined piece are slightly hazy, indicative of possible overseas storage, and a few scattered abrasions preclude a Gem grade. (#8873)

Sharply Struck 1913 Gem Ten Dollar

2773 **1913 MS65 PCGS.** The 1913 eagle is relatively common through near-Gem, but is becomes more elusive in MS65. The Gem example presented in this lot displays attractive orange-gold patination interspersed with splashes of yellow. A well executed strike brings out nice definition on the design elements. Well preserved save for a solitary mark at the Indian's temple. Housed in a first generation PCGS holder. Population: 46 in 65, 12 finer (6/07). (#8873)

2774 **1913-S AU53 PCGS.** This still-lustrous straw-gold piece has moderate wear on the left border of the eagle's wing. Marks are unimportant for the grade. One of just 66,000 examples coined. (#8874)

2775 **1913-S AU58 NGC.** The 1913-S is a key date of the pre-World War I portion of the series, since only 66,000 pieces were struck, and most exhibit signs of handling. The present representative displays unbroken cartwheel sheen, and evidence of friction is elusive. The reverse field is slightly subdued beneath TRUST. (#8874)

2776 **1914-D MS62 PCGS.** The flashy obverse has a distinctive sun-gold color, while the reverse has a slightly paler appearance. Well-defined with a handful of abrasions present in the left obverse field. An attractive example of an issue that becomes more elusive in finer grades. (#8876)

2777 **1914-D MS62 ANACS.** A moderately abraded piece with booming luster and a good strike. The final Denver Mint Indian eagle issue, although the facility struck the denomination again in 1984 as an Olympic commemorative. (#8876)

Reddish-Gold MS64 1914-D Ten Dollar

2778 **1914-D MS64 PCGS.** This sharply struck and thoroughly lustrous near-Gem has the occasional faint luster graze, but its quality for the grade is undeniable. A better-date Indian ten, especially relative to the abundant 1926 and 1932 issues. Purchased in the 1930s at face value by Karl Stecher Sr. from coins turned in by the public as per President Roosevelt's March 9, 1933 directive. (#8876)

2779 **1915 MS62 PCGS.** The 351,000 pieces struck for this issue would be the last eagles coined at Philadelphia for more than a decade, as production would not resume there until 1926. This well struck piece has pleasing luster and lovely lemon-yellow color on both sides. Lightly abraded overall, though the visual appeal approaches that of a Select piece. (#8878)

2780 **1916-S MS62 PCGS.** A satiny and well struck example that displays dusky antique-gold color over each side. Light, scattered abrasions preclude a Select grade. The 1916-S was the only eagle issue for that year, and four years would pass before San Francisco or any other mint would strike the denomination again. (#8880)

Choice AU 1920-S Indian Eagle Rarity

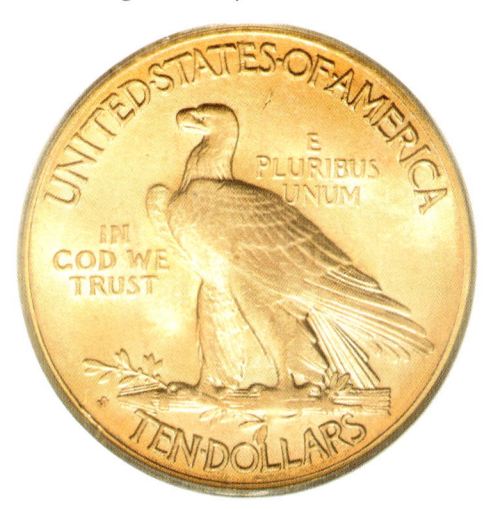

2781 **1920-S AU55 PCGS.** This issue is one of the five important rarities in the Indian eagle series, along with the two 1907 With Periods varieties, the 1930-S, and the 1933 issues. While there are other condition rarities, these five varieties are rare in all grades.

The mintage of this issue was 126,500 coins, seemingly large enough that examples should still be plentiful, except that this issue was not exported overseas like many others. Therefore, most or all of those struck were placed in circulation where survival was limited to the few pieces acquired by collectors during the 1920s. Any remaining coins were returned to the Treasury in 1933 and melted soon afterwards.

This example is a pleasing piece with nearly full luster and attractive orange-gold surfaces. Only a trace of highpoint wear is evident. The fields have a few faint hairlines that were most likely acquired during its brief stay in circulation. An attractive example, this piece should see considerable auction activity. (#8881)

Key 1920-S Ten Dollar, MS62
Third Rarest Issue in the Ten Dollar Indian Series

2782 1920-S MS62 NGC. The mintage of the 1920-S ten dollar is 126,500 pieces, certainly not an impressively low mintage for this series. However, the absolute rarity of the 1920-S points to the real use for ten dollar gold pieces as a trade medium for European and Central American banks. An interesting and somewhat lengthy passage from the Garrett-Guth reference explains in greater detail the rarity of the 1920-S:

> "Obviously, the three-year hiatus [since 1916] did little to drum up excitement for this series, and most of these entered circulation unnoticed soon after the time of issue. Europe was in disarray when these were struck; remaining banks were simply trying to survive and didn't have the ability or credit to hoard additional gold coins. As World War I came to an end in 1918, German troops returned home to devastation, and in a few years had to fight the insidious hyperinflation that wiped out any remaining savings in late 1923. Thus, survival of the 1920-S Indian Head eagle was strictly a matter of chance, and very, very few did survive in any grade."

Only 44 pieces have been certified by NGC and PCGS combined, minus an uncertain number of resubmissions. This low number of Mint State examples confirms this issue's status as the third rarest date in the series, trailing only the 1933 and the 1907 Rolled Rim.

This frosted example has even reddish patina over each side. The TY in LIBERTY are weakly impressed, as usual for this issue. Additionally, there is uniform striking weakness on the reverse on the eagle's feathers and the right (facing) leg. Magnification shows a number of small abrasions scattered over each side, but the only one worthy of individual mention is a shallow, vertical mark at the top of the eagle's tail feathers. A rare opportunity for the specialist to acquire this seldom-offered issue. (#8881)

2783 **1926 MS63 NGC.** In 1926, Philadelphia struck just over a million pieces, the highest mintage achieved for the denomination at a single Mint since 1910. This strongly lustrous Select piece offers pleasing detail and shimmering wheat-gold surfaces with a touch of frost on the highpoints. A copper spot appears near 6 o'clock on the reverse rim. (#8882)

2784 **1926 MS63 PCGS.** This is a lovely Select ten dollar that displays a gorgeous mix of apricot-gold and mint-green patination resting on intensely lustrous surfaces. An attentive strike emboldens the design elements, enhancing the coin's overall eye appeal. A few minute handling marks on each side account for the grade, though they are not as numerous as is usually the case for the issue (Jeff Garrett and Ron Guth, 2006). (#8882)

2785 **1926 MS64 PCGS.** Lovely lime-gold and rose toning is illuminated by intense, shimmering luster. The design motifs are boldly struck. A handful of minor abrasions on each side preclude a higher grade assessment. A popular issue for type purposes. (#8882)

2786 **1926 MS64 PCGS.** This butter-yellow near-Gem's soft luster distinguishes it from the more typical flashy appearance found on other examples. A well struck example of this popular type issue, one that has two grade-defining diagonal marks on the portrait. (#8882)

2787 **1926 MS64 PCGS.** Softly frosted luster illuminates the fine-grained surfaces of this boldly struck example. Each side displays pleasing lime-green and peach toning, as well as a handful of fine, grade-defining marks. A candidate for the similarly graded 20th century gold type set. (#8882)

2788 **1926 MS64 PCGS.** The date seems lightly doubled on 926. This beautifully lustrous orange-gold example displays adequate striking details and a few small abrasions that preclude the Gem grade assessment. A pleasing example of this available issue. (#8882)

2789 **1926 MS64 PCGS.** Hints of light green are included in the peach-gold patination covering highly lustrous surfaces. Sharply struck on the design features, further enhancing the coin's eye appeal. Some minuscule marks limit the grade. (#8882)

2790 **1926 MS64 NGC.** Intense luster and lovely peach-gold coloration compete for attention on the surfaces of this relatively high grade example. The second-highest mintage in the Indian Head gold eagle series makes this issue an ideal choice for type purposes. (#8882)

2791 **1932 MS63 PCGS.** A lustrous and nicely struck lemon-gold type coin from the final collectible year of the series. Minor distributed marks are typical for the grade. (#8884)

2792 **1932 MS64 PCGS.** Regardless of the reasons for the unusually high mintage for the 1932 eagle, that issue gives type collectors a golden opportunity. This near-Gem example displays pleasing detail and soft, shimmering luster. Lightly marked on the yellow-orange reverse. (#8884)

2793 **1932 MS64 PCGS.** Boldly struck and highly lustrous, with just a few minuscule surface blemishes. The essentially brilliant surfaces show subtle accents of lime-green and rose. (#8884)

2794 **1932 MS64 PCGS.** A softly lustrous, highly appealing Choice example of the highest-mintage eagle issue ever produced, solidly struck with a combination of apricot-gold and orange colors. A delightful piece that would fit well in a similarly graded type set. (#8884)

2795 **1932 MS64 PCGS.** The Indian's nostril is die doubled with a decent spread, a doubling class similar to that found on the 1984 Doubled Ear Lincoln cent. A carefully preserved and lustrous orange-gold type coin, crisply struck except for some softness near the eagle's shoulder. Housed in a green label PCGS holder. (#8884)

2796 **1932 MS64 PCGS.** This issue's generous mintage has made it a staple of dealers' cases. The well struck yellow-gold piece offered here has splashes of orange color at the margins and a tiny copper spot to the left of the chin. Modestly marked overall. (#8884)

2797 **1932 MS64 PCGS.** Glowing luster issues from yellow-gold surfaces, and a solid strike brings out excellent definition on the motifs. A few minor scuffs and marks define the grade. (#8884)

2798 **1932 MS64 PCGS.** Luscious orange-gold, rose, and mint-green coloration adorns the gleaming, highly lustrous surfaces of this Indian Head eagle. Just a handful of tiny marks, on each side, limit the grade. Survivors from this penultimate issue are the ultimate type coins for the series.
From The Vanek Collection. (#8884)

2799 **1932 MS64 PCGS.** A slightly frosty and well-defined Choice example of this popular type issue. The reverse is butter-yellow, while the obverse has a slightly lighter cast. Though over 4.4 million pieces were struck for this issue, the next year saw Roosevelt's mandatory recall of gold coinage. (#8884)

Gem 1932 Indian Eagle

2800 **1932 MS65 PCGS.** An ideal piece for the type collector who desires high quality at a reasonable price, this frosty Gem exhibits exceptionally brilliant yellow-gold luster with traces of bluish patina on each side. The surfaces have a few tiny marks that are consistent with the grade. (#8884)

Highly Attractive 1932 Gem Ten Dollar

2801 **1932 MS65 PCGS.** The 1932 ten dollar, with its plentiful numbers (4.463 million produced), is often sought as a type coin for the Indian Head design. Lovely peach-gold surfaces display dazzling luster, and the design elements are boldly impressed. Both sides are minimally abraded. (#8884)

LIBERTY DOUBLE EAGLES

2802 **1850—Scratched—ANACS. AU Details, Net XF40.** A green-gold example of the first collectible double eagle issue. Substantial luster is present, but the wingtips exhibit slight wear, and there are two thin horizontal pinscratches on the central left reverse. (#8902)

2803 **1850 AU50 NGC.** A luminous, lightly circulated example from the first year of issue with dusky antique-gold color overall and a few points of deeper color. Moderately abraded with slightly above-average detail and a scrape to the left of Liberty's chin. (#8902)

2804 **1850—Cleaned—ANACS. AU55 Details.** An interesting example from the first official Philadelphia double eagle issue. Though the lightly hairlined orange-gold fields are primarily glossy, a degree of original luster remains at the reverse periphery. Crisply struck with light, even wear on the devices and minor, scattered abrasions. (#8902)

Choice XF 1850-O Double Eagle

2805 1850-O XF45 NGC. As the first year of issue for the type and the first branch mint double eagle to be struck, the 1850-O is immensely popular with collectors. Unfortunately, this issue is rarely found with aesthetically pleasing qualities. As Douglas Winter notes in his *Gold Coins of the New Orleans Mint 1839-1909*: "Nearly every 1850-O double eagle has extensively abraded surfaces. These marks are deep and often very distracting." The current example is typical of the issue, with abraded surfaces throughout. The luster and strike, however, are surprisingly above average considering the assigned grade. (#8903)

Lustrous AU 1850-O Twenty

2806 1850-O AU50 PCGS. While CC-mint gold coins have a special cachet all their own, the C- and D-mint early gold from Charlotte and Dahlonega can seem simultaneously alluring and yet remote in time and place. New Orleans gold offers the best of both worlds, combining ready accessibility with the exotic appeal of branch mint gold. The 1850-O goes a step further, adding the attraction of a mintmarked piece from the introductory year of a new type. Most survivors of the issue grade Choice XF or lower and are plagued by heavy abrasions. The present AU example preserves more than half of its original mint luster, but the surfaces are typical in terms of abrasions, with myriad moderate contact marks on each side. Population: 15 in 50, 35 finer (6/07). (#8903)

2807 1851 AU53 NGC. A moderately abraded green-gold twenty with the undipped "dirty gold" appearance valued by specialists. The 1851 is surprisingly scarce in Mint State, despite a production of more than 2 million pieces. (#8904)

1851-O Twenty Dollar, XF45

2808 1851-O XF45 PCGS. The 1851-O is the most available New Orleans double eagle, although examples grading above AU are rare. The majority of extant examples are found in the VF to XF grade range and typically display heavily abraded surfaces. The current coin is above average in terms of eye appeal, with cleaner fields and more luster than one would expect on a Choice Extra Fine example. The strike is average, with weakness on stars 1 through 7 noted for accuracy. Traces of semiprooflike reflectivity are observed in the protected areas. (#8905)

Sharp 1851-O Twenty Dollar, AU58

2809 1851-O AU58 NGC. Douglas Winter, in his *Gold Coins of the New Orleans Mint, 1839-1909* (2006), says: "The 1851-O is the most common New Orleans double eagle in terms of overall rarity and the second most available in high grades." As such, the issue is popular as a type coin.

A well executed strike leaves excellent definition on the design elements of this high-end AU example. Orange-gold and mint-green hues enrich both sides, and the surfaces reveal just a few minute marks, unusual for a date that has a reputation for being heavily abraded (Winter, 2006). This piece is free of copper spots and grease stains, the latter of which frequently are found on extant specimens. Partially prooflike fields are noted when the coin is tilted under a light source. (#8905)

2810 1852 XF45 PCGS. Pale mint-green and coral toning embraces the surprisingly lustrous surfaces of this early Philadelphia Mint double eagle. Both sides of the coin are extensively abraded, but the degree of highpoint wear is less-than-expected for the grade. (#8906)

2811 1852 AU50 ANACS. Well struck with light, even wear evident on the devices. The butter-yellow surfaces display a degree of remaining luster, particularly at the margins. A moderately abraded, yet appealing example of this early double eagle issue. (#8906)

2812 1852 AU50 PCGS. Traces of luster reside in the recessed areas of this generally well struck twenty. Peach-gold surfaces reveal the expected number of marks for a large, heavy gold coin that saw limited circulation. A fairly high-mintage Philadelphia issue (2,053,026 pieces). (#8906)

2813 1852 AU53 NGC. Attractive yellow-gold surfaces display generally well defined design elements, as well as residual luster in the protected areas. We note fewer contact marks than what might be expected. The *S.S. Central America* and *S.S. Republic* wrecks contained about 130 1852 specimens. (#8906)

2814 **1852 AU55 NGC.** One of the more common Type One double eagles, the 1852 was struck in large numbers and survivors are represented in all grades. This is a moderately abraded, lightly worn coin that still shows a fair amount of luster. An appealing Choice AU example of this date.
From The Vanek Collection. (#8906)

Choice XF 1852-O Double Eagle

2815 **1852-O XF45 PCGS.** A particularly attractive 1852-O twenty considering the assigned grade, this example is well struck and displays original yellow-gold surfaces. The fields are slightly semiprooflike, as often found on this issue, yet not as abraded as most examples at this grade level. Although available in grades below AU condition, an 1852-O double eagle with eye appeal is truly special. (#8907)

1852-O Double Eagle, XF45 NGC

2816 **1852-O XF45 NGC.** With a mintage of 190,000 coins, the 1852-O is one of the more available double eagles produced by the New Orleans Mint. The example in this lot is characteristic of most early O-mint twenties, having an average strike and moderately abraded surfaces. Mint-made beveled rims, common to this issue, are also observed. The coloration is an attractive light yellow-gold. (#8907)

Choice AU 1852-O Double Eagle

2817 **1852-O AU55 NGC.** New Orleans double eagles are scarce, partly because most issues had low mintages, and partly because only a single O-mint issue was struck after 1861, the very rare 1879-O. This sun-gold example has copious iridescent luster, and aside from a few small ticks near the cheekbone, the surfaces are surprisingly void of bagmarks. (#8907)

Lustrous AU58 1852-O Twenty

2818 **1852-O AU58 PCGS.** As one of the more available Type One twenties, the 1852-O enjoys constant demand from gold type collectors. Few pieces are known in Uncirculated condition, with most collectors having to content themselves with a coin in one of the various states of AU. This piece has rich reddish tinted surfaces that add considerably to the overall visual appeal. Considerable mint luster remains on each side, with more obviously on the reverse than in the exposed obverse fields. Sharply struck throughout; there are no obvious or detracting marks on either side of this impressive O-mint twenty. (#8907)

2819 **1853—Repaired—NCS. AU Details.** Apricot-gold patination is imbued with whispers of mint-green, and the design features are nicely defined. Liberty's portrait and the obverse fields have been smoothed, perhaps attempting to remove numerous tiny pock marks. (#8908)

Pleasing 1853 Double Eagle, AU58

2820 1853 AU58 NGC. This high-end About Uncirculated double eagle displays considerable luster on peach-gold surfaces. An impressive strike brings out sharp definition on the design features, save for minor softness in portions of Liberty's hair. A few minute marks scattered about do not detract. The 1853 becomes tough to locate in Mint State, particularly at the choice level. (#8908)

2821 1854 Small Date AU50 PCGS. Luster brightens the stars, legends, and devices of this crisply impressed, mildly glossy, and only briefly circulated double eagle. Philadelphia double eagle mintages dropped annually between 1852 and 1856, as California-mined bullion began making its way to the U.S. Assay Office and San Francisco Mint. (#8911)

Almost Uncirculated 1854-S Twenty

2822 1854-S AU50 NGC. The San Francisco Mint struck twenties each year from 1854 through 1907, with the exception of an unexplained interruption in 1886. Not counting the 1866-S No Motto subtype and the 1861-S Paquet Reverse, the 1854-S boasts the lowest recorded mintage in the entire Liberty double eagle series. And of the 141,468 pieces struck in that inaugural year in San Francisco, the vast majority of the coins were released into circulation. There was also a significant hoard of high grade pieces that were salvaged in the 1970s. These coins show matte-like surfaces from the abrasive action of sea water, unlike this coin. Light friction is seen over the highpoints and there is a significant presence of mint luster around the devices. Lightly abraded with the most obvious marks located in the field to the right of the date. (#8913)

Challenging Choice AU 1855 Twenty

2823 1855 AU55 PCGS. Mintages of double eagles at Philadelphia dropped annually between 1851 and 1856, since an increasing quantity of California-mined gold was struck by the U.S. Assay Office or the fledgling San Francisco Mint. This partly lustrous representative has distributed small marks but is free from heavy abrasions. (#8914)

Choice AU 1855 Double Eagle

2824 1855 AU55 NGC. This Choice AU 1855 twenty is refreshingly original. Lustrous surfaces abound, especially on the reverse where the cartwheels are virtually uninterrupted. A few scattered marks are observed on the obverse, the largest being a 3-mm mark to the left of the date. The defect in the field to the left of star 12 appears to be a mint-produced strike-through. Garrett and Guth consider the 1855 double eagle to be a "true condition rarity," as stated in their *Encyclopedia of U.S. Gold Coins*, and add that "nearly all of the known coins for the date are low grade." Census: 64 in 55, 80 finer (6/07). (#8914)

2825 1855-S XF45 PCGS. Moderately marked with substantial remaining details and showing a great deal of luster for the grade. A slightly scarcer Type One double eagle. (#8916)

2826 1855-S AU53 NGC. Distinct green-gold surfaces are splashed with traces of coppery-orange toning. Both sides have numerous tiny surface marks, not unusual for these large gold coins that served in the channels of Western commerce. (#8916)

2827 1856 AU55 NGC. A still-lustrous pre-Civil War piece that has elegant antique-gold and butter-yellow color over each side, along with minor copper spots on the reverse. Well struck with only light abrasions and minimal wear on the devices. (#8917)

2828 1856 AU55 NGC. The peripheral elements are well-defined, though the modestly worn devices exhibit slight weakness. The luminous wheat-gold surfaces of this briefly circulated piece display light, scattered abrasions and a vertical ruby copper streak at the eagle's tailfeathers. (#8917)

2829 1856-S XF45 NGC. This Choice XF twenty displays luster clinging to the areas around the design elements, along with generally well defined motifs. Peach-gold surfaces are lightly marked. (#8919)

2830 1856-S AU50 NGC. Bright apricot-gold surfaces retain wisps of luster in the recesses. Generally well defined, save for lightly worn areas of Liberty's hair. Evenly distributed minute contact marks are not offensive. (#8919)

2831 1856-S AU53 PCGS. Attractive apricot-gold color bathes both sides of this AU53 specimen. This is complemented by well impressed design elements, and a fair amount of luster in the recessed areas. The normal assortment of marks are visible on both faces. (#8919)

Conditionally Elusive 1856-S Double Eagle MS63

Gem S.S. *Central America* 1857-S Twenty

2832 1856-S MS63 NGC. The surfaces of this Select Mint State specimen are unusually bright and flashy. The rich golden-yellow coloration is imbued with lime-green accents in the fields. All of the design elements are crisply defined, and surface marks seem minimal for the grade. At one time, this date was notoriously scarce in Mint State, but the discovery of several shipwrecks containing hundreds of '56-S double eagles has modified the availability of this San Francisco Mint issue. Even so, examples remain extremely elusive in any grade finer than MS62. Census: 5 in 63, 2 finer (5/07). (#8919)

2833 1857-S Spiked Shield MS65 PCGS. Variety 20A. SSCA 2965. A remarkably unabraded Gem kept from an even finer grade by some dusky gray patina from 7 to 8 o'clock on the obverse, and from 4 to 10 o'clock on the reverse. An outstanding example of this famous shipwreck hoard issue. Lustrous, crisply struck, and housed in its initial gold label PCGS holder. Included with the lot is a red California Gold Marketing Group box, a faux book, and a certificate of authenticity signed by S.S. *Central America* expedition leader Tommy Thompson. The S.S. Central America sank on September 12, 1857, with approximately 435 lives lost. The wreck was located after several years effort in 1988, yielding a large bounty of double eagles. (#70000)

Impressive MS65 1857-S Twenty
Ex: S.S. *Central America*

2834 **1857-S Bold S MS65 PCGS.** Ex: *S.S. Central America*. 20B. It is truly remarkable that modern technology was able to rescue so many coins that were previously thought to be lost, circulated, melted, or otherwise unavailable to collectors. The prospect of owning a Gem Type One double eagle was simply not realistic for most collectors a generation ago, not only because of the cost of the few pieces that were known but because of the unavailability of these coins in high grade. The luster on this piece is as bright and frosted as the day it was minted 150 years ago. The luster is rich orange-gold and deepens significantly to reddish gold around the perimeter of the reverse. Fully struck in all areas. As one would expect from a coin in this grade, there are no mentionable abrasions on either side of this magnificent Type One twenty. (#70001)

2835 **1857-S AU55 NGC.** Variety 20C, confirmed by the small spikes (as made) along the left edge of Liberty's neck. Orange-tinged luster outlines design elements. A trivial rim ding is noted on the obverse at 11 o'clock. (#70002)

2836 **1857-S AU55 NGC.** Variety 20C. A well struck and original representative with dusky sun-gold toning. No relevant marks are present. The prior generation holder has a small chip on lower left corner, with no effect on the coin itself.
Ex: Stack's, (Henry Da Costa Gomez Collection, 6/04), lot 3419, which realized $1,495. (#70002)

2837 **1857-S XF45 NGC.** Variety 20D. The 1 and 7 are bold, and the flag of the 1 is repunched. This crisply struck '57-S has minor highpoint wear, but luster is extensive for the grade, particularly on the reverse. (#70003)

Near-Prooflike 1857-S Double Eagle, AU55
Ex: S.S. *Central America*

2838 **1857-S Bold 7, Faint S AU55 PCGS.** Ex: *S.S. Central America*. Variety 20D. SSCA 0756. This is a wonderful Choice AU example from the *S.S. Central America* treasure. The surfaces retain evidence of reflectivity, and this must have been a gorgeous prooflike piece when it was struck. (#70003)

2839 **1857-S AU53 PCGS.** Variety 20F, identified in part by the defective left serif on the U in UNITED and the open top on the E in AMERICA. This is a partly lustrous representative with a small reverse rim nick at 12:30 and the expected moderate marks on the left obverse. (#70005)

Scarce Choice AU 1858 Twenty

2840 **1858 AU55 NGC.** Luster emerges from the devices and peripheries of this lower mintage Philadelphia twenty. Liberty's cheek displays slight wear, but there are no mentionable marks. The last year of the initial obverse hub, which uses an L punch in place of the proper I punch within LIBERTY. (#8923)

2841 **1858-O Fine 15 NGC.** Well worn on the obverse but showing quite a bit more remaining detail on the reverse. The light orange-tan surfaces are free of sizeable marks. Each side has a few bits of dark verdigris. (#8924)

2842 **1858-S AU53 NGC.** Moderately worn on the highpoints with attractive coloration and a few scattered abrasions on each side. A great deal of luster remains evident, for an AU coin. A reasonably available issue at this grade level. (#8925)

2843 **1858-S AU53 ANACS.** Both sides of this bright yellow-gold example have minor surface marks that are expected at this grade level. It is an attractive coin for this date that has avoided massive treasure discoveries. (#8925)

2844 **1858-S AU55 PCGS.** Struck too late to emerge from the *S.S. Central America* shipwreck, yet too early to be a major player in the *S.S. Brother Jonathan* hoard. Luster dominates protected areas of this moderately abraded green-gold representative. Population: 35 in 55, 38 finer (4/07). (#8925)

2845 **1859-S AU50 PCGS.** Luster forms a bright band across the peripheries of this attractive double eagle. A cluster of thin marks beneath the hairbun determines the grade. Certified in an old green label holder. (#8928)

2846 **1859-S AU50 NGC.** Bright peach-gold surfaces display traces of luster in the protected areas of this AU50 specimen. Generally well defined, with no more than the expected number of marks usually found on these large, heavy coins. (#8928)

Lustrous AU53 1862-S Twenty

2860 **1862-S AU53 PCGS.** This Civil War S-mint issue was formerly rare in high grades, but recoveries from both the *S.S. Brother Jonathan* and *S.S. Republic* have made it more plentiful in high grade than previously. This example offers gorgeous luster coruscating from the yellow-orange surfaces, with moderate scattered abrasions throughout both sides and light, grade-consistent wear. Population: 40 in 53, 78 finer (6/07). (#8938)

Pleasing Choice AU 1862-S Double Eagle

2861 **1862-S AU55 PCGS.** While minted in substantial numbers, the 1862-S twenty is surprisingly difficult at all grade levels and downright scarce in AU. It is well struck with only traces of highpoint wear and surprisingly intense luster for the grade. A few moderate blemishes are noticeable on the obverse. This is a lovely Choice AU example of the 1862-S double eagle that is highly recommended to the discriminating bidder. In an old green label holder. (#8938)

2862 **1863-S AU53 NGC.** This piece shows a substantial amount of luster, as might be expected on an AU coin. The design elements are well struck expect for the lower obverse stars. The surfaces show only faint highpoint wear, but a high number of small to moderate abrasions are noted on both sides. (#8940)

2863 **1863-S AU53 PCGS.** This pleasing AU53 double eagle retains considerable luster in its recesses, and gives off peach-gold coloration. The design features exhibit good definition, and each side possesses a uniform scattering of minute marks. (#8940)

Attractive 1863-S Double Eagle AU55

2864 **1863-S AU55 PCGS.** The design elements of this Choice AU survivor are generally bold, except for noticeable flatness on obverse stars 4 through 7, and on selected parts of the eagle. The pale green coloration yields to gleaming coral-gold luster near the devices. Scattered abrasions and traces of highpoint wear on the eagle's wingtips and on Liberty's hair detail define the grade of the piece. (#8940)

2865 **1864-S XF45 NGC.** A lightly circulated and appealing representative of this Civil War issue, well struck with remnants of luster at the margins of the yellow-gold surfaces. Minor, scattered abrasions appear on each side. (#8942)

2866 **1864-S AU50 PCGS.** Bright peach-gold surfaces yield a fair amount of luster and exhibit good detail on the design elements. Each side reveals an even distribution of light marks, none of which are worthy of individual mention. Prior to the discoveries of the *S.S. Brother Jonathan* and the *S.S. Republic*, the 1864-S was found mostly in VF to XF condition (Jeff Garrett and Ron Guth, 2006). (#8942)

2867 **1864-S AU50 ANACS.** Light, even wear affects the still-lustrous butter-yellow surfaces of this wartime San Francisco issue. Scattered abrasions appear in the fields and on the devices, with the most notable mark appearing in Liberty's hair. (#8942)

2868 **1864-S AU50 NGC.** This piece is much more attractive than the average AU50 example, perhaps because of the shimmering luster and the lovely rose and green-gold toning that adorns both sides. Typically worn on the highpoints, with mostly small marks that seem consistent with NGC's grade determination. (#8942)

Historic 1864-S Twenty, AU55

2869 **1864-S AU55 NGC.** Struck during the waning years of the Civil War, this 1864 S-mint double eagle is a tangible connection to a tumultuous time in our nation's history. Fortunately for modern day collectors, examples of this date are available above XF, thanks almost entirely to treasures recovered from the *S.S. Brother Jonathan* and the *S.S. Republic*. This is an attractive coin for the grade that retains generous portions of mint luster on each side. Rich reddish-gold color. (#8942)

MS61 1864-S Twenty, Ex: S.S. Brother Jonathan

S.S. Republic 1865 Double Eagle, MS63 ★ NGC

2870 **1864-S MS61 PCGS.** Ex: *S.S. Brother Jonathan* 355. Fictional character Brother Jonathan was the early 19th century equivalent of Uncle Sam, a personification of the United States. The *S.S. Brother Jonathan* made its first voyage on November 11, 1850. It sank on July 30, 1865, near the Oregon coastline, with a loss of approximately 200 lives. The wreck was discovered on September 30, 1992 by Deep Sea Research, Inc.

This satiny peach-gold example is generally well struck, with minor softness on a few letters in STATES OF. There are no heavy marks, which is unusual for an MS61 double eagle. An outstanding souvenir from one of the three most famous American numismatic shipwrecks (the other two were the *S.S. Central America* and *S.S. Republic*.)
Ex: The S.S. Brother Jonathan Treasure Coins (Bowers and Merena, 5/99), lot 358, which realized $6,900. (#8942)
From The Vanek Collection.

2871 **1865 MS63 ★ NGC.** Ex: *S.S. Republic*. The *S.S. Republic* sank on October 18, 1865, and was the most recent major shipwreck recovery of U.S. gold coins. Previous hoards emerged from the *S.S. Yankee Blade* (1854), *S.S. Brother Jonathan* (1865) and the *S.S. Central America* (1857). The 1865 twenty was the primary haul from the *S.S. Republic*, but the extraordinary demand for attractive Type One double eagles has quickly removed most examples from the marketplace. The present piece has an immaculate reverse, the quality of which must be seen to be believed. The obverse does have a few minor marks, mostly on the portrait and the lower left field. A well struck piece with booming luster. This lot is accompanied by a presentation box, booklet, DVD, and certificate of authenticity from Odyssey Marine Exploration, Inc. (#8943)

2872 **1865-S AU55 NGC.** This Choice AU55 twenty dollar displays great luster for a coin that has seen some circulation. Brass-gold surfaces exhibit well defined motifs, and just a few minute contact marks. (#8944)

2847 **1859-S AU53 NGC.** Luster dominates the borders and devices of this moderately abraded and lightly circulated double eagle. The 1859-S is collectible in AU, but Mint State pieces are rare. (#8928)

2848 **1859-S AU55 NGC.** The yellow-orange surfaces of this briefly circulated San Francisco example display short copper streaks at the margins. Well struck with scattered abrasions evident in the still-lustrous fields. (#8928)

2849 **1859-S AU55 PCGS.** This Choice AU double eagle has rich honey-gold color with smooth, satiny surfaces and nearly full luster. The typical 1859-S is heavily abraded and lower quality than this piece. (#8928)

2850 **1860 AU50 PCGS.** This original canary-gold Liberty twenty has the luster extent of a higher grade, and the sharpness is also pleasing. A thin vertical mark is noted on the right reverse field. Encapsulated in a green label holder. (#8929)

2851 **1860—Cleaned—ANACS. MS60 Details.** Bright peach-gold surfaces reveal fine hairlines under high magnification, and exhibit sharply struck motifs. Detracting contact marks are absent. Certified populations indicate most survivors are in XF and AU grade; Uncirculated pieces appear to be somewhat elusive. Do not be intimidated by the ANACS disclaimer, as the cleaning is relatively light. (#8929)

Lustrous AU58 1860-S Twenty

2852 **1860-S AU58 NGC.** 1860 S-mint double eagles were struck for the sole purpose of serving the growing needs of commerce through widespread circulation. And circulate they did! Most examples known today are in the VF to XF grade range. With fewer than 30 Uncirculated examples believed extant, including a handful salvaged from at least two shipwrecks, a near-Mint 1860-S twenty is a completely acceptable conciliation for most collectors. This is a sharply defined example that retains almost complete mint luster. Lightly abraded with the most obvious abrasion being a luster scrape in the right obverse field. (#8931)

1860-S Double Eagle, MS60 Details

2853 **1860-S—Scratched, Cleaned—ANACS. MS60 Details** The 1860-S double eagle saw heavy circulation. Jeff Garrett and Ron Guth write that: "The remaining examples are mostly Very Fine or Extremely Fine." This MS60 Details specimen reveals fine obverse hairlines on apricot-gold surfaces, and sharply defined design elements. A short, shallow scratch runs through star 1 into the field. (#8931)

2854 **1861 AU58 PCGS.** A high-mintage, common issue in most grades. Yellow-gold surfaces are laced with wisps of light tan, and retain ample luster. The design elements are well defined throughout. A few inoffensive marks are visible on each side. (#8932)

Scarce 1861 Select Twenty Dollar

2855 **1861 MS63 PCGS.** The 1861 mintage of 2,976,453 pieces is one of the highest of the Liberty Head double eagle series, making it a common issue in most grades. Mint State pieces are generally available through the MS62 level. In this regard, Jeff Garrett and Ron Guth, in their *Encyclopedia of U.S. Gold Coins*, indicate that "Nearly 500 examples of the date were found on the S.S. *Republic*. Most were in grades from AU58 to MS62." MS63 coins, such as the offering in this lot, are scarce, with fewer than 60 specimens having been certified by PCGS and NGC. Higher-grade examples are rare.

Intense luster radiates from this Select example, and a solid strike leaves sharp definition over most of the design elements. Peach-gold surfaces are relatively well preserved, revealing just a few minute contact marks that define the grade. Some light die striations are noted in the fields. Population: 30 in 63, 16 finer (4/07). (#8932)

Phenomenally Lustrous MS64 1861 Twenty

2856 1861 MS64 NGC. The absolutely gorgeous, coruscating radiant luster is more characteristic of an S-mint Morgan dollar than what one usually sees on Type One Libertys. Moreover, while the generous mintage of nearly 3 million pieces makes this the most available Type One Liberty and the one that collectors turn to for type purposes, in Choice condition the issue is actually quite rare (Garrett and Guth, 2006). As testament to that assertion, NGC and PCGS as of this writing (6/07) have certified only 33 pieces in MS64, with 15 finer—and that small population includes the nearly 500 examples found aboard the *S.S. Republic!*

Aside from the phenomenal luster, the present example offers attractive orange-gold coloration and a bold strike. Mentionable abrasions are nil. Competition should be deservedly fierce for this piece. Census: 22 in 64, 10 finer (6/07). (#8932)

Appealing AU53 1861-S Double Eagle

2857 1861-S AU53 PCGS. The 1861-S double eagle is a doubly popular gold issue, firstly for its association with the fabulous 1861-S Paquet Reverse pieces, and secondly for its Civil War connection. Most pieces found grade AU or less, and Mint State pieces are quite rare. As of (6/07), NGC and PCGS combined have certified only about three dozen Uncirculated coins in all grades, despite the recovery of a smattering of Mint State examples aboard the *S.S. Republic* and *S.S. Brother Jonathan*.

This piece offers a pleasing amount of original mint luster over the deeply mellow apricot-gold surfaces. While there are a few moderate abrasions consistent with the grade, only a couple of deeper nicks before Liberty's face require singular mention, while failing to detract from the significant eye appeal. (#8935)

Pleasing 1861-S Twenty Dollar, AU55

2858 1861-S AU55 PCGS. The 1861-S twenty, with a mintage of 768,000 pieces, is found in relatively abundant quantities, especially in Extremely Fine and the lower levels of About Uncirculated. Choice AU specimens, such as the offering in the present lot, are more difficult to locate, and Mint State pieces are rare. This example displays bright yellow-gold surfaces that retain a good amount of luster, and most of the design features exhibit sharp definition. A few minute marks consistent with the grade are scattered over each side. (#8935)

2859 1862-S AU50 PCGS. This double eagle from the time of the Civil War displays quite a bit of luster, for a lightly circulated piece, along with even khaki-gold coloration. It is moderately marked and typically worn across the design's highest points, for the grade. A scarce S-mint twenty that is seldom seen at any grade level, despite additions to the extant population from several shipwrecks. (#8938)

Pleasing 1865-S *Brother Jonathan* Double Eagle, MS64

2873 1865-S MS64 NGC. Ex: *Brother Jonathan.* Jeff Garrett and Ron Guth (2006) note that more than 500 1865-S double eagles were found on the wreck of the *S.S. Brother Jonathan*, ranging in grade from About Uncirculated to Mint State 66. This near-Gem representative exhibits pleasing luster emanating from brass-gold surfaces. Most of the design elements benefited from a relatively sharp strike, though typical softness is visible in some of the star centers. A few minor obverse marks define the grade. NGC *Brother Jonathan* Census: 57 in 64, 54 finer (5/07). (#8944)

Reddish-Tinged, Lustrous MS64 1865-S Twenty
Ex: *Brother Jonathan*

2874 1865-S MS64 PCGS. Ex: *Brother Jonathan.* The double eagle in this lot was just months old when the *S.S. Brother Jonathan*, a 220-foot side wheeler steamship, sank off of the California coast in July of 1865. Seemingly lost forever were 204 souls and a treasure that some believe was actually a Civil War Army payroll. Through the efforts of modern day treasure hunters, this and many other gold coins were liberated from their watery grave 131 years later, thus providing collectors with a previously rare opportunity of owning a high grade example of this Civil War era S-mint twenty. The surfaces display the frosted texture one would expect from a San Francisco product, and both sides are enveloped in deep reddish-gold color. Sharply struck throughout. PCGS has graded only 22 coins finer (6/07). (#8944)

2875 1866 AU50 PCGS. IN GOD WE TRUST was added to the reverse die in 1866, and on some pieces, the legend is strongly die doubled (FS-801). The present piece represents the non-doubled variety, and it may actually be scarcer than FS-801. Luster glimmers from protected areas, and there are no distracting marks. (#8949)

Surprisingly Lustrous MS60 1866 With Motto Twenty

2876 1866 MS60 PCGS. Rarely available in mint condition and always of interest as the first year of the With Motto type. This MS60 has strong mint luster that is interrupted by numerous small to medium sized abrasions that are peppered over each side. Well, but not fully struck. Important and desirable to those who need an Uncirculated Type Two twenty. (#8949)

2877 1866-S Motto XF45 PCGS. The relatively high mintage 1866-S With Motto twenty dollar apparently saw extensive circulation, as most examples come well worn. The Choice XF specimen shown here displays apricot-gold patina imbued with traces of light green. Luster clings to the design elements, which are relatively well defined. A few minute contact marks are noted on each side. (#8950)

2878 1866-S Motto AU53 PCGS. At the suggestion of Reverend M.R. Watkinson, Congress passed the Act of March 3, 1865, mandating that all silver and gold coins carry the motto IN GOD WE TRUST. To fulfill this requirement for the double eagle, James Barton Longacre enlarged the oval of stars above the eagle's head and inserted the motto within its outline. Like many early branch mint double eagles, this piece displays numerous moderate to heavy bagmarks. It also shows much luster and minimal highpoint wear. Population: 26 in 53, 66 finer (4/07). (#8950)

Choice AU 1867 Double Eagle, Type Two

2879 1867 AU55 ICG. A lovely example of a coin that is elusive in Mint State grades, this Choice AU specimen displays mellow straw-gold surfaces that are only moderately abraded, more so on the obverse. As with other dates of this era, the 1867 twenties were used in international trade. Shipping overseas in bags resulted in a degradation of surface quality and most examples of this date are abraded. It is likely that this coin was an early strike using freshly prepared dies, as evidenced by the semiprooflike surfaces, especially on the reverse. When examined in the light at just the right angle, the fields are beautifully reflective. (#8951)

Elusive MS61 1867 Twenty

2880 1867 MS61 NGC. Since gold coins failed to circulate except on the West Coast in 1867, the mintage of 251,065 double eagles at Philadelphia was likely intended for export to Europe. Most of those pieces must have been eventually melted, given the scarcity of the 1867 in any grade. Between NGC and PCGS, only three pieces exceed the MS62 level, and those are certified MS63. This well struck and somewhat scuffy example has good luster and a single mentionable mark on the obverse rim at 7 o'clock. (#8951)

2881 1867-S AU53 NGC. Many 1867-S twenties saw heavy circulation or the melting pot (Jeff Garrett and Ron Guth, 2006). This AU53 example exhibits traces of luster in the recesses of the yellow-gold surfaces. The motifs show good detail, and the usual amount of light abrasions occur over each side. (#8952)

Attractive AU55 1867-S Twenty Dollar

2882 1867-S AU55 NGC. The 1867-S double eagle in this lot is a picture-perfect AU55. Attractive yellow-gold surfaces are highlighted by subtle tinges of red-gold color in the protected areas of the recessed design elements. The lustrous surfaces and minimal surface distractions combine with honest wear to define the grade of Choice AU. (#8952)

2883 1868-S AU50 PCGS. This is a scarce issue in AU, the condition of the coin in this lot. Orange-gold surfaces reveal luster in the protected areas, along with well detailed design elements. We note a scattering of light marks on the obverse. (#8954)

2884 1868-S—Cleaned—ANACS. AU53 Details. Jeff Garrett and Ron Guth (2006) write that "although the 1868-S double eagle is readily found in grades of Very Fine or Extremely Fine, the date becomes scarce in About Uncirculated condition." This AU53 Details specimen displays luster in the recesses of the yellow-gold surfaces, and nice definition in most of the design elements. Some fine hairlines show up under magnification when the coin is rotated beneath a light source, more so on the obverse. This is really a decent coin, as the cleaning is light. (#8954)

2885 1868-S—Scratched—ANACS. AU55 Details. A well struck yellow-orange example that exhibits considerable original luster, particularly on the reverse. A series of scratches above and behind Liberty's head account for the net grade, and a rim bruise appears at the top of the obverse. Still, a desirable example of this post-war San Francisco issue. (#8954)

2886 1869 AU53 NGC. Well struck with minimal highpoint wear but a high number of small to moderate abrasions over each side. A substantial degree of luster remains evident on the straw-gold surfaces. (#8955)

2887 1869-S AU50 NGC. This is a plentiful date in VF and XF grades, but scarce in higher grades. The mintage was quite substantial, but like other issues of the San Francisco Mint, nearly all of them entered circulation. This example is clearly abraded like most, but it has excellent luster and good eye appeal. (#8956)

1870 Double Eagle, Lustrous AU55

2888 1870 AU55 NGC. A low mintage of 155,150 coins combined with a low rate of survival accounts for the scarcity of the 1870 Philadelphia double eagle issue. The current example displays attractive yellow-gold color with lustrous surfaces that are slightly abraded, which is typical for this issue. A minor rim nick at 11 o'clock on the obverse is noted for the sake of accuracy, although it does not distract from the eye appeal of this scarce coin. (#8957)

2889 1870-S AU50 NGC. Jeff Garrett and Ron Guth (2006) note that while "the 1870-S was minted in large numbers, most were exported or destroyed. The coin that did survive is mostly Very Fine or Extremely Fine." Honey-gold patination adorns this AU specimen that sees traces of luster in the recesses. Well struck and lightly abraded. (#8959)

2890 1870-S AU55 NGC. Some of the hair details and the stars on the lower left of the obverse reveal some weakness, but the remaining elements are nicely struck. A copper-gold patina bathes both sides of this lightly abraded piece. Overall, this is a nice AU coin.
Ex: Paramount Sale (9/71), lot 1575, where it brought $81. (#8959)

Low Mintage 1871 Twenty, AU55

2891 1871 AU55 PCGS. The 1871 double eagle is clearly an underrated coin. Out of a relatively small mintage of 80,120 coins, the lowest of all Type Two Philadelphia issues, few coins survive in AU condition or better. Those examples that are extant are often found with abraded surfaces or other impairments. The numbers attest to this fact: As of (6/07), PCGS has certified 24 pieces in AU55, with only 15 finer. However, one must assume that the population figures are artificially high due to resubmissions. The current example is only slightly abraded and displays honey-gold color over lustrous surfaces. A small mint-made rim defect at 3 o'clock on the reverse is noted. (#8960)

Challenging Mint State 1871 Liberty Twenty

2892 **1871 MS60 NGC.** The 1871 is rare in Mint State for several reasons. It has a mintage of only 80,120 pieces. It was struck after the famous 1857 to 1865 gold-laden shipwrecks. It was struck prior to the large-scale export of U.S. gold to foreign bank holdings. Few collectors could afford to set aside twenty dollar pieces in 1871, and those who had the ability to do so selected proofs instead of business strikes. This sun-gold example is typically abraded on the left obverse, and displays light hairlines on the reverse field. Census: 2 in 60, 9 finer (5/07). (#8960)

2893 **1871-S AU50 PCGS.** Honey-gold patination covers both sides of this AU specimen, and sharp definition is apparent on the design elements. A few light contact marks are evenly distributed over both sides. (#8962)

2894 **1871-S AU55 NGC.** An orange-gold cast enriches both sides of this well struck '71-S, and each displays a fair amount of luster. We note a number of circulation marks on the obverse. Jeff Garrett and Ron Guth (2006) mention of this issue that: "Quantities were shipped overseas, and significant numbers are known today." (#8962)

2895 **1872 AU58 NGC.** Dynamically prooflike fields are the hallmark of this pleasing near-Mint double eagle. Well struck and moderately abraded, with mere traces of highpoint friction on each side. A lower mintage issue that becomes scarce in Mint State. (#8963)

Choice XF 1872-CC Twenty Dollar

2896 **1872-CC XF45 NGC.** All pre-1874 Carson City twenties are scarce, particularly those that have escaped cleaning or tooling. This almond-gold representative has its share of luminous luster, especially on the reverse. A few small marks are noted above the arrowheads, but the overall appearance is clean. (#8964)

Elusive 1872-CC Twenty Dollar, AU53

2897 **1872-CC AU53 PCGS.** Most 1872-CC double eagles seen at auction over the last 15 or so years are in grades Very Fine or Extremely Fine. High grade examples are very rare (Jeff Garrett and Ron Guth, 2006). This AU53 example displays yellow-gold surfaces with traces of luster in the protected areas. Sharp definition is visible on the design elements, and the minuscule marks scattered are not worthy of individual mention. (#8964)

2898 **1872-S AU58 PCGS.** This is a very attractive high-end AU that retains considerable luster on peach-gold surfaces. The design features are well defined throughout. Lightly marked, with none worthy of individual mention. (#8965)

2899 **1873 Open 3 MS60 NGC.** This lustrous Type Two Liberty twenty has a good strike, and the reverse is only moderately abraded. The obverse has a profusion of wispy marks, customary for the designated grade. (#8967)

2900 **1873 Open 3 MS61 NGC.** The 1873 Open 3 is often called upon to represent the Type Two design, which bears the Motto IN GOD WE TRUST but abbreviates DOLLARS with D. Lustrous and crisply struck with distributed obverse marks. (#8967)

2901 **1873 Open 3 MS61 PCGS.** Apricot-gold surfaces show soft luster, and a number of light contact marks and scuffs. Relatively sharp definition is noted on the design features. (#8967)

2902 **1873 Open 3 MS61 PCGS.** Apricot-gold surfaces exhibit glowing luster and well defined motifs. The reverse is relatively well preserved, while the obverse reveals a scattering of minute contact marks. The Open 3 is scarcer than the Close 3 variety. (#8967)

2903 **1873 Open 3 MS62 PCGS.** FS-101. LIBERTY and the coronet beads are lightly die doubled, with the widest spread on the leg of the R. This assertively struck caramel-gold Type Two coin has sweeping luster and the expected number of minor obverse grazes. (#8967)

2904 **1873 Open 3 MS62 PCGS.** A well struck and unworn orange-gold representative of this classic issue. The light to moderate abrasions present on the obverse are largely absent on the reverse. Although always available for a price, the 1873 Open 3 is a popular type coin, since the 11-year reign of the Type Two design was after the shipwreck hoards and before the large-scale export of gold. (#8967)

2905 **1873-S Closed 3 AU58 PCGS.** Bright peach-gold surfaces yield a considerable amount of luster, and exhibit well impressed design elements. Minute marks scattered over obverse and reverse are consistent with the grade level. (#8969)

2906 **1873-S Closed 3 MS60 ANACS.** A well struck butter-yellow example of this Type Two double eagle that exhibits strong luster. Scattered abrasions affect both sides, though the overall visual appeal suggests a finer grade than MS60.
From The Vanek Collection. (#8969)

Difficult 1873-S Open 3 Twenty AU58

2907 **1873-S Open 3 AU58 PCGS.** Because of the distance between the two coasts, the new Open 3 double eagle dies from Philadelphia took their time reaching the San Francisco Mint. By the time of arrival, most 1873-S twenties needed for the year had already been coined. Some Open 3 pieces were struck, but the issue is undeniably scarce. This is a moderately abraded and partly lustrous near-Mint example. (#8979)

Near-Mint 1873-S Open 3 Twenty

2908 **1873-S Open 3 AU58 NGC.** Well-defined for the issue with minor friction on the highest parts of the design. The lightly abraded yellow-gold fields retain nearly all of their original luster. The Open 3 logotype replaced the Closed 3 logotype, which came under criticism as looking like an 8. (#8979)

2909 **1874-CC VF35 NGC.** Noticeable remaining luster persists on this slightly glossy honey-gold Carson City twenty. Liberty's hair exhibits wear, but the eagle's wings exhibit most of their initial plumage. (#8971)

AU Type Two 1874-CC Twenty

2910 **1874-CC AU50 PCGS.** Luster connects the reverse peripheral legends, and forms a halo around each obverse star. Moderate marks here and there are unimportant for the grade. Liberty's hair shows light wear, and the shield lines are incompletely brought up, but the eagle's wings are bold. (#8971)

Charming and Lustrous AU50 1874-CC Double Eagle

2911 **1874-CC AU50 PCGS.** In 1874 the Carson City Mint revved up production to more than 100,000 pieces, specifically 115,085 coins, the first time a yearly emission was in the six-figure range. As the more-plentiful mintage was not all needed locally, it achieved wider distribution and a higher survival rate in high grades than earlier CC double eagles. This piece boasts splendid luster clinging to the charming yellow-gold surfaces, which show considerable prooflikeness under a light veil of field chatter characteristic of a short stay in circulation. Certified in a green-label holder. (#8971)

Lustrous and Attractive 1874-CC Twenty, AU53

2912 **1874-CC AU53 ANACS.** A lustrous and clean example of this generally available CC-mint double eagle, the first of the denomination from that mint that can be readily encountered. Both sides display attractive yellow-gold, pristine surfaces with far fewer bagmarks than might be expected. The surfaces are fairly prooflike, and a couple of reeding marks on Liberty's cheek are the only singular distractions. A nice piece for the grade. (#8971)

Lightly Circulated 1874-CC Twenty, AU55

2913 **1874-CC AU55 PCGS.** Jeff Garrett and Ron Guth (2006) say of the 1874-CC twenty that "over the last two decades, large groups have surfaced in European and South American holdings. However, nearly all of those examples have been heavily circulated." This lightly circulated example retains ample luster in the recessed areas of the peach-gold surfaces. Generally well defined, save for the usual softness in Liberty's hair. A few minute marks are noted. (#8971)

2914 **1874-CC—Cleaned—ANACS. AU55 Details.** Peach-gold surfaces exhibit a bright obverse that reveals light hairlines, and both sides display some luster, much more so on the reverse. The design elements are better struck than is typical for the issue, though the surfaces fit the profile of the typical '74-CC example, where the obverse is heavily marked, while the reverse is cleaner (Douglas Winter, 2001). AU examples are quite rare. (#8971)

2915 **1874-S AU58 NGC.** Although both sides of this near-Mint example are lightly abraded, the surfaces exhibit frosty yellow luster with faint traces of pink toning. (#8972)

Lustrous MS62 1875 Twenty Dollar

2916 **1875 MS62 PCGS.** The 1875 is one of the more available P-mint Type Two twenties. Several hundred Mint State coins may exist today, but only a couple of dozen are known finer than this MS62. The surfaces show bright, flashy mint luster, and there are the expected numerous, small abrasions on the obverse that account for the grade. Sharply defined throughout. (#8973)

2917 **1875-CC XF40 NGC.** Well detailed with glimpses of mint luster near the devices, and evenly worn highpoints on each side. Small abrasions pepper the light green-gold and coral surfaces. (#8974)

2918 **1875-CC—Cleaned—ANACS. AU55 Details.** Many 1875-CC twenty dollar pieces exhibit strike weakness, particularly on Liberty's hair, the stars, and the shield (Douglas Winter, 2001). The specimen in this lot exhibits better-than average definition in these areas, except for softness in portions of Liberty's hair. Peach-gold surfaces display luster in the recessed areas, and reveal some fine hairlines. Small contact marks are scattered about, especially on the obverse. (#8974)

2919 **1875-CC AU55 PCGS.** An original Carson City twenty with plentiful luminous luster. The fields are only moderately abraded, although the cheek has a few conspicuous marks. (#8974)

Pleasing Near-Mint 1875-CC Double Eagle

2920 **1875-CC AU58 NGC.** One of the more available Carson City issues of the Liberty Head double eagle series. This example is boldly struck and seems fully lustrous. It is mildly abraded on both sides and shows a trace amount of highpoint friction on the central devices. (#8974)

Ebullient 1875-CC Twenty Dollar MS61

2921 **1875-CC MS61 PCGS.** The reverse of this lustrous and attentively struck CC-mint Type Two twenty is remarkably free from scuffs. The left obverse is somewhat abraded, but the orange-gold toning leads to pleasing eye appeal. The portrait highpoints display subtle ice-blue patina. Encapsulated in a green label holder. (#8974)

2922 **1875-S AU58 NGC.** Boldly struck, except for the first two obverse stars, with brassy coloration and numerous small marks on each side. A lustrous near-Mint example from the final year of the "TWENTY D" type of double eagle. (#8975)

2923 **1875-S MS60 ANACS.** Peach-gold surfaces display pleasing luster for the grade, as well as nicely defined motifs. An evenly distributed number of light abrasions account for the grade. (#8975)

Scarce 1875-S Type Two Twenty MS62

2924 **1875-S MS62 NGC.** Booming luster illuminates this better date yellow-gold Liberty twenty. The left obverse shows the faint scuffs expected of the grade, while the reverse and the right obverse are surprisingly smooth for the MS62 level. Type Two double eagles are scarce in Mint State, and when encountered, are usually the 1873 Open 3 or 1876-S issues. (#8975)

1875-S Twenty Dollar MS62

2925 **1875-S MS62 PCGS.** This evenly struck and fully lustrous twenty is generally clean for the grade, although the cheek is abraded. Hard to find any better, undoubtedly due to indifferent bag storage and transport long ago. A popular Type Two issue. Population: 83 in 62, 16 finer (6/07). (#8975)

2926 **1876 MS61 NGC.** Heavy Motto. A lustrous pumpkin-gold example with fewer noticeable marks than expected of the MS61 grade. The final year of the Type Two design, which is scarce in Mint State relative to Type Three. (#8976)

2927 **1876 MS61 PCGS.** Light Motto. This ephemeral reverse subtype is only found on certain 1876 double eagles, although collectors prize the date more as an example of the Type Two design. A lustrous piece that has moderate obverse marks and a relatively clean reverse. (#8976)

2928 **1876-CC—Scratched, Cleaned—ANACS. AU50 Details.** Semi-bright yellow-gold surfaces are imbued with whispers of mint-green, and traces of luster reside in the protected areas. Magnification is necessary to view some fine hairlines; a short scratch occurs on Liberty's jaw, and a fainter one on the neck. While the '76-CC has the highest mintage figure for any Carson City double eagle (138,441 pieces), it is not the most common twenty from this mint (Douglas Winter, 2001). (#8977)

Pleasing 1876-CC Double Eagle, AU53

2929 **1876-CC AU53 PCGS.** A small patch of hairlines in the left obverse field is perhaps the grade-limiting factor of this 1876-CC double eagle, which boasts a pleasing natural patina, attesting to its originality. When viewed at an angle under a light source, delicate prooflike surfaces emerge and the visual effect is pleasing. Because most of this issue was exported overseas in bags, the typical survivor will display abraded surfaces. The current example, possessing only slightly abraded surfaces, is above average in terms of eye appeal, especially considering the assigned grade. (#8977)

2930 **1876-CC AU55 NGC.** The final Type Two double eagle issue minted at Carson City also has the most generous mintage for the production run. This modestly worn example displays slightly soft detail on the devices, though the yellow-orange fields retain plenty of reflective luster. Scattered light to moderate abrasions affect the obverse, but the reverse is comparatively clean. (#8977)

Near-Mint State 1876-CC Twenty

2931 **1876-CC AU58 NGC.** The orange-gold surfaces of this near-Mint State piece remain semiprooflike, and moderate abrasions are seen on both sides, with only a few ticks on Liberty's cheek requiring singular mention. A couple of gray-gold haze spots are seen on the highpoints. The 1876-CC double eagle offers the double allure of a Centennial-year and CC-mint issue. (#8977)

1876-CC Type Two Twenty, AU58

2932 **1876-CC AU58 ICG.** The 1876-CC saw a record mintage for a CC-mint Type Two (or other type) double eagle, those with TWENTY D. in the denomination, as a result of peak outflows of gold for coinage in Nevada during the salad days of the Comstock Lode. A total of 138,441 double eagles were produced during this U.S. Centennial year, making the issue a doubly perennial favorite. What a pity the Mint chose not to issue a commemorative gold double eagle for the Bicentennial in 1976! This example offers much prooflikeness remaining over surfaces that show a few abrasions consistent with light circulation. (#8977)

2933 **1876-S AU58 NGC.** An outstanding pink-gold specimen, this near-Mint double eagle is sharply struck and attractive, despite a few minor surface marks. (#8978)

2934 **1876-S AU58 NGC.** The intense mint luster displayed on each side of this golden-rose example is suggestive of a Mint State coin. Highpoint wear is minimal, as numerous small to moderate marks appear on both sides of the coin. The final year of issue for the Liberty type with the denomination displayed as "TWENTY D." (#8978)

2935 **1876-S MS61 NGC.** This evenly struck piece has unencumbered luster and a smattering of pinpoint carbon on the upper reverse. All 1876-S twenties are from the Heavy Motto hub, unlike their Philadelphia counterparts. (#8978)

2936 **1876-S MS61 PCGS.** This lustrous example has blended pale lime and butter-gold toning. A well struck and moderately abraded representative of this popular Centennial-year issue. (#8978)

2937 **1876-S MS61 NGC.** An interesting piece from the final year of the Type Two double eagles, well struck with lovely luster and softly shimmering yellow-orange surfaces. Minimally marked for the grade with a small copper spot near Liberty's throat. (#8978)

2938 **1876-S MS61 PCGS.** This lustrous butter-gold type coin appears at first glance to merit a higher grade, particularly since the reverse is only lightly abraded. Further evaluation locates a shallow, broad graze on the jaw. (#8978)

2939 **1876-S MS61 PCGS.** San Francisco struck nearly 1.6 million double eagles in this centennial year, including this solidly struck, unworn survivor. The strongly lustrous yellow-orange surfaces display attractive luster. Moderately abraded overall with a vertical abrasion at the center of Liberty's neck. (#8978)

Type Two 1876-S Twenty MS62

2940 1876-S MS62 NGC. San Francisco's place as the country's prime Mint for gold production continued in 1876, as its double eagle mintage was more than twice that of Philadelphia and Carson City combined. This shining example, peach-gold with splashes of yellow in the fields, has strong peripheral detail, though the lightly abraded devices show slight weakness. (#8978)

MS62 Type Two 1876-S Twenty

2941 1876-S MS62 NGC. This crisply struck and thoroughly lustrous Centennial-year twenty has scattered minor field marks, as expected of the grade, but the portrait is relatively clean. A popular issue since it represents the scarcer Type Two design, which has IN GOD WE TRUST but abbreviates the denomination as TWENTY D. (#8978)

2942 1877 MS61 ICG. The surfaces are intermingled with deep honey-gold and lighter yellow-gold color. Both sides are heavily abraded, but there is no sign of wear. First year of issue for the Type Three design modification. (#8982)

AU53 1877-CC Double Eagle

2943 1877-CC AU53 NGC. Doug Winter, in his *Gold Coins of the Old West*, ranks the 1877-CC as the ninth rarest of the 19 Carson City double eagle issues. Most survivors are found in VF and XF condition, with true AU examples scarce. Even with the repatriation of several overseas hoards in recent decades, the 1877-CC twenty is rarely seen in Mint State. For this reason, most collectors must settle for attractive AU examples of this date. The current coin provides that opportunity. Displaying delicate yellow-gold coloration and sufficiently lustrous surfaces, this example is visually pleasing. The abraded surfaces found on this example are typical for the issue. NGC has graded 78 examples in AU53 (6/07). (#8983)

Pleasingly Original 1877-CC Twenty, AU53

2944 1877-CC AU53 PCGS. This 1877-CC double eagle stands out among similarly graded examples in that the surfaces display fewer distracting abrasions than usual. As with other dates in this series, large quantities of twenties were exported overseas to facilitate international trade. The methods used to transport these large gold pieces centered more on convenience than preservation of the coins. Soft gold, heavy coins, haphazard handling, and long voyages translate into coins with heavily abraded surfaces. For collectors today, this means that finding an 1877-CC twenty with clean fields is like finding the proverbial needle in a haystack. The present example is one such piece. The assigned grade is accurate, if not a bit conservative, but the aesthetic qualities of this refreshingly original Carson City twenty is worth a premium to experienced collectors. (#8983)

2945 1877-S MS61 NGC. A splendid Mint State representative, and not often seen so fine. This piece has lovely orange and yellow-gold luster. (#8984)

2946 1878 MS61 NGC. A semi-prooflike Liberty twenty with lustrous fields and devices. The strike is sharp, and the scattered small marks on both sides are appropriate for the grade. (#8985)

Choice XF 1878-CC Twenty
Original Surfaces

2947 1878-CC XF45 PCGS. Ex: Rainy Day Collection. Garrett and Guth comment that the 1878-CC double eagle is among the rarer Nevada issues and they point out that production of Carson City twenties dropped off sharply this year. But why? There are three principal reasons. First, 1878 was the year of the Bland-Allison Act, and it meant that the mints turned much of their attention to churning out silver dollars, as a virtual flood of silver ore came from the Comstock Lode. Second, the production of gold in the American West was dwindling as the yellow ore became more difficult to mine profitably. Third, the "bimetallism battle" caused by Bland-Allison forced gold coins out of circulation in most parts of the country: the profit motive made the hoarding of gold tempting for anyone who understood the arbitrage opportunities. Gold circulated mainly in the West, where hard money had always been more appealing than paper. Much of the allure of a slightly circulated coin such as this is to imagine what it witnessed. Was it spent for pony supplies at Fort Carson? Did it change hands on the poker tables of Dodge City? If only it could tell us!

The surfaces show even wear over each side. Minimally abraded, the coin has lovely rose tinted gold color with an accent of lilac over the highpoints. (#8986)

Captivating Near-Mint 1878-CC Double Eagle

Doubled Die Reverse 1878-S Twenty, MS62

2950 **1878-S MS62 ANACS.** Doubled Die Reverse, as noted on the ANACS encapsulation. The doubling is most prominent at IN GOD WE TR and E PLURIBUS UNUM, although traces of doubling can also be seen on the scrollwork surrounding the eagle and the arrow feathers. The *Cherrypickers' Guide* fourth edition does not list this piece, but it deserves a place therein, as the doubling is quite prominent. This piece displays nice yellow-gold surfaces with good luster and a few light abrasions consistent with the grade assigned. (#8987)

2948 **1878-CC AU58 PCGS.** Variety 1-A. This variety is distinguished by the long, nearly vertical die scratch that runs along the length of Liberty's neck and is one of two varieties for this lower-mintage issue, one that had a significantly small production run than that of the previous year, with a total mintage of just 13,180 pieces. Winter (2001) ranks it "among the scarcest double eagles" from Carson City.

This attractive example, largely yellow-gold with a touch of deeper color at the highpoints, which exhibit minor, yet grade-defining friction. The fields display frosty luster with a hint of granularity, and the devices exhibit the strong strike found on most representatives. A noteworthy piece that lands just outside Condition Census territory. Population: 8 in 58, 7 finer (5/07). (#8986)

2949 **1878-S AU58 PCGS.** This high-end AU S-mint representative retains considerable luster, and exhibits sharply defined motifs. Peach-gold surfaces display the normal amount of minute contact marks. (#8987)

San Francisco Branch Mint

Finest Known 1879-S Twenty Dollar, MS64

2951 **1879-S MS64 PCGS.** While the 1879-S as a date is not generally thought of as rare, like a long list of Liberty Head double eagles in high grade, it is conditionally quite elusive. Unlike most Liberty Head double eagles, however, it is rare in any Mint State grade. The issue in the past has been underrated, due to its large emission exceeding 1.2 million pieces, but *in grades above MS62 the issue is surpassingly rare. The present example is the single highest graded of the issue at either NGC or PCGS, and it is the finest by two grade points that we have ever had the privilege of offering.*

The current NGC and PCGS population data eloquently tell the story: While NGC has certified 33 pieces in MS62, there is not a single piece graded MS63, much less one in MS64. (Even the 1897-S's sibling, the famously rare 1879-O double eagle with a mintage of 2,325 pieces, shows one example graded MS63 at NGC.) PCGS has certified 44 examples of the 1879-S in MS62, yet there are only three specimens certified MS63 (or—as always—one piece submitted three times). Finally, in MS64, the present example is the only one so certified.

Once considered a common Type Three double eagle, the 1879-S in recent years has seen a burgeoning awareness of its true rarity in the numismatic marketplace. Heritage has offered a total of only 11 MS62 examples of the 1879-S in the past dozen or so years. While in the mid-1990s the selling price was only slightly higher than generic pieces, 10 years later the average price for an MS62 had increased fifteenfold. In 2004's *Type Three Double Eagles 1877-1907*, the authors made the following observations: "The 1879-S Double Eagle can be located in any circulated grade without much difficulty although nice About Uncirculated coins are not nearly as common as their current price level would indicate. This is a scarce date in Uncirculated with a great majority of the known specimens grading Mint State-60. It becomes rare in Mint State-61 and any 1879-S Double Eagle grading Mint State-62 or better is very rare."

Bowers' *Guide Book of Double Eagles* probably understates the elusiveness of the issue in MS62 by saying, "The 1879-S is another easy winner in the double eagle sweepstakes—with examples being readily available in just about any grade desired from VF to MS-62. Higher level coins are in another category, however, and are very elusive." Of course, on the latter point he is absolutely correct.

The latest (and most encyclopedic) gold coin reference available, Jeff Garrett and Ron Guth's *Encyclopedia of U.S. Gold Coins 1795-1933*, offers the following comments: "Although the mintage for the 1879 New Orleans issue was tiny, the San Francisco Mint produced an abundant number of coins. Many were shipped overseas for international trade. Large numbers have returned in recent decades. Most are just Extremely Fine or About Uncirculated, and the issue is actually scarce in Mint State. In choice condition the 1879-S double eagle is very rare. Some high-grade examples seen are partially prooflike. Amazingly, two NGC MS-62 examples sold for more than $29,000 each in early 2005."

The present example boasts a bold strike, with full radial details seen on each peripheral star, and none of the mentionable weakness so often seen on the highpoints of Liberty's hair. The surfaces offer intense luster over medium orange-gold surfaces that show a hint of reflectivity in the fields. For such a large gold coin, the surfaces are remarkably free of all but a few smallish abrasions that are consistent with the near-Gem grade level. This beautiful and rare coin is bound to catch the attention of Registry Set collectors and connoisseurs of the finest rare-date gold. Population: 1 in 64; there are none finer (6/07). (#8991)

2952 **1880 AU58 NGC.** A bright sheen of essentially complete mint luster is seen over both sides of this near-Mint double eagle. Well struck with deep rose-gold toning and minimal highpoint wear. Both sides of the piece are moderately abraded. A quite elusive and expensive issue in Mint State. (#8992)

2953 **1880-S MS61 PCGS.** A softly lustrous, unworn example of this higher-mintage San Francisco issue, solidly struck with muted apricot-gold and wheat colors. The surfaces display myriad light marks that combine to limit the grade. (#8993)

Conditionally Scarce 1880-S Twenty MS62

2954 **1880-S MS62 PCGS.** Well struck with semi-prooflike fields that show just a slight degree of cloudiness. Both sides of the piece have a mildly scuffy appearance that limits the grade. The '80-S is a conditionally scarce issue in Mint State, despite its substantial mintage of 836,000 coins. Only twelve examples have been graded finer than MS62, by PCGS and NGC combined (6/07). (#8993)

2955 **1881-S MS61 ICG.** Apricot-gold surfaces are laced with whispers of red and mint-green, especially on the reverse, and an attentive strike brings out fairly sharp definition on the design elements. The luster flow, particularly on the obverse, is slightly interrupted by small contact marks. (#8995)

Conditionally Difficult MS62 1881-S Twenty

2956 **1881-S MS62 PCGS.** Booming luster brightens this moderately abraded and powerfully impressed S-mint twenty. The 1881-S is plentiful in certified AU58 to MS61 grades, but because of indifferent contemporary storage and shipment, only a single example (a PCGS MS64) has been certified above the MS63 level by either major service. Population: 75 in 62, 17 finer (4/07). (#8995)

AU53 1882-CC Twenty Dollar

2957 **1882-CC AU53 NGC.** Despite a relatively low mintage of 39,140 pieces, the 1882-CC is reasonably available in AU or lower grades. This lustrous representative possesses light yellow-gold surfaces that are lightly abraded, as is often the case for the issue. A thin, circular die crack is observed around most of the reverse's periphery, further adding to the charm of this piece. NGC has certified 65 coins as AU53 (6/07). (#8997)

Choice AU 1882-CC Double Eagle

2958 **1882-CC AU55 NGC.** A charming and original Choice AU CC-mint twenty. A halo of luster outlines individual stars, and a band of luster connects the reverse legends. Despite brief circulation, this coin has no detracting marks. The 1882-CC was the first Carson City issue since 1879, although eagles and half eagles were annually produced within that four-year span. (#8997)

Radiant 1882-CC Double Eagle, AU55

2959 **1882-CC AU55 NGC.** As Rusty Goe points out in his splendid *The Mint on Carson Street*, double eagle coinage in Carson City falls into three time periods, with 1882 marking the beginning of the second period and the first coinage since 1879. Only 39,140 pieces were produced of the 1882-CC, and today the average survivor grades AU53 or so. This Choice AU example offers glorious radiant luster over moderately abraded yellow-gold surfaces. Certified in an old-style NGC holder. (#8997)

2960 **1882-S MS62 PCGS.** This shining orange-gold example has pleasing detail overall, though the last star displays weakness. By marks alone, the MS62 grade seems harsh, though the upper reverse displays a rim bruise as well. Still, an attractive example of this San Francisco issue. (#8998)

Popular 1883-CC Twenty Dollar, AU58

2961 1883-CC AU58 PCGS. Ample luster remains on peach-gold surfaces that are imbued with traces of light tan, and excellent definition is noted on the design features. The few minute marks scattered about do not disturb. The 1883-CC, with a mintage approaching 60,000 pieces, is a popular Carson City Mint issue. Population: 68 in 58, 53 finer (4/07). (#8999)

2962 1883-CC AU58 NGC. The yellow-orange surfaces retain most of their original soft luster, though light friction is present on the well-defined devices. This mid-date Carson City double eagle offers an unusually clean appearance, with few abrasions overall. Fewer than 60,000 pieces were struck. (#8999)

Near-Mint 1883-CC Twenty

2963 1883-CC AU58 PCGS. Abundantly lustrous and well struck for the issue, this 1883-CC twenty has the eye appeal of a Mint State example. According to *Gold Coins of the Old West* by Doug Winter and Lawrence Cutler, this is variety 2-A (identifiable by a peculiar, small raised dot to the right of the 3 in the date). The authors state this variety is possibly less available than the other known variety of this popular date. Population: 69 in 58, 53 finer (6/07). (#8999)

2964 1883-S MS62 PCGS. The yellow-orange fields of this lightly abraded S-mint double eagle have a slightly brassy quality. This crisply struck example displays a degree of olive copper staining at Liberty's face and throat. (#9000)

2965 1883-S MS62 PCGS. In his 1988 *Encyclopedia*, Breen states "tall S [only] as on silver dollars," but the majority of '83-S twenties (including the present piece) have his "small squat S," which he believed was struck from leftover 1880-S reverse dies. This lustrous example is sharply struck and has the expected number of moderate obverse marks. (#9000)

2966 1883-S MS62 PCGS. According to Jeff Garrett and Ron Guth (2006), large quantities of this issue were shipped for international trade, and were carelessly handled and bagmarked. This lustrous MS62 specimen, while showing some minute, grade-defining marks, is better preserved than most. Peach-gold surfaces exhibit exceptionally well defined motifs. (#9000)

2967 1883-S MS62 PCGS. Well struck except for the rather mushy mintmark. Bright satiny luster shines from the obverse and reverse surfaces. The scattered marks and luster grazes displayed by this San Francisco Mint product are as expected for the grade. (#9000)

2968 1883-S MS61 Prooflike NGC. The '83-S is plentiful with cartwheel luster, but examples with prooflike fields are highly elusive. Obverse abrasions include a pinscratch near star 4. Census: 2 in 61 Prooflike, 2 finer (6/07). (#79000)

2969 1884-CC VF35 PCGS. Ex: Rainy Day Collection. Bright yellow-gold surfaces project a greenish cast, and still possess traces of luster in the protected areas. Well defined and minimally abraded for the grade. (#9001)

2970 1884-CC XF45 PCGS. This is a pleasing example for the grade that is typically worn for the grade and displays few abrasions. Light-green and pastel orange colors are blended over both sides. A slight degree of luster still clings to the devices. (#9001)

2971 1884-CC—Cleaned—ANACS. AU55 Details. This olive-gold Carson City twenty is cloudy from hairlines, but luster is unmistakable within protected areas, and there are no singularly mentionable marks. (#9001)

2972 1884-CC AU55 NGC. Lustrous and well struck, with a touch of wear on Liberty's hair bun and pleasing peach-gold coloration. A few faint pinscratches and small milling marks are noted on each side, along with some wispy hairlines in the fields. An appealing Choice AU example. (#9001)

Exceptional 1884-CC Double Eagle, AU58

2973 1884-CC AU58 NGC. According to Douglas Winter (2001), 1884-CC double eagles are nearly always abraded, and copper spots and grease stains are not uncommon. The high-end AU specimen in the present lot possesses a uniform distribution of small marks on the obverse, while the reverse is relatively clean for a large, heavy gold coin. Peach-gold surfaces show a good amount of luster, and are completely devoid of spots or stains. This piece will fit quite nicely in a high-grade type set.
From The Vanek Collection. (#9001)

Distinctive 1884-CC Double Eagle, MS61

2974 1884-CC MS61 PCGS. Variety 1-A. One of the few Carson City gold issues for which a Mint State example is not automatically a condition rarity, the 1884-CC double eagle has long been popular with collectors. This frosty, attractive example displays bold central detail. The sun-gold fields have strong peach and orange overtones, though they also display a number of scattered, grade-defining abrasions. Population: 57 in 61, 35 finer (5/07). (#9001)

Mint State 1884-CC Twenty

2975 1884-CC MS61 NGC. Booming luster sweeps this solidly struck CC-mint twenty. The reverse rim is abraded near 6:30, but the fields and devices show only faint grazes along with a few minor marks. Grover Cleveland, an opponent of the Carson City Mint, was elected to his first term in 1884. (#9001)

2976 1884-S MS62 PCGS. Green-gold fields encompass the orange devices. Lustrous and crisply struck with a couple of moderate, inconspicuous marks on the portrait. (#9002)

Low Mintage Condition Rarity
AU58 1885-CC Twenty

2977 1885-CC AU58 NGC. Due to the death of Mint Superintendent James Crawford on March 8, Carson City produced only silver dollars and double eagles, both with low mintages, before curtailing operations for the rest of 1885. The double eagle mintage was a mere 9,450 coins, and Rusty Goe, author of *The Mint on Carson Street*, estimates that only 40 to 50 pieces exist today in AU condition.

For an AU coin, the typically numerous surface blemishes are unusually superficial, especially on the obverse. There are noticeable hairlines in the obverse fields, but the luster remains quite vigorous for the assigned grade. A conditionally scarce offering from an issue that becomes downright rare and prohibitively expensive in Mint State. Census: 53 in 58, 13 finer (6/07). (#9004)

Mint State Details 1885-CC Twenty

2978 **1885-CC—Scratched—ANACS. MS60 Details.** At first glance, this lustrous and attractive Carson City twenty appears to grade MS62, or even finer, since the fields are generally clean and the cheek lacks the usual scuffs. Further evaluation locates a wispy mark behind the hairbun, and a hair-thin pinscratch above the WEN in TWENTY, but in-person examination should confirm the quality and opportunity of the present lot. Only 9,450 pieces were struck. (#9004)

Select 1885-S Liberty Twenty

2979 **1885-S MS63 PCGS.** This lustrous Liberty twenty has olive-gold borders and apricot fields and devices. The strike is bold, with only slight blending of detail within the hair. The reverse field is surprisingly clean, and the portrait lacks the conspicuous abrasions often seen on these large bag-stored gold coins. (#9005)

2980 **1888 MS62 PCGS.** Well struck, with honey-gold surfaces that exude soft luster. A few small scuffs, especially on the obverse, limit the grade. This issue becomes scarce to rare in finer grades. (#9008)

2981 **1888-S MS62 PCGS.** Well struck and highly lustrous, with lovely peach and lime-gold toning. A slightly scuffy appearance on the obverse reduces the grade. *From The Vanek Collection.* (#9009)

Delightful Choice AU 1889-CC Twenty

2982 **1889-CC AU55 NGC.** An unusually large survival rate for this low-mintage issue prevents it from being unobtainable in high grade. Only 30,945 business strikes were made after the Carson City Mint's four-year hiatus, but Rusty Goe estimated in 2003 that 3.5%-4% of the original mintage survived in all grades, "with more continuing to be added on an annual basis." This piece joins a large contingent of AU coins at both services, boasting semiprooflike, delightful orange-gold surfaces that are minimally abraded for the grade. (#9011)

2983 **1889-S MS62 PCGS.** Swirling luster gives this piece a very flashy appearance. The yellow-gold coloration is also quite appealing. Well struck with scattered small marks that prevent a higher grade. (#9012)

2984 **1889-S MS62 PCGS.** The top of the 89 in the date is lightly repunched. A lustrous and original green-gold twenty with a clean reverse. Encapsulated in a green label holder. *From The Vanek Collection.* (#9012)

2985 **1889-S MS62 PCGS.** This sun-gold twenty exhibits unbroken luster, and is smooth for the grade despite minor marks on the cheek. Certified in a green label holder. *From The Vanek Collection.* (#9012)

2986 **1890 MS61 PCGS.** This is a lower mintage issue (75,995 coins) that is somewhat scarce in Mint State and rarely seen above the MS62 grade level. The current example is boldly struck and intensely lustrous with alluring yellow-gold coloration and a normal number of trivial surface blemishes for the grade. (#9013)

2987 **1890-CC AU50 PCGS.** Lustrous for the grade and only moderately abraded. TWENTY and PLURIBUS are lightly die doubled. A popular Carson City gold type coin. Housed in a green label holder. (#9014)

2988 **1890-CC AU53 NGC.** Luster individually outlines the obverse stars, and dominates protected areas of the reverse. Lightly abraded for a briefly circulated Carson City double eagle. TWENTY is lightly die doubled north, as often seen on the '90-CC. (#9014)

2989 **1890-CC AU53 NGC.** Luster brightens Liberty's hair and the eagle's wings. Less abraded than is customary for a briefly circulated double eagle. TWENTY and PLURIBUS are lightly die doubled, the usual reverse for this popular Carson City issue. *From The Vanek Collection.* (#9014)

2990 **1890-CC AU53 NGC.** A lightly circulated example of this later Carson City double eagle that has hints of butter-yellow against the still-lustrous orange-gold surfaces. Well struck save for softness on the obverse stars and with light abrasions present on the cheek. (#9014)

2991 **1890-CC AU53 NGC.** This piece is bright and attractive, showing light coloration and substantial luster on both sides. Traces of highpoint rub and numerous wispy field hairlines define the grade. (#9014)

2992 **1890-CC AU55 ANACS.** A well executed strike leaves sharp detail on the design elements of this Choice AU Carson City issue. Both sides retain a fair amount of luster, and present the viewer with yellow-gold coloration that possesses a greenish cast. Small contact marks are scattered about, particularly on the obverse; these are fewer than ordinarily found on this issue. Moreover, copper spots, grease marks, and areas of discoloration, which also frequently plague this issue, are completely absent from this example. (#9014)

Lustrous AU58 1890-CC Double Eagle

2993 **1890-CC AU58 PCGS.** The relatively large emission of 91,209 business strikes, and large-scale exportations of double eagles in the 1890s combine to make this one of the more abundant CC-mint double eagles in high grade. The green-gold surfaces are highly lustrous on this piece, and a thorough perusal with a strong loupe locates few distracting abrasions of any size. A nice coin for the grade and issue. A light die crack encircles much of the reverse at the peripheral stress points. (#9014)

Borderline Uncirculated 1890-CC Twenty

2994 1890-CC AU58 PCGS. The mint luster is virtually complete, subdued only on Liberty's cheek. The fields and devices are less abraded than on many Mint State pieces, ant the present coin has excellent eye appeal for the AU58 level. TWENTY and PLURIBUS are lightly die doubled, as often seen for this popular Carson City issue. (#9014)

2995 1890-S MS62 PCGS. This suitably struck and lustrous Liberty twenty is primarily olive-gold, although the centers exhibit salmon-pink patina. Generally smooth despite a couple of moderate marks near the chin and the right border of the shield. (#9015)

2996 1890-S MS62 ICG. The intensely lustrous surfaces are fully brilliant, with pleasing light coloration. Small marks pepper each side of the coin, without spoiling its eye appeal. The scarcest San Francisco Mint double eagle issue of the 1890s. (#9015)

Refinery House, Philadelphia Mint, 1901

Appealing 1891-CC Double Eagle, AU53

2997 1891-CC AU53 NGC. The initial year of CC-mint coinage, 1870, and 1891 are responsible for the two lowest-mintage CC double eagles, but there the similarity ends. The 1870 is a great and expensive rarity, but the 1891-CC can be obtained, for a price, in any grade up through the lower Uncirculated levels. This AU53 specimen is about a typical grade for survivors, but it offers generous eye appeal, a combination of the pleasing surfaces that are only lightly abraded, the radiant luster still present, the yellow-gold coloration, and a remarkable absence of singular distractions. A nice coin, both for the grade and for the issue. (#9017)

2998 1891-S MS61 ANACS. Medium S. A boldly impressed and lustrous example of this popular Type Three issue. Less abraded than is usual for the grade. E PLURIBUS UNUM is lightly die doubled. (#9018)

2999 1891-S MS63 PCGS. Medium S. E PLURIBUS UNUM and the arrows are lightly die doubled. Lustrous and well struck with an uncommonly clean reverse. The obverse is also less abraded than expected for the MS63 level. (#9018)

Sharply Defined, Lustrous MS64 1891-S Twenty

3000 1891-S MS64 PCGS. The primary significance of the 1891-S is its availability as a pre-1900 Type Three twenty in mint condition. The MS64 level is generally as fine as the '91-S can be found as only two pieces have been graded finer (both by NGC). This coin has the bold mint luster one would expect from an S-mint with a glint of semi-prooflikeness in the fields and a light overlay of reddish patina. It also is sharply defined in all areas. Minimally abraded, as one would expect from an MS64. Population: 65 in 64, 0 finer (6/07). (#9018)

3001 1892-CC AU50 NGC. A well-defined, briefly circulated representative that retains plenty of flash in the yellow-orange fields. Despite a number of marks in the fields, the portrait is clean for the issue and the grade.
From The Vanek Collection. (#9020)

3002 1892-CC AU55 PCGS. A briefly circulated representative from the penultimate Carson City double eagle issue, this 1892-CC piece has boldly impressed, lightly worn devices that show a handful of copper spots. Scattered abrasions appear in the brassy fields. (#9020)

3003 1892-CC AU55 NGC. Considerable semi-prooflike luster brightens this charming Carson City double eagle. The upper obverse stars are softly impressed, but the devices display only slight wear. A few marks near obverse star 12 fail to distract. The 1892-CC is less rare than the 1891-CC or 1893-CC, but is significantly scarcer than the 1890-CC. (#9020)

Appealing Near-Mint State 1892-CC Twenty

3004 1892-CC AU58 NGC. As is the case with many Saint-Gaudens double eagles, this mintmarked Liberty twenty was formerly considered a major rarity, and yet today it is fairly available because of recent importations. Only light abrasions dot the surfaces of this strictly graded near-Mint State piece, and considerable prooflikeness remains on the appealing surfaces, primarily yellow-gold tinged with reddish-gold in the recesses. (#9020)

Attractive AU58 1892-CC Double Eagle

3005 1892-CC AU58 PCGS. A delightful piece that has much the same look as a Mint State coin, yet is far more affordable. Both sides of this yellow-orange example have practically complete luster, and the sharply struck devices exhibit only a touch of friction. A beautiful example of this late-date Carson City double eagle. (#9020)

Scarce Mint State 1892-CC Double Eagle

3006 1892-CC MS60 NGC. Boldly struck on the central design elements, with some softness noted on the obverse and reverse dentils, as well as on the obverse peripheral stars. The fields are bright and somewhat reflective. Numerous small to moderate marks define the grade. A scarcer issue in Mint State which has become more available during the past decade, according to Jeff Garrett and Ron Guth. (#9020)

Reflective Mint State 1892-CC Double Eagle MS61

3007 1892-CC MS61 PCGS. Although not certified as a prooflike example by PCGS, both sides have fully reflective, mirrored fields. The mintage was 27,265 coins, and at one time this date was considered a rarity, although many examples have been brought back from overseas holdings. This example has faint green and pink overtones with medium yellow-gold color. The surfaces are lightly abraded, yet still quite attractive. Population: 40 in 61, 43 finer (4/07). (#9020)

3008 1892-S MS63 PCGS. A well-defined later 19th century example of Longacre's enduring double eagle design, apricot-gold with a splash of orange on the reverse. Subtly lustrous with few marks for the grade and considerable visual appeal. (#9021)

3009 1892-S MS63 PCGS. Many 1892-S double eagles, along with other San Francisco twenty dollar issues of the era, were shipped to Europe or South America for international trade (Jeff Garrett and Ron Guth, 2006), making this date readily available in all but the highest Mint State grades. This Select example exhibits yellow-gold color with a faint green cast, and pleasing luster. A sharp strike emboldens the design features. A few obverse contact marks and scuffs limit the grade. (#9021)

Colorful MS64 1892-S Twenty

3010 **1892-S MS64 NGC.** A couple of small groups of 1892-S twenties entered the marketplace in the early 1990s, which account for many of the better-grade examples known today of this issue. This is a particularly attractive coin that displays rich pinkish-gold and lilac coloration. Sharply struck with a few small field marks, especially on the reverse, and light abrasions on the cheek of Liberty. Census: 46 in 64, 4 finer (5/07). (#9021)

3011 **1892-S MS62 Prooflike NGC.** The luminous apricot-gold fields are moderately abraded. Well struck and attractive for the grade. Only a minuscule fraction of the Mint State survivors are prooflike. Census: 3 in 62 Prooflike, 0 finer (5/07).
From The Vanek Collection. (#79021)

Choice Mint State 1893 Type Three Liberty

3012 **1893 MS64 NGC.** A delightful near-Gem example of this late-19th century emission, one with a moderate mintage by Philadelphia Mint standards of 344,200 pieces. The mellow orange-gold surfaces show a noteworthy lack of mentionable abrasions, and radiant cartwheel luster enlivens each side. In *Type Three III Double Eagles: A Numismatic History and Analysis* by Michael Fuljenz and Douglas Winter, the authors note that "of all the common Philadelphia issues from the 1890's, the 1893 is the most difficult to locate with choice surfaces." Census: 48 in 64, 3 finer (6/07). (#9022)

3013 **1893-CC XF45 NGC.** This was the final double eagle issue from the Carson City Mint, and a mere 18,402 pieces were produced. This example has a surprising amount of remaining detail for the grade, and may represent an upgrade candidate. Surface marks are not obtrusive, and bits of luster cling to the devices. (#9023)

Bright, Attractive 1893-CC Twenty, AU58

3014 **1893-CC AU58 NGC.** Few 1893-CC twenties saw actual circulation. Most were apparently shipped to Europe, and have only returned to this country over the past 30 years. This piece shows slight friction from handling and nearly complete mint luster. Bright and sharply struck, there is just a hint of the reddish color usually seen on these pieces. (#9023)

Exceptional 1893-CC Twenty Dollar, AU58

3015 **1893-CC AU58 PCGS.** The 1893-CC is the final double eagle produced at the Carson City Mint. This high-end About Uncirculated example displays brassy-gold surfaces that retain considerable luster. The strike is exceptional, as sharp delineation is apparent on all of the design elements. This issue is usually heavily bagmarked (Douglas Winter, 2001). Fortunately, this lovely specimen does not fit that profile, as we see just a few minor grazes and marks. (#9023)

3016 **1893-S MS62 PCGS.** The lustrous surfaces display accents of lime-green and pastel peach coloration. The design elements are boldly detailed. Typically abraded for the MS62 grade level. (#9024)

Exemplary 1893-S Twenty, MS64
One of the Finer Pieces Known

3017 **1893-S MS64 NGC.** While abundant in lower grades, the cutoff of availability for the 1893-S is at the MS63 level. When the numbers certified in MS64 are combined from the two major services, it shows that only 53 coins have been graded the same as this piece (only one is finer). This example has especially pronounced, flashy mint luster and reddish tinted surfaces. Only the slightest abrasions are present and none are worthy of individual mention. (#9024)

3018 **1894-S MS63 PCGS.** A crisply struck piece from this later San Francisco issue, one of many that boast a mintage of over 1 million pieces. Both sides display strong luster and light abrasions on the vivid yellow-gold surfaces. (#9026)

3019 **1894-S MS63 PCGS.** Well struck with satin luster and lovely yellow-gold and peach toning. A few light marks define the grade. An appealing Select Uncirculated representative of this later San Francisco Mint issue. (#9026)

3020 **1895 MS63 PCGS.** Potent luster, a good strike, and clean fields confirm the quality of this Select representative. The faint grazes on the cheek are typical of the grade. (#9027)

3021 **1895 MS63 PCGS.** Pleasing luster emanates from peach-gold surfaces that display sharply impressed motifs. A few minor marks define the grade. (#9027)

3022 **1896 MS63 PCGS.** Apricot-gold patina adorns both sides of this Select twenty, and sharp definition characterizes the design features. Lustrous surfaces reveal some light grade-defining scuffs. (#9029)

3023 **1896 MS63 NGC.** A crisply struck example of this late 19th century double eagle issue, one of fewer than 800,000 pieces coined. The lightly abraded surfaces display rich sun-gold color with a dash of orange.
From The Vanek Collection. (#9029)

3024 **1896 MS62 Prooflike NGC.** The 896 in the date is repunched. Probably not Breen-7322, since that variety also shows recutting on the 1. The reflective canary-gold fields are abraded, but lack individually mentionable marks. Census: 5 in 62 Prooflike, 1 finer (5/07).
From The Vanek Collection. (#79029)

3025 **1896-S MS62 PCGS.** This is a highly lustrous example from the San Francisco Mint that displays sensational yellow-gold and peach toning and nicely preserved surfaces for the grade. (#9030)

3026 **1897-S MS63 NGC.** This is a fully brilliant and highly attractive example with rich honey-gold color that is accented by traces of pale pink toning. (#9032)

Conditionally Elusive 1897-S Twenty MS64

3027 **1897-S MS64 PCGS.** Most of the design elements are well struck and the highly lustrous surfaces display pleasing honey-gold and rose toning, imbued with underlying greenish field accents. A few wispy marks deny a finer grade assessment. This issue is scarce at the MS64 grade tier, and rare any finer. (#9032)

Scarce Near-Gem 1897-S Twenty

3028 **1897-S MS64 PCGS.** A crisply struck yellow-orange and lime Choice Liberty twenty with vibrant luster and a well preserved reverse. High-end for the grade, and difficult to improve upon since PCGS has certified only five pieces finer (5/07). (#9032)

3029 **1898 MS62 PCGS.** This date is somewhat of a condition rarity in higher Mint State grades, and even at the MS62 level it is not often exceeded, although PCGS has certified 119 better ones (6/07). This piece is fully brilliant and frosty with bright yellow and pink-gold color. (#9033)

3030 **1898 MS62 PCGS.** The bright, satiny surfaces have a distinctly matte-like, fine grain texture in the fields. Coruscating luster illuminates the yellow-gold and pink coloration. Relatively slight luster grazes and contact marks define the grade. (#9033)

Attractive Select 1898 Twenty

3031 **1898 MS63 PCGS.** The orange-gold devices are framed with lighter yellow-gold toning. Dazzling luster sweeps the relatively smooth fields, and the cheek displays only minor grazes. A better date with a low mintage of 170,395 pieces. Its S-mint counterpart has a production of more than 2.5 million pieces. PCGS has certified only seven examples finer (5/07). (#9033)

Elusive 1898 Double Eagle, MS64

3032 **1898 MS64 NGC.** According to Jeff Garrett and Ron Guth, the 1898 double eagle is: " ... seldom seen above MS62." Glowing luster exudes from surfaces that display rich apricot-gold color on this near-Gem specimen. A solid strike left its mark on the design elements, including virtually complete delineation in Liberty's hair strands. A few minor scuffs define the grade. Census: 21 in 64, 0 finer (6/07). (#9033)

3033 **1898-S MS63 PCGS.** The 89 in the date are lightly recut southeast. A lustrous green-gold Liberty twenty that boasts a clean cheek and good eye appeal. (#9034)

3034 **1898-S MS64 NGC.** Stars 7 to 10 are a bit soft, but the overall strike is sharp. This yellow-gold Choice Liberty twenty has pleasing luster and clean surfaces. The obverse is especially free from consequential contact. (#9034)

3035 **1898-S MS64 PCGS.** While a large population of this date exists at the MS64 grade level, PCGS has only certified 68 finer pieces. The frosty surfaces are smooth and nearly mark free with highly lustrous yellow and pink-gold color. (#9034)

3036 **1899 MS64 PCGS.** This charming green-gold near-Gem has a bold strike and is void of mentionable marks. The reverse rim exhibits infrequent traces of struck-in grease, as made. PCGS has certified a mere nine pieces finer (4/07). (#9035)

3037 **1899-S MS63 PCGS.** This piece looks finer than the assigned grade level would ordinarily imply. The intense luster and unusually vibrant lime-gold coloration are both unusually attractive. Well struck and minimally abraded, this is an outstanding Select Mint State double eagle. (#9036)

3038 **1899-S MS63 PCGS.** Potent luster sweeps this lightly abraded and well struck Type Three twenty. Most Mint State '99-S double eagles are significantly bagmarked, unlike the present lot. (#9036)

3039 **1899-S MS63 PCGS.** Glowing luster emanates from peach-gold surfaces that display sharply impressed design features. We note a few minute marks on the obverse that limit the grade. (#9036)

3040 **1900 MS63 PCGS.** A solid strike leaves sharp definition on the design features of this Select double eagle, and dazzling luster issues from green-gold surfaces. A few trivial marks define the grade. Housed in a green-label holder.
From the Reuben Reinstein Collection. (#9037)

3041 **1900 MS64 PCGS.** A sharply struck and carefully preserved near-Gem whose lustrous surfaces display hints of lime and pumpkin-gold toning. The 1900 was struck in quantity, yet PCGS has certified only 51 pieces finer (4/07). (#9037)

3042 **1900 MS64 PCGS.** A sharply struck and satiny peach-gold example of this final 19th century Philadelphia issue, minimally marked overall and attractive. The outer reverse displays a touch of orange color. (#9037)

3043 **1900 MS64 NGC.** A flashy and carefully preserved near-Gem with impressive eye appeal. Boldly struck and attractive. Although an available issue, the 1900 is about ten times scarcer than the 1904 in Mint State. (#9037)

3044 **1900-S MS62 PCGS.** Boldly struck overall with attractive, original coloration and outstanding luster for this overlooked turn-of-the-century date. Relatively few examples of this high-mintage issue have been certified at higher Mint State grade levels. (#9038)

3045 **1900-S MS63 PCGS.** Rich apricot-gold coloration adorns this highly lustrous Select S-mint representative, and an impressive strike leaves its mark on well defined motifs. A few minor marks preclude a higher grade. (#9038)

3046 **1900-S MS63 PCGS.** A wonderful Select example of this final 19th century San Francisco double eagle, solidly struck with vibrant luster. Light, well-distributed abrasions are noted on the vivid orange-gold surfaces. (#9038)

3047 **1900-S MS63 PCGS.** This is a relatively high-mintage issue of nearly 2.5 million pieces that becomes surprisingly scarce at grade levels finer than MS63. This example displays intense mint luster and attentively struck design features. Pretty lime-green and peach toning is especially noticeable on the reverse. (#9038)

3048 **1901 MS64 PCGS.** Crisply struck with shining luster and lovely yellow-gold surfaces with hints of apricot color. Light marks appear on the portrait, though these are consistent with the near-Gem designation. By the time this piece was struck, Longacre's portrait of Liberty had endured on the denomination for more than half a century. (#9039)

3049 **1901 MS64 PCGS.** Fully struck, each side displays blazing mint luster and bright yellow-gold color. A lovely MS64 type coin. (#9039)

Vibrant Gem 1901 Double Eagle

3050 **1901 MS65 PCGS.** With a mintage of just 111,430 pieces, the 1901 double eagle remains underappreciated as an issue, with practically no premium accorded to it through most Mint State grades. This beautiful and well-preserved piece has bold detail and powerful luster. The shining surfaces are predominantly orange-gold, though elements of peach are present in the fields. Extremely rare as a Premium Gem; NGC has graded no coins finer, while PCGS has certified just three (5/07). (#9039)

3051 **1902 MS61 PCGS.** A sharply defined example of this popular, low mintage issue. A few light field marks explain the grade as well as a small scrape on the upper reverse. (#9041)

3052 **1903 MS63 PCGS.** This Select 1903 twenty displays pleasing apricot-gold patination tinged with traces of mint-green. These attributes are complemented by radiant luster, accentuating the coin's overall eye appeal. A few light marks preclude a higher grade. The high quality of production and plentiful supply resulting from the uncovering of some large hoards make the 1903 a popular type coin. (#9043)

3053 **1903 MS64 PCGS.** A satiny sun-gold Type Three twenty that has a well preserved reverse and a clean portrait, aside from a solitary mark above the cheekbone. The strike is sharp throughout. (#9043)

3054 **1903 MS64 PCGS.** Despite a comparatively low mintage of just 287,270 pieces, the 1903 double eagle is accorded virtually no premium over its more available counterparts. This sharply struck yellow-gold example has strong luster and few marks overall. A lovely example of this underappreciated issue. (#9043)

3055 **1903 MS64 PCGS.** Philadelphia minted under 300,000 examples of this issue, though the next year would set a new record for double eagle production. This Choice example offers swirling luster and pleasing butter-yellow surfaces in addition to solidly struck devices. Fine, scattered marks deny a higher grade. (#9043)

3056 **1903 MS64 PCGS.** The Philadelphia Mint struck more than nine times as many double eagles in 1903 as it did the previous year, and 1904 would see an even greater jump. This well-defined piece displays attractive luster and minimally marked surfaces. A desirable example. (#9043)

3057 **1903 MS64 PCGS.** This is a sharply struck near-Gem that reveals a few minute obverse marks that define the grade. Both sides are awash in pleasing peach-gold luster. (#9043)

3058 **1903 MS64 PCGS.** Bright yellow-gold color and sharply struck throughout. A lustrous, high-end MS64. (#9043)

3059 **1903 MS64 PCGS.** Lustrous and well struck, with attractive light toning, this impressive near-Gem displays well struck design features and carefully preserved surfaces. The reverse is clean and blemish-free, while the obverse shows a few unimportant marks. (#9043)

3060 **1903 MS64 PCGS.** Fully struck and highly lustrous, with rich orange-gold toning and just a few minor, grade-limiting marks. An appealing near-Gem example of this issue, which becomes scarcer at the MS65 grade level.
From The Vanek Collection. (#9043)

Bright, Lustrous 1903 Twenty Dollar, MS65

3061 1903 MS65 PCGS. A common post-1900 date in the twenty dollar Liberty series, but a good alternative to much more frequently seen 1904. This piece displays bright mint luster with even orange-gold color. Only a couple of minor areas of softness are seen with intricate detailing on Liberty's hair and the eagle's feathers. (#9043)

3062 1903 MS64 Prooflike NGC. This piece is obviously Prooflike, with massively deep reflectivity in the fields. It also displays attractive mild frost on the central devices, and would probably qualify for the Cameo designation if it were a proof. Well struck and untoned with great eye appeal despite the trivial abrasions that keep it from being a Gem. Census: 4 in 64 Prooflike, 0 finer (5/07). (#79043)

3063 1903-S MS64 PCGS. Fully struck and highly lustrous, this near-Gem double eagle displays attractive honey-gold toning with rose highlights that are deeper and more noticeable on the reverse. Several faint grease streaks (as struck) are noted—one below 19 in the date and couple on the upper right reverse—which do not influence the technical grade of the piece. A few minor marks on Liberty's cheekbone and in the fields prevent a higher grade. PCGS has only graded eight examples of this issue finer (6/07). (#9044)

3064 1903-S MS64 PCGS. Lovely honey-gold toning and vibrant luster are hallmarks of this near-Gem double eagle. If not for a few stray marks, this high-end example might have qualified as a Gem. (#9044)

3065 1904 MS63 NGC. Unlike the usual representative of this generic issue, this example displays a dazzlingly frosty appearance on both sides. Well struck with light honey-gold toning and a few wispy blemishes on the obverse that define the grade. (#9045)

3066 1904 MS63 PCGS. Pleasing orange-gold luster adorns both obverse and reverse of this Select double eagle, and a sharp strike translates into excellent design definition. The grade is defined by a handful of minute marks scattered about.
From the Reuben Reinstein Collection. (#9045)

3067 1904 MS63 PCGS. Dazzling luster radiates from relatively smooth, peach-gold surfaces imbued with whispers of mint-green. Excellent definition results from a solid strike, further enhancing the coin's eye appeal. A sharp coin for the grade. Housed in a green-label holder.
From the Reuben Reinstein Collection. (#9045)

3068 1904 MS64 PCGS. A solidly struck representative that has pleasing luster and attractive yellow-orange color. With a generous mintage of over 6.2 million pieces, the 1904 is the issue of choice for many type collectors, and the near-Gem grade enjoys high popularity. (#9045)

3069 1904 MS64 PCGS. A decisively struck and flashy Choice example of the quintessential Liberty double eagle issue, lemon-gold with hints of deeper and lighter colors. Appealing with just a few too many marks for a finer grade. (#9045)

3070 1904 MS64 PCGS. A blend of sunset-orange and yellow-gold graces the shimmering surfaces. A well-defined and minimally marked representative of this ubiquitous 20th century issue. (#9045)

3071 1904 MS64 PCGS. The fields of this piece show a noticeable trace of semiprooflikeness on each side. As such, this should be of additional interest to collectors because of the extra flash. The fully struck surfaces are upper-end for the MS64 grade. (#9045)

3072 1904 MS64 PCGS. Sharply struck throughout with coruscating mint luster. Just a shallow mark on the cheek of Liberty from a Gem grade. (#9045)

3073 1904 MS64 PCGS. The 1904 double eagle is one of a handful of issues that defines "type gold," and as such, it remains a collector and investor favorite. This orange-gold twenty displays powerful, though not flashy luster and excellent detail. (#9045)

3074 1904 MS64 PCGS. An elegant appearance greets the viewer of this clean, richly toned double eagle. Well struck and highly lustrous, with few surface blemishes. A conservatively graded near-Gem. (#9045)

3075 1904 MS64 PCGS. This example is sharply struck and well preserved, with lime-gold surfaces that are minimally marked and close to Gem quality. The most common issue in the Liberty Head double eagle series, and an ideal choice for type purposes. (#9045)

3076 1904 MS64 PCGS. This attractive near-gem displays sharp definition and lustrous, peach-gold surfaces. Just a few minor marks preclude a higher grade. (#9045)

3077 1904 MS64 PCGS. Radiant luster is emitted from orange-gold surfaces. Sharply struck, with just a few minor grade-defining marks. (#9045)

3078 1904 MS64 NGC. A beautiful peach-gold twenty with a semi-prooflike obverse. The reverse exhibits potent cartwheel luster. Close to a higher grade despite minor contact on the upper left reverse. A shiny spot at 4 o'clock on the reverse is of mint origin. Housed in a prior generation holder. (#9045)

Lovely Gem 1904 Liberty Twenty

3079 1904 MS65 PCGS. Rich lime-green fields cede to orange centers. An attentively struck and impressively unblemished Gem, ideal for a high quality gold type set. The reverse is particularly smooth for the grade. Certified in a green label holder. (#9045)

Dazzling Gem 1904 Twenty

3080 1904 MS65 NGC. This expertly struck twenty has original peach and lime-gold toning. A yellow-gold beauty with a well preserved reverse and only a few minor marks on the portrait and the upper left obverse field. More double eagles were struck in 1904 than in any other year, but quality always finds a buyer. (#9045)

Impressive Gem 1904 Liberty Twenty

3081 1904 MS65 PCGS. A beautifully preserved orange and olive Gem that lacks the numerous marks usually encountered on Mint State Liberty twenties. The 1904 is (and will always be) common, but only a tiny fraction of survivors can compete with the quality of the present coin. (#9045)

Handsome Gem 1904 Double Eagle

3082 1904 MS65 PCGS. The 1904 is one of the most common dates of the Liberty Head double eagle series, and is often sought as a type coin. This Gem displays highly lustrous, apricot-gold surfaces with hints of mint-green. A sharp strike emboldens the design elements, and both sides are well preserved. (#9045)

Attractive 1904 Twenty Dollar MS65

3083 1904 MS65 NGC. The sleek, satiny surfaces display rich toning and pleasing luster. A couple of trivial marks near the tip of Liberty's nose fail to preclude the Gem grade assessment. An astonishingly high number of 1904 double eagles survive in high grades of preservation, making this issue the ideal choice for the type collector. (#9045)

Lustrous Gem 1904 Double Eagle

3084 1904 MS65 NGC. The appealing luster and exceedingly clean-cheeked Liberty are more reminiscent of a high grade Morgan dollar than what one normally thinks of in the quintessential Liberty Head Type Three coin, but here is such a piece. The peach-gold surfaces radiate coruscating cartwheel luster, and nary a distracting abrasion is found on either side. The bold strike more than fulfills the criteria for a Gem. Buy this superlative coin before it gets away! (#9045)

Premium Gem 1904 Double Eagle

3085 1904 MS66 NGC. Undoubtedly the most plentiful date in the entire Liberty double eagle series, this is an excellent choice for type collectors who desire the best possible quality for the price. An outstanding specimen, this Premium Gem has soft, frosty gold luster with hints of orange and iridescent toning. It is sharply struck, and the surfaces are pristine. (#9045)

3086 1904 MS62 Prooflike NGC. The glassy fields are extremely flashy and highly reflective. The design elements are sharply impressed throughout. Numerous superficial abrasions limit the numerical grade level, but the eye appeal of the piece remains high. The 1904 is the most common double eagle issue of all time, but Prooflike examples like this one are relatively few and far between. (#79045)

3087 1904 MS63 Prooflike NGC. A flashy canary-gold double eagle whose clean surfaces and crisp strike attest to the eye appeal. The 1904 is common, but prooflike examples comprise only a slender percentage of survivors. (#79045)

3088 1904 MS64 Prooflike NGC. The fields exhibit dazzling reflectivity, and the penetrating strike and unmarked surfaces further ensure the eye appeal. Census: 32 in 64 Prooflike, 10 finer (5/07). (#79045)

3089 1904-S MS64 ★ NGC. The fields are flashy and approach a Prooflike designation, although the obverse field has some cartwheel luster as well. The moderate reflectivity undoubtedly inspired the ★ designation from NGC. The cheek displays minor grazes. (#9046)

3090 1904-S MS64 PCGS. This appealing near-Gem is nicely detailed overall, even if some of the reverse motifs are softly defined. Lustrous and satiny, with lovely light coloration and just one noticeable mark, on Liberty's hair beneath the coronet. (#9046)

3091 1904-S MS64 PCGS. Though overshadowed by its Philadelphia counterpart, the 1904-S double eagle has a titanic mintage in its own right, in excess of 5.1 million pieces. This solidly struck representative offers strong luster and appealing yellow-orange coloration with a touch of haze over the fields. Lightly abraded, yet appealing for the grade. (#9046)

3092 1904-S MS64 PCGS. Pleasing luster radiates from both sides of this yellow-gold near-Gem, and a sharp strike brings out strong delineation in the design elements. (#9046)

Desirable Gem 1904-S Double Eagle

3093 1904-S MS65 PCGS. The high mintage 1904-S double eagle, with more than five million pieces originally produced, is well known as the most common Type III double eagle from the San Francisco Mint. Above the MS65 grade level, however, this issue is excessively rare, with a mere three examples certified at MS66 by the two major services, and none finer (6/07). The surfaces of the currently offered Gem are blessed with effulgent mint luster and alluring coloration. The design elements are sharply struck and surface marks are not excessive for the grade. (#9046)

Highly Attractive Gem 1904-S Double Eagle

3094 1904-S MS65 NGC. This is a highly attractive Gem double eagle, with deep golden-rose toning and intense, coruscating mint luster. All of the design elements are well struck and surface marks are minimal, although a shallow luster graze is noted in the upper left obverse field. Surprisingly, these San Francisco pieces sell for nearly the same price as an example from the Philadelphia Mint, from the same year and at the same grade level; even though many more of the P-mint coins have been certified at the MS65 grade level by NGC and PCGS.
From The Vanek Collection. (#9046)

3095 1904-S MS64 Prooflike NGC. This impressively reflective Choice Liberty twenty has a good strike, and the only a pair of thin marks behind the hairbun are worthy of singular mention. Census: 3 in 64 Prooflike, 0 finer (5/07). (#79046)

3096 1906 MS62 NGC. A better date twenty with a mintage of a mere 69,596 pieces. This lustrous sun-gold representative is surprisingly unabraded for the grade, with the exception of a brief curved obverse mark at 5 o'clock. (#9049)

Popular 1906-D Twenty Dollar, MS63

3097 1906-D MS63 NGC. The production of double eagles at the Denver Mint began in 1906. The 1906-D is very popular, as it is one of only two years in which Liberty Head twenties were struck at the new mint. Apricot-gold surfaces on this Select example emit glowing luster, and exhibit sharply struck design elements. A few minute obverse marks define the grade. (#9050)

3098 1906-S MS62 NGC. The highest-mintage of three issues for this penultimate year of the Liberty Head double eagle. This well-defined and shining piece has a number of small, scattered copper spots against yellow-orange surfaces that show light to moderate abrasions, including one that crosses the cheek.
From The Vanek Collection. (#9051)

Choice 1906-S Double Eagle

3099 1906-S MS64 PCGS. Well struck with intense mint luster and lovely honey-gold and rose coloration. Both sides display a few minor, well scattered abrasions. This is a scarce issue at the Choice Mint State level of preservation, and the combined efforts of PCGS and NGC have certified only seven pieces finer (5/07). (#9051)

Alluring 1906-S Double Eagle MS64

3100 1906-S MS64 PCGS. This attractive near-Gem is noteworthy for the sharpness of its overall striking detail. Highly lustrous and richly toned, it is an alluring example of this San Francisco Mint issue. According to Garrett and Guth (2006): "Although the 1906-S double eagle is reasonably available in average condition, choice examples become quite scarce."
From The Vanek Collection. (#9051)

3101 1907 MS64 PCGS. A boldly struck and original Choice Liberty twenty. Sea-green shades dominate the borders, while the radiant centers are yellow-gold. The reverse is well preserved, and the obverse is only lightly abraded. The 90 in the date is minutely repunched. Certified in a green label holder. (#9052)

Attractive Choice 1907-D Twenty

3102 **1907-D MS64 PCGS.** An impressive butter-gold near-Gem from the final year of this long-lived series. Luster shimmers across the smooth fields. The reverse is particularly unabraded. An inconspicuous nick on the tip of the chin determines the grade. (#9053)

Choice 1907-D Double Eagle

3103 **1907-D MS64 PCGS.** Orange-gold surfaces display strong luster, and just a few minor grade-defining marks. All of the design elements are well brought up by the dies. The second and final Denver Mint Liberty double eagle, which becomes scarce in attractive Mint State grades. (#9053)

1907-D Twenty Dollar MS64

3104 **1907-D MS64 PCGS.** The only Denver double eagle issue for the year, as no branch mint struck any Saint-Gaudens pieces in 1907. This solidly struck near-Gem displays rich sunset-orange color with a touch of peach at the margins. A small copper spot is noted near the rim at 4 o'clock on the highly lustrous reverse. (#9053)

Final Year 1907-D Twenty MS64

3105 **1907-D MS64 PCGS.** Dazzling luster and an intricate strike provide attractive eye appeal. This piece appears conservatively graded at first glance, although close evaluation locates concealed marks above the ear and beneath the jaw. The obverse die is lapped, causing prooflike areas near the ear similar to that seen on several proof Barber dates. Encapsulated in a green label holder. (#9053)

3106 **1907-D MS61 Prooflike NGC.** Distinctly reflective and decisively struck, this final-year D-mint piece displays a hint of haze against vibrant yellow-orange surfaces. Scattered moderate abrasions account for the grade. Census: 3 in 61 Prooflike, 9 finer (5/07). *From The Vanek Collection.* (#79053)

Breathtaking MS64 1907-S Liberty Twenty

3107 **1907-S MS64 NGC.** This piece would make an ideal type coin, as a near-Gem example of the last S-mint issue in the long-lasting Liberty Head double eagle series. Surprisingly for a mintage that exceeded 2 million pieces, Choice examples are scarce, the apparent result of indifferent storage. This specimen features gorgeous orange-gold surfaces that complement breathtaking luster, with an absolute minimum of abrasions. NGC has certified only 11 pieces finer (6/07). (#9054)

PROOF LIBERTY DOUBLE EAGLES

Challenging Proof 1901 Liberty Twenty

3108 **1901 PR60 NGC.** The 1901 has a proof mintage of 96 pieces, a reduction from the 124 proofs struck for the 1900. In his 1988 Encyclopedia, Breen stated, "Possibly 36-40 proofs survive, many impaired." Proofs, such as the present specimen, can be identified by the presence of four faint diagonal, parallel die lines between the TY in LIBERTY.

This needle-sharp proof twenty features darkly mirrored fields and moderately frosted motifs. By today's standards, the contrast may be sufficient to merit a Cameo designation, but no such notation is present, since the piece is certified in an older generation holder. As expected of the PR60 grade, the fields are moderately abraded, but there are no distracting marks. Overall, a worthy contribution to a gold proof type set.
From The Vanek Collection. (#9117)

Pleasing 1907 Liberty Head Twenty, PR53

3109 **1907 PR53 PCGS.** The 1907 issue is the final year for the Liberty Head double eagle. Jeff Garrett and Ron Guth (2006) write that "although the mintage for 1907 proofs (78 pieces) is fewer than for the issues of the previous few years, the number of survivors is about the same, at 40 to 50 coins. There are also several impaired examples known. Most examples also lack the cameo devices commonly seen on pre-1902 specimens." PCGS and NGC data corroborate the number of survivors, as those services have graded about 40 examples to date. This PR53 specimen displays apricot-gold surfaces that exhibit considerable field-motif contrast, especially when the piece is tilted under a light source, and mildly frosted design elements are exquisitely struck up. Minute contact marks are scattered about, somewhat more so on the obverse. Housed in a green-label holder. Pleasing overall eye appeal, despite the light circulation.
From The Vanek Collection. (#9123)

HIGH RELIEF DOUBLE EAGLES

AU55 Details 1907 High Relief Twenty

3110 **1907 High Relief, Wire Rim—Cleaned—ANACS. AU55 Details.** Both sides of this deep yellow-gold representative have noticeable hairlines from improper cleaning. However, it is still a desirable example of the coveted High Relief that should appeal to the budget-minded collector. (#9135)

1907 High Relief Wire Rim Twenty Dollar, Unc Details

3111 **1907 High Relief Wire Rim—Improperly Cleaned—NCS. Unc Details.** The scarce High Relief double eagles rank among the most coveted types in numismatics. On the present piece, fine hairlines are visible under magnification. Peach-gold surfaces exhibit apricot and red accents, and the strike is commanding. A small strike-through is noted on a ray southwest of the branch stem, and a wire rim encircles most of both sides. (#9135)

MS60 Details MCMVII High Relief

3112 **1907 High Relief, Wire Rim—Cleaned—Rims Damaged—ANACS. MS60 Details.** The wire rim that partially encircles the coin on each side has been rather badly bent up at seemingly random intervals, perhaps from an amateurish attempt to mount this in a jewelry holder at some time in the past. The fields are lightly hairlined, but the color is a consistent and attractive yellow-gold, save for a bit of darker coloration on the highpoints. Despite the minor distractions, the majesty of Saint-Gaudens' phenomenal design manages to shine forth. (#9135)

Bright, Attractive MCMVII High Relief, MS62

3113 **1907 High Relief, Wire Rim MS62 PCGS.** The allure of a rare coin is not just its technical state of preservation, and the degree of its closeness to perfection. Eye appeal is important to almost every collector, but many forget or do not realize the place and time from which a coin came. The always popular High Relief—of whatever variety, or whatever might be the state of its preservation—was born of genius 100 years ago this year. All collectors today are familiar to some extent with its story. But what of the year 1907? The man who engraved this coin died in the same year it was introduced. His double eagle was a dramatic break from the past, ground breaking in 1907. Other daring artists were at work: Henry Rousseau, Edvard Munch, Marc Chagall, and Pablo Picasso. Art Nouveau was sweeping the decorative art world; the Impressionist movement of the 1880s was beginning to be appreciated as it had not been in the heyday of its creative momentum; and experiments in the art of money were breaking ground—the brilliant proofs of the 19th century, for example, were just giving way to the experimental matte proofing technique, both in America and in Europe. A century ago, the world was looking both backward and forward. Artists found inspiration in the past, as did Saint-Gaudens from ancient coins. Technology was looking forward, and making history at the same time, for never in the remembered past had a coin of such luxurious appearance as this piece been created—not since the ancient artists of some 2,000 years past.

This MS62 High Relief has significant visual appeal. The surfaces are a bit bright, as might be expected from the grade, and are covered with even reddish patina. A few small, individually insignificant contact marks can be seen with magnification but are virtually imperceptible to the unaided eye. (#9135)

Lovely High Relief Saint-Gaudens MS63

3114 **1907 High Relief, Wire Rim MS63 PCGS.** A beautiful sun-gold representative of this American numismatic classic. Prolonged inspection and rotation beneath a loupe is unable to locate any grade-limiting marks, and in fact the luminous surfaces are impressively unperturbed. A small, curved lintmark (as produced) southwest of Liberty's chest is mentioned for pedigree purposes, and the reverse rim is raised at 2:30 and 9 o'clock. The strike is intricate throughout with the sole exception of Liberty's raised knee. Doubling from the multiple strikes is only apparent on the base of the LIB in LIBERTY. Encapsulated in a green label holder.
From The Vanek Collection. (#9135)

Gorgeous 1907 High Relief Twenty Dollar Wire Rim, MS64

3115 **1907 High Relief, Wire Rim MS64 NGC.** Soon after the initial production of the Ultra High Relief version of the Saint-Gaudens double eagle, it became apparent that they were unsuitable for circulation-strike coins. Paul Green, in an October 28, 2003 *Numismatic News* article, indicates that the Ultras would not stack properly, and that: "... they could never be produced in sufficient numbers for regular use ... because the dies cracked after managing just 19 or so coins." A lower but still High Relief version was then struck. These 1907 Roman Numeral High Reliefs came with either a flat or so-called wire rim. While not as rare as the Ultra High Relief type, the High Reliefs, with their bold designs and low mintage (12,367 pieces), are still extremely desirable.

Gorgeous satiny luster enlivens both sides of this near-Gem, and a solid strike imparts excellent detail to the design features. A few trivial handling marks on apricot-gold surfaces do not detract from the coin's overall eye appeal. A knife-like fin is noted on a good portion of both the obverse and reverse, though it is sometimes difficult to discern in the holder. (#9135)

Flashy MS64 MCMVII High Relief Twenty

3116 **1907 High Relief, Wire Rim MS64 NGC.** A piece that approaches Gem status in the quality of its surfaces as well as in the excellence of its eye appeal, the present example boasts lovely yellow-gold surfaces. Bright flashy luster radiates from each side of the coin, a type that never fails to stun and delight viewers with its sculptural details and timeless elegance. Close scrutiny with a loupe reveals a dearth of mentionable abrasions, save for a couple of small contact marks that are well hidden in the eagle's feathers, and a small tick on Liberty's face. A couple of tiny alloy spots are seen on the reverse. A pretty piece that merits inclusion in a fine collection. (#9135)

Breathtaking MS65 1907 High Relief Saint-Gaudens Twenty

3117 1907 High Relief, Wire Rim MS65 PCGS. What a pity that the very nature of this magnificent coin caused it to be minted in such relatively modest numbers! There is a beauty in every Saint-Gaudens double eagle, but not to the extent that beauty reigns on superb pieces made to match the original conception of the artist, in high relief, with all details struck boldly—to mesmerize the human eye!

Countless words have been written about this coin, but how many collectors have ever considered its symbolism, especially compared to the symbolism portrayed on the first double eagle, of the Liberty Head style? On the earlier coin, we see emblematic structure, familiar to most collectors and admired by nearly all. Yet, by its nature, it is static, formal, handsomely stark but without "life." Surrounding the left-facing head of Liberty are 13 stars, each of six points. The date in Arabic numerals appears below, easy to read. Otherwise, the obverse is void, an intentionally open field meant to offset the very concept of Liberty. On the reverse appear our nation's name and the denomination, spelled out clearly. The eagle here is diminutive, strictly emblematic, but "emblazoned" by short rays rising from its shoulders with a sort of halo of stars above the bird's head. The coin is a study in formality.

By contrast, Augustus Saint-Gaudens' Liberty approaches us! She is striding forward (into the future?). It is Liberty itself here that is "alive," while the government she represents is diminutive, at her skirt tips. The date is unimportant in this artistic scheme. It is not even readily readable, for it is in Roman numerals. The rays here are long and shine brightly! They gleam, they surround the concept of Liberty, they embolden the very nature of freedom. Numerous stars encircle, representing not only the states of the Union but outlining the proclamation of Liberty. And the reverse—oh, the reverse! Again, the rays blaze away, shine below and lift the American eagle, now no longer a mere emblem but animated, flying, and free! As the United States of America herself was, in 1907, on the verge of becoming an international power, for the first time ever, our wings were about to carry us into a bright and bold future—as indeed our national pride proclaims on this golden coin. It was important, too, that it was a gold coin, money in any language, and for all time.

This Wire Rim example is poised at the threshold of perfection. The thick, satiny surfaces glow with mint luster. There are no contact marks visible to the unaided eye, and the striking definition is complete on each side. A magnificent High Relief and a coin that will surely take bidders' breath away. (#9135)

Select 1907 High Relief Double Eagle, MS63

3118 1907 High Relief, Flat Rim MS63 PCGS. A sharply detailed Select Mint State example of the ever-popular MCMVII High Relief double eagle, this piece has fully brilliant greenish-gold color and satiny luster. Traces of swirling die polish can be seen in the fields on both sides, typical of most or all surviving examples of this issue.

The High Relief double eagle ranks as the most beautiful American coin ever produced, in the opinion of most collectors and numismatists. The artistry and talent of Augustus Saint-Gaudens created a coin design that may never be equaled again. (#9136)

SAINT-GAUDENS DOUBLE EAGLES

3119 1907 Arabic Numerals MS64 PCGS. The yellow-gold surfaces of this Choice example border on lemon-gold at the margins. A well-defined and pleasing example of this No Motto issue that has minor, yet grade-defining marks on each side. (#9141)

3120 1907 Arabic Numerals MS64 PCGS. The first year of issue was an eventful one for the Saint-Gaudens double eagle design, modified several times and due for further changes in 1908. This version features a lower relief on both sides, with the initial Roman numerals changed to the Arabic style. This is a satiny and boldly struck representative that shows scattered light marks on each side. A brief two-year type with no motto. (#9141)

3121 1907 Arabic Numerals MS64 PCGS. A green-gold and apricot near-Gem from the initial year of the Saint-Gaudens design. Smooth aside from a thin mark on the extended arm. The Capitol building is razor-sharp. (#9141)

3122 1907 Arabic Numerals MS64 PCGS. This green-gold Choice Saint-Gaudens is from the scarcer year of the two-year No Motto type. Thorough evaluation locates occasional groups of field marks. Encapsulated in a green label holder. (#9141)

3123 1907 Arabic Numerals MS64 PCGS. Bright, intense luster is the hallmark of this beautiful near-Gem. Olive-orange toning adorns the well preserved surfaces. A popular type from the first year of issue that is considerably more affordable than a High Relief, one of its 1907 counterparts. (#9141)

3124 1907 Arabic Numerals MS64 NGC. Philadelphia was the only mint to produce the lowered-relief Arabic Numerals variant of the 1907 Saint-Gaudens double eagle. Scattered marks appear in the fields of this radiant yellow-orange piece, one that offers pleasing luster and solid definition on the devices.
From The Vanek Collection. (#9141)

3125 1907 Arabic Numerals MS64 PCGS. A powerful strike leaves exquisite detail on this near-Gem double eagle, including the panes of the Capitol building and the eagle's plumage. Apricot-gold surfaces imbued with tinges of lime-green are awash in luster, and reveal just a few minor marks totally consistent with the grade level. This issue was saved in large numbers by the public and by European banks. (#9141)

3126 1907 Arabic Numerals MS64 NGC. This near-Gem from the first year of the Saint-Gaudens double eagle series displays effulgent satiny luster and lovely orange-gold toning with rose overtones. The design elements are well struck and there are only a few scattered marks that prevent an even higher grade. (#9141)

3127 1907 Arabic Numerals MS65 PCGS. Attractive apricot and orange-gold coloration bathes both sides of this Gem double eagle. An impressive strike brings out sharp definition on the design elements, including separation in the panes of the Capitol building, and on Liberty's fingers and toes. Intensely lustrous surfaces reveal just a few light marks within the confines of the grade designation. (#9141)

3128 1907 Arabic Numerals MS65 PCGS. This sun-gold Gem has comprehensive cartwheel sheen, and careful examination beneath a glass finds only an inconspicuous mark beneath the center of the eagle's front wing. The strike is precise on the Capitol building, and other device highpoints are evenly brought up. As often seen on the No Motto type, the eagle's beak is strike doubled. (#9141)

3129 1907 Arabic Numerals MS65 PCGS. First year of issue and always of interest as such. However, the quantity of 1907 twenties that have been found in high grade make this an obtainable type coin also. This coin actually appears finer than the stated grade with superb mint luster and virtually abrasion-free surfaces. (#9141)

3130 1907 Arabic Numerals MS65 PCGS. Rich, variegated orange-gold and yellow color is interspersed over each side of this nicely frosted Gem. Fully struck as well with no mentionable abrasions. (#9141)

3131 1907 Arabic Numerals MS65 PCGS. Sharply defined, each side has deep, frosted mint luster. Additionally, there are no noticeable abrasions, and both obverse and reverse are covered with even reddish-golden patina. (#9141)

3132 1907 Arabic Numerals MS65 PCGS. The much-modified Saint-Gaudens design had more or less assumed final form by this iteration, but it would require modification yet again the following year, as Congress overrode President Theodore Roosevelt's strong distaste for associating the Deity with money to have IN GOD WE TRUST placed on the denomination. This piece boasts intensely lustrous orange-gold surfaces, with a premium appearance and an equally compelling strike. (#9141)

3133 1907 Arabic Numerals MS65 NGC. Exceptional color characterizes this Gem 1907. While not meaning to overlook the clean surfaces, thick mint luster, and strong strike, the color really dominates on this coin. (#9141)

3134 1907 Arabic Numerals MS65 NGC. Thick, softly frosted mint luster covers both sides of this lovely Gem 1907. While most of the coin displays medium rose-gold color, the reverse has accents of lilac over the highpoints. Sharply struck. (#9141)

3135 1908 No Motto MS65 PCGS. A pleasing Gem representative of this two-year type, well struck with subtly lustrous peach-gold surfaces. A trace of orange-peel texture is present in the fields. Between a mintage of over 4 million pieces and a sizable survival rate, the 1908 No Motto double eagle is one of the most available issues for the design. (#9142)

3136 1908 No Motto MS65 PCGS. Bright yellow-gold color shimmers over each side of this lustrous Gem. Fully struck. (#9142)

3137 **1908 No Motto MS65 PCGS.** Lustrous and well preserved, with lovely honey-gold coloration and boldly struck design elements. Only trivial marks are found on either side. The No Motto type was only produced for two years, ensuring its popularity among collectors of the Saint-Gaudens double eagle series. (#9142)

3138 **1908 No Motto MS65 NGC.** Long Rays Obverse. A satiny and smooth Gem with pleasing sharpness on the Capitol building, the face, and the eagle's leg feathers. A briefly produced type, as IN GOD WE TRUST was added later in 1908. (#9142)

3139 **1908 No Motto MS66 NGC.** Short Rays Obverse. This desirable Premium Gem offers scintillating luster and exquisite preservation. Fully struck on the Capitol building, and Liberty's fingers and nose also have uncommon definition. (#9142)

3140 **1908 No Motto MS66 NGC.** Long Rays Obverse. This beautiful olive and yellow-gold Premium Gem has scintillating luster and a remarkably preserved obverse. The reverse is smooth aside from minor rim contact near 9 o'clock, and an inconspicuous thin mark on the front wing. The obverse features a wire rim, a telltale indication of the penetrating strike. (#9142)

3141 **1908 No Motto MS66 PCGS.** Fully struck and extraordinarily clean, even for an MS66. This would make an excellent type coin for some lucky collector. (#9142)

3142 **1908 No Motto, Wells Fargo MS66 PCGS.** A quintessentially attractive representative from one of the most famous single-issue hoards in numismatic history. The subtly lustrous peach-gold surfaces are carefully preserved overall, though a mark is noted on the eagle's wing. Housed in a green label holder. (#99142)

3143 **1908 No Motto, Wells Fargo MS66 PCGS.** Short Rays obverse. A handsome khaki-gold Premium Gem with impressively unabraded fields and devices. The strike is attentive, since any incompleteness is limited to the eagle's leg. Housed in a green label holder. (#99142)

Superb 1908 Wells Fargo Double Eagle

3144 **1908 No Motto, Wells Fargo MS67 PCGS.** Satiny yellow-gold luster is typical of the Wells Fargo Double Eagles. These coins laid in storage for several decades before their numismatic recovery a few years ago. While examples are still plentiful in the marketplace today, this is good news for the type collector who wants an amazing quality Saint-Gaudens Double Eagle. (#99142)

3145 **1908-D No Motto MS64 PCGS.** The fine-grain surface textures on each side of this piece are easy to see with the aid of bright mint luster. Straw-gold coloration and few surface marks complete the description of this near-Gem, from the second year of the Saint-Gaudens double eagle design. (#9143)

3146 **1908-D No Motto MS64 PCGS.** Lustrous and appearing quite fine overall for the assigned grade level. The surfaces display brassy coloration and some strictly trivial contact marks that are noticeable mainly on the lower reverse. A scarcer issue from the second year of the Saint-Gaudens double eagle series. (#9143)

3147 **1908-D No Motto MS64 NGC.** The matte-like surfaces exhibit shimmering luster and a slight reddish tint on both sides. Uniformly bold definition is noted on every design element. A handful of trivial surface blemishes limit the grade. This issue becomes very scarce any finer. (#9143)

3148 **1908 Motto MS63 PCGS.** A satiny low mintage twenty with rich green-gold and peach toning. The Capitol building is well struck, and there are fewer marks than customary for the grade. Certified in a green label holder.
From The Vanek Collection. (#9147)

3149 **1908 Motto MS63 NGC.** Lovely lime-gold coloration and shimmering luster ensure the alluring eye appeal of this Select Mint State double eagle. A normal number of small marks define the grade. (#9147)

Attractive Near-Gem 1908 With Motto Double Eagle

3150 **1908 Motto MS64 PCGS.** Unlike its No Motto counterpart (4,271,551 coins produced), the 1908 Motto double eagle is a scarce issue from a low mintage (156,258 pieces). This attractive near-Gem is lustrous and attentively struck, with uniformly bold details on each side. A few minor marks and luster grazes prevent a higher grade, but the coin retains a substantial degree of overall eye appeal. (#9147)

3151 **1908-D Motto MS64 PCGS.** Lustrous and boldly struck, and lacking any severe marks, this is a high-end representative for the grade. A pleasing amalgam of lime-gold and peach toning decorates the fine-grain surfaces.
From The Vanek Collection. (#9148)

3152 **1908-D Motto MS64 NGC.** The pleasing double eagle is noteworthy for being essentially blemish-free on both sides. Just a faint luster graze is noted on the upper left obverse, near 10 o'clock. Boldly struck and lustrous with beautiful coloration. An exceptionally clean example of this scarce and underrated issue. (#9148)

1908-S Saint-Gaudens Twenty, AU55

3153 **1908-S AU55 NGC.** At first glance, this 1908-S double eagle has the appearance of a Mint State coin. However, close inspection reveals slight rub on the highpoints of the design elements. The dazzling luster in the fields remains undisturbed on this orange-gold beauty. Boasting the lowest mintage of any Saint-Gaudens twenty, excepting the High Relief issues, the 1908-S is a challenge to locate in high grade. NGC has certified 60 examples in AU55 (6/07). (#9149)

Near-Mint State 1908-S Twenty

3154 1908-S AU58 NGC. This low-mintage issue is usually found in circulated or low Mint State grades, with most pieces averaging about Choice AU. This near-Mint State piece features the gorgeous luster characteristic of the issue, with light abrasions and wear attesting to a short spate in circulation. Good value for the AU58 grade. (#9149)

3155 1909 MS62 ANACS. The non-overdate variety of this lower mintage issue. A typically struck yellow-gold example with bright, moderately marked surfaces. (#9150)

Select Mint State 1909/8 Double Eagle

3156 1909/8 MS63 ICG. The 1909/8 Saint-Gaudens twenty is celebrated as the only overdate in the series. In the early years of the Mint, devices (stars, letters and numbers) were individually punched into each working die. In 1909, and for many years prior, the date was an integral part of the hub. A die sinker, for whatever reason, used both 1908 No Motto and 1909 obverse hubs to prepare a working die, which required multiple impressions to complete. While not a traditional overdate (a previously used working die that is modified for use in a subsequent year), the 1909/8 adds some spice to this popular series. This honey-gold specimen is lustrous and completely worthy of the assigned grade. The only distraction that requires mention is a nick on the eagle's left wing. (#9151)

Sharply Detailed Gem 1909 Overdate Twenty

3157 1909/8 MS65 NGC. The 1909/8 has long enjoyed a place of honor in U.S. numismatics as the only overdate in the popular and widely collected Saint-Gaudens Double Eagle series. Several hundred examples surfaced in Europe in the 1960s and 1970s, but the vast majority of those coins were circulated to one degree or another. Even the coins that were Mint State, like most Uncirculated survivors in today's market, grade no finer than MS63. Gems are of the utmost rarity, and there are just 23 examples certified MS65 by NGC and PCGS combined, with a mere 10 finer (3/07).

This issue has a peculiar "look" for a P-mint double eagle struck in 1909. Since the obverse die was leftover from the 1908 No Motto series, the design elements on that side are not as sharply detailed as those on the 1909 perfect date examples. However, we stress that this lovely Gem possesses ample evidence of having received a powerful strike from the dies. Both sides are fully lustrous with a rich, frosty texture that highlights the rich orange-gold coloration. We are hard pressed to find more than one or two scattered bagmarks on both the obverse and the reverse; but, if we had to select a pedigree marker, we would use a horizontal scuff at the top of the sun on the reverse. We cannot overstate the importance of the present lot among advanced gold specialists, and this coin that is fully deserving of a premium quality bid. Census: 9 in 65, 7 finer (5/07). (#9151)

Rare MS66 1909/8 Twenty

3158 1909/8 MS66 NGC. The 1909/8 was the only overdate produced in the Saint-Gaudens double eagle series. It was first discovered in 1910, and written up by Edgar H. Adams in the June 1910 issue of *The Numismatist* (Vol. XXIII, No. 5). Adams' interpretation of the 1909/8 overdate is presented here in its entirety:

> "Overstruck dates are those where the die of one year has been altered to do service for the succeeding one. The last figure in the date is usually gouged out and replaced by the new one, but seldom is this operation conducted so skillfully that traces of it are not left. Of course the reason for this is to save money in the making of the dies, and the practice has by no means been abandoned altogether, for careful scrutiny of the Saint-Gaudens piece of 1909 will reveal traces of what seems to have been the alteration of the figure 8 to 9."

Today we understand that an overdate is not produced in the manner related by Adams in 1910. Gold specialist Roger Burdette goes into a more in-depth explanation of the 1909/8 double eagle:

> "Sometime in late 1908 the die sinkers prepared working dies in the usual manner. This required several strikes (more like "squeezes") from a hydraulic press of the working hub to produce a complete working die. This process occurred over several days, and for a coin the diameter of a double eagle, may have required a total of four or more strikes to complete a single working die. Evidently, one of the die sinkers accidentally got his hands on a 1908 hub and used that to make some impressions. He then switched back to the correct 1909 hub and completed the working die."

Burdette goes on to say:

> "Normally, the sharp-eyed engraver Charles Barber would have checked working dies before releasing them to the coiner. But much of Barber's attention may have been given to the new sunken relief gold half- and quarter-eagles designed by Bela Pratt, and the overdated die went to the coining department. The finished obverse die for this curious numismatic variety was used and finally discarded. Apparently no one in the coining department realized that a 1909/8 overdate had been created. If they did, no action to condemn the coins was taken."

The peach-gold surfaces of the Premium Gem in this lot exhibit dazzling luster, and possess a pleasing grainy finish. The strike is well executed, and manifests itself in sharp definition on the panes of the Capitol building, Liberty's face, fingers, and toes, and the eagle's plumage. The few minute marks that are present on each side do not distract, and are well within the parameters of the grade designation. NGC and PCGS combined have certified, to date, only ten examples in MS66, and none finer (5/07). (#9151)

Scarce 1909-D Twenty MS62

3159 1909-D MS62 PCGS. This satiny apricot-gold double eagle is sharply struck, particularly on the Capitol building. Attractive for the grade despite an abrasion near 9 o'clock on the obverse border. Only 52,500 pieces were struck, the third-lowest Motto production. Certified in a green label holder.
From The Vanek Collection. (#9152)

Notable Near-Gem Large D/Small D 1909-D Double Eagle

3160 1909-D MS64 PCGS. Large D Over Small D. Most extant 1909-D double eagle survivors returned to the United States from decades overseas, largely spent in banks in France and Switzerland, with at least a few coming from a Central American source as well. These pieces solidify this issue's status as "merely" a semikey, despite its low mintage of just 52,500 pieces.

This sharply struck coin shows rich, original orange-gold and lilac coloration and soft, frosty luster. The mintmark appears to be the elusive Large D Over Small D variant that was discovered and first publicized in the Norweb III Sale. There is a portion of the smaller mintmark visible at the upper left. The inner right curve also appears to be present; otherwise, the mintmark is wide. An interesting variety, perhaps underappreciated due to this issue's all-around desirability. (#9152)

Choice Mint State 1909-D Double Eagle

3161 1909-D MS64 PCGS. This is a highly lustrous near-Gem specimen with brilliant orange-gold color and frosty surfaces. Both sides are well-detailed. The primary obverse design motif has slightly lighter pink color. A few faint abrasions can be seen on each side, but none are immediately obvious.

The 1909-D double eagle is quite scarce. The mintage was limited to 52,500 coins, and many of those actually entered circulation. Few high quality survivors have been identified. In fact, PCGS has only certified 26 finer quality pieces (6/07) since it began grading coins some 20 years ago. (#9152)

3162 1909-S MS61 ANACS. The surfaces of this piece exhibit frosty luster and faint pink toning over yellow-gold surfaces. Both sides have myriad abrasions that are expected for the grade.
From The Vanek Collection. (#9153)

3163 1909-S MS63 ANACS. This bright S-mint displays pleasing luster on peach-gold surfaces that are lightly abraded. Excellent definition is noted on the design elements. (#9153)

3164 1909-S MS64 PCGS. Fully struck with bright, coruscating mint luster. This coin exemplifies why the '09-S is so popular with collectors. (#9153)

3165 1909-S MS64 PCGS. An upper-end example of this popular hoard date. Fully struck with strong mint luster. A loupe will be necessary to find the abrasions that limit the grade on this sharp coin. (#9153)

3166 1909-S MS64 NGC. This crisply impressed and thoroughly lustrous Choice Saint-Gaudens twenty lacks mentionable marks, and has much cleaner fields than the usually encountered example. Encapsulated in a prior generation holder.
From The Vanek Collection. (#9153)

Conditionally Scarce Gem 1909-S Twenty

3167 1909-S MS65 PCGS. Despite its relatively high mintage, this issue is scarce at or above the Gem level of preservation. This example is lustrous and richly toned, with variegated shades of orange-gold, steel-gray, lilac, and rose displayed over the two sides. The striking details seem adequate, even if a bit soft near the lower obverse border. (#9153)

Lustrous MS65 1909-S Twenty

3168 1909-S MS65 NGC. The discovery of the hoard of 1909-S twenties in El Salvador in 1989 greatly increased the number of better-grade examples of this issue. It also had a significant effect on the supply of Gems, as several hundred have qualified at that level. This is an especially attractive coin that has rich reddish-golden color and strong mint frost. Fully struck also. (#9153)

3169 1910 MS64 PCGS. The lustrous surfaces of this near-Gem Saint are predominantly yellow-gold, though the fields have lime accents and an area near Liberty's head exhibits milky patina. A well struck example that displays strong circumstantial evidence of time spent overseas. (#9154)

3170 1910 MS64 PCGS. This scarcer, early P-mint is seldom located finer than MS64. The rich yellow-gold mint luster shows a light overlay of reddish patina. Only the slightest luster grazes prevent an even higher grade. Fully struck in all areas. (#9154)

3171 1910 MS64 PCGS. Rich honey-gold toning and intense luster are the hallmarks of this alluring near-Gem. A few minuscule blemishes are found in the obverse fields, and a faint pinscratch extends from just behind the eagle's mouth across the shoulder area.
From The Vanek Collection. (#9154)

3172 1910 MS64 PCGS. Sharply defined with excellent luster characteristics. A few luster grazes limit the upper potential of this attractive near-Gem. (#9154)

Sharp 1910 Twenty, MS65

3173 **1910 MS65 PCGS.** Sharp design definition and frosty yellow-gold luster are the hallmarks of this lovely Gem. A few scattered surface marks are evident, defining the grade. This is an elusive issue in the higher grades, with just three finer examples certified by PCGS (6/07). (#9154)

3174 **1910-D MS63 ANACS.** A lovely prewar Saint-Gaudens twenty with comprehensive luster and a precise strike. The obverse is uncommonly clean for the grade, as is the reverse despite a single thin mark beneath DOLLARS. (#9155)

3175 **1910-D MS64 PCGS.** Boldly struck with vibrant luster and carefully preserved surfaces. Unusually vivid apricot-gold toning adorns some of the coin's surfaces, while mint-green and rose accents are also noted. A few minor field marks on the obverse and a small abrasion above the eagle's head limit the grade. *From The Vanek Collection.* (#9155)

3176 **1910-D MS65 PCGS.** The satiny mint luster has taken on a lovely, even overlay of light reddish patina over both obverse and reverse. A fully struck example and rarely encountered finer. (#9155)

3177 **1910-D MS65 PCGS.** This is a very appealing Gem, displaying as it does radiant luster and an attentive strike. Exquisite definition is noted on all of the design elements, and rich apricot-gold color adorns minimally abraded surfaces. (#9155)

3178 **1910-D MS65 PCGS.** Fully struck, each side is covered with thick, satiny mint luster. Rarely encountered any finer than MS64. (#9155)

3179 **1910-D MS65 PCGS.** Pleasing, lustrous surfaces that are more suggestive of a 1924 than a coin from this decade. The devices are fully struck, and there are no mentionable marks on either side. Light, even reddish patina. (#9155)

3180 **1910-S MS64 PCGS.** In contrast to Philadelphia and Denver, which each struck fewer than 500,000 double eagles in 1910, San Francisco coined over 2 million pieces. The yellow-orange example offered here is a distinctive representative of this available issue. The lustrous fields and well struck devices display a few grade-defining abrasions, including a handful on the robe. (#9156)

3181 **1910-S MS64 PCGS.** A radiantly lustrous near-Gem that exhibits boldly struck design elements. Apricot-gold surfaces reveal some minor grade-defining marks. Most of the 1910-S mintage was melted in the 1930s (Jeff Garrett and Ron Guth, 2006). (#9156)

3182 **1911 MS64 PCGS.** The lustrous surfaces of this near-Gem 1911 double eagle display uncommonly vivid yellow-orange color. A well-defined example of this lower-mintage early issue, which had an original production run of under 200,000 pieces. (#9157)

3183 **1911-D/D MS63 ANACS.** Breen-7383. Bold repunching is visible on the mintmark. Attractive apricot-gold patina bathes both sides of this MS63 twenty dollar, and a solid strike brings out excellent definition on the design elements. Attractive surfaces yield a somewhat pebbly finish, especially on the reverse. The few minute marks scattered about do not disturb. (#9158)

3184 **1911-D/D MS64 NGC.** FS-501. The mintmark is repunched. This example has a splendid appearance that is enhanced especially by beautifully deep orange-rose color. The fields display a dramatic pebbly texture (as struck) that is actually quite attractive. Well struck with minimal marks for the grade. (#9158)

3185 **1911-D/D MS64 PCGS.** FS-501. The mintmark is repunched east. This boldly impressed and lustrous near-Gem displays original lemon and lime tints. Both sides are impressively free from marks. *From The Vanek Collection.* (#9158)

3186 **1911-D/D MS64 ANACS.** FS-501, formerly FS-1911.5. Breen-7383. The mintmark is clearly repunched east. A lustrous canary-gold twenty with pleasing preservation and a bold strike. (#9158)

3187 **1911-D MS65 PCGS.** This shimmering green-gold double eagle is impressively smooth aside from faint obverse grazes near 3 o'clock. Well struck on the Capitol building, torch fingers, and face. (#9158)

Illustrious MS66 1911-D/D Saint, Ex: Duckor/Akers

3188 **1911-D/D MS66 PCGS.** Ex: Duckor/Akers. FS-501, Repunched Mintmark. The illustrious pedigree says much, but one does not hesitate to note the coruscating cartwheel luster, the delicious peach-gold coloration accented with mint-green, and the near-full strike over frosty and pristine surfaces. Were it not for a stray mark or two on the reverse mint device, this piece might qualify for a Superb Gem grade. As it stands, it is one of the few mintmarked Saint-Gaudens issues fairly obtainable in so high a Mint State grade, with the 1915-S and 1916-S close behind in terms of availability. As a huge bonus on so nice a coin, the mintmark is nicely and prominently repunched east, practically the poster child for this available but popular variety. Are those drumbeats the sound of bidders lining up? (#9158)

3189 **1911-S MS64 PCGS.** This satiny yellow-gold near-Gem has surprisingly few abrasions, and the highpoints of the striding Liberty are only slightly shiny. A good value relative to higher grades. (#9159)

3190 **1911-S MS64 PCGS.** Blushes of mint-green add to rich apricot-gold patination, through which pleasing luster radiates. Exceptionally well struck, with just a few minor marks limiting the grade. (#9159)

3191 **1911-S MS64 NGC.** This S-mint piece displays 46 stars around the obverse and the same number of stars on the edge, a number that would change to 48 as the continental United States took on its present-day form. A well struck near-Gem that offers soft, pleasing luster and displays few marks in the yellow-gold fields. *From The Vanek Collection.* (#9159)

3192 **1911-S MS64 PCGS.** Frosty and bright, with yellow-gold toning and a normal number of minor abrasions for the grade. The surfaces have a finely granular texture, and the devices are boldly struck. (#9159)

3193 **1911-S MS64 PCGS.** A medley of apricot-gold and gray-green patina bathes lustrous surfaces of this near-Gem twenty. A solid strike brings out excellent definition on Liberty's face, fingers, and toes, the panes on the Capitol building, and the eagle's plumage. Devoid of significant marks; small toning spots are located on the reverse. (#9159)

Pleasing Gem 1911-S Double Eagle

3194 **1911-S MS65 PCGS.** Vibrant luster and rich sun-gold toning confirm the charm of this well preserved and original Gem. The obverse center has a couple of small splashes of rose-red patina. Attentively struck and conditionally scarce. As of (5/07), only 20 pieces have been certified finer by PCGS. (#9159)

Radiant Gem 1911-S Twenty

3195 **1911-S MS65 PCGS.** In MS65 the present 1911-S is the finest grade easily obtainable, as NGC and PCGS have each certified only a couple of dozen pieces in higher grades—20 at PCGS and 34 at NGC (6/07). Radiant luster emanates from the frosty orange-gold surfaces, and the few marks noted on Liberty's torso are both minor and grade-consistent. The strike is bold, and the overall appearance is pleasing and high-end. (#9159)

Accented Gem 1911-S Twenty Dollar

3196 **1911-S MS65 PCGS.** Bright, swirling mint luster is seen over both sides and the orange-gold color has an accent of lilac over the figure of Liberty. A lovely, fully struck Gem example of this popular, better date early S-mint. As of (5/07), PCGS has certified a mere 20 pieces finer, approximately one for every year of the firm's operation. (#9159)

1911-S Twenty Dollar MS65

3197 **1911-S MS65 PCGS.** Original surfaces with frosted orange-gold luster that is overlaid with hints of lilac on the highpoints of the devices. The strike is impressive throughout, including the Capitol building, the torch fingers, Liberty's face, and the eagle's breast feathers. An attractive example of this better Saint-Gaudens issue. (#9159)

3198 **1912 MS62 PCGS.** Yellow-gold save for a few russet freckles along the right reverse border. The left obverse field has a few minor marks, but this shimmering example will represent this lower mintage issue. (#9160)

3199 **1912 MS63 PCGS.** Consistent light apricot toning fails to impede the energetic cartwheel luster. This attentively struck Select twenty has good eye appeal for the grade. (#9160)

3200 **1912 MS63 PCGS.** This sharply struck green-gold Select twenty has clean fields and a few moderate marks on the eagle. Philadelphia was the only facility to strike the denomination in 1912. Certified in a green label holder.
From The Vanek Collection. (#9160)

Lustrous 1912 Near-Gem Twenty

3201 **1912 MS64 PCGS.** Technically, the 1912 double eagle is a new type created by the addition of two stars placed below the date near the oak leaves. This was done to represent the addition of New Mexico and Arizona to the Union. Apricot-gold luster radiates from both sides of this near-Gem, and a well executed strike sharpens the design elements. Scattered light marks limit the grade. (#9160)

Outstanding 1912 Double Eagle, MS65

3202 1912 MS65 PCGS. The 1912 double eagle is a scarce date, and a condition rarity in Gem or finer quality, as indicated by the current PCGS population data. This example, like most, is sharply struck with essentially full obverse and reverse details. The surfaces are brilliant with frosty yellow-gold luster, and both sides are essentially mark-free. Attractive pink overtones add to its aesthetic appeal.

When New Mexico and Arizona joined the United States early in 1912, new obverse dies were prepared with two additional stars along the border, bringing the star count up to 48. This is technically a new design type, and 1912 represents the first year of issue. Population: 25 in 65, 5 finer (6/07). (#9160)

3203 1913-D MS63 PCGS. This Select D-mint representative displays pleasing luster and bright apricot-gold coloration tinged with hints of yellow and mint-green. An attentive strike manifests itself in sharp definition on the design elements, especially on the fingers of Liberty's left (right facing) hand and toes, and the eagle's plumage. A few minor marks define the grade. (#9162)

3204 1913-D MS64 NGC. This pumpkin-gold near-Gem has vibrant luster and a decisive strike. The obverse is well preserved, and the reverse is clean despite moderate marks concealed on the eagle. Housed in a prior generation holder. (#9162)

Pleasing Gem 1913-D Double Eagle

3205 1913-D MS65 PCGS. Solid detail and delightful wheat-gold color characterize this attractive Denver double eagle. The luster is pleasing, and marks are few. Though the 1913-D is the most available of the double eagles of 1913, with nearly 400,000 pieces struck, finding an attractive Gem can be a challenge, and anything finer is exceedingly elusive; PCGS has graded only three pieces finer (5/07). (#9162)

Desirable 1913-D Double Eagle, MS65

3206 1913-D MS65 PCGS. Both the Philadelphia and San Francisco Mint issues of this date are rarities in Gem quality, thus the similarly dated Denver Mint double eagle is the logical choice for those collectors who desire one example from each year of issue. This sharply detailed piece has frosty orange-gold luster. Just three finer pieces have been certified by PCGS (6/07). (#9162)

Flashy 1913-D Gem Double Eagle

3207 1913-D MS65 PCGS. Most examples of the 1913-D double eagle survived in European or South American bank vaults before returning to the States over the past four decades. MS63 and MS64 coins are sufficiently available, but the number of Gems drops dramatically (Jeff Garrett and Ron Guth, 2006). Blazing luster envelops this MS65 specimen, and apricot-gold color graces both sides. Sharply struck, with just a few minor marks that likely preclude an even higher grade.
From The Silver Fox Collection. (#9162)

3208 1913-S MS61 ANACS. Generally well struck for the issue, this MS61 '13-S specimen displays soft luster issuing from yellow-gold surfaces. Several minor contact marks are noted on the obverse. No alloy spots are seen on either side, which is unusual for this date. (#9163)

3209 1913-S MS62 PCGS. This MS62 specimen displays a better-than-average strike for the issue, and is devoid of the copper spots that plague the date. Lustrous surfaces reveal some minor obverse marks that define the grade. (#9163)

Lustrous MS63 1913-S Saint-Gaudens Twenty

3210 1913-S MS63 PCGS. A low mintage and lax quality standards at the San Francisco Mint in 1913 ensure that examples of this issue in high Mint State grades are few and far between. This piece shows a couple of small alloy spots intermixed among the golden-gray patination, and the strike—again typical for the issue—is fairly blunt on both Liberty's face and on the Capitol building. The radiant cartwheel luster, however, is superb and undiminished by the passage of time. (#9163)

Low Mintage, Radiant 1913-S Twenty, MS64

3211 1913-S MS64 PCGS. Coins of the 1913-S issue, the second-lowest mintage of the 1908-1933 era, are available in grades up through MS64, but higher-graded pieces are few indeed. The present orange-gold example boasts radiant luster emanating from the well struck surfaces, but a couple of scrapes on Liberty's head and in the obverse field prevent a Gem grade. PCGS has certified only 20 pieces finer (6/07). (#9163)

Upper-End MS64 1913-S Twenty Dollar

3212 1913-S MS64 PCGS. With a negligible total of 20 coins graded higher at PCGS (6/07), some of which are likely resubmissions, collectors find themselves vying for near-Gem examples of this low mintage double eagle. The fact that the Smithsonian Institution's specimen is considered only an MS63 supports the aforementioned claim. This is a highly attractive, lustrous MS64. Most of each side is deep cherry-red in color with a pronounced accent of lilac over the figure of Liberty. Definitely an upper-end coin and worth a premium. (#9163)

Charming Gem 1913-S Saint-Gaudens, Low Mintage Rarity

3213 1913-S MS65 PCGS. Although small hoards of the 1913-S Saint-Gaudens twenty have been imported in recent decades, the low mintage and a subsequent low survival rate for Choice and Gem pieces ensure that such coins as the present Gem will always be in ceaseless demand. The original mintage was only 34,000 coins, an emission second lowest of the 1908-1933 series and exceeded only by the 1908-S, at 22,000 pieces. This example offers remarkably distraction-free surfaces, a combination of the bold strike, the prodigious luster, and the deep, attractive orange-gold coloration. Few pieces indeed can match the numeric grade of this charming Gem, and fewer still can provide a match in aesthetic terms. Population: 17 in 65, 1 finer (6/07). (#9163)

3214 1914 MS62 NGC. The 1914 has the lowest mintage of any Philadelphia Mint Motto Saint-Gaudens, although, of course, its survival rate is higher than a number of the postwar issues with greater productions. Satiny and lightly abraded with faint flatness on the highpoints. (#9164)

Eye-Appealing 1914 Saint-Gaudens Twenty, MS63

3215 **1914 MS63 PCGS.** A lovely example of this fairly low-mintage issue, with radiant cartwheel luster emanating from the pretty yellow-gold surfaces. While there are a few too many small ticks to qualify for a finer Mint State grade, this piece is sure to please its next owner, as its eye appeal is considerable. (#9164)

3216 **1914-D MS64 NGC.** Excellent frosty luster adorns this near-Gem, which is complemented by sharply impressed devices. Peach-gold surfaces reveal just a few minute marks. (#9165)

3217 **1914-D MS64 PCGS.** Sharply struck, the bright yellow-gold surfaces show a slight accent of reddish patina on each side. (#9165)

3218 **1914-S MS64 PCGS.** This sun-gold near-Gem has effusive luster and few marks. Generally sharply struck, although the 4 in the date is slightly soft. (#9166)

3219 **1914-S MS64 PCGS.** This lustrous canary-gold example has a well preserved obverse, and only moderate contact on the sun limits the reverse in grade. Crisply struck and attractive. (#9166)

3220 **1914-S MS64 PCGS.** The 1914-S is one of the most common dates in the Saint-Gaudens series, as large numbers have shown up from overseas hoards. This pleasing near-Gem displays dazzling luster, and a mix of orange-gold and yellow-gold color on minimally abraded surfaces. A sharp strike imparts great detail to Liberty's features, the Capitol building, and the eagle's feathers. (#9166)

3221 **1914-S MS65 PCGS.** This honey-gold beauty has splendidly smooth fields and devices. The Capitol building is fully struck, and only a small section of the sun lacks a crisp impression. A quality example from this pivotal year in World history. (#9166)

3222 **1914-S MS65 PCGS.** Splashes of pumpkin-gold compete for territory with green-gold iridescence. A meticulously struck and carefully preserved Gem that provides rich luster and good eye appeal. (#9166)

3223 **1914-S MS65 NGC.** Intense luster radiates from peach-gold surfaces that exhibit sharply impressed design features, including excellent delineation on Liberty's hand and foot and the eagle's plumage. A few minute marks do not detract in the least. A great high-grade type coin from this readily available issue. (#9166)

3224 **1915 MS63 NGC.** This lustrous and lower mintage Saint-Gaudens twenty has minor distributed marks, but the eye appeal is attractive for the grade. A well struck piece with original green-gold surfaces. (#9167)

Near-Gem 1915 Saint-Gaudens Twenty

3225 **1915 MS64 PCGS.** This is a wonderful near-Gem with brilliant yellow-gold luster and traces of faint pink overtones. A few insignificant abrasions on each side keep it out of the elusive Gem category. The date is scarce in all grades, and it is a condition rarity in higher grades. PCGS has only certified 32 finer Gem examples (6/07). (#9167)

3226 **1915-S MS64 PCGS.** The 1915-S double is a collector favorite because of its quality and availability. Excellent delineation characterizes this near-Gem, as do bright luster and a mix of peach-gold and mint-green coloration. A few minor marks prevent Gem status. (#9168)

3227 **1915-S MS64 NGC.** This attractive near-Gem is satiny on the obverse, but very flashy and bright on the reverse. The design features are crisply defined throughout, and surface marks are minimal for the grade. A very appealing Choice Mint State representative. *From The Vanek Collection.* (#9168)

3228 **1915-S MS64 NGC.** Lovely luster and a hint of orange-peel texture distinguishes the obverse of this vibrant yellow-gold example. A well-defined Choice piece that is appealing with only inoffensive, scattered marks. (#9168)

3229 **1915-S MS65 PCGS.** Pale lime and peach endow this shimmering and exactingly struck Gem. Void of unattractive marks, and a small gray spot beneath the eagle's leg is of little concern. (#9168)

3230 **1915-S MS65 PCGS.** Rich apricot-gold patination bathes lustrous surfaces on this gorgeous Gem. Exquisite motif delineation results from an attentive strike. A few trivial marks of no consequence. (#9168)

3231 **1915-S MS65 PCGS.** This Gem example possesses considerable "flash," as each side is awash in coruscating luster. A powerful strike emboldening the design elements complements this attribute. Yellow-gold surfaces are well preserved for the grade designation. (#9168)

3232 **1916-S MS64 PCGS.** Rich peach-gold patina with light green undertones adorns both sides of this near-Gem. Excellent definition appears on the design features, including Liberty's face, fingers, and toes, as well as the Capitol dome and the eagle's plumage. A handful of small marks define the grade. According to Jeff Garrett and Ron Guth (2006), a large hoard of Mint State examples uncovered in 1983 increased the supply of this issue for collectors. (#9169)

3233 **1916-S MS64 PCGS.** This highly lustrous near-Gem exhibits exquisite strike definition, especially on Liberty's face, fingers, and toes, and on the panes of the Capitol building. Pretty apricot-gold color adorns both faces. (#9169)

3234 **1916-S MS64 PCGS.** Apricot-gold surfaces exhibit sharply defined motifs and pleasing luster. A few minute contact marks limit the grade. This issue was scarce until a hoard of 4,000 pieces was discovered in South America (Jeff Garrett and Ron Guth, 2006) (#9169)

3235 **1916-S MS65 PCGS.** Peach-gold surfaces reveal traces of apricot, and emit radiant luster. Sharply struck, with just a few minute marks. (#9169)

3236 **1916-S MS65 NGC.** This is a gorgeous olive-rose double eagle with carefully preserved surfaces that are illuminated by a pleasing sheen of softly frosted mint luster. The design elements are generally bold, and there are few surface marks on either side. *From The Vanek Collection.* (#9169)

3237 **1920 MS63 PCGS.** This sun-gold Select twenty has sweeping luster and moderately abraded fields. The Capitol building is well struck, and the remainder of the devices are bold save for minor incompleteness on Liberty's raised knee. (#9170)

3238 **1920 MS63 PCGS.** Vibrant luster and variegated green-gold and amber toning adorn the surfaces of this Select Mint State double eagle. A typical number of small abrasions are scattered over each side, for the grade.
From The Vanek Collection. (#9170)

1920 Saint-Gaudens Twenty MS64

3239 **1920 MS64 PCGS.** The lemon-gold surfaces are lustrous, and the strike is good aside from a portion of the eagle's leg. The Capitol building is needle-sharp. Small marks are distributed, but none individually distract. PCGS has certified a solitary MS65 finer (5/07). (#9170)

Conditionally Scarce 1920 Twenty MS64

3240 **1920 MS64 PCGS.** A lovely near-Gem representative of this mid-date issue, one with a mintage of just 228,250 pieces. The well-defined piece has yellow-orange surfaces with small copper spots on each side. Minimally marked save for a single abrasion on the eagle's wing. PCGS has graded a single coin finer (5/07). (#9170)

3241 **1922 MS64 PCGS.** The 1922 is common in relation to the 1922-S, but becomes scarce when compared with the 1923 to 1928 Philadelphia issues. This highly lustrous near-Gem has a pleasantly mark-free obverse. An interesting mint-made retained lamination is present on the reverse at 7:30. (#9173)

3242 **1922 MS64 PCGS.** This is an absolutely gorgeous near-Gem with much greater eye appeal than normal for the grade. The rich orange-gold toning and shimmering mint luster are more attractive than ordinarily encountered for any Saint-Gaudens issue. Surface marks are nearly nonexistent, while a grease streak (as struck) that rests on Liberty's lower abdomen seems to prevent a higher grade. (#9173)

3243 **1922 MS64 PCGS.** The borders show moderate incompleteness of strike, but the major devices are precisely brought up. Lustrous, lightly marked, and encapsulated in a green label holder. (#9173)

3244 **1922 MS65 PCGS.** Rich khaki-gold patina embraces this vibrantly lustrous and boldly struck Gem. Only lightly abraded, although a few minor rose and ebony alloy spots are present. Perhaps two dozen times scarcer than the 1924 in the MS65 grade. (#9173)

Scarce 1922-S Double Eagle, MS62

3245 **1922-S MS62 PCGS.** Despite a mintage of more than 2.5 million coins, this date is scarce in all grades. The vast majority of the original mintage disappeared during the wholesale melting of gold coins during the 1930s. Although the surfaces have minor abrasions and a few faint hairlines, this is an attractive orange-gold specimen with deeper olive toning along the borders. (#9174)

Elusive Choice 1922-S Saint-Gaudens

3246 **1922-S MS64 PCGS.** For ten years, the 1922-S could be obtained at face value from the Treasury. Few took the offer, and after Roosevelt's 1933 gold recall, the 1922-S emerged as a scarcity. The 1922-S has approximately double the mintage of the 1922, yet is much more difficult to locate. This lustrous yellow-gold near-Gem has pleasing preservation for an MS64, although a star is incused above Liberty's extended arm. Encased in a green label holder.
From The Vanek Collection. (#9174)

3247 **1923 MS64 PCGS.** A nicely struck yellow-orange near-Gem that has subtle, pleasing luster. Minor abrasions between the rays on each side are appropriate for the grade. (#9175)

3248 **1923-D MS65 PCGS.** Crisply defined design elements complement the radiant luster exuding from peach-gold surfaces. Some trivial marks do not negate the Gem classification. (#9176)

3249 **1923-D MS65 NGC.** A delightful yellow-gold example with subtle glints of wheat and canary color. Well-defined with soft, pleasing luster on each side of this mid-date D-mint double eagle. Minor marks are noted at Liberty's waist and legs.
From The Vanek Collection. (#9176)

3250 **1923-D MS65 NGC.** A sharp strike is brought out by the intense orange-gold luster on both sides of this Gem. A few tiny surface chips are visible on the obverse. (#9176)

3251 **1923-D MS66 PCGS.** This lustrous and intricately struck premium Gem has pleasing olive-gold and orange tones, and has remarkably few tiny contact marks. An impressive addition to an advanced cabinet of double eagles. (#9176)

3252 **1923-D MS66 NGC.** A highly lustrous Premium Gem with exquisitely struck design elements. Wheat-gold surfaces are impeccably preserved. (#9176)

3253 **1923-D MS66 ANACS.** This beautiful Saint-Gaudens twenty has remarkably smooth fields, and in addition, the reverse is well preserved. An infrequent and tiny alloy spot is noted, and minor contact is present beneath Liberty's knee and mouth. (#9176)

3254 **1924 MS63 PCGS.** Original apricot-gold toning deepens toward the rims. A cluster of small marks is located beneath Liberty's extended arm, but the piece is otherwise well preserved. The front of the first generation holder is scuffy, but this has no effect on the coin itself.
From the Reuben Reinstein Collection. (#9177)

3255 **1924 MS63 PCGS.** An attractive canary-gold type coin that benefits from an exceptionally sharp strike. Faint obverse luster grazes are fewer in number than expected of the grade. Encapsulated in a prior generation holder.
From the Reuben Reinstein Collection. (#9177)

3256 **1924 MS64 PCGS.** A boldly struck sun-gold type coin with potent cartwheel shimmer and minor obverse field luster grazes. (#9177)

3257 **1924 MS64 PCGS.** This shimmering pumpkin-gold double eagle is remarkably unabraded for the MS64 level. A strong bid will be required to secure this conservatively graded type coin. Encapsulated in a first generation holder.
From the Reuben Reinstein Collection. (#9177)

3258 **1924 MS65 PCGS.** Shimmering luster and beautiful light coloration ensure the eye appeal of this Saint-Gaudens double eagle. A handful of small marks on the reverse and a minor abrasion on Liberty's left (facing) leg, above the knee, fail to prevent the Gem grade assessment. (#9177)

3259 **1924 MS65 PCGS.** The obverse has lime fields and an orange center. The reverse has even apricot toning. A lustrous type coin with minimal contact. (#9177)

3260 **1924 MS65 PCGS.** Refreshingly unabraded fields and blazing cartwheel sheen confirm the quality of this pumpkin-gold Gem. The top of the sun has minor grazes, but the eagle is well preserved. (#9177)

3261 **1924 MS65 PCGS.** The obverse of this Gem has a hint of satin in the fields, but the reverse displays pure, sparkling brilliance. An immensely appealing lemon-gold example that should prove well-suited to a type or date set. (#9177)

3262 **1924 MS65 PCGS.** One of the most available double eagle issues in Gem grade, the 1924 is one of the most popular choices for type collections. The surfaces of this strongly lustrous yellow-gold example exhibit splashes of orange color in the fields. (#9177)

3263 **1924 MS65 PCGS.** The surfaces of this type Gem have a slight brassy quality. Solidly struck with a hazy appearance on the obverse, though the reverse displays less cloudy fields and devices. (#9177)

3264 **1924 MS65 PCGS.** The impressive lemon-gold toning is nearly comprehensive, although the obverse has an occasional area of pale aqua patina. This lustrous and exactingly struck Gem is clean for the grade despite a small rim depression on the reverse at 9 o'clock. (#9177)

3265 **1924 MS65 PCGS.** Strong, uniform definition occurs over both sides of this lustrous Gem. Peach-gold surfaces reveal just a few trivial marks. (#9177)

3266 **1924 MS65 PCGS.** Sharply struck, with olive-gold lustrous surfaces. there are no significant marks to report. (#9177)

3267 **1924 MS65 PCGS.** Pretty peach-gold color embraces both sides of this Gem. Sharply struck, with no mentionable marks on highly lustrous surfaces. (#9177)

3268 **1924 MS65 PCGS.** Sharply struck with satin luster and pleasing mint-green, gold and rose toning. A few trivial blemishes are noted on each side, but they are not inconsistent with the Gem grade designation. (#9177)

3269 **1924 MS65 NGC.** A rich satiny sheen enlivens the lime-gold and peach surfaces. The design motifs are crisply defined. Minimal surface marks are found on either side of this lovely Gem. (#9177)

3270 **1924 MS65 NGC.** Lovely soft mint frost radiates from the yellow-gold and pink surfaces of this attractive Gem example. Surface marks are minimal. This extremely common date is always an excellent choice for type purposes. (#9177)

3271 **1924 MS65 PCGS.** An apricot-gold Gem with sweeping luster and a good strike. The reverse is well preserved save for a few ticks on the front wing. An abrasion is noted beneath the R in LIBERTY. (#9177)

3272 **1924 MS65 PCGS.** An original green-gold Gem that has impressively clean fields and only minor marks on Liberty. Inconspicuous contact on the eagle's wings denies a higher grade. (#9177)

3273 **1924 MS66 PCGS.** The 1924 is and will always be available in typical Mint State grades. But Premium Gems are scarce, because of the soft gold alloy, large diameter, and indifferent bag storage of the issue. A loupe locates the occasional tiny mark, but the lustrous lime-gold surfaces are relentlessly undisturbed overall. (#9177)

3274 **1924 MS66 NGC.** Sharply struck design elements and glowing luster add up to outstanding eye appeal on this Premium Gem. Peach-gold surfaces are minimally abraded. Jeff Garrett and Ron Guth (2006) write that "this date is believed to be the most common of the entire series." (#9177)

3275 **1924 MS66 ANACS.** Orange and green-gold shadings alternate across this shimmering and precisely struck gold type coin. An attractive representative that lacks mentionable contact. (#9177)

3276 **1924 MS66 PCGS.** This lustrous Premium Gem has all of the eye appeal that one could ever ask for. A shimmering, softly frosted sheen highlights the beautiful peach and lime-gold coloration. The design features are boldly struck, save for weakness on IN and the lower obverse foot and stars. A couple of small, insignificant marks are noted on the eagle's wings. (#9177)

Appealing, Condition Scarcity 1924 Twenty, MS67

3277 **1924 MS67 NGC.** While the 1924 is one of the most common dates of the series, MS67 pieces, as we have here, are somewhat tougher to locate. Sharply struck design elements complement highly lustrous surfaces that are devoid of mentionable marks. Pleasing apricot-gold patina covers each side, further enhancing the coin's great eye appeal. A mere two finer specimens have been certified. (#9177)

Exceptional MS67 1924 Saint-Gaudens Twenty

3278 1924 MS67 ANACS. The surfaces are wonderfully free from the abrasions that normally plague Saint-Gaudens twenties. Each side is also sharply struck. The mint luster is thick and frosted but initially appears somewhat subdued because of the presence of light patina over each side. (#9177)

Well Defined 1924-D Double Eagle, MS62

3279 1924-D MS62 PCGS. Many 1924-D double eagles were consigned to the melting pots. Most survivors, according to Jeff Garrett and Ron Guth (2006), " ... have worn dies around the peripheries, as quality control was lacking." This MS62 specimen shows little evidence of worn peripheries. Indeed, the rim and most of the margin elements appear solidly defined, as do the central devices. Lustrous surfaces reveal a few too many marks for a higher grade. (#9178)

Exuberantly Lustrous 1924-D Twenty, MS64

3280 1924-D MS64 PCGS. A number of late-series Saint-Gaudens mintmarked pieces are now less rare than formerly, due to the discovery of small mini-hoards overseas that eventually made their way back to the United States. The 1924-D is one such. As Q. David Bowers wrote in *The Numismatic Sun* #5 (winter/spring 2005), "Most *rare* coins keep getting rarer as the years pass, but notable exceptions are certain of the Saint-Gaudens double eagles of the 1920s and 1930s. Most of the mintmarks of this era as well as the later (1929 and afterward) dates were exceedingly rare in the 1950s, less rare in the 1960s, and are widely collectible today. The explanation is that foreign reserves have been tapped, including sources not known earlier."

In the case of the 1924-D, today the issue must be considered as more of a conditional rarity than an absolute, as PCGS has certified well over 100 examples in MS64, yet only eight coins finer, as always including the inevitable duplications (6/07). This piece offers exuberant luster over the deep apricot-gold surfaces, with tinges of mint-green and hazel near the rims. The strike is precise and intricate, and only a few light contact marks on Liberty's torso and the sun on the reverse appear to limit a finer grade. (#9178)

Desirable 1924-S Double Eagle, MS62

3281 1924-S MS62 PCGS. Like many dates in the series that are scarce or rare today, nearly all of the nearly 3 million coins minted were melted a decade later. In the past 50 years, small quantities have returned from European holdings, and these are the coins available today. Jeff Garrett and Ron Guth write: "During the 1940s and 1950s, it was generally believed that fewer than a half-dozen examples of this date existed!" This example is a pleasing satiny Mint State piece with light yellow-gold luster and good eye appeal. The surfaces are consistent with the grade. (#9179)

Satiny MS63 1924-S Double Eagle

3282 1924-S MS63 PCGS. At one time in the not-too-distant past, the 1924-S was regarded as one of the premier rarities in the Saint-Gaudens series. Although its rarity ranking has slipped following the immigration of a few hundred pieces from European bank vaults over the past 40 years, the 1924-S is still an important mintmarked Saint-Gaudens issue from the 1920s. This satiny-textured example displays noticeably fewer abrasions than the typical Uncirculated survivor. Its apricot-gold surfaces exhibit nice luster and sharply struck design elements. (#9179)

Attractive 1924-S Near-Gem Double Eagle

3283 1924-S MS64 PCGS. The 1924-S comes with a mintage of nearly 3 million pieces, most of which succumbed to the melting pots of the 1930s. The coins available to collectors today, mostly in the lower grades of Mint State, survived in overseas banks, returning to the United States in the 1950s and 1960s (Jeff Garrett and Ron Guth, 2006).

The near-Gem specimen presented in the current lot displays rich apricot-gold color and glowing luster. A well executed strike manifests itself with sharp definition on most of the design elements, accentuating the coin's eye appeal. A few light obverse marks limit the grade. Population: 88 in 64, 3 finer (4/07). (#9179)

Colorful and Lustrous MS64 1924-S Twenty

3284 1924-S MS64 PCGS. The 1924-S was apparently one of the issues in the Saint-Gaudens series that was simply not set aside in any appreciable numbers by collectors in this country. When large-scale melting of many Saints began in 1937, it appears that the only survivors were held in Swiss and Paris bank vaults. In the Adolphe Menjou Sale in 1950, Abe Kosoff estimated that only five coins were extant. Then the coins slowly began to be released from the vaults in Europe. The '24-S is still a scarce and desirable coin, and it is especially worthwhile in MS64 condition.

This particular coin has frosted mint luster that is thicker in texture than usually seen on this issue. The color is a pronounced reddish-gold with a couple of streaks of yellow-gold on the reverse. Sharply struck in all areas. There are no mentionable abrasions on either side of this impressive coin. Population: 88 in 64, 3 finer (6/07). (#9179)

3285 1925 MS63 NGC. A well executed strike manifests itself in sharp definition on Liberty's face, fingers, and toes, as well as on the Capitol building and the eagle's plumage. Glowing luster radiates from peach-gold, lightly abraded surfaces.
From the Reuben Reinstein Collection. (#9180)

3286 1925 MS64 PCGS. Well struck and attractively preserved with rich peach-gold patina. Thorough evaluation locates a small number of tiny copper-red alloy spots. Certified in a first generation holder.
From the Reuben Reinstein Collection. (#9180)

3287 1925 MS65 PCGS. The 1925 is an available later Saint-Gaudens issue, though it is off the radar for many type collectors due to the presence of 1924 and 1927 pieces. This slightly frosty yellow-gold example has lovely luster and above-average detail. (#9180)

3288 1925 MS65 PCGS. An intriguing Gem, this piece has satiny pinkish-gold luster on the obverse and frosty greenish-gold luster on the reverse. (#9180)

3289 1925 MS66 PCGS. This common date is available through MS66, while higher date pieces are elusive. This Premium Gem displays bright luster and sharply struck design elements. A few trivial obverse marks do not distract. (#9180)

3290 1925 MS66 PCGS. Rich orange-gold patination covers highly lustrous surfaces. Sharply struck, with no significant marks. Nice overall appeal. (#9180)

Pleasing, Lustrous Mint State 1925-S Twenty

3291 1925-S MS60 NGC. Most of the enormous original mintage exceeding 3.7 million coins was melted in the gold coin recall of the 1930s, and today the few coins seen are largely just shy of Mint State. This strictly Uncirculated piece offers pleasing luster over deep orange-gold surfaces with a few too many light bagmarks to qualify for a higher Mint State grade. The mintmark appears to be lightly repunched. (#9182)

Lustrous 1925-S Double Eagle, MS63

3292 1925-S MS63 PCGS. Many of the rarest Saint-Gaudens double eagles have high mintages, including the '25-S. All of these rarities, usually from Denver or San Francisco, were subject to massive destruction by the government in the 1930s, after President Franklin D. Roosevelt took the country off the gold standard. In most cases, the coins were struck but never released. They remained in Mint or Treasury vaults since the time of issue, ending up in the melting pot during the mid to late 1930s.

This example is one of the few coins actually released. It was either set aside by a collector in the late 1920s, or it spent several decades in Europe before its return. While each side has a few scattered surface marks that are consistent with the grade, the surfaces are fully brilliant with satiny orange-gold luster. Population: 72 in 63, 22 finer (6/07). (#9182)

3293 1926 MS65 NGC. Brilliant green-gold luster is exhibited on both sides of this sharply defined, frosty Gem. (#9183)

Fascinating 1926-S Twenty, MS62

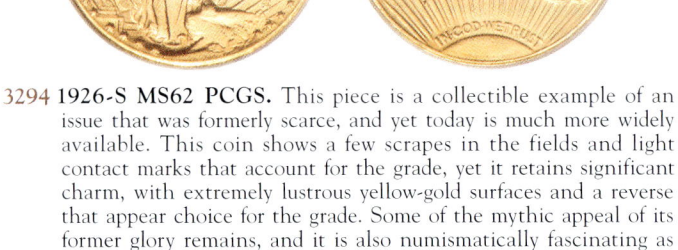

3294 1926-S MS62 PCGS. This piece is a collectible example of an issue that was formerly scarce, and yet today is much more widely available. This coin shows a few scrapes in the fields and light contact marks that account for the grade, yet it retains significant charm, with extremely lustrous yellow-gold surfaces and a reverse that appear choice for the grade. Some of the mythic appeal of its former glory remains, and it is also numismatically fascinating as the only U.S. gold coin of any denomination dated 1926-S. (#9185)

Lustrous MS62 1926-S Twenty

3295 1926-S MS62 PCGS. Formerly considered a great rarity, the 1926-S in more recent times has seen a number of specimens repatriated from overseas hoards, mostly in the lower Mint State grades. This piece shows the typically high production standards of the issue, with a bold strike and frosty, lustrous surfaces that show a few grade-consistent abrasions. (#9185)

Enticing Select 1926-S Double Eagle

3296 1926-S MS63 PCGS. Despite a mintage of over 2 million pieces, the 1926-S is less available in all grades than its P-mint counterpart. This strongly lustrous yellow-gold example has hints of green-gold color in the fields. The strike is sharp, and only light, scattered marks affect the obverse, though the reverse has slightly more significant abrasions. Still, an appealing representative. (#9185)

Frosted MS63 1926-S Twenty

3297 **1926-S MS63 PCGS.** Found in substantial numbers in European holdings, the 1926-S is now one of the most frequently encountered mintmarked issues from the 1920s. This piece has rich frosted surfaces and shows a noticeably deeper orange hue around the margins. Sharply struck. Each side has only slight abrasions, none of which deserve individual mention. (#9185)

Desirable Select Mint State 1926-S Twenty

3298 **1926-S MS63 PCGS.** This is a desirable Select Mint State example of the '26-S Saint-Gaudens, an issue that was heavily produced to the extent of two million plus pieces, but later was heavily melted, probably in the 1930s. Well struck with thick mint luster and pleasingly deep rose-gold toning. A moderate number of small abrasions define the grade.
From The Vanek Collection. (#9185)

3299 **1927 MS65 PCGS.** Most of the design elements are well defined, and the gleaming luster illuminates lovely honey-gold toning. Aside from a few stray nicks, the surfaces are unharmed. A fine Gem example of the Saint-Gaudens type. (#9186)

3300 **1927 MS65 PCGS.** Delicate lime-green and rose toning adorns the lustrous surfaces of this Gem example. Typically well struck with a mere handful of scattered, trivial coin-to-coin marks. (#9186)

3301 **1927 MS65 PCGS.** This well struck piece displays strong luster, and the fields give off a subtle glow. Cherry-red copper stains on the eagle's lower wing give this type coin a distinctive appearance. (#9186)

3302 **1927 MS65 PCGS.** A lustrous and well-defined Gem representative of this ever-present later double eagle issue, predominantly yellow-orange with areas of ruby copper spotting. Small dots appear in the left and right obverse fields, while the reverse has a sizable patch just below the eagle's breast. (#9186)

3303 **1927 MS65 NGC.** A subtly lustrous and solidly struck yellow-orange representative of this ubiquitous double eagle issue, carefully preserved with a touch of haze in the fields. Minor marks to the left of Liberty preclude an even finer grade. (#9186)

3304 **1927 MS65 PCGS.** Though several issues have higher mintages, the 1927 has become the type issue of choice for many collectors. This vibrant yellow-orange Gem has the strong visual appeal that makes the date so prized, with strong detail, vivid color, and exemplary luster. (#9186)

3305 **1927 MS65 PCGS.** Gorgeous apricot-gold and mint-green patina enriches both sides of this radiantly lustrous Gem. The design elements benefit from a well executed strike, and both faces are devoid of significant marks. Its high availability and great eye appeal make the 1927 a favorite type coin. Housed in a green-label holder. (#9186)

3306 **1927 MS65 PCGS.** This lovely green-gold and rose double eagle exhibits pleasing mint frost over each side, and minimally disturbed surfaces. The striking details are generally bold and the overall eye appeal of the piece is outstanding. This coin would make an ideal representative for a Gem type set.
From The Vanek Collection. (#9186)

3307 **1927 MS65 NGC.** Highly lustrous with clean surfaces and a pleasingly bright appearance. The light green-gold and peach toning is especially attractive. (#9186)

3308 **1927 MS65 NGC.** The utterly brilliant surfaces display lovely lime-green and peach toning. Lustrous and carefully preserved, neither side of the coin reveals any severe blemishes or abrasions. A small mark on Liberty's upper left (facing) thigh is noted only for the sake of accuracy. One of the two most common Saint-Gaudens issues, the 1927 is often used for type purposes. (#9186)

3309 **1927 MS65 NGC.** The 1927 was a well produced issue in the Saint-Gaudens series that has proven to have a large number of high grade survivors. This Gem is lustrous, boldly struck, and well preserved. A typically attractive and technically impressive example of this prolific date. (#9186)

3310 **1927 MS65 PCGS.** A splendidly mark-free Gem with exceptional eye appeal for the MS65 grade. The 1927 will never be rare, but this crisply struck example will nonetheless please its next owner. (#9186)

3311 **1927 MS65 PCGS.** A blush of orange-red adorns the center of this lustrous Gem. The designer's monogram is indistinct, but the strike is otherwise crisp. (#9186)

3312 **1927 MS66 PCGS.** A flashy Premium Gem that displays a blend of vibrant orange-gold and delicate wheat-gold colors on each side. Crisply struck with excellent surface quality, and an immensely appealing candidate for the type collector. PCGS has graded just 12 pieces finer (5/07). (#9186)

3313 **1927 MS66 PCGS.** Ex: Brahin. This is a flashy pumpkin-orange and rose example that displays ample luster and excellent striking detail throughout. A few nicks and shallow field grazes are noted under magnification, but are not readily apparent otherwise. A lovely Premium Gem double eagle of unimpeachable technical and visual quality. (#9186)

3314 **1927 MS66 NGC.** While not particularly scarce in Premium Gem quality, this date is a major condition rarity in Superb preservation. Both sides have soft, frosty honey-gold luster with pristine surfaces. (#9186)

3315 **1928 MS64 PCGS.** A crisply struck khaki-gold near-Gem with vibrant luster and a good strike. A small mark on the forehead, but generally clean for the grade. In a first generation holder.
From the Reuben Reinstein Collection. (#9189)

3316 **1928 MS65 PCGS.** Though Philadelphia produced over 8.8 million double eagles in 1928, a far greater percentage of those pieces were melted compared to earlier issues. This strongly lustrous example displays above-average luster and pretty yellow-orange coloration. Well-defined with strong visual appeal. (#9189)

3317 **1928 MS65 PCGS.** Though the 1928 has the highest mintage of any Saint-Gaudens issue, it has less representation in the certified populations than a number of other issues. This yellow-gold example has powerful luster and crisp detail. Two distinctive features are a mark in the right obverse field and a copper streak through the sun's rays on the reverse. (#9189)

3318 **1928 MS66 NGC.** A splendid, virtually unblemished example of one of the most collectible U.S. type coins. It is unusual to encounter a double eagle this nice with such clean surfaces. Bright, frosty luster. (#9189)

3319 **1928 MS66 NGC.** This is a splendid Premium Gem with amazing luster and frosty yellow surfaces. Both sides have wisps of light orange toning. (#9189)

PROOF SAINT-GAUDENS DOUBLE EAGLES

Enthralling 1912 Double Eagle, PR67

3320 1912 PR67 NGC. The U.S. Mint has a long history of interaction with the mints of Europe. Chief Engravers William Barber and George T. Morgan were employed in Great Britain prior to their work in the United States, and the technological advances made in Europe from the 1830s to the 20th century made their way across the Atlantic Ocean as well. Q. David Bowers, in his *Commemorative Coins of the United States* (1991), writes that "in 1905 the government sent [Chief Engraver Charles] Barber on a tour of European mints to study the procedures in use there. Upon his return to Philadelphia he implemented many changes that resulted in the Medal Department of the Mint's being one of the world's finest facilities."

Not every European concept found a warm welcome in the United States. The dulled, dark finish of the sandblast proof, however *en vogue* it might have been in Europe, was a shocking change from the brilliant proofs to which American numismatists were accustomed, and when the gold sandblast proofs of 1908 reached numismatists, complaints followed. After two years of the distinctive, brighter "Roman Gold" finish failed to quell its customers' criticism, the Mint returned to the sandblast finish in 1911. Predictably, demand plummeted, and production fell from 167 proofs in 1910 to 100 pieces in 1911. For the next year, 1912, the Mint released just 74 pieces.

The exquisitely preserved double eagle offered here makes tangible all of the strengths and perceived weaknesses of the sandblast proofs of 1912. Both sides display bold detail, which is particularly evident on Liberty's toes and the veins of the eagle's feathers. The delicately faceted, undisturbed surfaces display even khaki-gold coloration with only two small points of slightly deeper color, one in the left obverse field and one near 3 o'clock on the reverse rim. A spectacular survivor, one that ranks alongside the Trompeter, Morse, and Loewinger specimens, all Superb Gems. NGC has certified a lone piece graded PR68 ★, while PCGS has graded no coins above PR66 (5/07). (#9209)

Exceptional PR67 1913 Saint-Gaudens Twenty

3321 1913 PR67 NGC. As with any proof double eagle, examples from this year are rare in the truest sense of the word, as can be easily ascertained by its minuscule mintage of 58 coins, which is second lowest in the series. Unlike the previous two issues, a greater percentage of the mintage seems to have been set aside and survives today. Still, probably no more than 35-40 individual coins are probably extant today. This number of survivors is somewhat higher than in previous years, and it is also a more accurate estimation of the number of coins remaining. David Akers' estimate of 20-25 coins seems a bit on the low side, especially when more than 60 pieces have been certified by both NGC and PCGS (5/07).

As with most 1913 proofs, the matte surfaces on this coin exhibit a brownish-khaki coloration that is similar to the color seen on 1908 proofs, more so than on other dates in the series. The surfaces show a pronounced granularity, and when closely examined each of the thousands of individual granules sparkle in a random, diffuse manner. Even with the aid of magnification, the tiniest of surface flaws appear to be of mint origin. Whether this magnificent specimen could possibly be deserving of an even higher rating is up to the potential buyer. Either way, the importance of this classic 20th century gold issue cannot be underestimated and its technical and aesthetic merits are equally sound. Census: 10 in 67, 2 finer (5/07). (#9210)

TERRITORIAL GOLD

1853 900 Thous. Assay Office Twenty AU50

3322 **1853 Assay Office Twenty Dollar, 900 Thous. AU50 PCGS.** K-18, R.2. The subvariety without crossbars on the A's in AMERICA. This sharply struck straw-gold Assay Office twenty has lustrous borders and devices. Subtle thin marks are present near the fineness scroll, and a faded scratch approaches the Liberty scroll. Certified in a green label holder. Listed on page 356 of the 2008 Guide Book. *From The Vanek Collection.* (#10013)

Lustrous MS62 1853 Assay Office Twenty, K-18

3323 **1853 Assay Office Twenty Dollar, 900 Thous. MS62 NGC.** K-18, R.2. The U.S. Assay Office of Gold fulfilled a crucial role in the Old West of the days before the San Francisco Mint began operations in 1854 (of which it was the predecessor), producing about 2.5 million "double eagles" of this variety from March-October 1853. Partners Joseph R. Curtis, Philo H. Perry, and Samuel H. Ward agreed to provide the structure and equipment for the new federal mint, in reality an enlargement of the existing structure that proved completely inadequate. The Assay Office became history on December 14, 1853. The first gold coinage in the new mint occurred on April 3, 1854, with the first double eagles of the regular Longacre design.

The Donald Kagin standard reference comments that the K-18s were produced "... from some 30 different dies destroyed in the fire of 1906," with no estimate of how many die *marriages* were employed, or indeed if there were 15 obverses and 15 reverses, or one reverse and 29 obverses! Most of the K-18s are ".900 over .880" in the fineness legend, but the underdigits fade with die use and are sometimes indistinguishable. On this piece, there is an unrecognizable blob under the first digit, with the top of an 8 clear above the second digit, and nothing remaining under the last. Much more important, however, is the overall superlative condition of this piece, clearly among the few dozen finest from the original large emission. It is unusual to see cartwheel luster on a "Territorial" gold coin, but this piece is one such, with ample coruscating mint luster radiating from the greenish-gold surfaces. There are relatively few abrasions of mentionable size on either side, although a couple of rim irregularities on the obverse border are likely as struck. This piece is missing the top serif on the I in UNITED, and most of the bottom-left serif of the E in TWENTY. On the reverse, AY in ASSAY nearly join at the bottoms. Listed on page 356 of the 2008 Guide Book. Census: 51 in 62, 42 finer (6/07). (#10013)

3324 (1842-52) A. Bechtler Dollar, 27G. 21C.—Repaired, Whizzed—ANACS. AU50 Details. K-24, R.3. Repaired on the obverse border between 9 and 12 o'clock, and on the reverse between 1 and 4 o'clock. Hairlined and wavy with a whizzed texture above 27 G. A collectible example of a normally costly series. (#10040)

Choice VF 887 Thous. 1852 Humbert Fifty, K-11

3325 **1852 Humbert Fifty Dollar, 887 Thous. VF35 PCGS.** K-11, R.5. The last of fifty dollar slug varieties issued prior to the reorganization of the California mint as the United States Assay Office of Gold. The assay office was operated by Moffat & Co., which dissolved after its founder, John Little Moffat, left the firm in 1852. The new principles were Curtis, Perry, and Ward. Business continued as before, but the name of Augustus Humbert would no longer appear on the coins struck at the facility. This straw-gold slug has glimpses of rose-tinted luster within the wings, legends, and engine turning. The distributed marks are appropriate for 25 points of wear. Certified in a green label holder, and listed on page 353 of the 2008 Guide Book. (#10217)

Important, Appealing, and Rare 1855 Kellogg & Co. Twenty Dollar, K-3b, XF45

3326 **1855 Kellogg & Co. Twenty Dollar XF45 PCGS.** K-3b, R.5. Kellogg and Co. performed a valuable function in the Territorial gold arena by providing double eagles between the cessation of coinage at the U.S. Assay Office of Gold in late 1853 and the beginning of gold coin production at the San Francisco Mint (April 1854), as well as for a short time thereafter that extended into 1855.

This is an important example of this rare Territorial. The reverse arrows are short, and the O of CO is in Liberty's hair rather than on the coronet. Perhaps one-third to one-half of the original mint luster is still present, and while the surfaces show a number of moderate abrasions, none of them is especially bothersome. The yellow-gold surfaces that deepen to magenta-red at the obverse margins and over much of the reverse further enhance the enormous appeal. Listed on page 363 of the 2008 Guide Book. (#10225)

Gem Proof Restrike 1855 Kellogg Fifty

3327 **1855 Kellogg & Co. Fifty Dollar Gem Proof PCGS.** Struck on August 21, 2001, with a proof mintage on that date of only 84 pieces. The initials C.H.S. are seen on both the counterstamp and on the ribbon, and refer to the California Historical Society. Struck on gold alloy from ingots recovered from the S.S. *Central America*. An essentially pristine example, with exquisitely struck design elements. The frame and presentation box of issue is included, along with a Certificate of Authenticity, a colorful brochure titled "The King of Territorial Gold Coins," and a screwdriver for opening and closing the velvet frame. (#10228)

Gem Proof Restrike 1855 Kellogg Fifty

3328 **1855 Kellogg & Co. Fifty Dollar Restrike Gem Proof PCGS.** Struck on August 23, 2001, with a proof mintage on that date of 109 pieces. The exquisitely struck and thickly frosted motifs provide outstanding contrast with the glassy fields. A tiny spot is present between star 2 and the chin, and minuscule contact is detected beneath the scroll ends, but the preservation is otherwise immaculate. (#10228)

Popular Proof Restrike 1855 Kellogg Fifty Dollar

3329 **1855 Kellogg & Co. Fifty Dollar Restrike Gem Proof PCGS.** A brilliant, deeply mirrored cameo proof. Struck from melted down Kellogg & Humbert gold ingots recovered from the S.S. Central America, using transfer dies from the originals engraved by Ferdinand Gruner. The pieces were struck at the Presidio on a former San Francisco Mint coin press. The present flawless example was struck on August 31, 2001. The proof mintage for that date of 483 pieces. Accompanying the lot are the glass and velvet-lined frame, the certificate of authenticity, a screwdriver, a colorful brochure, and an outer gold-colored presentation case from the California Historical Society. (#10228)

Restrike Gem Proof 1855 Kellogg Fifty Dollar

3330 **1855 Kellogg & Co. Fifty Dollar Restrike Gem Proof PCGS.** Struck on the tragic date of September 11, 2001, with a mintage of 99 pieces for that date. An immaculate example with light die polish lines on the reverse. This relic medal was struck from the contents of gold ingots recovered from the S.S. Central America. Some of the ingots were too large to be readily sold intact, so the faces were shaved off and separately sold, while the remainder was melted to provide planchets for this issue and an 1850 Baldwin ten "restrike." The dies for the relic medal were "originated by transfer from the original 1855 dies," according to the certificate of authenticity. The frame and presentation box of issue also accompany, along with a brochure entitled "The King of Territorial Gold Coins." No screwdriver is present. (#10228)

Gem Uncirculated Restrike 1855 Kellogg Fifty

3331 **1855 Kellogg & Co. Fifty Dollar Restrike Gem Uncirculated PCGS.** Struck on Sept. 12, 2001, with an Uncirculated mintage of 200 pieces on that date. The final date of striking, since the S.S. Central America sank on Sept. 12, 1857. A relic medal struck from gold alloy reclaimed from S.S. Central America Kellogg & Humbert ingots. A pristine example with infrequent tiny freckles of peach patina. (#10228)

Impressive 36.40-Ounce Kellogg & Humbert Gold Ingot
Ex: *Central America*

3332 Kellogg & Humbert Gold Ingot. A disaster such as the sinking of a ship focuses the attention of people on what is truly important, life itself. It also brings out the best and worst in people. A passage from *America's Lost Treasure* is of interest and was written later by one of the survivors, William Chase:

> "Some of the men unbuckled their gold-stuffed belts and flung their hard-earned treasure upon the deck to lighten their weight. Chase claimed that he could easily have picked up thousands of dollars, if he thought he had a chance of reaching safety with this treasure. Shortly before eight o'clock, the *Central America*, with its decks now awash, was rapidly filling with water and sinking lower into the sea. In a dinner conversation earlier in the voyage Captain Herndon had told the Eastons that if his ship were ever to go down, he would go with it. Now, having done everything he could to save the women and children, and wondering if he could have done anything different to avoid the imminent tragedy, Captain Herndon retired to his quarters. Stoic and proud, he returned to the wheelhouse wearing his full-dress uniform."

Of the gold ingots that slipped to the bottom of the sea 150 years ago, the most plentiful were those from the well-respected firm of Kellogg & Humbert. More than 400 of these ingots were recovered in 1988. In spite of its considerable heft, the present piece is actually one of the smaller ingots recovered. The smallest from Kellogg & Humbert was 5.71 ounces and the largest weighed an amazing 933.94 ounces! At the time the Central America sunk, this particular ingot was valued at $620.77.

The ingot is 52 mm tall, 41 mm wide, and 30 mm deep. The top side reads: No 1028/36.40 OZ/825 FINE/$620.77. The individual ingot number is repeated at the top of the back side. The company imprint is neatly impressed on the right side. Two assay chips are out of opposing corners, as always. Bright overall with no traces of the rust that is often seen on these ingots.

CALIFORNIA FRACTIONAL GOLD

3333 **Undated Liberty Round 25 Cents, BG-224, R.3, MS64 PCGS.** A charming Period One piece that boasts lustrous, clean surfaces and a penetrating strike. The engraver likely had no access to numeral punches, which explains the crude appearance of the denominator.
From The Vanek Collection. (#10409)

3334 **1854 Liberty Octagonal 50 Cents, BG-308, R.4, MS64 PCGS.** A straw-gold representative with glimpses of milk-gray toning above the hair bun and near the coronet tip. Evenly struck, attractive, and housed in a green label holder. Population: 5 in 64, 0 finer (4/07).
From The Vanek Collection. (#10428)

Select 1855/4 Octagonal Dollar, BG-511

3335 **1855/4 Liberty Octagonal 1 Dollar, BG-511, High R.4, MS63 PCGS.** Mostly light green-gold, but the right obverse is golden-brown, and the right reverse border has a hint of orange-red. Well struck and satiny with smooth surfaces. Certified in a green label holder. Population: 9 in 63, 2 finer (4/07).
From The Vanek Collection. (#10488)

3336 **1853 Liberty Octagonal 1 Dollar, BG-530, R.2, AU55 PCGS.** A well struck straw-gold representative of this popular Period One variety. The surfaces are slightly subdued, but there are no relevant marks. Encapsulated in an old green label holder. (#10507)

3337 **1853 Liberty Octagonal 1 Dollar, BG-530, R.2, MS61 PCGS.** This evenly struck representative has only a single remotely mentionable mark, a hair-thin diagonal pinscratch above the 3 in the date. Otherwise, a subdued and smooth Period One dollar. (#10507)

3338 **1853 Liberty Octagonal 1 Dollar, BG-531, R.4, AU58 NGC.** This Period One octagonal dollar displays substantial luster, particularly across the portrait. The pale green-gold fields exhibit minor marks from brief non-numismatic handling. (#10508)

3339 **1855 Liberty Octagonal 1 Dollar, BG-533, Low R.4, MS62 Prooflike NGC.** Light plum-red toning visits the margins of this sharply struck and lightly abraded Period One octagonal dollar. The reverse legend includes the letters N and R; these represent the makers, Nouizillet & Routhier. (#710510)

Extremely Rare BG-703A Octagonal Quarter

3340 **1856 Liberty Octagonal 25 Cents, BG-703A, R.8—Reverse Scratched—NCS. Unc Details.** This extremely rare variety was first reported in the August 8, 1984 issue of Coin World. Only two survivors are listed in the second edition of Breen-Gillio, the discovery piece and the Roe plate coin. The present piece is neither of those. It is free from wear, but is subdued by a cleaning and has a thick cluster of vertical pinscratches near 3 o'clock. Nonetheless, an important opportunity for the dedicated collector of California small denomination gold. (#10960)

3341 **1864 Liberty Octagonal 25 Cents, BG-706, High R.5, MS64 NGC.** An impressive near-Gem with smooth, flashy fields and a consistent strike. Heavy clashed, but void of visible marks. Census: 2 in 64, 2 finer (6/07). (#10533)

3342 **1871 Liberty Octagonal 25 Cents, BG-714, R.3, MS65 NGC.** Large Liberty head with 9 stars, an undersized 4 in the fraction, and the D in DOLLAR partly embedded in the wreath. A pair of die cracks (as struck) connect the LL in DOLLAR with the 1s in the date. The orange peripheries surround prooflike, mint-green fields. The surfaces are free of distracting marks. (#10541)

3343 **1871 Liberty Octagonal 25 Cents, BG-714, R.3, MS66 NGC.** Orange and lime toning alternate across this gorgeously unabraded Premium Gem. The strike is consistent, and the eye appeal is exceptional. Census: 2 in 66, 0 finer (6/07). (#10541)

1872 Washington Octagonal Quarter Dollar MS66, BG-722

3344 **1872 Washington Octagonal 25 Cents, BG-722, Low R.4, MS66 PCGS.** Bright yellow-gold surfaces possess a greenish cast, and display noticeable field-motif contrast. Well struck, with nicely preserved surfaces. Walter Breen and Ron Gillio (2003) write: "It would seem that in 1872 Frontier switched to a Washington Head obverse to avoid too much resemblance to the design of the U.S. gold dollar." (#10549)

3345 **1867 Liberty Octagonal 25 Cents, BG-741, R.5, MS64 PCGS.** This flashy near-Gem has an exemplary obverse and a few tiny strike-throughs on the central reverse field. Housed in a green label holder.
From The Vanek Collection. (#10568)

3346 **1875 Liberty Octagonal 25 Cents, BG-777, Low R.7, MS63 PCGS.** A flashy green-tinged Select example of this rare variety. Well struck with a pleasing appearance. PCGS has certified only eight examples in all grades. Population: 1 in 63, 0 finer (1/07). (#10604)

3347 **1872 Indian Octagonal 25 Cents, BG-791, R.3, MS65 Prooflike NGC.** This mirrored California fractional gold piece is well preserved. The strike is sharp except for minor weakness on the fraction denominator. Slightly wavy, as made. Census: 7 in 65 Prooflike, 6 finer (5/07). (#710618)

3348 **1865 Liberty Round 25 Cents, BG-802, Low R.5, MS64 NGC.** Although undesignated as Prooflike, the fields are flashy and lack noticeable contact. Primarily lime-gold with hints of lilac patina on the highpoints of the portrait. Census: 1 in 64, 0 finer (6/07). (#10663)

3349 **1866 Liberty Round 25 Cents, BG-804, R.4, MS65 NGC.** The dies are rotated 180 degrees. The light-green fields are semi-prooflike and unmarked. The date and LLA in DOLLAR are incompletely struck due to die polish. A well preserved and conditionally scarce Gem example of this later Large Head type. Census: 2 in 65, 1 finer (6/07). (#10665)

Lustrous Liberty Round 25 Cents
MS66, BG-810, Low R.7
Among Finest Certified

3350 **1871 Liberty Round 25 Cents, BG-810, Low R.7, MS66 PCGS.** Highly lustrous surfaces display delicate yellow-gold and lime-green patination accented with traces of apricot. The design elements are well impressed, and both sides are devoid of disturbing marks. PCGS has graded just 11 examples of this variety, with the Premium Gem in this lot tied with two other pieces for the finest certified (6/07). (#10671)

3351 **1870 Goofy Head Round 25 Cents, BG-867, R.4, MS64 PCGS.** Peach, rose, and lime toning invigorate this shimmering, problem-free near-Gem. Probably scarcer than the R.4 suggested by the Second Edition of Breen-Gillio. Population: 9 in 64, 0 finer (4/07). (#10728)

3352 **1875 Indian Round 25 Cents, BG-878, R.3, MS64 Deep Mirror Prooflike NGC.** Die State II. Profoundly reflective fields contrast with the glowing portrait and wreath. Well struck and attractive. The reverse is slightly concave, as usual for this series. (#710739)

3353 **1876 Indian Round 25 Cents, BG-879, R.4, MS65 PCGS.** Straw-gold with a splash of honey-toning on the reverse field. A few letters in DOLLAR CAL are soft, because of metal flow toward the Indian head during the strike. Certified in a green label holder.
From The Vanek Collection. (#10740)

3354 **1876 Indian Round 25 Cents, BG-881, R.5, MS65 PCGS.** The lustrous lemon-gold display occasional ruby and ice-blue tints. A small spot separates the 76 in the date. The central reverse is slightly wavy, as made. (#10742)

Rare BG-960A 1868 Indian Half, MS63 Prooflike

3355 **1868 Indian Octagonal 50 Cents, BG-960A, High R.6, MS63 Prooflike NGC.** Mirrored fields and cameo frost on the wreath proclaim the eye appeal of this seldom-seen octagonal half dollar variety. Minor incompleteness of strike is noted on the central reverse. BG-960A is technically a late die state of BG-960. The reverse die was lapped, greatly weakening CAL. (#710829)

3356 **1871 Liberty Round 50 Cents, BG-1011, R.2, MS66 Prooflike NGC.** Prominently reflective fields and a mark-free appearance ensures the quality of this beautiful Period Two Premium Gem. Sharply struck aside from the base of the wreath.
From The Vanek Collection. (#710840)

3357 **1874/3 Indian Round 50 Cents, BG-1052, High R.4, MS65 Prooflike NGC.** Ex: Stecher Collection. This is an amazing prooflike Gem with extraordinary aesthetic appeal. The obverse field is deeply mirrored and the reverse is moderately mirrored, both sides showing excellent contrast between the fields and devices. This is the single finest piece designated prooflike by NGC, although Gem Deep Prooflike pieces have also been certified. (#710881)

3358 **1874/3 Indian Round 50 Cents, BG-1052, High R.4, MS65 Prooflike NGC.** Gorgeous yellow-gold surfaces display a noticeable cameo-like effect. Exceptionally well struck, save for slight softness in the A of DOLLAR. Census: 2 in 65 Prooflike, 2 finer as DPL (6/07). (#710881)

Prooflike 1860 BG-1102 Gold Dollar, MS64

3359 **1860 Liberty Octagonal 1 Dollar, BG-1102, R.4, MS64 Prooflike NGC.** Both sides of this piece are fully brilliant with light yellow-gold color. The fields are entirely reflective and mirrored, with reflective devices, resulting in little cameo contrast. The early "fractional" gold dollars from the first period of California small denomination gold pieces are among the most desirable pieces in the series. Census: 2 in 64 Prooflike, 0 finer (6/07). (#710913)

3360 **1869 Liberty Octagonal 1 Dollar, BG-1106, High R.4, MS62 PCGS.** Attractive orange-red shades adorn the borders, while the centers are yellow-gold. A few faint hairlines are present, and the LL in DOLLAR is typically brought up. Certified in a green label holder.
From The Vanek Collection. (#10917)

3361 **1869 Liberty Octagonal 1 Dollar, BG-1106, High R.4, MS61 Prooflike NGC.** Ex: Stecher Collection. Die State II. The G is absent beneath the portrait. Evenly struck and nicely mirrored with a couple of small strike-throughs (as made) near the right reverse border. An appealing Mint State example of this octagonal dollar variety. (#710917)

3362 **1874 Indian Octagonal 1 Dollar, BG-1124, High R.4, AU55 PCGS.** This green-gold Period Two octagonal dollar has witnessed brief non-numismatic handling, but luster outlines the wreath and legends. (#10935)

End of Auction

AND THE WINNER IS... HERITAGE!

Once again, Heritage is the proud winner of the prestigious NLG Award for Best Auction Catalog: Coins and Currency, presented this year to the Jules Reiver Collection Signature Catalog. A perfect blend of scholarship and design, this catalog will no doubt stand as an important reference work for years to come.

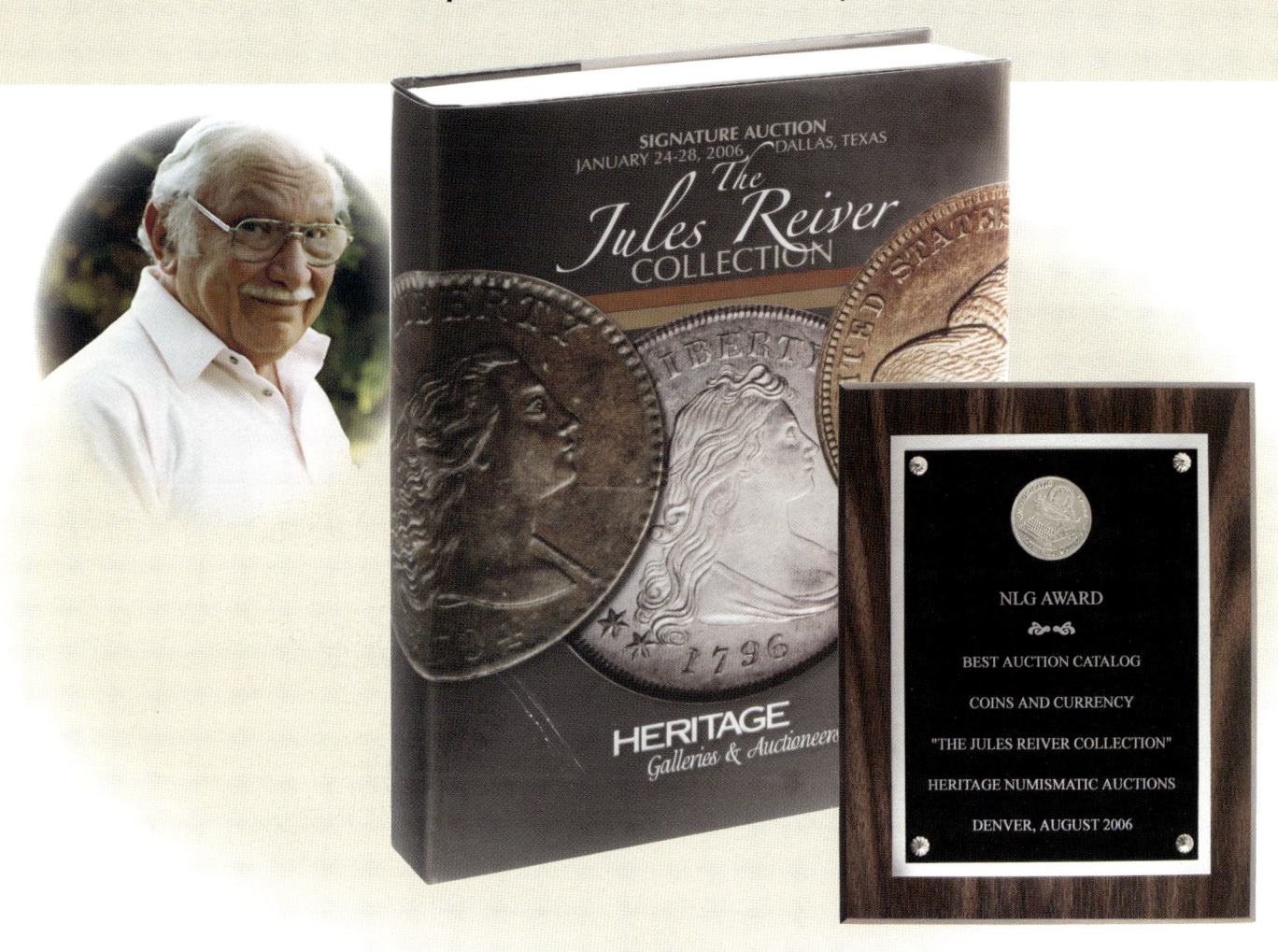

NLG AWARD

BEST AUCTION CATALOG

COINS AND CURRENCY

"THE JULES REIVER COLLECTION"

HERITAGE NUMISMATIC AUCTIONS

DENVER, AUGUST 2006

If you want your collection cataloged and presented with the same care that went into the Jules Reiver Collection Catalog, call one of our Consignment Directors today at 1-800-872-6467, ext. 222 for Coins and ext. 555 for Currency. We invite you to participate in one of our exciting upcoming auctions. Who knows, perhaps YOUR name could be on next year's NLG Award!

The World's #1 Numismatic Auctioneer

HERITAGE
Auction Galleries

Annual Sales Exceeding $500 Million • 300,000+ Online Registered Bidder-Members
1-800-U.S. Coins (800-872-6467) Ext. 222, 24-hour voice mail • or visit HA.com
3500 Maple Avenue, 17th Floor • Dallas, Texas 75219-3941
214-528-3500 • FAX: 214-443-8425 • e-mail: Consign@HA.com